Readings in Strategic Management

Readings in Strategic Management

Third Edition

Arthur A. Thompson, Jr.
The University of Alabama

William E. Fulmer
Graduate School of Business Administration
College of William and Mary

A. J. Strickland III
The University of Alabama

Homewood, IL 60430
Boston, MA 02116

© RICHARD D. IRWIN, INC., 1984, 1987, and 1990

Associate publisher: Martin F. Hanifin
Developmental editor: Elizabeth J. Rubenstein
Project editor: Paula M. Buschman
Production manager: Bette K. Ittersagen
Compositor: J.M. Post Graphics, Corp.
Typeface: 10/12 Times Roman
Printer: Malloy Lithographing, Inc.

Library of Congress Cataloging-in-Publication Data

Readings in strategic management / Arthur A. Thompson, Jr.,
    William E. Fulmer, and A.J. Strickland III.—3rd ed.
        p.   cm.
    Includes bibliographical references.
    ISBN 0-256-08280-4
     1. Strategic planning.   I. Thompson, Arthur A., 1940–
II. Fulmer, William E.   III. Strickland, A. J. (Alonzo J.)
    HD30.28.R418   1990   89–37683
    658.4′012—dc20   CIP

Printed in the United States of America
1 2 3 4 5 6 7 8 9 0 ML 6 5 4 3 2 1 0 9

Preface

During the past decade or so, business policy has expanded its status from being just an integrative course in the business curriculum to being a full-fledged discipline with a distinctive literature of its own. A large knowledge base is rapidly building on the concept of strategy, the tasks and process of strategy formulation and implementation, and all the ramifications of aligning the operations and culture of the enterprise to fit the requirements of strategy.

Important, insightful techniques for examining a company's competitive position, business strengths, industry attractiveness, and the makeup of multibusiness corporate portfolios have come to the fore. Formal strategy evaluations and annual strategy reviews are growing in use, having already risen to become a standard management practice in most large companies. There is heightened managerial application of such strategic concepts as driving forces, strategic groups, competitor analysis, key success factors, distinctive competence, strategic fit, switching costs, first-mover advantages, and strategic business units. Issues pertaining to strategy formulation and strategy implementation enjoy high priority on managerial action agendas. The whole strategic management cycle—from defining the business *to* strategy formulation *to* implementation and execution *to* evaluation of results *to* reformulation and fine-tuning of the game plan—is being intensively scrutinized by practitioners, consultants, and business school academics.

Although many instructors rely on text treatments and case analysis to teach their courses in strategic management, there is reason to supplement the "standard approach" with articles in the field of strategic management. For those instructors who see the value of incorporating samples of the strategic management literature into their course, *Readings in Strategic Management* attempts to provide a variety of current articles that reflect the thinking and research of academics and the state of the art as it is being practiced by consultants and managers.

This book contains 40 articles from a variety of up-to-date sources. Only 8 appeared in the second edition. Not only have almost two-thirds of the readings been published in the last three years, but the book reflects an international perspective—approximately 20 percent of the articles are by authors outside the

United States. More important, all are eminently readable and well matched to the level of most business policy/strategy texts.

The readings themselves are primarily of two types. One type, consisting of standard-length articles reprinted from first-tier journals, adds in-depth treatment to important topic areas covered in most business policy/strategy texts, thereby probing further into the details of particular techniques and exposing students to leading-edge research findings and conclusions. The second type includes shorter articles, drawn from practitioners' sources, that emphasize how strategic management concepts and tools relate directly to actual practice. In tandem, the two types of readings provide an effective and efficient vehicle for reinforcing and expanding text-case treatments and for giving students a flavor of both current literature and state-of-the-art strategic management applications.

ORGANIZATION OF THE READINGS

This book is divided into five sections. Each of the first four sections is organized around one of the major building blocks of strategy management. The fifth section is a new addition reflecting current thoughts about the important subject of business ethics. At the beginning of each section is a brief overview of the topics covered and of how each article fits into the scheme and structure of strategy management as well as an introductory statement about the content of each article. Each of the two types of articles mentioned earlier is included in each section.

Section 1 addresses the role of the general manager as chief architect and chief implementer of strategy. The lead article, by Robert D. Paulson of McKinsey and Co., emphasizes that "making it happen" is the real strategic challenge. James Brian Quinn then reports on his research findings on what the strategy formulation process is like in large corporations and how executives manage the process. The next two articles, one by an academic (Bob Hayes) and one by a consultant (Daniel Gray), report on some of the current criticisms of strategic planning. These articles are followed by Henry Mintzberg's reexamination of the question of why organizations really do need strategies. The last two articles reflect insights on management by two of America's best-known CEOs—Lee Iacocca of Chrysler and Jack Welch of General Electric.

The focus of Section 2 is the formulation and analysis of business level strategy. Henry Mintzberg's article exploring how strategies get made, as opposed to how they are supposed to get made, begins this section. The next two articles discuss approaches for understanding an organization's future environment. Ian Wilson provides a very readable description of GE's pioneering efforts in environmental scanning and the role it plays in strategy formulation. Steven P. Schnaars discusses the increasingly popular technique of scenario analysis. The next two articles explore aspects of generic strategies. Peter Wright examines three generic strategies—least-cost, differentiation, and niche. William Fulmer and Jack Goodwin examine some of the implications of a differentiation strategy. Next Malcolm Schofield and David Arnold examine strategies for mature businesses. In contrast, an interview with Victor Kiam explores growth strategies at Remington. The next two articles explore ways of developing a sustainable competitive advantage. Albert Isenman examines the strategic implications of suppliers and David Aaker looks at managing a firm's assets and skills. An international perspective is the focus of the next two articles. James Leontiades examines the impact of internationalization on competitive positioning and Michael Porter discusses the lag in competitive thinking that affects some U.S. managers as they try to compete globally.

Section 3 presents six articles that address some of the issues facing strategic managers in diversified companies. Setting the stage for this section is Michael Porter's discussion of the "dismal" track record of corporate strategies. Roland Calori draws on his study of 27 diversified companies to offer insights about how companies manage diversity successfully. The next two articles deal with the timely subject of acquisitions. Robert J. Perry offers "10 suggestions for acquisition success" and William Bain of Bain and Company, Inc., discusses 10 working principles that can help a firm that is seeking to diversify through acquisition. The last two articles in this section return to an international perspective. First, David Lei discusses the need for a broader definition of corporate strategy as U.S. companies enter the fight for global markets. Then, James Bolt discusses the factors most often evident in large corporations that have succeeded in the global business arena.

Section 4 takes an in-depth look at the problems and tasks of strategy implementation. First, L. J. Bourgeois and David Brodwin discuss the different roles and methods used by chief executive officers in developing and implementing strategies. Designing organizations to aid strategy implementation is the focus of an article by Ian C. MacMillan and Patricia E. Jones. Next Yvan Allaire and Mihaela Firsirotu propose a framework for devising and implementing "radical" strategies in large organizations. The linking of reward structures to strategic performance is discussed by Henry Migliore. Two Japanese authors, Tomasz Mroczkowski and Masao Hanaoka, discuss changes in the employment and promotion systems of Japanese companies as they position themselves to compete in the 1990s. The next two articles (by Bernard Reimann and Yoash Wiener; and Sebastian Green) discuss corporate culture and its implications for strategy formulation and implementation. John Butler discusses the role that the human resource management function can play in the implementation of a business strategy. This section concludes with a discussion of implementing intrapreneurship as a business strategy at the 3M Corporation.

The final section takes an in-depth look at business ethics. The first of six articles explores the issue of codes of ethics and ethical business behavior. The next two articles, one by a CEO and one by an academic, provide an interesting perspective on the current debate about business ethics. Doug Wallace and Julie Belle White then discuss an integrity audit and lessons learned from such an audit. The next two articles explore two U.S. companies' approach to ethics and values—Johnson & Johnson and the Boeing Company. This section concludes with Patrick Murphy's article on implementing business ethics.

ACKNOWLEDGMENTS

We wish to thank the various publishers and authors of the articles contained in this book. In addition, we wish to express a special thanks to Andrea Truax of the Graduate School of Business Administration, Harvard University, for her assistance.

Comments regarding coverage and content of this book will be most welcome. Please write us at Graduate School of Business Administration, College of William and Mary, Williamsburg, VA 23185, or P.O. Box 870225, Department of Management and Marketing, University of Alabama, Tuscaloosa, AL 35487.

Arthur A. Thompson, Jr.
William E. Fulmer
A. J. Strickland III

Contents

Part I

The General Manager and Strategy

This section addresses the role of the general manager as chief architect and chief implementer of strategy. The lead article, by Robert D. Paulson of McKinsey and Co., emphasizes "making it happen" is the real strategic challenge. James Brian Quinn then reports on his research findings on what the strategy formulation process is like in large corporations and how executives manage the process. The next two articles, one by an academic (Bob Hayes) and one by a consultant (Daniel Gray), report on some of the current criticisms of strategic planning. These articles are followed by Henry Mintzberg's reexamination of the question of why organizations really do need strategies. The last two articles reflect insights on management by two of America's best known chief executive officers—Lee Iacocca of Chrysler and Jack Welch of General Electric.

What this article is about: Leadership is an essential factor when a major change in corporate strategy is planned. As a role model for managers, the CEO should be dynamic, open to suggestions, innovative, and expert in the fine art of delegating. This article discusses the whys and hows of the general manager's personal role in leading the task of strategy implementation.

1–1 The Chief Executive as Change Agent

Robert D. Paulson

Robert D. Paulson is a director and manager of the
Los Angeles office of McKinsey & Co.

"Weak leadership can wreck the soundest strategy; forceful execution of even a poor plan can often bring victory." So wrote the Chinese general and philosopher Sun Zi in 514 B.C. Today, 25 centuries later, that axiom still holds in business.

Much has been written recently about the need for effective business strategies. A new phase, "strategic management," has even been coined to describe the stage of management sophistication in which the principal role of line executives is to develop and implement effective strategies. Yet very few large companies have reached this level of sophistication.

New strategies inherently involve significant change for an organization. Productive change on a large scale is one of the most arduous and demanding assignments faced by any chief executive officer. The CEO's chances of leading a major change successfully are much better if he understands how to exploit the forces for change that are latent in his organization. Also, the CEO must determine precisely what role he should play and how to design a specific plan of action.

Assume that a company has developed a powerful new strategy, based on creative insights drawn from a thorough knowledge of its industry. Before this strategy can be converted into effective action, a number of things must happen. First and foremost, the CEO must be an active leader. But that is not enough.

Constructive corporate staff work, a compatible organizational structure, appropriate management processes, and a supportive corporate environment will all be required to facilitate the needed change.

CHIEF EXECUTIVE LEADERSHIP

There seems to be universal agreement among strategic planners that the key to strategic change is the chief executive. At a recent planning conference, a corporate planner complained that his CEO did not actively support the planning effort and asked the group what he should do. The candid and immediate advice was to find another job in a company with a CEO who wanted to make things happen.

Chief executives can inadvertently discourage strategic change in many ways. Some of the more dangerous of these traps are:

Seeking False Uniformity. It is unproductive for the CEO of a diversified company to impose artificial uniformity on business-unit goals, organization structure, management activities, rewards, and strategies. This ignores the essential differences among businesses, the importance of clear priorities, and the need to tailor approaches to specific competitive situations.

Trying to Eliminate Risk. In an uncertain world, risk cannot be eliminated, but it can be anticipated and effectively managed. Unfortunately, many chief executives stifle new initiatives by creating the impression that they prefer to avoid risk. This encourages people to assume the role of auditors and fault-finders rather than change catalysts.

Trusting Tradition. Faced with fundamental changes in his major markets, a CEO cannot safely assume that his own line experience still applies. Nor can the chief executive safely neglect to question the validity of the hidden assumptions that underlie the strategic plans he is asked to approve.

Dominating Discussions. As his organization grows in size and diversity, the chief executive is forced to delegate authority. As he does so, his firsthand contact and "feel" for the business fade, and he must largely depend on subordinates for vital information. If he is to maintain open communications with them, he must learn to be comfortable discussing uncertain issues and to encourage executives to pass on the bad news as well as the good.

Delegating Strategy. The CEO must not delude himself that the task of developing strategies can be delegated to his staff. It is true that managers can develop strategies for their individual businesses, but the chief executive still needs to provide a clear and cohesive corporate strategy or vision for the whole organization. While his staff can supply analysis and support, the CEO himself must be intimately involved in developing his overall corporate strategy. Otherwise, he becomes little more than a chief operating officer, leaving the company to face the future on the basis of the collective (and potentially conflicting) strategies of the various business units.

Just as there are dangerous traps for the chief executive, there are also powerful levers that he or she can use to bring about strategic change. First, he should realize that what the organization sees him *do* will carry far more conviction than what it hears him *say*. To awaken and redirect his organization, the CEO has many powerful signals at his disposal. They include guiding the activities of his staff, controlling the allocation of his time, defining a specific vision for the future of the company, and constantly reinforcing this theme in discussions, explanations, and public statements.

STAFF ROLES

The activities of the corporate and group staffs have a major impact on the organization and its attitude toward strategic change.

A staff whose perceived role is to prevent mistakes and point out shortcomings can be a significant deterrent to real strategic management. One long-suffering division president dubbed the headquarters staff in his corporation "the seagulls": they flew in in the morning, he said, strutted around pecking at things, and flew away before sundown, leaving behind a small, distinctive, and unpleasant calling card. A much more positive, productive, and satisfying role for the corporate staff is to contribute substantially to the development of effective business-unit and corporate strategies, serving as direct support to both corporate and business-unit managers in areas of potential need, and focusing on important specific business issues rather than the routine operational matters. In some cases, staffs can serve as "centers of excellence," which contain the corporation's best thinkers on specialized issues of common concern.

Meeting behavior is an important indication of staff roles. Ceremonious, tightly controlled meetings resembling labor-management negotiations are a sure sign of unhealthy staff-line relationship. In some companies, staffs frankly regard it as their role to "make snowballs" for the boss to throw at proposals. Lively, action-oriented meetings, with discussion focused on a joint search for "unshakable facts," indicate that the staff is making a useful contribution.

Clear direction from the chief executive, rotation between line and staff duties, formal training, and clear agreement on the specific roles of the staff can all contribute to a constructive corporate staff environment.

STRATEGICALLY FOCUSED ORGANIZATION

The important link between organization and strategy has long been recognized. Some authorities argue that organization should follow strategy; others, that strategy is inevitably shaped by organizational characteristics and boundaries. For the practical manager, however, the point is that they must be compatible. For example, there is often a strategic advantage in grouping similar businesses. Not only can shared resources frequently be better exploited, but line executives and staffs can be given a much broader field to search for strategic options.

Equally often, however, organizational constraints have discouraged or defeated strategic change. Organizations built on personalities or tradition tend to produce strategies that are parochial or extrapolations of the past. Frequently, organizational change is essential in the diversified company seeking to realize the potential synergies presented by new market or technological opportunities.

TAILORED MANAGEMENT PROCESSES

Line managers tend to take their cues from the way the company sets business objectives, monitors performance, and evaluates and rewards individuals. Failure by the CEO to take into account the motivational effects of these practical signals is likely to make down-the-line managers excessively short-term oriented and cautious in their relations with corporate management.

In setting objectives, the business-unit goals, required resources, and measurement standards should be openly negotiated between corporate management and the business-unit heads, so that business plans become, in effect, contracts between corporate and business-unit management. If top corporate management changes the business unit's performance targets, it must also be willing to revise the resources that will be provided. Likewise, both parties should continue to be concerned about whether the "contract" has been fulfilled.

In many companies, measurement and control systems put a premium on short-term financial performance, thus encouraging what many observers see as the unconscious "harvesting" of U.S. businesses. Equal attention should be given to the achievement of such nonfinancial business objectives as market-share growth, new product development, product quality, and customer satisfaction. Measurement and control systems should measure progress in developing the most important competitive skills, and they should be tailored to fit the business plans and the natural time cycle of the business.

The basis of management evaluation also provides an important signal for strategic change. Middle-level managers in some companies feel that "corporate" evaluates them on their ability to exceed their forecasts, to mask any sign of competitive weakness, and to avoid risks. This naturally fosters a short-term orientation and an unwillingness to take initiatives. It also tends to result in unrealistically conservative financial plans.

Incentives can be a powerful lever for strategic change. A survey of more than 50 major corporations disclosed that inappropriate incentives are regarded as the most common weakness in the entire management system. Natural reluctance to engage in subjective evaluations or explain unpleasant news leads chief executives to rely on short-term-oriented, mathematically based incentives, which in turn lead to a standardized and shortsighted approach to strategy development. Some of the most effective incentive systems, designed around the concept of multiyear planning to achieve both financial and business objectives, clearly allow for differences among business units and their respective managers and different performance periods. Thus, incentives for the aggressive manager of a high-growth business should encourage building for the long term, while the manager of a mature or declining business should be rewarded primarily for maximizing and sustaining near-term performance.

Finally, the incentive system must be well understood by the recipients. Too many chief executives wrongly believe that "our people know where they stand." Unless recipients clearly understand how their individual rewards have been calculated, they will tend to focus on well-known, easily calculable financial criteria (that is, making budget).

SUPPORTIVE CORPORATE VALUES

In virtually every large organization, there is a shared point of view about "who we are, where we are going, and how we will get there." These values, beliefs, or corporate philosophies constitute a set of subtle but powerful levers for strategic change.

Texas Instruments is one of many possible examples of an organization strongly shaped by a set of clearly articulated shared values. In the words of president Fred Bucy: "The image we want is of a high-technology innovator—it's the key to our strategy." In support of this overriding objective, reports *Business Week* (September 18, 1979), "TI stresses a strong spirit of belonging, strong work ethic, competitive zeal, company loyalty, and rational decision making." Working in teams, people are motivated by peer pressure and peer recognition. And top management, to make it clear that ideas are wanted from all TI employees, systematically encourages innovative thinking in a variety of ways.

Corporate values like these, which encourage risk taking, cooperation, substantive analysis, and competitive spirit, enhance the capacity and the readiness of an organization to undergo strategic change. Our research suggests that these shared values are an important factor distinguishing excellent companies from the also-rans.

In total, there are many ways to help an organization accept and successfully carry out strategic change. The challenge for chief executives and planners is to use these levers to bring about a coordinated and effective change program.

ACHIEVING STRATEGIC CHANGE

In any large organization, new goals or a new strategy to achieve existing goals will create anxiety and tension. Managers will be expected to learn new skills, and individual businesses or staffs will gain or lose relative power. Familiar habits are challenged, and the uncertainty of the external world is highlighted.

Organizing and controlling a program of strategic change is a difficult task. However, a study of several successful programs reveals a number of effective basic ways to initiate and guide needed change.

Since early successes are critical to the continued effectiveness of a long-term change program, it is well to begin in areas that offer a high probability of success and relatively fast results. In this way, senior management can create positive reinforcement for the organization and build overall confidence.

Change should be seen as a gradual process. There are few examples of organizations gaining a new leader and immediately undergoing a successful strategic change. Unless there is a real threat to corporate survival, such upheavals should be avoided.

In the process of change, it is very useful to create "heroes" within the organization. An effective chief executive will often single out one or more promising line executives, provide encouragement and support, and highlight how effective their new approaches have been. Within this kind of public re-inforcement, the organization will recognize a new role model.

A program of strategic change requires both top-down direction and bottom-up support. Senior management can point out the need for change and single out key issues, but the creative analysis, support, and implementation must come from the individual business units. Sometimes a vital stimulus can be provided by adding new people with a fresh perspective, through either promotion or outside recruitment.

Once a change program is launched, it is important that the chief executive and his staff members continue to probe deep into the organization to judge the effectiveness of the program and spot needed refinement. Another effective technique is to consciously describe the history of the organization to show that past practices were sensible once but that external conditions now require a new approach. Finally, competitive setbacks or market changes should be exploited to encourage and accelerate change. Under the guidance of senior managers and a staff that is effective at sensing the organization's mood, providing examples, and educating, a program of strategic change can be remarkably effective.

ESSENTIAL ROLES OF CEO AND CPO

One of the most important elements of an effective program of strategic change is a partnership between the chief executive officer and the chief planning officer (CPO). Their roles are complementary. It is the CEO's task to define the corporate vision and to provide personal leadership; in times of strategic change, the organization must be able to look to him as the "Moses" leading it through the wilderness toward a vision that is clear only to a few. Only if he involves himself in the early stages of strategy development will he be able to shape and redirect plans before they become rigid. Early involvement will also give him oppor-tunities to motivate his subordinates to deepen their knowledge and understanding of their businesses.

For his part, the senior planning executive should support the CEO by con-tinuously scanning the corporation and its environment with a view to generating or soliciting new options that can be evaluated and tested. To conserve the chief executive's time and to ensure that it is applied to the areas of greatest strategic leverage, the chief planner must be an effective counselor to the CEO, advising him where and how to influence the organization and helping to shape its attitudes and practices. He has other, equally important roles: monitoring performance against plan and providing direct support to the various business units and the other staffs as they address strategic issues. In a sense, his staff serves as a resource pool for the entire corporation.

Although pace and effectiveness of strategic change cannot be judged in quantitative terms, there are useful criteria by which it may be assessed. Some of the more important hallmarks of progress include the following seven factors:

1. Strategies are principally developed by line managers with direct, constructive support by the staff.
2. Real strategic alternatives are openly discussed at all levels within the corporation.
3. Corporate priorities are relatively clear to senior management but permit flexible response to new opportunities and threats.
4. Corporate resources are allocated based on these priorities and in view of future potential as well as historical performance.
5. The strategic roles of business units are clearly differentiated; so are the performance measures applied to their managers.
6. Realistic responses to likely future events are worked out well in advance.
7. The corporate staff adds real value to the consideration of strategic issues and receives cooperation from most of the divisions.

A coordinated program of change in pursuit of a sound and relevant strategy, under the active direction of the chief executive and the chief planner, can lead to significant progress. While this may only begin a long-term program, it should yield benefits far out of proportion to the time and effort invested.

Effective strategic management will be an essential competitive skill in the 1980s. With limited resources to beat aggressive competitors in shrinking world markets, chief executives will need more effective strategies. Many new planning tools are being developed to encourage more creative and effective strategies; but to achieve the benefits they make possible, chief executives will still have to "make it happen."

What this article is about: Top managers in large organizations develop their major strategies through processes that formal approaches to planning inadequately explain. The dominant patterns in the successful management of strategic change in large organizations are incremental and evolutionary.

1–2 *Managing Strategic Change*

James Brian Quinn

*James Brian Quinn is the William and Josephine Buchanan
Professor of Management at the Amos Tuck School of
Business Administration, Dartmouth College.*

*Just as bad money has always driven out good, so the talented general manager—
the person who makes a company go—is being overwhelmed by a flood of so-
called professionals, textbook executives more interested in the form of management
than the content, more concerned about defining and categorizing and quantifying
the job, than in getting it done. . . . They have created false expectations and
wasted untold man-hours by making a religion of formal long-range planning.*[1]

H. E. Wrapp, *New York Times*

Two previous articles have tried to demonstrate why executives managing strategic change in large organizations should not—and do not—follow highly formalized textbook approaches in long-range planning, goal generation, and strategy formulation.[2] Instead, they artfully blend formal analysis, behavioral techniques,

---

Reprinted from "Managing Strategic Change," by James Brian Quinn, *Sloan Management Review 21,* no. 4. pp. 3–20, by permission of the publisher. Copyright © 1980 by the Sloan Management Review Association. All rights reserved.

[1]See H. E. Wrapp, "A Plague of Professional Managers," *New York Times,* April 8, 1979.

[2]This is the third in a series of articles based upon my study on 10 major corporations' processes for achieving significant strategic change. The other two articles in the series are: J. B. Quinn, "Strategic Goals: Process and Politics," *Sloan Management Review,* Fall 1977, pp. 21–37; and J. B. Quinn, "Strategic Change: 'Logical Incrementalism'," *Sloan Management Review,* Fall 1978, pp. 7–21. The whole study was published as a book entitled *Strategies for Change: Logical Incrementalism* (Homewood, Ill.: Dow Jones-Irwin, 1981). All findings purposely deal only with strategic changes in large organizations.

and power politics to bring about cohesive, step-by-step movement toward ends which initially are broadly conceived, but which are then constantly refined and reshaped as new information appears.[3] Their integrating methodology can best be described as "logical incrementalism."

But is this truly a process in itself, capable of being managed? Or does it simply amount to applied intuition? Are there some conceptual structures, principles, or paradigms that are generally useful? Wrapp, Normann, Braybrooke, Lindblom, and Bennis have provided some macrostructures incorporating many important elements they have observed in strategic change situations.[4] These studies and other contributions cited in this article offer important insights into the management of change in large organizations. But my data suggest that top managers in such enterprises develop their major strategies through processes which neither these studies nor more formal approaches to planning adequately explain. Managers *consciously* and *proactively* move forward *incrementally:*

- To improve the quality of information utilized in corporate strategic decisions.
- To cope with the varying lead times, pacing parameters, and sequencing needs of the "subsystems" through which such decisions tend to be made.
- To deal with the personal resistance and political pressures any important strategic change encounters.
- To build the organizational awareness, understanding, and psychological commitment needed for effective implementation.
- To decrease the uncertainty surrounding such decisions by allowing for interactive learning between the enterprise and its various impinging environments.
- To improve the quality of the strategic decisions themselves by (1) systematically involving those with most specific knowledge, (2) obtaining the participation of those who must carry out the decisions, and (3) avoiding premature momenta or closure which could lead the decision in improper directions.

How does one manage the complex incremental processes which can achieve these goals? The earlier articles structured certain key elements[5]; they will not be repeated here. The following is perhaps the most articulate short statement on how executives proactively manage incrementalism in the development of corporate strategies:

---

[3]See R. M. Cyert and J. G. March, *A Behavioral Theory of the Firm* (Englewood Cliffs, N.J.: Prentice-Hall, 1963), p. 123. Note this learning-feedback-adaptiveness of goals and feasible alternatives over time as organizational learning.

[4]See H. E. Wrapp, "Good Managers Don't Make Policy Decisions," *Harvard Business Review,* September–October 1967, pp. 91–99; R. Normann, *Management for Growth,* trans. N. Adler (New York: John Wiley & Sons, 1977); D. Braybrooke and C. E. Lindblom, *A Strategy of Decision: Policy Evaluation as a Social Process* (New York: Free Press, 1963); C. E. Lindblom, *The Policy-Making Process* (Englewood Cliffs, N.J.: Prentice-Hall, 1968); and W. G. Bennis, *Changing Organizations: Essays on the Development and Evolution of Human Organizations* (New York: McGraw-Hill, 1966).

[5]See, respectively, Quinn, "Strategic Goals," and Quinn, "Strategic Change."

Typically you start with general concerns, vaguely felt. Next you roll an issue around in your mind till you think you have a conclusion that makes sense for the company. You then go out and sort of post the idea without being too wedded to its details. You then start hearing the arguments pro and con, and some very good refinements of the idea usually emerge. Then you pull the idea in and put some resources together to study it so it can be put forward as more of a formal presentation. You wait for "stimuli occurrences" or "crises," and launch pieces of the idea to help in these situations. But they lead toward your ultimate aim. You know where you want to get. You'd like to get there in six months. But it may take three years, or you may not get there. And when you do get there, you don't know whether it was originally your own idea—or somebody else had reached the same conclusion before you and just got you on board for it. You never know. The president would follow the same basic process, but he could drive it much faster than an executive lower in the organization.[6]

Because of the differences in organizational form, management style, or the content of individual decisions, no single paradigm can hold for all strategic decisions.[7] However, very complex strategic decisions in my sample of large organizations tended to evoke certain kinds of broad process steps. These are briefly outlined below. While these process steps occur generally in the order presented, stages are by no means orderly or discrete. Executives do consciously manage individual steps proactively, but it is doubtful that any one person guides a major strategic change sequentially through all the steps. Developing most strategies requires numerous loops back to earlier stages as unexpected issues or new data dictate. Or decision times can become compressed and require short-circuiting leaps forward as crises occur.[8] Nevertheless, certain patterns are clearly dominant in the successful management of strategic change in large organizations.

CREATING AWARENESS AND COMMITMENT—INCREMENTALLY

Although many of the sample companies had elaborate formal environmental scanning procedures, most major strategic issues first emerged in vague or un-defined terms, such as "organizational overlap," "product proliferation," "ex-

---

[6]See J. B. Quinn, *Xerox Corporation (B)* (copyrighted case, Amos Tuck School of Business Administration, Dartmouth College, Hanover, New Hampshire, 1979).

[7]See O. G. Brim, D. Class, et al., *Personality and Decision Processes: Studies in the Social Psychology of Thinking* (Stanford, Calif.: Stanford University Press, 1962).

[8]Crises did occur at some stage in almost all the strategies investigated. However, the study was concerned with the attempt to manage strategic change in an ordinary way. While executives had to deal with precipitating events in this process, crisis management was not—and should not be—the focus of effective strategic management.

cessive exposure in one market," or "lack of focus and motivation."[9] Some appeared as "inconsistencies" in internal action patterns or "anomalies" between the enterprise's current posture and some perception of its future environment.[10] Early signals may come from anywhere and may be difficult to distinguish from the background "noise" or ordinary communications. Crises, of course, announce themselves with strident urgency in operations control systems. But, if organizations wait until signals reach amplitudes high enough to be sensed by formal measurement systems, smooth, efficient transitions may be impossible.[11]

Need Sensing: Leading the Formal Information System

Effective change managers actively develop informal networks to get objective information—from other staff and line executives, workers, customers, board members, suppliers, politicians, technologists, educators, outside professionals, government groups, and so on—to sense possible needs for change. They purposely use these networks to short-circuit all the careful screens[12] their organizations build up to "tell the top only what it wants to hear." For example:

> Peter McColough, chairman and CEO of Xerox, was active in many high-level political and charitable activities—from treasurer of the Democratic National Committee to chairman of the Urban League. In addition, he said, "I've tried to decentralize decision making. If something bothers me, I don't rely on reports or what other executives may want to tell me. I'll go down very deep into the organization, to certain issues and people, so I'll have a feeling for what they think." He refused to let his life be run by letters and memos. "Because I came up by that route, I know what a salesman can say. I also know that before I see [memos] they go through 15 hands, and I know what that can do to them."[13]

---

[9]For some formal approaches and philosophies for environmental scanning, see W. D. Guth, "Formulating Organizational Objectives and Strategy: A Systematic Approach," *Journal of Business Policy,* Autumn 1971, pp. 24–31; and F. J. Aguilar, *Scanning the Business Environment* (New York: Macmillan, 1967). For confirmation of the early vagueness and ambiguity in problem form and identification, see H. Mintzberg, D. Raisinghani, and A. Theoret, "The Structure of 'Unstructured' Decision Processes," *Administrative Science Quarterly,* June 1976, pp. 246–75.

[10]For a discussion of various types of "misfits" between the organization and its environment as a basis for problem identification, see Normann, *Management for Growth,* p. 19.

[11]For suggestions on why organizations engage in "problem search" patterns, see R. M. Cyert, H. A. Simon, and D. B. Trow, "Observation of a Business Decision," *Journal of Business,* October 1956, pp. 237–48; for the problem of timing in transitions, see L. R. Sayles, *Managerial Behavior: Administration in Complex Organizations* (New York: McGraw-Hill, 1964).

[12]For a classic view of how these screens operate, see C. Argyris, "Double Loop Learning in Organizations," *Harvard Business Review,* September–October 1977, pp. 115–25.

[13]See Quinn, *Xerox Corporation (B).*

To avoid undercutting intermediate managers, such bypassing has to be limited to information gathering, with no implication that orders or approvals are given to lower levels. Properly handled, this practice actually improves formal communications and motivational systems as well. Line managers are less tempted to screen information and lower levels are flattered to be able "to talk about the very top." Since people sift signals about threats and opportunities through perceptual screens defined by their own values, careful executives make sure their sensing networks include people who look at the world very differently than do those in the enterprise's dominating culture. Effective executives consciously seek options and threat signals beyond the status quo. "If I'm not two to three years ahead of my organization, I'm not doing my job" was a common comment of such executives in the example.

In some cases executives quickly perceive the broad dimension of needed change. But they still may seek amplifying data, wider executive understanding of issues, or greater organizational support before initiating action. Far from accepting the first satisfactory (satisficing) solution—as some have suggested they do—successful managers seem to consciously generate and consider a broad array of alternatives.[14] Why? They want to stimulate and choose from the most creative solutions offered by the best minds in their organizations. They wish to have colleagues knowledgeable enough about issues to help them think through all the ramifications. They seek data and arguments sufficiently strong to dislodge preconceived ideas or blindly followed past practices. They do not want to be the prime supporters of losing ideas or to have their organizations slavishly adopt "the boss's solution." Nor do they want—through announcing decisions too early—to prematurely threaten existing power centers which could kill any changes aborning.

Even when executives do not have in mind specific solutions to emerging problems, they can still proactively guide actions in intuitively desired directions—by defining what issues staffs should investigate, by selecting principal investigators, and by controlling reporting processes. They can selectively "tap the collective wit" of their organizations, generating more awareness of critical issues and forcing initial thinking down to lower levels to achieve greater involvement. Yet they can also avoid irreconcilable opposition, emotional overcommitment,[15] or organizational momenta beyond their control by regarding all proposals as "strictly advisory" at this early stage.

As issues are clarified and options are narrowed, executives may systematically alert ever wider audiences. They may first "shop" key ideas among trusted

---

[14]Cyert and March, *Behavioral Theory of the Firm*, suggest that executives choose from a number of satisfactory solutions; later observers suggest they choose the first truly satisfactory solution discovered.

[15]See F. F. Gilmore, "Overcoming the Perils of Advocacy in Corporate Planning," *California Management Review*, Spring 1973, pp. 127–37.

colleagues to test responses. Then they may commission a few studies to illuminate emerging alternatives, contingencies, or opportunities. But key players might still not be ready to change their past action patterns or even be able to investigate options creatively. Only when persuasive data are in hand and enough people are alerted and "on board" to make a particular solution work might key executives finally commit themselves to it. Building awareness, concern, and interest to attention-getting levels is often a vital—and slowly achieved—step in the process of managing basic changes. For example:

> In the early 1970s there was still a glut in world oil supplies. Nevertheless, analysts in the General Motors Chief Economist's Office began to project a developing U.S. dependency on foreign oil and the likelihood of higher future oil prices. These concerns led the board in 1972 to create an ad hoc energy task force headed by David C. Collier, then treasurer, later head of GM of Canada and then of the Buick Division. Collier's group included people from manufacturing, research, design, finance, industry-government relations, and the economics staff. After six months of research, in May of 1973 the task force went to the board with three conclusions: (1) there was a developing energy problem; (2) the government had no particular plan to deal with it; (3) energy costs would have a profound effect on GM's business. Collier's report created a good deal of discussion around the company in the ensuing months. "We were trying to get other people to think about the issue," said Richard C. Gerstenberg, then chairman of GM.[16]

Changing Symbols: Building Credibility

As awareness of the need for change grows, managers often want to signal the organization that certain types of changes are coming, even if specific solutions are not in hand. Knowing they cannot communicate directly with the thousands who could carry out the strategy, some executives purposely undertake highly visible actions which wordlessly convey complex messages that could never be communicated as well—or as credibly—in verbal terms.[17] Some use symbolic moves to preview or verify intended changes in direction. At other times, such moves confirm the intention of top management to back a thrust already partially begun—as Mr. McColough's relocation of Xerox headquarters to Connecticut (away from the company's Rochester reprographics base) underscored the company's developing commitment to product diversification, organizational decentralization, and international operations. Organizations often need such symbolic moves—or decisions they regard as symbolic—to build credibility behind a new

---

[16]See J. B. Quinn, *General Motors Corporation: The Downsizing Decision* (copyrighted case, Amos Tuck School of Business Administration, Dartmouth College, Hanover, New Hampshire, 1978).

[17]See E. Rhenman, *Organization Theory for Long-Range Planning* (New York: John Wiley & Sons, 1973), p. 63. Here the author notes a similar phenomenon.

strategy. Without such actions even forceful verbiage might be interpreted as mere rhetoric. For example:

> In GM's downsizing, engineers said that one of top management's early decisions affected the credibility of the whole weight-reduction program. "Initially, we proposed a program using a lot of aluminum and substitute materials to meet the new 'mass' targets. But this would have meant a very high cost, and would have strained the suppliers' aluminum capacity. However, when we presented this program to management, they said, 'Ok, if necessary, we'll do it.' They didn't back down. We began to understand then that they were dead serious. Feeling that the company would spend the money was critical to the success of the entire mass-reduction effort."[18]

Legitimizing New Viewpoints

Often before reaching specific strategic decisions, it is necessary to legitimize new options which have been acknowledged as possibilities, but which still entail an undue aura of uncertainty or concern. Because of their familiarity, older options are usually perceived as having lower risks (or potential costs) than newer alternatives. Therefore, top managers seeking change often consciously create forums and allow slack time for their organizations to talk through threatening issues, work out the implications of new solutions, or gain an improved information base that will permit new options to be evaluated objectively in comparison with more familiar alternatives.[19] In many cases, strategic concepts which are at first strongly resisted gain acceptance and support simply by the passage of time, if executives do not exacerbate hostility by pushing them too fast from the top. For example:

> When Joe Wilson thought Haloid Corporation should change its name to include Xerox, he first submitted a memorandum asking colleagues what they thought of the idea. They rejected it. Wilson then explained his concerns more fully, and his executives rejected the idea again. Finally, Wilson formed a committee headed by Sol Linowitz, who had thought a separate Xerox subsidiary might be the best solution. As this committee deliberated, negotiations were under way with the Rank Organizations and the term Rank-Xerox was commonly heard and Haloid-Xerox no longer seemed so strange. "And so," according to John Dessauer, "a six-month delay having diluted most opposition, we of the committee agreed that the change to Haloid-Xerox might in the long run produce sound advantages."[20]

---

[18]See Quinn, *General Motors Corporation.*

[19]See R. M. Cyert, W. R. Dill, and J. G. March, "The Role of Expectations in Business Decision Making," *Administrative Science Quarterly,* December 1958, pp. 307–40. The authors point out the perils of top management advocacy because existing policies may unconsciously bias information to support views they value.

[20]See J. H. Dessauer, *My Years with Xerox: The Billions Nobody Wanted* (Garden City, N.Y.: Doubleday, 1971).

Many top executives consciously plan for such "gestation periods" and often find that the strategic concept itself is made more effective by the resulting feedback.

Tactical Shifts and Partial Solutions

At this stage in the process, guiding executives might share a fairly clear vision of the general directions for the movement. But rarely does a total new corporate posture emerge full grown—like Minerva from the brow of Jupiter—from any one source. Instead, early resolutions are likely to be partial, tentative, or experimental.[21] Beginning moves often appear as mere tactical adjustments in the enterprise's existing posture. As such, they encounter little opposition, yet each partial solution adds momentum in new directions. Guiding executives try carefully to maintain the enterprise's ongoing strengths while shifting its total posture incrementally—at the margin—toward new needs. Such executives themselves might not yet perceive the full nature of the strategic shifts they have begun. They can still experiment with partial new approaches and learn without risking the viability of the total enterprise. Their broad early steps can still legitimately lead to a variety of different success scenarios. Yet logic might dictate that they wait before committing themselves to a total new strategy.[22] As events unfurl, solutions to several interrelated problems might well flow together in a not-yet-perceived synthesis. For example:

> In the early 1970s at General Motors there was a distinct awareness of a developing fuel economy ethic. General Motors executives said, "Our conclusions were really at the conversational level—that the big car trend was at an end. But we were not at all sure sufficient numbers of large car buyers were ready to move to dramatically lighter cars." Nevertheless, GM did start concept studies that resulted in the Cadillac Seville.
>
> When the oil crisis hit in fall 1973, the company responded in further increments, at first merely increasing production of its existing small car lines. Then as the crisis deepened, it added another partial solution, the subcompact "T car"—the Chevette—and accelerated the Seville's development cycle. Next, as fuel economy appeared more salable, executives set an initial target of removing 400 pounds from B–C bodies by 1977. As fuel economy pressures persisted and engineering feasibilities offered greater confidence, this target was increased to 800–1,000 pounds (three mpg). No step by itself shifted the company's total strategic posture until the full downsizing of all lines was announced. But each partial solution built confidence and commitment toward a new direction.

---

[21]See H. Mintzberg, *The Nature of Managerial Work* (New York: Harper & Row, 1973). Note that this "vision" is not necessarily the beginning point of the process. Instead it emerges as new data and viewpoints interact; Normann, *Management for Growth.*

[22]See Mintzberg, Raisinghani, and Theoret, "Structure of Unstructured Decision Process." Here the authors liken the process to a decision tree where decisions at each node become more narrow, with failure at any node allowing recycling back to the broader tree trunk.

Broadening Political Support

Often these broad emerging strategic thrusts need expanded political support and understanding to achieve sufficient momentum to survive.[23] Committees, task forces, and retreats tend to be favored mechanisms for accomplishing this. If carefully managed, they do not become the "garbage cans" of emerging ideas, as some observers have noted.[24] By selecting the committee's chairman, membership, timing, and agenda, guiding executives can largely influence and predict a desired outcome, and can force other executives toward a consensus. Such groups can be balanced to educate, evaluate, neutralize, or overwhelm opponents. They can be used to legitimize new options or to generate broad cohesion among diverse thrusts, or they can be narrowly focused to build momentum. Guiding executives can constantly maintain complete control over these "advisory processes" through their various influences and veto potentials. For example:

> IBM's Chairman Watson and Executive Vice President Larson had become concerned over what to do about: third-generation computer technology, a proliferation of designs from various divisions, increasing costs of developing software, internal competition among their lines, and the needed breadth of line for the new computer applications they began to foresee. Step by step, they oversaw the killing of the company's huge Stretch computer line (uneconomic), a proposed 8000 series of computers (incompatible software), and the prototype English Scamp computer (duplicative). They then initiated a series of "strategic dialogues" with divisional executives to define a new strategy. But none came into place because of the parochial nature of divisional viewpoints.
>
> Larson, therefore, set up the SPREAD Committee, representing every major segment of the company. Its 12 members included the most likely opponent of an integrated line (Haanstra), the people who had earlier suggested the 8000 and Scamp designs, and Learson's handpicked lieutenant (Evans). When progress became "hellishly slow," Haanstra was removed as chairman and Evans took over. Eventually the committee came forth with an integrating proposal for a single compatible line of computers to blanket and open up the market for both scientific and business applications, with "standard interface" for peripheral equipment. At an all-day meeting of the 50 top executives of the company, the report was not received with enthusiasm, but there were no compelling objections. So Larson blessed the silence as consensus saying, "OK, we'll do it"—i.e., go ahead with a major development program.[25]

---

[23]Wrapp, "Good Managers Don't Make Policy Decisions," notes that a conditioning process that may stretch over months or years is necessary in order to prepare the organization for radical departures from what it is already striving to attain.

[24]See J. G. March, J. P. Olsen, S. Christensen, et al., *Ambiguity and Choice in Organizations* (Bergen, Norway: Universitetsforlaget, 1976).

[25]See T. A. Wise, "I.B.M.'s $5 Billion Gamble," *Fortune,* September 1966, pp. 118–24; and T. A. Wise, "The Rocky Road to the Marketplace," part 2: "I.B.M.'s $5 Billion Gamble," *Fortune,* October 1966, pp. 138–52.

In addition to facilitating smooth implementation, many managers reported that interactive consensus-building processes also improve the quality of the strategic decisions themselves and help achieve positive and innovative assistance when things otherwise could go wrong.

Overcoming Opposition: "Zones of Indifference" and "No Lose" Situations

Executives of basically healthy companies in the sample realized that any attempt to introduce a new strategy would have to deal with the support its predecessor had. Barring a major crisis, a frontal attack on an old strategy could be regarded as an attack on those who espoused it—perhaps properly—and brought the enterprise to its present levels of success. There often exists a variety of legitimate views on what could and should be done in the new circumstances that a company faces. And wise executives do not want to alienate people who would otherwise be supporters. Consequently, they try to get key people behind their concepts whenever possible, to co-opt or neutralize serious opposition if necessary, or to find "zones of indifference" where the proposition would not be disastrously opposed.[26] Most of all they see "no lose" situations which will motivate all the important players toward a common goal. For example:

> When James McFarland took over at General Mills from his power base in the Grocery Products Division, another serious contender for the top spot had been Louis B. "Bo" Polk, a very bright, aggressive young man who headed the corporation's acquisition-diversification program. Both traditional lines and acquisitions groups wanted support for their activities and had high-level supporters. McFarland's corporatewide "goodness to greatness" conferences . . . first obtained broad agreement on growth goals and criteria for all areas.
>
> Out of this and the related acquisition proposal process came two thrusts: (1) to expand—internally and through acquisitions—in food-related sectors and (2) to acquire new growth centers based on General Mills' marketing skills. Although there was no formal statement, there was a strong feeling that the majority of resources should be used in food-related areas. But neither group was foreclosed, and no one could suggest the new management was vindictive. As it turned out, over the next five years about $450 million was invested in new businesses, and the majority were not closely related to foods.

---

[26]For an excellent overview of the process of co-optation and neutralization, see Sayles, *Managerial Behavior*. For perhaps the first reference to the concept of the "zone of indifference," see C. I. Barnard, *The Functions of the Executive* (Cambridge, Mass.: Harvard University Press, 1938). The following two sources note the need of executives for coalition behavior to reduce the organizational conflict resulting from differing interests and goal preferences in large organizations: Cyert and March, *Behavioral Theory of the Firm;* and J. G. March, "Business Decision Making," in *Readings in Managerial Psychology,* ed. H. J. Leavitt and L. R. Pondy (Chicago: University of Chicago Press, 1964).

But such tactics do not always work. Successful executives surveyed tended to honor legitimate differences in viewpoints and noted that initial opponents often shaped new strategies in more effective directions and became supporters as new information became available. But strong-minded executives sometimes disagreed to the point where they had to be moved or stimulated to leave; timing could dictate very firm top-level decisions at key junctions. Barring crises, however, disciplinary steps usually occurred incrementally as individual executives' attitudes and competencies emerged vis-à-vis a new strategy.

Structuring Flexibility: Buffers, Slacks, and Activists

Typically there are too many uncertainties in the total environment for managers to program or control all the events involved in effecting a major change in strategic direction. Logic dictates, therefore, that managers purposely design flexibility into their organizations and have resources ready to deploy incrementally as events demand. Planned flexibility requires: (1) proactive horizon scanning to identify the general nature and potential impact of opportunities and threats the firm is most likely to encounter, (2) creating sufficient resource buffers—or slacks—to respond effectively as events actually unfurl, (3) developing and positioning "credible activities" with a psychological commitment to move quickly and flexibly to exploit specific opportunities as they occur, and (4) shortening decision lines from such people (and key operating managers) to the top for the most rapid system response. These—rather than precapsuled (and shelved) programs to respond to stimuli which never quite occur as expected—are the keys to real contingency planning.

The concept of resource buffers requires special amplification. Quick access to resources is needed to cushion the impact of random events, to offset opponents' sudden attacks, or to build momentum for new strategic shifts. Some examples will indicate the form these buffers may take.

> For critical purchased items, General Motors maintained at least three suppliers, each with sufficient capacity to expand production should one of the others encounter a catastrophe. Thus, the company had expandable capacity with no fixed investment. Exxon set up its Exploration Group to purposely undertake the higher risks and longer-term investments necessary to search for oil in new areas, and thus to reduce the potential impact on Exxon if there were sudden unpredictable changes in the availability of Middle East oil. Instead of hoarding cash, Pillsbury and General Mills sold off unprofitable businesses and cleaned up their financial statements to improve their access to external capital sources for acquisitions. Such access in essence provided the protection of a cash buffer without its investment. IBM's large R&D facility and its project team approach to development assured that it had a pool of people it could quickly shift among various projects to exploit interesting new technologies.

When such flexible response patterns are designed into the enterprise's strategy, it is proactively ready to move on those thrusts—acquisitions, innovations, or resource explorations—which require incrementalism.

Systematic Waiting and Trial Concepts

The prepared strategist may have to wait for events, as Roosevelt awaited a trauma like Pearl Harbor. The availability of desired acquisitions or real estate might depend on a death, divorce, fiscal crisis, management change, or an erratic stock market break.[27] Technological advances may have to await new knowledge, inventions, or lucky accidents. Despite otherwise complete preparations, a planned market entry might not be wise until new legislation, trade agreements, or competitive shakeouts occur. Organizational moves have to be timed to retirements, promotions, management failures, and so on. Very often the specific strategy adopted depends on the timing or sequence of such random events.[28] For example:

> Although Continental Group's top executives had thoroughly discussed and investigated energy, natural resources, and insurance as possible "fourth legs" for the company, the major acquisition possibilities were so different that the strategic choice depended on the fit of particular candidates—e.g., Peabody Coal or Richmond Insurance—within these possible industries. The choice of one industry would have precluded the others. The sequence in which firms became available affected the final choice, and that choice itself greatly influenced the whole strategic posture of the company.

In many of the cases studied, strategists proactively launched trial concepts— Mr. McColough's "architecture of information" (Xerox), Mr. Spoor's "Super Box" (Pillsbury)—in order to generate options and concrete proposals. Usually these "trial balloons" were phrases in very broad terms. Without making a commitment to any specific solution, the executive can activate the organization's creative abilities. This approach keeps the manager's own options open until substantive alternatives can be evaluated against each other and against concrete current realities. It prevents practical line managers from rejecting a strategic shift, as they might if forced to compare a "paper option" against well-defined current needs. Such trial concepts give cohesion to the new strategy while enabling the company to take maximum advantage of the psychological and informational benefits to incrementalism.

SOLIDIFYING PROGRESS—INCREMENTALLY

As events move forward, executives can more clearly perceive the specific directions in which their organizations should—and realistically can—move. They can seek more aggressive movement and commitment to their new perceptions, without undermining important ongoing activities or creating unnec-

---

[27]Cyert and March, *Behavioral Theory of the Firm*, also note that not only do organizations seek alternatives but that "alternatives seek organizations" (as when finders, scientists, bankers, etc., bring in new solutions).

[28]See March, Olsen, Christensen, et al., *Ambiguity and Choice in Organizations*.

essary reactions to their purposes. Until this point, new strategic goals might remain broad, relatively unrefined, or even unstated except as philosophic concepts. More specific dimensions might be incrementally announced as key pieces of information fall into place, specific unanswered issues approach resolution, or significant resources have to be formally committed.

Creating Pockets of Commitment

Early in this stage, guiding executives may need to actively implant support in the organization for new thrusts. They may encourage an array of exploratory projects for each of several possible options. Initial projects can be kept small, partial, or ad hoc, neither forming a comprehensive program nor seeming to be integrated into a cohesive strategy. Executives often provide stimulating goals, a proper climate for imaginative proposals, and flexible resource support, rather than being personally identified with specific projects. In this way they can achieve organizational involvement and early commitment without focusing attention on any one solution too soon or losing personal credibility if it fails.

Once under way, project teams on the more successful programs in the sample became ever more committed to their particular areas of exploration. They became pockets of support for new strategies deep within the organization. Yet, if necessary, top managers could delay until the last moment their final decisions blending individual projects into a total strategy. Thus, they were able to obtain the best possible match among the company's technical abilities, its psychological commitments, and its changing market needs. By making final choices more effectively—as late as possible with better data, more conscientiously investigated options, and the expert critiques competitive projects allowed—these executives actually increased technical and market efficiencies of their enterprises, despite the apparent added costs of parallel efforts.[29]

In order to maintain their own objectivity and future flexibility, some executives choose to keep their own political profiles low as they build a new consensus. If they seem committed to a strategy too soon, they might discourage others from pursuing key issues which should be raised.[30] By stimulating detailed investigations several levels down, top executives can seem detached yet still shape both progress and ultimate outcomes—by reviewing interim results and specifying the timing, format, and forums for the release of data. When reports come forward, these executives can stand above the battle and review proposals

---

[29]Much of the rationale for this approach is contained in J. B. Quinn, "Technological Innovation, Entrepreneurship, and Strategy," *Sloan Management Review,* Spring 1979, pp. 19–30.

[30]See C. Argyris, "Interpersonal Barriers to Decision Making," *Harvard Business Review,* March–April 1966, pp. 84–97. The author notes that when the president introduced major decisions from the top, discussion was "less than open" and commitment was "less than complete," although executives might assure the president to the contrary.

objectively, without being personally on the defensive for having committed themselves to a particular solution too soon. From this position they can more easily orchestrate a high-level consensus on a new strategic thrust. As an added benefit, negative decisions on proposals often come from a group consensus that top executives can simply confirm to lower levels, thereby preserving their personal veto for more crucial moments. In many well-made decisions people at all levels contribute to the generation, amplification, and interpretation of options and information to the extent that it is often difficult to say who really makes the decision.[31]

Focusing the Organization

In spite of their apparent detachment, top executives do focus their organizations on developing strategies at critical points in the process. While adhering to the rhetoric of specific goal setting, most executives are careful *not* to state new goals in concrete terms before they have built a consensus among key players. They fear that they will prematurely centralize the organization, preempt interesting options, provide a common focus for otherwise fragmented opposition, or cause the organization to act prematurely to carry out a specified commitment. Guiding executives may quietly shape the many alternatives flowing upward by using what Wrapp refers to as "a hidden hand." Through their information networks they can encourage concepts they favor, let weakly supported options die through inaction, and establish hurdles or tests for strongly supported ideas with which they do not agree but which they do not wish to oppose openly.

Since opportunities for such focusing generally develop unexpectedly, the timing of key moves is often unpredictable. A crisis, a rash of reassignments, a reorganization, or a key appointment may allow an executive to focus attention on particular thrusts, add momentum to some, and perhaps quietly phase out others.[32] Most managers surveyed seemed well aware of the notion that "if there are no other options, mine wins." Without being Machiavellian, they did not want misdirected options to gain strong political momentum and later have to be terminated in an open bloodbath. They also did not want to send false signals that stimulated other segments of their organizations to make proposals in undesirable directions. They sensed very clearly that the patterns in which proposals are approved or denied will inevitably be perceived by lower echelons as precedents for developing future goals or policies.

---

[31]See March, "Business Decision Making."

[32]The process tends to be one of eliminating the less feasible rather than of determining a target or objectives. The process typically reduces the number of alternatives through successive limited comparisons to a point where understood analytical techniques can apply and the organization structure can function to make a choice. See Cyert and March, *Behavioral Theory of the Firm*.

Managing Coalitions

Power interactions among key players are important at this stage of solidifying progress. Each player has a different level of power determined by his or her information base, organizational position, and personal credibility.[33] Executives legitimately perceive problems or opportunities differently because of their particular values, experiences, and vantage points. They will promote the solutions they perceive as the best compromise for the total enterprise, for themselves, and for their particular units. In an organization with dispersed power, the key figure is the one who can manage coalitions.[34] Since no one player has all the power, regardless of that individual's skill or position, the action that occurs over time might differ greatly from the intentions of any of the players.[35] Top executives try to sense whether support exists among important parties for specific aspects of an issue and try to get partial decisions and momenta going for those aspects. As "comfort levels" or political pressures within the top group rise in favor of specific decisions, the guiding executive might, within his or her concept of a more complete solution, seek—among the various features of different proposals—a balance that the most influential and credible parties can actively support. The result tends to be a stream of partial decisions on limited strategic issues made by constantly changing coalitions of the critical power centers.[36] These decisions steadily evolve toward a broader consensus, acceptable to both the top executive and some "dominant coalition" among these centers.

As a partial consensus emerges, top executives might crystallize issues by stating some broad goals in more specific terms for internal consumption. Finally, when sufficient general acceptance exists and the timing is right, the goals may begin to appear in more public announcements. For example:

> As General Mills divested several of its major divisions in the early 1960s, its annual reports began to refer to these as deliberate moves "to concentrate on the company's strengths" and "to intensify General Mills' efforts in the convenience foods field."

---

[33]For more detailed relationships between authority and power, see H. C. Metcalf and L. Urwick, eds., *Dynamic Administration: The Collected Papers of Mary Parker Follett* (New York: Harper & Row, 1941); and A. Zalenik, "Power and Politics in Organizational Life," *Harvard Business Review*, May–June 1970, pp. 47–60.

[34]See J. D. Thompson, "The Control of Complex Organizations," in *Organizations in Action* (New York: McGraw-Hill, 1967).

[35]See G. T. Allison, *Essence of Decision: Explaining the Cuban Missile Crisis* (Boston: Little, Brown, 1971).

[36]See C. E. Lindblom, "The Science of 'Muddling Through,'" *Public Administration Review*, Spring 1959, pp. 79–88. The author notes that the relative weights individuals give to values and the intensity of their feelings will vary sequentially from decision to decision; hence the dominant coalition itself varies with each decision somewhat.

Such statements could not have been made until many of the actual divestitures were completed and a sufficient consensus existed among the top executives to support the new corporate concept.

Formalizing Commitment by Empowering Champions

As each major strategic thrust comes into focus, top executives try to ensure that some individual or group feels responsible for its goals. If the thrust will project the enterprise in entirely new directions, executives often want more than mere accountability for its success—they want real commitment.[37] A significantly new major thrust, concept, product, or problem solution frequently needs the nurturing hand of someone who genuinely identifies with it and whose future depends on its success. For example:

> Once the divestiture program at General Mills was sufficiently under way, General Rawlings selected young "Bo" Polk to head up an acquisition program to use the cash generated. In this role Polk had nothing to lose. With strong senior management in the remaining consumer products divisions, the ambitious Polk would have had a long road to the top there. In acquisitions, he provided a small political target, only a $50,000 budget in a $500 million company. Yet he had high visibility and could build his own power base, if he were successful. With direct access to and the support of Rawlings, he would be protected through his early ventures. All he had to do was make sure his first few acquisitions were successful. As subsequent acquisitions succeeded, his power base could feed on itself—satisfying both Polk's ego needs and the company's strategic goals.

In some cases, top executives have to wait for champions to appear before committing resources to risky new strategies. They may immediately assign accountability for less dramatic plans by converting them into new missions for ongoing groups.

From this point on, the strategy process is familiar. The organization's formal structure has to be adjusted to support the strategy.[38] Commitment to the most important new thrusts has to be confirmed in formal plans. Detailed budgets, programs, controls, and reward systems have to reflect all planned strategic thrusts. Finally, the guiding executive has to see that recruiting and staffing plans are aligned with the new goals and that—when the situation permits—supporters and persistent opponents of intended new thrusts are assigned to appropriate positions.

---

[37]Zalenik, "Power and Politics in Organizational Life," notes that confusing compliance with commitment is one of the most common and difficult problems of strategic implementation. He notes that often organizational commitment may override personal interest if the former is developed carefully.

[38]See A. D. Chandler, *Strategy and Structure: Chapters in the History of the Industrial Enterprise* (Cambridge, Mass.: MIT Press, 1962).

Continuing the Dynamics by Eroding Consensus

The major strategic changes studied tended to take many years to accomplish. The process was continuous, often without any clear beginning or end.[39] The decision process constantly molded and modified management's concerns and concepts. Radical crusades became the new conventional wisdom, and over time totally new issues emerged. Participants or observers were often not aware of exactly when a particular decision had been made[40] or when a subsequent consensus was created to supersede or modify it; the process of strategic change was continuous and dynamic. Several GM executives described the frequently imperceptible[41] way in which many strategic decisions evolved:

> We use an iterative process to make a series of tentative decisions on the way we think the market will go. As we get more data we modify these continuously. It is often difficult to say who decided something and when—or even who originated a decision. . . . Strategy really evolves as a series of incremental steps. . . . I frequently don't know when a decision is made in General Motors. I don't remember being in a committee meeting when things came to a vote. Usually someone will simply summarize a developing position. Everyone else either nods or states his particular terms of consensus.

A major strategic change in Xerox was characterized this way:

> How was the overall organization decision made? I've often heard it said that after talking with a lot of people and having trouble with a number of decisions which were pending, Archie McCardell really reached his own conclusion and got Peter Mc-Colough's backing on it. But it really didn't happen quite that way. It was an absolutely evolutionary approach. It was a growing feeling. A number of people felt we ought to be moving toward some kind of matrix organization. We have always been a pretty democratic type of organization. In our culture you can't come down with mandates or ultimatums from the top on major changes like this. You almost have to work these things through and let them grow and evolve, keep them on the table so people are thinking about them and talking about them.

Once the organization arrives at its new consensus, the guiding executive has to move immediately to ensure that this new position does not become inflexible. In trying to build commitment to a new concept, individual executives often surround themselves with people who see the world in the same way. Such people can rapidly become systematic screens against other views. Effective executives therefore purposely continue the change process, constantly intro-

---

[39]See K. J. Cohen and R. M. Cyert, "Strategy: Formulation, Implementation, and Monitoring," *Journal of Business,* July 1973, pp. 349–67.

[40]March, "Business Decision Making," notes that major decisions are "processes of gradual commitment."

[41]Sayles, *Managerial Behavior,* notes that such decisions are a "flow process," with no one person every really making the decisions.

ducing new faces and stimuli at the top. They consciously begin to erode the very strategic thrusts they may have just created—a very difficult, but essential, psychological task.

INTEGRATION OF PROCESSES AND OF INTERESTS

In the large enterprises observed, strategy formulation was a continuously evolving analytical-political consensus process with neither a finite beginning nor a definite end. It generally followed the sequence described above. Yet the total process was anything but linear. It was a grouping, cyclical process that often circled back on itself, with frequent interruptions and delays. Pfiffner aptly describes the process of strategy formation as being "like fermentation in biochemistry, rather than an industrial assembly line."[42]

Such incremental management processes are not abrogations of good management practice. Nor are they Machiavellian or consciously manipulative maneuvers. Instead, they represent an adaptation to the practical psychological and informational problems of getting a constantly changing group of people with diverse talents and interests to move together effectively in a continually dynamic environment. Much of the impelling force behind logical incrementalism comes from a desire to tap the talents and psychological drives of the whole organization, to create cohesion, and to generate identity with the emerging strategy. The remainder of that force results from the interactive nature of the random factors and lead times affecting the independent subsystems that compose any total strategy.

An Incremental—Not Piecemeal—Process

The total pattern of action, though highly incremental, is not piecemeal in well-managed organizations. It requires constant, conscious reassessment of the total organization, its capacities, and its needs as related to surrounding environments. It requires continual attempts by top managers to integrate these actions into an understandable, cohesive whole. How do top managers themselves describe the process? Mr. Estes, president of General Motors, said:

> We try to give them the broad concepts we are trying to achieve. We operate through questioning and fact gathering. Strategy is a state of mind you go through. When you think about a little problem, your mind begins to think how it will affect all the different elements in the total situation. Once you have had all the jobs you need to qualify for this position, you can see the problem from a variety of viewpoints. But you don't try

---

[42]See J. M. Pfiffner, "Administrative Rationality," *Public Administration Review,* Summer 1960, pp. 125–32.

to ram your conclusions down people's throats. You try to persuade people what has to be done and provide confidence and leadership for them.

Formal-Analytical Techniques.   At each stage of strategy development, effective executives constantly try to visualize the new patterns that might exist among the emerging strategies of various subsystems. As each subsystem strategy becomes more apparent, both its executive team and top-level groups try to project its implications for the total enterprise and to stimulate queries, support, and feedback from those involved in related strategies. Perceptive top executives see that the various teams generating subsystem strategies have overlapping members. They require periodic updates and reviews before higher-echelon groups that can bring a total corporate view to bear. They use formal planning processes to interrelate and evaluate the resources required, benefits sought, and risks undertaken vis-à-vis other elements of the enterprise's overall strategy. Some use scenario techniques to help visualize potential impacts and relationships. Others utilize complex forecasting models to better understand the basic interactions among subsystems, the total enterprise, and the environment. Still others use specialized staffs, "devil's advocates" or "contention teams" to make sure that all important aspects of their strategies receive a thorough evaluation.

Power-Behavioral Aspects: Coalition Management.   All of the formal methodologies help, but the real integration of all the components in an enterprise's total strategy eventually takes place only in the minds of high-level executives. Each executive may legitimately perceive the intended balance of goals and thrusts differently. Some of these differences may be openly expressed as issues to be resolved when new information becomes available. Some differences may remain unstated—hidden agendas to emerge at later dates. Others may be masked by accepting so broad a statement of intention that many different views are included in a seeming consensus, when a more specific statement might be divisive. Nevertheless, effective strategies do achieve a level of understanding and consensus sufficient to focus action.

Top executives deliberately manage the incremental processes within each subsystem to create the basis for consensus. They also manage the coalitions that lie at the heart of most controlled strategy developments.[43] They recognize that they are at the confluence of innumerable pressures—from stockholders, environmentalists, government bodies, customers, suppliers, distributors, producing units, marketing groups, technologists, unions, special-issue activists, individual employees, ambitious executives, and so on—and that knowledgeable people of goodwill can easily disagree on proper actions. In response to changing pressures and coalitions among these groups, the top management team constantly forms and reforms its own coalitions on various decisions.[44]

[43]See R. James, "Corporate Strategy and Change—The Management of People" (monograph, University of Chicago, 1978). The author does an excellent job of pulling together the threads of coalition management at top organizational levels.

[44]See Cyert and March, *Behavioral Theory of the Firm,* p. 115.

Most major strategic moves tend to assist some interests—and executives' careers—at the expense of others. Consequently, each set of interests serves as a check on the others and thus helps maintain the breadth and balance of strategy.[45] To avoid significant errors, some managers try to ensure that all important groups have representation at or access to the top.[46] The guiding executive group may continuously adjust the number, power, or proximity of such access points in order to maintain a desired balance and focus.[47] These delicate adjustments require constant negotiations and implied bargains within the leadership group. Balancing the focuses that different interests exert on key decisions is perhaps the ultimate control top executives have in guiding and coordinating the formulation of their companies' strategies.[48]

Establishing, Measuring, and Rewarding Key Thrusts

Few executives or management teams can keep all the dimensions of a complex evolving strategy in mind as they deal with the continuous flux of urgent issues. Consequently, effective strategic managers seek to identify a few central themes that can help to draw diverse efforts together in a common cause.[49] Once identified, these themes help to maintain focus and consistency in the strategy. They make it easier to discuss and monitor proposed strategic thrusts. Ideally, these themes can be developed into a matrix of programs and goals, cutting across formal divisional lines and dominating the selection and ranking of projects within divisions. This matrix can, in turn, serve as the basis for performance measurement, control, and reward systems that ensure the intended strategy is properly implemented.

Unfortunately, few companies in the sample were able to implement such a complex planning and control system without creating undue rigidities. But all did utilize logical incrementalism to bring cohesion to the formal-analytical and power-behavioral processes needed to create effective strategies. Most used some approximation of the process sequence described above to form their strategies

---

[45]Lindblom, "The Science of 'Muddling Through,' " notes that every interest has a "watchdog" and that purposely allowing these watchdogs to participate in and influence decisions creates consensus decisions that all can live with. Similar conscious access to the top for different interests can now be found in corporate structures.

[46]See Zalenik, "Power and Politics in Organizational Life."

[47]For an excellent view of the bargaining processes involved in coalition management, see Sayles, *Managerial Behavior*, pp. 207–17.

[48]For suggestions on why the central power figure in decentralized organizations must be the person who manages its dominant coalition, the size of which will depend on the issues involved, and the number of areas in which the organizations must rely on judgmental decisions, see Thompson, "Control of Complex Organizations."

[49]Wrapp, "Good Managers Don't Make Policy Decisions," notes the futility of a top manager trying to push a full package of goals.

at both subsystem and overall corporate levels. A final summary example demonstrates how deliberate incrementalism can integrate the key elements in more traditional approaches to strategy formulation.

In the late 1970s, a major nation's largest bank named as its new president and CEO a man with a long and successful career, largely in domestic operating positions. The bank's chairman had been a familiar figure on the international stage and was due to retire in three to five years. The new CEO, with the help of a few trusted colleagues, his chief planner, and a consultant, first tried to answer these questions: "If I look ahead seven to eight years to my retirement as CEO, what should I like to leave behind as the hallmarks of my leadership? What accomplishments would define my era as having been successful?" He chose the following as goals:

1. To be the country's number one bank in profitability and size without sacrificing the quality of its assets or liabilities.
2. To be recognized as a major international bank.
3. To improve substantially the public image and employee perceptions of the bank.
4. To maintain progressive policies that prevent unionization.
5. To be viewed as a professional, well-managed bank with strong, planned management continuity.
6. To be clearly identified as the country's most professional corporate finance bank, with a strong base within the country but with foreign and domestic operations growing in balance.
7. To have women in top management and to achieve full utilization of the bank's female employees.
8. To have a tighter, smaller headquarters and a more rationalized, decentralized corporate structure.

The CEO brought back to the corporate offices the head of his overseas divisions to be chief operating officer (COO) and to be a member of the Executive Committee, which ran the company's affairs. The CEO discussed his personal views concerning the bank's future with this committee and also with several of his group vice presidents. Then, to arrive at a cohesive set of corporate goals, the Executive Committee investigated the bank's existing strengths and weaknesses (again with the assistance of consultants) and extrapolated its existing growth trends seven to eight years into the future. According to the results of this exercise, the bank's foreseeable growth would require that:

1. The bank's whole structure be reoriented to make it a much stronger force in international banking.
2. The bank decentralize operations much more than it ever had.
3. The bank find or develop at least 100 new top-level specialists and general managers within a few years.
4. The bank reorganize around a "four-bank" principle (international, commercial, investment, and retail banks) with entirely new linkages forged among these units.

5. These linkages and much of the bank's new international thrust be built on its expertise in certain industries, which were the primary basis of its parent country's international trade.

6. The bank's profitability be improved across the board, especially in its diverse retail banking units.

To develop more detailed data for specific actions and to further develop consensus around needed moves, the CEO commissioned two consulting studies: one on the future of the bank's home country and the other on changing trade patterns and relationships worldwide. As these studies became available, the CEO allowed an ever wider circle of top executives to critique the studies' findings and to share their insights. Finally, the CEO and the Executive Committee were willing to draw up and agree to a statement of 10 broad goals (parallel to the CEO's original goals but enriched in flavor and detail). By then, some steps were already underway to implement specific goals (e.g., the four-bank concept). But the CEO wanted further participation of his line officers in the formulation of the goals and in the strategic thrusts they represented across the whole bank. By now 18 months had gone by, but there was widespread consensus within the top management group on major goals and directions.

The CEO then organized an international conference of some 40 top officers of the bank and had a background document prepared for this meeting containing: (1) the broad goals agreed upon, (2) the 10 major thrusts that the Executive Committee thought were necessary to meet these goals, (3) the key elements needed to back up each thrust, and (4) a summary of the national and economic analyses the thrusts were based upon. The 40 executives had two full days to critique, question, improve, and clarify the ideas in this document. Small work groups of line executives reported their findings and concerns directly to the Executive Committee. At the end of the meeting, the Executive Committee tabled one of the major thrusts for further study, agreed to refined wording for some of the bank's broad goals, and modified details of the major thrusts in line with expressed concerns.

The CEO announced that within three months each line officer would be expected to submit his own statement of how his unit would contribute to the major goals and thrusts agreed upon. Once these unit goals were discussed and negotiated with the appropriate top executive group, the line officers would develop specific budgetary and nonbudgetary programs showing precisely how their units would carry out each of the major thrusts in the strategy. The CEO was asked to develop measures both for all key elements of each unit's fiscal performance and for performance against each agreed-upon strategic thrust within each unit. As these plans came into place, it became clear that the old organization had to be aligned behind these new thrusts. The CEO had to substantially redefine the CEO's job, deal with some crucial internal political pressures, and place the next generation of top managers in the line positions supporting each major thrust. The total process, from concept formulation to implementation of the control system, was to span three to four years, with new goals and thrusts emerging flexibly as external events and opportunities developed.

CONCLUSIONS

In recent years, there has been an increasingly loud chorus of discontent about corporate stragetic planning. Many managers are concerned that, despite elaborate strategic planning systems, costly staffs for planning, and major commitments of their own time, their most elaborately analyzed strategies never get implemented. These executives and their companies generally have fallen into the trap of thinking about strategy formulation and implementation as separate, sequential processes. They rely on the awesome rationality of their formally derived strategies and the inherent power of their positions to cause their organizations to respond. When this does not occur, they become bewildered, if not frustrated and angry. Instead, successful managers in the companies observed acted logically and incrementally to improve the quality of information used in key decisions; to overcome the personal and political pressures resisting change; to deal with the varying lead times and sequencing problems in critical decisions; and to build the organizational awareness, understanding, and psychological commitment essential to effective strategies. By the time the strategies began to crystallize, pieces of them were already being implemented. Through the very processes they used to formulate their strategies, these executives had built sufficient organizational momentum and identity with the strategies to make them flow toward flexible and successful implementation.

What this article is about: Several reasons are briefly explored for why companies practicing strategic planning are falling behind competitors, largely of foreign origin, who place much less emphasis on strategic planning. Of particular concern to the author is the emphasis on "grandiose strategic leaps" rather than step-by-step improvements and ignoring the capabilities of the organization.

1–3 Why Strategic Planning Goes Awry

Robert H. Hayes

Robert H. Hayes is professor of management and technology at Harvard Business School.

Let's face it. Strategic planning, as practiced by most American companies, is not working very well. This is embarrassing, because we essentially invented the idea, and have poured more resources into it than any other country in the world.

The whole purpose of strategic planning is to help a company get from where it is to where it wants to be, and in the process to develop a *sustainable* advantage over its competitors. Yet a growing number of industries and companies find themselves more vulnerable strategically today than when they started. Not only have they fallen short of the goals they set for themselves, they find themselves falling behind competitors, largely of foreign origin, who place much less emphasis on strategic planning.

How can we explain this?

One or more of three reasons are usually cited: most companies do not really engage in planning but simply play out an annual ritual; planning is carried out largely by outside consultants and corporate staff personnel, and therefore is becoming increasingly divorced from the realities of the business; and plans, once developed, tend to be too inflexible and constraining in rapidly evolving competitive environments. Cummins Engine, for example, was led to diversify by the expectation that its core business was dying. Instead, diversification siphoned off resources that were needed to exploit the continued vitality of the old one.

I would add two other reasons: planning's top-down orientation has empha-

---

sized the development of grandiose strategic leaps, rather than the patient step-by-step improvements that are difficult for competitors to copy; and planning has led companies into competitive positions opposite to those desired because they were, in effect, doing it backwards.

The traditional strategic planning process is based on an "ends-ways-means" model. First, one is supposed to establish corporate objectives (ends). Given those objectives, one develops a strategy (ways) for attaining them. Then one marshals the necessary resources (means).

Most companies, unfortunately, base these plans on 5- to 10-year time frames. This makes it almost impossible for them to create a truly strategic difference—one that leads to a competitive advantage that is difficult to copy and, therefore, sustainable. Goals that can be achieved within five years are usually either too easy or are based on buying and selling something. Anything that a company can buy is probably available for purchase by its competitors.

Focusing on major milestones also induces a top-down, "strategic leap" mentality in an organization. Such "leaps" might take a variety of forms: a product redesign, a factory modernization or expansion, a relocation, acquiring a supplier of a critical material or component, or adopting a new manufacturing technology.

Such big steps are highly visible and usually require a major expenditure of funds. Therefore, much staff development is required, and the expertise of many highly specialized people—financial analysts, strategic planners, legal experts, and outside consultants—must be tapped. In such companies, the corporate staff is regarded as the elite, and assignments of line managers to staff positions are typically felt to be promotions. This strategy does not require outstanding, highly trained people at lower levels in the organization. Their job is simply to operate the structure that top management and its staff of experts have created.

Increasingly, though, companies are succeeding by eschewing such strategic leaps and seeking competitive advantage through continual incremental improvements. This requires a very different kind of organization. Small improvements seldom involve major capital authorization requests, so there is little need for staff assistance or the advice of outside experts. Rather than putting huge resources into developing elaborate plans and projects, these companies expect most improvements to bubble up, in entrepreneurial fashion, from the lower ranks.

This approach requires a great deal of "low-level expertise" (not expertise *of* a low level, but expertise *at* low levels). Developing such expertise is a long process. Great effort must be spent on recruiting workers and managers who are both loyal and trainable. Once hired, the capabilities of these people must be continually improved and expanded, both through formal education and through job assignments that provide a broad understanding of the company's products, production systems, and competitive environment.

Such companies do not believe that many of the problems they face can be solved by top management, either because the information and expertise needed for dealing with them is lower in the organization or because the problems are continually evolving over time. Therefore, the role of top management is not to spot and solve problems as much as to create an organization that can spot and solve its own problems.

Most companies fall somewhere between these extremes. But our companies tend to favor "strategic leaps," while those of our two most powerful competitors, West Germany and Japan, tend to seek "incremental improvements" within an existing structure and technology. They are the tortoise, we are the hare.

In the fable, of course, the tortoise won the race. When this happens in business, it is usually because a new breakthrough is not available exactly when it is needed. That is, we often see major competitive advantages nibbled away by competitors that gradually adapt themselves to the new technology and then push it beyond the limits we were able to achieve (as is happening in the semiconductor industry today). When this happens, we would like to make another leap. But what if our labs and strategists reach into their hats and find nothing there?

This is essentially the trap that our home electronics producers fell into. While they frantically sought to develop flat-screen television and set up labor-intensive factories in low-wage countries, their Japanese competitors were learning—step-by-step—how to automate production in Japan. Over a period of more than 15 years, Japanese companies patiently reduced the cost of Ampex's pioneering videotape recorder to one-hundredth of its original cost, so they could introduce the first consumer VCR.

An obvious response would be to adopt an incremental approach, but this is hard for a company that has configured itself around the expectation of major breakthroughs. Entrepreneurship at the bottom cannot be "ordered" from the top—particularly when, as usually happens, top-down, staff-dominated planning and control systems have caused most of the entrepreneurs to leave.

The traditional approach to strategic planning also errs in its treatment of the third element: means—the resources necessary to implement the chosen strategy. Although many different types of resources will generally be required, most strategic planning focuses primarily on financial wherewithal, ignoring the capabilities of the organization.

A-M International, for example, developed an exciting strategic plan: It would turn to high technology to revitalize its aging office equipment product line. This led it to buy high-technology companies and hire new managers to run them. But it neglected to ensure that its factories could make reliable, high-precision products and that its field organizations could sell and service the new products. The new strategy led to disaster because such capabilities cannot be bought. They must be grown from within.

The problems with strategic planning may run even deeper, to the underlying assumption that responsibility for organizational success lies primarily on the shoulders of top management. We need to realize that other approaches can be equally, if not more, effective.

One such approach is to turn the ends-ways-means logic on its head: means-ways-ends. A road map is useful if one is lost in a highway system, but not in a swamp whose topography is constantly changing. A simple compass—that indicates the general direction and allows you to use your own ingenuity in overcoming difficulties—is far more valuable.

Let's think about how such a logic might work.

First, it suggests that a company begin by investing in developing its capabilities along a broad front (means). New technologies and techniques are acquired and experimented with. Small, information-gathering subsidiaries are set up in strategic locations like Japan and Korea. R&D activity is spread more widely throughout the organization. Workers and managers are given cross-functional assignments so that they develop a broad understanding of the company's markets, technologies, and factories.

If American electronics companies had followed this approach 15 years ago, they wouldn't have discontinued the internal production of integrated circuits—because chip design is becoming interchangeable with systems design. Nor would American semiconductor companies have stopped producing much of their own manufacturing equipment—even though every advance in their product requires equal advance in the production process.

Second, as these capabilities develop and as technological and market opportunities appear, managers well down in the organization are encouraged to exploit matches wherever they occur (ways). Top management's job is to facilitate this kind of entrepreneurial activity, provide it with resources from other parts of the company, and, where feasible, encourage cooperative activities.

In short, the company doesn't first develop plans and then seek capabilities; it builds capabilities and then encourages the development of plans for exploiting them. Rather than trying to develop optimal strategies that assume a static environment, it seeks opportunistic improvements in a dynamic environment.

Such a "reverse" logic tends to be most effective in rapidly changing competitive environments. Fixed objectives are likely to lose their attractiveness over time as the company and its competitive environment evolve. A common vision, however, will keep people moving ahead, around unforeseen obstacles and beyond the stated (largely because they were visible) immediate objectives.

In such organizations *everybody* is assumed to be responsible for the organization's prosperity. Its success rests on its ability to exploit opportunities as they arise, its ingenuity, its capacity to learn, its determination, and its persistence. The obvious analogy is with guerrilla warfare.

Sometimes, of course, companies must change their objectives, decide to enter a new business, or abandon an old one. Such decisions seldom bubble up from the bottom; they must flow from the top. The trick is to manage such discontinuities without undermining lower-level managers. When a guerrilla army decides that the only person with any real authority is the supreme leader, its field commanders lose their credibility. And as the balance of power begins to shift, more and more is likely to be drained from lower levels. As the "counters" gain ascendancy over the "doers," the best doers are likely to become counters. Or they go elsewhere, where they can do it their way.

The struggle between American companies and their foreign competitors can be likened to a battle between a bunch of hares trained in conventional warfare and equipped with road maps, and a bunch of tortoises that are expert in guerrilla tactics and armed with compasses. Unfortunately, the battle is taking place in a swamp, and the ends-ways-means logic that got the hares into such a situation is unlikely to get them out.

They may have to replace it—or at least supplement it—with a reverse logic. Rather than building elaborate strategic plans around forecasts of an unworkable future, they might ask themselves why they were so successful when planning occupied little of their time, but their industrial capabilities were the envy of the world.

What this article is about: In spite of recent criticisms of formal strategic planning, most corporate executives and business-unit managers continue to practice—and value—strategic planning. The concept itself isn't the problem, according to the executives surveyed and interviewed. Rather, planning systems often break down because of faulty preparation and implementation. Well-managed companies can overcome these problems by involving line managers in the planning process, defining business units correctly, outlining action steps in detail, and integrating the strategic plan with other organizational controls.

1–4 *Uses and Misuses of Strategic Planning*

Daniel H. Gray

*Daniel H. Gray is president and chief executive officer of
Gray-Judson, Inc., a consulting firm based in Boston that
specializes in strategic management.*

There's nothing wrong with formal strategic planning—if you do it right.

Some writers on management today claim that strategic planning is on the wane—or at least on the defensive. Is yet another management fad about to fade away? Are we seeing still another example that shows the folly of trying to manage in "too rational" a way? Consider all those companies that have spent so much money on strategic planning yet still have problems. And look at all those impressive plans that fall apart during implementation.

Though it seems as if strategic planning is on the way out in some companies because of faulty diagnosis of its defects, I would say, on the basis of my research and experience, that reports of its demise are exaggerated and premature.

Strategic planning as many textbooks describe it may not be around much longer but not for the reasons most critics give. If formal strategic planning vanishes in a few years, it will be because wherever it is undertaken it either gets better or it gets worse, depending on how well it's done: If you do it poorly, either you drop out or you rattle around in its mechanics; if you do it well, you evolve beyond strategic planning to strategic management.

Strategic planning is usually seen, on adoption, as a separate discipline or a management function. It involves the allocation of resources to programmed activities calculated to achieve a set of business goals in a dynamic, competitive environment. Strategic management, on the other hand, treats strategic thinking as a pervasive aspect of running a business and regards strategic planning as an instrument around which all other control systems—budgeting, information, compensation, organization—can be integrated. This interdependency usually comes to light when a business has trouble implementing the results of a free-standing strategic planning process.

These distinctions and definitions emerged from a year-long research project that focused on where things most often go wrong in "good" strategic planning systems and what has been learned about shoring up these weak spots. In this research, my colleagues and I have contacted a broad sample of business-unit heads, corporate planning directors, and chief executive officers engaged in strategic planning in American multibusiness corporations. We used a questionnaire to pinpoint where things have gone wrong and conducted 14 executive seminars to search for remedies (see Figures 1 and 2). To date there have been 300 respondents to the questionnaire and 216 participants in the day-and-a-half seminars.

At this point we can report the following findings:

- First, most companies in our sample remain firmly committed to strategic planning, even though 87 percent report feelings of disappointment and frustration with their systems.
- Second, 59 percent attribute their discontent mainly to difficulties encountered in the implementation of plans.
- Third, when multibusiness executives compare their experiences, 67 percent trace their implementation problems to the design of their systems and the way they manage them.

While implementation failures have for some been the cause of frustration and withdrawal, such experiences have helped others learn to run their planning systems better. Consider the "Gamma Corporation," a provider of upscale women's garments, jewelry, luggage, and cosmetics, whose growth curve had flattened out. To recover, it acquired a related but embryonic service business with apparel and cosmetic appendages. The service business became a new Gamma profit center, while its appendages were assimilated into kindred profit centers of the parent. The corporate requirement that the new service business match the profit and cost control performance of the established business made rapid sales growth an imperative.

The hotshot, upscale marketer who was given the entrepreneurial opportunity to make something of the service unit tried to accomplish this through dress

---

FIGURE 1   Topics and Responses in the Evaluation of Strategic Planning Systems in U.S. Multibusiness Companies

Topic	*Response*
Source of greatest frustration or disappointment	Implementation difficulties
Other areas of major concern	Skills of line managers Adequacy of information
Rating of current planning system on a scale of 1 to 10, from worst to best	56% in 6-7-8 range Mode: 7 Mean: 5.5
Nature of planning output	General direction or thrust for strategic action
Locus of planning responsibility	Line managers: 78%
Relation to budget process	Planning first, budgeting afterward: 55%
Sources of market information	In-house: 80%
Number of strategic business units (SBUs)	Range from 6 to 48
Basis of unit definition	Product lines: 57%
Relation of SBUs to profit centers	Coincide: 51%
How unit goals and objectives are set	Top-down: 33% Bottom-up: 67%
Who owns an SBU's cash flow	Corporation: 83%
Unit strategy development process	Interdepartmental group give-and-take: 34%
Linkage of planning to other controls	More to budgets than anything else: 42%
Impact of strategic planning on organizational structure	Structure often adapted to support strategy: 70%
Relationship of executive bonuses to strategic performance	Financial results only: 60% Financial and strategic mix: 22%
Authority of groups or divisions over SBU planning	Not significant: 68% Controlling: 32%
Corporate resource allocation process when resource requests exceed resources available	Perceived as unfair: 49% Perceived as fair: 37%

---

pattern and cosmetic giveaways. When sister profit centers blocked this move, he missed his targets and quit. The Gamma strategy to rejuvenate a low-growth company with a vigorous new synergistic service acquisition was the company's maiden voyage into strategic planning. The verdict at corporate headquarters was that the plan "fell apart through poor implementation."

FIGURE 2   Executive Seminar Participants

Management Level			Industry Type		
Corporate executives	91	42%	Service businesses	89	41%
Corporate planning directors and staff	85	39	Manufacturing businesses	111	52
Business-unit managers	40	19	Government agencies	16	7
Total	216	100%	Total	216	100%

After an extensive audit of this implementation failure, Gamma executives perceived that their strategy had been deeply flawed well before implementation: the company had made only a financial evaluation of the acquisition candidate. The new retail service unit was a poorly designed strategy center. It was lodged in the same organization with mature wholesale product businesses. Its best strategic options were preempted by an inappropriate financial strategy. There was no portfolio strategy to reconcile the new unit with others. The new unit head was not allowed to behave entrepreneurially. The company had no detailed action plan to mesh the new and old business strategies.

The Gamma Corporation and many other companies have stuck to their strategic plans in spite of their frustrations. Their persistence is rooted in the needs that led them to adopt strategic planning in the first place. They have come to realize that steering a business by financial controls alone is not enough. However vital the bottom line, balance sheet feedback is too lumpy, too stripped of connotative information, and often too late. Financial plans must be augmented and supplemented by strategic plans if managers are to make more timely and accurate midcourse corrections in response to external change. The competitive penalty for inability to adapt along the way is too great for most companies to do without strategic planning.

Another reason that companies persist in planning despite disappointment is evident in the way many respondents to our questionnaire rated their planning systems. On a scale of 1 to 10 (1 meaning worst and 10 meaning best), the modal rating (7) accounted for 27 percent of all responses. This rating was assigned to any system considered to be excellent for clarification of where one wants to go but not very good in execution. This finding suggests a view of planning as a two-part process—a strategy development part and a strategy execution part. One can then look with approval on strategy development and with disapproval on strategy execution. This allows strategy developers to view themselves as the victims of the poor work of implementers lower down in the organization and to overlook the crucial role that strategy development plays in determining whether a plan can be implemented.

COMMON PROBLEMS AND WORKABLE SOLUTIONS

When chief executives, corporate planning directors, and business-unit heads in our sample got together to discuss common problems, we observed that they tended to have second thoughts about how good their planning systems are, what is wrong with them, and where and how to put things right. (For a sample of what they said, see Box, p. 44.) Two-thirds of what these managers called implementation difficulties were, on closer scrutiny, attributed to these six preimplementation factors:

1. Poor preparation of line managers.
2. Faulty definition of business units.
3. Vaguely formulated goals.
4. Inadequate information bases for action planning.
5. Badly handled reviews of business-unit plans.
6. Inadequate linkage of strategic planning with other control systems.

The uncovering of these design and management errors can lead to new insights about how to avoid many implementation problems. In this article, we examine several of them. There are undoubtedly more to be uncovered in the ongoing search for the most effective principles of strategic planning. (see Figure 3 for some suggestions.)

Involve Line Managers

It does little good to allocate planning responsibility to line managers if they receive no or poor preparation for this key role.

At a major aerospace and automotive supplier, for example, managers complained that a sophisticated planning system had failed to "come alive" and that formal business-unit plans were lying "unused in bottom drawers." Recently, four years into their system and just after making a major acquisition, the company convened more than 40 heads of strategic business units (SBUs) to teach them the skills that strategic planning requires. Picture a week-long conference in posh surroundings: visiting management gurus doing star turns; reprints of landmark cases describing classic acquisition assimilation problems; workshops where messages from the participants to the corporate hierarchy could be hammered out; and, at the end of the week, a flying visit from the CEO to talk about his vision of the future. Total cost: more than $250,000. Result: last-minute watering-down of the messages, a 60-day fade-out of the experience, and no significant change in behavior.

It is now widely accepted that strategic planning is a line-management function in which staff specialists play a supporting role. Yet many companies have done little to prepare line managers for this kind of leadership. When they are left to grope for the operational meaning of concepts like "strategic mind-set," "issue formulation," "conflict management," and "portfolio role," they feel ill at ease.

FIGURE 3   Some Principles for Strategic Planning

Strategic planning is a line management function for which training in strategic analysis and participative skills is usually necessary.

Strategic business units need to be defined so that one executive can control the key variables essential to the execution of his or her strategic business plan.

A unit's concept of the business it is in must above all be formulated from the outside-in so that it can most effectively engage the dynamics of its strategic environment.

Action plans for achieving business objectives are the key to implementing and monitoring strategy. They require extensive lower-level participation and special leadership skills. Action plans are complete when underlying assumptions, allocation of responsibilities, time and resource requirements, risks, and likely responses have been made explicit.

Participative strategy development, a prerequisite for successful strategy execution, often requires cultural change at the upper levels of corporations and their business units.

The strategic planning system and other control systems designed to guide managerial and organizational behavior must be integrated in a consistent whole if business strategies are to be executed well.

Productivity improvement programs are best treated as aspects of strategic business plans since productivity takes on significantly different meanings as the strategic balance between marketing and production shifts.

Well-managed organizations must be both centralized and decentralized—centralized so that strategies and control systems can be integrated and decentralized so that units in each strategic environment can act and be treated with appropriate differentiation.

Over time, good strategic planning, once considered a separate activity, becomes a mind-set, a style and a set of techniques for running a business—not something more to do but a better way of doing what has always had to be done.

Strategic planning seems more like a burden imposed from above than a better way of running their units. Not surprisingly, some of these line managers adopt a modest, mechanical approach to their planning duties. Then staff planners may creep back in to lend a hand and help fill the void.

Line managers in charge of business units say they want coaching in the skills required to guide strategy debates. They want to know how to draw department heads out of their specialized frames of reference and into a general management view of trade-offs between functions. They want to know what questions will be asked and what challenges to expect when they send their business plans up for approval.

Some companies have tried to help their unit heads by offering them quick-fix management development courses—often with disappointing results. A great deal of management development training is still carried on with generic or

---

WE'VE COME TO PRAISE STRATEGY PLANNING, NOT TO BURY IT

Quotes from postseminar self-evaluation sheets

We expected too much of strategic planning and were disappointed. Now we know that planning is part of a larger process, and mastering *that* is fulfilling our expectations.

—Corporate planning officer, insurance company

I can't conceive of doing business without a strategy and a plan. Every company has to do it. Either you get to be good at it, or you do it poorly and suffer the consequences.

—Chief executive officer, diversified manufacturer

What we had was a kind of strategic rain dance—war cries, smoke signals, sacrificial offerings. We're much more thorough and disciplined now—more analytical and more demanding of ourselves.

—President, retail division, clothing business

We actually used to tell ourselves our planning system was OK, even though we admitted it fell apart in implementation. That was our way of telling ourselves that the trouble was not at the top.

—Head of a strategic business unit in a 17-unit corporation

The way to get into a planning bind is to go at everything piecemeal. . . . First the organization chart—that's done. . . . Then the plan—that's done. . . . Then the budget—that's done. . . . The bonus system—that's done. . . . All that hard work and then nothing fits.

—Executive vice president, health-care holding company

When you have two rival plans—a strategic business plan and a financial plan—either you dovetail them or before long the strategic plan and the will to do it are dead.

—Financial director, department store chain

---

hypothetical case materials and with packages of received wisdom presented to groups of peers. Such training may be valuable, but it usually does not replicate the real conditions facing the line-management strategist.

A better practice is to focus on real problems in managers' own companies so as to see the trouble in its current strategic context. This opportunity to learn how to be more flexible and adaptive (and to learn about learning) should be offered not as a gift but as part of a transaction—this assistance in exchange for that change in behavior. It should be offered to groups representing the various functions and levels whose cooperation is needed to solve tough problems.

An example of a company that successfully involved line managers in planning is a manufacturer of electronic components in the Sunbelt. Facing an urgent need to offset price declines with cost reductions, the company assembled a 25-person training squad of managers ranging from the level of superintendent to that of divisional chief operating officer. With the help of a process facilitator and with engineering, marketing, and personnel staff on call, the training squad was charged to explore the rationale, the feasibility and cost, the potential savings, and the cultural consequences of four options—asset reduction, productivity gain sharing, plant rationalization, and operator training—and then to recommend a remedial action program. Four of the 12 lowest ranking members of the team would be chosen for promotion and training roles in their own or other plants. In the end, the squad's plan was accepted, three men were promoted, and divisional operating costs dropped 17 percent in the ensuing six months.

Define the Business Unit

Even when its boundaries are strategically correct, a business unit is vulnerable to an outmoded conceptualization of the business it is in. Consider the difference between being a brewer of beer and being a seller of beer in English pubs. Under either category, the assets, products, markets, people, and functions are the same; but there is a world of difference in the kind of strategy developed, the direction of people's energies, the priorities of action, the indicators to be monitored, and the places where profit is taken. In one case, beer production is all-important; in the other, beer is fourth or fifth in importance in the customer's purchase decision. In an aging, oligopolistic industry with excess capacity, Courage Breweries' shift from a supply-side mind-set to a consumer-lifestyle mind-set helped break open a stalemated industry's market-share equilibrium and improve profits.

How a strategy center or an SBU conceives of its business can have a significant bearing on its strategic behavior and its competitive clout. Management's attitude toward a business is as important as its boundaries. For example, a manufacturer of rubber and plastic control devices and assemblies saw its business flatten out under a definition of itself as a company that supplies "these specific products to these specific industries." While continuing to make large batches of flow valves and gaskets for automobile and appliance makers, the manufacturer began to diagnose and treat the precision-molding process control problems of manufacturers in general. To its single-tier, high-volume, production-driven product line the company added an R&D and marketing-driven premium-price line.

If a multibusiness fails to define its strategy centers or its strategic business units correctly, the best planning techniques available can't undo the damage. When strategic planning is newly installed, it is often assumed that the organizational units already in place should handle the planning. These units, however, may owe their boundaries to many factors that make them inappropriate to use as a basis for planning: geography, administrative convenience, the terms of old acquisition deals, product lines, traditional profit centers, a belief in healthy internal competition, or old ideas about centralization and decentralization.

Frequently these familiar rationales for unit boundaries make for poor strategy centers. That they could be wrong may not occur to executives who take organizational structure as a given before planning begins. But strategic planning teaches its more successful practitioners that the main purpose of organization (including both structure and process) is to support the development and execution of strategy. Thus organization should come after strategic planning.

The following principles should guide the definition of business units:

- Include within the jurisdiction of the strategy center all variables the unit head needs for executing the strategy. For example, it may not be wise to require a manager charged with opening up new markets for a cluster of products to buy manufacturing and distribution services from sister profit centers.
- Leave the unit head free to take profits where strategy dictates. Hence nothing smaller than a strategy center should be a profit center.
- Let external rather than internal forces shape unit boundaries. If competitive forces require a larger unit than normal spans of control would dictate, go with the larger unit.
- When separate units are strategically appropriate for external reasons but must, for economies of scale, share central facilities and services, let them share, but keep them as separate units. A Texas chemical company, for example, decided against combining the planning processes of its generic and specialized businesses. Although they share a common infrastructure, their customers and competitors are so different that the managers of these businesses could never agree on a common strategy.

While the application of these principles of unit definition is crucial to good strategy development and execution, they can conflict with one another. As a practical matter, therefore, these principles cannot serve as absolutes. In the end, boundary setting is an executive judgment call but not a purely subjective one. The final judgment can be either adaptive, in which case the boundaries line up with the realities of the prevailing strategic game, or willful, in which case the company accepts the risks of trying to change the way the external game is played.

Failure to address the unit definition question at all or to address it without giving due weight to the external environment can lead to serious problems. Looking first at the environment, however, is by itself no guarantee of success. A rule often used in unit boundary setting is one product, one manager. This is meant to ensure direct accountability and single-minded strategic concentration on the fate of the product. The penalty for this approach, however, can be the loss of opportunities for discretionary profit taking, synergistic manipulation of related products, marketing cooperation, and economies of scale. The result is often the creation of too many business units too narrow to compete effectively.

Move beyond General Goals

Implementation is bound to go awry if strategy formulation goes no further than defining general thrusts and end-point goals. Consider a public utility that adopted a strategy of "energy conservation, high earnings, diversification, and excellence." These four goals were so general that the person in charge of managing each one could unwittingly be at cross-purposes with the others. Field personnel cuts made to improve earnings eliminated the very people needed to run a new diversification venture aimed at saving energy through home and factory audits and retrofits. At the same time, the pursuit of engineering "excellence" led to the purchase of materials that were too durable to mesh with the utility's plan for capacity replacement.

Approximately 7 out of 10 companies in our sample do not carry the formulation of strategy much beyond some general statement of thrust such as market penetration or internal efficiency and some generalized goal such as excellence. Having only generalizations to work with makes implementation very difficult. Targets don't mean much if no one maps out the pathways leading to them. After this kind of half-baked strategy is handed over for execution, subordinates who have not been in on the formulation of the strategy are left to deal with its cross-impacts and trade-offs when they bump into them. If told only that the name of the strategic game is high quality and prompt delivery, various people in an organization—designers, inspectors, schedulers, piece workers, and salespeople—may each reconcile these two factors differently. Subordinates' efforts are often parochial and improvisational; the way they carry out an undefined strategy is often unsatisfactory—if they elect to complete it at all.

Make More Detailed Action Plans

The cure for half-baked strategy is action detailing, but this task often baffles and irritates many executives. Only one in three of the companies in our study has a process or a forum for the interfunctional debate and testing of unit strategies. Their procedures for action detailing and other kinds of reality testing are often nonexistent or merely rudimentary. Action detailing of a sort is carried on in some places as a part of operational planning, but it usually follows strategic planning and takes the strategy as given. Planning in detail should be used as a further test of a strategy's feasibility.

One way to combine operational and strategic planning is to begin an advocacy process as soon as agreement on strategic thrusts has been reached. An interfunctional task force is set up for each thrust—with strong representation from middle management. Each team can identify and analyze the options for reaching a particular objective and then rough out the major action steps necessary to accomplish the option that it will advocate to the unit strategy team.

The team's job is to explain and defend what it considers the best way of bringing this option to life. Each team must deal with time frame, risk analysis, allocation of responsibility, resource requirements, organization obstacles, and monitoring devices. In mapping out and testing strategic options, managers begin to think explicitly about assumptions, alternatives, contingencies, and what competitive reactions to expect. Failure to come to grips with these details can undermine the execution of the strategy.

When senior executives are invited to try their hands at action detailing, they often find it an uncomfortable exercise. They tend to offer as action steps what are really no more than wishes or desired results—such as "upgrading front-line supervision," "introducing services that appeal to the customer," or "eliminating wasteful practices." Good action detailing, however, requires the participation of middle and lower management and the work force. Top management knows the direction; those below know the terrain. Not only is lower-level participation essential to working out practical steps, but it is also highly desirable. Through such participation, managers generate the kind of understanding, ownership, commitment, and motivation necessary for successful implementation. The alternative, which is to try to push strategic planning out into the organization and down through the ranks by exhortation and other forms of one-way "communication," has only minimal effect.

Companies trapped in half-thought-out planning may lack the information and motivation necessary to good strategy execution. These companies may avoid the front-end costs of participation, discussion, and explicit detailing, but they pay the cost of not seeing their options, not reaching their goals, and spending days bogged down in implementation.

Manage the Face-Off

Even when all the steps in the strategy development process are taken according to the principles of best practice, strategic plans can be ruined and the whole system undermined at the final review stage. The issue is how good the design and management of the planning cycle is when the business units' proposed plans hit the corporate screen. We call this crucial encounter managing the face-off.

The face-off is a moment of inevitable, healthy conflict. Not only do all the units' resource requests frequently exceed what headquarters is prepared to provide, but their aggregate performance promises are often less than the corporation as a whole requires. Since performance requirements come from an analysis of capital markets while performance promises arise from strategies for dealing with each business unit's particular environment, this conflict is not surprising.

What should happen at the face-off is reconciliation, which often involves queuing, downsizing, redirection, and recycling. What actually does happen is often rather primitive: exhortation, backdoor dealing, across-the-board cuts, moving the goalposts, and mandated performance promises. In other words, the units' plans are force-fit in various ways into the corporate plan. At this stage of the game, companies normally focus their attention more on the numbers in the business plan than on the strategies. For example, one general manager responsible for an aging product described scaling down his profit projections after a rival company had captured a 4 percent market share in five months with a generic commodity substitute. This manager's boss, however, ordered the higher profit figures restored and asked him how he expected to win the marketing wars with "negative thinking." Unfortunately, this example is typical. Numbers are often altered at the face-off so as to close the gap without any discussion of the need to revise the risk assessments, competitive reactions, probability estimates, and other problems lying beneath the numbers.

Even if all the units have done their strategic planning very well up to the time of final review, think of the consequences for the next round of planning if they tack new financial projections arbitrarily onto strategies whose predicted effects in a particular competitive environment have already been calculated to be lower. The obligatory promise that headquarters extracts from a subunit may close the gap for a while, but it will undercut and degrade the next round of planning and budgeting. The force-fit at the face-off is an invitation to play games and a clear signal that scrupulous planning is considered a waste of valuable time.

Only a small minority of the companies we studied (13 percent) say they have a satisfactory process for managing the face-off. A little over one-third report some attempt at "rigorous trade-off analysis among business units." Among corporate controls, strategic planning is often the new kid on the block. Some executives see strategic planning as challenging financial controls and think of the face-off as the place where financial management supersedes strategic management. In these companies, financial strategy is not reconciled with other strategies but preempts them as the final arbiters of corporate resource allocation.

Integrate Plans and Controls

A strategic planning system can't achieve its full potential until it is integrated with other control systems such as budgets, information systems, and reward systems. The badly designed, poorly managed face-off is a manifestation of a deeper problem—the "compartmentalization syndrome," which treats various control systems as freestanding and strategically neutral.

While most executives who have adopted strategic planning see it as an indispensable tool, they tend to treat it at first as just another addition to an array of control devices. Before long they may discover that one control is at odds with another. Then the notion of linking these different controls arises, and that is as close as most companies in our study have come to a concept of integrated control. The three linkage problems they frequently identified have to do with plans and budgets, plans and information systems, and plans and reward systems.

Plans and Budgets. The conflict between strategic plans and budgets is the most commonly perceived area of dissonance. Managers tend to view the annual planning and budgeting sequence as logically connected but not integrated in fact. While the best strategic planning starts from an environmental analysis and then works in the unit's ability to respond, budgeting usually proceeds by making incremental adjustments to the previous year's internal departmental budgets. This practice allows the momentum of last year's (possibly obsolete) business strategy and this year's functional strategies to determine the funding of this year's business-unit plan.

The absence of strategic action planning often thwarts those who want to integrate plans and budgets. Not until a company has formulated explicit action steps can it cast fixed capital, working capital, operating expense, and revenue and head-count implications in the form of strategy-based budgets. Most CEOs yearn for such budgets so that they can see how their strategies, not just their departments, are doing. But the same CEOs often report that they are told such budgets are not possible without disrupting the whole accounting system.

Plans and Information Systems.   Many strategic planners in the units and at the top of multibusiness corporations express concern about the adequacy of their planning information bases and decision support systems. They worry about linking poor information bases with sophisticated computers. Even accurate, timely, and accessible information will not help the planner if it leads to an inappropriate strategy.

For example, a manufacturer of components for automobiles, appliances, medical equipment, and the like once developed a sophisticated data base for manpower planning that it can no longer use. The company's well-stocked management information system displays on demand how many machinists—white and black, male and female, high school educated and not—live within 30 minutes' commuting distance of its plant in New Jersey. The trouble is, the competition has changed, so that the company cannot be globally cost-competitive unless it bases its production in Europe or Asia.

Like many businesses, this company based its strategy on data that had accumulated in response to questions raised by its financial managers and its technical and professional specialists, whose expertise was too narrow. The information system drove the strategy instead of the other way around. Strategy is what makes a fact relevant or irrelevant, and a relevant fact significant or insignificant.

Corporate CEOs and their business-unit heads are the ones who must raise the issues, ask the questions, and formulate the business definitions, missions, objectives, and strategies that will drive their decision support systems. With today's information technology, it is possible to move in the right or the wrong strategic direction with great speed.

Plans and Reward Systems.   When companies design reward systems as separate, freestanding controls, they may overlook the fact that such controls are not strategically neutral. For example, a strategy for competitive survival required a Tennessee manufacturer of temperature control devices to put expensive new assets in place to bring out a new version of a fading product. Its management had less than a year to realize the six-figure bonuses they would receive under a three-year average ROI payout formula. The head-on collision of a strategy that increased the asset base at the expense of reducing executive bonuses delayed the strategy's implementation for five months.

Many companies have witnessed the quiet destruction of a two- or a three-year strategy while their executives protected their first-year profit-sharing bonuses. It is folly to appeal to managers' self-interest with rewards for behavior other than the kind the strategic business plan calls for, and it is naive to expect them to override the powerful incentives that reward systems evoke.

THE PRIMACY OF STRATEGIC PLANNING

No organizational arrangement, control system, or productivity program is strategically neutral. Strategic planning becomes the device for consistently lining up such factors.

Among companies exploring the problem of integrated control systems, the idea is taking shape that strategic planning can serve as the core control instrument of a business enterprise, with other controls adjusted and adapted to facilitate the execution of strategy. Why this emphasis on strategic planning? Because of all control devices, it is the one that is driven by the business environment. Strategic planning comes before the final results are known, determines whether profit will be taken now or later, and decides which facts are relevant. While financial controls are obviously indispensable, the feedback they give is often too aggregated, too homogenized, and too late—not to mention too conservative of past business practices.

With strategic planning, the concept of integrated, or fused, controls goes further than the reconciliation of budgets, rewards, and decision support systems. As the unifying role of strategy in running a business becomes clear, we see that getting control over the productivity of a business is not strategically neutral either. It is apparent that in embryonic and growth industries productivity should refer to such things as market response time and market penetration, even if the price of these achievements is some internal inefficiency or postponed profit.

A leading paint manufacturer once lost volume by holding a price umbrella over its competitors and then seeking to restore falling margins through a productivity drive in every department of every plant. The company learned that the price cuts it made to restore volume and raise plant utilization above the break-even point did eight times as much for productivity as a $3 million waste elimination campaign had done earlier.

Seen as part of strategy, productivity is not exclusively concerned with physical input and output ratios or even with current net revenue. Productivity is keyed to the intended outcome of a business plan. Sometimes the intended outcome is profit today, in which case productivity may mean moving down the experience curve. Sometimes the goal is profit tomorrow, in which case productivity may mean preempting rivals and buying shares for future payback. Traditional corporate productivity czars presiding over programs that treat all business units alike can kill growth units before they ever get to the mature stage, when low-cost strategies are appropriate.

Finally, effective strategic planning that reflects the importance of integrated controls also takes organizational structure into account. For example, their strategic planning experience is enabling some executives to rethink the age-old problems of whether to centralize or decentralize management. Everyone knows that centralization inhibits the motivation of decision makers on the periphery of large organizations. In a multibusiness setup, centralization can lead to passive or reactive unit leadership. It is also widely understood that decentralization frequently leads to highly energetic policies and behaviors that may be suboptimal from the corporate viewpoint. Many companies trying to escape this apparent dilemma have swung back and forth between centralization and decentralization.

Now there appears to be a way out: multibusiness strategic planning clearly calls for both centralization and decentralization. No strategic corporate portfolio management and resource allocation rationale can exist without bringing the family of unit heads together at the center. Similarly, differentiated unit strategies cannot be executed in varying business environments without a process for local advocacy and local discretion in execution. In short, the planning process demands both integration and differentiation. These terms may be more useful and revealing than centralization and decentralization because they leave strategic planners free to decide what needs to be integrated at the center as well as what needs to be differentiated on the periphery and free to set up whatever organizational arrangements best facilitate strategy development, reconciliation, execution, and adaptation.

From this line of reasoning it is a short step to the conclusion that strategic planning, at its leading edge, is really just an aspect of strategic management. From this perspective it no longer makes sense to question people about the merits of their planning systems. What matter is whether their mind-sets, their plans, their practices, and their overall controls are coordinated and fit together harmoniously. In the most effective companies I've observed, strategic planning is no longer an added managerial duty. It is a way of thinking about a business and how to run it.

What this article is about: This article reconsiders the question of why organizations really do need strategies, and also shows how some long-held beliefs explain why organizations do not, as well as do, need strategies. It considers the needs for strategy to set direction, focus effort, define the organization, and provide consistency.

1–5 The Strategy Concept II: Another Look at Why Organizations Need Strategies

Henry Mintzberg

*Henry Mintzberg is professor of management
at McGill University*

In a previous article, I proposed five definitions of strategy—as a plan, ploy, pattern, position, and perspective. Drawing on these, I wish to investigate here the question of why organizations really do need strategies. In discussing some of the conventional reasons as well as other ones—to set direction, focus effort, define the organization, provide consistency—I will consider how they may suggest not only why organizations *do* need strategies, but also why they *don't*.

SETTING DIRECTION

Most commentators, focusing on the notions of strategy as deliberate plan and market position, argue that *organizations need strategy to set direction for themselves and to outsmart competitors, or at least enable themselves to maneuver through threatening environments.* In its boldest (and baldest) form: "The main role of strategy is to evolve a trajectory or flight path toward that bull's eye."[1] If its strategy is good, such commentators argue, then the organization can make various mistakes, indeed can sometimes even start from a weaker position, and still come out on top. Chandler quotes one of the men responsible for Sears Roebuck's great success: "Business is like war in one respect—if its grand

SOURCE: *California Management Review*, Fall 1987, pp. 25–32.

[1]B. Yavitz and W. H. Newman, *Strategy in Action: The Execution, Politics, and Payoff of Business Planning* (New York: The Free Press, 1982), p. 7.

strategy is correct . . . any number of tactical errors can be made and yet the enterprise proves successful."[2] In a similar vein, Tilles explains that:

> When Hannibal inflicted the humiliating defeat on the Roman army at Cannae in 216 B.C., he led a ragged band against soldiers who were in possession of superior arms, better training, and competent 'noncoms.' His strategy, however, was so superior that all of those advantages proved to be relatively insignificant.[3]

The assumption here is that the competitor with the better strategy will win, or, as a corollary, that the competitor with a clear strategy will beat the one that has none. Strategy, it is suggested, counts for more than operations: What really matters is *thinking* it through; *seeing* it through, while hardly incidental, is nonetheless secondary. "Doing the right thing" beats "doing things right" is the expression for such strategic thinking, or to take the favorite example of the opposite, "rearranging the deck chairs on the *Titanic*."

Sound strategic thinking can certainly explain a good deal of success, in fact, more success than it should, since it is always easy, after the fact, to impute a brilliant strategy (and, behind it, a brilliant strategist) to every great victory. But no shortage of failure can probably be attributed to organizations that got their strategy right while messing up their operations. Indeed, an overdose of strategic thinking can impede effectiveness in the operations, which is exactly what happened on the *Titanic*. The ship did not go down because they were rearranging the deck chairs at all, but for exactly the opposite reason: They were so busy glorying in the strategy of it all—that boat as a brilliant conception—that they neglected to look out for icebergs.

As for the assumption that any strategy is always better than none, consider an oil company executive in 1973, just as the price of oil went up by a factor of four. What strategy (as plan) should he have pursued when his whole world was suddenly upset? Setting oneself on a predetermined course in unknown waters is the perfect way to sail straight into an iceberg. Sometimes it is better to move slowly, a little bit at a time, looking not too far ahead but very carefully, so that behavior can be shifted on a moment's notice.

The point is not that organizations don't need direction, it is that they don't need homilies. It stands to reason that it is better to have a good strategy, all things being equal. But all things are never equal. The *Titanic* experience shows how a good strategy can blind an organization to the need to manage its operations. Besides, it is not always clear what a good strategy is, or indeed if it is not better at times to proceed without what amounts to the straitjacket of a clear intended strategy.

---

[2] A. D. Chandler, *Strategy and Structure: Chapters in the History of the Industrial Enterprise* (Cambridge, Mass.: M.I.T. Press, 1962), p. 235.

[3] S. Tilles, "How to Evaluate Corporate Strategy," *Harvard Business Review*, July/August 1963, p. 111.

FOCUSING EFFORT

A second major claim, looking inside the organization, is that *strategy is needed to focus effort and promote coordination of activity*. Without strategy, an organization is a collection of individuals, each going his or her own way, or else looking for something to do. The essence of organization is *collective action,* and one thing that knits individual actors together is strategy—again, through providing a sense of direction. Alfred Sloan notes in his memoirs a justification of the consolidated product-line strategy developed at General Motors under his leadership: "Some kind of rational policy was called for . . . it was necessary to know what one was trying to do," especially with regard to duplication across certain product lines.[4] Of course, by so focusing effort and directing the attention of each part within the integrated whole, the organization runs the risk of being unable to change its strategy when it has to.

DEFINING THE ORGANIZATION

Third, *strategy is needed to define the organization*. Strategy serves not only to direct the attention of the people working within an organization, but also to give the organization meaning for them as well as for outsiders. As plan or pattern, but especially as position or perspective, its strategy defines the organization, providing people with a shorthand way to understand it and to differentiate it from others. Christensen et al. discuss "the power of strategy as a simplifying concept" that enables certain outsiders (they are referring here to independent directors, but the point applies to any interested outsider) "to *know* the business (in a sense) without being *in* the business."[5] Of course, that "little knowledge" can be "a dangerous thing." But there is no denying that strategy does provide a convenient way to understand an organization.

In the early 1980s, the business press was very enthusiastic about General Electric. A reading of the reports of journalists and financial analysts suggests that what really impressed them was not what General Electric had done up to that point but that its new chief executive had articulated a clear, intended strategy for the firm. Thus Kidder, Peabody opened a December 21, 1983 newsletter with the statement: "General Electric is in the process of becoming a somewhat simpler company to understand," the result of the CEO's statement that it would focus on three major segments—core businesses, high technology, and services. Later they explained that "One of the main reasons we have been recommending General Electric for the past three years is the dynamic, creative, motivational

---

[4]A. P. Sloan, *My Years at General Motors* (New York: Doubleday, 1963), p. 267.

[5]C. R. Christensen, D. R. Andrews, J. L. Bower, R. G. Hamermesh, and M. E. Porter, *Business Policy: Text and Cases,* 5th ed. (Homewood, Ill.: Richard D. Irwin, 1982), p. 834.

leadership that the youthful Jack Welch . . . has provided. . . . His energy, enthusiasm, and ability to articulate a tight and viable corporate strategy are very impressive." No analyst can ever hope to understand much about a company so diversified and complex as General Electric, hence a clear, articulated strategy becomes a surrogate for that understanding.

The important question is whether a simplified strategy for such a complex system helps or hinders its performance—and the question is not meant to be rhetorical. On one hand, such a strategy cannot help but violate the immense complexity of the system, encouraging various dysfunctional pressures from outsiders (directors, for example, who may try to act on their "little knowledge") or even from insiders (chief executives, for example, who try to exercise control over divisions remote from their understanding by putting them into the simplistic categories of "dog" or "cash cow"). On the other hand, the enthusiasm generated by a clear strategy—a clear sense of mission—can produce a host of positive benefits. Those stock analysts not only helped to raise General Electric's stock price, they also helped to fire up the enthusiasm of the company's suppliers and customers, as well as the employees themselves, thereby promoting commitment which can improve performance. Thus, strategy may be of help, not only technically, through the coordination of work, but also emotionally, through the development of beliefs.

Imagine an organization without a name. We would not even be able to discuss it. For all purposes—practical and otherwise—it would not exist. Now imagine an organization with a name but with no strategy, in any sense—no position, no perspective, no plan (or ploy), not even any pattern consistent in its behaviors. How would we describe it or deal with it? An organization without a strategy would be like an individual without a personality—unknown, and unknowable. Of course, we cannot imagine such an organization. But some do come close. Just as we all know bland people with hardly any personality, so too do we know organizations with hardly any sense of strategy (which Rhenman labels "marginal organizations"[6]).

Most people think of such organizations as purely opportunistic, flitting from one opportunity to another,[7] or else as lethargic, with little energy to do anything but allow inertia to take its course (which may suggest strategy as pattern but not as plan). But we need not be so negative about this. Sometimes, lack of strategy is temporary and even necessary. It may, for example, simply represent a stage in the transition from an outdated strategy to a new, more viable one. Or it may reflect the fact that an environment has turned so dynamic that it would be folly to settle on any consistency for a time (as in the oil companies in 1973).

In one study,[8] a film company that began with a very clear direction lost it

---

[6]E. Rhenman, *Organization Theory for Long-Range Planning* (New York: Wiley, 1973).

[7]H. I. Ansoff, *Corporate Strategy* (New York: McGraw-Hill, 1965), p. 113.

[8]H. Mintzberg and A. McHugh, "Strategy Formation in an Adhocracy," *Administrative Science Quarterly* 30 (June 1985), pp. 160–97.

over time. It never really had formal plans; at best there existed broad leadership intentions in the earliest years. But it did have a very clear position and a very distinct perspective, as well as rather focused patterns, the latter at least at certain periods in its history. But over time, the position eroded, the perspective clouded, and the patterns multiplied, so that diffusion replaced definition. The insiders become increasingly frustrated, coming to treat their organization more like a shell under which they worked than a system of which they were an integral part. As for the outside influences, lacking any convenient means to define the organization, they attacked it increasingly for irrelevance. Ironically, the organization turned out a number of brilliant films throughout all this, but—contrary to General Electric yet reinforcing the same conclusion—what it did do proved less important than what it did not exhibit, namely, strategy as a clear sense of direction.

PROVIDING CONSISTENCY

A return to the notion of strategy as a "simplifying concept" may provide the clearest reason as to why organizations seem to need strategies. *Strategy is needed to reduce uncertainty and provide consistency (however arbitrary that may be), in order to aid cognition, to satisfy intrinsic needs for order, and to promote efficiency under conditions of stability (by concentrating resources and exploiting past learning).*

Psychologist William James once described the experiences of the infant as a "blooming, buzzing confusion." According to Ornstein, who so quotes him, that is due to "the lack of a suitable categorizing scheme in which to sort experiences consistently."[9] An organization without a strategy experiences the same confusion; its collective cognition can become overloaded, its members having no way to deal with experiences consistently. Thus, strategy is a categorizing scheme by which incoming stimuli can be ordered and dispatched.

In this sense, a strategy is like a theory; indeed, it *is* a theory (as in Drucker's "theory of the business"[10])—a cognitive structure (and filter) to simplify and explain the world, and thereby to facilitate action. Rumelt captures the notion well with the comment that "The function of strategy is not to 'solve a problem', but to so structure a situation that the emergent problems are solvable."[11] Or, as Spender puts it (and so specifies how ambitious is research on the process of

---

[9]R. F. Ornstein, *The Psychology of Consciousness* (New York: Freeman, 1972), p. 74.

[10]P. F. Drucker, *Management: Tasks, Responsibilities, Practices* (New York: Harper & Row, 1974).

[11]R. P. Rumelt, "Evaluation of Strategy: Theory and Models," in *Strategic Management: A New View of Business Policy and Planning*, ed. D. E. Schendel and C. W. Hofer (Boston: Little Brown, 1979), p. 199.

strategy making): "Because strategy-making is a type of theory building, a theory of strategy-making is a theory of theory-building."[12]

But, like every theory, strategy is a simplification that necessarily distorts the reality. Strategies and theories are not reality themselves, only representations (that is, abstractions) of reality in the minds of people. Thus, every strategy must misrepresent and mistreat at least some stimuli; that is the price of having a strategy. Good strategies, like good theories, simply minimize the amount of distortion.

"Strategy," notes James Brian Quinn, "deals . . . with the unknowable."[13] But it might perhaps be more accurate to write that strategy assumes the unknowable can be made knowable, or at least controllable. As such, it is important to emphasize that strategy is a concept rooted in *stability*.[14] No one should be fooled by all the attention to change and flexibility. When Miller and Friesen write that "Strategy is essentially a dynamic concept. It describes a modus operandi more than a posture, a process more than a state,"[15] they are not talking about strategy at all but about the process of making strategy. Strategy is not about adaptability in behavior but about regularity in behavior, not about discontinuity but about consistency. Organizations have strategies to reduce uncertainty, to block out the unexpected, and, as shown here, to *set* direction, *focus* effort, *define* the organization. Strategy is a force that *resists* change, not encourages it.

Why then do organizations seem to have such an overwhelming need for consistency? In other words, why the obsession with strategy? To some extent, this is a human need per se. Consistency provides us with a sense of being in control (and nowhere is this better illustrated than in the prescriptive literature of strategic management, although those of us who feel compelled to study strategy as a pattern in behavior may be accused of the same thing). That is presumably why some psychologists have found that people claim to discover patterns even in streams of random numbers.[16] Moore makes this point well: Strategy is "a relief from the anxiety created by complexity, unpredictability, and incomplete knowledge. As such, it has an element of compulsion about it."[17]

---

[12]J. C. Spender, "Commentary," in *Strategic Management: A New View of Business Policy and Planning,* ed. D. E. Schendel and C. W. Hofer (Boston: Little Brown, 1979), p. 396.

[13]J. B. Quinn, *Strategies for Change: Logical Incrementalism* (Homewood, Ill.: Richard D. Irwin, 1980), p. 163.

[14]D. J. Teece, "Economic Analysis and Strategic Management," *California Management Review* 26/3 (Spring 1984), p. 88; R. E. Caves, "Economic Analysis and the Quest for Competitive Advantage," *AEA Papers and Proceedings* 74/2 (May 1984), pp. 127–28.

[15]D. Miller and P. H. Friesen, "The Longitudinal Analysis of Organizations: A Methodological Perspective," *Management Science* 28/9 (1982), p. 1020.

[16]R. N. Taylor, "Psychological Aspects of Planning," *Long Range Planning* 9/2 (1976), p. 70.

[17]D. G. Moore, *Managerial Strategies and Organization Dynamics in Sears Retailing,* Ph.D. thesis, University of Chicago, 1954, p. 34.

But there is more to the need for consistency than that. Above all, consistency is an efficient response to an environment that is stable, or at least a niche that remains lucrative.

For one thing, strategy enables the organization to concentrate its resources and exploit its opportunities and its own existing skills and knowledge to the very fullest. Strategies reflect the results of organizational learning, the patterns that have formed around those initiatives that have worked best. They help to ensure that these patterns remain fully exploited.

Moreover, once established, strategies reduce the need to keep learning in a broad sense.[18] In this respect, a strategy works for an organization much like instinct works for an animal: It facilitates fast, almost automatic response to known stimuli. To be efficient, at least in a stable environment, means to get on with things without the need to think them through each time. As Jonsson notes about "myth," his equivalent to what we call strategy as perspective:

> The myth provides the organization with a stable basis for action. It eliminates uncertainty about what has gone wrong, and it substitutes certainty: we can do it, it is up to us . . . the riskiness disappears when you 'know' what has to be done. If there is much at stake and you are uncertain as to what is wrong, action is inhibited. If you are certain about what should be done, action is precipitated.[19]

To rethink everything all the time, as Jonsson implies, is unproductive. The person who gets up every morning and asks, "Do I really want to remain married?" or even, "I wonder if it is better today to wash before I brush my teeth," will eventually drive himself crazy, or at least work himself into inaction. The same will be true of the organization that is constantly putting its strategies into question. That will impede its ability to get on with things. (A colleague makes this point best with his proposed epitaph: "Here lies RR: he kept his options open.")

We function best when we can take some things for granted, at least for a time. And that is a major role of strategy in organizations: It resolves the big issues so that people can get on with the little details—targeting and serving customers instead of debating which markets are best, buying and operating machines instead of wondering about different technologies, rearranging deck chairs and looking for icebergs. This applies not only at the bottom of the hierarchy, but all along it, right to the very top. Most of the time, the chief executive, too, must get on with managing the organization in a given context; he cannot continually put that context into question.

---

[18]J. S. Bruner, J. J. Goodnow, and G. A. Austin, *A Study of Thinking* (New York: Wiley, 1956), p. 12.

[19]S. A. Jonsson and R. A. Lundin, "Myths and Wishful Thinking as Management Tools," in *Perspective Models of Organization,* ed. P. C. Nystrom and W. H. Starbuck (New York: North Holland Publishing, 1977), p. 43.

There is a tendency to picture the chief executive as a strategist, conceiving the big ideas while everyone else gets on with the little details. But his job is not like that at all. A great deal of it has to do with its own little details—reinforcing the existing perspective ("culture" is the currently popular word now) through all kinds of mundane figurehead duties, maintaining the flow of information by developing contacts and disseminating the resulting information, negotiating agreements to reinforce existing positions, and so on.[20]

The problem with all this, of course, is that eventually situations change, environments destabilize, niches disappear. Then all that is constructive and efficient about an established strategy becomes a liability. That is why, even though the concept of strategy is rooted in stability, so much of the study of strategy making focuses on change. But while prescription for strategic change in the literature may come easy, management of the change itself, in practice, especially when it involves perspective, comes hard. The very encouragement of strategy to get on with it—its very role in protecting the organization against distraction[21]—impedes the organization's capacity to respond to change in the environment. As Kuhn notes, in discussing the paradigms of communities of scholars, "Retooling is expensive."[22] This is especially true when it is not just machines that have to be retooled, but human minds as well. Strategy, as mental set, can blind the organization to its own outdatedness. Thus we conclude that strategies are to organizations what blinders are to horses: they keep them going in a straight line, but impede the use of peripheral vision.

And this leads to our final conclusion, which is that strategies (and the strategic management process) can be vital to organizations, both by their presence *and* by their absence.

---

[20]H. Mintzberg, *The Nature of Managerial Work* (New York: Harper and Row, 1973).

[21]Christensen et al., Business Policy: Text and Cases, 5th ed.

[22]T. S. Kuhn, *The Structure of Scientific Revolutions*, 2nd ed. (Chicago: University of Chicago Press, 1970), p. 76.

What this article is about: From his 1988 book, *Talking Straight,* the author discusses some of his principles of management and how to understand life in a corporation.

1–6 Management by Nagging

Lee Iacocca

*Lee Iacocca is chairman and
chief executive officer of Chrysler Corporation*

Whenever the subject of management comes up, everybody—and I mean everybody, right down to the janitor—seems to have some mystical approach to it. By now there have been about as many books written on management as there have been on diets—and, I might add, with about the same measure of success. There's probably even a grapefruit management book in the works somewhere.

How good are all those diet books? Well, none of them delivers unless you remember to do one thing: Don't eat so much. It's still the only way to lose weight. In the end, if you don't follow through on a few simple principles, what good is reading all those books?

The same is true of management. I got so much reaction to the management tips in my last book that I went back and reread them to see why all these testimonials were crossing my desk. All I'd done was toss out a few broad concepts—my quarterly review system, my firm belief in communications—and yet people were writing from all over the world to tell me they had turned their hardware store or their Good Humor route into a stunning success. I said to myself: I'd better try to figure out what my theory of management is. So here's my contribution to the never-ending debate.

If you make believe that 10 guys in pinstriped suits are back in a kindergarten class playing with building blocks, you'll get a rough picture of what life in a corporation is like. Grown men in a meeting will do anything—absolutely anything—to avoid being shown up. If someone doesn't know the facts about a subject, he'll ad-lib, just like a kid. Instead of saying "I'll have to get that for you, boss; I don't have the answer right at hand," he'll try to fake it. He's scared

---

that if he confesses he doesn't know, the boss will think he's not as sharp as the other little kids in class and maybe he'll miss nap time. As a result, he'll embarrass himself and babble like an idiot.

Only the boss can set a tone that lets people feel comfortable enough to say those magic words, "I don't know." Followed by: "But I'll find out." Business, after all, is nothing more than a bunch of human relationships. It's one guy comparing notes with another: "Here's what I'm doing. What are you doing? Is there some way I can help you—and you can help me?"

Whenever I talk about this subject, I feel like a 5-year-old myself. People are always saying to me: "But there's got to be something mysterious. There must be a formula." There really isn't. Start with good people, lay out the rules, communicate with your employees, motivate them, and reward them if they perform. If you do all those things effectively, you can't miss.

There are two broad management subjects that business people will argue about until long after I'm dead. One is the role of the staff (or planners) versus the line guys (or doers). The other subject is consensus management versus arbitrary one-man rule.

First things first. Staff, to reduce it to its simplest terms, is what supports the boss. I don't mean who brings the coffee, but who furnishes the information that helps the boss make decisions. The important question that every manager has to answer for himself or herself is: How much staff do I need to run my organization? In some businesses, often one good secretary will do. At Ford, either because of the family's mentality or the Harvard Business School mentality, you had to plan and analyze down to the last gnat's hair. Before you made a move, you had to examine every alternative and research every factor to be sure you didn't make a mistake. That was the ultimate sin. Ford is so chock-full of staffs that it even has a super staff—the Corporate Strategy and Analysis Staff—that oversees all the other staffs!

I don't care how successful Ford or anyone else might be with that approach; it's not the kind of environment that gives big business a good name. After a while, such companies have a hard time attracting young, entrepreneurial people, because there's just no room for guts management and instinct when you're loaded down with a lot of second-guessing.

My problem at Chrysler is exactly the opposite. I have a ridiculously small staff. My line guys are so aggressive that they may make multimillion-dollar mistakes before I've had one alternative to look at. Frankly, I'm so lean on staff that it sometimes scares me. That's why I've recently installed a few staff people, notably Tom DeNomme, who's listed on the chart as my vice president of corporate strategy.

His real title should be Devil's Advocate. He tosses out an idea a minute, some of them a bit off the wall, in order to keep me in constant turmoil. It can get crazy sometimes, but I like it that way because I don't have—or want—a purchasing staff, a marketing staff, an engineering staff, and a manufacturing staff to ride herd on the operating guys who are doing all the work.

My feeling is that if I'm going to err, I'd always err on the side of leanness, because the decision making is faster. Of course, if you get too lean, you'll wind up making momentous decisions with no more information than what the weather is like outside. But you don't need a bloody bureaucracy to make sure everybody's ass (especially the boss's) is covered in case of a screwup.

When it comes time to make decisions, you shouldn't get too old over them. Sure, they won't all be perfect. In fact, some of them will be duds. Learn from them, but don't stop trying. The introverts of the world, the nonrisk-takers, are probably that way because they got burned young. Maybe they made the wrong move in a marbles tournament or a game of checkers and now they're never going to take a risk again. That's no way to live—and it's certainly no way to make a profit.

The big fuss about consensus management is another issue that boils down to a lot of noise about very little. The consensus advocates are great admirers of the Japanese management style. Consensus is what Japan is famous for. Well, I know the Japanese fairly well: They still remember Douglas MacArthur with respect and they still bow down to the Emperor. In my dealings with them, they talk a lot about consensus, but there's always one guy behind the scenes who ends up making the tough decisions.

It doesn't make sense to me to think that Mr. Toyoda or Mr. Morita of Sony sits around in committee meetings and says, "We've got to get everybody in this organization, from the janitor up, to agree with this move." The Japanese do believe in their workers' involvement early on and in feedback from employees. And they probably listen better than we do. But you can bet that when the chips are down, the yen stops at the top guy's desk, while we're wasting time trying to emulate something I don't think really exists.

Business structures are microcosms of other structures. There were no corporations in the 15th century. But there were families. There were city governments, provinces, armies. There was the church. All of them had, for lack of a better word, a pecking order.

Why? Because that's the only way you can steer clear of anarchy. Otherwise, you'll have somebody come in one morning and tell you: "Yesterday I got tired of painting red convertibles, so today I switched to all baby-blues on my own." You'll never get anything done right that way.

What's to admire about consensus management anyway? By its very nature, it's slow. It can never be daring. There can never be real accountability—or flexibility. About the only plus that I've been able to figure out is that consensus management means a consistency of direction and objectives. But so much consistency can become faceless, and that's a problem too. In any event, I don't think it can work in this country. The fun of business for entrepreneurs, big or small, lies in our free-enterprise system, not in the greatest agreement by the greatest number.

Another thing that a lot of management experts advocate importing from the Far East is the notion that the boss should be one of the boys. Democratic as that philosophy may sound, I don't think it's very practical. If the boss lets his hair down too much, he ends up like Rodney Dangerfield. No respect.

And yet, the boss can't be aloof either. A lot of the guys in the *Fortune* 500 seem to feel it's beneath their station even to talk to their own work force. Someone who's got 200,000 people working for him and who makes a million dollars a year begins to believe his position and his power make him infallible. He forgets to listen. He gets caught up in the clack of all the yes-men around him.

My style, I hope, falls somewhere between those extremes. For example, I go the National Automobile Dealers Association convention every year. In fact I haven't missed one in 30 years. Why? Because my presence tells the dealers in the best way possible that I think they're a vital part of the company. My being with them for a few days is the most effective investment I can make, and so I'm there religiously. I shake hands with the dealers and try to tell them how much I appreciate all their efforts.

By the way, that goes for everybody on the team. Once in a while you've got to show them you care. I have a minimum of four press conferences; I even care for the reporters (how about that!). I have formal management meetings with our top 500 people four times a year. I visit our top bankers twice a year. You cannot call on these people only when you're in a jam. Handling crises is a hell of a lot easier if you've already got some rapport with the people who can help you solve them.

At Chrysler we've initiated an idea that works quite well. Every Monday, the top operating people have a meeting to go over basic operations. Before they discuss any business, they bring in someone from a lower level who has been named the winner of the week for his or her performance, and offer their congratulations for a job well done. Word gets around, and other people start thinking, I'd like to be invited too. They see that it's real recognition, right from the top.

Delegation versus the one-man band is another hot topic in management circles these days. The Harvard Business School says "Delegate," so people dutifully do it. But all too many of them never bother to get involved afterwards with the people they delegate to. This is where Reagan ran into trouble in the Iran crisis. The other extreme, of course, is the strong-willed leader who never lets go of anything, who has to be in on every decision. For instance, Donald Trump, the real-estate tycoon, signs every check in his organization. Every check. He's a fanatic about knowing where each and every penny is going. Obviously, that style works for him, but in a big organization it sure can slow things down.

In the end, you've got to take a little of each approach. Alone with yourself, you have to look in the mirror and analyze your strengths and weaknesses. The stuff you're good at you can hang on to, but the stuff you're lousy at, you delegate. Then you try to learn from the person you delegated to.

As for me, I delegate plenty, but I still have a hard time keeping my hands off the marketing and design areas of the business. I want to be there, because I like them. And so I drive the people in those departments nuts. I've just got to stop carrying on this way!

Let's say you've done a good job delegating. Even if the people to whom you've assigned responsibilities are top-notch, you must let them know that you remember what you gave them and that you're keeping track, for everyone's sake.

Charlie Beacham at Ford was a great delegator. And by and large he picked terrific people. If I ever questioned some of his choices, he'd snap back, "Well, I picked you. What the hell are you complaining about?" But after he delegated, he used to drive his people crazy. He didn't need to know every last fact, but when he'd drop into your office, sit on your desk, and say, "How are you doing? I haven't seen you in three months, but your truck sales stink," you'd snap to attention pretty quick.

I used to label that "management by nagging." A lot of business people might say, "Boy, I wouldn't want someone like that over me." But Charlie had such an engaging personality that he could get away with it. When he walked out, even though he'd just shoved a spear into you, you were still happy that he'd come to see you.

I learned that technique from him, and so I've always managed hands-on. If you ask my crew, they'll probably tell you that I'm a pretty good nagger in my own right. If I've got a fault, it's probably that I manage hands-on too much. You shouldn't get so antsy that your own people don't even have time to find out where the bathroom is.

It's also very important to be flexible. I don't want to quote you the old cliche, "Management's an art, not a science," but dammit if it isn't the truth. Some heads of companies maintain that they have a system and they don't care who they stick into it. They'll say, "Let's put No. 1573–8 in that slot," as if they're assigning a prisoner to a cell. I don't see how you can manage that way. You have to adapt to personalities or you're finished.

By the time people get to a company, they're pretty well molded. Time and again, I've tried to change people who are over 21, and I don't think I've succeeded with a single one. Over the years, I've been stuck with people who had some rotten work habits, and so I thought I'd pump some energy into them. Although I'm a pretty good salesman and can often be very persuasive, they wouldn't budge. Not one inch. Why? Their parents and their grade school teachers got to them before I did.

Charlie Beacham was right on the mark when he told me: "Don't try to change anyone. Use your energies on something better. You might win over 1 in 100, but you'll take such a long time finding him that you'll go crazy trying."

What does that mean? You have to take people with all their warts. And then, to make the system work, you have to discipline them a little bit. You have to say, "Okay, I don't care how you grew up or what you are—here's the way we're going to run this ball club. And here are the plays. If you don't like them, it's going to show. By that time, you won't have to get off the team—I'll throw you off."

Once you've laid down the rules, you have to sit back and trust your people, even though you won't know for a while if they'll come through on the battlefield. You can never be sure with live ammunition if the lieutenant is going to take you up the hill or turn around and run like a scared rabbit.

That's why the worst threat to a company, I'm convinced, is when you take a chance on someone who winds up being in over his head. He doesn't know how to admit he can't cope, and as he screws up he ends up screwing up everybody around him.

On the other hand, you have to be able to gamble on unproven talent, or everything stagnates. One of the most important ways I keep in touch with bright lights is through the technique of "skip" meetings. I don't know who coined the term, but the idea is that you're skipping levels of management to chat with someone you normally might never hear from. This means that the chairman of the board gets to have a relaxed talk with someone several levels removed from him.

I began skip meetings many years ago, because the system had gotten so big that I was talking only to my top two or three people. Oh, I heard from plenty of people in endless committee meetings. But those meetings were so highly structured you could almost smell that the system had already filtered or homogenized what they could say. I didn't want to wreck the system or go around the organization, but I wanted to stop being insulated at the top of the pyramid.

So every few weeks I call in a department manager or a top engineer or a plant manager and meet with him one-on-one. These people are known as the high-pos—or high potentials—who, unless they mess up, will be running the company 5 or 10 years from now. When they come in, they're usually a little reticent, praying they don't spill coffee on me or knock over a vase. I relax them by telling them this is not a performance review and everything's off the record and strictly confidential. Otherwise, they'd all run for cover.

My questions are always simple. How do you get along with the rest of the system? Does it work? Do you know what's coming up and going down? Once I start firing away, I find that they loosen up pretty quickly.

If you handle things right, the idea takes hold. I'd been doing skip meetings for many years when suddenly I noticed some of my other top people doing them too. Now members of our executive committee have picked up the habit.

After a year's worth of skip meetings, I may not remember who told me what, but I manage to get a feel for whether things are going right and whether the engine's hitting on all cylinders. I also get to know, close up, a lot of our best middle managers, whom otherwise I would never even meet.

I'll give you an example. I had been trying to put in a system of brand management under which every brand of car would have one person accountable for giving that brand an identity to the public. The manager would have control of the Plymouth car line and its marketing, for example, a full three years before the product was due to come to market.

At first we only put our toe in the water. We appointed a brand manager for product and a brand manager for marketing, and we told them: You two are going to be like Siamese twins. Live with each other. Get together day and night.

Turned out, the idea was a fiasco. How did I find out? Because in a lot of the skip meetings, people told me it wasn't working. I heard the same things over and over again. There should be one guy, not two. Also, the current two weren't able to get access to the company's resources early enough to have real responsibility. They were stuck on the outside like cheerleaders. That's how I discovered that we had to take the system apart and give the brand managers genuine power.

Whether it's through skip meetings or other means, it's absolutely essential to let your people express themselves. And that means letting them make mistakes. You've got to allow them to walk into your office and say, "Boss, I blew it." That's called growing.

I'm reminded of the guy who says to the football player, "Geez, your team won the Super Bowl—how do you feel about it?"

"Terrific," the player says. "A dream come true."

Then the first guy says, "Yeah, but you didn't play. You were on the bench the whole 60 minutes."

"Well, that's true," the player says, "but I was suited up and felt like part of the team."

That's not my approach. My feeling is that there's nothing like playing. Being active is the key. I like to get my people into the game.

Last year I decided to reorganize Chrysler for that reason alone. I came to the conclusion that I wasn't using all my people to their fullest potential. I was deep in talent, but it was arranged in such a monolithic way that I couldn't get some of the second-level people into the flow of things. That's when I said to myself: "I've got so much on my plate. Why don't I use some of these guys more? Why am I standing on the ceremony of an organizational chart?"

I decided to make a number of my second-tier people more accountable. At the same time, I also wanted to deploy them so that they'd be closer to the marketplace. I didn't need them to talk among themselves but to talk to the people who buy from us. And so I divvied up the company into manageable pieces and told these executives to go play the game to the hilt. It's now their show. Make it or break it.

When you try something like that, you have to be cautious or you'll bruise some mighty big egos. In reorganizing things, I had to switch some areas of responsibility. One lesson I learned a long time ago is that once you've given a guy turf in a hierarchy, the minute you openly take away any of it, even if it's one lousy blade of crab grass, he gets miffed.

I suppose I can't blame anyone who reacts like that, because I was the same way in my career. When Henry Ford named me head of the Ford division, I was given everything but the assembly plants. Now I didn't know a damn thing about assembly plants, but I did know that the guy I was replacing used to have them. So even though I was being given the opportunity of a lifetime, I was ticked off that Henry didn't have the confidence in me to give me the assembly operations. I needed those plants like a hole in the head, but I was offended anyway.

In my own company I've had situations where a guy's plate was so full that the food was spilling onto the floor, but if I lightened his load, he saw it as a threat to his power and forgot completely what the objectives of the company were.

I know right away when someone's mad, because he'll use the standard ploy to tip me off: You go to see the head of personnel and ask what your benefits are and what you would get if you retired tomorrow. Naturally word gets back to the boss. I have to confess it's a maneuver that I once used myself. The tricky part if you're the boss is that you can never be sure whether the guy's trying to deliver a message or whether he's just playing chicken with you.

When all is said and done, management is a code of values and judgments. And that's why, in the end, you have to be yourself. Which brings me to the best rule of management: Pick a style that you're comfortable with and stick with it. You can have role models, but don't try to be somebody else. Be yourself, stay natural, and dammit, smile once in a while!

What this article is about: In a speech presented at the General Electric Annual Meeting of Share Owners, Waukesha, Wisconsin, April 27, 1988, John Welch stated management's task should be aimed at liberating, facilitating, unleashing the human energy and initiative of people.

1–7 Managing for the Nineties

John F. Welch, Jr.

*John F. Welch, Jr., is Chairman and
Chief Executive Officer of
General Electric Company*

Good Morning . . . and welcome.

No annual meeting would feel right without a few numbers, preferably a few *good* numbers. Despite the unpleasantness of October—from which our stock has not yet recovered—1987 was a fine year for your company. Net earnings of $2.915 billion were up 17 percent; sales were up 12 percent and now approach $40 billion. October 19th didn't cause a hiccup in the company's business performance. Earnings growth in our last two quarters has averaged 17 percent.

But putting the numbers aside for a moment, this morning I would like to take a little of your time for a look back on the decade before we turn our faces toward the '90s. Retrospection, dwelling on the achievements and events of the past, is not something we spend much time on at GE. But just a few minutes of it might help us put our view of the future in context.

Seven years ago we stood before you, our share owners . . . before the financial community . . . before our employees . . . and sketched a vision that was unusual in that it had little of the soaring rhetoric and boundless optimism that often affect new teams impatient to take the field.

At the beginning of the decade, we saw two challenges ahead of us, one external and one internal. Externally, we faced a world economy that would be characterized by slower growth with stronger global competitors going after a smaller pie.

In the context of that environment we had one clear-cut major competitor:

SOURCE: GE Executive Speech Reprint.

Japan, Inc. . . . powerful . . . innovative . . . and moving aggressively into many of our markets.

Internally, our challenge was even bigger. We had to find a way to combine the power, resources, and reach of a big company with the hunger, the agility, the spirit, and the fire of a small one.

Our experience during the late '70s in grappling with world competition etched very clearly on our minds the belief that companies that held on to marginal businesses—or less than world-competitive operations of *any* sort—wouldn't be around for very long. That analysis led us to a strategy that said we had to be number one or number two in each one of our businesses . . . or we had to see a way to get there . . . or exit if we couldn't. The product businesses had to achieve global leadership positions in cost, quality, and technology. Our services businesses had to define and attain leading niche positions in the broad spectrum of markets they served. That was—this is—our strategy: simple, even stark.

Our internal challenge was infinitely more complex and difficult. As we set out to make this big company with its power, resources, and reach move and act like a small one, we tried to keep in mind the desirable characteristics the best small companies seem to share. First, they communicate better. Without the din and prattle of bureaucracy, people listen as well as talk; and since there are fewer of them they generally know and understand each other.

Second, small companies move faster. They know the penalties for hesitation in the marketplace.

Third, in small companies, with fewer layers and less camouflage, the leaders show up very clearly on the screen. Their performance and its impact are clear to everyone.

And, finally, small companies waste less. They spend less time in endless reviews and approvals and politics and paper drills. They have fewer people; therefore they do only the important things. Their people are free to direct their energy and attention toward the marketplace rather than fighting bureaucracy.

To win externally during the 80s, we believed we needed to develop these internal characteristics. So we embarked on a mission: to keep the good things inherent in this big company we had, and there were many of those, but combine them with the attractive small company features I've just described.

Now, how we went at this can be described from two totally different perspectives. One perspective would use words like "downsizing," "reducing," "cutting." We think that view misses the point. We see our task as a totally different one aimed at liberating, facilitating, unleashing the human energy and initiative of our people.

Sure we saved. Simply by eliminating the company's top operating level, the sectors, we saved $40 million. But that was just a bonus that pales in importance to the sudden release of talent and energy that poured out after all the dampers, values, and baffles of the sectors had been removed. We can say without hesitation that almost every single good thing that has happened within this company over the past few years can be traced to the liberation of some individual, some team, or some business.

So we reduced the number of management layers in the company to get closer to the individual—the source of that creative energy we needed.

In reducing these layers, we are trying to get the people in the organization to understand that they can't do everything they used to do. They have to set priorities. The less-important tasks have to be left undone. Trying to do the same number of tasks with fewer people would be the antithesis of what we set out to achieve: a faster, more focused, more purposeful company.

As we became leaner, we found ourselves communicating better, with fewer interpreters and fewer filters.

We found that with fewer layers we had wider spans of management. We weren't managing better. We were managing less, and *that* was better.

We found that the leaders—people with a vision and a passion—soon began to stand out. And when they did, we found our own self-confidence growing to the point that we began to delegate authority further and further down into the company. Businesses were allowed to develop their own pay plans and incentives that made sense for *their* marketplaces. They were given the freedom to spend significant sums on plant and equipment on their own, based on *their* needs, *their* judgment, *their* view of their marketplace. Freeing people to move rapidly and without hesitation makes all the difference in the world. At the corporate level it permitted us to move in the RCA merger, the Medical Systems/Consumer Electronics deal, the sale of Utah International and, most recently, in the Roper acquisition.

At the business level, it results in greater product and service innovation and more new ventures, all done within the business, without worrying about the corporate view—the corporate second-guess.

But it is when this freedom reaches *all* the way down through the organization and the energy at the *individual* level is released that truly great things begin to happen. In our Major Appliance business in Louisville a few years ago, people on the assembly line suddenly found two levers in front of them. One lever stopped the line. The other sent a part on its way *only* after an individual was satisfied that it was perfect. The line workers suddenly became the final authority on the quality of their work. The cynics scoffed when this system was proposed, predicting chaos or production at a snail's pace.

What happened? Quality increased enormously and the line ran faster and smoother than ever.

There in Louisville and elsewhere around the company, we have found what we believe is the distilled essence of competitiveness—the reservoir of talent and creativity and energy that can be found in each of our people. That essence is liberated when we make people believe that what they think and do is important . . . and then get out of their way while they do it.

We are nowhere near succeeding totally in achieving this ambiance. But with what we have seen so far of the energy that can be released by good people, we are convinced it is the factor that has driven our results in the 80s—and those results have been terrific.

From 1981 to 87 our earnings have grown 10 percent per year—triple the rate of the S&P 400 companies. Over the same period our stock has increased in value 19 percent per year compounded versus 11 percent for that same S&P 400. GE has come from eleventh in total market value to third—from $13 billion to close to $40 billion. By virtually every measurement, we have outdistanced the aggregate performance of our peers.

Our team's 28 straight quarters of earnings growth is good. But what encourages us most about the overall results is that our biggest annual earnings increases have been . . . and will be . . . in 87 and 88. The short-term–long-term management question, raised so often about American business, is not an issue at GE.

Nevertheless, there's a tendency now in everyone to want to pause, to relax, to be a little easier on ourselves. But we can't. In the 50s, 60s, and 70s the domestic business cycle permitted periods of consolidation—a breather every now and then. No more. We're all in the global arena now and there isn't even the usual one-minute break between rounds in this battle.

In 81, as I mentioned, Japan was our main competitive threat; and we've been going up against them all over the globe throughout the decade. But now the world is even tougher and more crowded. Korea and Taiwan have become world-class competitors, as hungry and aggressive as Japan was in 81. Europe is on fire with a new entrepreneurial spirit and leadership that is among the world's best. Many of its most aggressive companies, like Electrolux and ASEA of Sweden, Philips of Holland, and Siemens and Bayer of Germany, are after our markets through acquisitions and joint ventures . . . just as we are going after theirs.

At the same time, the Japanese are more sophisticated and aggressive than ever—building sourcing plants outside Japan, including dozens just over the Mexican border.

The environment we described seven years ago as tough, as we looked at the '80s, looks relatively easy compared to the one we see ahead of us today.

The 90s will be a white-knuckle decade for global business . . . fast . . . exhilarating . . . with sudden falls for many and victory for others. We are more confident than ever that we can win in this environment. We plan no major course corrections, just more on the same continuum of competitiveness propelled by individuals who have formed a consensus to win.

We approach the 90s with a business system, a method of operating, that allows us to routinely position each business for the short and long term so that while one or more are weathering difficult markets, the totality is always growing faster than the world economy.

No one in the world has a set of powerful businesses like ours. They've never been stronger. And big, bold moves are enhancing their global competitiveness: plastics by expansion in the United States, Europe, and the Far East . . . GEFS' numerous domestic acquisitions . . . Aircraft Engine with its European partnership . . . Factory Automations' worldwide venture with Fanuc of Japan . . . Medical Systems' French and Japanese acquisitions . . . NBC's new station and programming initiatives . . . joint ventures by Lighting in the Far East and, most recently, Roper's acquisition by Major Appliance. The list of moves goes on and on and will continue at an even faster pace. Our business strategy, grounded in reality, has *become* real. Our businesses *are* number one or two in their marketplaces.

To go with our business strategy, we've got a management system now in place and functioning that supports that strategy—one that is lean, liberating, fast-moving—an organization that facilitates and frees and, above all, understands that the fountainhead of success is the individual, not the system.

This management system, designed to draw out the best in the 300,000 individuals who make up this company, *is* drawing it out. *We're a long way from having those levers of responsibility in front of every workstation and desk in this company, but that is our ultimate objective.* We *know* where competitiveness comes from. It comes from people—but only from people who are free to dream, to risk, free to act.

Liberating those people, every one of them, is the great challenge we've been grappling with all over this company. And from what we've seen of the ocean of talent, initiative, and creativity that is unleashed when we have the self-confidence to turn it loose, we are convinced your company is more than a match for anything the world can throw at us.

With your support, we will continue to grow in the 90s. We'll continue to win . . . and win bigger than ever.

Part II

Business Strategy Formulation

The focus of this section is the formulation and analysis of business-level strategy. Henry Mintzberg's article exploring how strategies get made, as opposed to how they are supposed to get made, begins this section. The next two articles discuss approaches for understanding an organization's future environment. Ian Wilson provides a very readable description of GE's pioneering efforts in environmental scanning and the role it plays in strategy formulation. Steven P. Schnaars discusses the increasingly popular technique of scenario analysis. The next two articles explore aspects of generic strategies. Peter Wright examines three generic strategies—least-cost, differentiation, and niche. William Fulmer and Jack Goodwin examine some of the implications of a differentiation strategy. Next Malcolm Schofield and David Arnold examine strategies for mature businesses. In contrast, an interview with Victor Kiam explores growth strategies at Remington. The next two articles explore ways of developing a sustainable competitive advantage. Albert Isenman examines the strategic implications of suppliers and David Aaker looks at managing a firm's assets and skills. An international perspective is the focus of the last two articles. James Leontiades examines the impact of internationalization on competitive positioning and Michael Porter discusses the lag in competitive thinking that affects some U.S. managers as they try to compete globally.

What this article is about: In theory, corporate strategy is all reason, analysis, and planning. In practice, it is as much an art as a science. Some of the best strategies emerge over time, guided by executives whose feel for the business is like a potter's feel for clay.

2–1 *Crafting Strategy*

Henry Mintzberg
*Henry Mintzberg is Professor of Management
at McGill University*

Imagine someone planning strategy. What likely springs to mind is an image of orderly thinking: a senior manager, or a group of them, sitting in an office formulating courses of action that everyone else will implement on schedule. The keynote is reason—rational control, the systematic analysis of competitors and markets, of company strengths and weaknesses, the combination of these analyses producing clear, explicit, full-blown strategies.

Now imagine someone *crafting* strategy. A wholly different image likely results, as different from planning as craft is from mechanization. Craft evokes traditional skill, dedication, perfection through the mastery of detail. What springs to mind is not so much thinking and reason as involvement, a feeling of intimacy and harmony with the materials at hand, developed through long experience and commitment. Formulation and implementation merge into a fluid process of learning through which creative strategies evolve.

My thesis is simple: The crafting image better captures the process by which effective strategies come to be. The planning image, long popular in the literature, distorts these processes and thereby misguides organizations that embrace it unreservedly.

In developing this thesis, I shall draw on the experiences of a single craftsperson, a potter, and compare them with the results of a research project that tracked the strategies of a number of corporations across several decades. Because the two contexts are so obviously different, my metaphor, like my assertion, may seem farfetched at first. Yet if we think of a craftsperson as an organization of one, we can see that he or she must also resolve one of the great challenges

SOURCE: *Harvard Business Review*, July–August 1987, pp. 66–75.

the corporate strategist faces: knowing the organization's capabilities well enough to think deeply enough about its strategic direction. By considering strategy making from the perspective of one person, free of all the paraphernalia of what has been called the strategy industry, we can learn something about the formation of strategy in the corporation. For much as our potter has to manage her craft, so too managers have to craft their strategy.

At work, the potter sits before a lump of clay on the wheel. Her mind is on the clay, but she is also aware of sitting between her past experiences and her future prospects. She knows exactly what has and has not worked for her in the past. She has an intimate knowledge of her work, her capabilities, and her markets. As a craftsperson, she senses rather than analyzes these things; her knowledge is "tacit." All these things are working in her mind as her hands are working the clay. The product that emerges on the wheel is likely to be in the tradition of her past work, but she may break away and embark on a new direction. Even so, the past is no less present, projecting itself into the future.

Tracking Strategy

In 1971, I became intrigued by an unusual definition of strategy as a pattern in a stream of decisions (later changed to actions). I initiated a research project at McGill University, and over the next 13 years a team of us tracked the strategies of 11 organizations over several decades of their history. (Students at various levels also carried out about 20 other less comprehensive studies.) The organizations we studied were: Air Canada (1937–1976), Arcop, an architectural firm (1953–1978), Asbestos Corporation (1912–1975), Canadelle, a manufacturer of women's undergarments (1939–1976), McGill University (1829–1980), the National Film Board of Canada (1939–1976), Saturday Night Magazine (1928–1971), The Sherbrooke Record, a small daily newspaper (1946–1976), Steinberg Inc., a large supermarket chain (1917–1974), the U.S. military's strategy in Vietnam (1949–1973), and Volkswagenwerk (1934–1974).

As a first step, we developed chronological lists and graphs of the most important actions taken by each organization—such as store openings and closings, new flight destinations, and new product introductions. Second, we inferred patterns in these actions and labeled them as strategies.

Third, we represented graphically all the strategies we inferred in an organization so that we could line them up to see whether there were distinct periods in their development—for example, periods of stability, flux, or global change. Fourth, we used interviews and in-depth reports to study what appeared to be the key points of change in each organization's strategic history.

Finally, armed with all this strategic history, the research team studied each set of findings to develop conclusions about the process of strategy formation. Three themes guided us: the interplay of environment, leadership, and organization; the pattern of strategic change; and the processes by which strategies form. This article presents those conclusions.

In my metaphor, managers are craftspersons and strategy is their clay. Like the potter, they sit between a past of corporate capabilities and a future of market opportunities. And if they are truly craftspersons, they bring to their work an equally intimate knowledge of the materials at hand. That is the essence of crafting strategy.

In the pages that follow, we will explore this metaphor by looking at how strategies get made as opposed to how they are supposed to get made. Throughout, I will be drawing on the two sets of experiences I've mentioned. One, described in the insert, is a research project on patterns in strategy formation that has been going on at McGill University under my direction since 1971. The second is the stream of work of a successful potter, my wife, who began her craft in 1967.

Ask almost anyone what strategy is, and he will define it as a plan of some sort, an explicit guide to future behavior. Then ask what strategy a competitor or a government or even he himself has actually pursued. Chances are he will describe consistency in *past* behavior—a pattern in action over time. Strategy, it turns out, is one of those words that people define in one way, and often use in another, without realizing the difference.

The reason for this is simple. Strategy's formal definition and its Greek military origins notwithstanding, we need the word as much to explain past actions as to describe intended behavior. After all, if strategies can be planned and intended, they can also be pursued and realized (or not realized, as the case may be). And pattern in action, or what we call realized strategy, explains that pursuit. Moreover, just as a plan need not produce a pattern (some strategies that are intended are simply not realized), so too a pattern need not result from a plan. An organization can have a pattern (or realized strategy) without knowing it, let alone making it explicit.

Patterns, like beauty, are in the mind of the beholder, of course. But anyone reviewing a chronological lineup of our craftsperson's work would have little trouble discerning clear patterns, at least in certain periods. Until 1974, for example, she made small, decorative ceramic animals and objects of various kinds. Then this "knickknack strategy" stopped abruptly, and eventually new patterns formed around waferlike sculptures and ceramic bowls, highly textured and unglazed.

Finding equivalent patterns in action for organizations isn't that much more difficult. Indeed, for such large companies as Volkswagenwerk and Air Canada, in our research, it proved simpler! (As well it should. A craftsperson, after all, can change what she does in a studio a lot more easily than a Volkswagenwerk can retool its assembly lines.) Mapping the product models at Volkswagenwerk from the late 1940s to the late 1970s, for example, uncovers a clear pattern of concentration on the Beetle, followed in the late 1960s by a frantic search for replacements through acquisitions and internally developed new models, to a strategic reorientation around more stylish, water-cooled, front-wheel-drive vehicles in the mid-1970s.

But what about intended strategies, those formal plans and pronouncements we think of when we use the term *strategy*? Ironically, here we run into all kinds of problems. Even with a single craftsperson, how can we know what her intended strategies really were? If we could go back, would we find expressions of intention? And if we could, would we be able to trust them? We often fool ourselves, as well as others, by denying our subconscious motives. And remember that intentions are cheap, at least when compared with realizations.

Reading the Organization's Mind

If you believe all this has more to do with the Freudian recesses of a craftsperson's mind than with the practical realities of producing automobiles, then think again. For who knows what the intended strategies of a Volkswagenwerk really mean, let alone what they are? Can we simply assume in this collective context that the company's intended strategies are represented by its formal plans or by other statements emanating from the executive suite? Might these be just vain hopes or rationalizations or ploys to fool the competition? And even if expressed intentions exist, to what extent do others in the organization share them? How do we read the collective mind? Who is the strategist anyway?

The traditional view of strategic management resolves these problems quite simply, by what organizational theorists call attribution. You see it all the time in the business press. When General Motors acts, it's because Roger Smith has made a strategy. Given realization, there must have been intention, and that is automatically attributed to the chief.

In a short magazine article, this assumption is understandable. Journalists don't have a lot of time to uncover the origins of strategy, and GM is a large, complicated organization. But just consider all the complexity and confusion that gets tucked under this assumption—all the meetings and debates, the many people, the dead ends, the folding and unfolding of ideas. Now imagine trying to build a formal strategy-making system around that assumption. Is it any wonder that formal strategic planning is often such a resounding failure?

To unravel some of the confusion—and move away from the artificial complexity we have piled around the strategy-making process—we need to get back to some basic concepts. The most basic of all is the intimate connection between thought and action. That is the key to craft, and so also to the crafting of strategy.

Virtually everything that has been written about strategy making depicts it as a deliberate process. First we think, then we act. We formulate, then we implement. The progression seems so perfectly sensible. Why would anybody want to proceed differently?

Our potter is in the studio, rolling the clay to make a waferlike sculpture. The clay sticks to the rolling pin, and a round form appears. Why not make a cylindrical vase? One idea leads to another, until a new pattern forms. Action has driven thinking: A strategy has emerged.

Out in the field, a salesman visits a customer. The product isn't quite right, and together they work out some modifications. The salesman returns to his company and puts the changes through; after two or three more rounds, they finally get it right. A new product emerges, which eventually opens up a new market. The company has changed strategic course.

In fact, most salespeople are less fortunate than this one or than our craftsperson. In an organization of one, the implementor is the formulator, so innovations can be incorporated into strategy quickly and easily. In a large organization, the innovator may be 10 levels removed from the leader who is supposed to dictate strategy and may also have to sell the idea to dozens of peers doing the same job.

Some salespeople, of course, can proceed on their own, modifying products to suit their customers and convincing skunkworks in the factory to produce them. In effect, they pursue their own strategies. Maybe no one else notices or cares. Sometimes, however, their innovations do get noticed, perhaps years later, when the company's prevalent strategies have broken down and its leaders are groping for something new. Then the salesperson's strategy may be allowed to pervade the system, to become organizational.

Is this story farfetched. Certainly not. We've all heard stories like it. But since we tend to see only what we believe, if we believe that strategies have to be planned, we're unlikely to see the real meaning such stories hold.

Consder how the National Film Board of Canada (NFB) came to adopt a feature-film strategy. The NFB is a federal government agency, famous for its creativity and expert in the production of short documentaries. Some years back, it funded a filmmaker on a project that unexpectedly ran long. To distribute his film, the NFB turned to theaters and so inadvertently gained experience in marketing feature-length films. Other filmmakers caught onto the idea, and eventually the NFB found itself pursuing a feature-film strategy—a pattern of producing such films.

My point is simple, deceptively simple: strategies can *form* as well as be *formulated*. A realized strategy can emerge in response to an evolving situation, or it can be brought about deliberately, through a process of formulation followed by implementation. But when these planned intentions do not produce the desired actions, organizations are left with unrealized strategies.

Today we hear a great deal about unrealized strategies, almost always in concert with the claim that implementation has failed. Management has been lax, controls have been loose, people haven't been committed. Excuses abound. At times, indeed, they may be valid. But often these explanations prove too easy. So some people look beyond implementation to formulation. The strategists haven't been smart enough.

While it is certainly true that many intended strategies are ill conceived, I believe that the problem often lies one step beyond, in the distinction we make between formulation and implementation, the common assumption that thought must be independent of (and precede) action. Sure, people could be smarter—but not only by conceiving more clever strategies. Sometimes they can be smarter by allowing their strategies to develop gradually, through the organization's actions and experiences. Smart strategists appreciate that they cannot always be smart enough to think through everything in advance.

Hands and Minds

No craftsperson thinks some days and works others. The craftsperson's mind is going constantly, in tandem with her hands. Yet large organizations try to separate the work of minds and hands. In so doing, they often sever the vital feedback link between the two. The salesperson who finds a customer with an unmet need may possess the most strategic bit of information in the entire organization. But that information is useless if he or she cannot create a strategy in response to it or else convey the information to someone who can—because the channels are blocked or because the formulators have simply finished formulating. The notion that strategy is something that should happen way up there, far removed from the details of running an organization on a daily basis, is one of the great fallacies of conventional strategic management. And it explains a good many of the most dramatic failures in business and public policy today.

We at McGill call strategies like the NFB's that appear without clear intentions—or in spite of them—emergent strategies. Actions simply converge into patterns. They may become deliberate, of course, if the pattern is recognized and then legitimated by senior management. But that's after the fact.

All this may sound rather strange, I know. Strategies that emerge? Managers who acknowledge strategies already formed? Over the years, our research group at McGill has met with a good deal of resistance from people upset by what they perceive to be our passive definition of a word so bound up with proactive behavior and free will. After all, strategy means control—the ancient Greeks used it to describe the art of the army general.

Strategic Learning

But we have persisted in this usage for one reason: learning. Purely deliberate strategy precludes learning once the strategy is formulated; emergent strategy fosters it. People take actions one by one and respond to them, so that patterns eventually form.

Our craftsperson tries to make a freestanding sculptural form. It doesn't work, so she rounds it a bit here, flattens it a bit there. The result looks better, but still isn't quite right. She makes another and another and another. Eventually, after days or months or years, she finally has what she wants. She is off on a new strategy.

In practice, of course, all strategy making walks on two feet, one deliberate, the other emergent. For just as purely deliberate strategy making precludes learning, so purely emergent strategy making precludes control. Pushed to the limit, neither approach makes sense. Learning must be coupled with control. That is why the McGill research group uses the word *strategy* for both emergent and deliberate behavior.

Likewise, there is no such thing as a purely deliberate strategy or a purely emergent one. No organization—not even the ones commanded by those ancient Greek generals—knows enough to work everything out in advance, to ignore learning en route. And no one—not even a solitary potter—can be flexible enough to leave everything to happenstance, to give up all control. Craft requires control just as it requires responsiveness to the material at hand. Thus deliberate and emergent strategy form the end points of a continuum along which the strategies that are crafted in the real world may be found. Some strategies may approach either end, but many more fall at intermediate points.

Effective strategies can show up in the strangest places and develop through the most unexpected means. There is no one best way to make strategy.

The form for a cat collapses on the wheel, and our potter sees a bull taking shape. Clay sticks to a rolling pin, and a line of cylinders results. Wafers come into being because of a shortage of clay and limited kiln space in a studio in France. Thus errors become opportunities, and limitations stimulate creativity. The natural propensity to experiment, even boredom, likewise stimulate strategic change.

Organizations that craft their strategies have similar experiences. Recall the National Film Board with its inadvertently long film. Or consider its experiences with experimental films, which made special use of animation and sound. For 20 years, the NFB produced a bare but steady trickle of such films. In fact, every film but one in that trickle was produced by a single person, Norman McLaren, the NFB's most celebrated filmmaker. McLaren pursued a *personal strategy* of experimentation, deliberate for him perhaps (though who can know whether he had the whole stream in mind or simply planned one film at a time?) but not for the organization. Then 20 years later, others followed his lead and the trickle widened, his personal strategy becoming more broadly organizational.

Conversely, in 1952, when television came to Canada, a *consensus strategy* quickly emerged at the NFB. Senior management was not keen on producing films for the new medium. But while the arguments raged, one filmmaker quietly went off and made a single series for TV. That precedent set, one by one his colleagues leapt in, and within months the NFB—and its management—found themselves committed for several years to a new strategy with an intensity unmatched before or since. This consensus strategy arose spontaneously, as a result of many independent decisions made by the filmmakers about the films they wished to make. Can we call this strategy deliberate? For the filmmakers perhaps; for senior management certainly not. But for the organization? It all depends on your perspective, on how you choose to read the organization's mind.

While the NFB may seem like an extreme case, it highlights behavior that can be found, albeit in muted form, in all organizations. Those who doubt this might read Richard Pascale's account of how Honda stumbled into its enormous success in the American motorcycle market. Brilliant as its strategy may have looked after the fact, Honda's managers made almost every conceivable mistake until the market finally hit them over the head with the right formula. The Honda managers on site in America, driving their products themselves (and thus inadvertently picking up market reaction), did only one thing right: they learned, firsthand.[1]

Grass-Roots Strategy Making

These strategies all reflect, in whole or part, what we like to call a grass-roots approach to strategic management. Strategies grow like weeds in a garden. They take root in all kinds of places, wherever people have the capacity to learn (because they are in touch with the situation) and the resources to support that capacity. These strategies become organizational when they become collective, that is, when they proliferate to guide the behavior of the organization at large.

Of course, this view is overstated. But it is no less extreme than the conventional view of strategic management, which might be labeled the hothouse approach. Neither is right. Reality falls between the two. Some of the most effective strategies we uncovered in our research combined deliberation and control with flexibility and organizational learning.

Consider first what we call the *umbrella strategy*. Here senior management sets out broad guidelines (say, to produce only high-margin products at the cutting edge of technology or to favor products using bonding technology) and leaves the specifics (such as what these products will be) to others lower down the organization. This strategy is not only deliberate (in its guidelines) and emergent (in its specifics), but it is also deliberately emergent in that the process is consciously managed to allow strategies to emerge en route. IBM used the umbrella strategy in the early 1960s with the impending 360 series, when its senior management approved a set of broad criteria for the design of a family of computers later developed in detail throughout the organization.[2]

Deliberately emergent, too, is what we call the *process strategy*. Here management controls the process of strategy formation—concerning itself with the design of the structure, its staffing, procedures, and so on—while leaving the actual content to others.

Both process and umbrella strategies seem to be especially prevalent in businesses that require great expertise and creativity—a 3M, a Hewlett-Packard, a National Film Board. Such organizations can be effective only if their implementors are allowed to be formulators because it is people way down in the hierarchy who are in touch with the situation at hand and have the requisite

---

[1]Richard T. Pascale, "Perspective on Strategy: The Real Story Behind Honda's Success," *California Management Review,* May-June 1984, p. 47.

[2]James Brian Quinn, IBM (A) case, in James Brian Quinn, Henry Mintzberg, and Robert M. James. *The Strategy Process: Concepts, Contexts, Cases* (Englewood Cliffs, N.J.: Prentice-Hall, 1987).

technical expertise. In a sense, these are organizations peopled with craftspersons, all of whom must be strategists.

The conventional view of strategic management, especially in the planning literature, claims that change must be continuous: the organization should be adapting all the time. Yet this view proves to be ironic because the very concept of strategy is rooted in stability, not change. As this same literature makes clear, organizations pursue strategies to set direction, to lay out courses of action, and to elicit cooperation from their members around common, established guidelines. By any definition, strategy imposes stability on an organization. No stability means no strategy (no course to the future, no pattern from the past). Indeed, the very fact of having a strategy, and especially of making it explicit (as the conventional literature implores managers to do), creates resistance to strategic change!

What the conventional view fails to come to grips with, then, is how and when to promote change. A fundamental dilemma of strategy making is the need to reconcile the forces for stability and for change—to focus efforts and gain operating efficiencies on the one hand, yet adapt and maintain currency with a changing external environment on the other.

Quantum Leaps

Our own research and that of colleagues suggest that organizations resolve these opposing forces by attending first to one and then to the other. Clear periods of stability and change can usually be distinguished in any organization: While it is true that particular strategies may always be changing marginally, it seems equally true that major shifts in strategic orientation occur only rarely.

In our study of Steinberg Inc., a large Quebec supermarket chain headquartered in Montreal, we found only two important reorientations in the 60 years from its founding to the mid-1970s: a shift to self-service in 1933 and the introduction of shopping centers and public financing in 1953. At Volkswagenwerk, we saw only one between the late 1940s and the 1970s, the tumultuous shift from the traditional Beetle to the Audi-type design mentioned earlier. And at Air Canada, we found none over the airline's first four decades, following its initial positioning.

Our colleagues at McGill, Danny Miller and Peter Friesen, found this pattern of change so common in their studies of large numbers of companies (especially the high-performance ones) that they built a theory around it, which they labeled the quantum theory of strategic change.[3] Their basic point is that organizations adopt two distinctly different modes of behavior at different times.

Most of the time they pursue a given strategic orientation. Change may seem continuous, but it occurs in the context of that orientation (perfecting a given

---

[3]See Danny Miller and Peter H. Friesen, *Organizations: A Quantum View* (Englewood Cliffs, N.J.: Prentice-Hall, 1984).

retailing formula, for example) and usually amounts to doing more of the same, perhaps better as well. Most organizations favor these periods of stability because they achieve success not by changing strategies but by exploiting the ones they have. They, like craftspersons, seek continuous improvement by using their distinctive competencies in established courses.

While this goes on, however, the world continues to change, sometimes slowly, occasionally in dramatic shifts. Thus gradually or suddenly, the organization's strategic orientation moves out of sync with its environment. Then what Miller and Friesen call a strategic revolution must take place. That long period of evolutionary change is suddenly punctuated by a brief bout of revolutionary turmoil in which the organization quickly alters many of its established patterns. In effect, it tries to leap to a new stability quickly to reestablish an integrated posture among a new set of strategies, structures, and culture.

But what about all those emergent strategies, growing like weeds around the organization? What the quantum theory suggests is that the really novel ones are generally held in check in some corner of the organization until a strategic revolution becomes necessary. Then as an alternative to having to develop new strategies from scratch or having to import generic strategies from competitors, the organization can turn to its own emerging patterns to find its new orientation. As the old, established strategy disintegrates, the seeds of the new one begin to spread.

This quantum theory of change seems to apply particularly well to large, established, mass-production companies. Because they are especially reliant on standardized procedures, their resistance to strategic reorientation tends to be especially fierce. So we find long periods of stability broken by short disruptive periods of revolutionary change.

Volkswagenwerk is a case in point. Long enamored of the Beetle and armed with a tightly integrated set of strategies, the company ignored fundamental changes in its markets throughout the late 1950s and 1960s. The bureaucratic momentum of its mass-production organization combined with the psychological momentum of its leader, who institutionalized the strategies in the first place. When change finally did come, it was tumultuous: the company groped its way through a hodgepodge of products before it settled on a new set of vehicles championed by a new leader. Strategic reorientations really are cultural revolutions.

Cycles of Change

In more creative organizations, we see a somewhat different pattern of change and stability, one that's more balanced. Companies in the business of producing novel outputs apparently need to fly off in all directions from time to time to sustain their creativity. Yet they also need to settle down after such periods to find some order in the resulting chaos.

The National Film Board's tendency to move in and out of focus through remarkably balanced periods of convergence and divergence is a case in point.

Concentrated production of films to aid the war effort in the 1940s gave way to great divergence after the war as the organization sought a new raison d'être. Then the advent of television brought back a very sharp focus in the early 1950s, as noted earlier. But in the late 1950s, this dissipated almost as quickly as it began, giving rise to another creative period of exploration. Then the social changes in the early 1960s evoked a new period of convergence around experimental films and social issues.

We use the label "adhocracy" for organizations, like the National Film Board, that produce individual, or custom-made, products (or designs) in an innovative way, on a project basis.[4] Our craftsperson is an adhocracy of sorts too, since each of her ceramic sculptures is unique. And her pattern of strategic change was much like that of the NFB's, with evident cycles of convergence and divergence: a focus on knick-knacks from 1967 to 1972; then a period of exploration to about 1976 which resulted in a refocus on ceramic sculptures; that continued to about 1981, to be followed by a period of searching for new directions. More recently, a focus on ceramic murals seems to be emerging.

Whether through quantum revolutions or cycles of convergence and divergence, however, organizations seem to need to separate in time the basic forces for change and stability, reconciling them by attending to each in turn. Many strategic failures can be attributed either to mixing the two or to an obsession with one of these forces at the expense of the other.

The problems are evident in the work of many craftspersons. On the one hand, there are those who seize on the perfection of a single theme and never change. Eventually the creativity disappears from their work and the world passes them by—much as it did Volkswagenwerk until the company was shocked into its strategic revolution. And then there are those who are always changing, who flit from one idea to another and never settle down. Because no theme or strategy ever emerges in their work, they cannot exploit or even develop any distinctive competence. And because their work lacks definition, identity crises are likely to develop, with neither the craftsperson nor their clientele knowing what to make of it. Miller and Friesen found this behavior in conventional business too; they label it "the impulsive firm running blind."[5] How often have we seen it in companies that go on acquisition sprees?

The popular view sees the strategist as a planner or as a visionary, someone sitting on a pedestal dictating brilliant strategies for everyone else to implement. While recognizing the importance of thinking ahead and especially of the need for creative vision in this pedantic world, I wish to propose an additional view of the strategist—as a pattern recognizer, a learner if you will—who manages

---

[4]See my article "Organization Design: Fashion or Fit?" HBR January-February 1981, p. 103; also see my book *Structure in Fives: Designing Effective Organizations* (Englewood Cliffs, N.J.: Prentice-Hall, 1983). The term *adhocracy* was coined by Warren G. Bennis and Philip E. Slater in *The Temporary Society* (New York: Harper & Row, 1964).

[5]Danny Miller and Peter H. Friesen, "Archetypes of Strategy Formulation," *Management Science*, May 1978, p. 921.

a process in which strategies (and visions) can emerge as well as be deliberately conceived. I also wish to redefine that strategist, to extend that someone into the collective entity made up of the many actors whose interplay speaks an organization's mind. This strategist *finds* strategies no less than creates them, often in patterns that form inadvertently in its own behavior.

What, then, does it mean to craft strategy? Let us return to the words associated with craft: dedication, experience, involvement with the material, the personal touch, mastery of detail, a sense of harmony and integration. Managers who craft strategy do not spend much time in executive suites reading MIS reports or industry analyses. They are involved, responsive to their materials, learning about their organizations and industries through personal touch. They are also sensitive to experience, recognizing that, while individual vision may be important, other factors must help determine strategy as well.

Manage Stability.   Managing strategy is mostly managing stability, not change. Indeed, most of the time senior managers should not be formulating strategy at all; they should be getting on with making their organizations as effective as possible in pursuing the strategies they already have. Like distinguished craftspersons, organizations become distinguished because they master the details.

To manage strategy, then, at least in the first instance, is not so much to promote change as to know *when* to do so. Advocates of strategic planning often urge managers to plan for perpetual instability in the environment (for example, by rolling over five-year plans annually). But this obsession with change is dysfunctional. Organizations that reassess their strategies continuously are like individuals who reassess their jobs or their marriages continuously—in both cases, people will drive themselves crazy or else reduce themselves to inaction. The formal planning process repeats itself so often and so mechanicaly that it desensitizes the organization to real change, programs it more and more deeply into set patterns, and thereby encourages it to make only minor adaptations.

So-called strategic planning must be recognized for what it is: a means, not to create strategy, but to program a strategy already created—to work out its implications formally. It is essentially analytic in nature, based on decomposition, while strategy creation is essentially a process of synthesis. That is why trying to create strategies through formal planning most often leads to extrapolating existing ones or copying those of competitors.

This is not to say that planners have no role to play in strategy formation. In addition to programming strategies created by other means, they can feed ad hoc analyses into the strategy-making process at the front end to be sure that the hard data are taken into consideration. They can also stimulate others to think strategically. And of course people called planners can be strategists too, so long as they are creative thinkers who are in touch with what is relevant. But that has nothing to do with the technology of formal planning.

Detect Discontinuity.   Environments do not change on any regular or orderly basis. And they seldom undergo continuous dramatic change, claims about our "age of discontinuity" and environmental "turbulence" notwithstanding. (Go tell people who lived through the Great Depression or survivors of the seige of

Leningrad during World War II that ours are turbulent times.) Much of the time, change is minor and even temporary and requires no strategic response. Once in a while there is a truly significant discontinuity or, even less often, a gestalt shift in the environment, where everything important seems to change at once. But these events, while critical, are also easy to recognize.

The real challenge in crafting strategy lies in detecting the subtle discontinuities that may undermine a business in the future. And for that, there is no technique, no program, just a sharp mind in touch with the situation. Such discontinuities are unexpected and irregular, essentially unprecedented. They can be dealt with only by minds that are attuned to existing patterns yet able to perceive important breaks in them. Unfortunately, this form of strategic thinking tends to atrophy during the long periods of stability that most organizations experience (just as it did at Volkswagenwerk during the 1950s and 1960s). So the trick is to manage within a given strategic orientation most of the time yet be able to pick out the occasional discontinuity that really matters.

The Steinberg chain was built and run for more than half a century by a man named Sam Steinberg. For 20 years, the company concentrated on perfecting a self-service retailing formula introduced in 1933. Installing flourescent lighting and figuring out how to package meat in cellophane wrapping were the "strategic" issues of the day. Then in 1952, with the arrival of the first shopping center in Montreal, Steinberg realized he had to redefine his business almost overnight. He knew he needed to control those shopping centers and that control would require public financing and other major changes. So he reoriented his business. The ability to make that kind of switch in thinking is the essence of strategic management. And it has more to do with vision and involvement than it does with analytic technique.

Know the Business. Sam Steinberg was the epitome of the entrepreneur, a man intimately involved with all the details of his business, who spent Saturday mornings visiting his stores. As he told us in discussing his company's competitive advantage:

"Nobody knew the grocery business like we did. Everything has to do with your knowledge. I knew merchandise, I knew cost, I knew selling, I knew customers. I knew everything, and I passed on all my knowledge; I kept teaching my people. That's the advantage we had. Our competitors couldn't touch us."

Note the kind of knowledge involved: not intellectual knowledge, not analytical reports or abstracted facts and figures (though these can certainly help), but personal knowledge, intimate understanding, equivalent to the craftsman's feel for the clay. Facts are available to anyone; this kind of knowledge is not. Wisdom is the word that captures it best. But wisdom is a word that has been lost in the bureaucracies we have built for ourselves, systems designed to distance leaders from operating details. Show me managers who think they can rely on formal planning to create their strategies, and I'll show you managers who lack intimate knowledge of their businesses or the creativity to do something with it.

Craftspersons have to train themselves to see, to pick up things other people miss. The same holds true for managers of strategy. It is those with a kind of peripheral vision who are best able to detect and take advantage of events as they unfold.

Manage Patterns. Whether in an executive suite in Manhattan or a pottery studio in Montreal, a key to managing strategy is the ability to detect emerging patterns and help them take shape. The job of the manager is not just to pre-conceive specific strategies but also to recognize their emergence elsewhere in the organization and intervene when appropriate.

Like weeds that appear unexpectedly in a garden, some emergent strategies may need to be uprooted immediately. But management cannot be too quick to cut off the unexpected, for tomorrow's vision may grow out of today's aberration. (Europeans, after all, enjoy salads made from the leaves of the dandelion, America's most notorious weed.) Thus some patterns are worth watching until their effects have more clearly manifested themselves. Then those that prove useful can be made deliberate and be incorporated into the formal strategy, even if that means shifting the strategic umbrella to cover them.

To manage in this context, then, is to create the climate within which a wide variety of strategies can grow. In more complex organizations, this may mean building flexible structures, hiring creative people, defining broad umbrella strat-egies, and watching for the patterns that emerge.

Reconcile Change and Continuity. Finally, managers considering radical de-partures need to keep the quantum theory of change in mind. As Ecclesiastes reminds us, there is a time to sow and a time to reap. Some new patterns must be held in check until the organization is ready for a strategic revolution, or at least a period of divergence. Managers who are obsessed with either change or stability are bound eventually to harm their organizations. As pattern recognizer, the manager has to be able to sense when to exploit an established crop of strategies and when to encourage new strains to displace the old.

While strategy is a word that is usually associated with the future, its link to the past is no less central. As Kierkegaard once observed, life is lived forward but understood backward. Managers may have to live strategy in the future, but they must understand it through the past.

Like potters at the wheel, organizations must make sense of the past if they hope to manage the future. Only by coming to understand the patterns that form in their own behavior do they get to know their capabilities and their potential. Thus crafting strategy, like managing craft, requires a natural synthesis of the future, present, and past.

Author's note: Readers interested in learning more about the results of the tracking strategy project have a wide range of studies to draw from. Works published to date can be found in Robert Lamb and Paul Shivastava, eds., *Advances in Strategic Management,* Vol. 4 (Greenwich, Conn.: Jai Press, 1986), pp. 3–41; *Management Science,* May 1978, p. 934; *Administrative Science Quarterly,* June 1985, p. 160; J. Grant, ed., *Strategic Management Frontiers* (Greenwich, Conn.: Jai Press, 1988); *Canadian Journal of Administrative Sciences,* June 1984, p. 1; *Academy of Management Journal,* September 1982, p. 465; Robert Lamb, ed., *Competitive Strategic Management* (Englewood Cliffs, N.J.: Prentice-Hall, 1984).

What this article is about: The primary purpose of strategic planning is to optimize the fit between the business and its current and future environment and environmental scanning is an important element in such planning. General Electric's approach to environmental scanning is described.

2–2 *Environmental Scanning and Strategic Planning*

Ian H. Wilson

*Ian H. Wilson is an executive
with the General Electric Company*

At the outset I should make clear my own conviction about the basic linkage between environmental scanning and strategic planning. The primary purpose of strategic planning, as I see it, is to optimize the "fit" between the business and its current and future environment—to enable the business to operate with maximum congruence, and minimum friction, with the changing expectations and conditions of an uncertain world. By the term *environmental scanning* I mean to encompass both the monitoring of current events in the business environment *and* the forecasting of future trends. And by *environment* I mean the *totality* of the external conditions and trends in which the business lives and moves and has its being—the market and competitive situation, economic and technological trends, and (increasingly) social and political developments.

From the above assertion about the purpose of strategic planning, two further statements derive:

1. Environmental scanning of the total business environment becomes an essential and integral part of strategic planning. It sets up the contextual framework within which planning can then logically proceed.
2. A business strategy that is adequate to meet the totality of these changing conditions must, in truth, be a strategy for the *total* business. That is, it should encompass not merely a market strategy, but also a technology strategy, a human resources strategy, a financial strategy, a public policy/government relations strategy, and so on.

SOURCE: This article is reprinted from *Business Environment/Public Policy: 1979 Conference Papers* (St. Louis: American Assembly of Collegiate Schools of Business, 1980), pp. 159–63.

If we put these two statements together, we can see the emergence of a holistic/systemic approach to planning, that is, viewing the environment as a whole and as integral to planning, and planning for the business as a total system.

With this as preface, we can now look a little more closely at the nature and role of environmental scanning. For all practical purposes, most corporate "long-term" planning currently focuses on a "window in time" three to five years from the present. This is not true for all businesses; nor does it mean that some exploratory thinking and planning does not extend to a more distant time horizon. However, when assessing the actionable implications and strategic options for the corporation, most attention tends to get focused on a time horizon about five years out.

Both conceptually and practically, there are two different approaches to this "window in time." On the one hand, it is possible, by analyzing the macro sweep of long-term trends, to take a leap into the future, developing alternative scenarios for the future 10 to 15 years hence, and then, calculating backward by a process of deductive reasoning, to develop hypotheses as to corporate implications for the intermediate period. On the other hand, one can focus attention on the micro picture, monitoring events as they occur, assembling the jigsaw of evidence into a coherent picture, and then projecting forward by a process of inductive reasoning to create a picture of the future five years out.

These two approaches, it should be noted, are more appropriately viewed as complements than as alternatives. Environmental scanning can make its soundest contributions to planning when it provides perspectives from both macro/long-term and micro/short-term analyses. For one thing, the longer term scenarios are, at best, hypotheses as to plausible futures. The trajectory of these scenarios must be constantly compared with the trajectory of actual events to determine what revision to the planning assumptions may be required.

To the extent that environmental scanning involves a forecasting element, it can be said to constitute an early warning system whose purpose is to buy lead time, to identify emerging issues in sufficient time for adaptive, "non-crisis" action to be taken by the corporation. So, while the system may be absorbing and analyzing current data, it should never lose its future focus.

In 1967 General Electric established a Business Environment Studies component to analyze long-term social and political trends in the United States and their implications for the corporation. Four years later, in 1971, we commenced the first cycle of our new strategic planning system, a key element of which—in fact, the starting point for the cycle—was the long-term environmental forecast. In looking over our experience with these ventures, I derive the following characteristics for a successful environmental scanning system.

1.   It must be *holistic* in its approach to the business environment, that is, it should view trends—social, economic, political, technical—as a piece, not piecemeal. Ecology and general systems theory both point to the maxim that "everything is related to everything else"; and Jay Forrester has demonstrated the dangers of applying linear, segmented thinking to analysis of any closed, complex system—a corporation, a city, or a society—with its dynamic, interacting parts and constantly operating feedback loops. The scanning system should, therefore, be comprehensive in its scope and integrative in its approach (cross-impact analyses and scenarios are remarkably useful techniques in this regard).

2. It must also be continuous, *iterative* in its operation. In a fast-changing world, it makes little sense to rely on one-shot, or even periodic, analyses of the environment. Only constant monitoring, feedback, and modification of forecasts can be truly useful. Carrying on the radar analogy, I call this a "cybernetic pulsing through the future." The system must be designed to deal with *alternative futures*. In an uncertain environment we can never truly know the future, no matter how much we may perfect our forecasting techniques. It is highly misleading, therefore, to claim (or believe) that an early warning system can predict *the* future. What it can do—and do effectively, if well designed—is to help us clarify our assumptions about the future, speculate systematically about alternative outcomes, assess probabilities, and make more rational choices.

3. It should lay heavy stress on the need for *contingency planning*. This is a necessary corollary to the preceding point. In fact, there is (or should be) a strong logical connection in our thinking among uncertainty, alternatives, and contingencies: the three concepts are strongly bound together. In the final analysis, of course, after considering alternatives, we have to commit to a plan of action based on our assessment of the most probable future. But those lesser probabilities—even the "wild card" scenarios—should not be neglected, for they represent the contingencies for which we should also, in some degree, plan. A commitment to contingency planning is, it seems to me, the essence of a flexible strategy.

4. Most important, the environmental scanning system should be an *integral part of the decision-making system* of the corporation. Speculation about alternative futures makes no real contribution to corporate success if it results merely in interesting studies. To contribute, it must be issue-oriented and help make today's decisions with a better sense of futurity; but it can do this *only* if the planning and decision-making system is designed to include the requirement of such monitoring and early warning.

The positioning of environmental scanning/analysis with respect to other planning and analysis activities is shown in Figure 1. This schematic diagram serves to demonstrate the fact that analysis of current and future environmental trends is, at least conceptually, the starting point for the strategic planning process. Within that process, issues analysis is central. Strategic planning should have as its focus identification of the key strategic issues[1] confronting the business (issues that arise from the interaction of the business with environmental forces) and the development of strategies to deal with these issues. Contingency planning

---

[1]A "strategic issue" can be defined as a major opportunity or threat which could critically affect the long-term future of the business. An issue may be immediate or emerging, internal or external in origin, concerned with any facet of the business—competitive, marketing, technological, human resources, financial, and so on.

FIGURE 1

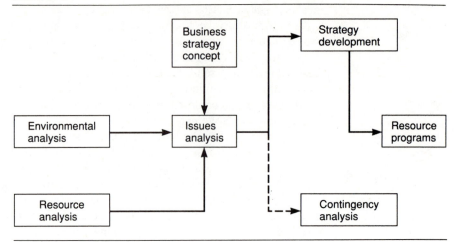

and analysis is also important for strategic positioning in an uncertain environment.

Over the past 10 years the techniques of environmental monitoring and forecasting have grown in scope and sophistication. By 1976 General Electric and The Future Group had developed the FUTURSCAN system, which is a state-of-the-art combination of:

- Futurcasts data bases (potential future events).
- Delphi technique.
- Trend-impact analysis—how events move trends.
- Cross-impact analysis—how events move one another.
- Probabilistic system dynamics—how events and trends shape alternative futures.
- Scenarios.

Essentially the system operates in six stages:

1. Prepare background.
    Assess overall environmental factors for the industry (or market, society, etc.) under investigation.
    Demographic and lifestyle.
    General business and economic.
    Legislative and regulatory.
    Scientific and technological.
    Develop crude "systems" model of the industry.
2. Select critical indicators.
    Identify the industry's key indicators (trends).
    Undertake literature search to identify potential future events impacting the key trends.

Nominate Delphi panel participants whose expert opinion is credible in evaluating the industry's future.

3. Establish past behavior for each indicator.
    Establish the historical performance for each indicator.
    Enter data into the data base of the Trend Impact Analysis program.
    Analyze reasons for past behavior of each trend.
        Demographic and social.
        Economic.
        Political and legislative.
        Technological.
    Construct Delphi panel interview.

4. Verify potential future events.
    Interrogate Delphi panel.
        Evaluate past trends.
        Assess the potential impact of future events.
        Assess the probability of future events.
        Forecast future values.
    Specify and document assumptions for forecasts.
    Specify and document rationale for projected values.

5. Forecast each indicator.
    Operate the Trend Impact Analysis and Cross Impact Analysis programs on the literature search and Delphi output to establish the range of future values.
    Analyze forecast results.

The detailed operation of the FUTURSCAN system is a topic for another paper.[2] Here it is simply worth noting that the value of utilizing such a multidimensional analysis of the future environment lies in the fact that:

- It makes explicit *all* the environmental assumptions on which corporate planning and policymaking should be based.
- It integrates the "social" factors and the "business" factors into the planning framework.
- It confronts future corporate problems as a system of interrelated issues and pressures, with all their attendant complexities and "trade-offs."
- It identifies the spectrum of probable future constraints *and opportunities* for corporate performance.
- It provides an opportunity, early in the planning cycle, for determining needed corporate responses to changing conditions.

---

[2]See, for instance, the article on this topic by L. H. Cullum in *Business Tomorrow* 1, no. 3 (World Future Society, 1978).

What this article is about: Scenario analysis is an increasingly popular way to look at the future business environment. This paper provides a critical assessment of the literature on scenario analysis. It summarizes what is currently known about this approach to forecasting, and offers some guidelines regarding the construction and use of scenarios. It also offers a comparison and evaluation of many of the techniques that have been proffered to generate scenarios, suggesting which are worthwhile and which are not.

2–3 *How to Develop and Use Scenarios*

Steven P. Schnaars

*Steven Schnaars is Associate Professor of Marketing
at Baruch College, the business school of the
City University of New York*

For many years, it was widely believed that the greatest potential for obtaining accurate forecasts lay in the development of complex, quantitative models. It was thought that with just a little more time, a few more equations, and a lot more dollars, these models would be able to provide forecasts that were much more accurate than those produced by more mundane methods. This has not turned out to be the case. A multitude of comparative forecasting studies has clearly shown that such models are usually no more accurate than much simpler approaches,[1,2] As a result, many users of forecasts have become disillusioned with forecasting models that, under the guise of scientific analysis, attempt to predict the future from fancy mathematical manipulations of historical data. This as much as anything has fostered a growth market for scenario analysis.

Scenario analysis is not a new technique. Herman Kahn was writing scenarios as far back as the 1950s.[3] What is new is that the remarkably poor record of forecasters, even those armed with impressive credentials and gigantic computers, has become more obvious. If it ever was possible to accurately predict the future, it is surely a hazardous task today. Consequently, planners have recognized the importance of considering a number of plausible future environments that their firms may face, rather than relying on a single forecast that, in hindsight, may be grossly mistaken. This too has fostered a growth market for scenario analysis.

SOURCE: *Long Range Planning* 20 (February 1987), pp. 105–14.

Oddly, this new-found interest in the use of scenarios has not fostered a great deal of interest in researching the approach itself. The topic has been largely ignored by business researchers. In the words of one study, "Practice seems to be leading the literature."[4]

Most of what is known about scenario analysis comes from three rather distinct sources. The first and smallest body of research consists of empirical studies that have focused on related topics that offer some evidence as to the value of scenarios as a forecasting tool. This research is not tied to any one academic discipline, and is widely dispersed in the literature.

A second group of articles consists of descriptions of how scenario analysis is conducted at large firms. Most of these articles are written by corporate planners who have firsthand experience in the construction and use of scenarios. They offer many valuable heuristics regarding the construction of scenarios that are based on practical business opinions.

The final group of studies comes from the "futures research" literature. It offers a plethora of methods for constructing scenarios, some of which are reasonable, many of which are arcane and impractical, most of which have never been fairly tested. Many of these studies deal with cross-impact analysis, a scenario-generating technique that has received a great deal of attention over the past 15 years.

This paper reviews the literature on scenario analysis. It summarizes what is currently known about the method, as well as what people think they know about it. In addition, it offers some guidelines regarding the construction and use of scenarios as a forecasting tool. It also evaluates some of the myriad techniques that have been offered to generate scenarios, and suggests which are worthwhile, and which are not.

This paper does not attempt to chronicle all of the applications of scenario analysis (there are too many). Nor does it spend a great of time on the technical aspects of the more complex quantitative methodologies that have been preferred (since there are serious problems with the basic premise of these approaches). Overall, the goal of this paper is to find out where we are now, so that we can move forward in the future.

WHAT IS SCENARIO ANALYSIS?

Scenario analysis differs from most other approaches to forecasting in two important ways. First, it usually provides a more qualitative and contextual description of how the present will evolve into the future, rather than one that seeks numerical precision. Second, scenario analysis usually tries to identify a set of possible futures, each of whose occurrence is plausible, but not ensured. This combination of offering more than one forecast, and offering it in the form of a narrative, is deemed by advocates to be a more reasonable approach than trying to predict (to four significant decimal places) what *will* happen in *the* future.

Not everyone incorporates both aspects of this definition into their scenarios. Some adopt the narrative format, but offer only a single forecast. Others offer multiple forecasts, based on differing assumptions regarding the future environment, but do not present the results in the form of a stylized narrative. Both groups refer to the results of their efforts as scenarios.

Herman Kahn, the famous futurist, credits himself with coining the term *scenario*. His brand of scenario analysis embraces the stylized narrative, and is usually referred to as *scenario writing*.[5]

> As near as I can tell, the term scenario was first used in this sense in a group I worked with at the Rand Corporation. We deliberately chose the word to deglamorize the concept. In writing the scenarios for various situations we kept saying "Remember, it's only a scenario," the kind of thing that is produced by Hollywood writers both hacks and geniuses. (p. 112)

Scenario writing is a highly qualitative procedure. It proceeds more from the gut than from the computer, although it may incorporate the results of quantitative models. Scenario writing is based on the assumption that the future is not merely some mathematical manipulation of the past, but the confluence of many forces, past, present, and future that can best be understood by simply thinking about the problem.

As narratives, scenarios can either trace the evolution of the present into the future, or merely describe what the future will look like.[6,7] That is, they can be longitudinal or cross-sectional. The most widely quoted definition of scenarios, proposed by Kahn and Weiner,[8] focuses on longitudinal scenario analysis. They define scenarios as "A hypothetical sequence of events constructed for the purpose of focusing attention on causal processes and decision points" (p. 6).

Many researchers also use the term *scenarios* to describe any set of multiple forecasts. For example, Carlson and Umble[9] generate multiple forecasts of automobile sales from an econometric model using different assumptions regarding the future values of predictor variables. Such procedures are essentially quantitative and mechanistic, but still termed *scenario analysis* since more than one forecast is provided.

The idea of providing multiple forecasts has become a cornerstone of scenario analysis. It is an explicit recognition of the frailty of forecasting and the importance of underlying assumptions. It suggests that a forecast is only as accurate as its underlying assumptions, and that it makes more sense to consider a number of plausible assumptions, rather than a single one which may later turn out to be incorrect.

There is some strong empirical evidence to support this claim. A massive study by Ascher[10] reviewed past forecasts and concluded that the most frequent reason for errors was that they were predicated on erroneous underlying assumptions. He also found that the methodology used to construct the forecast was of trivial importance. This suggests that less attention should be paid to methodological issues, and more to the assumptions underlying a forecast; a point on which scenario analysis scores high.

Other reviews of historical forecast accuracy offer additional support. For example, Schnaars,[11] in a review of growth market forecasts published in the business press between 1960 and 1979, found that most of the technological forecasts of the late 1960s that foresaw fantastic innovations permeating nearly every aspect of life were predicated on the mistaken assumption that surging economic conditions and massive funding of the space program would continue unabated. Similar mistaken assumptions at other times (e.g., a continued dramatic rise in the price of oil) have caused the failure of other growth market forecasts.

THE USE OF SCENARIOS BY BUSINESS

Most of the evidence regarding the use of scenarios by U.S. industrial firms comes from a survey conducted by Linnenman and Klein.[4] They inferred that about 22 percent of the Fortune 1000 were using scenario analysis in the late 1970s. Roughly three-quarters of these firms had adopted the approach after the oil embargo sent corporate strategies sailing into oblivion. Meristo[12] reports that a survey of 1,100 European firms showed that many of these firms also adopted scenarios after the oil crisis.

In an earlier study, McHale and McHale[13] found scenario analysis to be a popular forecasting tool among organizations in the United States.

Armstrong[2] notes that an earlier, unpublished study by McHale found scenarios to be the most popular "futures research" tool among the 356 "organizations, institutional units, and individuals" that were polled.

In a follow-up study, Linneman and Klein[14] found that, between 1977 and 1981, the use of scenario analysis as a business forecasting tool had grown even further.

Clearly, the growing popularity of scenario analysis can be directly attributed to the "random shocks" of the 1970s. Less clear is whether the 1980s will be beset by similar disturbances, and if so, whether scenario analysis will prove superior to other forecasting approaches.

THE RELATIVE ACCURACY OF SCENARIO FORECASTS

The key question in scenario analysis is whether it works any better than alternative approaches. Schnaars[15] compared two unconditional forecasts prepared using scenario writing (optimistic and pessimistic) with two generated from a simple econometric model. The application was for one-quarter ahead forecasts of six types of U.S. auto sales (e.g., subcompacts, full-sized) in early 1983, a highly uncertain time since the economy was believed to be moving from recession to recovery. The scenario writing approach showed a slight advantage over the simple demand function. This advantage was most pronounced on forecasts of those series where uncertainty was high, and historical relationships were changing. Possibly, as Klein and Linneman[6] note, judgmental scenario writing is best able to anticipate those "historyless" events that are so pervasive in today's business environment.

THE SCOPE OF SCENARIOS

Scenarios have been constructed to study futures of varying levels of aggregation. At one extreme lies the "worldviews" popularized by Herman Kahn. Such forecasts are all-encompassing. Their goal is nothing less than to identify a set of plausible global futures and their consequences to man. Such efforts almost inevitably rely on scenario writing due to the large number of factors that must be considered.

Businesspersons, with an eye toward corporate planning, are usually attracted to more focused scenarios. These scenarios tend to focus more on those aspects of the environment that directly affect their products and markets. While this is a more feasible task, it carries the increasing danger that, as the scope of the scenario narrows, the accuracy of the scenarios will be affected by an event that was not considered. There appears to be a trade-off between the feasibility of considering a large number of factors and the validity of considering only a few.

A large number of industry-level scenario studies have been published in the business literature. For example, Wilson[16-18] discusses scenario generation at General Electric and its relation to marketing strategy. Zentner[19] lists some other applications. All told, the applications of scenario analysis far outnumber the investigations of the approach itself.

The greatest potential for the use of scenario analysis in business forecasting probably lies within this more narrow focus. Many industries, products, and markets are primarily affected by only a handful of factors that are fairly easy to identify but notoriously difficult to predict. Scenario analysis should perform well in such instances.

THE CONTENT OF SCENARIOS

There is some confusion in the literature as to what types of information scenarios should contain. Most authors equate scenarios with environmental forecasts, against which plans are laid. That is, the scenarios that identify plausible future environments that the firm might face. The firm then draws plans in light of these forecasts. In this sense, scenario analysis and planning are concerned with two distinct activities.

Other authors bundle into the scenarios themselves plans and the outcome of the plans.[20] *That is, the scenarios contain not only environmental forecasts, but how well a given plan will fare in it*. In this case, scenario analysis is complicated by the inclusion of additional uncertainties. Not only must potential future environments be identified, but the performance of plans must be estimated.

The content of scenarios should be determined by where the uncertainty lies. In some instances, it is the future course of the market itself that presents questions. In others, it is the market's response to strategic maneuvers. In each case the content of the scenarios would be different.

However, it is essential to keep the number of factors that are considered to a minimum. If too many factors are considered, scenario analysis becomes unwieldy and an exercise in speculation. *Scenario analysis seems best suited for those situations where a few crucial factors can be identified, but not easily predicted.*

TIME HORIZON

Scenario analysis has been used primarily in long-term forecasting. The characteristics of the approach—providing more than one forecast, each in the form of a purposely vague narrative—are best suited for more distant, less certain forecasting applications. However, there is no empirical evidence that scenarios are inappropriate over shorter time horizons.

Linneman and Klein[4] found that most of firms that used scenario analysis employed a five-year horizon. Planners at Xerox Corporation have stated that they extend their scenarios 15 years ahead.[21] Zentner,[22] of Shell Oil, notes that they generate scenarios with at least 15-year horizons, and frequently longer. He also notes that the content of their scenarios become progressively more vague as the time horizon lengthens.

It appears that the ideal time horizon of scenario analysis is specific to the industry, product, or market under consideration. A number of authors have observed that long-range and short-term forecasts are not absolute terms. Linneman and Kennell[23] suggest that the "acid test" for deciding on a time horizon is "How far in the future are you committing resources?" Similarly, Armstrong[2] defines a long-range forecast as "the length of time over which large changes in the environment can be expected to occur" (p. 5).

THE NUMBER OF SCENARIOS TO GENERATE

There seems to be a consensus in the literature that three scenarios are best. Some schemes propose only two, and some propose more than three, but the general feeling is that two tend to be classified as "good-and-bad," while more than three become unmanageable in the hands of users, resulting in their attending to only a subset anyway.

Wilson[17] offers one of the only caveats regarding the use of three scenarios. He suggests that in some instance *this number will result in users focusing mostly on the scenario that seems to represent the "middle ground."* This is particularly true when the future path of a quantifiable trend is under study. A graphical display of three scenarios would be categorized by the user as "high," "low," and "middle ground," with the middle projection being selected as the safest bet. He prescribes that in such cases the scenarios should be *distinctly "themed" to make them appear equally likely.*

Only two schemes actually propose generating only two scenarios. Beck[24] contends that at Shell U.K. "the fewer the better" (p. 18). He raises the same issue as above; that planners tend to dwell on the middle scenario when three are offered. Schnaars[15] also found that two scenarios to be preferable for a projection of automobile sales series.

Another dissenting viewpoint is offered by Mason,[25] and extended by Mitroff and Emshoff.[26] They propose a novel approach to scenario analysis based on dialectical methods that derives only two scenarios, a "best-guess" forecast and its "deadliest enemy." If nothing else, this approach forces a firm to confront the *"worst" case scenario,* and plan in light of it.

Industry seems to agree with the consensus. Linneman and Klein[4] found that more companies used three scenarios than any other number.

ARRAYING SCENARIOS

Scenarios are inevitably arrayed over some background theme. This gives the forecaster some criterion for selecting scenarios, and conveys to the user that each is part of a coherent set. Four background themes are commonly found in scenario studies.

Favorability to the Sponsor

The most widely used procedure is to array scenarios according to their favorability to the sponsor. This usually entails selecting a scenario that represents an "optimistic" prediction, and another that represents a "pessimistic" prediction. These then serve as alternatives for what Kahn calls a "surprise-free" or "baseline" scenario.

It should be noted that a surprise-free scenario is different from a "most likely" scenario. The former is a forecast based on the assumption of no unexpected changes, which may not be the most likely.

The central issue regarding this procedure for arraying scenarios is the same one that was mentioned in the previous section. Will planners attend to the surprise-free at the expense of the alternatives? If so, then the central objective of scenario analysis, to get planners to jointly consider a set of possibilities, is destroyed.

Probability of Occurrence

This scheme arrays scenarios according to their likelihood of occurrence. Usually, this means that one of the scenarios is labeled as most likely. The implication is that one scenario is more likely to occur, but that other outcomes are also possible. Vanston,[27] for example, uses a most likely scenario.

Quantitative methods of generating scenarios, such as cross-impact analysis, take this a step further. They actually attach probabilities to the scenarios they derive. The scenarios are then ranked by how likely they are to occur.[28]

Some judgmental schemes also assign probabilities to scenarios. For example, Edesess and Hambrecht[29] and deKluyer[30] adopt this procedure.

Many authors take issue with the practice of providing a most likely scenario. Kahn, Brown, and Martel,[31] Congressional Research Service,[32] and Zentner,[22] all feel that no most likely or "most probable" scenario should be offered. They contend that in *such instances planners will again focus on only the most likely scenario,* again defeating the objective of scenario analysis.

Another criticism, aimed particularly at the quantitative methods, is that in most business applications it is probably folly to attempt to assign probabilities to scenarios. Such estimates can be nothing short of misleading. The precision they imply is not warranted by either (1) the data that were used to derive them, or (2) the phenomenon they purport to predict. Scenarios are possibilities, not probabilities.

Finally, there is some persuasive empirical evidence that judgmental probability estimates are subject to a host of biases.[33] It is probably best not to assign probabilities to scenarios.

Single, Dominant Issue

In some applications there is a single dominant factor whose outcome is central to the item being forecast. Frequently, this dominant factor is the economy, or government policy. In such instances, scenarios can be arrayed over plausible outcomes for this dominant factor. For example, Dickson, Ryan and Smulyan[34] offer three scenarios for the future role of hydrogen as an energy source. Government funding is the crucial unknown. Each of their scenarios provides market estimates for differing levels of government interest.

Themes

In most business applications there is more than a single unknown. There are many issues which compete, combine, and interact with one another to characterize the future. Arraying scenarios according to this scheme tries to capture this. For example, Vanston et al.[27] offer three scenarios labeled "economic expansion," "environmental concern," and "technological domination." Each of these scenarios emphasizes a different aspect of the future environment. It also focuses attention on some of the disparate possibilities that have so frequently laid waste to even the best-drawn plans.

MacNulty,[35] Chapman,[36] and Linneman and Kennell[23] have all employed this scheme to array their scenarios.

METHODS OF CONSTRUCTING SCENARIOS

Most of the current methods of generating scenarios that are available today have their roots in the Rand Corporation of the 1950s. At that time, both Herman Kahn and Olaf Helmer worked on defense-related projects at Rand. Kahn pioneered scenario writing and Helmer developed the Delphi technique. Kahn's approach stressed the judgmental aspects of forecasting. He believed that the most important part was "simply to think about the problem" and engage in "systematic conjecture" (p. 5).[8] In contrast, Helmer focused on methodology. His Delphi technique attracted a great deal of attention, and spawned the currently popular Cross-impact Analysis. Both Delphi and Cross-impact are attempts to structure and formalize judgmental forecasting.

This division is still evident today. *Cross-impact analysis, which now exists in many versions, is still essentially concerned with methodological issues, while most other scenarios generating procedures try to provide guidelines for those who wish to write scenarios.*

Some Highly Qualitative Procedures

Kahn rejected the notion of quantitative model building, in favor of a more qualitative approach. His criticism was that quantitative models focus only on those aspects of a problem that are easily quantified and, therefore, represent only a partial formulation of the forecasting problem. He felt that when all of the clever mathematical manipulations were stripped away, model building "comes down to a simplistic intuition or an expression of bias rather than a careful synthesis and balancing of the analysis with more subtle qualitative considerations" (p. 99).[37]

Kahn's approach is deceptively simple. It identifies the basic trends underlying a forecasting problem, projects these trends to construct a surprise-free scenario, then alters some of these projections to create alternative futures—a stage he calls "Canonical Variations."[37]

Some scenarists are even stronger advocates of qualitative analysis. Godet[38] offers "Exploratory Prospective Analysis" as an alternative to more structured forecasting methods. He lambasts quantitative methods, and adds to Kahn's criticism the problems of inaccurate data and unstable relationships encountered by these models. His approach stresses a "holistic" and integrative analysis.

Durand[39] offers another highly qualitative approach. It too stresses intuitive analysis.

The primary problem with these procedures is that they rely so heavily on intuitive and subjective analysis that they are difficult to implement. There is really no procedure to follow. What they propose is abstract and difficult to apply in practice. It would be very hard for a planner to sit down and adopt their advice. In many respects these authors are more lucid in their criticism of quantitative methods than they are in explaining their alternative approaches.

Some Practical Procedures

Another set of qualitative procedures offers a more practical means of generating scenarios in a business environment. Essentially, these recipes provide a set of sequential steps that can be followed to construct scenarios. Table 1 compares a sampling of these procedures.

These procedures are similar in many respects. They all begin by identifying those factors that are expected to affect the forecasting situation at hand. They then postulate a set of plausible future values for each of these factors. Then, from the large number of possible combinations of the values of these factors, they select a few plausible scenarios.

It is on this last point that the procedures diverge. Each employs a different strategy for reducing the large number of possible scenarios to the few that are selected. Essentially, these strategies follow one of two paths. The first considers only a few key factors to start with. This greatly reduces the number of possible scenarios to select from. The other considers a larger number of factors but either constrains the possible values of these factors by setting the theme of the scenarios beforehand, or mentally integrating this larger number of factors into a consistent set of scenarios. Some examples should make this difference clearer.

Vanston et al.,[27] for example, rely on a deductive approach. This scheme first selects the dominant background themes for each of the scenarios (e.g., economic expansion, environmental concern, technological domination), and then forecasts each of the key factors in light of each of these themes. That is, the procedure is inherently deductive, the tone of the scenarios is set by their theme, and the forecasts are made to conform to this tone.

Conversely, the Linneman and Kennell[23] and Becker[7] procedures are inductive. They focus on only a few important "impacting" factors, and postulate possible future values for each of them. Linneman and Kennell then tally every possible combination of these values (e.g., low inflation, high unemployment, low consumer confidence), and select a set of three or four distinct, but plausible, scenarios from the total concatenation of variables. Becker follows a similar strategy.

MacNulty[35] and deKluyer[30] use a more intuitive approach to integrate the

TABLE 1 A Comparison of Selected Scenario-Generating Procedures

	Becker (1983)	deKluyver (1980)	Linneman and Klein (1977)	MacNulty (1977)	Vanston et al. (1977)	Wilson (1978)	Zentner (1975)
Number of scenarios	3	3	3 or 4	3 or 4	3–6	3 or 4	3
Length of scenarios	—	—	1 or 2 paragraphs	—	7–10 pages	—	<50 pages in all
Base scenario	Most likely	Most likely	None	Surprise-free	Most likely	Surprise-free	None
Alternative scenarios	Opt./pess.	Opt./pess.	Themed	Themed	Themed	Opt./pess.	Themed
Are probabilities assigned?	No	Yes	No	—	No	No	No
Does it use Cross-impact Analysis?	No	No	No	Yes	No	Yes	No
How is the number of factors reduced?	Considers only key factors	Considers only key factors	Considers only key factors	It is not	Considers many factors	Scoring by probability and importance	—
How are the scenarios selected?	Selects plausible combinations of key factors	Judgmental translation into opt./pess. and most likely	Selects plausible combinations of key factors	Judgmental integration of trends and intuition	To conform to the themes	Scenario writing and Cross-impact Analysis	—

factors into scenarios. Their procedures rely on a judgmental integration that is less mechanical, but also less descriptive.

Finally, McNamara,[40] Cazes,[41] and Gershuny[42] offer additional procedures for constructing scenarios.

The advantage of the deductive approach is that the factors can be combined into a set of consistent scenarios that capture the general theme of the future environment. The danger is that some unexpected combination of factors will be overlooked. The inductive approach allows all combinations to be considered, but since only a few factors are considered, an important one might be omitted. In short, the former approach risks the elimination of a key scenario, the later the omission of a key variable.

One possible solution would be to try both approaches. It would probably be a better strategy to employ the results of a number of simple methods, such as these, rather than spend a great deal of time on a single, complex method. Armstrong[2] has argued persuasively for a greater use of "eclectic" research in forecasting.

Cross-impact Analysis

Cross-impact Analysis emerged from early work on the Delphi Technique. Delphi was developed shortly after the end of World War II, but was first introduced in the published literature by Dalkey and Helmer.[43] Since then it has attracted a great deal of attention. Among other things, it has (1) become an accepted method of forecasting, (2) been soundly criticized by Sackman,[44] (3) been used to generate alternate scenarios,[45] and (4) spawned the development of Cross-impact Analysis.

According to most accounts, Cross-impact was first used to generate scenarios at Kaiser Aluminum in 1966. Gordon and Hayward[46] provide the first published account of the technique. Since then a plethora of articles in the futures research literature have offered refinements, alternatives, and, alas, criticisms of this method.

The basic philosophy of Cross-impact Analysis is that no development occurs in isolation. Rather, it is rendered more or less likely by the occurrence of other events. Cross-impact attempts to capture these "cross-impacts" from the judgmental estimates of experts.

There is no one method of Cross-impact Analysis. Instead, there are many techniques which pursue this same basic philosophy. Essentially, all rely on experts to provide some estimate of how likely it is that an event will occur by some given time period. They then ask how likely it is that the event will occur given the occurrence of some other event. These data (either for a single expert or an average or consensus of experts) are then input into a computer simulation or mathematical programming. The result is either a single most likely scenario or multiple scenarios ranked by probability.

A great deal of effort has been expended over the years in deciding how to stir the pot. For example, Enzer[47] argues that an "odds ratio" should be used to transform an expert's estimates into cross-impact probabilities, instead of the "quadratic" function suggested by Gordon and Hayward. Turoff[48] argues that a "log-odds ratio" is even better. Dupperin and Godet[28] disagree with all of these simulation approaches and propose SMIC-74, an approach based on mathematical programming that, believe it or not, can actually provide probability estimates for every possible scenario. Even Helmer has recognized that there are problems with existing models, and offers some additional mathematical refinements.[49]

These are all superfluous issues. The key problem with Cross-impact is that judgmental estimates are surely not amenable to any such mathematical machinations. As Kelly[50] notes, "To suggest that any method exists which might extract such blood from such stones is wishful thinking" (p. 342). McLean[51] adds, "In putting the emphasis on computation rather than conceptualization it tended to conceal the contradictions inherent in the approach" (p. 349).

Finally, Klein and Linneman[6] note that fancy methods have not been widely adopted. This should not be interpreted as a lack of innovativeness on the part of planners. Rather it is a commendation of their common sense.

In sum, the underlying idea of Cross-impact Analysis is a reasonable one. It recognizes that many events are interdependent. But researchers in this field have gone awry. They have focused too intently on the methodology of Cross-impact Analysis, at the expense of practical issues Those interested in using scenario analysis as a practical business-forecasting tool would be best advised to continue to avoid cross-impact procedures, and instead, adopt some of the helpful guidelines offered in the previous section.

HOW TO DEVELOP AND USE SCENARIOS

The literature on scenario analysis suggests some guidelines that can aid in the development and use of scenarios. Generally, these guidelines speak to two issues: (1) how to construct scenarios and (2) in what situations scenario analysis should be selected over other forecasting approaches. Some of these guidelines are presented below.

Herman Kahn was probably not far off the mark when he noted that the most important part of scenario analysis is simply to think about the problem. There appears to be no advantage to complex mathematical methods of constructing scenarios. Although we live in a world surfeit with automated processes, there is really no mechanical method of generating scenarios. To believe that there is, is to deceive yourself.

In particular, it is important to think about the assumptions that underlie the scenarios. Obtaining accurate assumptions is far more important than selecting the "best" method of constructing them. A forecast based on untenable assumptions is more likely to go awry than one that used the wrong model form.

While there may be no mechanical method of generating scenarios, there are some guidelines to follow. These guidelines answer some of the key questions regarding the construction of scenarios.

The most difficult issue in scenario analysis is how to reduce a large number of potential future outcomes to a few plausible scenarios. The number of possible scenarios grows quickly as the number of factors increases. Two methods have been proposed to handle this problem. Each approaches the problem in a different way, and is tailored to serve a different application.

In either case, avoid assigning probabilities to the derived scenarios. Such probabilities are misleading. They convey a sense of precision that is not there.

Besides, the *goal of scenario analysis is to generate a set of equally likely outcomes against which plans can be drawn, not a most likely scenario that may be attended to at the expense of the other, less likely outcomes.*

Instead of assigning probabilities, array scenarios using either the "optimistic/pessimistic" format (with or without a "surprise-free"), or "theme" them according to some possible dominant aspects of the future environment. Either of these procedures is superior to arraying the scenarios according to their likelihood of occurrence.

In most applications, two to four scenarios should suffice. A greater number tends to be confusing (and unworkable), and less than two (one) is a point-estimate forecast.

It is difficult to state whether two, three, or four is best. It probably depends on the specific application and the goals of the analysis. Most authors argue strongly that three scenarios are best, and point up a host of deficiencies with other numbers (e.g., two will be classified as "good" and "bad"). Others contend that there are problems with three scenarios (the one in the middle will be selected as the most likely and the others will be ignored), and suggest that two (or four) is the best number. Whatever the case, either two, three, or four scenarios can be strongly supported in business applications.

Scenarios should be limited to environmental forecasts. They should not include plans, or the response of the marketplace to plans. It is a difficult enough task to estimate the future environment, without attempting to bundle into the scenarios additional uncertainties. To do so is to render scenario analysis an exercise in sheer speculation.

Scenarios should also be targeted to applications of a narrow scope. It is important in scenario analysis to limit the number of factors that are considered. Ideally, scenario analysis should be applied to industries, products, and markets that are primarily affected by only a small number of factors that are fairly easy to identify, but very difficult to predict. These situations are more amenable to scenario analysis than those that are much wider in scope (e.g., worldviews), are affected by many more factors, and are hence more speculative.

Scenario analysis seems best suited for longer time horizons. Over longer time horizons, the accuracy of most forecasts deteriorates appreciably. This highlights the more contextual format of scenarios, as well as the fact that more than a single forecast is offered. This purposeful impreciseness is more attuned to the vagaries of longer time horizons.

Long term is a relative notion. It is not possible to state precisely at what point scenario analysis should be preferred to other forecasting methods. A rough rule of thumb might be to gauge how long it takes for changes in historical trends and relationships to occur in your industry. In applications such as stock prices, this time period might be measured in weeks. In more stable environments, it might be measured in years. Whatever the case, scenario analysis seems to offer the greatest advantage over quantitative methods when the assumptions of stability that underlie these models cannot be supported.

Scenario analysis offers the greatest advantage over other methods when uncertainty is high, and historical relationships are shaky. In such instances, traditional forecasting models, such as time-series and econometric models, will perform poorly since they focus solely on historical data.

Similarly, scenario analysis is ideally suited for those situations where the future is likely to be affected by events that have no historical precedent. Scenarios can include anticipations, whereas quantitative methods rely solely on historical patterns and relationships.

In short, scenario analysis seems to be more attuned to the current business environment. Many of the events that will undoubtedly affect business in the coming years are not discernible solely from the manipulation of historical data. This has been shown consistently over the past decade by the poor performance of quantitative forecasting models. Scenario analysis holds that a careful consideration of future possibilities is more valuable than even the most elegant of computations that will later turn out to be mistaken.

NOTES

1. Spyros Makridakis, et al. "The Accuracy of Extrapolation (time-series) Methods," *Journal of Forecasting* 1 (April–June 1982), pp. 111–53.
2. J. Scott Armstrong, *Long-Range Forecasting: From Crystal Ball to Computer* (New York: John Wiley, 1978).
3. Herman Kahn, *On Thermonuclear War* (London: Oxford University Press, 1960).
4. Robert E. Linneman and Harold E. Klein, "The Use of Multiple Scenarios by U.S. Industrial Companies," *Long Range Planning* 12 (February 1979), pp. 83–90.
5. Herman Kahn, *The Japanese Challenge*, (New York: Thomas Y. Crowell, 1979).
6. Harold E. Klein and Robert E. Linneman, "The Use of Scenarios in Corporate Planning," *Long Range Planning* 14 (October 1981), pp. 69–77.
7. Harold S. Becker, "Scenarios: A Tool of Growing Importance to Policy Analysts in Government and Industry," *Technological Forecasting and Social Change* 23 (March 1983), pp. 95–120.
8. Herman Kahn and A. J. Weiner, *The Year 2000* (London: Macmillan, 1967).
9. Rodney L. Carlson and M. Michael Umble, "Statistical Demand Functions for Automobiles and Their Use for Forecasting in an Energy Crisis," *Journal of Business* 53 (April 1980), pp. 193–204.
10. William Ascher, *Forecasting: An Appraisal for Policy-Makers and Planners* (Baltimore: Johns Hopkins University Press, 1978).

11. Steven Schnaars and Conrad Berenson, "Growth Market Forecasting Revisited: A Look Back at a Look Forward," *Calif. Mgmt. Review* 28 (Summer 1986), pp. 71–88.

12. Tarja Meristo, "The Multiple Scenario Approach—An Aid to Strategic Planning as Part of the Information Base," unpublished paper presented at International Symposium on Forecasting, Philadelphia, PA, June 7, 1983.

13. John McHale and M. McHale, "An Assessment of Futures Studies Worldwide," *Futures* 8 (1976), pp. 135–45.

14. Robert E. Linneman and Harold E. Klein, "The Use of Multiple Scenarios by U.S. Industrial Companies: A Comparison Study, 1977–1981," *Long Range Planning* 16 (December 1983), pp. 94–101.

15. Steven P. Schnaars, "A Comparison of Scenario Writing and Simple Econometric Models," unpublished paper presented at International Symposium on Forecasting, Philadelphia, PA, June 7, 1983.

16. Ian H. Wilson, "Futures Forecasting for Strategic Planning at General Electric," *Long Range Planning,* June 1973, pp. 39–42.

17. Ian H. Wilson, "Scenarios," in *Handbook of Futures Research,* ed. Jib Fowles (Westport, Conn.: Greenwood Press, 1978), pp. 22–47.

18. Ian H. Wilson, W. P. George, and P. J. Solomon, "Strategic Planning for Marketers," *Business Horizons* 21 (1978), pp. 65–73.

19. Rene D. Zentner, "Scenarios, Past, Present, and Future, *Long Range Planning* 15 (June 1982), pp. 12–20.

20. Russel L. Ackoff, *A Concept of Corporate Planning,* (New York: Wiley-Interscience, 1970).

21. Piercing Future Fog in the Executive Suite," *Business Week* 28 (April 1975), pp. 46–52.

22. Rene D. Zentner, "Scenarios in Forecasting," *Chemical and Engineering News,* October 6, 1975, pp. 22–34.

23. Robert E. Linneman and John D. Kennell, "Shirt-Sleeve Approach to Long-Range Plans," *Harvard Business Review* 55 (March–April 1977), pp. 141–50.

24. P. W. Beck, "Corporate Planning for an Uncertain Future," *Long Range Planning* 15 (August 1982), pp. 12–21.

25. Richard O. Mason, "A Dialectical Approach to Strategic Planning," *Management Science* 15 (April 1969), B-403–14.

26. Ian I. Mitroff and James R. Emshoff, "On Strategic Assumption-Making: A Dialectical Approach to Policy and Planning," *Academy of Management Review* 4 (January 1979), pp. 1–12.

27. John H. Vanston, Jr., W. P. Frisbie, S. C. Lopreato, and D. L. Poston, "Alternate Scenario Planning," *Technological Forecasting and Social Change* 10 (1977), pp. 159–80.

28. J. C. Dupperin and M. Godet, "SMIC—A Method for Constructing and Ranking Scenarios," *Futures* 7 (August 1975), pp. 302–12.

29. Michael Edesess and George A. Hambrecht, "Scenario Forecasting: Necessity, Not Choice, *Journal of Portfolio Management* 6 (Spring 1980), pp. 10–15.

30. Cornelis A. deKluyer, "Bottom-Up Sales Forecasting through Scenario Analysis," *Industrial Marketing Management* 9 (1980), pp. 167–70.

31. Herman Kahn, W. Brown, and L. Martel, *The Next 200 Years: A Scenario for America and the World,* (New York: William Brown, 1976).

32. Congressional Research Service, Library of Congress, *Long Range Planning,* Serial BB, U.S. Government Printing Office, May 1976.

33. Daniel Kahneman, Paul Slovic, and Amos Tversky, *Judgment under Uncertainty: Heuristics and Biases,* (Cambridge: Cambridge University Press, 1982).

34. E. M. Dickson, J. W. Ryan, and M. H. Smulyan, *The Hydrogen Energy Economy,* (New York: Praeger, 1977).

35. Christine A. Ralph MacNulty, "Scenario Development for Corporate Development," *Futures* 9 (April 1977), pp. 128–38.

36. Peter F. Chapman, "A Method for Exploring the Future," *Long Range Planning* 9 (February 1976), pp. 2–11.

37. Herman Kahn, "The Alternative World Future's Approach," in *New Approaches to International Relations,* ed. M. A. Kaplan (New York: St. Martin's Press, 1968).

38. Michel Godet, "Reducing the Blunders in Forecasting," *Futures* 15 (June 1983), pp. 181–92.

39. Jacques Durand, "A New Method for Constructing Scenarios," *Futures* 4 (December 1972), pp. 325–30.

40. James F. McNamara, "Trend Impact Analysis and Scenario Writing: Strategies for the Specification of Decision Alternatives in Educational Planning," *Journal of Educational Administration* 14 (October 1976), pp. 143–61.

41. Bernard Cazes, "The Future of Work: An Outline for a Method of Scenario Construction," *Futures* 8 (October 1976), pp. 405–10.

42. J. Gershuny, "The Choice of Scenarios," *Futures* 8 (December 1976), pp. 496–508.

43. Norman C. Dalkey and Olaf Helmer, "An Experimental Application of the Delphi Method to the Use of Experts," *Management Science* 9 (1963), pp. 458–67.

44. Harold Sackman, *Delphi Critique,* (Lexington, Mass.: D. C. Heath, 1975).

45. J. C. Derian and F. Morize, "Delphi in the Assessment of Research and Development Projects," *Futures* 5 (1973), pp. 469–83.

46. T. J. Gordon and H. Hayward, "Initial Experiments with the Cross Impact Matrix Method of Forecasting," *Futures* 1 (December 1968), pp. 100–116.

47. Selwyn Enzer, "Delphi and Cross-Impact Techniques: An Effective Combination for Systematic Futures Analysis," *Futures* 3 (March 1971), pp. 48–61.

48. Murray Turoff, "An Alternative Approach to Cross-Impact Analysis," *Technological Forecasting and Social Change* 3 (1972), pp. 309–39.

49. Olaf Helmer, "Reassessment of Cross-Impact Analysis," *Futures* 13 (October 1981), pp. 389–400.

50. P. Kelly, "Further Comments on Cross-Impact Analysis," *Futures* 8 (August 1976), pp. 341–45.

51. Mick McLean, "Does Cross-Impact Analysis Have a Future?" *Futures* 8 (August 1976), pp. 345–49.

What this article is about: Three different firms pursue three different but strategic options: RCA chose the least-cost option, Coca-Cola opted for differentiation, Rockford Headed Products, Inc., found a niche in its market. All were successful because they adjusted their strategy and repositioned their products as their product markets changed.

2–4 *The Strategic Options of Least-Cost, Differentiation, and Niche*

Peter Wright

*Peter Wright is a professor of management
at Southeastern Louisiana University, Hammond*

- RCA's television division commanded market leadership in America from the 1940s to the 1960s. With the decade of the 60s, however, foreign competition for the U.S. market began to exert a negative effect on RCA and other American television producers.
- Over the years Coca-Cola, the world's largest soft-drink producer, witnessed its competitors making inroads into its customer base. Competitors such as Royal Crown, Pepsico, and 7 Up jumped the gun on Coca-Cola and offered new products in innovative containers. These moves resulted in Coke's temporarily losing market share.
- For decades Rockford Headed Products, Inc. produced standard fasteners for general wholesalers. This small manufacturer chose local general distributors as its customers. The crucial weapon in this industry became price competition. And over the years Rockford's profitability turned into losses.

RCA, Coca-Cola, and Rockford, though to different degrees, all faced difficulties because of the changing competitive environment. By responding strategically to the environment changes, all three firms have done well. By continuously examining and reexamining their product-market scopes, these enterprises have made competitive forces work in their favor. Yet each company responded in quite a different way.

Reprinted from *Business Horizons*, March–April 1986. Copyright 1986 by the Foundation for the School of Business at Indiana University. Used with permission.

RCA's corporate managers realized that the competitive forces of cheaper imports had transformed the television industry into one with fairly standardized product-market dimensions. RCA considered two options. First, the firm could switch its product-market option away from mass merchandising, and toward high-quality television units, as Curtis Mathes had done successfully. Second—and this was RCA's choice—the firm could become price-competitive by expanding its TV production capacity to a world scale in order to capitalize on cheaper resources in various countries. RCA also has capitalized on the innovation capabilities of its world business units to improve its output technologically.

Coca-Cola's competitive response has been to broaden its product lines and to compete head-on with rival soft-drink companies. Because of its huge resources, Coca-Cola has been able to support its competitive moves successfully through massive advertising.

Rockford's financial losses resulted in a change of top management. At that point, most sales were of standardized fasteners. The new management switched the plant capacity away from standard fasteners and toward the production of technologically new, custom-made self-threading screws, which permitted faster assembly. The change resulted in a return to profitability. Specialized fasteners are normally sold directly to the end users, who purchase on the basis of customized specifications, on-time delivery, superior performance, and—last of all—price.

WHAT STRATEGIC OPTIONS ARE AVAILABLE?

These three cases point to the need for a periodic appraisal of the strategic options available to an enterprise. By viewing the firm from the perspective of strategic options, top management can structure a viable fit between an enterprise and its external environment.

A business unit's decision to compete with specific product-market dimensions links the business unit to one of three strategic options: least-cost, differentiation, and niche.

Least-Cost: The RCA Picture.   When a firm chooses to compete with uniform, standardized products, it is choosing the strategic option of least-cost. RCA chose this option, which emphasizes producing at very low per-unit costs. The competitive environment for businesses producing uniform products rewards primarily those firms that are able to offer low prices.

Differentiation: The Case of Coca-Cola.   When a business unit prefers to compete by offering unique products, it chooses the strategic option of differentiation. Its outputs must be considered exceptional. The competitive environment for unique products rewards enterprises that create demand for their products, even at relatively high prices, by convincing the consumer that the products are of superior value. Coca-Cola adopted this strategy.

Niche: The Rockford File.   Finally, when a business unit decides to fill a limited need, to offer a product that only a few buyers will purchase, it is selecting a special niche as its strategic option. The competitive environment for need-fulfilling outputs rewards those businesses that are willing to satisfy, at premium prices, the particular desires of small clusters of buyers. Rockford made this choice.

Each of these strategic options has distinct ramifications for a firm's international involvement. Each has implications for profitibility and innovation.

LEAST-COST

When a firm decides to provide uniform, standardized outputs that have substantial demand, it chooses the least-cost strategic option.[1] This option emphasizes producing a standardized product at very low per-unit costs. Ideally, firms that decide in favor of the least-cost option should be the larger ones in the industry or be willing to become so; they also should have greater access to resources than do their competitors. Such firms need functional support from finance, manufacturing, and at times R&D.[2] Their overriding objective should be to seek a high level of "experience" or cumulative volume of production.

The experience curve that conceptualizes cumulative volume of production allows lower per-unit costs through a combination of:

1. Substantial economies of scale.
2. Capital-labor substitution possibilities.
3. An incrementally increasing learning curve.[3]

Equally important for the least-cost strategic option is gaining access to low-cost inputs such as labor, energy, and freight. Firms that choose the least-cost option must be willing to strive for larger production capacities and market shares in their industries.

Firms that compete with least-cost strategies are confronted with a relatively elastic market demand that is likely to promote price concession policies.[4] Because the business entity and its competitors produce uniform goods, the firm

[1]See J. S. Bain, *Essays on Price Theory and Industrial Organization* (Boston: Little Brown, 1972), pp. 1–127; T. Flaherty, "Industry Structure and Cost Reducing Investment: A Dynamic Equilibrium Analysis" (Ph.D. diss., Carnegie-Mellon University, 1976), pp. 1–184.

[2]This point is made by J. S. Bain, *Industrial Organization* (New York: John Wiley & Sons, 1968), pp. 1–7.

[3]M. Porter, "How Competitive Forces Shape Strategy," *Harvard Business Review*, March–April 1979, pp. 137–44.

[4]See F. M. Scherer, *Industrial Market Structure and Economic Performance* (Chicago: Rand McNally, 1970); W. F. Mueller and L. G. Hamm, "Trends in Industrial Market Concentration, 1947–1970," *Review of Economics and Statistics* 56 (November 1974), pp. 511–20.

ordinarily expects competitive price pressures as buyers everywhere are drawn to those enterprises offering lower prices.

Industries subject to the least-cost option progressively have become global in order to achieve cumulative volume of production and gain access to low-cost inputs. Vernon mentions several examples of outputs that lend themselves to the least-cost strategy and are becoming "world products":

> The manufactured products that appear in the stalls and markets of Accra or Dar es Salaam are no longer very different from those in Djakarta or Cartagena or Recife . . . Electric batteries and electric bulbs are taking over the function of kerosene, wood, vegetable oils . . . the portable radio and the aspirin tablet are joining the list of life's universal necessities . . . middle-income automobiles, when judged by appearance and performance, are losing their last traces of national distinction, bicycles and ski equipment are universal commodities tailored to a global market.[5]

International Involvement

Like RCA, firms that produce standardized outputs which subject them to the least-cost option are forced in many instances to place business units strategically across the globe, in order to minimize costs. RCA, for example, located business units in such countries as Taiwan, Japan, Mexico, and Canada. These business units are managed interdependently with RCA units located in the United States. Each business unit performs complementary production or support functions. One may be a mass producer of components or parts. Other business units may assume support functions such as subassembly work, warehousing, or distribution on a massive scale. Each business unit is a link in the overall input-output strategy of RCA's world operations.

Enterprises that choose to compete through the least-cost strategy should strive for the efficiency of the firm's global system. Because coordination is crucial in such a system, the international involvement of the enterprise requires structuring multilateral relationships among its various global business units.

Ramifications for Profitability and Innovation

According to numerous studies conducted by various groups, per-unit costs typically fall by about one-third with every doubling in the number of outputs produced.[6] Because costs per unit decrease with greater production, the firm that produces the most should have the lowest marginal cost.

---

[5]R. Vernon, *Storm over the Multinationals* (Cambridge, Mass.: Harvard University Press, 1977), p. 20.

[6]See, for example, G. Allan and J. Hammond, *Note on the Use of Experience Curves in Competitive Decision-Making* (Cambridge, Mass.: Harvard Intercollegiate Clearing House of Cases, 1975), pp. 1–42; Boston Consulting Group, "Perspectives on Experience" (Boston, 1976), pp. 1–82.

Hence, the key to profitability when producing uniform products is to become a global market-share leader. Since the name of the game is price competition, higher profitability requires larger volumes of production and sales worldwide.

Such an assessment assumes a constant level of technology. Given this assumption, a firm's obvious course of action would be to add to production capacity and to gain market share at all costs. But business enterprises do not face a stable level of technology forever. Fortunately for RCA, its Japanese business units continually have developed innovative products (wide screens, thin picture tubes, recording capabilities) that then have been globally manufactured and distributed by RCA.

But firms in other industries have not always been so fortunate. For example, the largest producer of glass bottles for milk had developed the most stable and efficient technology for glass bottles. This firm had the most to lose, therefore, when technology shifted and waxed cartons replaced glass bottles as containers for milk. When demand for glass bottles was no longer there, the substantial investments made in plant and equipment for making glass bottles had to be written off.

For decades, American car manufacturers emphasized reducing costs through cumulative production volume. Management continuously attempted to stabilize technology and to reduce further the marginal cost of production. U.S. car markers did not consider technological innovations that dealt with variables other than reducing the manufacturing cost. Technological developments outside of America—in Japan and Germany—finally made Detroit realize that consumers preferred innovative cars. When American auto firms adopted aerodynamically efficient car bodies, transaxle and transverse mounted engines, and such fuel-saving parts as advanced plastic, graphite fibers, and dual-phased steel, the result was a car that was more reliable and less expensive to operate.

If a firm with standardized product-market scope, competing through the least-cost strategy, is to remain viable in the long run, it must also be willing to be a leader in technology. To be simultaneously a leader in technology *and* a least-cost producer is quite a challenge. Least-cost producers depend on a stable technology over time in order to cut manufacturing costs through cumulative volume of production. Reliance on a stable technology contradicts in many ways actively seeking innovations that might lead to the replacement of the present technology. The question is, *How do corporate managers balance the needs of a stable technology—and substantial investments in plant and equipment geared to that technology—against those needs to actively seek innovations that might replace present technology?*

History provides partial answers to this question. Any technology can be improved over time. But a point will be reached when further improvements in that technology will require prohibitively expensive inputs that will not improve product performance significantly. Exactly at such times, more emphasis should be placed on actively seeking innovations, at the cost of rendering obsolete the present stable technology. If one enterprise does not emphasize innovations at such critical times, others will. Instances abound in many industries.

For years NCR had the best and the cheapest mechanical cash register, which was the number one choice of the marketplace. Then Burroughs developed a fully integrated electronic cash register that was superior in performance. The demand shifted away from mechanical cash registers and toward electric cash registers.

The typewriter is another illustration of product improvements taking place throughout the years through shifts in technology. The mechanical typewriter was improved in many ways: it was made more sensitive to the touch, the keys were arranged for faster operator performance and less operator fatigue, and its size and weight were reduced. Underwood, the leading maker of mechanical typewriters, did not realize, however, that further improvements to the typewriter required a different technology—activating the keyboard electrically instead of mechanically. It was IBM that pioneered the electric typewriter, which essentially has replaced the mechanical typewriter.

Still a different technology has improved upon the electric typewriter. Because of its superior performance, the word processor, through its computer-assisted system, is likely to replace the electric typewriter. But IBM did not pioneer the word processor. Nor is IBM the current leader in the marketplace for word processors. Firms such as Wang and Olivetti have made IBM word processors the butt of industry jokes.

This brings us to an unfortunate ramification of innovation. With the onslaught of a new technology, a number of managers, engineers, scientists, and sometimes even plant foremen may have to be replaced. Personnel who for years have been committed to an existing technology tend to become dedicated to that technology. Hence, they probably are not best suited to developing and implementing innovative production methods that will yield technologically superior products.

DIFFERENTIATION

A firm that decides to offer products which are considered unique in the industry chooses the strategic option of differentiation.[7] Such firms need functional support from primarily the manufacturing and marketing sectors of their corporations.[8] This strategy emphasizes combining marketing and manufacturing efforts to allow for modifications in existing products and quick responses to changes in the nature or volume of demand. With unique outputs, low costs are not of

[7]See W. S. Comanor and T. A. Wilson, *Advertising and Market Power* (Cambridge, Mass.: Harvard University Press, 1974); M. Porter, *Competitive Strategy: Techniques for Analyzing Industries and Companies* (New York: Free Press, 1980), pp. 1–396.

[8]Robert Stobaugh and Piero Telesio, "Match Manufacturing Policies and Product Strategy," *Harvard Business Review*, March–April 1983, p. 118.

crucial importance. For products to maintain their distinguishable identities, the firms must bear the costs of their modification, packaging, distribution, and advertising. Because lower costs are not vital, smaller as well as larger firms may compete effectively with unique products.

Functional support from the manufacturing and marketing sectors helps a firm to position its unique products favorably so that it can make the most of the relatively inelastic market demand.[9] The relatively inelastic market demand for its outputs allows the firm, in turn, to set higher pricing policies and profit margins. Depending on the size of the business unit and the preference of its top managers, firms that compete through differentiation may choose smaller or larger market shares for their outputs.

International Involvement

When product-market choices yield unique outputs, as with Coca-Cola, planning for the firm's international involvement necessitates structuring independent relationships among its various world business units. That is, business units are created that function independently of each other on a market-by-market basis. Each independent business unit's market may have diverse product requirements, competitive forces, and economic/political risks. As long as return on investment remains acceptable, top managers allow local managers great autonomy in making decisions.

And whereas corporate entities with standardized product-market options have multilateral relationships among corporate groups, firms with unique product-market options tend to have bilateral relationships only between each business unit and company headquarters. The international involvement of firms competing through the strategy of differentiation may include exporting, licensing, joint ventures, and manufacturing. With this strategy, the world marketplace may be viewed as a potential area of activity.

Ramifications for Profitability and Innovation

Products that are considered unique are normally priced well above production costs. And their sales potential is relatively insensitive to price. Consequently, modifications in existing products and quick responses to changes in the nature

---

[9]See P. Wright, "Competitive Strategies for Small Businesses" in *Readings in Strategic Management*, ed. William Fulmer (Plano, Tex.: Business Publications, 1984), pp. 86–91; P. Wright, "Systematic Approach in Finding Export Opportunities," in *Managing Effectively in the World Marketplace*, ed. Harvard Graduate School of Business (New York: John Wiley & Sons, 1983), pp. 331–42.

of volume of demand far supersede considerations that would lower manufacturing costs.

Some centralized planning and implementation efforts are likely to boost profitability and innovation potentials of enterprises with unique products. For example, a degree of centralized engineering and R&D activities may provide useful inputs into the future product planning of any one business unit of the corporate entity. And some centralized efforts in advertising may save each business unit substantial sums. For instance, Coca-Cola is bottled in 115 countries. Part of its massive advertising is done by films, films made for use in many of the international markets. This centralized approach in film advertising alone saves Coca-Cola's world bottlers millions of dollars per year.[10]

For enterprises that compete through differentiation, innovations tend to arise from the local market demand and product development, as well as from unique market characteristics that may require offering special credit terms, packaging, promotion, and distribution services. Local market forces do not always influence all innovative aspects of a firm. For example, Coca-Cola provides the same product to all world markets. But though Coca-Cola's top managers do not allow various consumer tastes and preferences to affect the taste of the product, they do let local market forces influence credit terms, distribution, and promotion policies.

Manufacturers of home appliances, on the other hand, allow local market forces to influence their product-market scope heavily. Their rice cookers, as one instance, cook rice in substantially different form and quality, depending on local consumer tastes. Sometimes particular local preferences provide product ideas that can be implemented successfully in other regions. Originally intended for the Asian market, rice cookers that develop separate and fluffy grains of rice are now marketed in America as well.

With the least-cost strategic option, higher profitability correlated positively with greater production capacity and market share. With the differentiation option, however, according to a number of studies, higher profitability may correlate with either smaller or greater production capacity and market share.[11] In the mainframe computer manufacturing industry, for example, Burroughs, with less than 7 percent of market share, has had a high ROI (14 percent) with its unique products. IBM, also competing through differentiation, has also had a high ROI (20 percent), with a whopping 59 percent of market share.[12]

---

[10]Jay Leviton, "Coke's Big Market Blitz," *Business Week*, May 30, 1983, p. 61.

[11]See Carolyn Y. Woo and Arnold C. Cooper, "Strategies of Effective Low Share Businesses," *Strategic Management Journal*, July–Sept. 1981, pp. 301–18; Carolyn Y. Woo, "Market Share Leadership—Not Always So Good," *Harvard Business Review*, January–February 1984, pp. 50–54.

[12]R. G. Hamermesh, M. J. Anderson, and J. E. Harris, "Strategies for Low Market Share Businesses," *Harvard Business Review*, May–June 1978, pp. 95–102.

NICHE

When a business unit decides to offer existing products or technologically new or improved products that fulfill the needs of particular buyers in an industry, it has chosen the strategic option of niche.[13] Products of both the differentiation and niche options normally have well-known brands to distinguish them from the products of competitors. But though the unique products of the differentiation option are aimed at the whole industry, the need-fulfilling products of the niche option address specific clusters of buyers within an industry.

Firms using the niche strategic option need functional support primarily from their research and development, manufacturing, and marketing sectors.[14] While established products that have been in the marketplace for some time tend to rely primarily on marketing, technologically new or improved products depend primarily on R&D and manufacturing.

Low costs are less important with the niche option than with the differentiation option. Because, under the niche option, the firm will produce fewer units than under the differentiation option, per-unit costs tend to be higher. Technologically oriented product-market choices also require rapid product modifications and frequent and costly new-product introductions. These requirements make unfeasible lower manufacturing costs through larger volumes of production, particularly since accurate sales projections for innovative products are difficult to make.

Hence, business units competing through the niche option should be prepared to face and cultivate a highly inelastic market demand for their products.[15] Market demand for its outputs allows the firm to set higher pricing policies and profit margins than with the differentiation option. Under the niche option, larger and smaller firms with varying amounts of resources may compete effectively with need-fulfilling products.

International Involvement

Business units subject to the niche option have only limited opportunities for international involvement. Their markets are often restricted to advanced, high-income countries, though some exporting may be done to the developing nations. For example, Rockford's specialized fasteners are particularly appropriate for capital-intensive manufacturers that produce substantial volumes and implement

---

[13]P. Wright, "MNC-Third World Business Unit Performance: Application of Strategic Elements," *Strategic Management Journal*, August 1984, pp. 231–40.

[14]P. Wright, "Strategic Management within a World Parameter," *Managerial Planning*, ed. Henry C. Doofe (Oxford: Planning Executive Institute, 1985), pp. 33–37.

[15]Wright (note 13), pp. 231–40.

high value addition in their production process. Such manufacturers are usually found in the advanced countries.

International involvement may begin with exporting. It may culminate in establishing production units in select advanced, high-income countries, such as Canada, Germany, Sweden, Switzerland, England, and Japan. Because low costs are not of paramount importance, there is little incentive to adapt product technology to local factor costs.[16] Hence, the corporate headquarters of firms competing through the niche option would tend particularly to influence technology in all markets.

Ramifications for Profitability and Innovation

The niche strategic option emphasizes product outputs that fulfill the special needs of few buyers. Because need-fulfilling products present very high values to their consumers and are produced in lower numbers, the route to profitability is through very high profit margins and pricing policies. Higher profitability for need-fulfilling outputs tends to correlate negatively with production capacity and market share.[17] An executive of a toothpaste firm that specializes in treating gum diseases provides an example:

> We used to produce and sell $20 million per year and our return on investment was around 20 percent. Now we sell twice as much since we began expanding our market share. But we are lucky to have our return on investment break the single-digit range. The more customers we gain, it seems, the more we have to give price concessions.[18]

Innovative prospects of the niche strategic option tend to be brightest when R&D and manufacturing are emphasized. Although innovations may occur under any one of the options, the niche strategy, which revolves around smaller and more flexible production and R&D sectors, is best suited for making and responding to rapid technological advances. The task of R&D is to explore opportunities for superior outputs, and the mission of manufacturing is to remain flexible enough to accommodate specific demands for the products. For example, R&D provided the impetus for Rockford's technologically new, self-threading screw that permits faster assembly. And flexible manufacturing at Rockford has allowed the innovative fastener to be custom-made in size, strength, and coating for each customer.

Specific product-market choices tend to link an enterprise to the strategic options of least-cost, differentiation, or niche. But strategies are subject to change.

Select need-fulfilling products over time may be repositioned to compete as unique and subsequently standardized outputs. For example, the innovative,

[16]Stobaugh and Telesio, "Match Manufacturing," p. 20.
[17]M. Porter, *Competitive Strategy*, pp. 1–34.
[18]Quoted in Wright, "Competitive Strategies for," p. 88.

need-fulfilling computer of today, which is addressed to fewer buyers, eventually may be directed to larger portions of the market as a unique product. As its functions are superseded by more advanced technology, the same computer may carry a lower price tag and may be mass-produced for the price-sensitive consumer. The successful firm not only chooses a strategic option but also, as the product market changes, adjusts its strategy and repositions its products.

What this article is about: Low-cost leadership is merely one form of differentiation, and since only one firm can provide the lowest cost, other firms must choose other methods. A good place to start is with the customer.

2–5 Differentiation: Begin with the Consumer

William E. Fulmer and Jack Goodwin
*William E. Fulmer is a visiting professor
at the Graduate School of Business,
Harvard University, Boston, Mass.
Jack Goodwin is an associate professor
of business administration at the
Colgate Darden Graduate School of Business,
the University of Virginia, Charlottesville.*

One of the hottest buzzwords in business strategy today is "competitive advantage." Since the concepts of strategy are specific to competitive arenas, those speaking of competitive advantage are reinforcing the idea that strategies are designed to beat competitors. Consequently, managers are constantly searching for terminology, frameworks, and matrices that will help them better understand their companies' strategies as well as those of their competitors.

In the 1960s, the early work of the Boston Consulting Group focused on the importance of a low-cost position. The importance of market share was emphasized, because market share resulted from a firm's ability to move rapidly down the experience curve and thereby achieve the lowest-cost position in its industry.

By the late 1970s, Michael Porter was arguing that in addition to cost leadership, which he defined as a strategy by which the firm chooses to "become the low-cost producer in its industry," there was another "generic" strategy. He used the term "differentiation" to represent efforts by a company to "be unique in its industry along some dimensions that are widely valued by buyers."[1]

SOURCE: *Business Horizons*, September–October 1988, pp. 55–63.

[1]Michael Porter, *Competitive Strategy* (New York: The Free Press, 1980). In this article we consider only the generic strategies of low cost and differentiation. Porter's third generic strategy, focus, is not considered, since we are interested in the major players in industries and a focus player pursues only a narrow segment of the market. Furthermore, even focus players pursue either a low-cost or a differentiation strategy, if on a smaller scale.

Although there are some examples of firms successfully employing a highly differentiated strategy seemingly without much regard for cost (Hewlett-Packard in calculators, for example), and others that have dominated an industry for some period of time with a virtually undifferentiated product at the lowest possible cost (such as Texas Instruments), these easily perceived extremes are rare in practice.

A problem with the either/or approach is that most of us know firms that seem to fit both categories. For example, it has been our experience that many executives and MBA students, when analyzing the Crown Cork & Seal policy case, have difficulty deciding whether the firm has a low-cost or differentiated strategy. We think the confusion arises partially because Crown Cork & Seal is both a low-cost *and* a differentiated player in the metal-container industry.

Using the either/or approach of cost versus differentiation provides little help in distinguishing the players in most industries. Most firms cluster toward the middle of the low-cost/high-differentiation spectrum. For example, in the airline industry it has been very difficult to defend either a low-cost strategy (as People Express discovered) or a highly differentiated, unique strategy (as Atlanta Air and Presidential discovered). As a result, most of the major airlines offer a relatively similar product to the customer, both in characteristics and cost. In this middle ground, where most companies in many industries seem to fall, arises the greatest confusion about strategy.

WHY NOT BE BOTH?

Although Porter suggests that a firm can achieve both differentiation and low cost, his interpreters often seem to treat the two strategies as incompatible. But forcing firms to view the strategic choice as one of either low cost or differentiation significantly restricts management's competitive responses. With increased competition in the marketplace from low-cost countries, U.S. firms should look for ways to combine low cost and differentiation.

In reality, most firms' strategies reflect a trade-off between cost and other forms of differentiation. Figure 1 illustrates this behavior (relative product effectiveness is used as a surrogate for differentiation of the product). To achieve a given level of effectiveness, a firm must accept a minimum cost. In addition, consumers, regulatory agencies, and legislatures place minimum requirements on the effectiveness of any product. We usually refer to this as the minimum acceptable level of quality.

Given these restrictions, we would expect firm A to outperform firm B, since A achieves the same level of effectiveness at a lower cost (reflected in the selling price). Firm C, on the other hand, has chosen to differentiate itself (increase its effectiveness). Greater differentiation has been obtained at the expense of cost. The success of this strategy will depend on the consumer's willingness to pay a higher price for C's product to obtain the increased effectiveness. If this increase

FIGURE 1   The Differentiation Trade-off

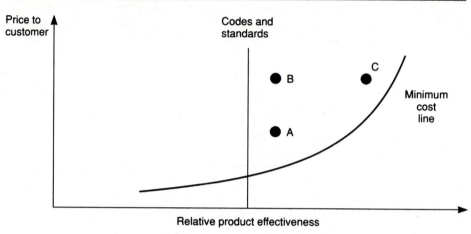

Adapted from John L. Colley, Jr., *Corporate and Divisional Planning: Text and Cases* (Reston, Va.: Reston Publishing, 1984).

in effectiveness is perceived by the customer as sufficient to justify the additional cost, then C's strategy will be successful.

Figure 1 suggests that it is impossible to achieve the same level of effectiveness as C at A's cost. In fact, the minimum cost frontier may be much flatter than that illustrated in Figure 1; more differentiation is not necessarily achieved through substantial increases in cost.

Our argument is based in part on experiences of U.S. manufacturers in their struggles with foreign competitors, particularly the Japanese. For years, most American manufacturers seemed to believe that cost and quality were conflicting priorities and that trade-offs between them were unavoidable. Recent experiences have shown this to be false. In fact, current practice indicates that improved quality can decrease, rather than increase, cost. With the advent of robotics, CAD/CAM, flexible manufacturing systems, and other technological advances, combinations of lower costs and higher levels of differentiation seem to be a reasonable expectation. Hall's research on strategy in hostile environments identifies Caterpillar and Philip Morris as companies achieving both low-cost and differentiated positions in their respective industries.[2] Other recent research also suggests that cost leadership and differentiation are independent and that each is a continuum.[3]

It is our contention that it is not only possible but essential to be both low

[2]William K. Hall, "Survival Strategies in a Hostile Environment," *Harvard Business Review*, September–October 1980, pp. 75–80.

[3]V. Govindarajan and Deven Sharma, "Generic Competitive Strategies: An Empirical Analysis," *1986 Decision Sciences Institute Proceedings*, pp. 1243–45.

cost and differentiated. In fact, since only one firm can be the true cost leader in a given industry, all other firms, if they are successful, are differentiated in some way. All firms, in essence, follow a differentiated strategy. Only one company can differentiate itself with the lowest cost; the remaining firms in the industry must find other ways to differentiate their products. This, then, is the focus of this article—how can companies differentiate themselves for competitive advantage?

FOCUS ON THE CUSTOMER

There are some relatively low-cost ways in which firms can differentiate themselves—with benefits that are far greater than the costs incurred. Peter Drucker suggests the place to start—the customer.

> To know what a business is we have to start with its *purpose*. Its purpose must lie outside of the business itself. In fact, it must lie in society since business enterprise is an organ of society. There is only one valid definition of business purpose: to create a *customer*.
>
> What the customer thinks he is buying, what he considers value, is decisive—it determines what a business is, what it produces, and whether it will prosper. And what the customer buys and considers value is never a product. It is always utility, that is, what a product or service does for him. And what is value for the customer is . . . anything but obvious.[4]

One problem with Drucker's statement is the difficulty of defining and measuring value. Value is a personal assessment of worth and therefore is unique to each individual customer. In addition, it is frequently influenced by events or activities beyond the control of the producer. Figure 2 illustrates the critical producer-customer interface that determines value and some of the factors influencing the customer's decision. But we need a better way of understanding and describing this relationship between producer and customer, a link between the customer's personal concept of value and that of the producer.

We have found the concept of customer bonding useful in creating value in customer's minds. We define customer bonding as *the process of tying a customer to a particular firm's product or service*. Although it can be done by effective advertising that ties a customer's self-perception to a particular product (Yuppies and BMW's), we believe a more enduring bond, loyalty, is built by good service at the producer-customer interface.

We have used a rough, three-level measure of bonding—high bonding, medium bonding, and low bonding—to study the performance of several businesses within an industry. The U.S. airline industry has been used as an illustration.

---

[4]Peter F. Drucker, *Management: Tasks, Responsibilities, Practices* (New York: Harper & Row, 1973), p. 61.

FIGURE 2   Producer-Customer Interface

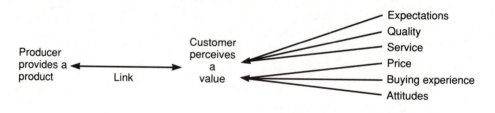

This industry is a good example of many firms bunched in the middle ground between the extremes of strategic choice. As a result, it is difficult to distinguish among the players in this industry using traditional strategic concepts.

THE AIRLINE INDUSTRY

The major players in the airline industry all pursue strategies based on structural factors. By routing all flights in a geographic region through a single city, the airline creates a hub-and-spoke configuration. This approach benefits the carrier in several ways. It eliminates thousands of potential routes in the network while still connecting all cities in the region that are served by the carrier. The airline can operate much more efficiently and dominate the geographic region through its ability to provide service to most or all of the airports in that region.

A hub-and-spoke strategy thus contributes to bonding by increasing availability. However, availability falls far short of providing an adequate measure of the strength of the bond between airline and customer. Another measure prominent in recent public discussions is on-time service. Once again, this measure does not seem to capture the essence of our concept. Perhaps the deficiency of these measures is that they ignore the personal touch. They address the *where* and *when* of travel but ignore the *how*. Airlines have used frequent-flyer programs and airport clubs to increase the personal touch, but these perks are utilized by a small percentage of customers. A study that British Airways conducted several years ago illustrates the problem.

In launching a "Customer First" campaign, British Airways (BA) administered a customer questionnaire to find out what factors customers consider most important in traveling by air and how BA compared to its competition. Two of the top four factors, care/concern and problem solving, were not surprising results. However, BA had never consciously thought about the other two factors considered most important by their customers: spontaneity and recovery—the ability to break out of the routine systems to accommodate a customer's individual

TABLE 1 The Number of Complaints to the Department of Transportation from January through September for Each 100,000 Passengers Flown

Airline	Complaints
World Airways[1]	15.06
People Express	7.76
Pan American	4.50
Trans World	4.21
Continental	3.76
United	2.77
Eastern	2.59
Republic	2.38
American	1.46
Northwest	1.46
USAir	1.45
Western	1.33
Piedmont	1.18
Delta	0.57
Southwest	0.51

[1]Stopped operating scheduled flights September 15.

SOURCE: *The Wall Street Journal*, November 10, 1986.

needs and the ability to recover after a mistake has been made. Both factors go beyond the mechanics of providing what is expected, the ability to get to your destination on time, and address the more personal issues: What does the airline do for you if there is potential for failure of service in a situation or after a failure of service has occurred?[5]

In an attempt to capture the personal nature of the concept, we used a weighted average of two measures as a proxy for bonding to compare the 13 largest U.S. airlines in late 1986. The measures are the number of complaints to the Department of Transportation from January to September 1986 for each 100,000 passengers flown (Table 1), and *USA Today's* 1986 survey of business travelers (Table 2). Table 3 combines the rank of each airline on both surveys and uses the combined score as a measure of bonding. This enabled us to split the 13 airlines into three roughly equal categories: high bonding, medium bonding, and low bonding.

Financial results for 1985 (Table 4) show a strong correlation between the level of bonding and financial returns. It is particularly interesting to note that revenue per employee increases as bonding decreases. This may indicate that

---

[5]Karl Albrecht and Ron Zemke, *Service America! Doing Business in the New Economy* (Homewood, Ill.: Dow Jones-Irwin, 1985), pp. 33–34.

TABLE 2 How Business Travelers Rated the Airlines

Airline	Rating
Delta	82
American	77
United	76
Northwest	73
Western	72
Piedmont	71
TWA	70
Republic	67
USAir	67
Continental	66
Pan Am	64
Eastern	58
People Express	47

Calculated from ratings of excellent, good, fair, poor for each airline. Excellent equaled 4 points; poor, 1 point.

SOURCE: *USA Today,* survey, reported September 15, 1986, p. 1E.

TABLE 3 Bonding Measurement for the 13 Largest U.S. Airlines

	Airline	DOT	USA Today	Combined Score
High bonding	Delta	1	1	2
	American	5	2	7
	Western	3	5	8
	Piedmont	2	6	8
Medium bonding	Northwest	5	4	9
	United	9	3	12
	USAir	4	8	12
	Republic	7	8	15
Low bonding	TWA	11	7	18
	Eastern	8	12	20
	Continental	10	10	20
	Pan Am	12	11	23
	People Express	13	13	26

TABLE 4   Financial Performance of 13 Largest U.S. Airlines by Category

Bonding Rank	Airline	*1985 Net Income as a Percentage of**			
		Revenues	Equity	Assets	Revenue per Employee (000)
1	Delta	5.5%	20.2	7.2	120.0
2	American	5.6	15.5	5.4	117.7
3	Western	5.1	27.9	7.1	127.5
3	Piedmont	4.4	13.3	4.5	95.7
Category I Averages		5.2	19.2	6.1	115.2
5	Northwest	2.8	7.7	3.2	159.6
6	United	(0.8)	(2.7)	(0.6)	84.0
6	USAir	6.6	12.3	6.0	125.9
8	Republic	10.2	88.4	13.8	114.1
Category II Averages		4.7	26.4	5.6	120.9
9	TWA	(5.2)	(35.8)	(7.0)	128.1
10	Eastern	0.1	2.4	0.2	117.2
10	Continental	4.7	75.7	4.7	122.3
12	Pan Am	1.5	11.5	2.1	142.0
13	People Express	(2.8)	(13.1)	(2.6)	130.4
Category III Averages		(0.3)	8.1	(0.5)	128.0

*1985 data were used, since *Fortune's* 1986 data reflected consolidation of several of the firms, making it difficult to use the rankings shown in Tables 1 and 2.

SOURCE: *Fortune*, June 9, 1986, pp. 138–39.

low-bonding organizations are trading efficiency for good service. If this is true, the other financial measures indicate that the trade-off is not a wise one.

We suspect that a similar relationship holds for traditional manufacturing companies. There is some evidence that American car companies have recognized the problem. It was recently reported in *The Wall Street Journal* that Ford Motor Company, recognizing narrowing price and quality differences between companies, has begun using a buyer-happiness index to award Merkur luxury-import franchises. However, in attempts to learn more about this program, we have been unable to find any Ford field representative who knows of the program's existence. Perhaps this lack of knowledge is symptomatic of the problem addressed here. Recognition of the need for stronger bonds with the customer is often not translated into real programs. (In a similar fashion, General Motors' Buick division is reportedly considering making such indexes a basis for distributing new models.[6])

[6]*The Wall Street Journal*, March 19, 1987, p. 1.

MANAGEMENT IMPLICATIONS OF BONDING

Although our analysis suggests that there are financial implications in the concept of bonding, we believe that the operating and strategic implications are at least as great—if not more important.

Operating Implications

The concept of bonding has significant implications for many operating issues. They involve most of the functional areas of the firm, encompass both human and technical problems, and have external as well as internal orientations. In spite of their diversity, they possess a common thread—a potential for influencing the customer—that relates them to the concept of bonding.

Culture. With the rapid transfer of technology, it is becoming increasingly difficult for companies in most industries to sustain competitive advantages based on superior product or process technology. Increasingly, companies are selling products with low perceived levels of differentiation. The attitude of managers and employees is often the one major distinguishing feature of competing products and companies. IBM, Procter & Gamble, Johnson & Johnson, and other firms have employed their customer-centered cultures with great success for many years.

A newsletter from the PIMS organization on "The Strategic Management of Service Quality" states:

> In his book *A Business and Its Beliefs,* Thomas Watson, Jr., writes, "'IBM means service' states exactly what we stand for. We want to give the best customer service of any company in the world." It was this perspective on the "soft" dimension of customer needs, so logical in hindsight, that was the trigger to IBM's rise to dominance.[7]

It was not only this belief that triggered IBM's success, but also its ability to inspire several hundred thousand employees to live by it. Procter & Gamble has been equally successful in developing a common set of values and beliefs that differentiates it from competitors in a market that is dominated by products we normally would consider commodities. An anecdote from Peters and Austin's *A Passion for Excellence* illustrates the point:

> A Procter & Gamble manufacturing manager remembers a call in the middle of the night. It came from a district sales manager, soon after this fellow (now a fifteen-year vet) had become a manager. "George, you've got a problem with a bar of soap down here." Down here, George explains (in 1983) was three hundred miles away. "George, think you could get down here by six-thirty this morning?" Our informant adds, "It

---

[7]Phillip Thompson, Glenn DeSouza, and Bradley T. Gale, "The Strategic Management of Service Quality," *PIMSLETTER 33*, p. 1.

sounded like something more than an invitation." And finally, he concludes, "After you've finished your first three-hundred-mile ride through the back hills of Tennessee at seventy miles an hour to look at one damned thirty-four cent bar of soap, you understand that the Procter & Gamble Company is very, very serious about product quality. You don't subsequently need a detailed two-hundred page manual to prove it to you."[8]

Johnson & Johnson's response to both Tylenol scares convinced customers that the company cared about them, and twice Tylenol did the impossible by recovering the lost market share.

Customer Involvement.   By involving the customer in the delivery of the service, firms have in some instances been able to reduce the cost of delivery while enhancing the quality of service. We are all familiar with the self-service approach and encounter it daily at fast-food restaurants, salad bars in full-service restaurants, mini-bars in hotels, direct-dial long-distance telephoning, and automatic teller machines (ATMs), to mention only a few examples. For this approach to be successful, the customer must perceive that the value of the service is enhanced in some way by his or her involvement.

The ATM provides an excellent example of the potential of this approach. An ATM gives the customer much greater access to the services of a bank. Access is available on a continual basis, a marked departure from the historical practice of limited banking hours. Thus, the service is significantly enhanced. What is not as apparent is the substantial decrease in the cost of the service to the bank. A bank's three greatest costs, after the cost of money, are bricks and mortar, people, and paper. All of these are largely eliminated with the ATM. It is widely accepted in banking that cost per transaction can be reduced 80 percent or more if a sufficient number of transactions can be moved from tellers to ATMs.

Of course, accessibility is not the only factor the bank's customers consider when selecting how, when, and where they bank. The challenge to the bank, and to other businesses using self-service applications, is to convince customers that the added value of the service offsets the additional cost to them. In addition to accessibility, the value-enhancing factors of increased customer involvement include time savings, confidentiality, accuracy, and quality control.

It is interesting to note that although customer involvement can increase bonding, it can also reduce human interaction. By becoming more "personal," we do not necessarily become more "human." The term "personal" does not refer to the amount of human interaction but to the extent that personal needs of customers are satisfied. The ATM enables a bank to respond to some customer needs more effectively and address a broader range of needs than previously possible.

---

[8]Tom Peters and Nancy Austin, *A Passion for Excellence* (New York: Random House, 1985), pp. 30–35.

Decentralization.   Because the customer is the key, the organization must be structured to facilitate better service. In most cases, this means a decentralized organization with considerable authority delegated to people close to the customer. You want your people to run the business as if it were their own.

Today's popular business folklore is filled with tales of organizations that have gained tremendous competitive advantage by pushing authority to lower levels. We could name company after company that has successfully employed a decentralized structure. However, no one has better explained why this strategy works than Robert Townsend in his classic *Up the Organization.* In explaining decision making in the organization, Townsend makes the analogy: "The Charge of the Light Brigade was ordered by an officer who wasn't there looking at the territory."[9]

People who interact with the customer, frequently those at the lowest levels in the organization, have the greatest possible visibility. Bill Marriott, Jr., notes, "We receive over a thousand customer forms and letters every day . . . and the most complimentary . . . are those written by guests who are impressed by our people and by some small thing that one of our staff went out of his or her way to do for them." Interaction with the customer gives employees a different perspective. They typically are the first to know when something is wrong, what customers' needs are, and how best to satisfy them. The organization that delegates the authority to act decisively in fulfilling these needs and solving the customers' problems often succeeds; the one that doesn't often fails.

Managing Supply and Demand.   The adept use of capacity is a formidable competitive weapon in any business. Often the proper balance of supply and demand is singled out as a special problem in service organizations. However, in today's world of just-in-time inventories and outsourcing of components, this skill has become equally important in manufacturing. In either type of industry, the ability to meet demand when it occurs with a high-quality product is central to the bonding concept. This is often more difficult than it seems.

Airlines have been particularly active in managing this problem, since additions to their capacity are extremely expensive and come not in single units but usually in blocks of 100 or more seats. In supplying this capacity, airlines are restricted again by their inability to divide capacity into units smaller than the size of their aircraft. A number of practices have been used to deal with the problem. Reservation systems assist in anticipating demand levels and planning for both the appropriate size of aircraft to be assigned to a particular route and the proper number of flights between two cities. Pricing is widely used to encourage customers to fly in periods of low demand rather than in peak-demand periods. By using dynamic yield-management programs, airlines can increase or reduce the number of seats sold for various prices, depending on the level of customer demand at various price points. In addition, a few airlines have shared

---

[9]Robert Townsend, *Up the Organization* (New York: Alfred A. Knopf, 1970), p. 45.

capacity on a regular basis by leasing aircraft to another airline when the lessor's demand was low and the lessee's demand was high.

Standardization of Key Operating Policies. Although at first glance standardization seems to conflict with decentralization, it is our contention that key operating policies should be standarized so people close to the customers can be free to provide customized service. This is not to say that people interacting with the customer should not be consulted in the establishment of the policies. They are more likely to feel ownership of the policies if they have been involved.

The Marriott Corporation is an oft-cited example of an organization that follows this operating principle very effectively:

> The company became one of the industry's most efficient by applying a tightly centralized system of policies, procedures, and controls to the slightest operational detail. Every job has a manual that breaks down the work into a mind-boggling number of steps. A hotel maid, for instance, has 66 things to do in cleaning up a room. . . .[10]

Electronic Data Systems Corporation has standardized not only training programs but also purchasing procedures for such ordinary items as raised flooring, air conditioning, power sources, and other routine equipment needed in a reliable computer environment. In addition, all of its regional data centers are as standarized as possible; even capacity level is standarized. As one official says, "If you have something go down and you don't have the specialist at hand to shoot the problem, he can look at the way it's done at another place and duplicate it."

This level of standardization normally has several positive results. Need for supervision is significantly reduced, so the cost of providing good service is lowered. The burden of making many decisions is removed from the person delivering the service, so more time can be devoted to providing the personal touch required for bonding. Finally, organizations that focus on detail to this extent spend little time correcting mistakes and invariably place more emphasis on training for good service.

Substituting Information for Assets. With the rapid improvements in information technology, some firms have been able to use information in innovative ways to better serve the customer and gain competitive advantage. By substituting more accurate and timely information for inventory and fixed assets, firms have been able to reduce costs and be more responsive to customer needs at the same time.

Italian-based Benetton, the world's largest manufacturer of knitware, has used the rapid collection and communication of information—in conjunction with a highly responsive manufacturing system—to operate its retail stores with substantially less inventory than its competitors. Its stores have no back-room storage. What is on the shelf is the only inventory in the store. By tracking sales very closely and identifying the items in greatest demand, the manufacturing

---

[10]Thomas Moore "Marriott Grabs for More Room," *Fortune,* October 31, 1983, p. 108.

system is able to respond rapidly to replenish the hot sellers. Not only are customers served better, but the critical performance measures of any retail operation, inventory turnover and sales per square foot, are maximized.

Strategic Implications

As pointed out earlier, Michael Porter has identified two generic strategies for successful major players in an industry—low cost and differentiation. We have tried to suggest that those who would view these as either/or options greatly limit their strategic choices.

As we tried to point out with the airline example, there is a basic difficulty in distinguishing among differentiation strategies within many industries, especially those industries in which most of the major firms seem to be offering fairly similar products. We believe the concept of customer bonding provides an extra dimension that makes such distinctions possible. For example, in the early 1980s, although Delta and Eastern airlines had fairly similar route structures, planes, and staff levels, Delta clearly had a closer bond with flyers—an almost family bond. To a lesser degree, American and United had similar routes—but American's innovation and high-quality service seemed to suggest a more professional and dependable operation to many travelers.

Clearly, supplying a custom-made or unique product is the ultimate in a differentiated strategy. Custom products have a natural advantage in bonding—attention to personal needs and desires. Nevertheless, some firms that have chosen low-cost strategy, producing even a standard, commodity-type product, have been very successsful in bonding. For example, although Kimberly Clark's newsprint division sells a commodity, it provides sufficient personal attention to its regular customers that it is able to avoid many of the price-cutting tactics of its competitors and yet keep its customers coming back, even when newsprint can be purchased at a lower price from a competitor. Crown Cork & Seal, by being close to its customers and providing them with an array of services, is able to maintain relatively high margins and returns in what is largely a commodity business. Thus, bonding can be combined with both low-cost and differentiated strategies.

All successful strategies are differentiation; cost is just one of the factors in which a firm can be different from the competition. If differentiation is considered in this manner, as a series of factors or dimensions in which a company can be better than or outperform the competitors, then only one company can be the best, or the industry leader, in any one dimension. For example, only one airline has the best food; only one has the friendliest employees; and only one is on time most frequently. With automobile manufacturers, only one has the best gas mileage; only one has the best repair service. Bonding occurs when a firm is able to identify and establish a leadership position in one, or more likely several, of these dimensions while meeting the other dimensions at some satisfactory level.

CREATING THE BOND

Although there are many ways to bond customers to a particular company's products (including effective advertising), and although some practices will be unique in various industries, in general the greater the personal attention to customers, the more enduring the bond. Service to the customer is the key issue. However, service to the customer is not the same as customer service. Service to the customer may mean not only providing special services but also making the product convenient to acquire, easy to use, and reliable over time. At a basic level it means showing a willingness to help customers solve problems and just being concerned or friendly. In the words of Peters and Austin:

> As IBM's Buck Rodgers . . . correctly (unfortunately) observes, "It's a shame, but whenever you get good service, it's an exception, and you're excited about it. It ought to be the other way around." We agree. Common decency, common courtesy toward the customer ("Guest") is indeed the exception. Economists may not buy it as the ultimate barrier to competitor entry or as a crucial form of sustainable strategic advantage, but such disparate actors (and extremely successful competitors) as IBM and McDonald's certainly do.[11]

Yet *The Wall Street Journal* recently reported that despite the furor over the poor quality of service, American companies are spending only $2.58 per employee to improve their dealings with the public—and most of the money goes to train workers to sell more or to calm complaining customers.[12]

Satisfying Expectations

We have found the concept of the psychological contract helpful in understanding how bonding takes place and why it is so important. This concept has traditionally been used to examine the relationship between an employer and its employees. We have applied it to the seller-customer relationship. In this exchange the customer comes to the seller with a set of expectations concerning the transaction. If these expectations are not fulfilled by the seller, the contract is violated and the seller has failed to complete a satisfactory transaction (create a happy customer). Hence, the seller must understand the nature of customers' expectations and how to satisfy them.

Gronroos has suggested that management of this process, in his terminology "service quality," is two-dimensional.[13] Customers are concerned with *what* is exchanged as well as *how* it is exchanged. Gronroos refers to the what of the

---

[11]Peters and Austin (note 8), p. 44.
[12]*The Wall Street Journal*, March 17, 1987, p. 1.

transaction as the "technical quality dimension" and the how of the transaction as the "functional quality dimension." Sellers must be aware of both dimensions to adequately meet the expectations of their customers. For example, patients are highly unlikely to continue to see a physician if the physician always has dirty hands, even if the physician has outstanding professional qualifications. The technical quality dimension is clearly fulfilled, but the functional dimension is not.

This dichotomy provides a framework for analysis of the expectations of customers. We believe that many firms focus the majority, if not all, of their attention on the technical quality dimension. Executives frequently point out how tremendous improvements in their products have made them as good as or superior to the competition. Furthermore, these improvements can be documented and demonstrated. Nevertheless, the irrational customers fail to recognize the improvements and do not purchase the products. There is no reason to doubt the truth of the executives' statements. What can be questioned is the functional dimension of their service quality. Has enough care and attention been given to the delivery of the product?

Another interesting aspect of the service dilemma revealed in the executives' comments is their reliance on truth and fact. Whether the superiority of the product is real or not is of no consequence. The perception of the customer concerning the product is *the only reality of any significance*. Thus, managers are compelled to take proactive measures that address both dimensions of service quality and perceptions of service to shape and influence expectations. Their success in doing so can be the difference in gaining or losing competitive advantage.

Consequences of Bonding

The TARP (Technical Assistance Research Programs, Inc.) studies cited in Albrecht and Zemke's *Service America* highlight the grave consequences of poor customer bonding through inferior service. The results include:

- For every complaint received, the average business has 26 customers with a problem. Six of these customers have "serious" problems.
- The average customer with a problem tells 9 or 10 people. Thirteen percent of the problem customers tell more than 20 others.
- Noncomplainers are less likely to do business with the offending firm than complainers.

---

[13]Christian Gronroos, *Strategic Management and Marketing in the Service Sector* (Lund, Sweden: Studentlitteratur ab, 1984). Gronroos' research and conclusions were directed at firms in the service sector. Nevertheless, we believe that they are equally applicable in the manufacturing environment because of the mix of tangible and intangible attributes in most products. For additional reading in this area see Theodore Levitt, *The Marketing Imagination* (New York: The Free Press, 1983).

Perhaps the most disturbing finding in the TARP studies is that customers share so few of their complaints with businesses. Being close to the customer takes on a new meaning in light of these revelations. An active program to respond positively to complaining customers is obviously necessary, but it cannot discern the expectations and perceptions of a firm's customer base.

The positive results of good service and a high level of bonding seem to be as encouraging as the negative results are discouraging. According to Albrecht and Zemke, a loyal customer in the auto industry represents an average revenue of $140,000 over his or her lifetime. A similar figure for supermarkets is estimated to be $22,000 over a five-year period. Hence, the customer's value must be viewed in terms of revenues (and profits) that result over the long term. The value of bonding and the potential rewards would therefore appear to justify dedicating considerable resources to managing the bonding process.

The concept of bonding can help us understand the relationship that businesses have with their customers—obviously a key to their continued success and prosperity. What is needed now is a way to operationalize the concept. To achieve this goal it will be necessary to measure bonding. It is not likely that a universal measure of bonding for all companies or industries will ever be developed. However, a company might be able to establish a reasonably accurate surrogate for the level of bonding by monitoring repeat business. In addition, answers to the following questions, asked of customers on a regular basis, would provide valuable insight to the firm's progress in this area:

- Would you recommend this product to a close friend or relative? Why?
- Would you buy this product again? Why?

Other information relevant to this process and worthy of examination would be what the firm does in situations where mistakes have been made and the customer's expectations have not been met. In the British Airways study cited above, recovery was one of the customers' top concerns. It suggests that the customers don't expect perfection, but they do expect that errors will be corrected. Thus it is necessary to check if errors *are* being corrected, if they are corrected *before* the customer complains, and how much time elapsed before the correction took place.

These suggested measures are tentative at best. When more precise measures are developed, they will be invaluable in assisting managers to gain and maintain competitive advantage through stronger customer bonding.

What this article is about: This article addresses the strategic implications and challenges of markets where change and uncertainty are a consequence of maturity and fragmentation rather than growth. It provides a strategic framework that is particularly relevant to the regeneration of British manufacturing industry.

2–6 Strategies for Mature Businesses

Malcolm Schofield and David Arnold

*Malcolm Schofield is Director of Studies for the
Management Development Group at
Ashridge Management College.
David Arnold is a member of the Marketing
and Strategic Management Group at Ashridge.*

Organizations facing maturity within their major markets should ideally recognize certain symptoms and invest early in strategic analysis and new-policy formulation. However, experience shows frequent failure to recognize the complexity of the aging process both at the onset of maturity and through to eventual market decline.

The paper argues that it is too simplisitic to assume a common set of market and customer characteristics applicable to large-volume, no-growth product markets. While the life-cycle concept is used as the basic analytical form, it has been developed to relate practically and more closely to the conditions found in many major markets today. Guidelines are provided for four strategic options, detailing initiatives appropriate for different stages of market maturity. The importance of recognizing the stage which a particular market has reached is emphasized and supported by practical examples.

THE LIFE CYCLE

Life cycles are applicable at various levels, to brands, product markets, industries, and economies. The "life cycle" concept most appropriate to strategy formulation is probably *market*-based, that is, examining whether or not cus-

SOURCE: *Long Range Planning* 21, no. 5 (October 1988), pp. 69–76.

tomers and demand are increasing, stable, or declining in volume. A *market* life cycle is the level of aggregation which perhaps best captures the changing nature of the business environment. Strategic initiatives may be taken at any stage, but timing considerations are paramount. Consider the range and complexity of market conditions, both approaching and during a period of maturity (stable demand).

The traditional life-cycle concept offers four distinct phases in introduction, growth, maturity, and decline. For most organizations, maturity is the most important phase—while introduction and growth may be short-lived conditions, maturity can continue almost indefinitely. For managers in these organizations, the challenge is to preserve market share in maturity, and to ensure that the onset of decline never happens.

Maturity is also the most complex phase, the only period during which the sales curve turns around. A closer perspective on maturity produces some interesting characteristics, applicable to four further distinct phases:

- Late growth.
- Early maturity.
- Mid-maturity.
- Late maturity.

These distinctions recognize the fact that the fundamental market conditions alter radically *during* the single phase of maturity, spanning the period from growth to decline. Each phase is considered in terms of its more common characteristics.

Late Growth: "Prepare for Maturity"

It is price and its level of significance which is of particular interest in this phase. The most commonly held view—that severe price competition is limited to the maturity phase, during which it intensifies as the competitive pressures increase, is oversimplistic. Placed under careful scrutiny, price often appears as a positive stimulation to demand in growth, and conversely is often viewed as of lesser importance as customers become more discerning and discriminating. In Figure 1, the hatched portion represents the part of the marketplace where price is the prime purchasing consideration. A peak is reached in early maturity, and thereafter it falls away substantially until the late appeal to the laggard first-time purchasers or more frequent user counteracts some real decline elsewhere.

Price competitiveness is normally associated with buyers' markets—supply exceeding demand. However, these examples will illustrate how frequently the optimum demand is dependent upon price emphasis and advantage during growth.
Air Travel. European air fares are widely recognized as excessive when compared with international travel. In contrast, following deregulation, U.S. domestic air fares are substantially lower (per passenger mile). There is, for the present, inhibited potential demand in Europe, demand boosted by lower fares in the States, bringing for the latter increased revenues and a revitalized industry.

FIGURE 1

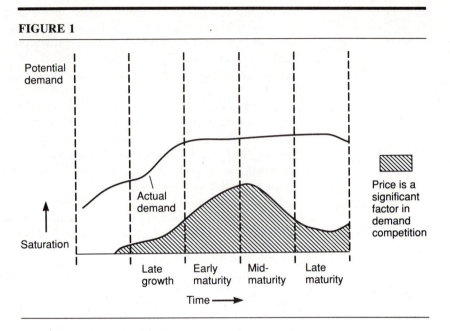

A recent relaxation of rules on routes between Britain and Ireland, cutting return fares by 25 percent, has led to a 30 percent increase in passengers.

Video Cassette Recorders.   Following rapid growth in Europe, the market slumped in 1984 from a 6 million unit demand to 4.5 million. Quota systems protect European manufacturers, import licenses issued only on the basis of the difference between "anticipated demand," that is, 4.5 million units and indigenous capacity, that is, 2 million units. The quota shared by Japanese and South Korean manufacturers was substantially reduced overall and by manufacturer (the South Koreans had not previously enjoyed a proportion of the quota). None had an incentive to lower prices, as their volumes were fixed. As a consequence, "high prices" failed to stimulate additional demand.

Package Holidays (inclusive tours).   The market for overseas package holidays from the United Kingdom grew year on year from 1975 to 1984 in spite of the 1980–1982 recession. Stimulated by increases in leisure time, higher disposable income, renewed expectations, and word of mouth, the market seemed destined for continued growth. However, the early booking pattern for the 1985 summer program showed a 20 percent year-on-year fall, rationalized in a dozen different ways, for example, the miners' strike, violence in Spain, demand failed to recover until price bargains stimulated late bookings. The year overall ended 10 percent lower than one year earlier. The major companies addressed the problem aggressively, heralding the 1986 program with dramatically lower prices. Thomson, the market leader, launched Skytours as its fighting brand. As a consequence, demand was boosted by an additional 2 million holidays, a 30 percent increase on 1985. The pattern was repeated for the 1987 season.

Attainment of market potential is therefore very much a function of price initiatives during late growth. Yet earlier life-cycle theory tends to argue low price sensitivity in growth and high price sensitivity in maturity. *Price* excepted, "late growth" characteristics follow the traditional pattern. *Customers,* both pre- and postpurchase, have acquired knowledge of alternative product "offerings" and in some instances are able to translate features into needs that are relevant to them personally. The market is likely to be broad in focus and homogeneous in preference—a video recorder is a video recorder is . . . , but not commodity-based. *First-time buyers,* that is, primary demand, are still a significant proportion of total sales. *Competition,* while intensifying, is more outward looking, that is, toward customers, than internecine, that is, toward other suppliers. There is still room for, and encouragement of, the newcomer, providing significant advantage to customers is evident. *Market share* is important—the broad market leaders pulling away from the competitive "pack"—pressure upon the middle-sized operator with a high manufacturing/support/distributive overhead and relatively lower volumes supporting it. A need to show strength begins to influence strategic positioning. There is a reluctance to invest heavily in *innovation*—either new products or new technologies. Earlier investment has still to be recouped in earnings recovery. *Promotion* enjoys a growing proportion of total expenditure as companies attend to awareness as the key statistic in volume growth, "Our products are superior, they are just not sufficiently known or talked about." *Brand* or *corporate loyalty* is increasing, with tender rather than deep roots. It is, however, important as an endorsement and an insurance policy against error and mistake in first-time purchase.

Above all, then, the management challenge is to achieve market saturation. Too many organizations are living through a maturity phase at a demand level which is in fact below their actual market potential. Some, like those, realize later on that they have not fully understood their own industry's demand curve. In most cases, as classic microeconomic theory suggests, price is the key to realizing full market potential.

Early Maturity: "Change Habits and Emphasis"

The battle is now in earnest and producing casualties. Customers flattered by lower prices, greater availability, and choice, frequently delay purchase, pursuing the "best offer" available. Economic factors, particularly expectations in relation to exchange rates and inflation, may confuse the picture and encourage a prompt response, that is, buy now or pay more later. However, the underlying tendency is toward a considered purchase exploring all the available alternatives before final choice. Price is still important for new and first-time buyers. Greater product awareness and competence elsewhere force a polarization of the market, the more discerning and astute buyers forming a distinctive segment, not necessarily large or dominant.

New markets promising growth are difficult to define, particularly in either shape, size, and characteristics. General classifications suffice, for example, slow growth, erratic growth, high growth. They offer the same singular opportunity to every current or prospective supplier. Mature markets, on the other hand, are easier to define but invariably complex in structure. The accepted subdivision of a market is by sector or segments. Concentration upon the substrata (markets within markets) can provide the basis for:

• More strategic options.
• Better strategies.

Sectors/segments may be seen as:

• Growing or declining.
• Large or small in relative terms.
• Competition free or competitive intensive.

To use an analogy, the exciting search is for "thermals," sectors which are large, fast growing, and relatively unoccupied. The bonus is to "rise" or build a business through market buoyancy, the product (glider) not requiring promotion (propulsion) for anything other than initial launch. "Thermals" do not last forever; hence there is a need to scan the market regularly and in advance for the next opportunity. While the market as a whole is not growing, new sectors within it are both emergent and buoyant. There is a need for careful judgment as to whether these sectors are likely to be short-lived or ultimately may propel a company from late entry to market dominance. The following examples may help to identify early maturity.

Specialist Distribution.   Retail multiples experienced phenomenal growth within the U.K. market throughout the 1970s. Organizations covering both the grocery and consumer durable sector grew at the expense of the independents and the more conservative big operators, for example, co-ops, mail order. Specialist distribution companies, for example, Geest Organization, Christian Salvesen, and Transport Development Group grasped opportunities commensurate with that growth. Such a "coat tail" strategy relied upon continued growth. However, by the mid-1980s further growth became difficult—most regions well represented, offering a choice in any retail sector, for example, groceries: Tesco versus J Sainsbury versus Asda. The critical strategic choice is to spot the winners for the 1990s, for example, which retailers will emerge on top on the basis not of superior price advantage but preferred and chosen on the basis of all-round superiority. Once spotted, these growth customers and their associated suppliers are going to require extensive sophisticated distribution systems and services, for example, automated warehouse, automatic stock replenishment. Each will demand high levels of investment initially, with the reward to be reaped in the medium term. The risk is either backing the losers or entering into investment decisions providing "white elephant" facilities.

Minicomputers.   In retrospect, the 1970s were the decade of the minicomputer, preceded by mainframes, followed by personal computers (PCs). Minicomputer companies managed to establish firm footings in the commercial marketplace against mainframe competition. Then as a group they were slow to react to the PC. To quote from *Computing* (November 1986): "They supposed that the niches they had created for themselves were large enough to shield them from the impact of PC." Failure to monitor the growing discernment and computer competence of prospective new users led to an underestimation of the desire of PCs as the ideal solution. Minicomputers were sold either direct to commercial users or through systems houses. Personal computing was seen as "tied up," the domain of the mini maker. At the same time mainframes were being upgraded and forming a convenient alliance with networks of PCs. As a consequence, minicomputer specialists, for example, Data General, Prime, have had no option but to accept the squeeze and move "up market," increasing power, adding features, and appealing to specialist users where price is not the main purchasing criterion. Successful minis are now supported by specialized software appealing to selected markets, for example, CAD/CAM, finance and banking. Digital Equipment (DEC) was the first away, using power, new technology, and motivating capabilities to build a distinctive, competitive "up market" edge. Similarly, Hewlett-Packard has developed a niche in the printer markets, with a laser-based device for desktop publishing. Other options include PC compatibility. For the mini maker, the day of specific clear choice has now arrived.

Lager Beers.   While the consumption of alcoholic drinks rises modestly, certain sectors are growing fast, while others decline. Lager with wine, vodka-based long drinks, prepared cocktails, and new exotics have gained. Bitter, whisky, and the majority of fortified wines have experienced declining volumes. The underlying trend to lighter (and therefore perceived as less unhealthy) alcoholic drinks has provided the growth "thermal" for a launch of a wide range of draught, canned, and bottled lagers. It is now possible to buy established lager brands from Australia (Fosters, Castlemaine XXXX), India (Kingfisher), Kenya (Tusker), and the United States (Budweiser), as well as a steady proliferation of European brewery and retailer own-label brands. The market shows signs of maturity, is global in nature, and is now discerning in taste. Price variation for comparable strength and volume is already significant. The strategic issues now facing the major brewers and distributors are:

- Brand identity and perceptions.
- Brand positioning in relation to
     consumer taste and preference, and
     competing brands.
- Market segmentation.

Major brands (Skol, Heineken) can no longer benefit from natural market growth. What growth exists, say in the U.K. market, has now to be shared with a multiplicity of newer brands.

Fragrances.   A world market of $7 billion in scent and related products, while substantial in total and growing in parts, has now reached maturity in its key markets—Europe and the United States. Life-style preferences toward more natural products, and the changing role of women, have contributed to the lack of growth. But the market is substantial and increasingly more international in character—it has become intensely competitive. Some 40 new scents (brands) are launched each year. Average profit margins have probably halved in the past 15 years. The United States, accounting for 40 percent of the total world market, is the most competitive. To quote from an *Economist* review (November 1986): "Behind increasingly overpowering smells and increasingly overpowering marketing campaigns . . . behind all the new products, is a shift in the way women buy perfume. Whereas 20 years ago they would tend to stick with one brand for years, nowadays they chop and change with the fashion and may own several brands at the same time . . . women are beginning to baulk at paying high prices . . . there is a growing market in so called 'knock-off' scents."

Thus the market is going global in one dimension and polarizing price/exclusivity in another. Marketing and packaging have become more important than smell and use. It demands strategic courage and single-mindedness and above all a clear, well-communicated, and consistent image.

Four examples have provided an insight into markets displaying early symptoms of maturity. The most important characteristic is the onset of fragmentation in the market. There are important strategic issues to be addressed and choices to be made. For those organizations able to identify "thermals" of demand within the market, growth in maturity is a real possibility. *This growth to maturity* phase is perhaps the most critical to identify, for continued or realized success. Failure to spot the symptoms or to react strategically to them may well lead to irretrievable product decline in full maturity. A superficial response—change in marketing tactics, for example, increased media advertising, a new distribution channel, may help but is more likely to confuse the position. It is a time for thorough review, a brief pause, and then single-minded execution of a clear strategy aimed at dominance of a specific sector within the total market.

Mid-Maturity: "Customers Come First"

Markets and demand vary in nature from fads to steady unspectacular repetitive responses. The difference is of time scale and is influenced by living standards, wealth, and the desire for modernity (the best that is available and affordable). In life-cycle terms, some markets go through maturity in weeks, others take years and provide sound and profitable business opportunities for the market-driven, customer-aware organization.

The significance and intensity of a particular need is the major determinant of market durability. The current TV market, while mature, with replacement demand affected by high product reliability, benefits from a desire for more individual home entertainment—a TV set in every room. If the underlying social and economic trends are supportive, mature markets may well provide many years of sustained demand. The trick is knowing the market well, keeping close to particular customers, with sufficient innovation and new product development to retain goodwill and word-of-mouth recommendation. The following examples are representative of markets in mid-maturity.

Washing Machines. The first machines were introduced in the 1920s with dramatic growth experienced in the period 1945 to 1965. Market maturity was postponed twice by technology—the advent of the twin-tub machine improving drying capability and the automatic freeing time for other things. By 1975 the market was totally dependent upon replacement demand and threatened by high-volume European manufacturers—AEG, Zanussi. The market is now therefore well into maturity—a steady annual demand of 3 million units being 98 percent replacement. New technology has changed the product balance in favor of combination washer/dryer front-loading machines. With over 12 European manufacturers still competing for market share, Hotpoint, which is U.K.-based and part of GEC, dominates with 34 percent of the total market. Yet their products are higher priced than competition. Equally, Hotpoint entered the new technology-based growth segment—the combined washer/dryer—later than three significant competitors. Within six months, with a premium-priced product, they captured 20 percent of this segment, which in turn now accounts for one-third of the total market.

Success has been achieved through the execution and strengthening of clear strategics adopted at the onset of maturity over 10 years ago. They are:

- High product reliability supported by the best U.K.-based after-sales service operation and five-year parts warranty.
- Maintained margins, discouraging excessive price cutting.
- Market concentration, upon specific major domestic appliances, that is, home laundry, refrigerators, dishwaters.

Reputation counts for everything in a replacement market.

Daily Newspapers. Newspapers are now among the most profitable businesses in America. One in four of all American dailies, accounting for 45 percent of total circulation, are owned by 14 big newspaper groups. The successful have benefited from new technology, stable newsprint prices, and, above all, local monopoly. In the United Kingdom, the market structure is fundamentally different—higher readership per capita but national circulation, that is, one market. The key to profit is advertising revenue attraction which is, in turn, a function of

- Reader profile.
- Circulation.

This is a classic mid-maturity market, with circulation neither growing nor declining, and having already remained stable for some time. New readers have to be poached from competitors. Thus many newspapers suffered falling circulation as first Rupert Murdoch (News International), then Robert Maxwell

(Mirror Group) combined positive aggressive management, forcing productivity improvements, with popular innovative changes to newspaper format and content. That the industry promised little more than headaches was the general view at the end of 1985. Nevertheless, undaunted, two new national dailies were launched in 1986. They were

- *Today,* launched March 1986 by Eddy Shah.
- *The Independent,* launched October 1986 by Andreas Whittam Smith.

Examination of the key strategies implemented in each case illustrates the dos and don'ts of late entry into mature markets.

(1) *Today*—Eddy Shah chose:

- High-tech printing.
- A cheap multicolored newspaper.
- Targeted readership at top end of popular (tabloids) and lower end of "serious."
- Target circulation of 1 million plus, break-even 750,000, offering prospective page rates per buyer at half that of the *Daily Mail.*
- A copy selling price of 20p.

(2) *The Independent*—Andreas Whittam Smith chose:

- Top journalists and journalism, the best available.
- A new, clear, high-quality typeface.
- Targeted readership, taking particularly from *The Times* and *Daily Telegraph.*
- Targeted stable circulation of 375,000 to prosper, attracting the independent-minded discerning reader. The paper is nonpolitical.
- A copy selling price of 25p.

Today achieved only half a million circulation and soon, needing a further capital injection of £15m, sold out to the Lonhro Group. Whittam Smith's relatively modest but clearly focused strategy appears by far the more successful.

The high barriers to entry, and therefore the high entry costs, were attacked in two quite separate ways. Shah used *new technology*—an expensive route which requires a higher market share for breakeven. Whittam Smith attacked through innovation, offering a better product in customer terms (not production terms); high-caliber journalists, new design, desktop layout. This less expensive route required half the volume share needed by *Today* to break even. *Today* had to build a broad appeal to achieve the volume, what one might call a blunt market entry compared with the sharp focus specific appeal which *The Independent* could afford.

There are many more examples, perhaps too many, of markets operating in mid-maturity. The 1980 to 1982 recession, followed by low economic growth and substantial industry and distributive channel restructuring, have all conspired to offer limited prospects for the traditional manufacturers and service companies. While the opportunity is confined, the threat is formidable and unrelenting. World competition, mergers, and aggressive predators from related activities all favor the customers who are increasingly more discerning, discriminating, and less loyal. But, on the positive side

- *Price is not important* to everyone and probably not to the majority.
- *Industries that evolve gradually* offer time and space for careful strategy selection.
- *Sustainable real or perceived advantage* in either cost or performance will attract new business if it is communicated effectively.
- *Geographical niches are vulnerable,* and if attacked selectively and with perseverence, on the basis of customer needs, profitable business will accrue.
- *The market is stable;* any sense of instability probably points to a lack of clear and consistent strategy relative to competition or trying to be all things to all people—the global mediocrity, which is the most common characteristic of the unsuccessful.
- *Matching capabilities and resources to particular market opportunities* is the underlying priority. As a rule of thumb, the more limited these are, the greater level of product/market concentration. The aim is to generate revenue through better margins and repeat orders rather than higher volume. Growth should then be achieved through existing product/market concentration applying discipline to any unplanned and superficially attractive proliferation of activities.
- *Niches once secured require fewer resources to defend them* than they do to obtain them in the first instance. Attack strategies, therefore, rely heavily on good timing—when significant advantage rests with the predator.

Late Maturity: "Choose between Withdrawal and Growth"

It is appropriate to distinguish between later maturity and decline. While both display similar characteristics, for example, establishment of commodity products, reduction in the number of suppliers, the simple but major differences are of size and stability. The late mature market is very substantial and subject to little change or movement in customer needs, attitudes, or preferences. It may be construed as boring, relationships between suppliers and customers entrenched and unexciting. There is, however, both the risk and the reward of complacency. As quality and performance tend to be taken for granted, focus once again turns on price. This is particularly true of component or service supply to Original Equipment Manufacturers (OEM). Pressure back from the end customer for price advantage is compounded up the manufacturing/distribution line. Some companies dependent upon markets in mid-maturity find their own particular sectors in late maturity, for example, tire and battery suppliers to the motor industry.

The barriers to entry into "late maturity markets" are usually formidable. In addition to physical requirements—plant, access to customers—the real disincentive to new entrants is apparent lack of business opportunity. This fact favors the existing supplier and reinforces market stability both in respect of new entrants and the likelihood of substitutes based upon new technology or new distribution channels. The following selected examples illustrate strategic considerations and options available to companies operating within late maturity markets.

Motor Tires.   The market is totally global and fiercely competitive. An estimated $30 billion of sales are shared between 10 major manufacturers (84 percent of the total) and a few national specialists. Goodyear and Michelin share just under half the total market. Tires last longer, and world demand is unlikely to rise above an annual new and replacement rate of 140 million. Goodyear can just claim market leadership. It boasts estimated profits of $400 million or 6 percent on sales. Rationalization, selective concentration upon growth geographical markets—(for example, Taiwan and India) and restored innovation have proved the right strategies for Goodyear. In contrast, Goodrich lost nearly $400 million on one-third of the turnover of Goodyear, and Firestone only broke even. Uniroyal, now merged with Goodrich, and Continental have both achieved success through market concentration, emphasizing performance rather than price.

Incandescent Light Bulbs.   While manufacturers have struggled to hold market share in the United Kingdom, a typical mature market, major multiple retailers (supermarket and DIY outlets) have dominated for nearly 10 years. "Own-label" products, for example, J Sainsbury, have been preferred by customers, looking for cheap, value-for-money replacement bulbs. A commodity market has prevailed.

Thorn EMI held, in 1986, a market share of 33 percent, the equivalent of 100 million light bulbs. Their brand "Thorn" had replaced "Mazda" shortly after acquiring the lighting subsidiary of AEI (GEC) 15 years ago. Thorn researched the market in 1986, concentrating upon customer attitudes, needs, and preferences for the product and, in particular, how it was packaged and displayed. They discovered, to their surprise, that customers:

• Held a higher brand awareness of "Mazda" than any other brand, except the market leader Osram.
• Preferred "light" colors in packaging, for example, white and yellow rather than brown and black, the shades used in most current packs.
• Could not easily find replacements for the 400 or so nonstandard light bulbs in use.

Thorn EMI listened to the customer and:

• Added the Mazda brand, dropping some minor brands.
• Redesigned the pack in light colors.
• Introduced a transparent "blister" pack for their range of 150 nonstandard bulbs supported by display stands and symbols to ease identification.

On launch in January 1987, sales reached 0.75 million within the first 14 days. Forward sales project 25 million light bulbs in the first full year, increasing the market share of all Thorn EMI brands from 33 to 44 percent. Major retailers have made a strategic decision to stock Mazda ranges in favor of "own-label" products. Reassessment of customer needs, support by innovative packaging, and display have produced excitement and restimulated a boring commodity market.

Large Industrial Motors. Although a major capital item, motors in size over 175 kW, are normally sold as a component to the Original Equipment Manufacturers (OEM). Pressure from OEMs for price concessions have been a significant feature in the world market, since the downturn in demand in the oil and petrochemicals sector in 1984. The major strategic issue for a motor manufacturer, determined to stay in business, is how to improve world competitiveness both addressing the keener price requirements and yet maintaining a profitable margin on the product. There is only one strategic option, to concentrate and then innovate. The dilemma is three-fold:

- Where to concentrate/specialize.
- How to sacrifice the badly needed volume of enquiries outside the area of concentration.
- How to convince the customer (OEM) who is not the user that rejection of some enquiries is in their interests.

As an illustration, choice of specialization following a detailed audit of competence and competition could be in the motor range of 1000 to 3000 kW concentrating upon certain use sectors, for example, public utilities. Specialization might then be *overt,* that is, communicated to both users and OEMs or *covert*—just used as the basis for strategy formulation and implementation. Whichever is chosen, the task of product innovation can begin with a focus on performance improvement in relation to particular applications.

The pressure for price concessions in late maturity can be met most effectively by a strategy of concentration on particular applications or uses supported by focused innovation.

STRATEGIC CONSIDERATIONS

Mature markets offer no easy routes to business growth and success to either the generalist or the specialist, the dominant or the new entrant. Strategic direction needs to be considered carefully and a clear choice made, implemented and supported by consistency of effort. That different conditions apply at four different stages of maturity has been argued and supported by examples. For a successful strategy to be identified, appreciation of the market conditions should help the selection process.

There are some overall ground rules that apply to mature markets. They are:

1. Be clear as to the market in which you are competing and wish to continue to compete.

2. Anticipate the changing phase of the market by recognizing the symptoms of change.
3. If the market is large and you are small (share of less than 5 percent), redefine the market more specifically. This may require an early decision to select and reject market sectors for concentration. Such a step is desirable anyway in maturity.
4. Put effort into strategic positioning before new product development and new promotional campaigns. It is important to
   a. Target particular customer groups.
   b. Understand better those customers particular needs and distinctive preferences.
   c. Position away from competition, offering a clear competitive advantage.
5. Remember price is only an important element in purchasing for certain customers and at particular stages of maturity.
6. A strategic closeness to customers is to be "market driven." The earlier this philosophy is adopted, the easier it will be to select the best strategy for either offensive or defensive action.
7. Innovation and a "market-driven" philosophy can be combined effectively at any stage of maturity, but particularly during late maturity in order to upset the status quo in your favor. This does, however, involve risk and demands concentration of resources and consistency in direction.

Seven ground rules have been provided. Their application must be carefully thought through in the context of the stage of maturity reached by the market. It is never too late to act decisively—it just becomes tougher and more demanding on those responsible for strategy formulation. It also usually requires more resources and effort in implementation. What is certain is that there is rarely success gained from the selection of a "wait and see" option. Any recovery related to economic cycles is almost certain to be negated by either changing technology or global competition.

CONCLUSION

Customers, competition, change, concentration, and creativity are all important aspects of markets that cease to offer growth prospects. There are no easy pickings and likely disaster for businesses placing their faith in market forces as the dictate for their direction. The external environment should be interpreted in terms of the life-cycle stages defined. Business should not be managed by assumption. Understanding the market, talking to the real customers, stalking competitors, and a clear focus are in. Pursuit of all possibilities and the acquisition of an "arsenal of excellence" are out. To borrow a phrase from Thomas Bonoma in *The Marketing Edge,* "If all of this sounds absurdly simple, the reason is that it is absurdly simple."

FURTHER READING

Articles

Bonoma, T. V., "Marketing Subversives," *Harvard Business Review* (November/December 1986).

Gluck, F. W., "Strategic Planning in a New Key," *The Mckinsey Quarterly* (Winter 1986).

Taylor, Bernard, "Corporate Planning for the 1990s," *Long Range Planning* 19 no. 6 (1986), pp. 13–18.

MacMillan, K., "Strategy Portfolio Analysis," *Journal of General Management* (Summer 1986).

Ghema, Pankaj, "Building Strategy on the Experience Curve," *Harvard Business Review* (March/April 1985).

Morden, A. R., "Market Segmentation and Practical Policy Formulation," *The Quarterly Review of Marketing* (Winter 1985).

Wind, Y. and Robertson, T. S., "Marketing Strategy: New Directors for Theory and Research," *Journal of Marketing* (Spring 1983).

Kanter, Rosabeth Moss, "The Middle Manager as Innovator," *Harvard Business Review* (July/August 1982).

Day, George S., "Customer Oriented Approaches to Identifying Product-Markets," *Journal of Marketing* (August 1982).

Hanan, M., "Reorganize Your Company Around Its Markets," *Harvard Business Review* (November/December 1974).

Books

Bonoma, T. V., *The Marketing Edge*. (New York: Free Press, 1985).

Kanter, R. M., *The Change Masters*. (London: Allen & Unwin, 1984).

Porter, M. E., *Competitive Strategy*. (New York: Free Press, 1980).

Porter, M. E., *Competitive Advantage*. (New York: Free Press, 1985).

Pinchot, G., *Intrapreneuring*. (New York: Harper & Row, 1985).

What this article is about: The author reveals his strategies for turning a company that lost $30 million in a four-year period to one with expected sales of $300 million for 1988.

2–7 Growth Strategies at Remington

An interview with Victor K. Kiam
Victor Kiam is President of Remington Products, Inc.

When Victor K. Kiam bought Remington Products, Inc., from conglomerate Sperry-Rand in 1979, the ailing consumer products company had lost $30 million in the prior three years. Market share was dwindling and sales declining. Today Remington is one of the fastest growing international small consumer products companies. Sales are expected to climb to $300 million for 1988, compared with $50 million in 1979.

What were Kiam's strategies? All overseas manufacturing was brought back to the United States and concentrated in the company's Bridgeport, Connecticut site. Kiam eliminated 79 executive positions. Annual product price increases and costly product modifications were canceled.

In 1988, the company spent $25 millon on advertising worldwide. Kiam's now famous "I like the product so much I bought the company" commercials are broadcast in 15 foreign languages in 31 countries, including Japan. One-third of Remington's sales comes from exports. Its market share has risen to over 40 percent and surpassed Norelco of the Netherlands, the industry's former leader.

Kiam sharpened his sales and marketing skills at Lever Brothers, selling Pepsodent toothpaste and Lifebuoy soap. Later he marketed bras and girdles at Playtex and then served as CEO of Benrus Watch Corporation. Kiam views himself as an entrepreneur. In his book, *Going for It!* Kiam says entrepreneurs are something like firemen—they are running into a situation everyone is trying to leave. "However," says Kiam, "just as the firefighter doesn't rush into a building and start spraying water helter-skelter, the entrepreneur must enter the turnaround with a well-drawn strategy."

SOURCE: *Journal of Business Strategy* (January–February 1989), pp. 22–26.

Kiam has capitalized on Remington's success with electric shavers by expanding the company's horizon with new products such as the Remington pool alarm, the Remington VIC VAC carpet cleaner, and the Lektro Blade® Razor.

Kiam has acquired Franzus Company, forming the largest travel appliance company in the United States. He plans to broaden its product line from travel applicances to small items such as travel kits that have widespread use. In addition to marketing consumer appliances and grooming products, Kiam recently bought the New England Patriots. Strategic plans for the football team are still in an incubation stage. But his revitalization of Remington is one of America's success stories. Executives who are planning to revitalize or expand their companies or products can profit from his example.

REVITALIZATION: PICK THE RIGHT COMPANY

The *Journal of Business Strategy:* *What recommendations do you have for someone who wants to revitalize a failing company?*

Victor K. Kiam: You don't go into a failing company unless it has certain assets that can provide the basis for the turnaround. Those assets could be a good product, good people, low-cost manufacturing, or almost anything.

There's got to be something that you believe will give you the base for the turnaround.

You can't simply say this company is losing money, it's in terrible shape, and I'm going to turn it around. You have to have something that you can hang your hat on, or you can't do it.

Remington had lost money and market share. But it had good people and a great product. When I compared the Remington shaver with all others, I realized it was sensational. So that was the cornerstone of the turnaround.

JBS: *Besides liking the shavers, what other elements attracted you to the company?*

Kiam: The international recognition of the Remington brand name, the amount of money that had been spent on it over the years, and the quality image were most attractive.

Even though the sales had gone down, the image of the company was that of a quality producer.

Another advantage came from a financial standpoint. What I was buying was mostly a current asset. It could be turned. At the same time I acquired Remington Products—a consumer business—the Sperry Corporation sold Remington Rand, which was a typewriter and office equipment division.

For Remington Rand, the buyers purchased mostly fixed assets that couldn't be turned over quickly. With Remington's consumer products, we could turn our inventory and reduce the amount of money we needed.

This was important because at the time we were paying interest rates of 23.5 percent. The people at Remington Rand were stuck with high-cost interest because the assets they purchased were plant equipment and they couldn't turn that.

ADVERTISING

JBS: *Was heavy advertising a major part of your turnaround strategy?*

Kiam: Ultimately, it was. But not in the first year. We didn't have enough money to spend on advertising. I have a philosophy about advertising: Either you have to run enough advertising or don't bother. If I can use a colloquialism, you can't be half pregnant.

What we did was give up running advertising in a large section of the country. We concentrated in specific areas. We changed the company's advertising philosophy. The company had been spending advertising money nationally at a very low level. We took that money and concentrated the bulk of it on the East and West Coasts and then gradually expanded it. We had enough money to make a decent penetration in the areas in which we started.

PRODUCTIVITY

JBS: *I understand that Remington has a unique incentive plan. Is it true that 65 percent of the paycheck is salary and the rest is based on incentives?*

Kiam: That's correct in the factory area. It could be even higher in some other areas. If you have an assembly line, incentives are based on how much piecework is done.

Clerical employees are evaluated on a more arbitrary basis. We look at the performance of individuals as well as performance of their division. This cannot always be measured in actual terms. You wouldn't want a bookkeeper to be paid according to the amount of paper work he puts out. We're getting sunk by paper anyway. So some incentives have to be arbitrary because you can't really measure them. But for about 75 percent of the people we can establish goals that can be measured. Top-level employees get more from their bonus than they get from a set salary. The results of our incentive program have been a 17 percent increase in productivity over the last four years.

JBS: *Remington has a reputation for high quality. What measures do you take to ensure quality products?*

Kiam: One measure is 100 percent inspection on the shavers. Another measure is that rejected items are counted against incentive pay for the responsible worker. So individual workers suffer financially just like the company does if the product doesn't measure up.

We also offer an extensive after-purchase service program. If there are any problems, we take care of them. We have 90 service centers and a consumer response department with a WATS line that will answer all questions and respond to all problems. We make sure that correspondence is answered within three days of receipt.

GROWTH

JBS: *I understand there's an exodus of businesses from Bridgeport, Connecticut, where Remington is headquartered. Do your plans to grow include moving?*

Kiam: No. We have very good people and we have a very good infrastructure here. We are, incidentally, the largest employer in the city of Bridgeport other than government employers. In Bridgeport, we have people with the skills that are required to manufacture shavers. If we were to go to Podunk, USA, where are we going to get toolmakers? Where are we going to get the experience that exists in Bridgeport?

When I got to Remington, the average length of employment was 14 years. Obviously with the growth of the firm—we've gone from 480 people to over 2,000 people—the average length of employment has gone down. But that core of 14-year veterans now consists of 20-year veterans. You can't replace that.

JBS: *When you bought Remington, you let a number of new-product engineers go. Growth in terms of new products was very slow. But now Remington is coming out with a host of new products. What role do you foresee for new-product development in the company's future plans?*

Kiam: If we have unique products—not just "me too" products that we can think of and develop—we'll bring them out. The reason we didn't bring out any new products in the first few years is that we had to concentrate on our core business, which was the shavers. We had limited financial resources, and we put our money where our mouth was. It's like the fellow who lives on a grass plot. His plot turns brown. All of a sudden he sees a beautiful green plot across the street. He takes that over. In all likelihood that will turn brown. You turn your brown plot green first before you go across the street.

JBS: *The press says that your new Lektro razor should be instrumental in helping you reach 1988's sales goal of $300 million. Why is the Lektro shaver different from previous products?*

Kiam: It's a razor with an electrified blade that's used with shaving cream. It's completely dissimilar from other electric shavers.

JBS: *Are you close to reaching your $300 million sales goal?*

Kiam: Our rate of sales worldwide is very, very strong. Our English business is up dramatically—about 100 percent so far. We've launched our own company in Germany. We'll have a better idea when all the figures are in from the Christmas season. Our sales now are right on plan.

JBS: *What about the Franzus Co., which you bought to expand your business in the travel appliance and accessory market—has this been a growth area for Remington?*

Kiam: A tremendous amount of effort is required to turn it around because there were a lot of difficulties when we took it over. There was no inventory when we got it. The company didn't have enough funding to go out with a letter of credit. It took us about three months to get back into an inventory posture. We took it over in June 1987. By the time we got the inventory and caught up with the back orders, it was November. It wasn't until then that we could ship all the items on an order. Now we're shipping every order complete.

Also, there were products being sourced from companies that couldn't deliver in large quantities on time. We had to find new supply sources for some of the items we didn't make. Obviously the field sales force was demoralized because products they sold could not be delivered. We had to rebuild the morale of the organization. This has been done. Sales are up now substantially.

JBS: *What are your plans for this company?*

Kiam: To build it into the largest travel appliance and travel accessory company in the United States and then the world.

GLOBAL EXPANSION

JBS: *What key strategies do you have to offer U.S. manufacturers who want to develop markets in other countries?*

Kiam: First, analyze which country is the most compatible in terms of accepting the product or service that you're selling. Then analyze the overall market. Go to the country yourself. If you're going to expand in another country, you won't be successful if you do it in a halfhearted way. Don't rely on consultants or trade groups to get you positioned in a country.

If you make ceramic cups, for example, you know that business cold. No trade group and no consultant really know your business. You know the frailties of the products; you know what is required for distribution and display. If you rely on some outside consulting organization, I don't think it will have the knowledge that is necessary to really do the proper job in that country.

Once you've penetrated one country, go to the next and take it country by country. I don't believe in a buckshot approach where you just send your product and your service wholesale around the world and hope that you're going to hit somebody on the head. You zero in on a particular area, concentrate, make a success, and use that success as a springboard to enter other areas.

JBS: *Would you use consultants to help you with the differences in culture?*

Kiam: No. Just go to a country. Do your own analysis and you can find out what you need to know. I go around the world twice a year. And Remington sells in almost every country in the world. We are as successful in the Philippines as we are in Germany or Japan.

JBS: *How do you go about getting a feel for the country?*

Kiam: Go there. Talk to the trade. Visit the stores. Talk to salespeople. Get reports on the market that are available through government agencies, advertising agencies, and other sources. Do an entire marketing plan for the country. Every country is different in some way. There are different nuances of distribution in Japan. There is a unique control factor of large companies in South America. You have to adapt your philosophy to the particular situation in which you find yourself.

JBS: *What are the biggest obstacles to overcome when selling overseas?*

Kiam: That varies by country. In some countries you might have high duties— that's what we face. Some countries we can't even sell in. In South Korea, our shavers are an embargoed product. The Philippines has a very high duty rate. Japan has a five-tier distribution system. In Europe it is quite prevalent to make commitments for television advertising by the end of September for all of the next year. You have to be very adaptable.

There isn't any single difficulty when expanding overseas. It's an analytical situation that must be looked at country by country. I think the worst difficulty that Remington had—and all America had—in selling products overseas was the strength of the dollar. If we let the dollar rise, as we unofficially did in the past, we just destroy our manufacturing base in the United States.

THE FUTURE

JBS: *Will you use some of the turnaround strategies you used at Remington to manage the New England Patriots?*

Kiam: None per se because the football team is a very successful entity, and it has performed very well. It has excellent coaches and good players. We won't be making changes in the team itself.

We may have to address changes in the financial area and in a few peripheral areas. We need to study the situation. You don't shoot from the hip in a takeover. Before I bought Remington, I studied it. As a result, at the time I took over, I knew exactly what I wanted to do.

One of the problems with a turnaround is that, in the beginning, certain strategies seem clearly the ones that should be followed. You go ahead and do them. But when you carry out these ideas, there are repercussions that you didn't expect. What you really have to do is look at the whole scheme and not just take one or two items and address them. You've got to look at the overall plan and the long-term strategy. When I say a long-term strategy, I mean about a year or two years out.

JBS: *What key strategic plans do you have for Remington?*

Kiam: I've got so many! It would take forever to answer. I think Remington has tremendous opportunities. I am working to achieve as many of them as possible, given the situation.

I think we can be a very large global company and compete with multinationals all over the world. We are the only U.S. shaver manufacturer. We have created unique items that have global markets. We can grow as long as we remember that quality is uppermost and that when you offer the consumer a product with a consumer benefit at a fair price, you can have success. We can do this because we're a private company. We don't have that Sword of Damocles—the 90-day reporting period—hanging over our necks. This lets us think long term.

As large as we grow, we will still have a company in which we believe the most important assets are our people. We continue to get good people and promote the people we have to higher levels. We're in the book *The 100 Best Companies to Work for in America*. We're the only leveraged buyout company in that book. We are a unique company. And we have a company in which everybody who works for us can be proud of their association.

What this article is about: After exploring the assumptions that underlie treating suppliers as adversaries or partners, the author discusses linking supply strategy to overall strategy.

2–8 Managing Suppliers: The Strategic Implications

Albert W. Isenman

A Canadian manufacturer of electronic devices entered into a supply contract with a Japanese maker of subassemblies, specifying a 5 percent defect rate, according to the company's usual purchasing practices. Sure enough exactly 5 percent of the subassemblies that began arriving were defective; conveniently, the defective devices were packaged separately from the good ones, and were labeled as such.

Astonished, the Canadian purchasing manager inquired about this anomaly, and was informed by the Japanese agent that his company was happy to supply the defectives but had been wondering why the Canadians *wanted* them in the first place.

A domestic auto-parts supplier, closely held by an American car manufacturer, provided a standard automobile component to a Japanese car maker as part of a well-known joint venture. Extra care was taken to ensure that the shipments abroad contained zero defects; even so, a portion of shipped goods were identified by the Japanese as substandard and were returned.

What happened to the defective parts? The American plant manager, whose bonus was tied to production volume, "salted" the defectives into shipments to the domestic parent, where they ultimately were installed in American cars.

Why do such perverse results occur so frequently? How can managers undertake and sustain symbiotic rather than parasitic relationships with suppliers? To answer these questions, let's examine the assumptions that underlie our understanding of the supply relationship.

SOURCE: *Strategic Planning Management*, December 1986; Commerce Communications, Inc.

SUPPLIERS AS ADVERSARIES

In conventional textbook treatments, managing the supplier is couched in terms of "minimizing your input costs," and assumes that you principally are concerned with prices and quantities while maintaining an arm's length bargaining position with your supplier.

For example, the classic "make-or-buy" decision (whether to acquire supplies on the open market or to integrate backward into production) requires you to consider the gain from recapturing the supplier's margin versus the investment costs of self-manufacture. Similarly, determining the optimal "economic order quantity" for inventories is a model for minimizing supply and inventory costs (subject to constraints of stockouts).

Hence, the adversarial view of suppliers suggests finding ways to minimize their bargaining power in order to obtain better terms. The following prescriptions are part of the adversarial recipe and often are suggested as ways to keep suppliers in line and supply agreements favorable:

1. Locate and exploit alternative sources of supply. This will reduce your dependency on any one supplier, and mitigate against the likelihood of a single source becoming a significant portion of your unit cost.
2. If only one or two suppliers exist, reduce their bargaining leverage over you by actively seeking or promoting the emergence of suppliers (e.g., plastic containers instead of glass).
3. Demonstrate that you are capable of integrating backward (by making some of your supplies yourself). Thus you have the potential of becoming a competitor to your supplier instead of simply a customer. In addition, your experience with self-manufacture gives you precise information about your suppliers' manufacturing and raw materials costs: Hence you will be an informed bargainer at contract time.
4. Whenever possible, exclude from your product's design any critical component not available from multiple sources.
5. Select suppliers that are smaller than you. Your purchases will be an important part of their revenues, making you very important to them; but they will lack the capacity to lean on you.

SUPPLIERS AS PARTNERS

The cooperative model of supplier relationships—often labeled a Japanese invention but common in Western Europe, too—assumes that you principally are interested in stability of supplies, consistency of quality, and maintaining a long-term but flexible relationship. This may require trading off absolutely low input costs when it gives you a competitive advantage in design, delivery, or features; or even if it is done to enable your supplier to survive and prosper. It recognizes, for instance, that your inventory decisions and delivery terms become part of the supplier's cost structure and affect the relationship itself in the long run. Managing suppliers as partners is a *negotiating* rather than a *bargaining* arrangement.

Advocates of cooperative relationships with suppliers emphasize practices that are rather different from the adversarial ones. While the price/quantity mix is important, it takes a back seat to policies that encourage a mutually beneficial relationship:

1. Consider longer-term contracts with suppliers rather than episodic discrete purchases. This has the advantage for both parties of building some certainty into the future of the supply relationship. In many instances, suppliers may be willing to enter into *exclusive* longer-term contracts, which has the added advantage of denying their supply to your competitors.

   Contracts need not build out strategic flexibility as some would complain: A well-prepared longer-term contract requires thinking through the contingencies and "what-ifs" that the future may bring (such as demand changes, product line extensions, service, and customization requirements of customers), and working out a mutual understanding of what both sides expect of one another in such eventualities.

   This will have implications for how you specify inventory and delivery terms, supply specifications, even the number, mix, and location of suppliers. Since this is precisely what strategic thinking is about, why not extend that intellectual habit to supplier management?

2. Invite your supplier to join you in "getting close to your customers." You are downstream, after all, from the supplier, and hence you are closer to the end-user. Your customer intelligence can be useful to the supplier in helping him serve your needs (and ultimately the customer's) more effectively.

   Additionally, a demonstrated strong supplier relationship itself can be a competitive advantage. For example, I know a large printing concern that specializes in consumer product packaging, both paper and plastic. When working with their customers (all large food, beverage, and tobacco companies), the firm takes care to involve their suppliers of paper, plastic, ink, and film color separations to produce the industry's best quality to customer specifications.

3. Share your supplier's risk. This is the "upstream" version of servicing and customizing for your customer's needs. For example, work closely with your suppliers to promote the introduction of quality improvements or manufacturing practices that may lower his (and your) costs. Sometimes this may even include investing in the supplying firm to assist in the acquisition of new technology or capacity expansion. Sears, for example, has long been an equity partner in firms that supply Kenmore appliances.

   This works in reverse, too: aluminum companies actively helped can manufacturers acquire the process equipment that accelerated the shift from three-piece steel cans to two-piece extruded aluminum containers. Many companies have undertaken joint ventures with their suppliers in research and development or to penetrate new markets.

MANAGING YOUR SUPPLIERS

What can we learn from the two models that can help you manage supplier relationships? It's unlikely that your situation exactly fits either model: If you are purchasing strictly commoditylike supplies and serving extraordinarily price-sensitive customers, your relationship may look very much like the classic adversarial bargaining situation. If, on the other hand, you face changing customer expectations, evolving technologies, or have a need for balancing stability with flexibility at the supply end, you may draw on elements of both models or begin to look very much like the cooperative model.

In any case, managers and planners should consider some of the following practices in order to help avoid pitfalls like the ones in our opening examples:

1. Develop a supplier intelligence capability. Firms have become quite sophisticated in customer and market research; more recently, analysis of competitors and competitive dynamics has come into vogue. Supplier analysis by comparison is in its infancy.

   Basic information about a supplying industry would certainly include:

   • The number, mix, and availability of alternative sources of supply or the possibility of locating suppliers of acceptable substitutes.
   • The amount that your purchases contribute as a percentage of the supplier's revenues. This is a proxy measure of how important you are to the supplier.
   • The supplier's interest in and capability of integrating forward into your industry; becoming your competitor.
   • The terms and conditions of suppliers' arrangements with your competitors.

   Other components of supplier intelligence suggest the kind of attention sophisticated firms give market and competitor analysis and would include:

   • What is the supplier's strategy? For example, if the supplier desires high growth or increased share while you are in a mature industry, you'll be less attractive to the supplier than a growing competitor unless you can demonstrate some unique potential that exploits the supplier's strategic capabilities.
   • What is the supplier's cost and manufacturing structure? Is the supplier equipped to customize, to meet your needs in terms of cost, delivery, and so on? The information is essential if one is an adversarial bargainer, but may also reveal potential competitive advantages.
   • Can the supplier give you a technical or design advantage? For example, are there ideas in the supplier's research pipeline that you could translate

into a market opportunity as a new product or as an improvement on a current product?

- What is the supplier's financial capacity? Is the supplier able to help you buffer your working capital and inventory requirements; or are there opportunities to solidify and stabilize your supplier relationship by offering such help to the supplier?

2. Link your supply strategy to your overall strategy. In one of our opening examples, the American car maker's practice of rewarding its vendor on price/volume considerations clearly was at odds with its intentions to boost product quality.

   Coordinating purchasing with your strategy is no different from linking other functional areas (sales, finance, etc.) with strategy, and bears similar pitfalls. Purchasing is a function and, in large complex organizations, purchasing agents may have particular parochial views or beliefs. And because purchasing is principally a *staff* function, purchasing managers (like human resource managers) frequently are excluded from strategy making and line of business decisions. And as we have seen, the reward system often motivates purchasing managers to treat vendors as adversaries, rather than managing them as partners.

3. Similarly, consider your supply strategy when other strategic decisions are made. For example, a decision to advance your process technology may have important implications for your supply relationship, such as changing delivery or packaging specifications, product form, inventory quantities and timing, or financial needs.

4. Finally, think about your suppliers as a *resource* with the potential to help you develop or sustain a competitive advantage:

   - By improving your cost position if your strategy is to be an industry price leader
   - By helping with features or design if product attributes are important to you
   - By managing inventory and delivery arrangements if service and availability are part of your strategic thrust.

The price/quantity mix is the classic economic treatment of the supplier/buyer relationship, the basis of all the "tools of the trade." But minding ps and qs is only part of thinking *strategically* about managing your suppliers.

What this article is about: Long-term success involves creating, managing, and exploiting assets and skills that competitors find difficult to match or counter. This involves a three-step process: (1) identify relevant skills and assets by observing successful and unsuccessful firms, key customer motivations, large value-added items, and mobility barriers; (2) select those skills and assets that will provide an advantage over competitors, will be relevant to the market, and will be feasible, sustainable, and appropriate for the future; and (3) develop and maintain those assets and skills and neutralize those of competitors.

2–9 Managing Assets and Skills: The Key to a Sustainable Competitive Advantage

David A. Aaker

*David Aaker is professor of marketing strategy
at the University of California at Berkeley*

According to one Xerox executive, a key sustainable competitive advantage in addition to the firm's technology has been its sales and service organization. It helped them to penetrate the medium and high end of the copier market during the 1960s.[1] Kodak plans to build upon its 200,000 store distribution system and the marketing clout of its yellow-and-black logo to penetrate the growing $2 billion battery market.[2] In each case, the firms developed, nurtured, and then exploited key assets and skills.

A business strategy, as suggested by Figure 1, involves the *way you compete*—what you do, the product strategy, positioning strategy, pricing strategy, distribution strategy, global strategy, manufacturing strategy, and so on. It also involves *where you compete*—the selection of the competitive arena, the markets, and the competitors. Competing the right way in the right arena can be extremely profitable, but only for a limited time. The assets and skills of the business, which are the *basis of competition*, provide the foundation of a sustainable competitive advantage (SCA) and long-term performance. Unless there is an

SOURCE: *California Management Review* (Winter 1989), pp. 91–106.

[1]Gary Jacobson and John Hillkirk, *Xerox, American Samurai* (New York: MacMillan, 1986), p. 275.

[2]What's Recharging the Battery Business," *Business Week*, June 23, 1986, p. 124.

FIGURE 1   Obtaining a Sustainable Competitive Advantage

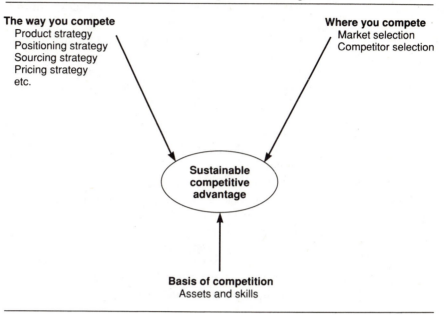

advantage over competitors that is not easily duplicated or countered, long-term profitability is likely to be elusive.

For an SCA to be truly sustainable it needs to be based upon assets or skills possessed by the business. An asset is something your firm possesses such as a brand name or retail location that is superior to the competition. A skill is something that your firm does better than competitors such as advertising or efficient manufacturing. Without the support of assets or skills it is unlikely that the SCA will be enduring. What a business does, the way it competes, and where it chooses to compete, is usually easily imitated. It is more difficult to respond to what a business is, to acquire or neutralize specialized assets or skills. Anyone can decide to distribute cereal or detergent through supermarkets but few have the clout to do it as effectively as a General Mills or Procter & Gamble. The right assets and skills can provide the needed barriers to competitor thrusts that make the SCA persist over time.

The essence of strategic management is the development and maintenance of meaningful assets and skills and the selection of strategies and competitive arenas such that those assets and skills form SCAs. Indicators of the strength of the assets and skills are thus required to measure performance and guide programs needed to improve assets and skills. The ability to produce high-quality products is a skill that could be monitored by quality goals such as a defect ratio to customer problem index. Clearly, such measures suggest that assets and skills go beyond simply stating that a firm is a "high-quality" firm or a "low-cost" business, although such statements of strategic thrusts or culture can be helpful.

Instead of a strategic focus upon assets and skills, U.S. management too often is driven by short-term measures such as sales, market share, ROI, or ROA. As a result, there is a temptation to overinvest in fast-payoff projects such as sales promotions (which have grown dramatically in the last 10 years) and to milk assets instead of creating new ones. For example, brand extensions are frequently used as a way to reduce the risk and investment required in new product introductions. Yet extensions can easily damage the brand by creating harmful associations or by clouding a previously well-defined image. Consider the decline of the Izod's alligator symbol following efforts to put it on just about anything.[3]

The short-term measures also encourage an underinvestment in the future. The reduction in expense items such as image advertising and new product development can provide an immediate impact on the bottom line while sacrificing asset enhancement that will pay off in the future. In contrast, the management of skills and assets provides an alternative to short-term financial measures that will provide the foundation for long-term success.

Four sets of practical questions can guide the implementation of a strategic focus upon the assets and skills of the business:

- What are the relevant skills and assets for your industry? What assets and skills either should be obtained or neutralized if you are to compete successfully?
- What is or should be the assets and skills that underlie your SCA? Of the set of relevant assets and skills, how do you select the optimal ones to develop, strengthen, or maintain?
- How can you go about creating assets and skills that will support SCAs?
- Finally, how can formidable assets and skills of competitors be neutralized?

WHAT ARE THE RELEVANT ASSETS AND SKILLS?

Most industries will have a set of relevant assets and skills, the presence or absence of which can directly affect the performance of a competitor. The first step in the management of assets and skills is to identify this set. Attention can then turn to selecting those assets and skills that should be associated with a business and identifying the assets and skills of competitors that should be neutralized.

[3]John L. Graham and Cathy Anterasian, "The Mouse that Roared," *Los Angeles Times*, May 8, 1988, p. IV 3.

WHAT BUSINESS MANAGERS SAY IS THEIR SCA

A sample of 248 managers of strategic business units (SBUs) from the Northern California area were contacted and asked what was the SCA of their business.[4] A total of 113 of these businesses were services such as consulting, financial services, real estate, airlines, hotels, law, insurance, retailing, venture capital, and restaurants. Another 68 were high-technology firms involved in products such as personal computers, software, information systems, lasers, medical instrumentation, and CAD/CAM equipment. The remaining 67 firms were in manufacturing or raw materials and included businesses in clothing, pharmaceuticals, air conditioning, chemicals, metal fabrication, garden supplies, oil, and specialty forging. The responses were recorded and coded into categories of assets and skills. The results, summarized in Table 1, provide some insights into the SCA construct.

For a subset of 95 of the businesses, a second SBU manager was independently interviewed. The result suggests that managers can identify SCAs with a high degree of reliability. Of the 95 businesses, 71 of the manager pairs gave answers that were coded the same and 20 more only had a single difference in the SCA list.

Table 1 shows a list of 31 SCAs, all assets or skills that were mentioned by at least 7 of the 248 respondents. This list provides a point of departure for determining what assets and skills are relevant.

By a significant margin, the most frequently named SCA was "quality reputation," undoubtedly reflecting the importance of the dimension to most markets. Given the incidence of quality in this SCA study, most business should probably consider the following questions:

- What are the quality dimensions in this industry?
- How should quality be measured?
- What are customers' perceptions of the quality of the competing businesses and how are these perceptions developed?

It is important to realize that quality, like many of the 31 dimensions, is itself complex and multidimensional. One writer, for example, suggested that product quality can include dimensions such as functional performance, "fit and finish," durability, incidence of defects, reliability, serviceability, features, or simply an overall "quality name."[5] A study of service quality found eight quality dimensions: the appearance of the facilities and people, service reliability, competence,

---

[4]The interviews were each conducted by a different MBA student who recorded the responses. The responses were coded by two different coders. The between coder reliability was .92. The coding was supervised by Shubra Sen, whose help is gratefully acknowledged.

[5]David A. Garvin, "Product Quality: An Important Strategic Weapon," *Business Horizons* 27 (May/June 1984), pp. 40–43.

TABLE 1 Sustainable Competitive Advantages of 248 Businesses

	High-Tech	Service	Other	Total
1. Reptuation for quality	26	50	29	105
2. Customer service/product support	23	40	15	78
3. Name recognition/high profile	8	42	21	71
4. Retain good management and engineering staff	17	43	5	65
5. Low-cost production	17	15	21	53
6. Financial resources	11	26	14	51
7. Customer orientation/ feedback/market research	13	26	9	48
8. Product line breadth	11	25	17	47
9. Technical superiority	30	7	9	46
10. Installed base of satisfied customers	19	22	4	45
11. Segmentation/focus	7	22	16	45
12. Product characteristics/differentiation	12	15	10	37
13. Continuing production innovation	15	20	10	35
14. Market share	12	14	9	35
15. Size/location of distribution	10	12	13	34
16. Low-price/high-value offering	6	20	6	32
17. Knowledge of business	2	25	4	31
18. Pioneer/early entrant in industry	11	11	6	28
19. Efficient, flexible production/ operations adaptable to customers	4	17	4	26
20. Effective sales force	10	9	4	23
21. Overall marketing skills	7	9	7	23
22. Shared vision/culture	5	13	4	22
23. Strategic goals	6	7	9	22
24. Powerful well-known parent	7	7	6	20
25. Location	0	10	10	20
26. Effective advertising/image	5	6	6	17
27. Enterprising/entrepreneurial	4	3	6	11
28. Good coordination	3	2	5	10
29. Engineering research development	8	2	0	10
30. Short-term planning	2	1	5	8
31. Good distributor relations	2	4	1	7
32. Other	6	20	5	31
Total	322	552	283	1157
Number of businesses	68	113	67	248
Average number of SCAs	4.73	4.88	4.22	4.65

trustworthiness, empathy, courtesy, and communication. Ultimately, of course, quality is defined by customer expectations.[6]

The second and seventh SCA both suggest customer orientation. A customer focus (perhaps like quality reputation) is something that nearly all organizations profess. The problem is to distinguish between lip service and a meaningful culture, an effective system, and motivated people that together can represent a set of assets and skills driving a customer-oriented business. Again customer orientation is complex and will take different forms in different contexts.[7]

The third ranked SCA was "name recognition/high profile," which often translated into a significant industry presence, high top-of-mind awareness, and the image of a substantial, committed player. Olivetti, for example, has used a "name" as the key to its strategy.[8] They became the world's third largest maker of personal computers (and the second largest in Europe) by making IBM clones under names such as AT&T in America and several other leading "names" in Europe.

Several of the assets and skills listed clearly represent barriers to competitors. "Product line breadth," for example, reduces the windows of opportunity for competitors. An "installed base of satisfied customers" is uniquely associated with a firm and is usually very costly and difficult to dislodge. A "pioneer or early entrant" is a historical heritage that can usually be attached to only one firm in the market. A "powerful well-known parent" and "location" are not easily duplicated. Over two-thirds of the SCAs are externally oriented and visible to the customer.

Suggestive differences arise when the list is analyzed for the high-tech and service firms. For high-tech firms, "technical superiority," which could include process technology as well as product technology, is listed relatively more frequently than in other industry contexts. For service firms, "the retention of good management" is relatively more frequently mentioned and low-cost production is relatively less frequently mentioned.

One finding of note is that businesses listed an average of 4.65 SCAs each. In reading the popular business press and books, the impression is often given that a successful business can be based upon doing some "one thing well" or having a single key asset. A firm can be a "quality company," an "R&D" company, an efficient manufacturing firm, a new product company, or a firm that excels in promotion and, thus, a single asset or skill could seem to be the basis for success. However, these results suggest that multiple strengths are needed in order to compete successfully and that assets and skills are defined at a more specific and detailed level.

---

[6]A. Parasuraman, Valarie A. Zeithaml, and Leonard L. Berry, "A Conceptual Model of Service Quality and Its Implications for Future Research," *Journal of Marketing*, 49 (Fall 1985), pp. 41–50.

[7]For a profile of a customer-driven organization, see David A. Aaker, *Developing Business Strategies*, 2nd ed. (New York: John Wiley & Sons, 1988), p. 212–13.

[8]"How Olivetti Cloned Its Way to the Top," *Business Week*, June 16, 1986, p. 82.

Four Questions

The list in Table 1 provides a set of assets and skills to consider. To identify the relevant assets and skills for a particular industry, however, it is useful to pose a series of four questions:

1. *Who are the successful businesses over time? What assets or skills have contributed to their success? Who are the businesses that have chronically low performance? Why? What assets or skills do they lack?*

By definition, assets and skills that provide SCAs should affect performance over time. Thus, businesses that differ with respect to performance over time should also differ with respect to their skills and assets. Analyzing the causes of the performance suggests sets of relevant assets and skills. The superior performers will usually have developed and maintained some key assets and skills that have been the basis for their performance. Conversely, weakness in several assets and skills relevant to their industry should visibly contribute to the inferior performance over time of the weak competitors.

For example, General Electric, the best performer in the CT scanner industry, has superior product technology and R&D, has a systems capability due to its related businesses, and has a strong sales and service organization due to its X-ray product line and an installed base. GE's largest competitor is Johnson & Johnson, which has been a chronic money loser for a decade because it lacks the synergistic combination of businesses, the product technology and R&D, and the sales and service organization.[9]

2. *What are the key customer motivations? What is really important to the customer?*

Customer motivations usually drive buying decisions and thus can dictate what assets and skills can potentially create meaningful advantages. In the heavy equipment industry, customers value service and parts back-up. Caterpillar's "24-hour parts service anywhere in the world" has been a key asset for them because of its importance to customers.

Sometimes motivations exist that are unmet by current offerings. Unmet motivations represent opportunities for the "outs" and threats for the "ins." For example, the successful Apple MacIntosh computer was developed in response to an unmet motivation for a user-friendly system. The technology surrounding the MacIntosh provides an enormous asset in an industry full of IBM clones.

An analysis of customer motivations can also identify assets and skills that a business will need to deliver. If the prime buying criterion for a snack is freshness, a brand will have to develop the skills to deliver that attribute. A business which lacks competence in an area important to the customer segment can be in trouble even if it has substantial other SCAs.

---

[9]"Changing a Corporate Culture," *Business Week*, May 14, 1984, pp. 130–37.

3. *What are the key activities providing customer value? What are the large cost components?*

Porter has suggested that the business identify its value-added activities—the distinct activities performed such as operations, marketing and sales, service, logistics, procurement, R&D, and human resource management.[10] The activities should then be analyzed as to their potential for having a high impact upon differentiation and whether they represent a significant or growing proportion of cost. In either case, the analysis should lead to an identification of assets and skills that would result in a meaningful advantage. Obtaining a cost advantage in a large value-added stage, for example, can represent a significant SCA, whereas a cost advantage in a lower value-added stages will have less leverage. Thus in the metal can business, transportation costs are relatively high and a competitor that can locate plants near customers will have a cost advantage—plant location then becomes a significant strategic asset.

4. *What are the mobility barriers in the industry?*

The cost and difficulty of creating assets and skills needed to support SCA represent the mobility barriers in an industry. Mobility represents both entry barriers and barriers to the movement from one strategic group or competitive arena to another. For example, in the oil-well drilling industry of the 1970s and early 1980s, barriers prevented firms from moving from shallow on-shore drilling to deep on-shore drilling to off-shore to foreign drilling.[11] Foreign, off-shore drilling requires specialized assets and skills in establishing and operating off-shore equipment, in dealing with foreign governments and firms, and in operating in different countries. The assets and skills that prevent entry into an industry or segment of an industry should be among those that are relevant to that industry.

SELECT ASSETS AND SKILLS TO DEVELOP, STRENGTHEN, OR MAINTAIN

Which assets or skills should be selected to develop or maintain? How much emphasis should be placed upon each? Clearly, a business needs to be selective. Limited resources will need to be focused upon those assets and skills that will support SCAs. Estimates of the costs and benefits will often be difficult. In making strategic judgments about assets and skills the following questions should be helpful. Is the asset or skill:

• Defined with respect to the competition? Will a competitive advantage result?
• Relevant to the market?

---

[10]Michael E. Porter, *Competitive Advantage* (New York: The Free Press, 1985), Chapter 2.

[11]Briance Macarenhus, and David A. Aaker, "Mobility Barriers and Strategic Groups," *Strategic Management Journal* (forthcoming 1989).

- Feasible and cost-effective?
- Going to result in an SCA that is sustainable?
- Appropriate to the future?

The Competitive Strength Grid

A competitive advantage must be both a point of difference and an advantage as defined with respect to the firms regarded as competitors. A skill that all competitors have will not be the basis for an SCA. For example, flight safety is important among airline passengers but if airlines are perceived to be equal with respect to pilot quality and plane maintenance, it cannot be the basis for an SCA. Of course, if some airlines can convince passengers that they are superior with respect to antiterrorist security, then an SCA could indeed exist.

To help provide the correct point of reference and summarize relevant information, it is usually helpful to scale your own firm and the major competitors or strategic groups of competitors (competitors who have similar strategies and characteristics) on the relevant assets and skills.[12] For each competitor, which are areas of strengths and which are weaknesses?

A competitor strength grid, as illustrated in Figure 2 for the gourmet frozen food industry, provides a compact representation of the results. The relevant assets and skills are listed in order of their importance to the extent that an ordering can be obtained. The principal competitors are then positioned on each dimension according to their relative strengths and weaknesses. The process can generate insight into the nature of the assets and skills, competitor capabilities, and a particular SBU's position relative to competitors.

In Figure 2, eight assets and skills are listed and seven main competitors in the gourmet frozen food industry in the mid-1980s are positioned. The grid suggests that Lean Cuisine is well positioned with the dominant market share, distribution, and advertising effort. However, other firms may have developed packaging advantages and there may be an industry gap with respect to quality.

It is often desirable, or even necessary, to conduct the analysis for submarkets or strategic groups and for different products. A firm may not compete with all the other firms in the industry but only those engaged in similar strategies and markets. For example, a competitor strength grid may look very different for the controlled calorie portion of the gourmet frozen food industry or the ethnic

---

[12]The competitive strength grid was first introduced in David A. Aaker, "How to Select a Business Strategy," *California Management Review* 26/3 (Spring 1984), pp. 167–75. The material on the gourmet frozen foods was drawn from work of students Alan Donald, Harvey Scodel, Dave Barnes, Jacquelyn Boykin, Joe Jimenez, Barbara May, and Jill Stewarts.

FIGURE 2 Competitor Strength Grid

Assets and Skills	Weakness									Strength
Product quality	W	V	B	A	G		L	M		
Market share/ share economies	V	B	W	A	G			M		L
Parent in related business		B	W		V	G	A		M	L
Package		V	W B			L	G		A	M
Low calorie position	V		G			M	B	A	L	W
Sales force/distribution	V		B			W	G	A	M	L
Advertising/promotion	V		B	G		W		A	M	L
Ethnic position	W			A	L	M		G	V	B

L Stouffer's Lean Cuisine (Nestle's—also makes Stouffer "Red Box" line)
M Le Menu (Campbell Soup—also makes Swanson's, Mrs. Paul's)
W Weight Watchers (Heinz)
A Armour Dinner Classic/Classic Lite (Con-Agra—also makes Banquet)
V Van deKamp Mexican Classic and other ethnic lines
B Benihana
G Green Giant Stir Fry Entrees (Pillsbury)

submarket. The relevant assets and skills may differ. The ethnic portion may not involve the asset "low calorie" position, for example. Further, the composition of the competitors and their relative strengths can change as well.

Relevant to the Market

An analysis of customer motivations should help evaluate as well as identify SCAs. In nearly all cases, an SCA should result in either a point of differentiation or a price advantage that is valued by the customer.

A case in point is the P&G Pringle experience. P&G developed a potato chip that was neither burnt or greasy, was of uniform shape and would "stack," had a package that protected the chips from breakage, and had a shelf life of over one year. P&G was the only firm that could really mount a national distribution and advertising effort for such a product. They had a series of substantial assets and skills to rely on. However, the customer was interested primarily in taste and had little concern with shelf life or breakability. Associating the product with "artificiality," consumer concluded that it had an inferior taste (despite the fact that blind taste tests indicated that it had a taste parity). As a result, the repeat purchase was weak and the product has had disappointing performance relative to expectations.

Feasible and Cost-Effective

Sometimes an objective analysis will conclude that the development of a desired asset or skill is so costly that it is simply not economically feasible. A competitor might be so entrenched with respect to a dimension such as quality or service or performance that the market would not find credible a claim that the competitor had been surpassed even if physical superiority had been achieved. Or there could be an implementation issue. The culture of the firm may simply not be compatible with creating a strong innovation strength, for example. The people, culture, systems, and rewards may all be geared to production and cost reduction in a way that would be impossible to change without doing substantial harm.

Sustainable

Will the resulting SCA be neutralized by the strategy of a competitor? There is little point to investing resources into assets and skills that can be easily neutralized by a competitor's strategy. A location advantage might be easily neutralized by an innovative logistical system. A distribution advantage that can be by-passed by using promotions or a different channel is not the basis of an SCA.

Another key consideration is whether competitors or potential competitors have the motivation to respond. Honda's reaction to the Yamaha challenge in motorcycles provides a vivid illustration of how a committed competitor can respond to emerging SCAs.[13] Through aggressive product introductions, capacity expansions, and the development of distribution strengths, Yamaha took over the leading position in Japan's motorcycle market at a time when Honda was diverted by its efforts to enter the automobile market. Yamaha publicly boasted that it would become number one worldwide. Honda's pride and historical commitment motivated it to counter with a wide variety of product options and lower price. The result of provoking Honda was nearly disastrous for Yamaha, which subsequently announced that it would be very happy to be number two.

A business should look for strategies that are sustainable when a competitor is inhibited or otherwise unable to respond. For example, a competitor might believe that a response to a low-end entry would result in cannibalizing an existing product line or tarnishing its image. A strategy of product breadth might leave no niche that would support an aggressive response by a competitor. A large competitor might be inhibited by antitrust laws and by a large installed base to respond to a niche strategy. Dominant firms like Anheuser-Busch, General Mo-

---

[13]James C. Abegglen and George Stalk, Jr., *Kaisha: The Japanese Corporation* (New York: Basic Books, 1985), pp. 45–50.

tors, and IBM are restricted by antitrust laws in the strategic options they can pursue. Further, they have to be sensitive to the impact upon their installed base of any strategic reaction to a competitor's strategy.

Relevant to the Future

Changing conditions can undercut strategies and the assets and skills upon which they are based. In many technical industries, for example, technology is of prime importance at the outset. The successful firms are those that can deliver the most advanced technology. The product then evolves in one of two directions. The product may become a commodity, in which case a key success factor for most firms tends to be achieving low production costs and an effective distribution system. Personal computers and low-cost copiers are examples of this. Or, the product may evolve toward a system, in which case it becomes important to participate in related businesses to control the system and to have a strong direct sales and service capability. The CT scanner and high-end copiers are examples.

It is thus important to anticipate what assets and skills will be needed as conditions evolve. Teece notes that innovator firms such as RC Cola in diet colas, Bowmar in pocket calculators, and DeHavilland in planes all were first with a successful innovative product but lacked the assets and skills to compete when others became established.[14] Pepsi-Cola, Texas Instruments, and Boeing had the complementary assets that were needed to compete after the initial phase of the product life. In these cases, the assets and skills needed were so crucial that the alternative to obtaining them (either internally or through a strategic alliance) was to lose nearly all the benefits of the innovation.

The task of projecting the environment and the needed assets and skills is not at all easy. Trends emerging from analyses of the customers, competitors, distribution channel, technology, and the industry environment need to be identified, monitored, and analyzed. The development of scenarios can be helpful because the realization of the new assets and skills that will be needed often emerges only from a picture of the future that is both rich and convincing.

HOW TO DEVELOP AND MAINTAIN SCAs

The creation of assets and skills can be difficult and costly. There is no right way or short-cut that will work in every situation, but the following should provide both useful suggestions as to how to proceed and additional insight into the SCA concept.

---

[14]David J. Teece, "Profiting from Technological Innovation: Implications for Integration, Collaboration, Licensing and Public Policy" *Research Policy* 15 (1986), pp. 285–305.

Link to Business Objectives

One key to the management of assets and skills is to link them to business objectives. An objective could thus be to create the asset of brand-name awareness or distribution coverage or the skill of low-cost production or providing high-quality service. Such objectives hopefully would dominate short-term financial objectives and provide a strategic focus to management of the operations.

The objectives need to be supported by measurable indicators of strength of assets and skills. Tom Peters provides examples of indicators of such assets and skills as quality, service, responsiveness, niches, creation, and innovation.[15] He notes that firms such as Ford, Tennant, and Perdue Farms use quality objectives as a basis for compensation. IBM measures customer satisfaction and analyzes complaints in order to help protect the loyalty of its installed base, perhaps its most important asset.

Fit with Strategies

Assets and skills will generate SCAs only in the context of the appropriate strategies and the right competitive environment. A large installed base facing substantial switching costs may be an SCA only if it is exploited. Micropro's Wordstar, the early leader in word processing, developed a new generation product, Wordstar 2000, that was sufficiently different from Wordstar so that its customers could switch to competitors almost as easily as they could learn the new Micropro product. As a result, Micropro's position eroded. Had it upgraded its basic Wordstar product instead, it might have held its position. Belatedly, it did introduce Wordstar Professional, an advanced program compatible with the original product.

The goal should be to develop strategies that exploit assets and skills. One long-time observer of Japanese firms notes that one key to their success is their creation and exploitation of competitive advantage.[16] Historically, an SCA of many Japanese firms was based upon low-cost manufacturing in part driven by low wages. This advantage supported aggressive pricing policies aimed at generating share dominance. More recently, some of these firms, finding the cost advantage eroding, have developed additional skills such as highly flexible factories that permit them to generate wide product lines without a cost premium. Their strategy is to exploit the manufacturing flexibility by creating a broad product line and segmenting the market to continue to pursue share growth. The point is that they have developed new assets and skills and then engaged in strategies that exploit those assets and skills.

[15]Tom Peters, *Thriving on Chaos* (New York: Alfred A. Knopf, 1987), see especially sections C-2, C-3, and S-1.
[16]Abegglen and Stalk, op. cit., pp. 10–11.

An SCA can often be leveraged by making it part of the positioning strategy. The distinction is between an asset or skill that is developed because its absence would create a problem or competitive opportunity and an asset or skill that is created to provide a visible consumer benefit. Thus, Maytag developed a product line and service system geared to delivering reliability and used that to position the firm with respect to the market. If the customers perceive the business with respect to its assets and skills, those assets and skills perform a marketing function as well. Further, the more visibility and commitment that are placed behind the assets and skills, the more likely that there will be supporting commitment and culture inside the business to maintain those assets and skills.

Routes to an SCA

The development of an SCA often requires not only insight and good management but also luck and/or substantial investment. For example, the creation and maintenance of American Express's 15 million cardholder base required an enormous expenditure of advertising and promotion funds. Although there are many routes to an SCA, a few are worth singling out because they illustrate the basic concept and because when they can be applied they can result in the development of assets and skills with a relatively modest investment.

Patent and Trade Secret Protection.   In some situations, patents can provide a substantial barrier to competitive response. Howard Head, who in the fifties revolutionized the ski industry with his metal skis, did the same thing to the tennis racket industry in the late 1970s by creating and obtaining a patent on the oversized Prince racket. The Prince market share went from zero in 1975 to 30.7 in 1981, while the total market for rackets collapsed from $183.7 million to 135.9 million.[17] Competitors proliferated products but could not compete with the basic Prince design because of the patent.

A study of 650 R&D executives attempted to determine the relative effectiveness of various means of protecting the returns from innovations such as patents, secrecy, lead time, and superior sales and service.[18] They found that patents tended to be more important in products than processes, as products are often patentable and are vulnerable to reverse engineering when patent protection is absent. Further, they found that patents are most useful in the chemical and drug areas where the product is easily analyzed and copied. Patents were found to be less of a factor in innovative industries such as computers and communications equipment where the environment is so dynamic that patents become obsolete.

---

[17]Walter McQuade, "Prince Triumphant," *Fortune,* February 22, 1982, pp. 84–90.

[18]Sidney G. Winter, "Knowledge and Competence as Strategic Assets," in *The Competitive Challenge: Strategies for Industrial Innovation and Renewal,* ed. David Teece (Cambridge, Mass.: Ballinger Publishing Company, 1987), pp. 159–84.

When patents are not strong enough to provide an adequate barrier, trade secret protection may protect an asset such as a process development or even an information system.[19] A trade secret can be protected by nondisclosure agreements, avoiding personnel turnover, and by avoiding access by vendor or customer firms.

Preemptive Strategies. A preemptive strategic move is the first implementation of a strategy into a business area that, because it was first, generates an asset or skill that creates a competitive advantage that is sustainable because competitors are inhibited or prevented from duplicating or countering it. A preemptive move can be directed at any element of strategy involving the supply systems, the product, the production system, the customers, or the distribution and service systems.[20] Thus, a key advantage of Red Lobster restaurants was their access to the best seafood sources and seafood distribution. A brand that enters a market first with a strong position upon a key dimension makes it more difficult for future competitors to engage in a similar strategy.

If key customers can be committed, competitors may be shut off from part of the market. For example, a hospital supply firm made substantial inroads against a dominant, established firm by offering to place computer terminals in hospitals to facilitate ordering emergency items. The terminals ultimately were used to order routine as well as emergency orders. Since hospitals had a need for only one such terminal, the established firm found its belated effort to duplicate the service frustrated—it had been preempted.

Exploiting Synergy. Synergy exists when the combination of two or more businesses provides either more customer value, less product cost, or less investment than would be the case if those businesses operated separately.[21] Thus, a firm that makes a printer, modem, and software in addition to a computer can furnish a systems solution which will provide customer value in selecting a system and in obtaining service. It could also provide reduced cost in that the lines could share a sales force and reduced investment if they could share manufacturing and warehousing facilities.

An advantage based upon synergy is likely to be sustainable because the firm itself is unique. No other firm will have the identical set of firm characteristics and profile of businesses. To the extent that the synergistic advantage is linked to the uniqueness of the firm it will be sustainable.

American Express decided that an important asset that they wanted to develop was their synergy among their bank, insurance, brokerage, and card operations.[22] As a result they developed the One Enterprise program to encourage the ex-

[19]Teece, op. cit., p. 287.

[20]Ian C. MacMillan, "Preemptive Strategies," *Journal of Business Strategy* (Fall 1983), pp. 16–26.

[21]For a discussion of the synergy concept see Aaker, *Developing Business Strategies*, op. cit., p. 242.

[22]Monci Jo Williams, "Synergy Works at American Express," *Fortune*, February 16, 1987, p. 80.

ploitation of the synergy. Significantly, each manager was evaluated on his or her contribution to the program; tied to the evaluation was compensation in the form of bonuses.

NEUTRALIZING COMPETITORS' ASSETS AND SKILLS

A key to winning is thus to create SCAs involving strategies that are based upon assets and skills. A companion approach to strategy development is to recognize the assets and skills of competitors and look for strategies that neutralize them by making them irrelevant.

An example of a firm that developed a strategy to neutralize competitor strengths was a small software firm that lacked a retail distribution capability or the resources to engage in retail advertising. It directed its efforts to value-added software systems firms, firms that sell total software and sometimes hardware systems to industries such as investment firms or hospitals. These value-added systems firms could understand and exploit the power of the product, integrate it into their system, and use it in quantity. The absence of a distribution channel or resources to support an advertising effort was thus neutralized.

CONCLUSION

Too often a concentration upon short-term profit measures sacrifices strategic position and long-term performance. The question is how to manage for the long term. One answer is to focus upon the assets and skills that provide the foundation for sustainable competitive advantage. The essence of strategic management then should be the development and maintenance of meaningful assets and skills, the selection of strategies and competitive arenas to exploit such assets and skills, and the neutralizing of competitors' assets and skills.

Managing assets and skills involves three steps. The first is the identification of relevant assets and skills by observing successful and unsuccessful firms, key customer motivations, large value-added items, and mobility barriers. Among those named by managers were product quality reputation, name recognition, and customer service/product support. The second step is to select those assets and skills to support a strategy that will provide an advantage over competitors, be relevant to the market, be feasible, be sustainable, and be appropriate to the future. The third step is to develop and implement programs and procedures to develop, enhance, or protect assets and skills. One key is the use of appropriate objectives and supporting measures. Another is to make sure that what a business does and where it competes supports and exploits its assets and skills and neutralizes the assets and skills of competitors.

What this article is about: A study of companies in three different industries—
auto, computers, and semiconductors—shows that growing internationalization
of business brings about major changes in the positioning of competitors and
the appropriate competitive strategies. Only after going through a financial crisis
did the companies studied emerge from national to international status.

2–10 Market Share and Corporate Strategy in International Industries

James Leontiades

James Leontiades is senior lecturer in international management,
Manchester Business School,
University of Manchester, England

Corporate strategy, with its emphasis on the adjustment of the firm to its environment, has obvious application for the study of international business. However, care must be taken that the concepts and principles forwarded under this
heading are suited to the special situation of the firm operating in an international
environment.

For example, evidence has been assembled to show that there is a positive
correlation between market share and profitability—a relationship that has considerable significance for strategic planning. This poses two problems for international firms which do not generally trouble the managers of domestic companies.

- *What is the geographic area encompassed by the market?* Should it be calculated nationally or is the *relevant* market (i.e., relevant for strategy formulation) international in scope? While the domestic national market may be
assumed as the basis for calculating market share for some firms in certain
industries, there are clearly others, for example, jet planes, microcircuits,
computers, and so on, where this assumption cannot be made.
- *Is the present geographic basis for calculating market share changing?* For
some companies, the relevant geographic market is changing, that is, expanding

from national to international. This entails questions of strategy related to the new situation posed by an enlarged market.

PURPOSE

The main thesis to be developed here is that the geographc scope of what is meant by the industry and its competitive environment cannot be assumed to be either stable over time or readily ascertainable. This implies that a national definition of market share/ROI (return on investment) can be dangerously misleading.

Some of the present evidence linking market share and ROI tends to be obscure on these points since (1) the precise geographic definition of the market is unstated and (2) the evidence showing a positive relationship between ROI and market share, as in Figure 1, is based on comparisons among U.S. companies. These may be unrepresentative. The exceptional size of the North American market may dominate the market share/ROI relationship to the point where it may swamp international efforts.

A broader aim is to investigate the changing nature of competition and strategy formulation in the more international industries. It is a priori evident that a

FIGURE 1   Relationship of Market Share to Profitability

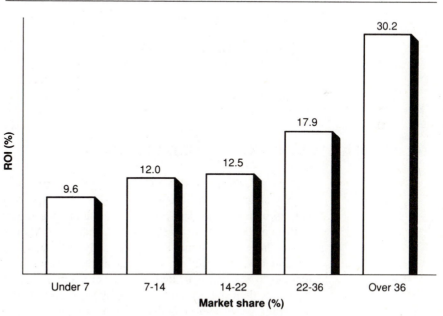

SOURCE: Schoeffler, Buzzell, and Heany, "Impact of Strategic Planning on Profitability," *Harvard Business Review*, March–April 1974.

significant number of industries are becoming increasingly international. We may postulate that industries are going through progressive developmental stages. We recognize that at one time industries that were subnational in terms of geographic coverage changed. National industries emerged with consequent implications for strategy. In more recent times, industries that are more international than national have emerged.

The questions and strategic decisions posed by the internationalization of an industry and its competitive sphere are quite different from those posed by the internationalization of a firm. In the case of the latter, the focus is on management decisions associated with company moves into new national environments. The internationalization of industry brings about basic changes in the firm's environment which pose questions for both domestic and international companies.

Some firms will adjust to the new situation better than others. We may speculate that the more international firms positioned to take maximum advantage of economies and efficiencies of the wider international market would do best in such industries. We may also hypothesize that, for this sort of firm, performance within any given national market (e.g., in terms of the market share/ROI relationship) would have less meaning.

We will now examine the market share/ROI performance on three pairs of firms. Each pair includes one of the following:

- *A major national competitor*. This refers to a company whose production and marketing operations are focused on a particular national territory. Its dominant strength in terms of production and marketing facilities lies within that national market, although this does not preclude the presence of some facilities, exports, or other operations in other countries.
- *A major international competitor*. This refers to a company with a major involvement in multiple national markets. This firm's national facilities and sales are only a part (often a small part) of an internationally integrated network of facilities and operations.

THE AUTOMOTIVE INDUSTRY: FORD VERSUS BL

Since 1967, the Ford Motor Company has operated its European facilities on a highly integrated pan-European basis. The firm's regional headquarters exercises control over a network of major manufacturing and assembly facilities located in Britain, Germany, France, Belgium, and Spain. Market research is coordinated across the major national markets to arrive at a standardized product line. Production is rationalized on a European basis, with the various national plants tending to specialize in high-volume production of components and products which are then shipped cross-nationally to be assembled and finally sold through the firm's various national distribution systems.

More than half of Ford's European and passenger car sales are outside the United Kingdom. The market share figures and profitability reported in Figures 2 and 3 refer to Ford's national subsidiary in Britain.

FIGURE 2   Ford/BL Market Share—U.K. Passenger Cars

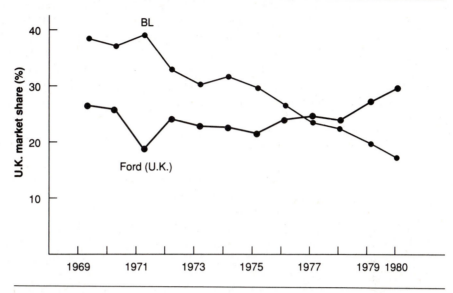

SOURCE: SMMT.

BL (formerly BLMC Ltd. and before that the British Leyland Motor Corporation) has a predominantly national orientation. The great majority of its car sales are within its British home market. Passenger car sales in the United Kingdom, as measured by new car registrations, now comprise about 80 percent

FIGURE 3   Return on Investment

	BL	Ford (U.K.)
1969	16%	18%
1970	6	11
1971	13	(loss)
1972	12	19
1973	16	28
1974	8	7
1975	(loss)	9
1976	20	31
1977	9	55
1978	8	35
1979	(loss)	49
1980	(loss)	24

SOURCE: *The Times 1000.*

of its total Western European sales. Throughout the past 12 years, the British national market has dominated its sales performance. Figure 2 shows that BL had the highest national market share in Britain from 1969 through 1975. However, Figure 3 indicates that Ford has the higher ROI for six of these eight years. Subsequently, Ford's market share exceeded that of BL and its ROI advantage improved still further over the national competitor. BL has received extensive government assistance in recent years. Financial crises have brought about a change in strategy, including a partnership with Honda, the Japanese automobile producer.

COMPUTERS: ICL VERSUS IBM

Historically, ICL has had the advantage over IBM in terms of national market performance. Figure 4 employs national (U.K.) market sales of ICL and IBM as a proxy for the relative market share of these two companies within the British market. Despite its smaller national market share, IBM's ROI performance averaged over 1978 to 1980 has been significantly better than ICL's. However, ICL's sales, both globally and within Western Europe, are much below those of IBM.

As with BL, the government has been forced to come to the assistance of the

FIGURE 4   IBM/ICL—ROI and Relative Market Share Position (average 1978–1980)

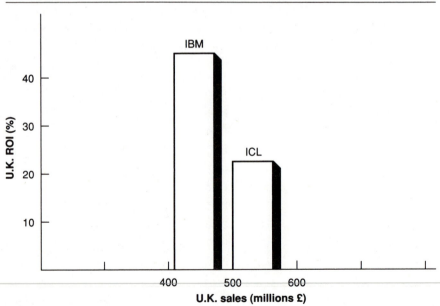

SOURCE: Annual Reports, *The Times 1000*.

national competitor. ICL incurred a net loss of £50 million during 1981. The government provided credit guarantees in the amount of £200 million which were used to implement a fundamental change in ICL strategy. This included a major shift in the firm's competitive positioning toward the rapidly growing market for small computers and telecommunications and away from mainframe computers, the traditional IBM strength.

SEMICONDUCTORS: TEXAS INSTRUMENTS VERSUS FERRANTI

In the semiconductor industry, Texas Instruments' British subsidiary enjoys a higher ROI than its national competitor, Ferranti Ltd., despite the higher national market share of the latter. (See Figure 5.) Ferranti has also had to resort to government help (in early 1974) to survive against international competition. Though it has recently improved its profitability and ceased to rely on government assistance, its ROI position relative to Texas Instruments–U.K. continues to deteriorate. (Texas Instruments–U.K. ROI during 1981 was over 90 percent.)

Competition for the mass markets in this fast-moving industry is based on high volume, technological leadership, and experience curve pricing. The national British market represents only a small fraction of world sales. The entire Western European market represents less than 15 percent of the total world

FIGURE 5 Texas Instruments/Ferranti—ROI and Relative Market Share Position (average 1978–1980)

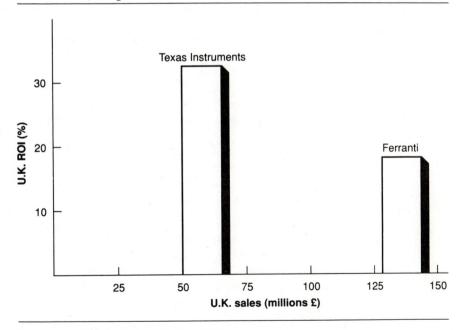

SOURCE: Annual Company Reports, *The Times 1000*.

market for semiconductors, still too small to provide economies of large-scale production.[1] Ferranti's total world sales in 1980 were approximately 10 percent of Texas Instruments' world total. Ferranti's present strategy concentrates on a specialized segment of this market, the so-called custom-built devices as opposed to the standardized, high-volume, mass-produced circuits.

COMMON FEATURES

While a sample of this size cannot "prove" anything, it is interesting that the above three comparisons have the following features in common:

1. The position of all three national competitors (BL, ICL, Ferranti) has been gradually eroded over the years. Each of these companies was at one time the leader in their respective national industries.
2. In all three situations, the U.K. industry viewed on a national basis has become increasingly less significant. Both markets and competition have become international in scope.
3. National market share does not appear to be positively correlated with national ROI, as per the relationship in Figure 1.
4. In all three situations, the international competitors, while smaller nationally, enjoyed the larger market share internationally (in terms of Western Europe or globally). Hence, any attempt to explain ROI as positively related to market share would have to rely on an international definition of the market.
5. All three international competitors operated on a supernational basis. That is, production, marketing, and research were rationalized across national boundaries as part of an international system aimed at securing maximum efficiencies of international scale and volume.
6. The national competitors have all encountered severe financial crises in recent years while their international competitors have prospered, the latter enjoying both higher national ROI and a growing national market share.
7. Subsequent to their financial crises, all three national competitors have undergone a fundamental reassessment and realignment of their competitive strategy.
8. All three of the national companies were at one time strong national firms considered to be leaders in their industry. The erosion of their position over time seems to be due to a basic change in the geographic scope of their industry and its marketplace, from national to international.

The last two points merit elaboration. In terms of strategy formulation, the reality to which the national competitors have had to adjust following their financial crises is, first, that their industry and competitive environment are now of international proportions. National barriers are no longer effective in segmenting the industry along national boundaries. Not only have trade barriers

---

[1]OECD Report, *Gaps in Technology*, 1968, p. 110.

been reduced between countries, but international firms have now developed an improved ability to operate internationally in a way that enables them to make use of their larger size to gain efficiencies of scale and their attendant advantages, especially in the high-volume markets.

Second, the national competitors find that in this wider competitive environment, their strategic posture vis-à-vis the larger international companies has significantly altered. The national firms now find themselves in a different competitive league. In regional (Western Europe) or global terms they are now "small" rather than "large" and their strategy has had to adjust accordingly.

FERRANTI'S EXPERIENCE

In this study of British electronics firms, Edmond Sciberras[2] found that these firms now fall into two distinct competitive leagues. The big-league firms are those major international companies (Texas Instruments, Phillips, Motorola, and others) that have the resources and sufficient capital and technological resources to compete in the high-volume mass markets for semiconductors. Small-league firms develop strategies based on avoidance of head-on competition with big-league companies, indicating strategies based on some form of specialization.

For example, Ferranti is now seen as belonging to the small league, representing a fundamental change in its strategic positioning vis-à-vis its competitors. Sciberras noted, "The answer to the problem of avoiding the competitive pressures of which Ferranti's experiences have made it so aware has been to opt out of the mass established competitive markets . . . and to specialize". He also observed, "The Company is very much aware of the competitive pressure upon it in the industry and seeks to avoid this pressure as far as possible. Its competitive awareness leads it to a policy of competitive avoidance through technology hive off and application of its specialized technology to custom markets".

ICL'S EXPERIENCE

ICL underwent a closely analogous transformation in its strategy after its 1981 financial crisis. Major elements of the new ICL strategy include:

1. A partnership agreement with Fujitsu, the large Japanese electronics firm, to supply ICL with microcircuits and related technology.
2. An agreement to market Fujitsu mainframe computers under an ICL brand name (Atlas) to compensate in some part for ICL's more limited effort in this area.
3. An agreement with the U.S. firm Three Rivers to produce its new small

---

[2]E. Sciberras, *Multinational Electronic Companies and National Economic Policies*, 1977, pp. 182 and 187.

computer. This is part of the new strategy reflected in the managing director's statement: "We will make ICL big in small systems."[3]

4. A change in policy to make the firm's new products plug-compatible with those of IBM.

The general strategy has been to use the firm's nationally based strengths, and particularly its U.K. and European marketing system, to forge links with foreign producers. These links have enabled ICL to shift the focus of its own efforts away from direct competition with the larger international firms, and to make more intensive use of its own resources in specialized areas. The latter will be in the high-growth small computer and telecommunications segments. The emphasis has moved away from direct "head to head" competition with IBM and other big-league firms.

The year 1982 saw a return to profitability. The overall change in strategy seems to be working, although it is still too early to say with any degree of certainty.

BL'S EXPERIENCE

BL has also changed its strategy. The partnership with Honda to develop new motor vehicles is a significant departure from past practice for a firm that prides itself on its Britishness. In other respects, however, BL has not followed the specialization strategies of ICL and Ferranti. Although a number of industry analysts have concluded that the firm's commercial future would be improved by concentration on its speciality products (e.g., Jaguar, Rover, Triumph), national policy considerations have constrained management's freedom in this direction.[4] BL still competes directly against the major international firms in its industry. Of the three national competitors, BL continues to operate at a loss.

COMPETITIVE STRATEGY IN INTERNATIONAL INDUSTRIES

The gist of the above analysis is that there has been a change in the definition of industry which has had a major impact on corporate strategy. Over time, industry has become progressively internationalized, to the point where the de-

---

[3]*The Scotsman*, June 21, 1982.

[4]Volume cars and specialist cars: Having accepted that BL should remain a major producer of cars, we considered whether it should continue as at present to cover the full range of the market from the "small/light" sector (represented by the Mini) to the luxury sector (represented by the Jaguar). In the past the more expensive models produced by BL (not only Jaguars, but also Rovers and Triumphs) have proved more profitable, and a less satisfactory return has been earned on volume cars, particularly the Mini. We therefore examined whether BL should adopt a strategy of abandoning the bottom end of the volume car market. This would mean in effect that no replacement would be brought forward for the Mini. We are strongly of the view that this would be the wrong strategy (U.K. Government Report, *British Leyland: The Next Decade*, 1975, pp. 15–16).

marcation of markets and environment is now international rather than national. This internationalization has brought about changes in the competitive leagues or groupings within industry.

The strategic significance of these competitive leagues has also been identified in a domestic context in research carried out by Hatten, Schendel, and Cooper.[5] In an analysis of the U.S. brewing industry, it was concluded that identification of homogeneous groups of companies (similar strategies within groups but differing between groups) was necessary for an understanding of industry strategy. For example, the authors found that "plant expansion was associated with increased profitability for the national brewers . . . though it is negative for other groups." The authors underlined the fact that strategies for the small firms do not apply to the large firms.

Michael Porter[6] sounds a similar theme when he points out that identifying the "strategic groups" within an industry is an important part of industry anaysis and strategy formulation.

In an international context, our study supports the importance of "leagues" or "strategy groups." The question of what league the firm belongs to is an important one for the strategist. However it also brings out the fact that the firm's league is subject to change over time as the industry becomes more international. Identifying what league a firm is in requires a perception of the geographic scope of the industry. One must determine whether it is national or international. This may not be readily apparent. Internationalization of the industry is a gradual process. Such recognition, with its implication for some firms that they have now become members of the "little league," may be resisted. In the three cases reviewed here, this perception of the changed nature of the industry came about only after financial crises for the three national competitors.

The story is a familiar one. The same theme is detectable in the development of the European industry for major household appliances such as washing machines and refrigerators. During the 1960s, a number of Italian producers of these goods expanded to achieve international scale. With the lowering of trade barriers, the industry became international on a regional basis. Firms that remained predominantly national producers found themselves relegated to the small league, as compared to the big-league Italian firms. A number were driven to financial collapse. Many were amalgamated and merged into other companies. National competitors that survived were forced to realign their strategies with the competition of the large Italian firms.

The same phenomenon overtook the U.S. television manufacturers. The orientation of Zenith, Motorola, and other U.S. producers was predominantly toward the national market. The United States accounted for the bulk of the business. In 1960, Japanese exports of television (monochrome) sets to the United States accounted for only 2 percent of total Japanese production. By 1970, the

---

[5]K. Hatten; D. Schendel; and A. Cooper, "A Strategic Model of the U.S. Brewing Industry: 1951–1971." *Academy of Management Journal*, 1978.

[6]M. Porter, *Competitive Strategy*, 1980, pp. 129–55.

Japanese were exporting more sets abroad (66 percent of production) than they were selling at home. Two-thirds of such exports went to the United States.[7] Eventually, the Japanese achieved economies of volume that enabled them to undercut the U.S. competitors. Those U.S. firms that survived clearly became little-league firms in a more international industry.

SWITCHING LEAGUES

Figure 6 employs Porter's U-shaped interpretation of the market share/ROI relationship to describe the switch of leagues discussed above. Porter argues that if the relationship between market share and ROI were extended to cover the smaller firms, one would find that it was U-shaped. This reflects the fact that many of the smaller firms and not just the giants enjoy high ROIs. It is the firms in between, neither large enough to enjoy the advantages of large size nor small enough to make use of advantages associated with small size, that are in trouble.[8]

In terms of the national competitors, their relative size would vary with the scope of the industry. As illustrated in Figure 6, within a national industry, the national competitors (such as those previously discussed) would find that they were large enough to qualify as big-league competitors.

However, if the market, for whatever reason, became international, many of these same firms would find their position changed. The successful ones would adjust their strategies and size to the new international environment, and gain a return to profitability. The less successful ones would (like BL) fall in between—enjoying neither the advantages of being small nor the advantages of being large.

The changeover of an industry from national to international scope is characterized by a major shakeout and industry realignment of company strategies. National competitors that do not adopt to the new competitive environment with its international competition are likely to go under. Two major options are open to them:

1. Attain the size and international organization necessary to join the big league. A good number of European national industries have taken this course, often with the assistance and blessings of government, to attain the larger size required in light of international competition. Many firms are presently engaged in such increases in size. The recipe here usually involves extensive mergers and amalgamations to attain the larger size required by changing industry conditions. The German firms Grundig and AEG are examples of firms currently caught up in this process.
2. Realign the firm's national strategy, based as it is on national competition in

---

[7]W. V. Rapp, "Strategy Formulation and International Competition." *Columbia Journal of World Business,* Summer 1973.

[8]Porter, p. 43.

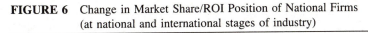

FIGURE 6   Change in Market Share/ROI Position of National Firms
(at national and international stages of industry)

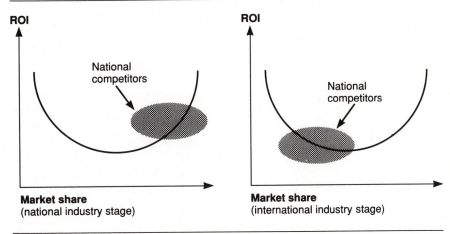

the national big league, to the new reality of international competition in the international little league.

BIG-LEAGUE AND LITTLE-LEAGUE STRATEGIES IN INTERNATIONAL INDUSTRIES

While it is not possible to outline the strategy appropriate to a group of firms in any detail, it is possible to point to a few common attributes that appear to be associated with strategies appropriate to big- and little-league competitors in industries that have become international.

The Big-League Firms

Strategies for the big-league firms in international industries are characterized by the following:

1. Pricing, production, and marketing aimed at high-volume mass markets defined on a multinational basis.
2. Design, research, and production aimed at making maximum use of economies of scale and accumulated volume.
3. Facilities of multinational firms engaged in these operations are operated as part of a single system, irrespective of national boundaries. This calls for an internationally integrated approach to production, marketing, and research.

4. The firm's environmental opportunities and competition are interpreted on a regional and/or global basis.
5. The firm cultivates an international image and reputation.

Little-League Competitors

Elements of little-league strategies include:

- Specialization. Adam Smith pointed out long ago that the degree of specialization was determined by the size of the market. Other things remaining the same, industry internationalization means a larger market for specialists. At the same time, it avoids direct competition with big-league firms. Specialization may take any one or all of the following forms:

    Specialization of product (e.g., Ferranti's specialization in custom-built integrated circuits). Specialization of technology. Certain technologies and subtechnologies do not lend themselves to the high-volume product targets of the major-league competitors; these may be licensed or otherwise acquired by little-league firms.

    Specialization by geography. One, in effect, concentrates company efforts in those countries that, because of tariffs, government regulations, or other reasons, are not subject to the full force of major-league competition.
- Extensive resort to partnerships, technology exchange agreements, joint ventures, and links with other organizations to make the most effective use of the limited resources available to the smaller firm.
- Maximum use of national strengths. This usually occurs in the firm's home as points of leverage to secure agreements such as those noted above. This often refers to strengths in national distribution and sale to government.
- Resort to complementarities with major-league firms (e.g., ICL's switch to products that are plug-compatible with IBM's).
- Internationalize. The larger international market for specialized products is available only to those firms geared to take advantage of it.
- Avoid big-league firms. Steer clear of head-on competition with international big-league firms.

CONCLUSION

The three industries in the above examples were all predominantly international, having changed rapidly in recent years. Hence, it was, perhaps, not surprising that no positive relationship between national ROI and national market share was found.

More significantly, it was evident in all three cases that the internationalization of the industry had brought about major changes in the positioning of competitors and the appropriate competitive strategies. These changes were apparently not perceived by the management of the three national companies. It was only after a financial crises that two of these three firms changed their strategies to take into account the enlarged nature of their industry. All three cases indicate that the definition of which customers and competitors are to be included within management's operative definition of the firm's industry and market cannot be taken as either given or obvious. Identification of the scope of the industry is itself part of the strategic problem and a key aspect of strategy formulation.

This study also tends to confirm the Hatten-Schendel-Cooper findings on the difficulty of generalizing about industry strategies. Within any industry, strategies appropriate to one strategic group (or league) may not be appropriate for another. Identification of which competitive league the firm is in can provide considerable insight regarding the appropriate strategy. Mistaken notions about which league the firm is in may adversely affect strategic planning.

Finally, in the context of industries changing from national to international, the above points are interrelated. Identification of the firm's competitive league requires that management first defines the geographic boundaries of the industry.

What this article is about: This is an interview with Michael E. Porter of Harvard Business School about his research that examines why nations succeed in particular industries, and the implications for both governments and companies. He also discusses a lag in competitive thinking among U.S. managements.

2–11 Where the Excellence Is, An Across the Board Interview with Michael E. Porter of the Harvard Business School

Susan Sanderson

Susan Sanderson, a former Conference Board researcher is now with the School of Management at Rensselaer Polytechnic Institute

Across the Board: *In a recent interview, you stated that American corporations have developed a bunker mentality. Could you tell us what you meant?*

Michael Porter: As I work with American companies, I sense a number of attitudes. The first is that top management sees a lot of negative forces out there in the world. And they feel that foreign countries are using unfair tactics. We poor American companies are disadvantaged and threatened, and we don't have the same advantages that are provided by the governments and capital markets in other countries.

I have found a lack of confidence in many American managements about their ability to succeed against Japanese or other foreign competitors. This grows out of all the popular press about the problems of American competitiveness, the publicity surrounding the Japanese as being the great managers while America is the next Britain. To some extent, our brash, we-can-do-anything confidence has been replaced by an attitude of "My God, what's wrong with us? We have all these disadvantages."

Across the Board: *You see our willingness to take risks evaporating?*

SOURCE: *Across the Board* (September 1987), pp. 23–31.

Porter: "Evaporating" is too strong a word. But I see much more of a mixed record, much more unevenness in risk-taking in the business community.

Across the Board: *What do you think is behind some of American business'*
major strategic failures?

Porter: Complacency is the biggest sin. Too many American companies have been willing to accept where they were, have been satisfied with their products and performance, and have not had the urge to continue to improve.

The automobile industry is a good example. That industry was coasting along, doing okay, and earning solid returns. Product development wasn't proceeding very rapidly. Quality wasn't improving. Productivity wasn't improving. But there was a self-satisfaction, a sort of a complacency, that provided a window of opportunity for competitors.

Continual improvement, by contrast, is the Japanese philosophy. The Japanese say, "We can always do better. We can always automate more. We can always enhance our product line." It's the same in Germany. There is tremendous attention paid to making the product even better, to eliminating all problems, to providing outstanding service.

Of course, you also have this attitude in some of the best American companies. For example, when Wal-Mart faced a competitive challenge from warehouse stores, instead of moaning and groaning about how unfair and doomed to failure warehouse stores were, they entered the warehouse-store business themselves. They said: "Let's try this and see whether it's a good idea. If it is, we'll enter in a big way ourselves."

The second problem with American companies is that too many have confused restructuring with strategy. There has been a tremendous effort in the past five years, which I think has been positive, to close factories, cut costs, and trim employment.

But cutting is only half of strategy. The real essence of international success is building. Building comes from improvements in quality, from new products, from new services. It comes fundamentally from innovation. I think that American industry is going to have to make the transition from cutting to building if it's ultimately going to succeed.

Another common error from a strategic point of view has been imitating instead of innovating. In America we're developed a very faddish approach to management. There is always some new concept that's going to solve all problems, whether it be quality circles, employee involvement, corporate culture, or sticking to your knitting. American companies also tend to copy one another in droves. Every bank adopts "relationship banking," every media company buys a television station. You can't achieve competitive advantage through being like your competitors. You've got to strive for ways to be different.

Finally, so much of the energy has been consumed in diversification and acquisitions that American companies have paid too little attention to making the core businesses succeed. It requires a long lead time to be out there trying to perform better in that basic business. It's been all too easy to show hollow growth and progress through making deals.

None of these problems is structural or inherent. I think there is every prospect for American industry to be successful internationally. But we have fallen into some bad habits.

Across the Board: *A lot of the recent restructuring is really "down-sizing" and cutting back. What aspects of restructuring do you see as positive? Which ones are going to make companies much more competitive?*

Porter: The most positive aspects of restructuring involve boosting quality and productivity through installing modern manufacturing systems, advanced ware-housing and logistical techniques, and the like. Just closing factories to reduce capacity, just cutting workers who have been redundant for a long time, just shrinking bloated middle-management ranks—that's not positive. That's just curing past mistakes. What lays the groundwork for future success is accelerating the rate of improvement in such areas as quality and productivity.

Across the Board: *General Motors has made a tremendous investment in au-tomated techniques, but the investment doesn't seem to have paid off. How would you explain GM's lack of success after investing more than $40 billion in new technology in the past four or five years?*

Porter: GM is an interesting case. They have indeed invested very heavily in reequipping and upgrading their facilities. The problem has been how to make all those new assets work.

Many would say that the biggest problem with General Motors is hundreds of thousands of entrenched middle managers who won't change. General Motors has lacked Ford's commitment to work more effectively with its employees, to unleash a positive attitude on the factory floor. What this shows is that the best equipment and the best factories won't necessarily produce the best products.

As a student of strategy, I would also say that General Motors retreated fundamentally from its historical strategy in the process of trying to reduce its costs. Historically, General Motors was a differentiator. That is, it had a broad line of cars consisting of distinct models serving all segments of the market. It tried to command a premium price in each of those segments by being a little better through such things as better styling and better dealers. General Motors lost sight of differentiation as it pursued the cost advantage of the Japanese. The company ended up homogenizing its cars, putting Chevy engines in Buicks—we all know the story.

I think that General Motors started out making the best response to the auto crisis of any of the Big Three companies. Ironically, though, it lost sight of its strategy in the process and was never able to bridge the gap between the in-vestments and their implementation.

Across the Board: *In your previous books, you talk about the role of government, but you have been primarily interested in the problems of the firm. Having served on John Young's Presidential Commission on Industrial Competitiveness, are you now more interested in what government can do to solve these problems?*

Porter: The book I'm working on now seeks to answer the question: Why do firms from particular countries succeed in particular industries? I'm trying to take another look, I hope a new look, at the theory of comparative advantage. What gives a country an advantage in a particular business? Why are the Germans so strong in chemicals and high-performance cars? Why are the Americans so dominant in health-related products? Why are the Japanese so strong in consumer electronics? We see a striking clustering of leaders in many industries in one or two particular countries. No country is successful in everything. I'm trying to understand why.

Across the Board: *How does your research approach differ from other studies that have been done?*

Porter: Most studies of international competitiveness of nations have been too macroeconomic in their orientation. They've tried to look at the country as a whole and make broad, general statements about a nation's competitiveness based on such macroeconomic variables as exchange rates, and to assume a vital role for government policy. My experience and research tell me that this is only part of the story, perhaps a small part.

The striking differences in the composition of economies in different countries suggests that there are important microeconomic factors at work. International success can be fully understood only by looking at a particular business and explaining a country's success in that business. I take a bottoms-up approach to competitiveness, whereas most of the research has been taking a top-down approach.

I have a growing conviction that the whole idea of a competitive nation is without any meaning. There are no competitive nations, only those that are competitive in some things and uncompetitive in others. The hope is that a nation can be competitive in enough industries to employ its work force and support a rising standard of living.

Across the Board: *How, specifically, did you go about investigating the factors in a country that promote competitiveness in a given industry?*

Porter: I picked a sample of countries that had wide variations in just about everything: government policy, size, location, culture, and so on. My final sample consists of 10 countries: West Germany, Japan, the United States, Sweden, Switzerland, Denmark, Italy, the United Kingdom, Singapore, and Korea.

In each country I've had a research team and a sponsor or a host. The Harvard Business School has funded the project, but I've also gotten support from various institutions around the world. In Germany it's the Deutsche Bank; in Japan it's Hitotsubashi University and MITI; in Sweden it's the Stockholm School of Economics; in England it's *The Economist*. The research assistants who are helping me conduct the work are nationals of the countries. I have been on a shuttle-diplomacy exercise all year, trying to sort this all out.

In each country I set out to do two things. The first was to use statistical data to identify every industry in the economy that, by various measures, was internationally successful. In my study, international success was a function of substantial exports or foreign investment based on skills and expertise created in the home country. For a large country such as Germany, there are hundreds of competitive industries. When I say industry, I'm talking about well-defined industries, such as tape recorders or high-performance cars, not broad aggregates, such as chemicals or steel.

Across the Board: *You seem to be saying that international trade and international investment are very closely linked.*

Porter: The old notion that trade and investment are separate phenomena is no longer true. Firms that compete globally use trade and foreign investment in tandem. They move goods and components around between countries and establish foreign plants or research centers as part of a global system.

Across the Board: *What conclusions have you reached about the theory of comparative advantage? Do you think it still applies?*

Porter: The classical theory of comparative advantage was based on the notion that a nation has an endowment of factors of production—land, labor, and capital—which differ across countries. This tended to give some nations a relative advantage in producing certain types of goods that were traded with other nations.

The more I observed international competition, the more it seemed that the classical model doesn't hold very well anymore. You don't need to have a steel industry in your country to buy steel. You don't need to have bauxite mines to be able to build an aluminum smelter. Markets are global and information flows freely. International firms can locate their plants anywhere in a nation. The link between the factors of production to capture the advantages of low-cost labor and the international success of a nation's companies seemed to have been broken.

At the same time, however, there is the strong country effect in practice. The leaders in many industries are all firms based in one or two countries. Thus, the paradox was: If it isn't the factor endowment suggested by the classical theory that determines why nations succeed in particular businesses, what is it?

Once we identified all the competitive industries in each country, we conducted interviews with government officials, bankers, and business leaders to try to get an overall picture of the economy. We also did analysis of the links among the competitive sectors. For each country we prepared what we call a clustering diagram that lays out all the competitive sectors on one big chart and shows where in the economy the pockets of success are.

One of the very strong findings of the research is that the competitive industries in an economy tend to be connected in a variety of ways. In Denmark, for example, virtually all the industries in which the country is internationally competitive have something to do with a cluster of food-related businesses. There are food products themselves, machinery to make food, chemicals used in processing food, and so on. There is another competitive cluster in Denmark in the area of housing and household products—furniture, chemicals to make furniture, various kinds of other household-related items. The same pattern holds in all economies, though in big countries, such as the United States, there are a whole lot of clusters.

The second step in the research was to select from the pockets of competitiveness in the economies representative industries to examine in detail. We then went back as far as the 14th century if we needed to, to understand why the industry started in that country, how it developed, how it grew, when it started exporting, and when it became internationally successful. Case studies were prepared for 8 to 20 industries in the country, depending on the size of the economy. In total there are roughly 120 of these longitudinal case studies.

Across the Board: *What have you concluded about the role of government in promoting competitiveness?*

Porter: The government's role is smaller than I expected when I started, and smaller than the conventional wisdom assumes. When you get away from the few highly visible industries that are studied over and over, such as cars and semiconductors, the role of government is frequently almost nonexistent.

Across the Board: *What are the real levers of competitiveness in an industry? Doesn't an advantage in labor, resources, or capital count heavily?*

Porter: It's important for a nation to possess relevant factors of production for the industry. But today the relevant factors of production are not inherited, they are created. They are such things as a particular pocket of scientific expertise, a particular kind of skilled work force, a particular kind of infrastructure or telecommunications system. Those sorts of things are created by both public investment and private investment. The important thing today is to understand how factors are created.

Another area—perhaps the most important of all—is the characteristics of the demand for the product or service in the home country. We find that the nature of local demand has a profound impact on the strategies chosen by the local firms, on the kind of products they produce, and, in turn, on their ability to succeed internationally. And a large home market is not necessarily an advantage. Sometimes it is, sometimes it isn't.

Across the Board: *Can you give examples?*

Porter: You might be shocked to know that Switzerland has a number of the world's leading companies in equipment for the production of paper products and the printing of newspapers. Hard to understand? It's not. Switzerland was the first country to face labor shortages after World War II. The newspapers there were the first to try to automate, while newspapers in most other countries were tied up in union restrictions. Also, the consumer in Switzerland or Germany demands that a paper doesn't have tears, rips, or smudges. If a torn paper is delivered, the customer will call up and say, "Take it back, I don't want it." Manufacturers had to come up with equipment that handled the papers without damaging them in the process.

Across the Board: *Don't you think that antitrust laws hamper American companies in global competition?*

Porter: On the contrary, I believe strongly that the current directions in antitrust policy have gone too far.

There's a view today that since competition is global, it doesn't matter if there are a lot of mergers in the home country. Yet in my study I found that the most competitive industries in a country were ones in which there were three or four (or more) domestic rivals fighting it out. The view that says you must merge to be efficient doesn't seem to hold.

Look at Germany's real strengths. There are many competing chemical companies, five automakers, and five or six firms manufacturing printing presses. Even in tiny Sweden, a country with eight million people, there are two car companies, two truck companies, and two major producers of mining equipment.

Across the Board: *One of the things that multinational firms seem to be trying to do today is expand their domestic markets by operating in other major countries and getting a window on new technology. Is it possible for any multinational to be really successful without operating in the three major markets—Europe, the United States, and Japan?*

Porter: First of all, we've got to make a distinction between a multinational and a global company. There are a lot of companies today that are multinational in the sense that they have facilities and other investments in many countries. But just being a multinational today isn't enough. To be successful, companies must find a way to integrate and get competitive advantage from their "multinationalness." In one of my books I make a distinction between global and "multidomestic" competition as a way of capturing this distinction.

One cannot be tied to manufacturing in any one country, to doing research in any one country, or to competing in any one country. There is really no excuse anymore for saying that local labor costs are too high, or that currency is overvalued. That's only a sign of inertia. The best companies view their strategies in global terms. But having said that, my research has shown the continued importance of the home country: the country where the strategy is set. What happens if you're in the wrong home country? The answer is that a company has got to use its multinationalness to overcome that.

Across the Board: *Any examples?*

Porter: Take Denmark, which has been very strong in anything related to fermentation. Novo Industries is number one or two in the world in insulin and industrial enzymes. Novo recognizes that Japan has become the major center of research in biotechnology, so Novo has been very aggressive in establishing research facilities in Japan. In electronics, many Japanese companies have long had outposts in Silicon Valley and the Route 128 area of Boston, where they do research.

If I wanted to summarize, in two words, what it takes to be internationally competitive, it's "constant innovation." That means constantly creating new products and new processes in a way that reflects evolving buyer needs. You don't do this by getting government subsidies and you don't generally succeed at this if you have government protection. In fact, that boomerangs. You get it by being exposed to the cold, harsh winds of competition.

Many companies don't realize this. They think it would be better to buy their competitors. They think that this would make them bigger and stronger to deal with foreign rivals. Over and over again, however, we see that it doesn't work that way. You're much better off having that local competitor and worrying about him all the time—trying to figure out how to keep doing a little bit better, a little bit better. That's the key to international success.

Across the Board: *What role do you see international joint ventures and strategic alliances playing in this?*

Porter: I'm somewhat bearish on alliances. I think that too many companies view strategic alliances as a way of solving their competitive problems. Although we don't have complete data on this, our observations tell us that many alliances are short-lived. There are some fairly obvious reasons for that. First, there is the organizational complexity of dealing with an independent company. Second, there's the natural tendency for one partner to become a competitor, or see itself as a competitor.

I believe that many companies have embraced alliances too quickly, and that probably too many of them have been formed. It's become another fad. The best alliances have a very narrow purpose. That is, they are built around a particular product, a particular country, a particular technology, or a particular problem. In some alliances, each side brings some significant long-term benefit to the party. But when there's asymmetry—when, say, one firm is bringing all the competitive assets and the other is bringing money—the alliance can dissolve very quickly.

A company must have within its own organization the capacity, the skills, and the resources in all the critical areas of business. You cannot rely on an alliance partner to provide them. An alliance can be a step along the way, if you will, but it's generally not a solution.

Across the Board: *Some firms are talking about becoming "fast followers" rather than innovators. They're less willing to put a lot of money into R&D, they want the Japanese and other people to do it. Do you think American firms can be good fast followers?*

Porter: The fast-follower approach has a long history of success. It demands that a firm set out to be the low-cost producer of products equivalent to those of the market leader. There is no reason that American companies can't pursue that strategy when appropriate. Some have done it for years, and always will. But in most industries, you have to question whether U.S. firms are equipped to be fast followers of Japanese firms.

We know that the root of much Japanese success is an ability to commercialize quickly; they have had an enormous advantage in terms of the time needed to develop and introduce new products, a great sense of teamwork, and a philosophy of continual improvement. It's hard to see how just adopting the fast-follower approach will mean that American companies acquire those strengths. If I were an American management team, the last thing I would do, except in a few cases, would be to abandon innovation and become a fast follower. The United States still has a compelling lead in terms of its scientific establishment, the university system, and access to capital for research.

It's easy to overstate the breadth and depth of America's competitiveness problem. I think that there are many interesting things going on in the United States. We continue to have a very vibrant and innovative economy. Our situation is not at all analogous to Britain's. Having said that, I think that there are many things that many companies need to do to improve their strategies and their attitudes, but I don't think the answer is to become a fast follower.

Across the Board: *You were recently in Japan. How are the Japanese dealing with the high value of the yen?*

Porter: Every American executive ought to go to Japan right now and see firsthand answers to this question. When the American dollar went through a long period of rise, one heard a lot of moaning and groaning in American industry. A certain amount of out-sourcing took place. But I would characterize the reaction as a very slow and very modest one.

By contrast, it's striking to see the Japanese reaction to the rising yen. Japanese are very much doomsday-oriented. They're always talking about how terrible their circumstances are. But there is an incredible drive and dedication to do something about it.

When the energy crisis hit in the 1970s, the Japanese made a herculean effort to reduce energy consumption. The same thing is happening today in response to the rising yen. Within weeks or months we saw companies adopting vigorous campaigns to improve productivity. We see very rapid movement of certain manufacturing activities to other nations. We see executives reducing their own salaries. At the same time, Japanese companies have made great efforts to upgrade quality and get into higher market segments, where pricing is not so crucial.

As I told my Japanese colleagues in a number of speeches this spring, I think the yen revaluation is the greatest thing that's happened to Japan in several years. Not only is it propelling them strategically to the next stage of the development of their economy, but it is creating the kind of shock necessary to make progress on the trade problem. It also has some faint hope of breaking a policy gridlock created by agricultural and housing interests, which have combined to keep land prices high, hold down the standard of living, and bleed off a lot of Japanese resources to support inefficient agricultural production. The government has never had enough power to break this gridlock. It may still not have enough power, because the Japanese government is very weak compared with even our government. But I believe that whatever unemployment is generated by out-migration of manufacturing and foreign investment of Japanese companies can easily be absorbed by the new activities that will grow out of a rising domestic standard of living. The Japanese response to the yen revaluation is a great lesson in how to manage companies.

A very similar thing happened in Germany in the early 1980s. The German trade balance shrank. Immediately, there was a national debate and soul-searching about what was wrong and what Germany needed to do. A whole series of reforms were put in place, in education and a variety of other fields. It was all front-page news. In America, our first trade problems cropped up in the early part of the 1970s, but it wasn't until, I'd say, January of this year that competitiveness became a premier issue. That was 15 years after the first signs of the problem.

Given the diversity of America, its breadth and size and political structure, perhaps it takes a long time to really galvanize behind something. Let's hope it's starting to happen.

Part III

Strategic Analysis in Diversified Companies

Section 3 presents six articles that address some of the issues facing strategic managers in diversified companies. Setting the stage for this section is Michael Porter's discussion of the "dismal" track record of corporate strategies. Roland Calori draws on his study of 27 diversified companies to offer insights about how companies manage diversity successfully. The next two articles deal with the timely subject of acquisitions. Robert J. Perry offers "10 suggestions for acquisition success" and William Bain of Bain and Company, Inc., discusses 10 working principles that can help a firm that is seeking to diversify through acquisition. The last two articles in this section return to an international perspective. David Lei discusses the need for a broader definition of corporate strategy as U.S. companies enter the fight for global markets, and James Bolt discusses the factors most often evident in large corporations that have succeeded in the global business arena.

What this article is about: The record of corporate strategy over the last 30 years has been dismal. A study of the diversification moves of prominent companies—including acquisitions, joint ventures, and start-ups—shows that they sold off more than they kept. To ensure a better record in the future, companies must move away from hands-off strategies like portfolio management to more hands-on collaborative efforts that build on interlocking strengths of the organization's diverse units.

3–1 From Competitive Advantage to Corporate Strategy

Michael E. Porter

*Michael E. Porter is Professor of Business Administration
at the Harvard Business School*

Corporate strategy, the overall plan for a diversified company, is both the darling and the stepchild of contemporary management practice—the darling because CEOs have been obsessed with diversification since the early 1960s, the stepchild because almost no consensus exists about what corporate strategy is, much less about how a company should formulate it.

A diversified company has two levels of strategy: business-unit (or competitive) strategy and corporate (or companywide) strategy. Competitive strategy concerns how to create competitive advantage in each of the businesses in which a company competes. Corporate strategy concerns two different questions: what business the corporation should be in and how the corporate office should manage the array of business units.

Corporate strategy is what makes the corporate whole add up to more than the sum of its business-unit parts.

The track record of corporate strategies has been dismal. I studied the diversification records of 33 large, prestigious U.S. companies over the 1950 to 1986 period and found that most of them had divested many more acquisitions than they had kept. The corporate strategies of most companies have dissipated instead of created shareholder value.

The need to rethink corporate strategy could hardly be more urgent. By taking over companies and breaking them up, corporate raiders thrive on failed corporate

SOURCE: *Harvard Business Review* (May–June 1987), pp. 43–59.

strategy. Fueled by junk bond financing and growing acceptability, raiders can expose any company to any takeover, no matter how large or blue chip.

Recognizing past diversification mistakes, some companies have initiated large-scale restructuring programs. Others have done nothing at all. Whatever the response, the strategic questions persist. Those who have restructured must decide what to do next to avoid repeating the past; those who have done nothing must awake to their vulnerability. To survive, companies must understand what good corporate strategy is.

A SOBER PICTURE

While there is disquiet about the success of corporate strategies, none of the available evidence satisfactorily indicates the success or failure of corporate strategy. Most studies have approached the question by measuring the stock market valuation of mergers, captured in the movement of the stock prices of acquiring companies immediately before and after mergers are announced.

These studies show that the market values mergers as neutral or slightly negative, hardly cause for serious concern.[1] Yet the short-term market reaction is a highly imperfect measure of the long-term success of diversification, and no self-respecting executive would judge a corporate strategy this way.

Studying the diversification programs of a company over a long period of time is a much more telling way to determine whether a corporate strategy has succeeded or failed. My study of 33 companies, many of which have reputations for good management, is a unique look at the track record of major corporations. (For an explanation of the research, see the insert "Where the Data Come From.") Each company entered an average of 80 new industries and 27 new fields. Just over 70 percent of the new entries were acquisitions, 22 percent were start-ups, and 8 percent were joint ventures. IBM, Exxon, Du Pont, and 3M, for example, focused on start-ups, while ALCO Standard, Beatrice, and Sara Lee diversified almost solely through acquisitions (Figure 1 has a complete rundown).

My data paint a sobering picture of the success ratio of these moves (see Figure 2). I found that, on average, corporations divested more than half their acquisitions in new industries and more than 60 percent of their acquisitions in entirely new fields. Fourteen companies left more than 70 percent of all the acquisitions they had made in new fields. The track record in unrelated acquisitions is even worse—the average divestment rate is a startling 74 percent (see Figure 3). Even a highly respected company like General Electric divested a very high percentage of its acquisitions, particularly those in new fields. Com-

---

[1]The studies also show that sellers of companies capture a large fraction of the gains from merger. See Michael C. Jensen and Richard S. Ruback, "The Market for Corporate Control: The Scientific Evidence," *Journal of Financial Economics,* April 1983, p. 5, and Michael C. Jensen, "Takeovers: Folklore and Science," HBR November–December 1984, p. 109.

panies near the top of the list in Figure 2 achieved a remarkably low rate of divestment. Some bear witness to the success of well-thought-out corporate strategies. Others, however, enjoy a lower rate simply because they have not faced up to their problem units and divested them.

I calculated total shareholder returns (stock price appreciation plus dividends) over the period of the study for each company so that I could compare them with its divestment rate. While companies near the top of the list have above-average shareholder returns, returns are not a reliable measure of diversification success. Shareholder return often depends heavily on the inherent attractiveness of companies' base industries. Companies like CBS and General Mills had extremely profitable base businesses that subsidized poor diversification track records.

I would like to make one comment on the use of shareholder value to judge performance. Linking shareholder value quantitatively to diversification performance works only if you compare the shareholder value that is with the shareholder value that might have been without diversification. Because such a comparison is virtually impossible to make, my own measure of diversification success—the number of units retained by the company—seems to be as good an indicator as any of the contribution of diversification to corporate performance.

My data give a stark indication of the failure of corporate strategies.[2] Of the 33 companies, 6 had been taken over as my study was being completed (see note on Figure 2). Only the lawyers, investment bankers, and original sellers have prospered in most of these acquisitions, not the shareholders.

PREMISES OF CORPORATE STRATEGY

Any successful corporate strategy builds on a number of premises. These are the facts of life about diversification. They cannot be altered, and when ignored, they explain in part why so many corporate strategies fail.

Competition occurs at the business-unit level. Diversified companies do not compete; only their business units do. Unless a corporate strategy places primary attention on nurturing the success of each unit, the strategy will fail, no matter how elegantly constructed. Successful corporate strategy must grow out of and reinforce competitive strategy.

Diversification inevitably adds costs and constraints to business units. Obvious costs such as the corporate overhead allocated to a unit may not be as important

---

[2]Some recent evidence also supports the conclusion that acquired companies often suffer eroding performance after acquisition. See Frederick M. Scherer, "Mergers, Sell-Offs and Managerial Behavior," in *The Economics of Strategic Planning*, ed. Lacy Glen Thomas (Lexington, Mass.: Lexington Books, 1986), p. 143, and David A. Ravenscraft and Frederick M. Scherer, "Mergers and Managerial Performance," paper presented at the Conference on Takeovers and Contests for Corporate Control, Columbia Law School, 1985.

FIGURE 1 Diversification Profiles of 33 Leading U.S. Companies

Company	Number Total Entries	All Entries into New Industries	Percent Acquisitions	Percent Joint Ventures	Percent Start-ups	Entries into New Industries that Represented Entirely New Fields	Percent Acquisitions	Percent Joint Ventures	Percent Start-ups
ALCO Standard	221	165	99%	0%	1%	56	100%	0%	0%
Allied Corp.	77	49	67	10	22	17	65	6	29
Beatrice	382	204	97	1	2	61	97	0	3
Borden	170	96	77	4	19	32	75	3	22
CBS	148	81	67	16	17	28	65	21	14
Continental Group	75	47	77	6	17	19	79	11	11
Cummins Engine	30	24	54	17	29	13	46	23	31
Du Pont	80	39	33	16	51	19	37	0	63
Exxon	79	56	34	5	61	17	29	6	65
General Electric	160	108	47	20	33	29	48	14	38
General Foods	92	53	91	4	6	22	86	5	9
General Mills	110	102	84	7	9	27	74	7	19
W.R. Grace	275	202	83	7	10	66	74	5	21
Gulf & Western	178	140	91	4	6	48	88	2	10
IBM	46	38	18	18	63	16	19	0	81
IC Industries	67	41	85	3	12	17	88	6	6

ITT	246	178	89	2	9	50	92	0	8
Johnson & Johnson	88	77	77	0	23	18	56	0	44
Mobil	41	32	53	16	31	15	60	7	33
Procter & Gamble	28	23	61	0	39	14	79	0	21
Raytheon	70	58	86	9	5	16	81	19	6
RCA	53	46	35	15	50	19	37	21	42
Rockwell	101	75	73	24	3	27	74	22	4
Sara Lee	197	141	96	1	4	41	95	2	2
Scovill	52	36	97	0	3	12	92	0	8
Signal	53	45	67	4	29	20	75	0	25
Tenneco	85	62	81	6	13	26	73	8	19
3M	144	125	54	2	45	34	71	3	56
TRW	119	82	77	10	13	28	64	11	25
United Technologies	62	49	57	18	24	17	23	17	39
Westinghouse	129	73	63	11	26	36	61	3	36
Wickes	71	47	83	0	17	22	68	0	32
Xerox	59	50	66	6	28	18	50	11	39
Total	3,788	2,644				906			
Average	114.8	80.1	70.3%	7.9%	21.8%	27.4	67.9%	7.0%	25.9%

NOTE: Beatrice, Continental Group, General Foods, RCA, Scovill, and Signal were taken over as the study was being completed. Their data cover the period up through takeover but not subseuqent divestments.

213

FIGURE 2 Acquisition Track Records of Leading U.S. Diversifiers Ranked by Percent Divested

Company	All Acquisitions in New Industries	Percent Made by 1980 and Then Divested	Percent Made by 1975 and Then Divested	Acquisitions in New Industries that Represented Entirely New Fields	Percent Made by 1980 and Then Divested	Percent Made by 1975 and Then Divested
Johnson & Johnson	59	17%	12%	10	33%	14%
Procter & Gamble	14	17	17	11	17	17
Raytheon	50	17	26	13	25	33
United Technologies	28	25	13	10	17	0
3M	67	26	27	24	42	45
TRW	63	27	31	18	40	38
IBM	7	33	0*	3	33	0*
Du Pont	13	38	43	7	60	75
Mobil	17	38	57	9	50	50
Borden	74	39	40	24	45	50
IC Industries	35	42	50	15	46	44
Tenneco	50	43	47	19	27	33
Beatrice	198	46	45	59	52	51
ITT	159	52	52	46	61	61
Rockwell	55	56	57	20	71	71
Allied Corp.	33	57	45	11	40	80

Company						
Exxon	19		20*	5	80	50*
Sara Lee	135	62	65	39	80	76
General Foods	48	62	62	19	93	93
Scovill	35	63	77	11	64	70
Signal	30	64	63	15	70	67
ALCO Standard	164	65	70	56	72	76
W.R. Grace	167	65	70	49	71	70
General Electric	51	65	78	14	100	100
Wickes	38	67	72	15	73	70
Westinghouse	46	68	69	22	61	59
Xerox	33	71	79	9	100	100
Continental Group	36	71	72	15	60	60
General Mills	86	75	73	20	65	60
Gulf & Western	127	79	78	42	75	72
Cummins Engine	13	80	80	6	83	83
RCA	16	80	92	7	86	100
CBS	54	87	89	18	88	88
Total	2,021			661		
Average per company†	61.2	53.4%	56.5%	20.0	60.0%	61.5%

*Companies with three or fewer acquisitions by the cutoff year.
†Companies with three or fewer acquisitions by the cutoff year are excluded from the average to minimize statistical distortions.
NOTE: Beatrice, Continental Group, General Foods, RCA, Scovill, and Signal were taken over as the study was being completed. Their data cover the period up through takeover but not subsequent divestments.

FIGURE 3 Diversification Performance in Joint Ventures, Start-ups, and Unrelated Acquisitions
Companies in same order as in Figure 2

Company	Joint Ventures as a Percent of New Entries	Percent Made by 1980 and Then Divested	Percent Made by 1975 and Then Divested	Start-ups as a Percent of New Entries	Percent Made by 1980 and Then Divested	Percent Made by 1975 and Then Divested	Unrelated Acquisitions as a Percent of Total Acquisitions	Percent Made by 1980 and Then Divested	Percent Made by 1975 and Then Divested
Johnson & Johnson	0%	†	†	23%	14%	20%	0%	†	†
Procter & Gamble	0	†	†	39	0	0	9	†	†
Raytheon	9	60%	60%	5	50	50	46	40%	40%
United Technologies	18	50	50	24	11	20	40	0*	0*
3M	2	100*	100*	45	2	3	33	75	86
TRW	10	20	25	13	63	71	39	71	71
IBM	18	100*	†	63	20	22	33	100*	100*
Du Pont	16	100*	†	51	61	61	43	0*	0*
Mobil	16	33	33	31	50	56	67	60	100
Borden	4	33	33	19	17	13	21	80	80
IC Industries	3	100*	100*	13	80	30	33	50	50
Tenneco	6	67	67	13	67	80	42	33	40
Beatrice	1	†	†	2	0	0	63	59	53
ITT	2	0*	†	8	38	57	61	67	64
Rockwell	24	38	42	3	0	0	35	100	100
Allied Corp.	10	100	75	22	38	29	45	50	0*
Exxon	4	0	0	61	27	19	100	80	50*
Sara Lee	1	†	†	4	75	100*	41	73	73
General Foods	4	†	†	6	67	50	42	66	83
Scovill	0	†	†	3	100	100*	45	80	100
Signal	4	†	†	29	20	11	67	50	50
ALCO Standard	0	†	†	1	†	†	63	79	81
W.R. Grace	7	33	38	10	71	71	39	65	65
General Electric	20	20	33	33	33	44	36	100	100
Wickes	0	†	†	17	63	57	60	80	75
Westinghouse	11	0*	0*	26	44	44	36	57	67
Xerox	6	100*	100*	28	50	56	22	100	100

FIGURE 3 *(concluded)*

Company	Joint Ventures as a Percent of New Entries	Percent Made by 1980 and Then Divested	Percent Made by 1975 and Then Divested	Start-ups as a Percent of New Entries	Percent Made by 1980 and Then Divested	Percent Made by 1975 and Then Divested	Unrelated Acquisitions as a Percent of Total Acquisitions	Percent Made by 1980 and Then Divested	Percent Made by 1975 and Then Divested
Continental Group	6	67	67	17	14	0	40	83	100
General Mills	7	71	71	9	89	80	65	77	67
Gulf & Western	4	75	50	6	100	100	74	77	74
Cummins Engine	17	50	50	29	0	0	67	100	100
RCA	15	67	67	50	99	55	36	100	100
CBS	16	71	71	17	86	80	39	100	100
Average per company‡	7.9%	50.3%	48.9%	21.8%	44.0%	40.9%	46.1%	74.0%	74.4%

*Companies with two or fewer entries.
†No entries in this category.
‡Average excludes companies with two or fewer entries to minimize statistical distortions.
NOTE: Beatrice, Continental Group, General Foods, RCA, Scovill, and Signal were taken over as the study was being completed. Their data cover the period up through takeover but not subsequent divestments.

or subtle as the hidden costs and constraints. A business unit must explain its decisions to top management, spend time complying with planning and other corporate systems, live with parent company guidelines and personnel policies, and forgo the opportunity to motivate employees with direct equity ownership. These costs and constraints can be reduced but not entirely eliminated.

Shareholders can readily diversify themselves. Shareholders can diversify their own portfolios of stocks by selecting those that best match their preferences and risk profiles.[3] Shareholders can often diversify more cheaply than a corporation because they can buy shares at the market price and avoid hefty acquisition premiums.

These premises mean that corporate strategy cannot succeed unless it truly adds value—to business units by providing tangible benefits that offset the inherent costs of lost independence and to shareholders by diversifying in a way they could not replicate.

[3]This observation has been made by a number of authors. See, for example, Malcolm S. Salter and Wolf A. Weinhold, *Diversification Through Acquisition* (New York: Free Press, 1979).

PASSING THE ESSENTIAL TESTS

To understand how to formulate corporate strategy, it is necessary to specify the conditions under which diversification will truly create shareholder value. These conditions can be summarized in three essential tests:

1. The attractiveness test. The industries chosen for diversification must be structurally attractive or capable of being made attractive.
2. The cost-of-entry test. The cost of entry must not capitalize all the future profits.
3. The better-off test. Either the new unit must gain competitive advantage from its link with the corporation or vice versa.

Of course, most companies will make certain that their proposed strategies pass some of these tests. But my study clearly shows that when companies ignored one or two of them, the strategic results were disastrous.

How Attractive Is the Industry?

In the long run, the rate of return available from competing in an industry is a function of its underlying structure, which I have described in another HBR article.[4] An attractive industry with a high average return on investment will be difficult to enter because barriers are high, suppliers and buyers have only modest bargaining power, substitute products or services are few, and the rivalry among competitors is stable. An unattractive industry like steel will have structural flaws, including a plethora of substitute materials, powerful and price-sensitive buyers, and excessive rivalry caused by high fixed costs and a large group of competitors, many of whom are state supported.

Diversification cannot create shareholder value unless new industries have favorable structures that support returns exceeding the cost of capital. If the industry doesn't have such returns, the company must be able to restructure the industry or gain a sustainable competitive advantage that leads to returns well above the industry average. An industry need not be attractive before diversification. In fact, a company might benefit from entering before the industry shows its full potential. The diversification can then transform the industry's structure.

In my research, I often found companies had suspended the attractiveness test because they had a vague belief that the industry "fit" very closely with their own businesses. In the hope that the corporate "comfort" they felt would lead to a happy outcome, the companies ignored fundamentally poor industry structures. Unless the close fit allows substantial competitive advantage, however, such comfort will turn into pain when diversification results in poor return. Royal

---

[4]See Michael E. Porter, "How Competitive Forces Shape Strategy," *HBR* (March–April 1979), p. 86.

BOX 1
Where the Data Come From

We studied the 1950–1986 diversification histories of 33 large diversified U.S. companies. They were chosen at random from many broad sectors of the economy.

To eliminate distortions caused by World War II, we chose 1950 as the base year and then identified each business the company was in. We tracked every acquisition, joint venture, and start-up made over this period—3,788 in all. We classified each as an entry into an entirely new sector or field (financial services, for example), a new industry within a field the company was already in (insurance, for example), or a geographic extension of an existing product or service. We also classified each new field as related or unrelated to existing units. Then we tracked whether and when each entry was divested or shut down and the number of years each remained part of the corporation.

Our sources included annual reports, 10K forms, the F&S Index, and Moody's, supplemented by our judgment and general knowledge of the industries involved. In a few cases, we asked the companies specific questions.

It is difficult to determine the success of an entry without knowing the full purchase or start-up price, the profit history, the amount and timing of ongoing investments made in the unit, whether any write-offs or write-downs were taken, and the selling price and terms of sale. Instead, we employed a relatively simple way to gauge success: *whether the entry was divested or shut down*. The underlying assumption is that a company will generally not divest or close down a successful business except in a comparatively few cases. Companies divested many of the entries in our sample within five years, a reflection of disappointment with performance. Of the comparatively few divestments where the company disclosed a loss or a gain, the divestment resulted in a reported loss in more than half the cases.

The data in Figure 1 cover the entire 1950–1986 period. However, the divestment ratios in Figure 2 and Figure 3 do not compare entries and divestments over the entire period because doing so would overstate the success of diversification. Companies usually do not shut down or divest new entries immediately but hold them for some time to give them an opportunity to succeed. Our data show that the average holding period is five to slightly more than ten years, though many divestments occur within five years. To accurately gauge the success of diversification, we calculated the percentage of entries made by 1975 and by 1980 that were divested or closed down as of January 1987. If we had included more recent entries, we would have biased upward our assessment of how successful these entries had been.

As compiled, these data probably understate the rate of failure. Companies tend to announce acquisitions and other forms of new entry with a flourish but divestments and shutdowns with a whimper, if at all. We have done our best to root out every such transaction, but we have undoubtedly missed some. There may also be new entries that we did not uncover, but our best impression is that the number is not large.

Dutch Shell and other leading oil companies have had this unhappy experience in a number of chemicals businesses, where poor industry structures overcame the benefits of vertical integration and skills in process technology.

Another common reason for ignoring the attractiveness test is a low entry cost. Sometimes the buyer has an inside track or the owner is anxious to sell. Even if the price is actually low, however, a one-shot gain will not offset a perpetually poor business. Almost always, the company finds it must reinvest in the newly acquired unit, if only to replace fixed assets and fund working capital.

Diversifying companies are also prone to use rapid growth or other simple indicators as a proxy for a target industry's attractiveness. Many that rushed into fast-growing industries (personal computers, video games, and robotics, for example) were burned because they mistook early growth for long-term profit potential. Industries are profitable not because they are sexy or high tech; they are profitable only if their structures are attractive.

What Is the Cost of Entry?

Diversification cannot build shareholder value if the cost of entry into a new business eats up its expected returns. Strong market forces, however, are working to do just that. A company can enter new industries by acquisition or start-up. Acquisitions expose it to an increasingly efficient merger market. An acquirer beats the market if it pays a price not fully reflecting the prospects of the new unit. Yet multiple bidders are commonplace, information flows rapidly, and investment bankers and other intermediaries work aggressively to make the market as efficient as possible. In recent years, new financial instruments such as junk bonds have brought new buyers into the market and made even large companies vulnerable to takeover. Acquisition premiums are high and reflect the acquired company's future prospects—sometimes too well. Philip Morris paid more than four times book value for 7-Up Company, for example. Simple arithmetic meant that profits had to more than quadruple to sustain the preacquisition ROI. Since there proved to be little Phillip Morris could add in marketing prowess to the sophisticated marketing wars in the soft-drink industry, the result was the unsatisfactory financial performance of 7-Up and ultimately the decision to divest.

In a start-up, the company must overcome entry barriers. It's a real catch-22 situation, however, since attractive industries are attractive because their entry barriers are high. Bearing the full cost of the entry barriers might well dissipate any potential profits. Otherwise, other entrants to the industry would have already eroded its profitability.

In the excitement of finding an appealing new business, companies sometimes forget to apply the cost-of-entry test. The more attractive a new industry, the more expensive it is to get into.

Will the Business Be Better Off?

A corporation must bring some significant competitive advantage to the new unit, or the new unit must offer potential for significant advantage to the corporation. Sometimes, the benefits to the new unit accrue only once, near the time of entry, when the parent instigates a major overhaul of its strategy or installs a first-rate management team. Other diversification yields ongoing competitive advantage if the new unit can market its product, through the well-developed distribution system of its sister units, for instance. This is one of the important underpinnings of the merger of Baxter Travenol and American Hospital Supply.

When the benefit to the new unit comes only once, the parent company has no rationale for holding the new unit in its portfolio over the long term. Once the results of the one-time improvement are clear, the diversified company no longer adds value to offset the inevitable costs imposed on the unit. It is best to sell the unit and free up corporate resources.

The better-off test does not imply that diversifying corporate risk creates shareholder value in and of itself. Doing something for shareholders that they can do themselves is not a basis for corporate strategy. (Only in the case of a privately held company, in which the company's and the shareholder's risk are the same, is diversification to reduce risk valuable for its own sake.) Diversification of risk should be only a by-product of corporate strategy, not a prime motivator.

Executives ignore the better-off test most of all or deal with it through arm waving or trumped-up logic rather than hard strategic analysis. One reason is that they confuse company size with shareholder value. In the drive to run a bigger company, they lose sight of their real job. They may justify the suspension of the better-off test by pointing to the way they manage diversity. By cutting corporate staff to the bone and giving business units nearly complete autonomy, they believe they avoid the pitfalls. Such thinking misses the whole point of diversification, which is to create shareholder value rather than to avoid destroying it.

CONCEPTS OF CORPORATE STRATEGY

The three tests for successful diversification set the standards that any corporate strategy must meet; meeting them is so difficult that most diversification fails. Many companies lack a clear concept of corporate strategy to guide their diversification or pursue a concept that does not address the tests. Others fail because they implement a strategy poorly.

My study has helped me identify four concepts of corporate strategy that have been put into practice—portfolio management, restructuring, transferring skills, and sharing activities. While the concepts are not always mutually exclusive, each rests on a different mechanism by which the corporation creates shareholder value and each requires the diversified company to manage and organize itself in a different way. The first two require no connections among business units; the second two depend on them. (See Figure 4). While all four concepts of strategy have succeeded under the right circumstances, today some make more sense than others. Ignoring any of the concepts is perhaps the quickest road to failure.

FIGURE 4   Concepts of Corporate Strategy

	Portfolio Management	*Restructuring*	*Transferring Skills*	*Sharing Activities*
Strategic prerequisites	Superior insight into identifying and acquiring undervalued companies	Superior insight into identifying restructuring opportunities	Proprietary skills in activities important to competitive advantage in target industries	Activities in existing units that can be shared with new business units to gain competitive advantage
	Willingness to sell off losers quickly or to opportunistically divest good performers when buyers are willing to pay large premiums	Willingness and capability to intervene to transform acquired units	Ability to accomplish the transfer of skills among units on an ongoing basis	Benefits of sharing that outweigh the costs
	Broad guidelines for and constraints on the types of units in the portfolio so that senior management can play the review role effectively	Broad similarities among the units in the portfolio	Acquisitions of beachhead positions in new industries as a base	Both start-ups and acquisitions as entry vehicles
	A private company or undeveloped capital markets	Willingness to cut losses by selling off units where restructuring proves unfeasible		Ability to overcome organizational resistance to business-unit collaboration
	Ability to shift away from portfolio management as the capital markets get more efficient or the company gets unwieldy	Willingness to sell units when restructuring is complete, the results are clear, and market conditions are favorable		

FIGURE 4 (*concluded*)

	Portfolio Management	*Restructuring*	*Transferring Skills*	*Sharing Activities*
Organizational prerequisites	Autonomous business units A very small, low-cost corporate staff Incentives based largely on business-unit results	Autonomous business units A corporate organization with the talent and resources to oversee the turnarounds and strategic repositionings of acquired units Incentives based largely on acquired units' results	Largely autonomous but collaborative business units High-level corporate staff members who see their role primarily as integrators Cross-business-unit committees, task forces, and other forums to serve as focal points for capturing and transferring skills Objectives of line managers that include skills transfer Incentives based in part on corporate results	Strategic business units that are encouraged to share activities An active strategic planning role at group, sector, and corporate levels High-level corporate staff members who see their roles primarily as integrators Incentives based heavily on group and corporate results
Common pitfalls	Pursuing portfolio management in countries with efficient capital marketing and a developed pool of professional management talent Ignoring the fact that industry structure is not attractive	Mistaking rapid growth or a "hot" industry as sufficieint evidence of a restructuring opportunity Lacking the resolve or resources to take on troubled situations and to intervene in management Ignoring the fact that industry structure is not attractive Paying lip service to restructuring but actually practicing passive portfolio management	Mistaking similarity or comfort with new businesses as sufficient basis for diversification Providing no practical ways for skills transfer to occur Ignoring the fact that industry structure is not attractive	Sharing for its own sake rather than because it leads to competitive advantage Assuming sharing will occur naturally without senior management playing an active role Ignoring the fact that industry structure is not attractive

Portfolio Management

The concept of corporate strategy most in use is portfolio management, which is based primarily on diversification through acquisition. The corporation acquires sound, attractive companies with competent managers who agree to stay on. While acquired units do not have to be in the same industries as existing units, the best portfolio managers generally limit their range of businesses in some way, in part to limit the specific expertise needed by top management.

The acquired units are autonomous, and the teams that run them are compensated according to unit results. The corporation supplies capital and works with each unit to infuse it with professional management techniques. At the same time, top management provides objective and dispassionate review of business-unit results. Portfolio managers categorize units by potential and regularly transfer resources from units that generate cash to those with high potential and cash needs.

In a portfolio strategy, the corporation seeks to create shareholder value in a number of ways. It uses its expertise and analytical resources to spot attractive acquisition candidates that the individual shareholder could not. The company provides capital on favorable terms that reflect corporatewide fund-raising ability. It introduces professional management skills and discipline. Finally, it provides high-quality review and coaching, unencumbered by conventional wisdom or emotional attachments to the business.

The logic of the portfolio management concept rests on a number of vital assumptions. If a company's diversification plan is to meet the attractiveness and cost-of-entry tests, it must find good but undervalued companies. Acquired companies must be truly undervalued because the parent does little for the new unit once it is acquired. To meet the better-off test, the benefits the corporation provides must yield a significant competitive advantage to acquired units. The style of operating through highly autonomous business units must both develop sound business strategies and motivate managers.

In most countries, the days when portfolio management was a valid concept of corporate strategy are past. In the face of increasingly well-developed capital markets, attractive companies with good managements show up on everyone's computer screen and attract top dollar in terms of acquisition premium. Simply contributing capital isn't contributing much. A sound strategy can easily be funded; small to medium-size companies don't need a munificent parent.

Other benefits have also eroded. Large companies no longer corner the market for professional management skills; in fact, more and more observers believe managers cannot necessarily run anything in the absence of industry-specific knowledge and experience. Another supposed advantage of the portfolio management concept—dispassionate review—rests on similarly shaky ground since the added value of review alone is questionable in a portfolio of sound companies.

The benefit of giving business units complete autonomy is also questionable. Increasingly, a company's business units are interrelated, drawn together by new technology, broadening distribution channels, and changing regulations. Setting strategies of units independently may well undermine unit performance. The companies in my sample that have succeeded in diversification have recognized the value of interrelationships and understood that a strong sense of corporate identity is as important as slavish adherence to parochial business-unit financial results.

But it is the sheer complexity of the management task that has ultimately defeated even the best portfolio managers. As the size of the company grows, portfolio managers need to find more and more deals just to maintain growth. Supervising dozens or even hundreds of disparate units and under chain-letter pressures to add more, management begins to make mistakes. At the same time, the inevitable costs of being part of a diversified company take their toll and unit performance slides while the whole company's ROI turns downward. Eventually, a new management team is installed that initiates wholesale divestments and pares down the company to its core businesses. The experiences of Gulf & Western, Consolidated Foods (now Sara Lee), and ITT are just a few comparatively recent examples. Reflecting these realities, the U.S. capital markets today reward companies that follow the portfolio management model with a "conglomerate discount"; they value the whole less than the sum of the parts.

In developing countries, where large companies are few, capital markets are undeveloped, and professional management is scarce, portfolio management still works. But it is no longer a valid model for corporate strategy in advanced economies. Nevertheless, the technique is in the limelight today in the United Kingdom, where it is supported so far by a newly energized stock market eager for excitement. But this enthusiasm will wane—as well it should. Portfolio management is no way to conduct corporate strategy.

Restructuring

Unlike its passive role as a portfolio manager, when it serves as banker and reviewer, a company that bases its strategy on restructuring becomes an active restructurer of business units. The new businesses are not necessarily related to existing units. All that is necessary is unrealized potential.

The restructuring strategy seeks out undeveloped, sick, or threatened organizations or industries on the threshold of significant change. The parent intervenes, frequently changing the unit management team, shifting strategy, or infusing the company with new technology. Then it may make follow-up acquisitions to build a critical mass and sell off unneeded or unconnected parts and thereby reduce the effective acquisition cost. The result is a strengthened company or a transformed industry. As a coda, the parent sells off the stronger unit once results are clear because the parent is no longer adding value and top management decides that its attention should be directed elsewhere. (See Box 2 for an example of restructuring.)

When well implemented, the restructuring concept is sound, for it passes the three tests of successful diversification. The restructurer meets the cost-of-entry

BOX 2
An Uncanny British Restructurer

Hanson Trust, on its way to becoming Britain's largest company, is one of several skillful followers of the restructuring concept. A conglomerate with units in many industries, Hanson might seem on the surface a portfolio manager. In fact, Hanson and one or two other conglomerates have a much more effective corporate strategy. Hanson has acquired companies such as London Brick, Ever Ready Batteries, and SCM, which the city of London rather disdainfully calls "low tech."

Although a mature company suffering from low growth, the typical Hanson target is not just in any industry; it has an attractive structure. Its customer and supplier power is low and rivalry with competitors moderate. The target is a market leader, rich in assets but formerly poor in management. Hanson pays little of the present value of future cash flow out in acquisition premium and reduces purchase price even further by aggressively selling off businesses that it cannot improve. In this way, it recoups just over a third of the cost of a typical acquisition during the first six months of ownership. Imperial Group's plush properties in London lasted barely two months under Hanson ownership, while Hanson's recent sale of Courage Breweries to Elders recouped £1.4 billion of the original £2.1 billion acquisition price of Imperial Group.

Like the best restructurers, Hanson approaches each unit with a modus operandi that it has perfected through repetition.

Hanson emphasizes low costs and tight financial controls. It has cut an average of 25 percent of labor costs out of acquired companies, slashed fixed overheads, and tightened capital expenditures. To reinforce its strategy of keeping costs low, Hanson carves out detailed one-year financial budgets with divisional managers and (through generous use of performance-related bonuses and share option schemes) gives them incentive to deliver the goods.

It's too early to tell whether Hanson will adhere to the last tenet of restructuring—selling turned-around units once the results are clear. If it succumbs to the allure of bigness, Hanson may take the course of the failed U.S. conglomerates.

---

test through the types of company it acquires. It limits acquisition premiums by buying companies with problems and lackluster images or by buying into industries with as yet unforeseen potential. Intervention by the corporation clearly meets the better-off test. Provided that the target industries are structurally attractive, the restructuring model can create enormous shareholder value. Some restructuring companies are Loew's, BTR, and General Cinema. Ironically, many of today's restructurers are profiting from yesterday's portfolio management strategies.

To work, the restructuring strategy requires a corporate management team with the insight to spot undervalued companies or positions in industries ripe for transformation. The same insight is necessary to actually turn the units around even though they are in new and unfamiliar businesses.

These requirements expose the restructurer to considerable risk and usually limit the time in which the company can succeed at the strategy. The most skillful proponents understand this problem, recognize their mistakes, and move decisively to dispose of them. The best companies realize they are not just acquiring companies but restructuring an industry. Unless they can integrate the acquisitions to create a whole new strategic position, they are just portfolio managers in disguise. Another important difficulty surfaces if so many other companies join the action that they deplete the pool of suitable candidates and bid their prices up.

Perhaps the greatest pitfall, however, is that companies find it very hard to dispose of business units once they are restructured and performing well. Human nature fights economic rationale. Size supplants shareholder value as the corporate goal. The company does not sell a unit even though the company no longer adds value to the unit. While the transformed units would be better off in another company that had related businesses, the restructuring company instead retains them. Gradually, it becomes a portfolio manger. The parent company's ROI declines as the need for reinvestment in the units and normal business risks eventually offset restructuring's one-shot gain. The perceived need to keep growing intensifies the pace of acquisition; errors result and standards fall. The restructuring company turns into a conglomerate with returns that only equal the average of all industries at best.

Transferring Skills

The purpose of the first two concepts of corporate strategy is to create value through a company's relationship with each autonomous unit. The corporation's role is to be a selector, a banker, and an intervenor.

The last two concepts exploit the interrelationships between businesses. In articulating them, however, one comes face-to-face with the often ill-defined concept of synergy. If you believe the text of the countless corporate annual reports, just about anything is related to just about anything else! But imagined synergy is much more common than real synergy. GM's purchase of Hughes Aircraft simply because cars were going electronic and Hughes was an electronics concern demonstrates the folly of paper synergy. Such corporate relatedness is an ex post facto rationalization of a diversification undertaken for other reasons.

Even synergy that is clearly defined often fails to materialize. Instead of cooperating, business units often compete. A company that can define the synergies it is pursuing still faces significant organizational impediments in achieving them.

But the need to capture the benefits of relationships between businesses has never been more important. Technological and competitive developments already link many businesses and are creating new possibilities for competitive advantage. In such sectors as financial services, computing, office equipment, entertainment, and health care, interrelationships among previously distinct businesses are perhaps the central concern of strategy.

To understand the role of relatedness in corporate strategy, we must give new meaning to this often ill-defined idea. I have identified a good way to start—the value chain.[5] Every business unit is a collection of discrete activities ranging from sales to accounting that allow it to compete. I call them value activities. It is at this level, not in the company as a whole, that the unit achieves competitive advantage.

I group these activities in nine categories. *Primary* activities create the product or service, deliver and market it, and provide after-sale support. The categories of primary activities are inbound logistics, operations, outbound logistics, marketing and sales, and service. *Support* activities provide the input and infrastructure that allow the primary activities to take place. The categories are company infrastructure, human resource management, technology development, and procurement.

The value chain defines the two types of interrelationships that may create synergy. The first is a company's ability to transfer skills or expertise among similar value chains. The second is the ability to share activities. Two business units, for example, can share the same sales force or logistics network.

The value chain helps expose the last two (and most important) concepts of corporate strategy. The transfer of skills among business units in the diversified company is the basis for one concept. While each business unit has a separate value chain, knowledge about how to perform activities is transferred among the units. For example, a toiletries business unit, expert in the marketing of convenience products, transmits ideas on new positioning concepts, promotional techniques, and packaging possibilities to a newly acquired unit that sells cough syrup. Newly entered industries can benefit from the expertise of existing units and vice versa.

These opportunities arise when business units have similar buyers or channels, similar value activities like government relations or procurement, similarities in the broad configuration of the value chain (for example, managing a multisite service organization), or the same strategic concept (for example, low cost). Even though the units operate separately, such similarities allow the sharing of knowledge.

Of course, some similarities are common; one can imagine them at some level between almost any pair of businesses. Countless companies have fallen into the trap of diversifying too readily because of similarities; mere similarity is not enough.

Transferring skills leads to competitive advantage only if the similarities among businesses meet three conditions:

1. The activities involved in the businesses are similar enough that sharing expertise is meaningful. Broad similarities (marketing intensiveness, for ex-

---

[5]Michael E. Porter, *Competitive Advantage* (New York: Free Press, 1985).

ample, or a common core process technology such as bending metal) are not a sufficient basis for diversification. The resulting ability to transfer skills is likely to have little impact on competitive advantage.

2. The transfer of skills involves activities important to competitive advantage. Transferring skills in peripheral activities such as government relations or real estate in consumer goods units may be beneficial but is not a basis for diversification.

3. The skills transferred represent a significant source of competitive advantage for the receiving unit. The expertise or skills to be transferred are both advanced and proprietary enough to be beyond the capabilities of competitors.

The transfer of skills is an active process that significantly changes the strategy or operations of the receiving unit. The prospect for change must be specific and identifiable. Almost guaranteeing that no shareholder value will be created, too many companies are satisfied with vague prospects or faint hopes that skills will transfer. The transfer of skills does not happen by accident or by osmosis. The company will have to reassign critical personnel, even on a permanent basis, and the participation and support of high-level management in skills transfer are essential. Many companies have been defeated at skills transfer because they have not provided their business units with any incentives to participate.

Transferring skills meets the tests of diversification if the company truly mobilizes proprietary expertise across units. This makes certain the company can offset the acquisition premium or lower the cost of overcoming entry barriers.

The industries the company chooses for diversification must pass the attractiveness test. Even a close fit that reflects opportunities to transfer skills may not overcome poor industry structure. Opportunities to transfer skills, however, may help the company transform the structures of newly entered industries and send them in favorable directions.

The transfer of skills can be one-time or ongoing. If the company exhausts opportunities to infuse new expertise into a unit after the initial postacquisition period, the unit should ultimately be sold. The corporation is no longer creating shareholder value. Few companies have grasped this point, however, and many gradually suffer mediocre returns. Yet a company diversified into well-chosen businesses can transfer skills eventually in many directions. If corporate management conceives of its role in this way and creates appropriate organizational mechanisms to facilitate cross-unit interchange, the opportunities to share expertise will be meaningful.

By using both acquisitions and internal development, companies can build a transfer-of-skills strategy. The presence of a strong base of skills sometimes creates the possibility for internal entry instead of the acquisition of a going concern. Successful diversifiers that employ the concept of skills transfer may, however, often acquire a company in the target industry as a beachhead and then build on it with their internal expertise. By doing so, they can reduce some of the risks of internal entry and speed up the process. Two companies that have diversified using the transfer-of-skills concept are 3M and Pepsico.

Sharing Activities

The fourth concept of corporate strategy is based on sharing activities in the value chains among business units. Procter & Gamble, for example, employs a common physical distribution system and sales force in both paper towels and disposable diapers. McKesson, a leading distribution company, will handle such diverse lines as pharmaceuticals and liquor through superwarehouses.

The ability to share activities is a potent basis for corporate strategy because sharing often enhances competitive advantage by lowering cost or raising differentiation. But not all sharing leads to competitive advantage, and companies can encounter deep organizational resistance to even beneficial sharing possibilities. These hard truths have led many companies to reject synergy prematurely and retreat to the false simplicity of portfolio management.

A cost-benefit analysis of prospective sharing opportunities can determine whether synergy is possible. Sharing can lower costs if it achieves economies of scale, boosts the efficiency of utilization, or helps a company move more rapidly down the learning curve. The costs of General Electric's advertising, sales, and after-sales service activities in major appliances are low because they are spread over a wide range of appliance products. Sharing can also enhance the potential for differentiation. A shared-order processing system, for instance, may allow new features and services that a buyer will value. Sharing can also reduce the cost of differentiation. A shared service network, for example, may make more advanced, remote servicing technology economically feasible. Often, sharing will allow an activity to be wholly reconfigured in ways that can dramatically raise competitive advantage.

Sharing must involve activities that are significant to competitive advantage, not just any activity. P&G's distribution system is such an instance in the diaper and paper towel business, where products are bulky and costly to ship. Conversely, diversification based on the opportunities to share only corporate overhead is rarely, if ever, appropriate.

Sharing activities inevitably involves costs that the benefits must outweigh. One cost is the greater coordination required to manage a shared activity. More important is the need to compromise the design or performance of an activity so that it can be shared. A salesperson handling the products of two business units, for example, must operate in a way that is usually not what either unit would choose were it independent. And if compromise greatly erodes the unit's effectiveness, then sharing may reduce rather than enhance competitive advantage.

Many companies have only superficially identified their potential for sharing. Companies also merge activities without consideration of whether they are sensitive to economies of scale. When they are not, the coordination costs kill the benefits. Companies compound such errors by not identifying costs of sharing in advance, when steps can be taken to minimize them. Costs of compromise can frequently be mitigated by redesigning the activity for sharing. The shared salesperson, for example, can be provided with a remote computer terminal to boost productivity and provide more customer information. Jamming business units together without such thinking exacerbates the costs of sharing.

Despite such pitfalls, opportunities to gain advantage from sharing activities have proliferated because of momentous developments in technology, deregulation, and competition. The infusion of electronics and information systems into many industries creates new opportunities to link businesses. The corporate strategy of sharing can involve both acquisition and internal development. Internal development is often possible because the corporation can bring to bear clear resources in launching a new unit. Start-ups are less difficult to integrate than acquisitions. Companies using the shared-activities concept can also make acquisitions as beachhead landings into a new industry and then integrate the units through sharing with other units. Prime examples of companies that have diversified via using shared activities include P&G, Du Pont, and IBM. The fields into which each has diversified are a cluster of tightly related units. Marriott illustrates both successes and failures in sharing activities over time.

Following the shared-activities model requires an organizational context in which business-unit collaboration is encouraged and reinforced. Highly autonomous business units are inimical to such collaboration. The company must put into place a variety of what I call horizontal mechanisms—a strong sense of corporate identity, a clear corporate mission statement that emphasizes the importance of integrating business-unit strategies, an incentive system that rewards more than just business-unit results, cross-business-unit task forces, and other methods of integrating.

A corporate strategy based on shared activities clearly meets the better-off test because business units gain ongoing tangible advantages from others within the corporation. It also meets the cost-of-entry test by reducing the expense of surmounting the barriers to internal entry. Other bids for acquisitions that do not share opportunities will have lower reservation prices. Even widespread opportunities for sharing activities do not allow a company to suspend the attractiveness test, however. Many diversifiers have made the critical mistake of equating the close fit of a target industry with attractive diversification. Target industries must pass the strict requirement test of having an attractive structure as well as a close fit in opportunities if diversification is to ultimately succeed.

CHOOSING A CORPORATE STRATEGY

Each concept of corporate strategy allows the diversified company to create shareholder value in a different way. Companies can succeed with any of the concepts if they clearly define the corporation's role and objectives, have the skills necessary for meeting the concept's prerequisites, organize themselves to manage diversity in a way that fits the strategy, and find themselves in an appropriate capital market environment. The caveat is that portfolio management is sensible only in limited circumstances.

A company's choice of corporate strategy is partly a legacy of its past. If its business units are in unattractive industries, the company must start from scratch. If the company has few truly proprietary skills or activities it can share in related diversification, then its initial diversification must rely on other concepts. Yet corporate strategy should not be a once-and-for-all choice but a vision that can evolve. A company should choose its long-term preferred concept and then proceed pragmatically toward it from its initial starting point.

Both the strategic logic and the experience of the companies I studied over the last decade suggest that a company will create shareholder value through diversification to a greater and greater extent as its strategy moves from portfolio management toward sharing activities. Because they do not rely on superior insight or other questionable assumptions about the company's capabilities, sharing activities and transferring skills offer the best avenues for value creation.

Each concept of corporate strategy is not mutually exclusive of those that come before, a potent advantage of the third and fourth concepts. A company can employ a restructuring strategy at the same time it transfers skills or shares activities. A strategy based on shared activities becomes more powerful if business units can also exchange skills. As the Marriott case illustrates, a company can often pursue the two strategies together and even incorporate some of the principles of restructuring with them. When it chooses industries in which to transfer skills or share activities, the company can also investigate the possibility of transforming the industry structure. When a company bases its strategy on interrelationships, it has a broader basis on which to create shareholder value than if it rests its entire strategy on transforming companies in unfamiliar industries.

My study supports the soundness of basing a corporate strategy on the transfer of skills or shared activities. The data on the sample companies' diversification programs illustrate some important characteristics of successful diversifiers. They have made a disproportionately low percentage of unrelated acquisitions, *unrelated* being defined as having no clear opportunity to transfer skills or share important activities (see Figure 3). Even successful diversifiers such as 3M, IBM, and TRW have terrible records when they have strayed into unrelated acquisitions. Successful acquirers diversify into fields, each of which is related to many others. Procter & Gamble and IBM, for example, operate in 18 and 19 interrelated fields, respectively, and so enjoy numerous opportunities to transfer skills and share activities.

Companies with the best acquisition records tend to make heavier-than-average use of start-ups and joint ventures. Most companies shy away from modes of entry besides acquisition. My results cast doubt on the conventional wisdom regarding start-ups. Figure 3 demonstrates that, while joint ventures are about as risky as acquisitions, start-ups are not. Moreover, successful companies often have very good records with start-up units, as 3M, P&G, Johnson & Johnson, IBM, and United Technologies illustrate. When a company has the internal strength to start up a unit, it can be safer and less costly to launch a company than to rely solely on an acquisition and then have to deal with the problem of integration. Japanese diversification histories support the soundness of start-up as an entry alternative.

My data also illustrate that none of the concepts of corporate strategy works when industry structure is poor or implementation is bad, no matter how related the industries are. Xerox acquired companies in related industries, but the businesses had poor structures and its skills were insufficient to provide enough competitive advantage to offset implementation problems.

An Action Program

To translate the principles of corporate strategy into successful diversification, a company must first take an objective look at its existing businesses and the value added by the corporation. Only through such an assessment can an understanding of good corporate strategy grow. That understanding should guide future diversification as well as the development of skills and activities with which to select further new businesses. The following action program provides a concrete approach to conducting such a review. A company can choose a corporate strategy by:

1.   Identifying the interrelationships among already existing business units.

A company should begin to develop a corporate strategy by identifying all the opportunities it has to share activities or transfer skills in its existing portfolio of business units. The company will not only find ways to enhance the competitive advantage of existing units but also come upon several possible diversification avenues. The lack of meaningful interrelationships in the portfolio is an equally important finding, suggesting the need to justify the value added by the corporation or, alternately, a fundamental restructuring.

2.   Selecting the core businesses that will be the foundation of the corporate strategy.

Successful diversification starts with an understanding of the core businesses that will serve as the basis for corporate strategy. Core businesses are those that are in an attractive industry, have the potential to achieve sustainable competitive advantage, have important interrelationships with other business units, and provide skills or activities that represent a base from which to diversify.

The company must first make certain its core businesses are on sound footing by upgrading management, internationalizing strategy, or improving technology. My study shows that geographic extensions of existing units, whether by acquisition, joint venture, or start-up, had a substantially lower divestment rate than diversification.

The company must then patiently dispose of the units that are not core businesses. Selling them will free resources that could be better deployed elsewhere. In some cases disposal implies immediate liquidation, while in others the company should dress up the units and wait for a propitious market or a particularly eager buyer.

3.   Creating horizontal organizational mechanisms to facilitate interrelationships among the core businesses and lay the groundwork for future related diversification.

Top management can facilitate interrelationships by emphasizing cross-unit collaboration, grouping units organizationally and modifying incentives, and taking steps to build a strong sense of corporate identity.

4.   Pursuing diversification opportunities that allow shared activities.

This concept of corporate strategy is the most compelling, provided a company's strategy passes all three tests. A company should inventory activities in existing business units that represent the strongest foundation for sharing, such as strong distribution channels or world-class technical facilities. These will in turn lead to potential new business areas. A company can use acquisitions as a beachhead or employ start-ups to exploit internal capabilities and minimize integrating problems.

5.   Pursuing diversification through the transfer of skills if opportunities for sharing activities are limited or exhausted.

Companies can pursue this strategy through acquisition, although they may be able to use start-ups if their existing units have important skills that can readily transfer.

Such diversification is often riskier because of the tough conditions necessary for it to work. Given the uncertainties, a company should avoid diversifying on the basis of skills transfer alone. Rather it should also be viewed as a stepping-stone to subsequent diversification using shared activities. New industries should be chosen that will lead naturally to other businesses. The goal is to build a cluster of related and mutually reinforcing business units. The strategy's logic implies that the company should not set the rate of return standards for the initial foray into a new sector too high.

6.   Pursuing a strategy of restructuring if this fits the skills of management or no good opportunities exist for forging corporate interrelationships.

When a company uncovers undermanaged companies and can deploy adequate management talent and resources to the acquired units, then it can use a restructuring strategy. The more developed the capital markets and the more active the market for companies, the more restructuring will require a patient search for that special opportunity rather than a headlong race to acquire as many bad apples as possible. Restructuring can be a permanent strategy, as it is with Loew's, or a way to build a group of businesses that supports a shift to another corporate strategy.

7.   Paying dividends so that the shareholders can be the portfolio managers.

Paying dividends is better than destroying shareholder value through diversification based on shaky underpinnings. Tax considerations, which some companies cite to avoid dividends, are hardly legitimate reasons to diversify if a company cannot demonstrate the capacity to do it profitably.

Creating a Corporate Theme

Defining a corporate theme is a good way to ensure that the corporation will create shareholder value. Having the right theme helps unite the efforts of business units and reinforces the ways they interrelate as well as guides the choice of new businesses to enter. NEC Corporation, with its "C&C" theme, provides a good example. NEC integrates its computer, semiconductor, telecommunications, and consumer electronics businesses by merging computers and communications.

It is all too easy to create a shallow corporate theme. CBS wanted to be an "entertainment company," for example, and built a group of businesses related to leisure time. It entered such industries as toys, crafts, musical instruments, sports teams, and hi-fi retailing. While this corporate theme sounded good, close listening revealed its hollow ring. None of these businesses had any significant opportunity to share activities or transfer skills among themselves or with CBS's traditional broadcasting and record businesses. They were all sold, often at significant losses, except for a few of CBS's publishing-related units. Saddled with the worst acquisition record in my study, CBS has eroded the shareholder value created through its strong performance in broadcasting and records.

Moving from competitive strategy to corporate strategy is the business equivalent of passing through the Bermuda Triangle. The failure of corporate strategy reflects the fact that most diversified companies have failed to think in terms of how they really add value. A corporate strategy that truly enhances the competitive advantage of each business unit is the best defense against the corporate raider. With a sharper focus on the tests of diversification and the explicit choice of a clear concept of corporate strategy, companies' diversification track records from now on can look a lot different.

Author's note: The research for this article was done with the able assistance of my research associate Cheng G. Ong. Malcolm S. Salter, Andrall E. Pearson, A. Michael Kechner, and the Monitor Company also provided helpful comments.

What this article is about: Diversity is the result of past diversification or merger. In the global competition and slow growth context of the 1980s, highly diversified companies have to manage diversity in order to benefit from it and to avoid its drawbacks. The benefits are compensation effects and cross-fertilization, and the drawbacks are dispersion of resources and internal inconsistencies. To balance integration and differentiation is the key success factor in managing highly diversified companies. This article is based on a field study among 27 diversified companies, most of them very successful, to find out how they manage diversity.

3–2 *How Successful Companies Manage Diverse Businesses*

Roland Calori and CESMA
*Professor Roland Calori is Head of the Business Policy Department
at Lyon Graduate School of Business
CESMA is the Centre d'Etudes Supérieures
en Management, Lyon, France*

From 1950 to 1975, product-market diversification of firms had been a major trend; highly diversified companies resulted from these cumulated diversification movements. These last 10 years, this trend has slowed down with the slowing down of growth and the globalization of the competition. Slow market growth makes it harder to get a share of a market (new entrants gain a share at the expense of the incumbent firms), and success in the global competition requires a "critical mass" for each competitor (consequently entry barriers and investments for holding position have risen up). Recent business stories tell more about cases of "recentrage," "refocusing," and "restructuring" (for instance see Bower[1]). This is probably also a symptom of problems in managing diversity.

In his pioneering work, Chandler[2] showed that structure follows strategy; more

SOURCE: *Long Range Planning* 21, no. 3 (June 1988), pp. 80–89.

Acknowledgments. The authors wish to acknowledge the important contribution of J. M. Ardisson of the Institut de Recherche de l'Entreprise, and all the participants from CESMA. They also wish to thank 3M France for their support of the study.

[1]J. L. Bower, *When Markets Quake: The Management Challenge of Restructuring Industry* (Boston, Mass.: Harvard Business School Press, 1986).

[2]A. D. Chandler, *Strategy and Structure* (Cambridge, Mass: M.I.T. Press, 1962).

precisely, companies which diversify their businesses tend to change their functional form structures into divisional form structures to manage several different businesses. On the other hand, Hall and Saias[3] have enlightened the influence of structure on strategy formulation. Strategy and structure should be consistent and designing the company's structure is a way to manage diversity.

Rumelt[4] studied the relationships between economic performance and diversity. He defined four generic types of business portfolio strategy: single business, dominant business, related business, and unrelated business (relatedness being defined in terms of products, markets, and technology). He demonstrated that related diversification outperforms the other diversification strategies, but the statistical relations were very weak.

Nathanson and Cassano[5] found that profitability decreases when "product diversity" increases, and that "market diversity" is not linked to profitability.

Then, should we believe in the Peters, and Waterman recipe for success: "Stick to the knitting"?[6]

Concerning mergers and acquisitions, Drucker[7] gave five rules: the acquired company should have a "common core of unity," there must be a contribution of skills to the acquired company, there must be a "temperamental fit," top management should be provided for the acquired company, and managers of both companies should receive substantial promotions from one company to the other. But according to Paine and Power,[8] Drucker's rules are conservative, there are many success stories violating them . . . the only key success factors are managers' information and skills and human relations during the implementation phase.

Some authors have focused on the organization of diversified companies; for instance Vancil and Lorange,[9] who worked on the strategic planning process, and Thietart and Horowitz,[10] who identified organizational success factors of diversified companies: decentralization and high commitment of the top management in the planning process (both factors related to profitability and growth).

---

[3]D. J. Hall, and M. A. Saias, "Les contraintes structurelles du processus stratégique," *Revenue Française de Gestion,* (Novembre/Décembre 1979), pp. 4–15.

[4]R. P. Rumelt, *Strategy, Structure, and Economic Performance,* Division of Research, Harvard University, 1974.

[5]D. Nathanson, and J. Cassano, "Organization, Diversity and Performance," *Wharton Magazine,* (Summer 1982), pp. 19–26.

[6]T. J. Peters, and R. H. Waterman, *In Search of Excellence* (New York: Harper & Row, 1982).

[7]P. F. Drucker, "The Five Rules of Successful Acquisition," *The Wall Street Journal,* October 15, 1981.

[8]F. T. Paine, and D. J. Power, "Merger Strategy: An Examination of Drucker's Five Rules for Successful Acquisitions," *Strategic Management Journal* 5, (April–June 1984), pp. 99–110.

[9]R. F. Vancil, and P. Lorange, "Strategic Planning in Diversified Companies," *Harvard Business Review* (January/February 1975), pp. 81–90.

[10]R. A. Thietart, and J. Horowitz, "Organiser la diversification," *Revue Française de Gestion,* (Mars/Avril 1980), pp. 30–35.

Daniels et al.[11] examined organization structures of 37 large U.S. multinationals which were highly diverse and involved abroad. They found five different structure types. The two more frequent ones are the "global product" and the "international divisions"; the most diverse companies (among which are the conglomerates) tend to have global product structures.

Godiwalla[12] has studied the planning systems in multinational companies following a multidomestic or a global strategy. He concluded that cultural, political, and legal differences make transfer of management "arts" and philosophies more difficult than the transference of management science and technology. Multinationals must blend their own goals with the host-country goals, aspirations, and culture if they are to be successful.

As a supplement to the current lines of research on the relations between diversity and performance, Prahalad and Bettis[13] use the concept of "dominant logic." The work of top management in diversified firms is a distinct skill and contributes to the success or failure. The top managers have cognitive schemas (resulting from their past experiences) influencing their decisions. The schema or the "dominant logic" of the "core business" should not influence the decisions on the other businesses if it does not fit. Consequently, a diversified firm should avoid businesses which need a different logic or create the capacity for multiple dominant logics (through sector-level executives, independent business units, new managers, etc.).

The "dominant logic" is something between managerial skills and corporate culture. Then, should the corporate culture be strong (i.e., homogeneous) as Peters and Waterman declared, or should business-level culture be dominant in diversified companies, as Sayles and Wright[14] argued?

Balancing centralization and autonomy, integration and differentiation seems to be the key management challenge of diversified companies. Our study was undertaken to gather more precise answers from the managers of diversified companies, and to find out some formulas of this "alchemy."

METHODOLOGY AND BASIC MODEL

We selected 200 large diversified companies established in France according to the Kompass directory (using two selection criteria: turnover and number of

[11]J. D. Daniels, R. A. Pitts, and M. J. Tretter, "Organizing for Dual Strategies of Product Diversity and International Expansion," *Strategic Management Journal* 6 (July–September 1985), pp. 224–37.

[12]Y. H. Godiwalla, "Multinational Planning—Developing a Global Approach," *Long Range Planning,* 19, no. 2 (1986), pp. 110–16.

[13]C. K. Prahalad, and R. A. Bettis, "The Dominant Logic: A New Linkage between Diversity and Performance," *Strategic Management Journal* 7 (November/December 1986), pp. 485–501.

[14]L. R. Sayles, and R. V. L. Wright, "The Use of Culture in Strategic Management," Center for Creative Leadership, *Issues and Observations* 5, no. 4 (November 1985), pp. 1–9.

business codes, and two quotas: product/services, French origin/foreign origin). Conglomerates with a single financial logic were not selected. Top managers were asked for in-depth interviews. Finally 27 companies participated in the study and our sample is relatively diverse (cf. Table 1): 12 French-origin industrial groups, 9 foreign-origin industrial groups, 4 French-origin service companies, 3 foreign-origin service companies (NB. ITT having significant business in both industrial and service sectors, is accounted for twice, in the partition).

From two to four members of the board of directors were interviewed in each company. Foreign-origin companies participated only through their French subsidiary, so there is certainly a bias coming from the partial perception from the subsidiary. Altogether 62 managers participated in the study.

Interviews lasted from 2 to 3 hours and were made up of four phases: a nondirective phase on the manager's perception of the diversity of the company, a directive phase on the diversity of the company (technologies, markets, required managerial skills, cultures), a nondirective phase on the company's formula for managing diversity, and a semidirective phase on the management of diversity in the company (current portfolio strategy, structure, human resources management, management of culture). Figure 1 gives a picture of our sketchy initial model.

For example, international job rotation is a way to manage diversity (it belongs

TABLE 1 Sample of Diversified Companies

	Origin	
Sector	*French (16)*	*Foreign (11)*
Industrial (21)	Salomon	Texas Instruments
	Empain Schneider	Du Pont de Nemours
	BSN	Olivetti
	Saint Louis Bouchon	Dow Chemical
	Schlumberger	Hewlett-Packard
	Moet Hennessy	Quaker
	L'Oreal	Staubli
	Rhone-Poulenc	3M
	Gerland	ITT
	Roussel Uclaf	
	CFP Total	
	Groupe Tapie	
Services (7)	Ecco	American Express
	Accor	Peat Marwick
	Société Lyonnaise des Eaux	ITT
	Europe 1 Communication	

FIGURE 1   A Model for the Management of Diversity

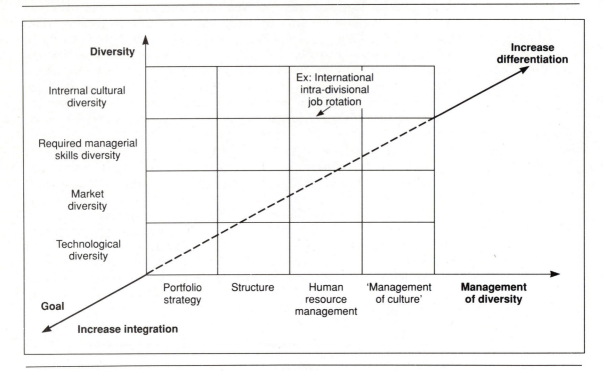

to the human resources management practices); it will reduce corporate internal cultural diversity and increase corporate integration and it might also increase innovation at the geographical business-unit level. All the management practices that we found in the field study could fit into this general model.

We shall present here only the major results concerning the whole sample; in the appendix, the case of 3M is briefly described in order to have a global view of the mix of the management practices of one company facing diversity.

Business Portfolio Strategy: Reaching the Critical Mass

Managing the business portfolio (with or without any "matrix") is an art as well as orcharding: There are conditions of success in pruning and grafting. Twenty-three companies in our sample are significantly changing their portfolio (January 1987); it is the most radical way to manage diversity just by changing it.

More than half of the companies in our sample are "refocusing" their portfolios: For example, Texas Instruments refocuses on semiconductor components, military applications, computers, and connectors, and ITT is refocusing on its most profitable businesses, particularly in the services sector. Many companies "refocus" to reach a critical mass in the priority businesses; for instance, it is the objective of Roussel Uclaf, which needs to reinforce its position on pharmaceutical specialties. The company's portfolio includes human health, veterinary products, phytosanitary products, chemicals, nutrition, perfumes, and spectacles. Roussel Uclaf is now looking for scale economies and sharing of resources (e.g., the same plant can produce human, animal, or vegetal specialties, and the same Research Analytic Service can serve several businesses), and the company is focusing on the "living world." According to M. Poite (Directeur de la Stratégie): "Markets are more and more open and international, new acquisitions are more and more difficult. As a consequence, large industrial groups are dividing the market, each competitor has to strengthen its position and focus on the main business to the prejudice of peripheral businesses." The problem is very similar to the one of R&D management: "A compromise should be found, considering the high uncertainty, budgets should be distributed among several programs, but a critical mass should also be reached on each program to increase the probability of success." Sometimes "refocusing" is the only way to correct past strategic diversification mistakes or bad surprises; then, this surgery should be done as early as possible. In our sample, we did not find any case of geographical "refocusing" and managers are very sceptical about the results of such movements. *The pure "refocus" strategy includes market and product extensions in the priority businesses as well as withdrawal from questionable businesses.* For instance, Quaker is involved in three broad business areas: grocery (breakfast, pet foods, energetic drinks), toys (Fisher Price), and sales by post (specialty retailing). Three criteria help in designing the portfolio of businesses: each brand must be leader or at least second on the market, differentiated consumer products, and high profitability. According to this philosophy and core businesses, Quaker sells some businesses in chemicals and restaurants but develops the cereal business (acquisition of Golden Grain) and the pet foods business (acquisition of Anderson Clayton) on a worldwide basis.

Several companies are still involved in diversification movements: Moet Hennessy, Salomon, American Express, Ecco, Société Lyonnaise des Eaux, and others. In most of the cases these *diversification movements are undertaken when the firm is already the leader in its core business:* Moet Hennessy was the world leader of champagne and cognac when it entered the horticultural market (acquisition of Delbart) and the perfume market (acquisition of Dior perfumes). Salomon diversified into ski shoes after dominating the ski fixations market; the more recent diversification into skis and golf (acquisition of Taylor Made) were not launched before Salomon had become the world co-leader in the ski shoes industry. At Salomon, this strategy can be partly explained by the wisdom and perfectionism of G. Salomon. Besides common sense, *"il ne faut pas lacher la proie pour l'ombre,"* there are some economic justifications for such a strategy. Diversification is generally a risky and costly operation, which should be balanced with the relative stability and profitability of the core businesses. In most of these cases, the financial resources of the candidates for diversification are sufficient to fund a massive entrance. Most of the current diversification movements of those companies fall into zone I of Figure 2, which gives a typology of

FIGURE 2   Typology of Diversification Movements

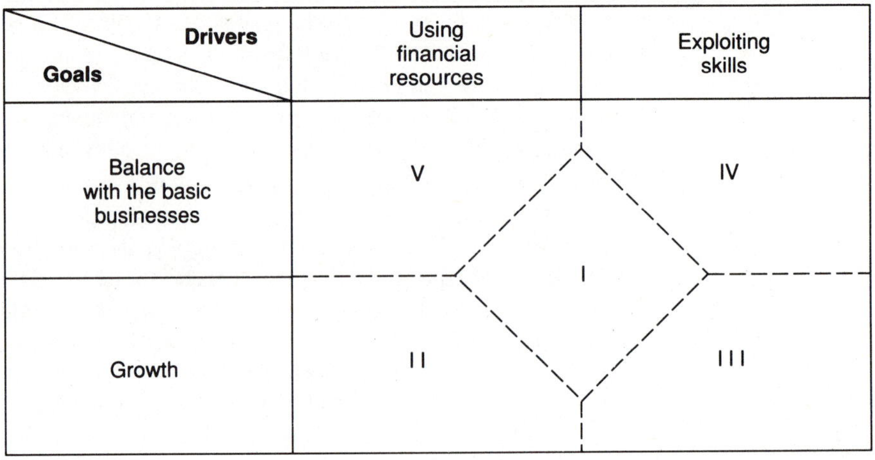

Goals \ Drivers	Using financial resources	Exploiting skills
Balance with the basic businesses	V	IV
Growth	II	III

(diamond in center labeled I)

diversification movements: *New businesses use available financial resources, exploit at least some managerial skills, and bring a better balance and growth.* The recent diversification of Salomon into the golf market exactly fits this scenario.

Preserving Some Consistency

The "traditional" measures of diversity (versus homogeneity) do not capture enough dimensions. Consistency does not mean necessarily relatedness of markets or technologies. The "Groupe Tapie" is involved in fashion clothes, sports equipment, managing the Marseilles football team, batteries, food, cosmetics, and weighing. Its consistency relies on common managerial skills: marketing general public products and companies recovery; the strong mediatic personality of its "boss," Bernard Tapie, is also a cement of this "*mosaique.*" Diversity versus homogeneity should be measured at three levels: technologies and markets, required managerial skills and company's vocation, and company's culture and top management image.

A highly diversified company can find its unity in the *relatedness of technologies* (generic technology). For instance, L'Oreal has related technologies in perfume and cosmetics, but if we consider markets, L'Oreal is extremely diversified, selling to hairdressers, hypermarkets, perfume shops, and pharmacies in more than 100 countries in the world. Besides, technologies might be different but related in a vertical chain as in the case of Total (oil prospecting, extraction, refining, and petrol distribution).

A highly diversified company may find its unity in the *relatedness of markets:* the same broad customer functions served (e.g., sports for Salomon) or the same broad customer group served. The Société Lyonnaise des Eaux has 34,500 employees working on water treatment and supply, street cleaning, distribution of energy, communication, cabling, funerary services, all worldwide; but all these businesses serve a relatively homogeneous customer group: local councils. In most of the cases in our study (American Express, Ecco, and Peat Marwick), diversified service companies keep some consistency in the customer group served; their diversification strategy relies more on international development and widening the lines of services sold to a relatively homogeneous group of customers.

Consistency can also be preserved on second-level dimensions: defining the *"vocation"* of the company and sticking inside its limits (e.g., "luxury products" for Moet Hennessy, "building and surfaces treatments" for Gerland, and "resources measurement and management" for Schlumberger) or preserving a common core of *managerial skills* ("marketing food products" for BSN, "human resources management" for Ecco, and "companies restructuring" for the Groupe Tapie).

At a more intangible third level, a *strong personality of the top manager* can be an essential element of unity of the diversified company, especially for the ones which cannot rely on the other elements: Antoine Riboud in BSN, Bernard Tapie in the Groupe Tapie, Georges Salomon in Salomon personify their companies and give a unique image inside and outside. Finally a *common culture* (shared values and the way people work and behave in the company), might be another key to preserve or build consistency. Dow Chemical, Hewlett-Packard, and Schlumberger have strong corporate cultures which facilitate integration and internal communication. On the other hand, such strong cultures might impede the integration of newly acquired businesses as in the Schlumberger case (acquisition of Fairchild in the semiconductor industry—1979).

Figure 3 gives an overview of these dimensions of diversity versus homogeneity and leverages to manage it. *All the diversified companies that we studied have at least one of these elements of consistency;* it is probably a condition of success.

Culture: Integration and Differentiation

Cultural diversity may arise from macrocultural differences linked with diverse geographical implantations, cultural diversity may be the consequence of different professional industrywide cultures, different historical backgrounds of the partners in mergers or acquisitions, or differences between the top managers' behaviors and styles.

Sometimes, "cultural diversity" is the main element of heterogeneity; for instance, Générale Sucrière (belonging to Saint-Louis Bouchon) is the result of the merger of nine French regional sugar refineries. For a few years it had to solve the problems of historical cultural differences among the partners. To build a sound corporate culture around three themes: "trust, vitality, and stability," Générale Sucrière is developing internal communication—a video journal, and,

FIGURE 3   Consistency Leverages

3rd level	Strong Personality of the Top Manager		Corporate Culture	
2nd level	Common Managerial Skills		Definition of the Company's Vocation	
1st level	Related Technologies		Related Markets	
	↗	↖	↗	↖
	One or a few generic technologies	Technologies related in a vertical chain	Same broad customer function	Same broad customer group

for its tenth anniversary, a book and a theater play on the company's short history.

Anyway, *very few companies in our sample actually "manage their culture(s)."* Some of them, like Du Pont de Nemours, are slowly modulating their strong corporate culture to adapt to national cultures. Other firms are preserving or strengthening their corporate culture. Among the 1,600 products of Dow Chemical, there are deep differences between basic chemicals (commodities) and pharmaceutical specialties (where the group has developed by acquisitions—for instance, acquisition of Merrell in 1982). Dow Chemical's strong corporate culture helps integration and communication; a written charter proclaims the "core values" (long-term profitability, growth, people are the source of success, high-quality products and services, innovation, and ecological responsibility) and the "values and traditions" (which tell the way people work there). Workshops and job rotation are other media for the diffusion and strengthening of the corporate culture which is slowly instilled into the newly acquired companies. For M. Pralus (Marketing Manager Europe), "We are all shaped into the Dow's mold which reduces the differences without rubbing them off. It develops common points, reflexes, common ways to solve problems, so that diversity is not a problem but a source of value." The top management symbolic behavior, internal publications, training, reward systems, and new staff integration are considered as the key vectors of the corporate culture. When acquisitions occur, the aculturation process is gradual: for example, when the Groupe Accor buys a new company, a "parrain" imbued with the Group's culture "goes part of the way" with the top managers of the new subsidiary. A proactive attitude toward culture is often dictated by a major change like radical diversification or restructuring as in the case of Empain Schneider.

A strong corporate culture (i.e., homogeneous and intense), serves a strong internal and external image and allows more decentralization without risking major divergences, but as Prahalad and Bettis have shown, a single dominant logic might not be adapted to all the businesses of a diversified company. In diversified companies, most managers agree on the necessity of a *coexistence of a "common cultural trunk"* and *"specific divisional cultures"*; BSN, American Express, Texas Instruments, Empain Schneider, Quaker, ITT, Schlumberger, Gerland, and Moet Hennessy, for instance, have this philosophy. In the Groupe Empain Schneider, the common cultural trunk is based on "the respect of individuals, profitability, trust, quality, and the respect of clients." Some business-specific values are grafted on this trunk; for instance, "integrity, commitment, and respect of the hierarchy" in SPIE Batignolles, the group's company involved in the building industry, and "technical excellence and flexibility" in Merlin Gerin, the Group's company involved in electromechanics. According to M. Guy de la Serre (Directeur Général Adjoint), "the Moet Hennessy community is far from homogeneous, with several businesses implanted in different countries. Each firm of the Group has its strong specific culture, related to its business environment and specific history. But, in spite of this cultural diversity, all those firms defend a common project based on identical *fundamental* values." In the Groupe Moet Hennessy, the common cultural trunk is based on "the permanent search for quality of the products and the management, human relations based on responsibility and initiative, and rewarding competences and services." In the Champagne branch, for example (Moet et Chandon), some specific cultural traits are grafted on this common trunk: "leadership, growth, competition, membership, and technical know-how."

Although we captured only the intended or promoted culture in each company, it is instructive to notice the great variety of cultural formulas between the 27 companies and to identify the most frequent values put forward. "Responsibility, innovation, and trust" seem to be particularly strong values in diversified companies, if we compare them to single business companies (cf. IRE[15]). "Quality, profitability, and flexibility" are also frequently put forward but are not specific to diversified companies.

We found that the service companies' managers feel particularly concerned with managing the corporate culture to strengthen and protect the corporate image. Quality and responsibility are two key values in the service sector; interactions between the suppliers and the clients and the relative intangibility of services explain this characteristic.

Managing culture "is difficult and takes a long time"; a written charter certainly is not sufficient, and values have to be translated into the managers' everyday behavior and human resources management practices.

---

[15]Institut de Recherche de l'Entreprise, "Values and Management Practices in Five Single Business Firms," Working paper, IRE, Lyon, November 1986.

Accessible Top Management, Task Forces, and Job Rotation

The management of diversity requires a very *accessible top management*. The open door policy, which is very typical of the "HP way," for instance, is a first management style principle which shortens the communication time. In the "HP way," no barrier and no sign of status should exist, "the managers must be free for the fellow workers"; landscape offices and open doors facilitate communication. However, to avoid any information flood, some autodiscipline will be a condition of success of this management style. The top management team should also leave the comfortable head offices and visit systematically the different subsidiaries and establishments in the world; it is a key principle in the Société Lyonnaise des Eaux where the members of the Board visit the subsidiaries at least once every three months. In the Groupe Tapie, Bernard Tapie himself visits the companies of the Group to solve marketing problems or participate in the strategic planning process. According to him, "A good manager should never stay in his office." The limited number of hierarchical levels is another way to preserve accessibility to the top management, as in Quaker. Besides, more formal and traditional top-down information on the corporate strategy can supplement this communication flow; BSN, for example, does a special effort to communicate its "Economic and Social double project."

Transversal *task forces* also are crucial leverages to improve communication in diversified companies. Most of the time, these task forces are spontaneous and ad hoc groups. They may be focused on improving quality as the Hewlett-Packard's "Total Quality Control" task forces. Some task forces are set up for the development and the launching of new products as in Roussel Uclaf. In Rhone-Poulenc, the task forces are grouped under five pilot committees (one for each sector, one for R&D, and one for marketing). At Texas Instruments, after a first reactive phase, "proactive" task forces were developed with "Quality Circles" and prevention techniques. "Quality Improvement Teams" are pluri-functional teams built up to solve a problem in a limited period of time. At the Société Lyonnaise des Eaux, transversal task forces are meeting points for the sales force and the marketing staff from diverse businesses and diverse geographical implantations, and as such they are an efficient alternative to a heavy matrix organization. All the diversified companies in our sample use task forces; companies like Accor, ITT, BSN, Moet Hennesy, L'Oreal, and Salomon strongly encourage them. According to the managers we met, task forces facilitate cross-fertilization and integration at two levels: the intradivisional level (most of the task forces are still intradivisional), and the interdivisional level (regional integration in the case of a "product form" general structure; product integration in the case of the geographical general structure); task forces are an essential means to supplement the general operational hierarchical structure in solving complex and multidimensional problems.

High job rotation is a third leverage for improving communication and managing diversity in diversified companies. International job rotation of the management staff is a must at American Express. At Total CFP, the mobility of the personnel is a key value. Total CFP is implanted in Africa, in the Middle East and Far East; international job rotation and, at a lower degree, functional job rotation are encouraged and planned. A formula gives the optimum number of years in a given job: "age of the employee divided by 10, plus or minus 1 year." A mobility clause is included in the recruitment contract, and carrier paths are designed for the development of managers with an alternation of functional positions in the head offices and operational positions in foreign countries' subsidiaries. At Texas Instruments, the staff mobility is considered as "a question of personal health," and rotations are managed by the "Job Opportunity System." At Hewlett-Packard, "a laboratory engineer should be ready to become a manufacturing engineer or a manager." BSN, Dow Chemical, Schlumberger, Rhone-Poulenc, ITT, Société Lyonnaise des Eaux, and others count on international and/or professional job rotation to breed managers, increase polyvalence, implant new ideas, and improve communication. However, in many companies in our sample, the *top manager at the national level is aboriginal;* ITT, Hewlett-Packard, Société Lyonnaise des Eaux, Texas Instruments, American Express generally respect this rule to match the company's image or management style with the host country; "international top managers" are placed at the "federal level" (for example, Europe).

Accessibility of the top management, task forces, and job rotation require highly adaptable and mobile managers. These practices have a double impact: They increase diversity through cross fertilization and innovation, and increase integration by developing individuals and improving vertical and transversal communication.

BALANCING CENTRALIZATION AND AUTONOMY

Three broad categories of general structures were identified: federations, divisional structure, and divisional matrix; however, most of the companies have hybrid structures adapted to the variety of the businesses. No structure type seems to outperform the others (cf. Stopford and Wells[16]). The identification of the functions represented in the "very light" headquarters of the federations (like Schlumberger, Empain Schneider, Société Lyonnaise des Eaux, Tapie, and Moet Hennessy) gives an idea of the minimum of integration needed: financial services, social relations, managers' development, corporate communication, and a part of strategic planning and juridical services.[17]

The degree of centralization versus decentralization and the respective roles

---

[16]J. M. Stopford, and L. T. Wells, *Managing the Multinational Enterprise* (New York: Basic Books, 1972).

[17]In such federations, the headquarters staff comprise between 0.4 and 1 percent of the total personnel.

and influences of the corporate headquarters and the business-level management on decision making has always been a key problem of diversified organizations.

Each company has its own formula for balancing centralization and autonomy. American Express, for instance, has the most atypical solution; the subsidiaries have a relative autonomy: The French subsidiary launched a new "sales by post" business (with the agreement of headquarters). However, such autonomy is limited by five rules to respect: growth, perfect quality, improve productivity, profitability, and strengthen the corporate image. Prices are settled on a world-wide basis, any "capital investment" must be accepted by New York and no employee (who has been in the company for more than 10 years) would be paid off without New York's consent.

Beyond this variety, a general statement can be made: there is a tendency for *"strategic control";* the corporate level has to give the go-ahead for strategic decisions, alliances are decided at the top, and reporting procedures on the strategic plan and budgets are rigorous (especially in American companies). The most frequent relation between a business unit and the corporate management is shown in Figure 4.

Although top managers often emphasize decentralization and although the strategic propositions often come from the business unit, this "strategic control" is a form of centralization. On the other hand, *operational decisions are systematically delegated to the business unit.*

At one end of the centralization/decentralization spectrum, there are companies

FIGURE 4 The Most Frequent Relation between Business Units and Top Management

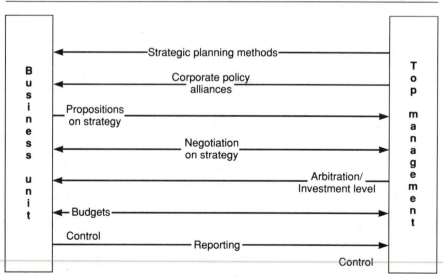

like BSN or Texas Instruments. At BSN, for example, "the cash flow produced by the business units ("departments") is managed by the Group. The corporate management plans investments, alliances, international strategy and new products." In the "preliminary objective" phase, business-unit managers propose several business strategy scenarios to the corporate management; they are considered as *"conseillers stratégiques du Groupe."* Then, the Group formulates corporate and business strategies and communicates strategic orientations to the business units. Finally, operational plans are elaborated by the business unit and communicated to the corporate level. At the other end of the spectrum, "federations" like Schlumberger, Empain Schneider, Société Lyonnaise des Eaux, Moet Hennesy, and Tapie certainly give more autonomy to the companies belonging to the federation. For instance, at Moet Hennessy, Y. Benard (Président du Directoire secteur Champagne) talks about two management principles: "Upward delegation" and "Subsidiarity": "Every executive manager has the full responsibility of his function and turns to his hierarchical boss only to ask for some advice if necessary." Fifty people work in the corporate headquarters (to compare with a total number of 7,000). Every year, each subsidiary presents its strategic plan (3- to 5-year horizons), and the corporate top management arbitrates business strategies to integrate them into a corporate strategy. Alliances and investment level are finally decided at the corporate level. The budget procedure follows; each profit center proposes its budget to the Holding which will arbitrate. The budget control exercised by the financial staff is rigorous (quarterly reports—deviations above 2 percent will lead to the revision of the budget). Quick and precise reporting is considered the counterpart of the participative process and of the relative decentralization. However, the general assumption, strategic control (as we defined it) and decentralization of operational decisions, is still valid.

Since the beginning of the 1980s, it seems that *there has been convergent movements toward more balanced power between corporate and business levels:* "federations" are looking for more robustness" and consistency; on the other hand, staff and line divisional structures have lightened their headquarters' staffs. The inverse organizational changes at Hewlett-Packard and at Texas Instruments illustrate this search for a balance. These last years, Hewlett-Packard has passed from a high decentralization and autonomy of the business units to a more centralized formula to improve cooperation between business units for product development and marketing. On the contrary, Texas Instruments, which was primarily centralized, has decentralized in the 1980s, giving to each business-unit manager the responsibility of R&D, manufacturing, and marketing (Product-Customer Centers).

Finally, *several degrees of centralization should coexist in one company according to the distance of each business to the core* (or dominant business). For instance, Roussel Uclaf did a morphological analysis of its businesses and found two main discriminant dimensions: communication intensity, and research and development intensity. Compared to the chemical products (low communication intensity and high R&D intensity), which are the core businesses of the company,

Rochas perfumes were very different according to key success factors and managerial skills (high communication intensity and low R&D intensity). In consequence, the Rochas subsidiary had been given a very broad autonomy, while chemical businesses were managed in a much more centralized way. According to the same logic, Merrell, the Dow Chemical subsidiary, acquired in 1979 and involved in pharmaceutical specialties, enjoys more autonomy than Dow's businesses in basic chemicals. Once again "hybrid," "tailor-made" organization formulas seem to be necessary to solve the complex problems of diversified companies.

CONCLUSIONS

We have tried to identify the dimensions of diversity and diversity management and to describe some dominant formulas for managing diversity in diversified companies.

Diversity should not impede reaching a critical mass in most of the company's businesses. Refocusing and new diversification should be done with a critical mass objective in mind.

The most diversified company should keep at least one element of consistency among the following: related technologies, related markets (first level), a delimited vocation, common managerial skills (second level), a corporate culture and a top manager who personifies the company (third level).

A common "corporate cultural trunk" should coexist with business-specific cultures.

Integration and innovation should be improved by the accessibility of the top management, transversal task forces, and job rotation.

The corporate level has "strategic control" on business strategies but operational decisions are systematically decentralized. Along the centralization/decentralization spectrum, there are convergent movements toward a more balanced power between the business unit and the corporate level. Finally, several degrees of centralization should coexist in one company according to the distance of each business to the core.

These conclusions are drawn from the analysis of the business portfolio strategy, the structure, the management of human resources, and the cultural traits of some diversified companies and they are inspired by the top managers' opinions on the key success factors.

After this limited exploratory study, these variables could be measured more precisely and possible relations with economic performance could be tested. We think that the major conclusion from this work is the crucial necessity of balancing forces. Managing a highly diversified company at the corporate level requires a consistent mix of decisions in four fields; strategy, structure, management of human resources, and culture; it certainly requires distinct managerial skills to succeed in the alchemy for balancing integration and differentiation.

Appendix: The 3M Case

To give an overview of the mix of leverages used in one company, we briefly describe the case of 3M.

3M is involved in 15 technologies (enduction, resins, optical systems, films, materials, electronic systems, etc.), 45 product lines (from the well-known Scotch Brite dishwashing pad to growing organic crystals in the weightlessness of space), in 55 countries, with nearly 100,000 people working in about 40 divisions. The key words of the company are diversification and cohesion; product innovation is the cornerstone of the diversification strategy. 3M France produces a part of the product line (mainly abrasives, adhesives, glues, and coatings) for Europe and manages the French market.

To encourage and preserve diversity, 3M has several recipes:

- The portfolio of businesses is diversified through new applications of the generic technological skills.
- There are many divisions divided into departments (corresponding to a product line in a geographical zone). The emergence of new departments is encouraged—departments sometimes merge and sometimes split to adapt to the environment.
- Structures are adapted to the local conditions of the environment; for instance, the bureaucratic business is grouped in a single division in Germany and split into three divisions in France.
- New projects are nurtured: an engineer may use 15 percent of his working time on his own personal ideas or projects; entrepreneurial product teams are encouraged. When the annual sales reach a certain point, a new department is created. Intrapreneurs and "pathfinders" are rewarded and their occasional failures are not sanctioned. The whole company takes up a challenge: "25 percent of the turnover must be done with products launched during the last 5 years."
- The 3M culture is based on innovation; the right of making mistakes for the ones who are in motion and the eleventh commandment: "Thou shalt not kill a new product idea" are two basic values which encourage diversity.
- Each department proposes its strategic plan and has a large autonomy on the operations as long as the financial goals of the company are met.

To avoid the drawbacks of an uncontrolled diversity, 3M has some regulation processes:

- A common core of genetic technological skills is preserved.
- 3M's competitive strategy recipe is based on differentiation: No subsidiary will follow a single-cost leadership strategy (cf. the dominant logic described by a Pralahad and Bettis[13]).
- The strength of 3M's corporate culture is a key element of consistency.
- Functional divisions have a technical responsibility. They give some homogeneity to the operations of the various departments or product division.
- The strategic planning process is international at the corporate level.
- A "corporate umbrella" is held on the institutional communication and the company's image (packaging, graphism, publications, and public relations).
- Ad hoc transversal interdivisional task forces deal with problems like distribution, image, quality improvement, and key customers.

- Some human resources projects may be launched, like the project of the French subsidiary based on *"l'esprit d'enthousiasme,"* to strengthen interdivisional communication and cooperation.

This dual management of diversity results in a balancing movement, diversity alternately increases and decreases.

3M is just one case of a successful highly diversified company. Most of the other companies in our sample are also successful and have their own formulas to manage diversity.

What this article is about: After examining some companies that have achieved sustainable improvements in their competitive position through acquisitions, the author distills a set of 10 principles that serves his clients well.

3–3 *Shopping for Companies*

William W. Bain, Jr.

*William W. Bain, Jr. is president of the
consulting firm of Bain & Company Inc.*

The business press is an avid chronicler of failed mergers and acquisitions. The resulting impression is that an executive who embarks on an acquisition is little better than a compulsive gambler throwing his money away trying to beat the house odds.

There are, of course, significant data supporting this viewpoint. Studies show that a dollar invested in an acquisition has only about a 30 percent chance of creating real economic value—and some who have looked at the record say the success rate is even worse. A craps game offers far better odds of winning.

Yet merger and acquisition activity continues at a high level. American companies laid down some $200 billion last year to make more than 2,500 acquisitions. In Europe, there has been a dramatic increase in M&As. Merchant banks in the United Kingdom, for example, have begun to assume the role of deal-maker first created by U.S. investment banks. The total value of deals there in 1985 was £7.1 billion, the highest total since 1972, adjusted for inflation.

Of course, the M&A-gambling analogy does not really hold up. Gamblers are always at the mercy of the house odds, while companies can actually turn the acquisition odds in their favor. A few years ago our firm took a close look at some companies that, through acquisitions, had grown, increased their profitability, and achieved sustainable improvements in their competitive positions. A short list of those that have built substantial corporate value this way would include Heileman Brewing, James River Corporation, Flowers Industries, and the Dun & Bradstreet Corporation in the United States, and such firms as Esselte, BTR, BSN, and Hanson Trust in Europe.

We have attempted to distill out the elements that made these companies

SOURCE: *Across the Board* (July–August 1986), pp. 44–49.

successful. Over the past two years, we have assisted clients in some 65 acquisitions in the United States and Europe, working on transactions that involved some $15 billion. Our role is not normally that of dealmaker. Typically, the first phase of our work involves setting strategy, screening acquisition candidates, evaluating them, and helping to determine the value. Structuring the exact terms of the offer and making the legally mandated inspections are areas in which investment bankers, law firms, and accountants have the appropriate expertise. We are often involved in the next stage: helping integrate the new company into the acquirer's strategy. We're still learning, but at this point I believe we do have a set of working principles that serve our clients well.

1. *Weigh an acquisition carefully against all other strategic options for creating long-term shareholder value.*

Mobil buys Montgomery Ward to establish a beachhead in a business with faster growth than oil. Coke buys Taylor Wine to get into a fast-growing business in which it can apply its vaunted marketing expertise. Fluor Corporation buys St. Joe Minerals to make good use of extra cash and diversify into a supposedly countercyclical industry.

Each company had plausible justification for making its acquisition. And each now almost certainly wishes it had figured out some other way to achieve its objective.

When an acquisition that looked plausible does not work well, it is usually because the acquisition was not consistent with the buyer's long-range strategic guiding principles. The point is, an acquisition may look like a good opportunity to accomplish some operating goal easily and quickly. But the chances of making the acquisition do what it is supposed to do are minuscule when the acquired company is a poor fit with the parent company's basic corporate strategy. That strategy, carefully thought through and defined, may dictate an entirely different kind of acquisition, or none at all.

The tremendous importance of core strategy is borne out by the experience of most companies that have built value through acquisitions. They have typically done it deliberately, over the long term.

At Dun & Bradstreet, acquisitions accounted for some 80 percent of the company's total revenues in 1984. The revealing figure here is that the acquisitions were made over 25 years. The success of the acquisition strategy at Dun & Bradstreet is seen in such figures as growth of the market-to-book value ratio, which in 1985 was two and a half times greater than that of the Standard & Poor's 400.

At BTR, a British conglomerate, growth in the earnings from base businesses was only 10.2 percent from 1973 to 1983, while acquisitions earnings grew by 22.7 percent. A planned, sequential acquisition program over a period of 16 years strengthened their core businesses and brought them into market leadership in new areas.

The key factor in the success of these and other firms is that they had a clear vision of their corporate strategy, they weighed their options, and they chose acquisition as the means of getting where they wanted to be.

2. *Actively look for a company to buy, rather than trying to save money and time by waiting for a seller to come to you.*

The typical merger or acquisition begins with an intermediary, usually an investment bank, approaching several prospective buyers to interest them in a company or a division of a company. Whatever the circumstances, the prospective acquirer is immediately at a disadvantage.

The company that is approached has been targeted by the seller, which probably has only a superficial understanding of the target company's business. Thus, there's a better than even chance that the firm for sale does not fit the prospective buyer's strategy. What is more, the company is for sale for a reason, which almost certainly ensures that an acquirer will be buying a headache of one kind or another.

The acquirer may not mind buying a certain type of headache, but there probably won't be time to make a thorough examination of the company to determine just what that headache is. Bendix, for example, took over Warner & Swasey in a high-pressure white-knight rescue—only to discover later that W&S was lagging far behind the Japanese in product development.

By contrast, if a company has an acquisition strategy, it can seek out the kinds of companies that fit that strategy and take its time in evaluating them. Sara Lee spent 16 months studying Hanes before buying the company—and the combination has been a success.

Even when a firm chooses not to make an active search, the process of setting strategy will give it a head start in making a quick, effective evaluation when an acquisition candidate presents itself.

3. *Invest plenty of effort in screening and establishing priorities among acquisition candidates.*

The screening process, done properly, can be a very large project. In a recent search, we began by screening thousands of companies on the basis of the business they were in, their size, and their market value. That left us a list of 219 possible candidates. We assigned each of them a priority on the basis of potential for market growth, profit improvement, and cost sharing; we also did a rough estimate of the probable price versus the net present value of future cash flow. That got us down to 59 companies. A management review and a close look at these companies' businesses left 35 possibilities. Detailed analysis of the companies, including their position versus their competitors, got the list down to 17. Of these, 12 were selected as attractive enough to contact about a possible merger.

That is the short description of the screening process. The "long form" would contain the details, such as a careful analysis of acquisition candidates' technological position, product quality, worldwide cost position, opportunities for cost sharing and profit improvement, and potential "experience-curve" advantages. We would also develop forecasts of costs and prices, capital needs, and future cash flow, and study such factors as the intentions of competitors and the regulatory environment in the particular business.

Of course, many companies do at least some of these analyses before making an acquisition—but too often, the analysis comes after the buyer has already been approached. The company cannot be sure it is looking at the best of all possible candidates, and the time for investigation is limited. Under pressure, the company may skew its basic strategic criteria to fit the acquisition, rather than make certain that the acquisition fits the strategy.

4. *Start with the knowledge that buying an industry leader will be extremely difficult. But don't settle for anything less than a company with a fighting chance to become a leader.*

If so many acquisitions run into problems, why not start with the rule, "Buy nothing but the best"? Because the best companies, with rare exceptions, are not for sale. To avoid spending a lot of time and money and winding up frustrated, firms looking for acquisition candidates should include probable availability as a criterion in early screening.

What is implied here, of course, is that the companies evaluated are going to be less than top performers. But that is almost always the case, as we have seen, if a company waits for a deal to come knocking. The advantage in the active approach is that the buyer can choose its problems—and opportunities. The rule of thumb is that a candidate must have a "fighting chance" of becoming an industry leader.

Indications of this fighting chance include one or more of the following: a high-quality product, widespread consumer recognition and acceptance, a strong technological position, clear opportunities to become the low-cost producer, long-term real market growth of at least 10 percent annually, a number of competitors with no one dominant, and a high barrier to market entry. Companies that have relatively low profit rates, despite high relative market share, are particularly good candidates.

5. *When you find a company with undervalued assets but whose business is completely unrelated to yours, think very, very carefully before grabbing this "bargain."*

One of the most seductive traps in acquisitions is the "asset bargain," in which a takeover candidate's raw-material reserves or other tangible assets can be picked up at a price below the current market. There are two problems with this approach. First, if the market has undervalued a company's tangible assets, there is probably a good reason, and that reason is seldom long in emerging: commodity prices plummet, or the industry runs into manufacturing overcapacity or some other difficulty.

The second problem is that the "undervalued-asset" argument is frequently used when the acquired company's business has no significant relationship to the acquirer's business. This is a problem because one of the key indicators of whether an acquisition will increase shareholder wealth is the degree to which the two companies' businesses are related. In a study of 68 mergers and acquisitions, market value of those involving unrelated businesses had declined by an average of 4 percent two years later.

6. *Make certain all the synergies of an acquisition are firmly based on shared economic systems and can be realized almost immediately.*

Our study showed that there was an increase in shareholder wealth when companies' businesses were related, but it was slight. When companies had related businesses and shared economic systems as well, the increase went up by some 3 percent over a two-year period. The seven-point improvement over unrelated acquisitions suggests an enormous improvement in rates of return, given the already large size of most of the acquiring companies.

There are obvious instances of shared economics that produce significant cost reduction. When companies share a customer base or distribution system, for example, functions can be combined to rationalize costs. Some of the most successful mergers, such as those between Nabisco and Standard Brands, and Norfolk & Western and Southern Railway, have been firmly grounded on shared economics. In fact, mergers within industries generally have a high potential for success because of cost sharing. The attractiveness and feasibility of such mergers is greatly increased, of course, under the federal government's current close interpretation of an antitrust law.

The comparatively good prospects for mergers within an industry have been demonstrated in airlines, oil, and other industries that have gone through deregulation. To survive in the newly competitive market, companies are virtually forced into mergers to improve their overall cost structure.

On the other hand, opportunities for good acquisitions within an industry don't always exist—which means that the principles of related businesses and shared economics must be applied creatively. For example, a number of public utilities, faced with slow growth in revenues, have successfully diversified. In one study, we found that the market-to-book value ratio of seven highly diversified utilities was an average of 20 percent higher than those of nondiversified utilities from 1975 to 1985, even though the diversifieds' return on sales and net plant investment was lower. These diversified utilities took advantage of their expertise and existing systems in such areas as monthly billing and crew/fleet scheduling to get into such businesses as transaction processing, time-sharing services, product marketing, fleet management, and energy-maintenance services.

"Shared economics," broadly interpreted, includes combining technology to achieve lower costs. Our own experience in this area has involved, among other things, working with a book publisher to acquire a printing firm whose advanced technology almost immediately resulted in lower costs.

The operative words here are "almost immediately." Convoluted schemes that promise ephemeral cost synergies down the road are not sufficient basis for a good acquisition, as the road often turns out to be a primrose path.

Of course, there are some successful "conglomerates," including several in Britain. Because the British government has raised formidable roadblocks to mergers that increase concentration in an industry, "acquisition houses" have put together groups of essentially unrelated businesses sharing few or no economic systems, and have managed to do it successfully. These companies may be the exception to the rule. But if they enjoy long-term success, it is more likely that they have followed a set of very fundamental principles in assembling their divisions.

7. *Go beyond the minimum "due diligence" by going inside the target to study its strategies and its competitive strengths and weaknesses.*

Believe it or not, many buyers never take a thorough look at what they are getting for their money. The typical due-diligence study lasts a week or so and may involve only cursory on-site inspections and discussions with the prospect's management personnel.

By contrast, our clients have often asked us to do in-depth internal studies lasting two or three months in order to get a complete understanding of the prospect's strategies, cost position, technical standing, research and development capability, and other characteristics. These "inside studies," done discreetly, can be a first step in a process of friendly acquisition and effective integration. With ample data on the company, the buyer is in a good position to discuss such matters as price and how the company will fit into an overall strategy.

Obviously, an internal study is not possible in all cases, especially in hostile takeovers. But even in those situations, an in-depth analysis can be done from the outside to help size up the target's strategies and competitive position.

8. *Early in your approach to an acquisition candidate, begin talking about your strategy and theirs, and how you intend to fit the two together.*

In our experience, the process of integrating an acquired company should begin early, even before the deal is completed. When the acquired company's management knows what their company's role is to be, and when the acquirer has their feedback on that role, the likelihood of harsh clashes later on is minimized.

Frank discussions at this point also can help smooth the path to a deal that is equitable for all parties. A buyer is unlikely to get a price that is a "steal," but a good relationship with the acquired company can prevent a bidding war.

Having arrived at a price based on information sharing, both companies understand that the price is justified only if the organizations can be integrated smoothly. One of our clients, which has been involved in a number of very successful acquisitions in recent years, adheres to the principle that it will realize the value of the transaction not by buying assets at a bargain price, but by doing a good job of integrating the acquired company.

9. *Determine how much you will pay for a company based on the value created by the merger, and don't get drawn into a bidding war that runs the price up beyond that level.*

Simply put, companies tend to pay too much for acquisitions. Between 1970 and 1983, acquiring companies paid premiums normally ranging 40 percent to 50 percent above the actual market value of companies they bought. The combined companies must create a great deal of added economic value to justify such premiums. Few manage to do it.

One reason companies pay too much is that they do not actively seek acquisition candidates, but wait for someone to approach them with a deal. The ensuing process will always maximize the price paid because, after all, the seller or the intermediary representing him is obligated to get the highest possible price for the company on the block. The typical scenario is a bidding war, with the price getting pumped up far above any reasonable level.

By contrast, when a company is an active buyer, it has time and can commit adequate resources to evaluating just what an acquisition is worth. It's not just a matter of valuing corporate assets. In our view, the proper method is to calculate the added value that can reasonably be expected to be achieved by combining the two companies, then use the net present worth of that added value to arrive at a price that gives both buyer and seller a share of the expected benefits.

Walking away when the price gets too high is not easy, but it can be done, as proved by such companies as Hanson Trust, which backed away from at least one acquisition when the price became unjustifiable.

10. *Rather than leave the acquiree alone to get used to the idea of being taken over, begin integrating the company as soon as the ink is dry.*

It seems logical: The buyer knows that the acquired firm will have problems because of intensified competition from without and feelings of insecurity from within. So the buyer takes a hands-off attitude, and even issues statements that may exaggerate the degree of autonomy the new subsidiary will have.

Our experience indicates, however, that this approach leads to early sorrow. In a study of 55 acquisitions, we found that 49 did not produce the first-year results that could reasonably have been expected. We believe that the honeymoon is responsible. It simply heightens the anxieties, uncertainties, and inward focus of the newly acquired company. The old corporate culture weakens, and there is nothing to replace it. Suddenly, in the middle of the year or two of grace that the buyer was going to give the acquired company, the problems become so intense that the buyer finds itself jumping in to fight fires, or standing by while the situation deteriorates.

A number of acquisitions have gained dubious distinction that way. Shortly after Midland Bank, of London, took over Crocker National Bank, the latter was reporting sharp losses, which most observers attributed to Midland's hands-off policy. When Prudential Insurance acquired Bache & Company, it reportedly left Bache almost entirely alone, recognizing the potential problems in trying to marry the two companies' vastly different cultures; Bache's early performance was not good. Phibro Corporation, a huge commodities trader, took over Salomon Brothers with the intention of achieving synergy between the two companies, with each operating autonomously under the holding company Phibro-Salomon. From all reports, the synergy did not materialize, and Phibro's subsequent poor performance evidently opened the way for Salomon to turn the tables and gain control of the parent company.

It is more effective—and realistic—to take immediate steps to begin integrating the new company. After all, the buyer has purchased the company as part of its strategy, and the new subsidiary should begin to play its role as soon as possible. Even before the detail is completed, a six-month integration plan should be prepared.

Of course, integrating will mean different things under different circumstances.

The buyer may want to give the acquiree a fair degree of autonomy, if that fits the buyer's strategy. For example, the British company Tilling preferred a "light touch" in managing its numerous divisions. That approach seemed to work well until the company ran into problems and was taken over by BTR, which is known for taking a firm hand in managing its acquisitions.

Integrating must be culturally sensitive. Too much interference has been cited as the cause of problems in such cases as Exxon-Vydec and Schlumberger-Fairchild.

But those are simply cautionary tales, and they do not alter the fundamental necessity of making a newly acquired firm understand and follow its role in the buyer's corporate strategy. The acquired company's management and employees may not like the new situation, but at least feelings of uncertainty are laid to rest.

There are some key steps in integrating the new company. One of the most important should be an "audit" to develop an independent data base on such factors as the acquisition's customers, competitors, and costs. This set of facts, agreed to by the buyer and the management of the acquisition, is the foundation for establishing the common goals they will be aiming for. And the plan to reach those goals should be put in motion without delay.

Of course, the most carefully wrought integration plan could turn out to be worthless. Charles A. Lamb, director of planning at Allied-Signal Inc., has stated the situation succinctly: "No integration process can overcome the problems of an acquisition that was ill conceived in the first place."

The principal reason that so many acquisitions are ill conceived is that most companies who make them are actually assuming a passive stance. The news media's fascination with takeover battles may give the opposite impression—but the fact is, some 85 percent of all acquisitions are initiated by the sellers. The company that makes an acquisition under these circumstances is like the shopper who goes to the supermarket without a grocery list. You spend more money than you intended, and you probably don't get what you need.

What this article is about: CIBA-GEIGY's experiences with acquisitions are summarized in the form of 10 suggestions to consider in an acquisition program. If these suggestions are followed, the author believes the result will be stronger, more profitable companies.

3–4 Ten Suggestions for Acquisition Success

Robert J. Terry

*Robert J. Terry is vice president for planning
and analysis of the CIBA-GEIGY Corporation*

Last summer, in the heat of the fierce bidding battle for Conoco, press criticism of acquisitions and mergers was also heating up. *Time* magazine expressed some "Big Doubts about Big Deals." *Newsweek* explored, "The New Urge to Merge," and wondered "Is Business Getting Too Big?" *Fortune* was a lonely holdout on the newsstand as it pleaded, "Don't Stop the Mating Game."

Some people are very critical of acquisitions and mergers, saying that they take money away from capital investment. "America is sinking in a productivity swamp," they say, "struggling against foreign competition . . . staggering under high interest rates and runaway inflation. And what are its largest corporations up to? They're not spending their money constructing factories . . . or creating jobs . . . or increasing R&D. Instead, they're gobbling each other up."

Fortunately, some economic observers have a more encouraging view. They say that acquisitions lead to economies of scale that improve productivity in the long run and eventually show up in lower prices for consumers.

So, to acquire or not to acquire: that is the question. Whether 'tis nobler to grow through acquisition . . . or to expand internally through increased R&D and capital investment. But do we have to make a choice? Can't we do both?

CIBA-GEIGY has done both. We spend 8 percent of our sales on R&D—more than most other chemical companies. But, during the 1970s, we also embarked upon an acquisition program. It was ambitious, and I think it was also successful.

I'd like to tell you about our acquisition program and share some of the lessons

SOURCE: Reprinted from *Managerial Planning* 31, no. 5 (September–October 1982), pp. 13–16. Copyright © 1982, by the Planning Executives Institute, Oxford, Ohio.

we've learned. I don't believe we have all the answers about acquisitions. But I do believe that we understand some of the questions. The reader may be able to benefit from our mistakes, as well as our successes.

CIBA-GEIGY itself is the product of a merger. It was formed in 1970 by combining two large Swiss chemical companies, CIBA and Geigy—companies of almost the same size but very different management styles. One of the reasons for the merger was the rising cost of research in both companies. Leaders of the two firms agreed that a merger could make their research expenditures more productive.

CIBA's strengths in pharmaceuticals and epoxy resins and Geigy's strengths in agricultural chemicals and polymer additives complemented each other. The result was a much stronger competitor in the international chemical industry.

In the United States, CIBA-GEIGY has four divisions—Agricultural, Pharmaceuticals, Dyestuffs and Chemicals, and Plastics and Additives—plus Airwick Industries, a subsidiary. Our U.S. sales are about a quarter of the worldwide total. Our parent would like us to increase this amount. That was part of the reason for the acquisition program that I'm about to describe.

During the 70s, CIBA-GEIGY made 19 acquisitions in the United States. The purchase prices ranged from under a million dollars to almost $100 million. Altogether we spent about $300 million on the program—rather meager in comparison to what Du Pont paid to acquire Conoco, but a significant amount for CIBA-GEIGY.

WHY THIS ACQUISITION PROGRAM?

First, we wanted to improve our competitive position by reducing our dependence on a few products. In 1975, a quarter of our sales came from one product—AAtrex, a corn herbicide. We expected a big loss of sales when our patent expired in 1976. Also, several of our other business, such as dyestuffs and epoxy resins, were becoming mature.

Second, we wanted to complement our internal R&D. As I noted earlier, we're strongly committed to basic chemical and pharmaceutical research. However, it seemed to us that, in many cases, it's cheaper to buy than it is to build, and it's faster too.

For instance, take our acquisition of the Hercules pigments business. We had been importing our pigments from Europe and were searching for an alternative. Our choices were to abandon the business—a business where we had research, technological know-how, and customers—or to build our own plants from scratch in the United States—or to go shopping. The first choice—abandonment—was unacceptable. The second—construction—made no sense financially. So we went shopping, and acquired the Hercules pigments operation.

The Hercules purchase, and most of our other acquisitions, were designed to complement internal strengths. We have R&D know-how in chemistry; we have experience in making specialty chemicals; and we have experience in marketing them. But we realized that this knowledge and experience would not necessarily enable us to make and sell hamburgers, for instance, because we clearly have no understanding of the fast-food industry.

Third, we wanted to cushion ourselves against the growing regulatory burden. Several of CIBA-GEIGY's core businesses—pharmaceuticals and agricultural chemicals, for instance—are highly regulated. In fact, the entire chemical industry is becoming one of the most regulated businesses in this country. Having other legs to stand on, where we don't have to satisfy an FDA or an EPA, helps to lighten the regulatory burden.

Those three reasons—a desire to reduce our dependence on a few products, a desire to complement our internal strengths, and a desire to expand into less regulated industries—sent us looking for suitable corporate partners.

How did our search work out? We're reasonably pleased with the results. We made some mistakes. But given the number of acquisitions we made, and the relatively short time in which we made them, winners still outnumber losers.

TEN SUGGESTIONS TO CONSIDER IN AN ACQUISITION PROGRAM

There are so many unknowns in the process of buying and selling companies that it can hardly be called a pure science. Anyone who's been involved in a successful acquisition has some pet theories about the process. Based on our experience, I've compiled 10 suggestions for those who may be considering an acquisition program.

First, *establish acquisition criteria*. And make sure everyone agrees on what those criteria are.

Buying a business is something like shopping in a supermarket. It helps to have a shopping list before you leave for the store. If you don't have a list, you may find yourself buying groceries, or businesses, that you don't need, just because they're available on the shelves. During the course of your acquisition program, you may stray, as we sometimes did, from the criteria on your shopping list, just as you sometimes buy an item or two on impulse at the market. But that's no excuse for not having a shopping list to start with.

At CIBA-GEIGY, we said our acquisition candidates should be in growing markets, should have patented products or well-known brand names in their field, should be able to benefit from our R&D know-how, should be product-oriented, rather than service-oriented, should have sales of at least $50 million, should be able to yield a return on investment of at least 15 percent, and should have a top purchase price of $400 million. Then, having made our shopping list, we headed for the acquisition supermarket.

Second, *if you think you see synergies, make sure they're real*.

Professor Rumelt of UCLA has published a study of acquisitions made by the 500 largest industrial companies over a 25-year period. He concluded that the best results were achieved by companies that diversified into areas of related skills or resources. The poorest results were achieved by companies that diversified into totally unrelated areas. An article in the current issue of *Fortune* magazine called "The Bottom Line on Ten Big Mergers of 1971" reached a similar conclusion.

An example of real synergism is Herbishield brand sorghum seed, which was developed jointly by our Agricultural Division and one of its acquisitions, Funk Seeds. Before Funk introduced Herbishield three years ago, sorghum growers couldn't use certain CIBA-GEIGY herbicides because they would damage the seed. Herbishield changed that. The sorghum seed is treated with a herbicide antidote, which protects the sorghum seedlings from the active ingredient in the herbicide. Funk has significantly increased its sorghum seed sales, and the Ag Division has increased its sales of herbicides to sorghum growers. Everybody's happy.

Another example of synergy is CIBA-GEIGY's investment in ALZA Corporation. ALZA's area of strength is in inventing unique drug delivery systems—a strength in research and technology. We teamed ALZA's strength with CIBA-GEIGY's strengths in pharmacology and in pharmaceutical marketing. The result: the first transdermal drug delivery system. It delivers the drug right through the skin and is used to combat motion sickness. We also have a second transdermal system on the market, containing nitroglycerin. Other new products combining unique ALZA delivery systems with CIBA-GEIGY drugs are in the development pipeline.

Third, *don't try to go into a completely new field* by telling yourself that good managers can manage anything. They can't. They can't because every industry has its own culture and it's own language. Perhaps any language can be learned, but by the time you learn it, the acquisition could be going down the drain.

We learned this lesson with Airwick's Pool Products business, which we'd acquired by accident rather than by plan. Airwick had acquired Pool Products shortly before we acquired Airwick itself. If came with the deal. But we were saddled with a business we didn't really want and didn't know anything about. We kept telling ourselves that swimming pool chemicals were somehow related to our other chemicals businesses, but they weren't. We never gave Pool Products the R&D it needed, and the financial results were disappointing. In the end we sold Pool Products to a company in the mainstream of that industry.

Fourth, *don't pay more for the acquisition than it's worth.* W. T. Grimm & Co. says that price premiums were averaging 41 percent above market price in 1975. That figure rose to 50 percent by 1980. Some were far above the averages.

To avoid this pitfall, put a ceiling on your acquisition budget. Then stick to it. Decide what return on investment you need to get. At CIBA-GEIGY, we make the same internal rate of return calculations for acquisitions as we do for capital investments.

Fifth, *don't think small.* We found that Charles S. Tanner Company, the little $12 million company we wanted to tuck neatly into our Dyestuffs and Chemicals Division, took almost as much overall effort as the acquisition of the $50 million

Airwick business. So you might as well go for the larger one—if it matches your acquisition criteria and if you can fold it into your operation smoothly.

There's a corollary to this. You don't have to be a big company to make an acquisition. CIBA-GEIGY has become 25 percent larger in the United States, and a lot stronger, through acquisitions. Keep in mind, too, that you don't have to buy an entire company. More business segments are being purchased, as opposed to whole companies. Five of our 19 acquisitions were parts of companies.

Sixth, *consider the quality of management in the acquired firm*. "Acquire and fire" is not a good policy. But don't just hold on to the managers you acquire—listen to them. They probably know their business a lot better than you do; at least in the beginning.

When Airwick first told us about its idea for Carpet Fresh—a powder that you sprinkle on the carpet, then vacuum up again, leaving a fresh, clean scent—there was a lot of disbelief among many members of CIBA-GEIGY's management. We didn't know much about consumer product market research and marketing. But we did have the good sense to listen to the management at Airwick. Carpet Fresh created a whole new product category—rug and room deodorizers. If imitation is the sincerest form of flattery, we're doing spectacularly. There's been a rash of "me-too" products, yet Carpet Fresh still holds a 43 percent share of the new $70 million category which it created.

Seventh, *don't overacquire*. Allow enough time to digest, integrate, and consolidate the acquisitions you make, particularly if you make a lot in a short period of time.

Our 19 acquisitions were made in three distinct phases. We bought two small companies during the early 70s. In 1974, after we decided to undertake a major acquisitions program, we bought Funk Seeds, Airwick, and Charles S. Tanner Company. Then we took a breather, partly dictated by the recession, but mostly to digest those sizable purchases. In the late 1970s we bought another 14 businesses. Now, once again, we're in a holding pattern. Looking back, our last push to diversify was too fast. We didn't allow enough time for some of our acquisitions to blend smoothly into our company. Our profits fell during the late 1970s, partly because of this too rapid acquisitions push. So we stopped short, consolidated, and put our house in order.

Eight, *be prepared for surprises*. In other words, allow for some acquisition indigestion. Have Tums or Rolaids handy. Sometimes the only way to spell relief is *d-i-v-e-s-t*.

One of our "tickets on the heartburn express" was Charles S. Tanner. Tanner had on the drawing board a new plant to produce EVA polymers. They, and we, thought the polymers would be very useful in the textile industry. When the plant was finished, it turned out that the textile industry didn't want the product. Most of the demand for the polymers was in the adhesives market. We recognized that our expertise is in textiles, not adhesives, so we sold Tanner to National Starch.

Another surprise was Hamblet and Hayes. It had leather tanning and finishing chemicals that we thought would complement our Dyestuffs and Chemicals Division sales to the leather industry. Hamblet and Hayes has done very well, but not because of its sales to the leather industry. The leather industry is in a slump. But the acquisition included an excellent chemical distribution business. That business has grown steadily since we acquired Hamblet and Hayes in 1978. So that acquisition surprised us too, but pleasantly.

Ninth, *have patience*—lots of it. It may take a long time to reach an acceptable level of profitability.

When we bought Airwick, there were practically no competitors for solid air fresheners. But almost before the ink was dry on the closing papers, S. C. Johnson introduced a competitive product to Airwick Solid—at a lower price. Airwick declined rapidly from a profitable business to a breakeven business. But then Airwick brought out some innovative products—Stick Ups, and then Carpet Fresh. By 1980, it had grown sixfold.

I've already related Funk Seeds' success with Herbishield. When we bought Funk, we found that the company was taking its research in an entirely different direction from the type of seed genetics which interested us. Now the company's on track with its research, and the synergy between Funk and our Ag Division has been proven. We're beginning to see financial success—eight years after the purchase.

Which brings me to my last piece of advice. *Don't hang on too long* hoping that losses will turn into profits. We didn't want the Pool business when we got it as part of the Airwick acquisition. But we kept it for seven years before we finally pulled the plug.

SUMMARY

To summarize these 10 points again briefly: Establish acquisition criteria. Make sure the apparent synergies are real. Don't try to diversify into a completely new field. Don't overpay. Don't think small. Consider the quality of management. Allow time for integration. Be prepared for surprises. Be patient, but don't hang on too long.

I stated earlier that I didn't have nice pat answers about whether to start an acquisition program. That's because there are no nice pat answers. What seems important to me in appraising acquisitions is the end result. Will there be increased productivity? Will there be a stronger competitive position? Will there be more effective R&D? Will there be a better bottom line? If the answers are yes, then the acquisition route may be the one to take.

Many acquisitions result in stronger, more profitable companies; companies that can delivery high-quality products at reasonable prices. Other corporate marriages are ill-conceived, poorly executed, almost destined to fail before they're consummated. "To acquire or not to acquire" is a question that all present-day Hamlets and their companies will have to decide for themselves.

What this article is about: This article analyses the strategic dimensions of global competition. As U.S. companies enter the fight for global markets, a broader definition of corporate strategy as it relates to developing competitive advantage is needed to provide managers with superior tools to improve their strategic thinking. Corporate-level strategy involves both a foreign policy as well as a domestic policy dimension, and a time dimension. The foreign policy dimension relates to the company's endeavours to find a workable balance between internal development and acquisitions for entering and exploiting new technologies on one's own. The final dimension relates to time, that is, understanding those conditions where changes in company strategy and structure are needed to help guide the company into the future. Examples are provided to illustrate these dimensions in action.

3–5 Strategies for Global Competition

David Lei

David Lei is Assistant Professor of International Management Studies at the University of Texas at Dallas

During recent years, many U.S. companies have substantially restructured not only their internal operations but also their vision of what constitutes a cohesive and effective strategy for competing on a global basis. The fierce level of competition from Japan, Western Europe, and other Far Eastern nations in every industry from processed foods to telecommunications is forcing U.S. companies to reexamine their traditional attitudes toward corporate and global strategies. Here are some recent examples of what some major manufacturers are doing to enhance their global competitive advantage.

- Texas Instruments has formed numerous strategic alliances with customers in Europe, the Far East, and the United States to focus their R&D in a way to improve their responsiveness to market demands.
- Philips N.V., the European producer and marketer of consumer electronics, has cooperated extensively with Matsushita of Japan in developing new products, such as compact discs and VCRs, to mutual benefit.

SOURCE: *Long Range Planning* 22, no. 1 (February 1989), pp. 102–109.

- Black and Decker's top management has refocused the company's product design and manufacturing efforts towards implementing a globalized strategy.
- IBM is simplifying its product designs and automating its key plants to produce on a low-cost global basis.

For those companies whose prosperity and survival have come to depend upon designing, producing, and selling their products and services to not only the United States but to much of the world, top management may have to rethink its conventional approaches in understanding and executing a workable set of strategies to meet the new challenge of global competition. Yet, strategy, especially corporate-level, is a difficult issue often construed in such vague terms as "distinctive competence," "globalizing," and "seeking focus." The central point of this article is to demonstrate that corporate strategy is a multidimensional concept that requires top management to consider the interplay of one's own efforts, that of potential competitors and partners, as well as that of time.

A NEW LOOK AT COMPETITIVE STRATEGY

The conventional approach to understanding and devising long-term strategy encourages managers to think of two distinct sets of strategies: corporate-level and business-level. Corporate strategy addresses the question of "What businesses should one compete in?" Business-level strategy, however, considers a different question of "How should we compete in a given business?" Applied in its simplest interpretation, corporate strategy implies that all top management needs to do is to choose those businesses that best fit the company and assimilate them.

Issues concerning global competitive advantage are key dimensions of corporate strategy for most large and medium-sized companies because they directly relate to their overall posture and performance over the long term as industries continue their trend of globalization. Thus, what constitutes corporate and business levels of strategy has blurred over time. As we are now witnessing the transformation of the modern industrial landscape with such advances as automation, worldwide sourcing, and joint ventures with foreign partners in key value-added activities, the concept and practice of separating corporate-level strategy from that of business-level may prove obsolete as the level of global competition intensifies. Increasingly it is the case that strategic business units (SBUs) and worldwide responsibility now depend upon a certain amount of corporate governance and cooperation with other SUBs to share risks, costs, and transfer skills from one to another, as costs and risks rise exponentially with each new global venture. Accordingly, top management has now come to exercise considerable influence in determining how business units will compete within their own product/market scope, since the entire company's fate is linked to each business unit's degree of success in the global environment. Global competition in every industry has blurred the distinction between corporate and business-level strategies as decisions and consequences emanating from one SBU may indeed alter the whole company's strategic complexion.

Multidimensional Complexity. Consequently, corporate strategy in companies with extensive global activities assumes a multidimensional character. The number of critical strategic dimensions which top management may need to consider not only involves the more traditional question of choosing the right businesses, but also encompasses what this author believes are the following critical strategic decisions that directly affect the company's long-term competitive state:

1. Strategic alliances: the use of joint ventures in sharing development and production costs and in penetrating new markets.
2. Internal development and acquisition of new technologies and businesses: searching for a balanced approach to entering promising growth areas.
3. Dynamic thinking through time: realizing the inherent fluidity and volatility of change in the global environment.

The use of strategic alliances is what this author terms the *foreign policy* dimension of strategy. It refers to knowing the motives and the long-term effects on one's own competitive posture when considering the selection of a foreign partner. Finding a balance between internal development and acquisitions relates to the company's *domestic policy* dimension of strategy. This dimension refers to the development of new technologies and products to achieve distinctive competence in a particular field or range of fields. Finally, the time element is something which American managers especially all too often neglect in their strategic thinking. The global environment promises much greater levels of uncertainty, volatility of change, as well as new opportunities to enter industries whose barriers were once thought insurmountable. This trichotomy does not imply that these dimensions are independent from one another, but rather they prove just as important as choosing which business to compete in.

THE FOREIGN POLICY DIMENSION: STRATEGIC ALLIANCES VIA JOINT VENTURES

Strategic alliances in the form of joint ventures offer tremendous potential and pitfalls for cooperation between global companies of different nationalities as we move into the 21st century. The higher costs and risks of R&D, production, financing, and market penetration brighten the prospects for expanded strategic alliances between global companies as top management believes that no company alone can manage all of the high risks associated with world-scale ventures. Yet, joint ventures raise several questions of great corporate strategic importance since this vehicle for cooperation can also seriously undermine the company's long-term competitiveness if management is not careful in defining and implementing its foreign policy.

Relationship with Corporate Strategy. Joint ventures are one critical dimension of global competition and corporate strategy because the company has undertaken a major watershed decision to include an external actor directly into its core operational activities. Instead of the more orthodox approach of "What businesses do we compete in," the question becomes more like "Should we involve an outsider in our businesses?" Perhaps because joint ventures have largely been viewed as either a market entry vehicle or platform to share risks, top management may have largely reduced the importance of this issue. Although joint ventures have considerable appeal as a means to share risks and markets, they could constrain the company's future strategy if the venture involves a leakage of either proprietary knowledge or some critical corporate core skill. Especially for those companies whose global competitive advantage arises from high technology, proprietary knowledge and processes, and specialized production and marketing techniques, the issue of joint ventures becomes ever more paramount, since prospective partners could very well gain a direct searchlight to learn about the company's core skills and strengths. The issue of joint ventures commands top management's full attention since they could reveal the company's key ingredients for its long-term competitiveness to a potential competitor later. This is not to say that companies should not consider joint ventures as a means to enter new markets; only that they should remain cognizant of some of the particular difficulties involved in retaining proprietary technologies and core skills.

Industry Structure and Global Ventures.   Joint ventures in theory convey many benefits to the partners involved. Within the context of global competition, joint ventures fall along two distinct categories. According to Porter and Fuller,[1] two distinct types of joint ventures may evolve. The first type, known as the X-type coalition, involves sharing complementary activities. An example would include an agreement between two auto manufacturers with one performing the design skills, while the other manufacturers the product itself. That is to say, X-type coalitions involve crossing over and cooperating across different activities in the chain of value-adding activities. The second type of coalition within which ventures occur is that of the Y type. This venture form involves two or more firms cooperating within the same basic activity in the value-added chain, for example, a joint production agreement (e.g., GM-Toyota), or a joint R&D venture (Boeing and Fuji Heavy Industries in aircraft).

The first category (X-type ventures) often concerns a manufacturer of new technologies and products that wishes access to another country's distribution channels and market. More specifically, this is the route many Japanese and U.S. firms have taken, as the Japanese partner wishes to avoid costly duplication of existing U.S. facilities. The recent agreement between Toyota and GM stems largely from Toyota's desire to have a factory in the United States to bypass possible protectionist legislation. N.V. Philips' agreement with Matsushita and other Japanese manufacturers to market Japanese-made products (e.g., compact disc players) under the Philips label is a clear example of such behaviour.

---

[1]M. E. Porter, and M. Fuller, "Coalitions and Global Strategy," in *Competition in Global Industries,* ed. M. E. Porter (Boston, Mass.: Harvard Business School Press, 1986).

CASE 1
Texas Instruments

Texas Instruments, one of the world's biggest manufacturers of semiconductors and related products, has undertaken major strides to become a global competitor in all of the markets it serves. Yet, to the fullest extent possible, TI has tried to operate as a wholly owned subsidiary wherever it has operations, even though it is explicitly seeking long-term alliances with their biggest customers. TI represents an interesting example of how a company can avoid losing its technologies to Japanese competitors through persistence and possession of a unique proprietary knowledge that helped it to eventually become one of a few U.S. companies to actually have wholly owned subsidiaries in Japan.

In 1964, TI believed that Japan would become a major competitor in the world's budding integrated circuit market. It first set up a marketing center in Japan and sought permission to build a wholly owned manufacturing center, something which MITI vehemently opposed. After four years' persistence, TI worked out an arrangement with Sony that resulted in a joint venture in which TI would buy out Sony's share after three years. In effect, TI's subsidiaries in Japan would be free from the constraint of joint-venture requirements. Now in 1987, TI has four major plants in Japan that produces important components and semiconductors for the rest of the company's worldwide operations.

Now, TI is engaging in a series of discussions with several other European and U.S semiconductor and computer manufacturers to build new custom chips for their specific needs. Although the specific mechanism of building strategic alliances may involve joint ventures, the company is committed to remain at the forefront of R&D and production of all processes that would eventually be used in conjunction with key customers to produce better products. TI's long-term alliances may involve major players in the telecommunications, computer, and even automotive industries.

Source: Interviews and discussions with TI managers; supplemented by articles and speeches from the company.

The other global rationale for joint ventures (Y-type ventures) is when a partner seeks another partner's technology or production skills. The recent decision to jointly design small cars between Ford and Mazda reflects this mutual need. In addition, Toshiba's recent decision to cooperate with Motorola in securing the latter's access to high-technology, specialized semiconductors gives the Japanese partner an edge over its domestic and foreign competitors by allowing it to bypass the costs needed to build the requisite strengths on its own. Recent deals between Boeing and a consortium of Japanese manufacturers interested in producing civilian (and possibly) military aircraft also result from the Japanese desire to seek American design and production skills in a highly lucrative market.

Economic Motives.   Joint ventures warrant top management's special attention just at a time when many European and American manufacturers are looking to this vehicle as the means by which to regain lost competitive advantage in many industries. Although both X- and Y-type ventures offer the recipient considerable short-term benefits, there are many dangers to watch out for, especially with long-term strategic motives.

In the case of X-type ventures, the need for vertical integration or to strengthen a weak link in one's own value-adding activities provides the strongest motive for seeking a prospective partner. Companies that find themselves weak in manufacturing often resort to X-type coalitions to compensate for inability to make the product or high expense associated with local production (e.g., Motorola and Toshiba for new chips). Long-term provision of feed stock or other supplies is a major source of X-type joint ventures.

For Y-type joint ventures, the primary economic motive, according to Porter and Fuller, hinges upon risk sharing and the pooling of resources for scale economies and learning-curve effects. Because the Y-type venture means that partners will be engaged in the same activity, there is greater potential for cross-fertilization and transfer of new knowledge which may enhance the competitiveness of both partners. Unlike X-type ventures, Y-type ventures usually occur when both partners are strong in the same activity, rather than the asymmetrical pattern found in the former agreement.

Foreign Policy and Dependence.   Unlike economic motives, which hinge directly upon the financial benefits accrued to partners from their venture activities,

---

CASE 2
Philips N.V.

Philips N.V. is one of the largest manufacturers and distributors of consumer electronics products in Europe and the United States. It is an unusual company by both European and U.S. standards because it seems to thrive on partnerships, coproduction, and joint ventures with different foreign companies. Nevertheless, the company still commits itself towards massive investment in product R&D and efficient production for its own purposes. One of Philips' most recent and potentially most successful joint ventures is that with AT&T to manufacture and network information transmissions systems throughout Europe, using the 5ESS/PRX switch. Philips receives access to some AT&T products, while AT&T enters European markets.

More important, Philips' greatest endeavor is to work out equitable partnership and technology-sharing agreements with Japanese firms, particularly Matsushita Electric. By sharing production and technology with the Japanese, Philips hopes to lead the world in standardizing design formats for new products such as compact discs and VCRs. Part of the success attributed to Philips' ability to cooperate with the Japanese is the fact that the company commands considerable European market share and also political clout within the EEC. More important, many of Philips' top management know their Japanese counterparts quite well, which lays the foundation for successful cooperation later.

there exists the more fundamental question of strategic or competitiveness motives for entering into joint ventures. This is where the greatest danger of relying upon joint ventures lies. More specifically, there may be direct costs associated with each of the joint ventures that may not surface until the venture is well on its way, but which top management should realize before potential damage spreads malignant effects within the company. Thus, over the long term, unless management recognizes the explicit and implicit vulnerabilities of joint ventures, the company's competitive strength may diffuse into the hands of a new competitor. Some companies may actually seek to engage prospective partners into a number of joint ventures as a means to collect intelligence data and to monitor their activities.

For example, joint ventures of the X type cede production and technology development away from the owning firm to the partner. The cases of American companies who unwittingly gave away such technologies as transistors, color television tubes, and other consumer electronics show how difficult it is for the U.S. firm to reenter the market after the technology is ceded away. Further, Y-type ventures may involve subtle damage to the stronger partner, as every link in the value-added chain from technology and core skills, even to marketing techniques, eventually become learned by the other firm. Thus, it is easy to see how the strategic use of joint ventures is to serve as a monitor or "mole" which can constantly measure the progress the partner firm is making in the development of new technologies. It is entirely conceivable that some companies, particularly Asian, may engage in joint ventures solely to listen to the developments of those whom they perceive as leaders in a given product or technology.

Foreign Policy in Action.   Robert Reich and Eric Mankin's[2] arguments that joint ventures, particularly with the Japanese, prevent the U.S. company from moving further down the experience curve and allow the Japanese to take advantage of U.S.-developed technology with surprising ease are especially worth noting. The experience of other European global companies such as N.V. Philips, Thomson, and Thorn-EMI all testify to the extreme difficulty of securing access to Japanese technology while their own strengths wither on the vine. A recent study by Doz, Hamel, and Prahalad suggested that Japanese firms do not enter joint ventures with the intention of working out issues and technical problems in an equitable manner, but to force the U.S. partner into a position of extreme dependency on the Japanese partner by undermining their core strengths and taking over their critical skills. Japanese-promoted joint ventures are designed to place the U.S. firm in a competitive *disadvantage* in the future by learning what the U.S. firm has done heretofore, and reducing their ability to develop new technologies. Joint ventures with Japan may not be the way for U.S. firms

---

[2]R. B. Reich and E. D. Mankin, "Joint Ventures with Japan Give Away Our Future, *Harvard Business Review* 64, no. 2 (March/April 1986), pp. 78–86.

to regain competitive dominance. The recent joint venture between Boeing and a consortium of Japanese firms to develop a 7Y7 (a future efficient commercial airliner) could bring all kinds of problems. Honeywell's disastrous performance in the computer business through its joint ventures with Bull of France and NEC of Japan offers another lesson to top management of the dangers of top management's not understanding the full ramifications.

INTERNAL DEVELOPMENT AND ACQUISITION POLICIES

A topic that bears directly upon global competitiveness concerns finding the right balance between internal development and acquisitions to build the basis for entering new technologies and businesses for the future. Internal development refers to a preference by the company to enter new technologies or businesses through growth by its own indigenous efforts, while an acquisitions-oriented approach depends upon top management's ability to use the newly introduced technology and acquired management to maximum advantage. The domestic-

---

CASE 3
Honeywell

Honeywell's recent retreat from the computer business reflects some of the big problems associated with a loosely managed joint venture. Established originally in 1962 with Bull of France and later with NEC of Japan in 1970, Honeywell's joint venture in France was designed as a means to secure entry both in Europe and France's original colonies throughout Africa. Over time, though, much of the production of the hardware associated with its line of computers moved from the United States to Europe and Japan. In 1986, Honeywell, Bull, and NEC agreed to create a consortium that would transfer much of Honeywell's original computer business to the two foreign partners.

What is especially telling about this example is that it reveals a U.S. manufacturer can eventually become little more than a distributor for other foreign companies' products. Within the new three-way company, Honeywell's role is to serve as the main distributor of NEC products in the United States, especially personal computers under the Honeywell label and central processing units for its largest computers. Moreover, NEC could perhaps even receive financial support from Honeywell to support its activities, thus even encroaching upon the company's financial reserves.

This is an example known all too well to several other U.S. industries, notably consumer electronics and machine tools, where in many cases the U.S. partner in the joint venture is nothing more than a replaceable distributor, while the Japanese partner retains all of the production advantages and technology development. These problems result form the U.S. partner's all-too-eager desire to receive new technologies from the Japanese as well as quick profits, with little substantive production undertaken by the U.S. partner in the end.

policy question reflects not so much a decision of whether it is necessary to enter new areas of technological growth, but rather how. In either case, internal development or acquisition aims to lead the company into new areas that could complement existing strengths well. It is domestic policy to the extent that partnerships or joint ventures are avoided.

A Search for Focus.   Although the topic of internal development and acquisitions has been around for a long time, its relevance to global competition becomes even more telling when one considers that the United States and other countries are in the midst of a new merger wave—one in which companies are trying to achieve focus and specialization. Unlike the mergers of the late 1960s and 1970s, where conglomerates and unrelated diversification proved popular and ultimately less than profitable, today's mergers and acquisitions represent a massive restructuring of American industry catalyzed by tidal waves of foreign competition. With many companies divesting themselves of businesses they know little about and repositioning themselves into those areas in which they have a better chance of competing, internal development and acquisition policies to achieve global competitive advantage have become salient and timely issues. Yet, U.S. management's ever-broadening push to seek specialization complements well the latest advances in manufacturing and product design technology that are now just surfacing. The issue of internal development has assumed a much more pronounced role within corporate strategy as advances in technology promise to erode away industry barriers and hindrances to serving several different markets simultaneously at low cost.

Internal versus External?   The choices of internal development and acquisitions have often been considered from an exclusive, either/or viewpoint rather than from a perspective which emphasizes balance and an understanding of the underlying industry structure. Rather, companies which have done very well around the world have used a combination of both policies to maximum advantage. For example, General Electric has encouraged the internal development of new businesses through intrapreneurship programs and hiving off new divisions when new products or technologies look profitable, while at the same time acquiring small companies that complement its own endeavours in entering new technologies, such as Calma—a specialized firm in the CAD/CAM area. AT&T has invested considerable sums in equity arrangements with such companies as Olivetti while simultaneously setting up new manufacturing and design centers around the world, along with several joint ventures. Rockwell International's celebrated purchase of Allen-Bradley, a manufacturer of automation equipment and industrial controls, has matched the company's own internally driven efforts to build cellular manufacturing facilities for its electronics and telecommunications products. Consequently, many companies which have traditionally relied on internal development for the basis of their future growth have also acquired growth companies whenever their technologies or products fit in with the parent's core skills. The scope of such acquisition activity, however, has tended to remain small and confined to businesses with which management feels comfortable or experienced.

CASE 4
Allen-Bradley

Allen-Bradley, a major manufacturer of industrial controls recently acquired by Rockwell International, has developed new advanced technologies which allow it to simultaneously combine economies of scale with economies of scope in manufacturing new control modules. Using computer-integrated manufacturing (CIM) and new plant layouts, A-B has mastered the technique of accommodating product variety with mass production efficiency. While every company can certainly meet a customer's tailored needs, only A-B can do so without actually shutting down the entire line and disrupting its work flow.

Rockwell's acquisition of A-B represents a major milestone for the parent company as well, especially with its major endeavors in cellular manufacturing and increasing inventory turnover. Both Rockwell and A-B have complementary strengths and their specialized talents will match nicely over the years as the telecommunications, industrial controls, sensor systems, and semiconductors industries become more related. Rockwell's careful acquisition as well as its own major investments in new plant and equipment shows how a company may simultaneously pursue both the internal and external modes of domestic policy without excessive reliance on either.

Industry Structure and Acquisition.   Corporate strategy of specialization requires top management to understand the versatility and idiosyncrasy of its company's core strengths and skills, and that of the underlying industry and technology upon which they are based. Focus brings not only potentially greater competence and experience in competing in any one or several products/markets, but also a need for innovative methods and strategies to enter into different but related markets, usually via new technologies spun off from existing businesses.

It is not surprising that companies such as General Electric, IBM, Siemens, Northern Telecom, and NEC have tended to shun large-scale acquisitions in competing abroad. These companies, whose sources of competitive advantage derive from long-standing R&D programs, proprietary knowledge, and specialized processes, cannot assimilate major acquisitions easily. Instead, the possession of such core strengths means that companies in industries such as pharmaceuticals, telecommunications, and office equipment must compete primarily by relying on their own internally developed products and technologies.

On the other hand, companies which rely extensively on acquisitions without a commensurately high level of internally generated skills and technologies have generally emphasized financial controls in lieu of building core skills. This has been the case with many U.S. conglomerates (e.g., ITT in Europe), which arguably have done less well in global competition than their internal development counterparts (e.g., Du Pont in Europe). Thus, an explicit strategy of specialization in itself does not imply that companies should exclusively pursue one path to growth and expansion over another, but rather recognize the importance of creating a home base of technology and products to fall back on when competition assumes an increasingly technological dimension. The implication is clear: Even carefully selected acquisitions cannot compensate for the lack of at least some home-grown development of core skills. This trend could prove even more important when the once-fixed boundaries of industry structure and the barriers to entry change with new technologies. Thus, the foundation for any successful domestic policy must first come from internally generated sources of strength and experience.

The Technology Imperative.   What promises to reward (and complicate) manufacturing and strategic planning in those companies pursuing internal development approaches to new businesses is the technology dimension. Critical to any discussion of internal development is the growing role that automation and flexible manufacturing systems (FMS) will play in most companies' manufacturing strategies in the near future. Automation, as IBM, GE, and other big and small manufacturers are finding, allows the company to drive down its manufacturing costs when new process technologies are implemented properly. When designed to incorporate the latest product designs that reduce the number of internal and complex parts, automation could offer the company considerable economies of scope, whereby the use of a limited set of fixed assets based in engineering, R&D, and production could turn out a greater number and mix of different (but related) product modifications, if not actual products themselves, in shorter time. By taking advantage of such concepts as group technology (modularity) and "smarter" production-based machines, a company can theoretically serve several distinct but related markets. Nonetheless, incorporating these new technological advances will require close attention from corporate management because of the many distinctly new problems they bring with them, such as difficulty in cross-business-unit cooperation, obsolescence of performance evaluation standards, and the need for closer functional integration within the plant's activities.

A New Way to Diversify.   Thus, advances in production technology and new product designs have bestowed on U.S. companies a new opportunity: the potential to garner the benefits of serving diversified markets with new products without acquiring another company in that market. For example, Du Pont's innovation of new chemical technologies has allowed it to compete not only in speciality chemicals, but also in supplying the carpet business with new synthetic fibers, medical supply houses with newly designed synthetic fluids, and the electronics industry with composite materials. Automation and economies of scope can, when properly understood and implemented, greatly enhance the competitive range and scope of the company's efforts to meet the needs of its worldwide markets and even make inroads into another competitor's (or industry's) domain. In theory, smart and flexible machines could be converted from making printer boards to personal computers within the same factory, thus avoiding the need to duplicate facilities. The focused factory concept will move away from rote, dedicated, rigid processes, to one based on a focused technology applied to many potential different market needs. Allen-Bradley's newest break-

CASE 5
IBM

IBM in the mid-1980s was bent upon preserving its manufacturing skills and cost efficiency despite enormous pressures from less costly Far Eastern producers and imitators. Using its own proprietary designs and manufacturing capabilities, IBM is upgrading its U.S. plants to outcompete Epson of Japan in producing dot-matrix printers for personal computers. A major upgrading of its Louisville, Kentucky plant was designed to become the cost leader in electronic typewriters.

The basis for IBM's cost-efficiency and automation drive was a tendency toward producing many different product configurations based on one or two central designs. For example, the typewriters as well as printers use common parts and common manufacturing facilities, thus saving time and inventory. Moreover, sub-assemblies were built within IBM's plants as much as possible without relying extensively on many different suppliers, such that plants produced many of the components as well as the final end product. Although the company still relied on some Japanese producers for its laser and color printers (e.g., Canon), IBM's strength and willingness to invest in its own customized machines and factories will give it considerable momentum for competing with anyone easily into the next decade.

through in making numerous types of industrial controls easily within one factory using automated equipment is just the beginning of a new trend that could sweep the world. The key to attaining this kind of flexible and sensitive manufacturing setup rests with top management's understanding not only of the engineering tasks associated with the organization of this technology, but also of the technology's unprecedented capability of breaking down many industry barriers once thought impenetrable.

Truly Global Products?   In addition, further advances in automation and more efficient product designs could move many companies toward fulfilling their dreams of a truly globalized product. Although Ford's World Car concept met considerable resistance in its early days in Europe, the company has begun to reap the benefits of its more advanced modular designs of such models as the Ford Taurus and the Mercury Sable which apparently has done quite well both in the United States and abroad. Black and Decker has effectively diversified away from its traditional niche of making small power tools toward that of serving the consumer appliance markets through both simpler designs and close cooperation with General Electric to access production facilities. Moreover, Black and Decker's commitment to remold the company into a globalized strategy may be paying off as its new design techniques apply well to both a broad spectrum of consumer products and different markets around the world.

In fact, the whole notion of making a standard global product may soon prove moot, as traditional physical obstacles to producing customized goods quickly on the assembly line melt away. One could easily envision a company very

---

CASE 6
Black and Decker

Black and Decker is one of the largest manufacturers of power tools and consumer household products. Its recent acquisition of some of the light consumer appliance businesses from GE helps buttress the company's position around the world. Ever since the early 1980s, B & D's top management has striven to globalize the company products to serve many different markets. The company has over 12 manufacturing and assembly sites around the world, selling to over 100 countries.

The basis for B & D's globalization plan is its emphasis on standardizing basic designs for its numerous products. To the extent possible, designs made for one country require very little modification in another, thus capturing economies of scale and specialization. Part of the difficulty surrounding this move has been the relatively large number of components required for some of B & D's earlier products which have now been streamlined and simplified. A newly introduced tight information system also links up the many subsidiaries with headquarters, thus furthering steps to rationalize product design and manufacturing.

---

rapidly broadening its product line and services to a wide portfolio of markets simply by tailoring its production processes to the market's particular needs— all without the kind of massive new investments in separate plants characteristic of decades earlier. Whether a truly standardized product for the world has arrived remains to be seen. What one can already see is the arrival of new process technologies and innovative methods to incorporate them into the plant floor that will shift traditional job shop production modes toward a more intermittent or even continuous flow configuration where product variety will prove more of a competitive asset than a hindrance to potentially smoother manufacturing and lower costs.

UNDERSTANDING THE NEW GLOBAL ENVIRONMENT

Probably the least understood aspect of corporate strategy is that relating to issues of time and space. Today's rapidly advancing technologies have accelerated the breakdown of traditional barriers to entry in many industries. Companies in the airlines and automobile industries, for example, have found themselves also in the position of indirectly being able to compete in some aspects of the information industry. The use of computers and information hook-ups in these two distinct industries have actually brought them closer to possible competition in an entirely new third area. Thus, one of the biggest prerogatives facing top management around the globe is to better understand how the time dimension can radically alter one's strategy. Those executives who can understand how industries evolve over time will be better equipped to take their companies into new markets than their counterparts whose thinking has remained static and ossified.

Time and Global Thinking.   What is most tricky about the time dimension is that it defies easy characterization or qualification, two features demanded by most companies' strategic planning departments. Unlike the physical, concrete issues such as R&D spending, joint venture partners, and other strategies, the time element is much more akin to a sense of a world view or global thinking and evolution. The success of implementing the first two dimensions of foreign policy and domestic policy depends upon an understanding of time as much as it does on the specific aspects of any given strategy. While it is arguable that any company could in theory duplicate the success that Philips or IBM has built around the world, those executives who are accustomed to thinking on a dynamic, worldwide basis already have one major advantage over their competitors.

It is at this point that U.S. managers may have their greatest difficulty in acclimatizing themselves to the global environment. A 1986 study of 100 executives performed by Egon Zehnder International revealed that about two-thirds of U.S. managers remained totally ignorant of foreign market opportunities. Moreover, U.S. executives still remained hesitant or fearful of committing resources to potentially new markets. Yet, despite these findings, it is important to define exactly what the time dimension means when competing globally.

Time, Strategy, and Structure.   There is little doubt that as communications, information, and transportation become much more widely available to everyone, companies wishing to compete globally must have a presence in every major market. Yet, all too often, managers have considerable difficulty seeing beyond their own market or area, with the usual consequences of poor organization, slow responsiveness, and inability to meet customer needs. Thus the biggest problem is to balance worldwide presence with cost competitiveness, especially when product life cycles are becoming increasingly shorter.

The time dimension exerts its greatest influence when one analyzes the necessary changes in strategy and structure required to compete in different environments. Understanding the time dimension means, on the one hand, knowing when one's strategy is most appropriate for managing and competing in a particular environment. Equally important, that strategy must have the full support of the company's planning processes, communications, incentive programs, and other dimensions of internal structure. To the extent that strategy and structure match each other over time, there is the basis for sustainable global competitive advantage. Consequently, the time dimension requires top management to know when to change course and when to modify their strategies according to the situations they face. Yet, any major change in strategy may necessitate some modification of internal structure too. The example of how Olivetti is determined to transform itself from an Italian computer manufacturer to a worldwide player in the information services industry shows how a company's top management team can make big strides in plotting a new direction for a once small company.

Thus, the greatest challenge offered by the time dimension is the willingness of top management to think about change and to redirect their company's efforts towards new areas of growth. Most executives around the world have a difficult time in conceiving of change as being productive and potentially beneficial—

CASE 7
Olivetti

Olivetti is taking major steps toward becoming both a European and a global producer of computers and information products. The company has invested heavily in joint ventures and equity agreements with many companies around the globe, but its underlying philosophy is to compete everywhere and anywhere around the world. Some of the most recent steps taken by Olivetti include the equity arrangement with AT&T to produce personal computers for the U.S. giant, acquisition of U.S. bank automation supplier Bunker Ramo, joint ventures with EDS Corporation, a specialist in information integration, and a joint venture with Canon of Japan to manufacture medium-sized computers in Europe, and acquisition of Triumph-Adler of West Germany, a manufacturer of typewriters and office automation equipment.

The basis for Olivetti's rapid and sustained involvement with these and other prospective companies reflects top management's willingness to build market share and presence in every major country. Moreover, Olivetti's management team seems to understand the issue of time quite well. They realize that perhaps this is the last chance for the company to gain the opportunity to become a major world player, first by becoming more European than Italian. Unless Olivetti acquires enough size and staying power in Europe, top management believes that their global competitiveness will dwindle over time.

Olivetti's commitment to global thinking and long-term planning is reflected through the company's emphasis on selling services and software, rather than computer hardware.

---

either because people are accustomed to working and thinking in a particular way, or because the previous strategy has worked so well that their ability to change becomes much reduced over time. Consequently, one of the greatest tests facing top management is how well they can smoothly redirect their company's efforts toward potentially new business opportunities.

FURTHER READING

Hout, T.; Porter, M. E.; and Rudden, E. "How Global Companies Win Out", *Harvard Business Review*," 60, no. 5 (September/October 1982), pp. 98–108.

Ohmae, K., *Triad Power: The Coming Shape of Global Competition*. New York: Free Press, 1985.

What this article is about: This paper was developed for use in an executive education program designed for a Fortune 200-sized firm aimed at preparing its executives for global competition. It identifies 10 statements that describe successful global competitors.

3–6 Global Competitors: Some Criteria for Success

James F. Bolt

James F. Bolt is founder and president of Executive Development Associates, a consulting firm based in Westport, Conn. that specializes in the development of customized executive education programs

No set of criteria has ever been developed to assess what makes a corporation a successful global competitor. No magic formula or convenient road map for the international executive exists.

That conclusion, reached after conversations with experts at academic and research organizations, is hardly surprising. No two global competitors are alike. The combinations of management styles, products, markets, strategies, countries, plants, and myriad other factors are virtually limitless. What works for one corporation might be disastrous for another. Some years ago, Pieter Kuin, then vice-chancellor of the International Academy of Management and a past president of Unilever, N.V., wrote in the *Harvard Business Review* that "The magic of multinational management lies not so much in perfection of methods or excellence of men as in developing *respect* for other nationalities and cultures and for the *determination* to succeed in foreign markets."[1] This observation is as valid today as it was more than a decade ago.

Yet, some broad criteria, the ones most often cited as necessary for a successful global competitor and most often evident in large corporations that have succeeded in the global business arena, can be isolated. These criteria can be broken, somewhat arbitrarily, into 10 separate statements.

SOURCE: *Business Horizons* (January–February 1988), pp. 34–41.

[1]Pieter Kuin, "The Magic of Multinational Management," *Harvard Business Review* (November–December 1972), p. 89.

1. *Successful global competitors perceive themselves as multinational, understand that perception's implications for their business, and are led by a management that is comfortable in the world arena.*

If there is one key criterion for successful global competitors, it is this one. In virtually all corporations global success is dependent on a corporate leadership that sees the world as a global village. Successful leaders all seem to understand that there are two distinct breeds of multinational corporations—the multidomestic corporation and the truly global corporation.

The multidomestic company pursues different strategies in each of its foreign markets. Each overseas subsidiary is essentially autonomous. In this type of arrangement, "A company's management tries to operate effectively across a series of worldwide positions with diverse product requirements, growth rates, competitive environments and political risks. The company prefers that local managers do whatever is necessary to succeed in R&D, production, marketing, and distribution, but holds them responsible for results."[2]

In effect, the company competes with local competitors on a market-by-market bases. Many successful American companies operate this way: Procter & Gamble in household products, Honeywell in controls, Alcoa in aluminum, and General Foods in consumer foods, for example.

The global company, on the other hand, pits its entire resources against its competition in a highly integrated way. Foreign subsidiaries and divisions are largely interdependent in both operations and strategy. Says one expert:

> In a global business, management competes worldwide against a small number of other multinationals in the world market. Strategy is centralized, and various aspects of operations are decentralized or centralized as economics and effectiveness dictate. The company seeks to respond to particular local market needs, while avoiding a compromise of efficiency of the overall global system.[3]

Many multinationals are moving in this direction. Those who have already arrived include IBM in computers; Caterpillar in large construction equipment; Timex, Seiko, and Citizen in watches; and General Electric, Siemens, and Mitsubishi in heavy electrical equipment.

The important thing is that successful global competitors have carefully considered the difference between multidomestic and global. Corporate leadership can show that it is serious by making sure that someone at the top is knowledgeable about and comfortable in the world arena. A Conference Board study some years ago found that the companies with foreign operations doing well invariably were led by chief executive officers who were "uncommonly well read, well traveled and took a very broad view of the world and the role of business in that world."[4]

---

[2]Thomas Hout, Michael E. Porter, and Eileen Rudden, "How Global Companies Win Out," *Harvard Business Review* (September–October 1982), p. 103.

[3]Hout, Porter, and Rudden (see note 2).

[4]*Organization and Central of International Operations* (New York: The Conference Board, 1978), p. 8.

2. *Successful global competitors develop an integrated and innovative global strategy that makes it very difficult and costly for other companies to compete.*

Perhaps the best evidence for this criterion was amassed by Thomas Hout, Vice President of the Boston Consulting Group; Michael E. Porter, professor at the Harvard Business School; and Eileen Rudden, Manager of the Boston Consulting Group's Boston office.[5]

The three authors argue that most successful global competitors "perceive competition as global and formulate strategy on an integrated worldwide basis." They develop "a strategic innovation to change the rules of the competitive game in its particular industry. The innovation acts as a lever to support the development of an integrated global system." The authors cite three cases to illustrate this point—Caterpillar, whose strategic innovation was in manufacturing; L. M. Ericsson, of Sweden, whose breakthrough was in technology; and Honda, where the innovative strategic thrust was in marketing.

The common denominator is that each of these highly successful global competitors altered the dynamics of its industry and pulled away from the other major players. Caterpillar achieved economies of scale through commonality of design. The competition could not match Caterpillar in either costs or profits. Consequently, the competition could not make the large investments required to catch up.

Ericsson, by developing a unique modular technology, created a cost advantage. Its global strategy turned electronics from a threat to Ericsson into a barrier to its competitors.

Honda unlocked the potential for economies of scale in production, marketing, and distribution through aggressive marketing. The only thing left for the competition was the small-volume specialty market.

In each case, there existed within the industry the potential for a worldwide system of products and markets. A company with an integrated global strategy (something all three companies had) could exploit that situation, which these three did.

3. *Successful global competitors aggressively and effectively implement their worldwide strategy, and they back it with large investments.*

That leads conveniently to our third criterion for success on the global stage: the determination and the ability to back the strategy with substantial long-term investments. The Caterpillar experience is a case in point. Caterpillar is the only Western company that matches its major competitor, Komatsu, in capital spending per employee. In fact, Caterpillar's overall capital spending is more than three times that of its Japanese competitor. And Caterpillar does not divert resources into other businesses or otherwise dissipate its financial advantage. With almost single-minded purpose, it pumps huge proportions of its profits back into its base business and dares the competition to try to match it.[6]

---

[5]Hout, Porter, and Rudden (see note 2), pp. 98–108.
[6]Hout, Porter, and Rudden (see note 2).

In *Competitive Strategy: Techniques for Analyzing Industries and Competitors,* Michael E. Porter points out that successful global competitors not only are willing to invest heavily, but (perhaps even more important) they are also willing to wait long periods of time before these investments pay off.[7] Porter adds that implementing such strategies takes time. The result, he says, can be major investment projects with zero or even a negative return on investment for periods that would be thought unacceptable a few years ago.

A case in point is the experience of Xerox Corporation. In the mid-1970s, the company's Japanese subsidiary, Fuji Xerox, fell on hard times. The oil shock hurt Japan's economy severely. Ricoh introduced a highly successful line of inexpensive, low-volume copiers. Xerox sales in the Far East plummeted, and the partnership reached a crossroads.

Had Xerox considered Fuji Xerox to be a basically Japanese subsidiary doing business only in that part of the world, it probably would have opted to scale back operations. But Xerox took a global approach, realizing that the partnership could be a powerful weapon in its worldwide battle with the Japanese. The company made large investments in technology, product development, and manufacturing capacity.

Although the investment did not become profitable for five years, it has since paid for itself many times over. Fuji Xerox is now the leader in its market. More important, Fuji Xerox supplies low-volume copiers for Xerox to market in much of the world—including the United States.[8]

4. *Successful global competitors understand that technological innovation is no longer confined to the United States, and they have developed systems for tapping technological innovation abroad.*

Another key in the battle for supremacy in international markets in technological innovation. In the late 1950s, more than 80 percent of the world's major innovations came from the United States. That percentage has steadily declined, and today less than half of the world's innovations can legitimately lay claim to the "made in America" slogan.[9]

How do the more successful global competitors respond to challenges on the worldwide technological front? Robert Ronstadt, associate professor of management at Babson College, and Robert J. Kramer, project director at Business International Corporation, sought to find answers in their landmark study three years ago. Their analysis was based on interviews with more than 50 American, European, and Japanese managers of multinationals, a mail survey of 240 corporations around the world, and data covering more than 100 foreign-based R&D investments.[10]

---

[7]Michael E. Porter, *Competitive Strategy: Techniques for Analyzing Industries and Competitors* (New York: Free Press, 1980).

[8]Jeff Kennard, "An American Expatriate View of Japanese Business," *Agenda: A Journal for Xerox Managers* (March 1983), pp. 4–10.

[9]Robert Ronstadt and Robert J. Kramer, "Getting the Most Out of Innovation Abroad," *Harvard Business Review* (March–April 1982), p. 94.

[10]Ronstadt and Kramer (see note 9), pp. 94–99.

Their data suggest that those companies who have done well in the international technological arena do some or all of the following:

- **Scanning and monitoring.** This includes reading journals and patent reports, meeting with foreign scientists and technical experts through conferences and seminars, and serving on advisory panels and study teams sponsored by the government and professional associations.
- **Connections with academia and research organizations.** Successful global enterprises actively pursue work-related projects with foreign academics, and they often make these associations with faculty members formal by using consulting agreements.
- **Programs to increase the company's visibility.** Many technological bonanzas go to companies with the right reputation. One common method of attracting attention is providing information to computer data banks that facilitate communication between prospective purchasers and vendors.
- **Cooperative research projects.** Many successful global enterprises enter into research projects with each other to broaden their contacts, reduce expenses, diminish the risk for each partner, or forestall the market entry of a competitor.
- **Acquiring or merging with foreign companies that have extensive innovative capabilities.** The two researchers found that the acquired company's innovative capability is not the primary reason for the merger. Nevertheless, significant technology may be acquired that can enhance an organization's ability to innovate abroad.
- **Acquisition of external technology by licensing.** A corporation may license in a technological innovation from another country, license out its own technology to others in the hope of getting access to improvements made by the licensee, or exchange its technology for another company's by cross-licensing.

Ronstadt and Kramer emphasize that "company-owned R&D labs located overseas provide the best opportunities for managers to internationalize their scanning operations and obtain foreign innovations or new technology . . . U.S. multinationals have spent untold time and money establishing extensive operations and resources abroad. The time has come for greater utilization of these resources—not just as sales outlets for domestic or foreign products but as sources of innovation in technology and management that will aid in the resurgence of U.S. industry and the world economy."[11]

5. *Successful global competitors operate as though the world were one large market, not a series of individual countries.*

Daniel J. Boorstin characterizes our age as driven by "the Republic of technology whose supreme law . . . is convergence, the tendency for everything to become more like everything else."[12] In business, this trend has pushed markets toward global commonality. Successful global competitors have embraced the

---

[11]Ronstadt and Kramer (see note 9), p. 99.

[12]Daniel J. Boorstin, *The Americans.* (New York: Random House, 1973), p. 284.

new phenomenon; they now sell standardized products in similar ways across increasingly larger portions of the planet.

Writing in the *Harvard Business Review,* Theodore Levitt says:

> The transforming winds whipped up by the proletarianization of communication and travel enter every crevice of life. Commercially, nothing confirms this as much as the success of McDonald's from the Champs Elysees to the Ginza, of Coca-Cola in Bahrain, and Pepsi-Cola in Moscow.[13]

The implications for all global competitors—consumer-goods producers and high-technology companies—are profound. American corporations, in particular, have built their success largely on giving their customers *precisely* what they say they want, even if that means higher costs. That philosophy has led many corporations to overreact to different national and regional tastes, preferences, and needs. There is powerful new evidence that this road is doomed to failure. Lynn W. Phillips, Dae Chang, and Robert D. Buzzell, in their as yet unpublished Harvard Business School working paper, document that this notion of being all things to all people dramatically drives cost up and quality down.[14]

Successful global competitors, on the other hand, have remembered Henry Ford and the Model T. They stress simplification and standardization. Much of the success of the Japanese is based on this approach. It is significant that Japanese companies operate almost entirely without the kinds of marketing departments and market research so prevalent in the West. John F. Welch, Jr., the chairman of General Electric, puts it this way: "The Japanese have discovered the one great thing all markets have in common—an overwhelming desire for dependable, world-standard modernity in all things, at aggressively low prices."[15]

This new reality is difficult for many American managers to comprehend. It runs counter to the methods that they have been taught and that have proved successful in the past. But companies that do not adapt to the new global realities lose to those that do adapt.

"Corporations geared to this new reality," according to Levitt, "benefit from enormous economies of scale in production, distribution, marketing, and management. By translating these benefits into reduced world prices, they can decimate competitors that still live in the disabling grip of old assumptions about how the world works."[16]

6. *Successful global competitors have developed an organizational structure that is well thought out and unique.*

Of all the subjects our research covered, the question of organization was the most vexing. There is simply no clear answer. If one examines the organization

---

[13]Theodore Levitt, "The Globalization of Markets," *Harvard Business Review,* (May–June 1983), p. 93.

[14]Lynn W. Phillips, Dae Chang, and Robert D. Buzzell, "Product Quality: Cost Production and Business Performance—A Test of Some Key Hypotheses," *Harvard Business School Working Paper* No. 83–13.

[15]John F. Welch, Jr., *Speech to the Foreign Policy Association,* New York City, November 28, 1983.

[16]Levitt (see Note 13), p. 92.

charts of most global competitors, it becomes clear that "there is no one way in which international companies organize their domestic and foreign activities"[17]

Most U.S.-based multinationals have at one time or another established international divisions to manage their overseas operations. As they grew, these same companies also sprouted several product-oriented divisions at home. In many cases, the result was a structural conflict between the geographic orientation of the international division and the product orientation of the domestic operations.

It is not surprising, therefore, that the international division has proved to be a transitory organization for many global competitors. As growth mushroomed in these companies, many of them abandoned their international divisions as such. J. William Widing, Jr., one-time vice president of Harbridge House, has identified three alternatives that are most often used:

- Worldwide product divisions, each responsible for selling its own products throughout the world.
- Divisions responsible for all products sold within a certain geographic area.
- A matrix consisting of either of these arrangements with a centralized functional staff, or a combination of area operations and worldwide product management.[18]

The literature on organization and multinationals is extensive. Much of it is opinion and conjecture. Still, some broad guidelines do emerge. Among them are the following:

- Corporations using the worldwide-product-division structure have grown about 50 percent faster than those using the area-division structure. Whether there is a cause-and-effect relationship is debatable, but there seems to be at least a preference for worldwide product divisions in situations involving rapid growth.
- The greater the diversity of product lines, the more likely it is that an American company will manage its foreign business through worldwide product divisions.
- The availability and depth of management resources is also important. The international division provides the easiest way to concentrate scarce managerial expertise for international operations. Worldwide product divisions provide the widest scope and latitude for individual decision making and risk taking. A geographic structure requires a large number of broad-gauged managers with considerable general management experience.
- Geographic divisions can concentrate most efficiently on developing close relationships with national and local governments. Worldwide product divisions do not fare as well in this regard.

---

[17]Joseph La Palombara, and Stephen Blank, *Multinational Corporations in Comparative Perspective,* (New York: The Conference Board, 1979).

[18]J. William Widing, Jr., "Reorganizing Your Worldwide Business," *Harvard Business Review* (May–June 1973), p. 156.

- Although the relative cost of operation varies, the matrix form tends to be the most expensive. It focuses extra attention on functional considerations and thus requires more staff personnel. Area divisions usually have the leanest staffs and, therefore, the lowest operating costs.

These and other guidelines are just that. "Organizational structure and reporting relationships present subtle problems for a global strategy," according to Hout, Porter, and Rudden. "Effective strategy control argues for a central product-line organization. Effective local responsiveness argues for a geographic organization with local autonomy. A global strategy argues for a product-line organization that has the ultimate authority, because without it the company cannot gain system-wide benefits. Nevertheless, the company still must balance product and area needs. In short, there is no simple solution."[19]

Echoing this sentiment, Levitt writes that "There is no one reliably right answer—no one formula by which to get it . . . . What worked well for one company or one place may fail for another in precisely the same place, depending on the capabilities, histories, regulations, resources, and even the cultures of both."[20]

7. *Successful global competitors have a system that keeps them informed of political changes abroad and the implications for their business.*

The world in which multinationals must operate is fraught with risk. Says Thomas A. Shreeve, a political analyst with the United States Department of State and a research associate at the Harvard Business School, "A new political party in power—or the new head of an old governing coalition—can easily decide to change the fundamentals for operating and investing by altering the regulation of licensing, for example, or so changing foreign equity restrictions, local participation requirements, or the basis of corporate taxation."[21]

Most successful global competitors have some system that attempts to read the winds of political change. As early as 1969, Gulf Oil formed an international policy analysis unit to keep senior executives appraised of political developments on a daily basis. Dow Chemical, General Motors, IBM, most large banks, and virtually all oil companies have people dedicated exclusively to political analysis.

But few multinational corporations seem satisfied with the way their systems function. Part of the problem is that most systems are designed to track dramatic events, such as the overthrow of a government or the taking of hostages. These types of events do not need to be monitored because they quickly become public knowledge, and because once they happen there is little the corporation can do. Corporations need systems that pay attention to small details that, when pieced together, provide advance information of what is likely to happen.

---

[19]Hout, Porter, and Rudden (see note 2), p. 107.

[20]Levitt (see note 13), p. 100.

[21]Thomas W. Shreeve, "Be Prepared for Political Changes Abroad," *Harvard Business Review* (July– August 1984), p. 111.

8. *Successful global competitors recognize the need to make their management team international and have a system in place to accomplish the goal.*

Most senior executives in large multinational corporations profess their commitment to bringing foreign managers into their inner circles. Yet, when one looks at the hierarchies of large global competitors, "the gap between their stated aims to have truly multinational executive personnel and the practice of actually having them is great . . . . And in the face of pressures from without and from within, it is becoming obvious that solving this human problem incurred in developing MNCs will be critical to the success of the enterprise in question."[22]

The crux of the problem seems to be a matter of attitude, not policy. For example, in determining who will receive incentive compensation, who will get a foreign assignment, or who has high management potential, the home-country executive is likely to rely on his own perception of who is the most competent and trustworthy, his compatriot down the hall or a foreigner thousands of miles away who he rarely sees. Given that choice, a variety of cultural and social biases often dictate the selection.[23]

Not surprisingly, then, most multinationals have a poor track record in integrating their management teams. One survey of 150 of the largest global competitors found that barely 1 percent of the senior headquarters positions were filled by foreign nationals, despite the fact that the average income generated by overseas operations was at least 20 percent of the companies' total income.[24]

Another survey found that "Executives we questioned in several successful companies closely associate paying greater attention to foreign nationals with improvement of corporate performance."[25] This same study, which was conducted by Howard V. Perlmutter, chairman of the Multinational Enterprise Unit at the Wharton School of Business and Daniel A. Heenan, then vice president for manpower planning and development at First National City Bank, identified four critical areas which need attention.

The first is headquarters and foreign service assignments. As one observer puts it: "They all love to talk about the Brazilian in London and the Indian in Belgium. But all that talk is for public consumption . . . the ultimate responsibilities still lie with the Americans." Those who have broken this pattern usually have done so with a two-pronged approach: a manpower-resource planning system that is dedicated to identifying and moving people across national boundaries, and a company godfather who is responsible for a handful of senior foreign executives. This role is normally reserved "for a person of considerable stature and influence in headquarters whose role is to ensure that people on overseas

[22]Howard V. Perlmutter, and David A. Heenan, "How Multinational Should Your Top Managers Be?" *Harvard Business Review* (November–December 1974), p. 123.
[23]Howard V. Perlmutter, "The Tortuous Evolution of the Multinational Corporation," *Columbia Journal of World Business* (January–February 1969), p. 9.
[24]Perlmutter and Heenan (see note 22), p. 124.
[25]Perlmutter and Heenan (see note 22), p. 124.

assignments are neither forgotten nor allowed to neglect the growth of their functional skills."[26] IBM is the most-often-cited example of this two-pronged approach.

The second critical area that needs to be addressed is compensation. Even today, only a handful of global competitors maintain truly multinational compensation programs for their managers. In many instances, foreigners with identical credentials and jobs receive one-half to one-third the total compensation package of their American counterparts. One expert explains the problem this way: "Without pay practices that offer equal monetary incentives for all managers, companies run the risk of not attracting and retaining high-quality professionals."[27]

A third key area is managerial inventories. The manpower lists from which candidates are assigned to key overseas and headquarters positions tend to be exclusive. While American expatriate managers are invariably included in these worldwide inventories, foreign nationals are not. If the manpower-planning lists contain only Americans, it should not be surprising that only Americans are found in prime international positions.

The fourth key area is performance-appraisal techniques. The Perlmutter-Heenan study found that the most successful global competitors had "adopted a worldwide performance appraisal system that assesses a manager's functional and administrative abilities plus his skills to operate in a global setting. The MNC executives we talked with suggest blending the best evaluative techniques from all over the world."[28]

Our research indicated that many multinationals who now have relatively good foreign representation among their senior executives began that process by placing a foreign manager in the hierarchy of personnel. That person tends to act as a catalyst and conscience when key operating assignments open up.

9. *Successful global competitors give their outside directors an active role in the affairs of the company.*

More and more multinationals are appointing local nationals to their foreign subsidiaries' boards of directors. Much of this trend is in response to foreign legislation that demands it. But the more sophisticated and successful global competitors realize that "The outside director who is also a citizen of the host country can play an important role in developing an atmosphere of trust in which they will be able to operate with a reasonable degree of freedom."[29]

Writing in the *Harvard Business Review*, Samuel C. Johnson and Richard M. Thomson offer some sage advice: "The chief executive of the MNC should not

---

[26]David A. Heenan, "The Corporate Expatriate," *Columbia Journal of World Business*, (May–June 1970), p. 49.

[27]David Young, "Fair Compensation for Expatriates," *Harvard Business Review* (July–August 1973), p. 117.

[28]Perlmutter and Heenan (see note 22). p. 130.

[29]*The Changing Role of the International Executive*, The Conference Board, SBP No. 119, p. 18.

delegate to others the selection of outside directors and the invitation to serve. His personal involvement will indicate the significance he ascribes to the position."[30]

Tasks the outside board members perform that are most often considered positive contributions include the following:

- Becoming familiar with the operation of the business and keeping abreast of local economic, legal, and political developments, so he or she can anticipate changes affecting business not only in his or her home country, but in the entire region or continent as well.
- Making certain that the subsidiary follows objectives and policies established by the parent and communicated to him or her through memoranda and discussions with the corporation's officers.
- Counseling the parent company regarding local compensation standards, trade-union regulations, and other personnel matters.
- Periodically appraising the performance of the subsidiary's management (primarily through review of its financial reports).
- Counseling the subsidiary's management on its relations with financial institutions, governmental bodies, and the public.
- Offering advice and counsel on broad political and social trends that may have a significant impact on long-range planning.
- Helping to ensure that the subsidiary behaves as a responsible member of the community.

Successful global competitors seem to have two things in common in their use of local nationals on their boards of directors. First, they are selected by the chief executive officer and have his confidence, support, and trust. Second, they are not just figureheads. They are effective contributors. Says one source: "If he (the outside director) is doing his job properly, he will have his hands full. The onus is on him to be vigorous and informed. The responsibility of the parent company is to listen and react."[31]

10. *Successful global competitors are well-managed.*

This may seem self-evident, but it bears mention. It would be foolhardy to think that a corporation could successfully expand beyond its own national borders if its domestic management house was not in order.

There are numerous ways of course, to assess a corporation's management effectiveness—not the least of which are healthy financial statements that show relative freedom from debt and consistent revenue and profit growth. We have elected to include here for the basis of discussion the eight attributes which bestselling authors Thomas J. Peters and Robert H. Waterman, Jr. used in *In Search of Excellence.* They are:

---

[30]Samuel C. Johnson, and Richard M. Thomson, "Active Role For Outside Directors of Foreign Subsidiaries," *Harvard Business Review* (September–October 1974), p. 14.

[31]Johnson and Thomson (see note 30), p. 14.

- **A bias for action.** While these companies may be analytical in their approach to decision making, they are not paralyzed.
- **Close to the customer.** They learn from the people they serve. Many of the innovative companies got their best product ideas from customers. That comes from listening, intently and regularly.
- **Autonomy and entrepreneurship.** The innovative companies develop many leaders and many innovators throughout the organization.
- **Productivity through people.** Excellent companies treat the rank and file as the root of quality and productivity gain. They do not have we/they labor attitudes.
- **Hands-on, value-driven.** The basic philosophy of an organization has far more to do with its achievements then do technical or economic resources.
- **Stick to the knitting.** The odds for excellent performance strongly favor those companies that stay reasonably close to businesses they know.
- **Simple form, lean staff.** The underlying structural forms in the excellent companies are elegantly simple. Top-level staffs are lean; it is not uncommon to find a corporate staff of fewer than 100 people running multibillion-dollar enterprises.
- **Simultaneous loose-tight properties.** The excellent companies are both centralized and decentralized.[32]

Any corporation seeking to expand globally would do well to ask itself how well it measures up to the Peters-Waterman criteria for excellence. At the very least, they provide some useful food for thought.

As we said at the outset, these 10 criteria for global successful competitiveness are somewhat arbitrary. Each reader could probably add to the list or refine it. Nevertheless, any corporation seeking to expand globally can help itself succeed by taking inventory against these 10 criteria.

---

[32]Thomas J. Peters, and Robert H. Waterman, Jr., *In Search of Excellence*, (New York: Harper & Row, 1982), pp. 89–318.

Part IV

Managing Strategy Implementation

This section takes an in-depth look at the problems and tasks of strategy implementation. First, L. J. Bourgeois and David Brodwin discuss the different roles and methods used by chief executive officers in developing and implementing strategies. Designing organizations to aid strategy implementation is the focus of an article by Ian C. MacMillan and Patricia E. Jones. Next Yvan Allaire and Mihaela Firsirotu propose a framework for devising and implementing "radical" strategies in large organizations. The linking of reward structures to strategic performance is discussed by Henry Migliore. Two Japanese authors, Tomasz Mroczkowski and Masao Hanaoki, discuss changes in the employment and promotion systems of Japanese companies as they position themselves to compete in the 1990s. The next two articles (by Bernard Reimann and Yoash Wiener, and Sebastian Green) discuss corporate culture and its implications for strategy formulation and implementation. John Butler discusses the role that the human resource management function can play in the implementation of a business strategy. This section concludes with a discussion of implementing intrapreneurship as a business strategy at the 3M Corporation.

What this article is about: In studying the management practices of a variety of companies, the authors have found that their approaches to strategy implementation can be categorized into one of five basic descriptions. In each one, the chief executive officer plays a somewhat different role and uses distinctive methods for developing and implementing strategies.

4–1 *Putting Your Strategy into Action*

L. J. Bourgeois III and David R. Brodwin

*Jay Bourgeois is Assistant Professor of Strategic Management,
Graduate School of Business,
Stanford University
David R. Brodwin is a member of the strategic management
practice at Arthur D. Little, Inc.,
San Francisco*

Most discussions of strategic planning focus on how to formulate strategy. There are several tools and techniques in widespread use. Management consulting firms offer strategic planning on a commodity basis, and business school programs are adorned with methodologies for choosing the "best" strategy.

By contrast, scant attention has been given to how to implement those strategies. Yet many people have recognized that problems with implementation in many companies have resulted in failed strategies and abandoned planning efforts. This paper will identify many of these implementation problems and then offer you some remedies for them.

Our discussions will provide suggestions that can help managers be more successful in three general areas:

- Developing strategies that can realistically be implemented, given not only the marketplace but also the politics, culture, and competence of your firm.
- Putting your strategies into action.
- Revising strategies continually so you can take advantage of new opportunities and respond to threats.

SOURCE: *Strategic Management Planning* (March–May 1983).

FIVE WAYS COMPANIES IMPLEMENT STRATEGY

In studying the management practices of a variety of companies, we have found that their approaches to strategy implementation can be categorized into one of five basic descriptions. In each one, the chief executive officer plays a somewhat different role and uses distinctive methods for developing and implementing strategies. We have given each description a title to distinguish its main characteristics.

The first two descriptions represent traditional approaches to implementation. Here the CEO formulates strategy first, and then thinks about implementation later.

1. *The Commander Approach*—The CEO concentrates on formulating the strategy, giving little thought to how the plan will be carried out. He either develops the strategy himself or supervises a team of planners. Once he's satisfied that he has the "best" strategy, he passes it along to those who are instructed to "make it happen."
2. *The Organizational Change Approach*—Once a plan has been developed, the executive puts it into effect by taking such steps as reorganizing the company structure, changing incentive compensation schemes, or hiring staff.

The next two approaches involve more recent attempts to enhance implementation by broadening the bases of participation in the planning process:

3. *The Collaborative Approach*—Rather than develop the strategy in a vacuum, the CEO enlists the help of his senior managers during the planning process in order to ensure that all the key players will back the final plan.
4. *The Cultural Approach*—This is an extension of the collaborative model to involve people at middle and sometimes lower levels of the organization. It seeks to implement strategy through the development of a corporate culture throughout the organization.

The final approach takes advantage of managers' natural inclinations to develop opportunities as they are encountered.

5. *The Crescive Approach*—In this approach, the CEO addresses strategy planning and implementation simultaneously. He is not interested in planning alone, or even in leading others through a protracted planning process. Rather, he tries, through his statements and actions, to guide his managers into coming forward as champions of sound strategies.

In studying these five approaches we noticed several trends. First, the two traditional methods are gradually being supplanted by the others. Second, companies are focusing increasingly on organizational issues involved in getting a company to adapt to its environment and to pursue new opportunities or respond to outside threats. Finally, we see a trend toward the CEO playing an increasingly indirect and more subtle role in strategy development.

Method 1: The Commander

The typical scenario depicting the most traditional approach to strategy formulation and implementation is as follows: After the CEO approves the strategic plan, he calls his top managers into a conference room, presents the strategy and tells them to implement it.

The CEO is involved only with formulating the strategy. He assumes that an exhaustive analysis must be completed before any action can be taken, so the CEO typically authorizes an extensive study of the firm's competitive opportunities. In general, focusing on the planning succeeds in at least giving the CEO a sense of direction for his firm, which helps him make difficult day-to-day decisions and also reduces uncertainty within the organization.

However, this approach can be implemented successfully only if several conditions are met. First, the CEO must wield a great deal of power so he can simply command implementation. Otherwise, unless the proposed strategy poses little threat to organizational members, implementation cannot be achieved very easily.

Second, accurate information must be available to the strategist before it becomes obsolete. Since good strategy depends on high-quality information, it is important that critical information entering the firm at lower levels is being compiled, digested, and transmitted upward quickly.

Third, the strategist must be insulated from personal biases and political influences that can impinge on the plan. Managers are likely to propose strategies favorable to their own divisions but not necessarily to the corporation as a whole.

One problem with this approach is that it often splits the firm into "thinkers" and "doers," and those charged with the doing may not feel that they are part of the game. The general manager must dispel any impression that the only acceptable strategies are those developed by himself and his planning staff, or he may find himself faced with an extremely unmotivated, uninnovative group of employees.

Method 2: Organizational Change

With this approach, the CEO makes the strategy decisions and then paves the way for implementation by redesigning the organizational structure, personnel assignments, information systems, and compensation scheme.

This method goes beyond the first one by having the CEO consider how to put the plan into action. The CEO basically uses two sets of tools: (1) changing the structure and staffing to focus attention on the firm's new priorities and (2) revising systems for planning, performance measurement, and incentive compensation to help achieve the firm's strategic goals.

The first set of tools—changing the organizational structure and staffing—has been the traditional approach espoused in most business strategy texts. Generally, the organizational structure should reflect the diversity of the firm's strategies. For example, if a company's strategy calls for worldwide coordination of manufacturing in order to capture cost efficiencies, the CEO would implement a "functional" organization for production, while a strategy calling for selling diverse product lines to various markets would demand a divisional organization of separate profit centers.

The second set of tools involves adjusting administrative systems. Various planning, accounting, and control tools, such as those governing capital and operating budgets, can be used to help achieve desired goals. For example, if the firm's strategy calls for investing certain businesses and harvesting others, or for channeling profits from one national unit into funding others, these goals should be featured prominently in the capital budgeting procedures so that business-unit managers can effectively plan their resource requests and others can effectively evaluate them.

Performance measures should be designed so that they target meaningful short-term milestones in order to monitor progress toward strategic goals. The incentive compensation scheme should then be tied into the clear-cut numerical terms of the performance measures. At a minimum, the general manager must ensure that the current compensation plan isn't thwarting the achievement of the strategy in ways such as rewarding short-term profitability at the expense of longer-term growth.

One company, with which the authors are familiar, clearly illustrates the problems which can arise when performance measures and administrative systems are inappropriate. This firm—a major diversified manufacturer—concluded that a steady stream of new products was the most important factor in maintaining the stock price at the desired level, yet the performance measures and management reports imposed on the division heads stressed quarterly profit above all else.

Unlike the first approach, in this method the CEO doesn't merely command his subordinates to put the plan into action. He supervises the implementation and may only reveal the strategy gradually, rather than in one bold proclamation.

However, it usually is inadequate for the CEO simply to tack "implementation" onto "strategy." This approach doesn't deal with problems of obtaining accurate information nor does it buffer the planner from political pressures. Also, as in the first approach, imposing the strategy downward from the top executives still causes motivational problems among the "doers" at lower levels.

In addition, another problem can develop when the CEO manipulates the systems and structures of the organization in support of a particular strategy. The general manager may be losing important strategic flexibility.

Some of these systems, particularly incentive compensation, take a long time to design, install, and become effective. If a dramatic change in the environment suddenly demands a major shift in the strategy, it may be very difficult to change the firm's course, since all the "levers" controlling the firm have been set firmly in support of the now-obsolete game plan.

In the interest of retaining strategic flexibility in situations where environmental uncertainty is high, it may prove more advisable in the long run to refrain from using some of the tools described above. For example, many high-technology firms, which rely on the rapid development and introduction of a continuous stream of technological innovations, avoid imposing bureaucratic administrative systems which would cripple their ability to create strategic change.

CONCLUSION

Dependence upon the Commander Approach has significant limitations. Yet it is the approach to strategy implementation with which all too many line managers are familiar. Strategy implementation is most divorced from strategy formulation under this approach.

But, with a set of powerful implementation tools at his or her disposal, the executive using the Organizational Change Approach can implement more difficult strategies or plans in a wide variety of organizations.

The strategist who has used either of these two traditional approaches eventually confronts a basic dilemma: How do I make realistic strategic decisions based on accurate and unbiased information, and then set up an administrative system to put those decisions into action over the long run? Of course, these goals should also be achieved without hurting managers' motivation, stifling creativity, or creating an inflexible bureaucracy.

As we pointed out, these approaches split the firm into thinkers and "doers," while confronting the planner or strategist with some dilemmas: How can you ensure sound strategic decision making based on accurate and unbiased information? And how can you execute those long-term decisions without hurting managers' motivation, stifling creativity, or creating an inflexible bureaucracy. We'll offer three possible solutions to these questions.

Method 3: The Collaborative Approach

In contrast to the two earlier approaches in which the chief executive makes most of the strategic and organizational decisions, the Collaborative Approach extends strategic decision making to the organization's top management team. The purpose here is to get the top managers to help develop and support a good set of goals and strategies.

In this model, the CEO employs group dynamics and "brainstorming," techniques to get managers with different points of view to contribute to the strategic process. Our research indicates that in effective top management teams the executives will have conflicting goals and perceptions of the external environment, so the CEO will want to extract whatever "group wisdom" is inherent in these different perspectives.

The typical scenario depicting this approach should be familiar to readers: With key executives and division managers, the CEO embarks on a week-long planning retreat. At the retreat, each participant presents his own ideas of where the firm should head. Extensive discussions follow, until the group reaches a consensus around the firm's longer-range mission and near-term strategy. Upon returning to their respective offices, each participant charges ahead in the agreed-upon direction.

In relying on collaboration among top executives, this approach depends on the skillful structuring of group interaction. This can take a variety of forms. For example, the consulting firm of Arthur D. Little engages in a process designed to gain team consensus on which generic strategies "fit" their particular industry situation.

We have employed another variant of the Collaborative Method which involves *teaching* analytical tools to the top management team. These variations all involve managers' participation in contrast to the typical approach used by consulting firms, in which top managers rely on outsiders to provide a final report and recommendations.

A number of corporations now use some type of Collaborative Method. General Motors formed "business teams" in 1980 which consisted of managers from different functional areas; the role of the team was simply to bring out different points of view on whatever strategic—usually product-focused—problem was identified.

The CEO of a wholly owned Exxon subsidiary informed us that *his* job was not to make and implement strategy. Instead, he was responsible for assembling a team of competent managers—most more competent than he in their respective functional fields—which could, jointly, collaborate in the formation of strategies.

The Collaborative Approach overcomes two key limitations of the previous two methods. By incorporating information from executives who are closer to the line operations and by engaging several points of view, it helps provide better information than the CEO alone would have. Also because participation breeds commitment, this method helps overcome any resistance from top managers—which improves the possibility of successful implementation.

However, what the Collaborative Approach gains in team commitment may come at the expense of "strategic perfection." That is, it results in a compromise that has been negotiated among players with different points of view. The strategy may not be as dynamic as one CEO's vision, but it will be more politically feasible.

A second criticism of the Collaborative Approach is that it is not "real" collective decision making from an organizational standpoint, because the managers—the organizational elite—cannot or will not give up centralized control. In effect, this approach still retains the wall separating thinkers from "doers," and it fails to draw upon the resources of personnel throughout the organization.

Our fourth approach to strategy implementation overcomes that shortcoming.

Method 4: Cultural Approach

The Cultural Approach extends the benefits of collective participation into lower levels of the organization in order to get the entire organization committed to the firm's goals and strategies.

In this approach, the CEO sets the game plan and communicates the direction in which the firm should move, but he then gives individuals the responsibility of determining the details of how to execute the plan. To a large extent, the Cultural Approach represents the latest wave of management techniques promulgated to (and, in some cases, enthusiastically adopted by) American managers seeking the panacea to our current economic woes in the face of successful Japanese competition.

The implementation tools used in building a strong corporate culture range from such simple notions as publishing a company creed and singing a company song to much more complex techniques. The complex—and usually effective—involve implementing strategy by employing the concept "third-order control."

Since implementation involves controlling the behavior of others, we can think of three levels of control. First-order control involves direct supervision. Second-order control involves using rules, procedures, and organization structure to guide the behavior of others (as in the Organizational Change Approach described in the last issue). Third-order control is a much more subtle—and potentially more powerful—means of influencing behavior through shaping the norms, values, symbols, and beliefs that managers and employees use in making day-to-day decisions.

The key distinction between managers using the Cultural Approach and those simply engaged in "participative management," is that these executives understand that corporate culture should serve as the handmaiden to corporate strategy, rather than proselytize "power equalization" and the like for its own sake.

Some of the tools used in the Cultural Approach involve some readily identifiable personnel practices, such as long-term employment, slow promotion of employees, less-specialized career paths, and consensus decision making. For many managers, the Cultural Approach will also lead to change in their management "style"; it will involve much more interaction where subordinates will be seen as "partners."

The Cultural Approach begins to break down the barriers between thinkers and "doers." Examples of the successful application of this model are numerous. Hewlett-Packard is a much-heralded example of a company where the employees share a strong awareness of the corporate mission. They all know that the "HP Way" encourages product innovation at every level and at every bench. Matsushita starts each day at 8:00 A.M. with 87,000 employees singing the company song and reciting its code of values.

Once an organizational culture is established that supports the firm's goals, the chief executive's implementation task is 90 percent done. With a cadre of committed managers and workers, the organization more or less "carries itself" through cycles of innovation in terms of new products and processes at the workbench, followed by assimilation and implementation at the lower levels.

The most visible cost of this system also yields its primary strength: the consensus decision making and other culture-inculcating activities consume enormous amounts of time. But the payoff can be speedy execution and reduced gamesmanship among managers. At Westinghouse, as William Coates, executive vice president of the corporation construction group, described it, "We spend a lot of time trying to get a consensus, but once you get it, the implementation is instantaneous. We don't have to fight any negative feelings." (*Fortune*, June 15, 1981).

Based on our assessment of the nature of the companies generally held up as examples of this approach to strategic management, we have reached some tentative conclusions about the organizational characteristics for which it is best suited. The Cultural Approach works when power is decentralized, where there are shared goals between the organization and its participants, and where the organization is stable and growing.

This last point may be the key: There must be sufficient organization slack (i.e., unused resources) to absorb the cost of installing and maintaining the culture. Consider some of the example firms: Hewlett-Packard, IBM, Matsushita, and Intel. These tend to be high-growth firms. As *Fortune* magazine describes Intel's experience, "To lessen the threat of change, Intel promised not to fire any permanent employee whose job was eliminated. The company's phenomenal sales growth, 29.3 percent in 1980, helps absorb everyone who wants to stay."

The Cultural Method has several limitations. For one, it works only with informed and intelligent people (note that most of the examples are firms in high-technology industries). Second, it consumes enormous amounts of time to implement. Third, it can foster such a strong sense of organizational identity among employees that it becomes almost a handicap—that is, it can be difficult to have outsiders at top levels because the executives won't accept the infusion of alien blood.

In addition, companies with excessively strong cultures often will suppress deviance, impede attempts to change, and tend to foster homogeneity and inbreeding. The intolerance of deviance can be a problem when innovation is critical to strategic success. But a strong culture will reject inconsistency.

To handle this conformist tendency, companies such as IBM, Xerox, and GM have separated their ongoing research units and their new-product development efforts, sometimes placing them in physical locations far enough away to shield them from the corporation's culture.

Homogeneity can stifle creativity, encouraging nonconformists to leave for more accepting pastures and thereby robbing the firm of its innovative talent. The strongest criticism of the Cultural Approach is that it has such an overwhelming indoctrinal air about it. It smacks of faddism and may really be just another variant of the CEO-centered approaches (i.e., the previously discussed Commander and Organizational Change Approaches). As such, it runs the risk of maintaining the wall between thinkers and "doers."

Preserving that thinker/"doer" distinction may be the Cultural Approach's main appeal. It affords executives an illusion of control. But you should also realize that holding tight the reins of control (a natural tendency in turbulent times, we have observed) may result in some lost opportunities—opportunities encountered by line managers in their day-to-day routines.

How can executives capitalize on their line managers' natural inclinations to want to develop opportunities as they encounter them on the firing line? The answer to this question is contained in the fifth implementation method, the Crescive Approach.

Although each of the approaches discussed can be effective in certain companies and business environments, none has proved adequate for complex companies in highly diversified or rapidly changing environments. The best way to implement strategy in this challenging situation is by what we have identified as the "Crescive Approach." The name means "growing," indicating that under this method the CEO cultivates or allows strategies to "grow" from *within* the company instead of imposing the strategies of top management onto the firm.

Method 5: The Crescive Approach

Here's a scenario depicting the Crescive Approach:

> As a general manager, you have just received a proposal to pursue continued development of a new product. You evaluate the report, deflate some overly optimistic figures, and consider the manager's track record. The product offers attractive profit potential and seems to fit the general direction you envision for the firm, so you approve the proposal.

The Crescive Approach differs from others in several respects. First, instead of strategy being delivered downward by top management or a planning department, it moves upward from the "doers" (salespeople, engineers, production workers) and lower middle-level managers. Second, "strategy" becomes the sum of all the individual proposals that surface throughout the year. Third, the top management team shapes the employees' premises—that is, their notions of what would constitute strategic projects. Fourth, the chief executive functions more as a judge, evaluating the proposals that reach his desk, than as a master planner.

Why Did the Crescive Approach Arise?   At first, the Crescive Approach may sound too risky. After all, it calls for the chief executive to relinquish a lot of control over the strategy-making process, seemingly leaving to chance the major decisions which determine the long-term competitive strength of the company.

To understand why the Crescive Approach is sometimes appropriate, you need to recognize five constraints that impinge on the chief executive as he sets out to develop and implement a strategy.

1.   *The chief executive cannot monitor all significant opportunities and threats.* If the company is highly diversified, it is impossible for senior management to stay abreast of developments in all of the firm's different industries. Similarly, if an industry is shifting very quickly (e.g., personal computers), information collected at lower levels often becomes stale before it can be assimilated, summarized, and passed up the ranks. Even in more stable industries, the time required to process information upward through many management levels can mean that decisions are being made based on outdated information.

As a result, in many cases, the CEO must abandon the effort to plan centrally. Instead, an incentive scheme or "free-market" environment is established to encourage operating managers to make decisions that will further the long-range interests of the company.

2. *The power of the chief executive is limited.* The chief executive typically enjoys substantial power derived from the ability to bestow rewards, allocate resources, and reduce the uncertainty for members of the organization. Thus, to an extent, the executive can impose his or her will on other members of the organization.

However, the chief executive is not omnipotent. Employees can always leave the firm, and key managers wield control over information and important client relationships. As a result, the CEO must often compromise on programs he wishes to implement.

Research indicates that new projects led by managers who were coerced into the leadership role fail, regardless of the intrinsic merit of the proposal. In contrast, a second-best strategy championed by a capable and determined advocate may be far more worthwhile than the optimum strategy with only lukewarm support.

3. *Few executives have the freedom to plan.* Although it is often said that one of the most important jobs of an executive is to engage in thoughtful planning, research shows that few executives actually set aside time to plan. Most spend the majority of their work days attending to short-range problems.

Thus, any realistic approach to strategic planning must recognize that executives simply don't plan much. They are bombarded constantly by requests from subordinates. So they shape the company's future more through their day-to-day decisions—encouraging some projects and discouraging others—than by sweeping policy statements or written plans. This process has been described as "logical incrementalism" because it is a rational process that proceeds in small steps rather than by long leaps.

4. *Tight control systems hinder the planning process.* In formulating strategies, top managers rely heavily on subordinates for up-to-date information, strategic recommendations, and approval of the operating goals.

The CEO's dependence on his subordinate managers creates a thorny control problem. In essence, if managers know they'll be accountable for plans they formulate or the information they provide, they have an incentive to bias their estimates of their division's performance.

A branch of decision science called "agency theory," suggests how this situation should be handled. First, if the CEO wants his managers to deliver unbiased estimates, he cannot hold them tightly accountable for the successful implementation of each strategic proposal. Without such accountability, he places great emphasis on commitment as a force for getting things done.

Second, in order to assess the true ability and motivation of any subordinate, the CEO must observe him over a long period of time on a number of different projects. Occasional failures should be expected, tolerated, and not penalized.

One means to promote the ongoing flow of strategic information is to establish a special venture capital fund to take advantage of promising ideas that arise after the strategic and operating plans have been completed. Like the IBM "Fellows" or the Texas Instruments "Idea" programs, this approach allows opportunities to be seized and developed by their champions within the company.

5. *Strategies are produced by groups, not individuals.* Strategies are rarely created by single individuals. They are usually developed by groups of people, and they incorporate different perspectives on the business. The problem with group decisions is that groups tend to avoid uncertainty and to smooth over conflicts prematurely.

To reduce the distortions that can result from group decision making, the CEO can concentrate on three tools: first, encouraging an atmosphere that tolerates expression of different opinions; second, using organization development techniques (such as group dynamics exercises) to reduce individual defensiveness and to increase the receptivity of the group to discrepant data; and third, establish separate planning groups at the corporate level and the line organization.

How the CEO Can Use the Crescive Approach. As the preceding discussion indicates, the CEO of a large corporation simply cannot be solely responsible for forming and implementing strategy. The Crescive Approach suggests that the CEO can solicit and guide the involvement of lower-level managers in the planning and implementation process in five ways:

1. By keeping the organization open to new and potentially discrepant information.
2. By articulating a general strategy of superordinate goals to guide the firm's growth.
3. By carefully shaping the premises by which managers at all levels decide which strategic opportunities to pursue.
4. By manipulating systems and structures to encourage bottom-up strategy formulations.
5. By approaching day-to-day decisions as part of strategy formulation in the "logical incrementalist" manner described above.

One of the most important and potentially elusive of these methods is the process of shaping managers' decision-making premises. The CEO can shape these premises in at least three ways. First, the CEO can emphasize a particular theme or strategic thrust ("We are in the information business") to direct strategic thinking. Second, the planning methodology endorsed by the CEO can be communicated to affect the way managers view the business. Third, the organizational structure can indicate the dimensions on which strategies should focus. A firm with a product-divisional structure will probably encourage managers to generate strategies for domination in certain product categories, whereas a firm organized around geographical territories will probably evoke strategies to secure maximum penetration of all products in particular regions.

CONCLUSION

The five approaches to developing and implementing strategy represent a range from which you can choose the techniques most suited to your particular situation. Through extensive interviews, most managers indicated to us that one of these five approaches is predominant in their companies, although often one or two of the other approaches may also pay a limited role.

In the few cases where two different approaches played equally strong roles in the same company, an explanation could be found in the history and makeup of the company. For example, one company we studied was active in two distinct industries: Its aerospace divisions, based in California, used a crescive strategic management process, while its automotive operation, headquartered in the Midwest, used a planning system incorporating elements of both the Commander and the Change Approaches.

Our research suggests that the Commander, Change, and Collaborative Approaches can be effective for smaller companies and firms in stable industries while the Cultural and Crescive alternatives are used by more complex corporations.

To conclude, a summary of the five approaches, the strategic question each addresses, and the CEO's role in each is given in the accompanying table. The choice of method should depend on the size of the company, the degree of diversification, the degree of geographical dispersion, the stability of the business environment, and, finally, the managerial style currently embodied in the company's culture.

The Five Approaches to Strategic Management

Approach	*The CEO's Strategic Question*	*CEO's Role*
I. Commander Approach	"How do I formulate the optimal strategy?"	Master Planner
II. Change Approach	"I have a strategy in mind—now how do I implement it?"	Architect of Implementation
III. Collaborative Approach	"How do I involve top management in planning so they will be committed to strategies from the start?"	Coordinator
IV. Cultural Approach	"How do I involve the whole organization in implementation?"	Coach
V. Crescive Approach	"How do I encourage managers to come forward as champions of sound strategies?"	Premise Setter and Judge

What this article is about: The ability of corporations to defend or take market share from competitors varies with the corporations' strengths and weaknesses, many of which spring from their own structures. The challenge is not to design organizational structures that are perfect, but to design structures that are better than those of competitors.

4–2 *Designing Organizations to Compete*

Ian C. MacMillan and Patricia E. Jones
Ian C. MacMillan is a professor at New York University
Patricia E. Jones is a staff manager at AT&T

In 1979, Kiechel[1] claimed that 90 percent of American corporations have been unable to develop and execute successful strategies. He cited implementation as a critical issue, which has become the new rallying cry for growing numbers of managers and consultants.[2] In this article we go a step further and claim, as Davis[3] has done, that lack of success in implementing strategies has, in many cases, been due to a complete lack of a competitive organization design. The challenge of developing such a design can be likened to the challenge facing the general who has prepared a superb campaign strategy and must now design the army that will execute that strategy. Without the correct assembly of different battle units and their support services, the campaign cannot proceed, let alone achieve victory. By design we mean not only the selection of the organization structure but also the design of the support systems, planning systems, and control systems that deliver the strategy via the structure.

"TRADITIONAL" DESIGN

Among others, Galbraith[4] and Nadler and colleagues[5] have done much to develop guidelines for "traditional" organizational design. Their three basic steps are:

1. Determine organization design "imperatives," that is, the demands and constraints placed on the organization by its environment and its strategy.

Reprinted by permission from; *Journal of Business Strategy* (Spring 1984) 4, no. 4, pp. 11–26.

2. Design an organizational structure to meet these imperatives.
3. Manage the implementation of the design carefully and systematically.

We contend that these steps have to satisfy an essential prerequisite—that they be carried out in a competitive context. Nearly all organizations are engaged in some form of competition, if not for customers, then for scarce resources such as funds or staff. Previous authors have largely ignored competition, mentioning it only briefly as but one facet of the environment. The result can easily be a design that strives to homogenize the system and develop similar structural units with common policies, procedures, and measurement and reward systems, all of which are of little avail if the different parts of the organization are being attacked by very different competitors in very different environments.

FIGURE 1   Questions for the Competitive Design Process

1. What is the organization's strategy?
   - What is its contribution to society?
   - What is its strategic role?
   - By what strategy will the above be accomplished?
   - What critical functions will drive the strategy?
   - What are the key success factors?

2. How will we know that the strategy has been accomplished?
   - What strategic accomplishments spell success?
   - In pursuing this strategy, what ideology should shape our decisions?
   - What changes are necessary to achieve the strategic accomplishments?

3. How will competitors be impacted?
   - Who are target competitors?
   - What are their strategic strengths and weaknesses?
   - What are their design weaknesses?

4. What major task groupings are feasible design alternatives?
   - What groupings address the needs of the marketplace?
   - What groupings address the competitive advantages?
   - What are the vulnerabilities of each of these feasible groupings?
   - Can we accomplish the strategy without major reorganization?

5. What linkages are necessary between groupings?
   - What mechanisms link key groupings to critical functions?
   - What linkages address key vulnerabilities?

6. What support systems are needed?
   - Have necessary support systems been identified?
   - What new management and functional skills are needed?

7. What execution problems can be anticipated?
   - Have key events been simulated?
   - Has stakeholder impact been identified and managed?
   - Have problem owners been assigned?

THE FOUNDATION OF COMPETITIVE DESIGN

The reality is that every design has imperfections. Once this is acknowledged, one can further acknowledge that the organization is better served by designing to be competitive rather than striving for the holy grail of perfection in efficiency. Competitive design is an extension of the above three basic steps, expanded to take into account the competitive nature of the environment. Figure 1 lists a set of questions that has proven helpful in the competitive design process. Appropriately addressing these questions provides the foundation upon which an effective competitive design can be built. Thereafter, it is possible to use the more traditional organizational design guidelines, which are put forth in the current literature on the topic, to complete the design. In this article, we shall not pursue the more traditional detail, but rather will focus on discussing the questions outlined in Figure 1.

1. What Is the Organization's Strategy?

Rothschild[6] has developed a detailed and helpful list of questions to aid in the strategic analysis process. Any analysis, however, should answer at least the following:

What Will the Organization's Contribution to Society Be?   In other words, what gives it the right to exist in society? It is important here to identify what need is being satisfied by the organization *from the point of view of society*. For instance, in its early days, IBM recognized that its societal contribution was not to "manufacture and sell computers," but to solve data storage, retrieval, and processing problems of large organizations. This question not only puts the business into a societal perspective, it also helps the business to recognize that there are many ways of satisfying its societal need. It is also a useful question for support departments to ask with respect to their corporation.

What Is the Strategic Role?   In other words, what strategic purpose must the organization accomplish for itself? MacMillan[7] has identified eight role choices, depending on the organization's position in a larger corporate portfolio: build aggressively, build gradually, build selectively, maintain aggressively, maintain selectively, prove viability, divest/liquidate, and competitively harass. (The missions associated with each role are summarized in Figure 2).

By What Strategy Will the Above Be Accomplished?   A business strategy must be selected to accomplish the above challenges. This involves selecting an array of products or services, targeting them at selected markets, and making use of selected competitive advantages. Thus, in the 1950s, IBM elected to build aggressively in the medium-to-large business market, the government market, and the medium-to-large educational market by supplying an array of mainframe computers with modest modularity and with a full range of peripheral devices. They elected advanced (but not cutting-edge) products, cutting-edge technology, and high operational reliability of product as key competitive advantages.

FIGURE 2 Possible Strategic Accomplishments for Strategic Roles

Role	Action Required	Relative Accomplishments	Absolute Accomplishments
Build aggressively	Build share on all fronts as rapidly as possible.	Rapid growth in share—all markets. Leadership in technology, service.	Limits on losses and negative cash flows.
Build gradually	Steady sustained increase in share of entire market.	Sustained growth in share—all markets. Leadership in quality, service.	Limited losses. Sustained cost reductions.
Build selectively	Increased share in carefully selected markets.	Share growth in selected markets. Leadership in customer satisfaction. Superiority in market research.	Growth in profits and profitability. Growth in cash flow.
Maintain aggressively	Hold position in all markets and generate profits.	Hold market share in all markets. Relative cost leadership—fixed and variable. Technology leadership—in product and process.	Improve asset utilization. Growth in profitability and cash flow. Improve expense-to-revenue ratio. Reduce force levels.
Maintain selectively	Select high-profit markets and secure position.	Overall share reduction. Hold market share in selected markets. Improve relative profitability. Distribution, service leadership.	Minimum investment. Improve asset utilization and cash flow. Reduce fixed cost/sales.
Prove viability	If there are any viable segments, maintain selectively, divest rest.	In this exhibit, see the sections to the left called "Maintain Selectively" and "Divest/Liquidate."	Minimize drag/risk to organization. Growth in profits and cash flow.
Divest/liquidate	Seek exit and sell off at best price.	Reduce share except for highly selective segments. Enhance value added via technical leadership.	Minimize investment. Reduce fixed costs. Improve profitability. Maximize selling price. Reduce work force levels.
Competitively harass	Use as vehicle to deny revenues to competitors.	Attack competitor's high-share business but do not gain share. Relative price never above that of target competitors.	Minimize fixed costs. Sustained reduction of variable costs. Limits on losses and negative cash flows.

What Critical Functions Will Drive the Strategy?   If the strategy is to be achieved, a limited number of functions must be performed and performed well, as Rothschild[6] indicates. In fact, these functions must be performed well for the company to attain the competitive advantage it seeks. And it is these functions that dictate where major resource allocations and trade-offs are to be made. For instance, IBM's commitment to advanced technology and to the operational reliability of the product on site caused development and service functions to take a critical role in the early days. Marketing and finance, although aggressive and powerful, generally had to take a back seat in trade-offs involving performance reliability of their computers versus introduction of new technology, or new product releases, or inventory allocations to customers. As a result, IBM today continues to extract a premium price based on its image of reliability and superb service.

What Are the Key Success Factors?   These will vary from company to company, but generally they include exceptional management of several of the following: product design, market segmentation, distribution and promotion, pricing, financing, securing of key personnel, research and development, production, servicing, maintenance of quality/value, or securing key suppliers. For example, companies in the grain-trading business simply will not survive if they do not have exceptional sourcing and delivery logistics as well as superior options and contract management. Once the key strategic decisions are made, answers to the next important set of questions define the major design parameters of the strategic control system.

2. How Will We Know When the Strategy Is Accomplished?

The critical challenge in designing a strategic control system is to create a system that is self-controlling; that can respond autonomously to environmental challenges, but in which the various subunits still pursue their assigned strategic roles, according to their designated strategy. It has been our experience that this is accomplished by detailed attention to strategic accomplishments and ideology.

What Strategic Accomplishments Spell Success?   In competitive design, those charged with executing strategy should at least be able to gauge when they have been successful. Success is best monitored by specifying the set of accomplishments that will demonstrate that the organization has achieved what is set out to do—namely, pursue the strategic role, via the selected strategy. Therefore, we need to specify clearly what will indicate that the role itself has been accomplished, as well as indicate the means by which it was accomplished. For instance, IBM's accomplishment of an aggressive build role via its selected strategy could be demonstrated in the late 1960s by the following accomplishments:

- It had a major share of *all* markets it had elected to serve.
- Growth had exceeded that of all major competitors (in other words, IBM was also gaining share).

- Profits were increasing and cash flows were positive.
- It was acknowledged worldwide as having the most up-to-date equipment—both mainframe and peripherals.
- It was acknowledged worldwide as having superior product reliability and service.

Thus, there was no question that IBM had been successful in its aggressive build mission (a role that calls for substantial gains in share in all markets) and that this had been done via IBM's selected strategy of providing advanced products with unequaled operational reliability and service.

An imperative in the specification of strategic accomplishments is the selection of the *minimum* number of key criteria which management will pursue in the actual execution of strategy. Having too many criteria is a drawback since each additional criterion inhibits the flexibility and adaptability of those charged with strategy execution. Yet there should also be a sufficient number of criteria to ensure that the single-minded pursuit of one or two criteria is not carried out to the detriment of the long-term health of the organization.

Particularly important is the selection of at least one relative criterion and at least one leadership criterion. Absolute criteria are inclined to encourage an inward orientation, with attention to performance compared to past history rather than the current competition. By relative criteria we mean measuring performance relative to competitors', while leadership criteria are criteria in which our performance exceeds that of all competitors. Those criteria selected should be selected in such a way as to steer the organization toward fulfilling its selected role. In our experience, the relative criteria set the strategic direction by forcing the organization to focus on its competitive performance, while the absolute criteria set limits on the extent to which relative performance can be single-mindedly pursued to the long-run detriment of the organization. Finally, the leadership criteria force the organization to focus on the desired competitive advantage. Figure 2 lists some typical criteria that have been selected by firms in past competitive designs.

Having selected the criteria, the final challenge is the selection of appropriate measures of accomplishment. Absolute criteria and relative criteria generally pose less of a problem than leadership criteria, but for all criteria the important thing is to find measures that are objective or external, rather than subjective and internal. It is all too easy for the organization to convince itself that it is a technology or quality or service leader if it listens only to itself or its loyal distributors and customers. However, leadership is in the eyes of the market, and it may be necessary to survey the market to establish whether the "leadership" is a fabrication of the organization's imagination. For example, AT&T, through its Telephone Survey Attitude Measurement (TELSAM) system, focused on customer evaluations of its service quality—in order to objectively assess its service performance.

Another problem arises with the need for appropriate measures. Often a direct measure cannot be obtained. For example, cost leadership and, particularly, technology leadership are difficult to assess because hard data about the competitors are rarely available. It may be necessary to come up with imaginative surrogate measures which are indicators of the actual performance. One high-technology equipment manufacturer used the following as indicators of technology leadership:

- Ratings of its research and development department compared to those of its two leading competitors. Ratings were done by customers, suppliers, investment bank analysts, and three leading universities.
- Relative number of patents (compared to leading competitors) applied for in the past five years, and past two years.
- Relative number of new models introduced by the company compared to its leading competitors, and ratings of these models by key firms in the served market (*not* only its own customers).
- Number of research and development job offers to recent scientific postgraduates that were "lost" to competitors, compared to number of research and development job applicants "captured" from competitors.

Note that it may be possible for each of these measures individually to be "subverted" by a devious development department, or for each of these measures to give false signals as to the true status of the firm's technology leadership. However, the reality was that senior management stressed that the spirit of the measures was more important than each individual measure itself. The firm's development staff was aware that in spirit it was expected to achieve technology leadership and would be judged more on the "gestalt," of the above measures than on any individual measure.

For strategic control it is direction and commitment that are important, not precision of the measurement. With a limited number of criteria to steer the organization in the desired strategic direction, management is free to pursue this direction, responding autonomously to competitive conditions as they occur.

In order to create a self-controlling environment in which relatively autonomous decisions can be made, it is necessary to design and disseminate suitable ideology to guide such decision making.

What Should the Ideology Be?   Development of a suitable ideology has been discussed by many authors. By ideology we do not mean the corporate culture, which is a passive manifestation of corporate beliefs. Ideology is an explicitly generated, consciously managed, and clearly disseminated set of values by which senior management will judge the quality of internal behavior, attitudes, and external interactions of the organization and its members.

Peters and Waterman,[8] in their study of excellent companies, identified a number of factors that need to be included in ideology. These components of ideology were made more explicit in the analysis of several companies by MacMillan.[9] The fundamental principles held by the organization should broadly specify the following:

- Scope—what constitutes desirable types of products and markets?
- Drivers—which shall be the critical functions?
- Style—what style of management shall prevail?

- Ethics—what are the determinants of ethics?
- Attitude to risk taking—how much risk is encouraged?
- Attitude to competition—how aggressively should competition be pursued?
- Attitude to customers and channels—are they regarded as intelligent decisio. makers or people who are easily manipulated?
- Attitude to employees—are they considered robots or intelligent contributors?
- Attitude to external groups—what is the attitude toward various special interest groups, government, and so on?
- Self-image—how does the company feel about its control over its destiny?

The underlying philosophy is that once managers in the organization have internalized these key principles, the autonomous decisions they make in response to competitive or environmental challenges, while addressing the specific challenge, will also stay within the boundaries of behavior desired by the organization as a whole.

This set of explicit principles, plus the strategic accomplishments, creates a framework for autonomous but self-controlling responses by the managers to the competitive environment. Discussion of the problems and the management of this strategic control system can be found in the material cited above and will not be discussed here.

With the foundation of the strategic control system in place, it is necessary to consider what changes are required to effect these accomplishments.

What Changes Are Necessary to Achieve the Strategic Accomplishments?   If major strategic shifts must be made, this will certainly necessitate major changes: in staffing, in support systems, and particularly in skills required. It is imperative to identify what changes will be necessary for two reasons: First, change must be managed internally, or the organization will revert to past practices; second, such changes have to be supported by the external (and internal) stakeholders, and the process of generating their support will also have to be managed. The organization designer therefore must identify what the most critical changes will be if the strategy is to be accomplished; these changes then become the focus of the change management process, which is extensively discussed in the literature,[5] and will not be discussed here.

The answers to the set of questions covered so far are equivalent to the military specification of mission. The "senior officers" responsible for conducting this specific secondary task have been apprised of how their action is to fit into the overall campaign, what key results must be achieved, what resources will be available, and what guidelines they should use to shape their tactical decisions. The next set of questions involves assessing the design of the "enemy"—namely, the competition.

3. How Will Competitors Be Impacted?

In reality, no strategy impacts all competitors evenly. In fact, a good indicator that a strategy has not been thoroughly thought through is when the strategists cannot pinpoint which of the competitors will bear the main brunt of the impact of their strategy.

Who Are the Target Competitors?   If the strategy formulation process did not start with target competitors in mind, the analysis of the impact of strategy on the competitors will highlight those companies that *will* be target competitors—namely, those that bear the brunt of the strategic attack. Responses of these competitors and their capacity to respond need to be evaluated. This assessment results from determining the competitors' strategic and design weaknesses.

What Are the Target Competitors' Strategic Weaknesses?   This question ensures that we have in fact identified the *real* target competitors. These are competitors whose strategic weaknesses render them most vulnerable to our strategy. If we have a strategy that is based on a competitive advantage in distribution and service, then clearly the brunt of our attack will be borne initially by those firms that are weak in these areas, not those that are strong. (On the other hand, if *none* are weak, then we are not undertaking an attack, but a defense; essentially, we are playing catch-up.)

What Are the Design Vulnerabilities of the Target Competitors?   It is also important to analyze the organization design of the competition, particularly the structure of the competition. This analysis could provide some interesting opportunities for an aggressive competitive design. At each level in the organization, work can be grouped in one of three basic ways: by activity (typically, a functional design), by output (typically, a product division), or by client (typically, a market segment division). The first few levels of design are critical; each combination of groupings at these levels brings with it substantial strengths and weaknesses. For example, a computer firm had for years been successfully organized by activity/output. Within the marketing department (activity), sales of its two product (output) groups—large and small computers—were organized separately. However, in the 1970s, the distinction between large and small computers started to blur. The result was that salespeople from each product group were calling on the same customers, creating customer confusion and irritation. "Turf" wars started between competing sales forces, service difficulties increased, and eventually the company became vulnerable to a small-computer competitor which designed its structure around key accounts under the marketing function (thus using an activity/client structure).

Competitors are in business to defend or take market share from the organization, and their ability to do so varies with their individual strengths and weaknesses, *many of which spring from their own structure*. One tool for assessing potential design advantages has been presented in the appendix to this article. First, consider how target competitors have grouped work at the top two layers, and then identify the potential strengths and weaknesses inherent in these particular groupings. Then, when we are considering alternative groupings for our own design, we can select combinations of groupings that recognize the competition's strengths. And, if we are fortunate, we can also take advantage of their weaknesses.

For example, if the target competitor is organized by activity/activity, then by grouping by output/user-client we will create a much higher sensitivity to market needs. Because of its organization, the competitor inherently will have a much slower response to these needs. This is the situation in which AT&T found itself in the late 1970s when MCI attacked specific high-density routes, and focused on specific client segments on these routes (business and consumer).

Note that the more usual case where the target competitor does happen to be grouped effectively does not preclude us from grouping our own organization in the same way. In fact, we are even more obliged to design effectively. There may be weaknesses in other parts of the design, such as the linking mechanisms (specific arrangements designed to facilitate and control the flow of critical information between groups, such as standing committees, product managers, liaison officers, or task forces) that the competitor uses (or does not use). For instance, direct responsibility to respond to our strategy may not fall within the jurisdiction of one particular department, as happened when Merrill Lynch "raided" the commercial banks' big retail customers by offering to these consumers one-stop cash management accounts. The banks had several departments which were affected, no single one of which had the authority to respond.

Alternatively, other support systems of competitors, such as their planning, control, and reward systems, standard operating procedures, or even ideology, shape the rate at which they become aware of, and respond to, strategic moves we make.[7] The organization that can build superior linking mechanisms or major support systems into its own structure may yet capitalize on the design vulnerabilities of a competitor whose major groupings mirror its own.

With the competitors' design strengths and vulnerabilities identified, it is possible to turn to the design of our own organizational structure. There are many considerations that go into designing the formal organizational structure: work grouping, linking, job design, methods and practices, standards and measurements, physical work environment, human resource management systems, reward systems, and support systems. All of these must reflect the organization's strategy and its competitive environment. It is here that it becomes all too easy to lose the *competitive* imperatives in the detail. In competitive design, it is the top few layers of the organization that are vital, and the key decisions are in the areas of grouping and linking. These are discussed next.

4. What Major Task Groupings Are Feasible Design Alternatives?

The first key decision addresses major task groupings.[11] It is here that the organization designer may be tempted to design with the focus on the internal activities rather than on the external challenges of the organization. The questions that follow force an external focus.

What Groupings Address the Needs of the Marketplace?   The organization is in business to deliver products or services to the target markets. The first step in grouping should thus address how the organization plans to serve, and compete in, the selected markets. The strategic and competitive analyses recommended above suggest what factors should be considered.

FIGURE 3   Key Groupings for Industrial Foods Manufacturer

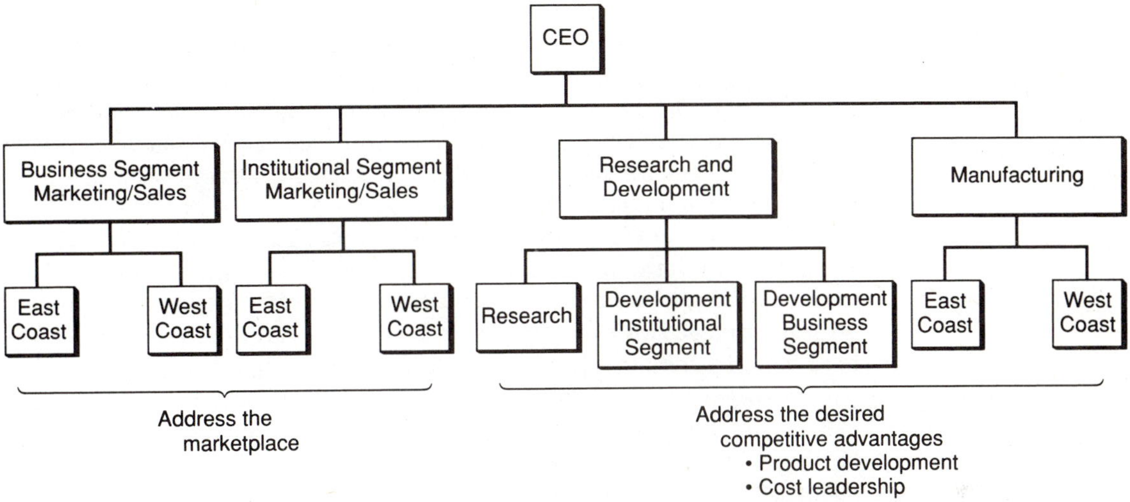

For example, an industrial foods firm decided that in order to compete with its larger competitors, it had to keep prices competitive. At the top level, this called for a function design (activity). However, the firm's business and institutional markets were drastically different, and each required very different and specialized marketing skills. So, management elected to segment the marketing efforts by client (see Figure 3) at the next level. At the third level, the marketing for each segment was grouped geographically to reflect discerned regional differences on the East and West Coasts. Thus, the marketing activity was grouped according to a client/client grouping (see appendix). Had the regional sensitivity been identified in the strategy as the key difference, their second- and third-level groupings (in marketing) might have been reversed.

What Groupings Address the Competitive Advantages?   The next grouping decision must address the organization's desired competitive advantages. Continuing our example in Figure 3, the industrial foods firm selected two areas in which it felt it had to develop a competitive advantage: product development and cost leadership. In order to retain competitive prices, the firm maintained its activity groupings for basic research and development and for manufacturing. It decided on an activity/client design for research and development and another form of activity/client design for manufacturing. Some interesting points emerge as we look at these subgroupings. Under research and development, two development functions were established: one in support of the business segment, the other in support of the institutional segment. While it may be argued that such a grouping reduces efficiencies available from economies of scale, it produced an organization capable of responding quickly to needs and changes in each market segment, thereby *designing in* effectiveness. If serving particular market segments well with rapid and market-responsive product introductions is key to the success of the organization, then effectiveness must take priority over efficiency. Also, note that the research function was separated from the development function. The "blue sky" nature of basic research would be ill-served by grouping it with the shorter-term development function.

However, there remained the problem of keeping the research function in line with the rest of the organization and with the demands of this environment. This called for effective linkages[12] and the company created a formal linking position: product managers for each market, who interacted constantly with the development function on the subject of new products.

The next area of interest was in manufacturing. The geographical groupings at the second level were in response to the need for a price leadership position: Economies of scale were essential, so each regional plant manufactured products for both markets. However, the market focus within these plants was maintained once more by the product managers, whose linking role here was to manage conflicts between the needs of marketing and those of manufacturing.

Note that if the firm had been a much smaller one, such a structure may have highlighted the impossibility of price leadership *and* product leadership as competitive advantages in a small firm. Such a discovery in the design phase is not at all inconceivable, and may lead the organization to reexamine its selected strategy.

What Are the Vulnerabilities of Each of These Feasible Groupings?   The best grouping mix is one that enables the organization to most effectively maximize its strengths and minimize its vulnerabilities vis-à-vis the competition. At this point in the design process, several structures might seem feasible. However, some alternatives can be eliminated by weighing the advantages and disadvantages of the various groupings, as reflected in the appendix. Some of these vulnerabilities could be defused with appropriate linking mechanisms (which will be addressed in the next section), but none should be tolerated that interfere with the organization's ability to effectively address the needs of the marketplace; this automatically disqualifies a potential grouping.

Can We Accomplish Our Strategy without Major Reorganization?   If one of the feasible groupings closely resembles the current method of grouping, this should become a prime candidate for final selection, particularly if this grouping structure seems to have relatively minor vulnerabilities vis-à-vis those of the key competitors. The reason for this is that a major reorganization is also a tremendous source of trauma for the company. Enormous amounts of time, energy, talent, and competitive vigor are consumed as the new structure is developed under the new set of relationships. It is estimated that it takes a minimum of three years to "recover" from a major reorganization. So, if it is at all possible, it is preferable to try to use the existing groupings, supported if necessary by well-conceived new linking mechanisms (which we discuss next) in order to avoid the disruption created by reorganizing. Once again, the pragmatic challenge is not to design systems that are perfect but systems that are merely better than those of the competitors and that are appropriate to the strategy.

5. What Linkages Are Necessary between Groupings?

The very act of grouping certain functions together will also mean that certain natural work flows are separated. For instance, it may be appropriate to divide production into two geographically separate plants, even if some of the production of one plant is needed at the other. But if there are no coordinating or linking mechanisms, disruptions or exceptions at the first plant can create problems for the second. Linking mechanisms must be designed to coordinate and control critical interfaces. The focus at this stage should be on those interfaces that are critical to the organization's strategic and competitive success. Figure 4 lists the key mechanisms that have been used to link interfaces. The details of how to use such linking mechanisms are not discussed here since they are freely available in the literature.[5,12] We have, however, tried to indicate the circumstances under which each should be employed by focusing on the nature of the disruptions/exception conditions which create the need for intergroup coordination. For instance, if the expected disruptions are not likely to be serious and will occur frequently, and their nature is fairly predictable, the most appropriate linking mechanism is the appointment of formal liaison people in each department who will coordinate actions when these disruptions occur. A typical example would be to assign a plant foreman the responsibility of coordinating the acquisition of supplies from another of the company's plants. To do this, he would coordinate his activities with those of the foremen in the other plant. Sequential dependence means that one group depends on the input of another, such as in a production line. With reciprocal dependence, the output of one group becomes the input of another, which in time provides input back to the first. Typical reciprocal situations are relations between units that use equipment and units

FIGURE 4   Key Linking Mechanisms*

Exception Conditions			Grouping Interdependency	Linking Mechanism
Impact	Predictability	Frequency		
Low	High			Rules
Low	Low	Low		Contact
Low	Low	High		Liaison
High	High	Low		Contingency plan
High	Low	Low		Task force
High	High	High		Teams
High	Low	High	Sequential	Integrating role
High	Low	High	Reciprocal	Matrix

NOTE: Critical to success of linking mechanisms is to ensure that they take place at the correct level with correct delegation.
*Adapted from Reference 12.

that maintain equipment (airlines, railroads). Another reciprocal situation is the relationship between the design, production, and marketing departments as new products and their supporting production systems are developed.

For the purposes of Figure 4, the following definitions apply:

- Task force: A group is selected from various activities to tackle a specific intergroup problem. It is automatically disbanded after the problem is solved.
- Team: A group is selected from various activities in the organization to respond to *recurring* problems that cross over group boundaries. It is a permanent coordinative arrangement that is disbanded only by a higher level in the hierarchy.
- Integrating role: An individual is charged with formal responsibilities for coordinating between two groupings. A common example is the product manager whose task it is to see that specific products get adequate attention from the marketing, production, and service functions.
- Integrating department: A department with independent resources and staff whose task is to ensure coordination between different functions. A typical example is an expediting department in a manufacturing firm whose task is to coordinate between marketing and production. In a defense contracting firm, an expediting department might coordinate between specific projects and the various technical departments supplying skills to execute the projects.
- Matrix structure: A person simultaneously reports to and has responsibility for a number of managers, each in charge of different activities or resources which must be coordinated. In addition, below this matrix manager is a structure in which competing tasks must be executed. The classic example is the project manager in a construction company who is required to report both to operations (for project programs) and to the technical manager (for staffing requirements) while managing a specific project under her control. In effect, the matrix manager absorbs conflicts between groupings and thus shields the subordinates from the intergroup conflicts, so allowing the subordinates to pursue their tasks without such disruptions. The matrix structure is extremely difficult to operate and should be avoided in favor of a simpler linking mechanism.

What Mechanisms Will Link Key Groupings to Critical Functions? As mentioned above, the critical functions are those that must deliver the competitive advantage and the strategic role. Here, the designer must build linking mechanisms to ensure that these critical functions perform their tasks and at the same time remain responsive to the markets being served. In our example of the industrial foods company, it is futile for the development department to create new products that the market does not want. It is also fatal for the manufacturing department to seek cost reductions if this means the company would have to deny an appropriate variety of products to the market or reduce the availability or reliability of supply to the customers in order to reduce inventory and scheduling costs.

The research and development function *must* deliver new products appropriate to the market, and the manufacturing function *must* accomplish cost reductions appropriate to the marketing effort. To accomplish this, the company in our example created teams in which a senior marketing manager from each segment worked with a senior development manager and a senior manufacturing manager. It was the charter of these teams, together with any ad hoc members co-opted as deemed appropriate, to *drive* the coordinated development of new products and processes, and the coordinated development of cost-reduction programs, in directions that were appropriate to the markets being served.

What Linkages Address Key Vulnerabilities?   Every structure has its vulnerabilities. Vulnerabilities arising from the organization's structure can be reduced, if not eliminated, with the design and installation of additional linkages. Some of the grouping alternatives identified in the previous step will lend themselves easily to the design of linkages that overcome vulnerabilities. This will weed out the less desirable grouping options. For instance, the industrial foods company was aware that its fundamental design was an activity/client one. The key vulnerability was from low-cost competitors who might undercut prices to secure price-sensitive clients. This is why the firm *had* to select continuous cost reduction as a key strategic imperative, and why teams of marketing, development, and production managers were created to pursue cost reductions on a continuous basis.

6. What Support Systems Are Needed?

The grouping and linking decisions which shape the organization's formal structure still do not adequately address the requirements for a complete design. Nadler[5] and Peters and Waterman,[8] among others, point out the need for additional, highly interrelated support systems and the need for congruence between these components if the organization is to perform effectively.

Have Necessary Support Systems Been Identified?   If the questions above have been answered adequately, it is now possible to use the more traditional approaches to organization design to plan the necessary support systems. The idea is to design detailed planning, control, and reward systems focused on the pursuit of the strategic accomplishments and the ideology established in earlier stages.

What New Skills Will Be Needed to Produce the Accomplishments?   It is critically important to identify what changes in the skill mix may be required if the strategy is to be accomplished, since there is usually a substantial lag between recognition of a required change in skill mix and its accomplishment. Furthermore, the required skill mix may extend well beyond the traditional boundaries of the business: IBM during its aggressive build phase in the 1950s and 1960s was astute enough to recognize that it was vital to develop the programming skills of potential clients, and so spent millions of dollars on educating and training its clients' employees worldwide. To accomplish this, IBM's own capabilities to devise and deliver such training required development. The result was a huge program to train programming instructors and software applications instructors within IBM.

The management attitudes and skills needed to carry out a particular strategic role may also call for a change in the human resource management systems. Selection, promotion, and compensation guidelines must be designed and installed to encourage the development of the needed attitudes and skills. Without systems that support the strategic role, traditional American business values[13] such as the tendency to maximize short-term profits and minimize risk, will quite naturally take precedence, whether or not they suit the role.

If the strategy is to be effective, it may also be important to recognize the skill requirements of suppliers and distributors. For decades, the large U.S. auto manufacturers had a formidable advantage against foreign competition due to their networks of dealers who offered service and repair capabilities. It was only by designing highly reliable vehicles that Japanese auto producers considerably reduced the need for such service skills, thus defusing the advantage of domestic producers.

To get a better idea of the importance for implementation of required change in the skill mix, it is useful to ask what the impact on strategic accomplishment will be if there is a shortfall in the skill categories needed to support a particular strategy. One electrical equipment manufacturer estimated that a 10 percent shortfall in trained repair technicians would be enough to both severely damage its service reputation and also virtually destroy a proposed aggressive maintenance strategy which had been based on distribution and service leadership. This discovery precipitated a major reallocation of senior management attention to internal technical training and a substantial redirection of corporate resources and support for technical training in regional public school systems.

7. What Execution Problems Can Be Anticipated?

Answers to this last set of questions reduces the organization's exposure to major implementation pitfalls to which so many of the most well-conceived strategies and designs fall prey.

Have Key Events Been Simulated?   By this we mean "walking through" the major events that the organization must be able to handle if its strategy is to be executed. This is in essence a reality check, an attempt to answer the question "Will it work?" This analysis must be done, and done in detail, if the emerging design is to effectively implement the strategy.

The first step is to identify and then list the key challenges the organization is likely to encounter. A good place to look for the identification of these key challenges is in the organization's strategy. If, for example, the organization seeks to achieve market leadership via new-product introductions, then a new product is a major event and should be walked through the proposed design to make sure that the design is set up to handle the identification, development, and introduction of new product ideas as well as the responses of distributors, customers, and competitors to its introduction.

Another important check is to identify competitive triggers. For example, if a target competitor counterattacks, how will the proposed design identify and respond to this move? Once the key inputs are identified, the progress of each can be traced through each design alternative.

From the simulations will emerge conflicts, redundancies, or misunderstandings about groupings, questions about how coordination and control mechanisms will function, and any missing or incomplete functions. Based on the results, further grouping alternatives will be ruled out entirely, or other new or different linking mechanisms will be designed. At this point, if more than one design alternative remains, the final choice can be made by checking each against the answers to Questions 1 to 3, choosing the one that best meets the resulting strategic and competitive imperatives. Specifically ask: Have all the strategic and competitive imperatives been met?

Has Stakeholder Impact Been Identified and Managed?   The impact of the design on stakeholders cannot be ignored. Strategic accomplishment may be considerably delayed by resistance from key stakeholders, or considerably facilitated by their active support. The extent to which stakeholders will be impacted as the strategy is executed needs to be analyzed, and major threats or opportunities emanating from stakeholder reaction must be identified and managed. Specific plans for managing both positive and negative stakeholder reactions must be made and appropriate action taken before the first move, as well as throughout the implementation phase.

Have Problem Owners Been Assigned?   A very effective mechanism, invented by IBM, has been the identification and appointment of problem owners for implementation. All major problem areas for implementation identified in the prior simulation—for example, technical difficulties, motivation problems, human resource management challenges, and stakeholder resistance—are assigned to a "problem owner" who acknowledges and accepts the responsibility for managing this problem area. Problem owners are not necessarily given resources and authority, but they are held accountable for managing all problems that may arise in their problem area during implementation. They do have the right to veto (if they *have to*) any move that negatively impacts their problem area. Two benefits are obtained with this mechanism: The problem owners themselves receive important developmental experience, and the organization receives the smoothest possible change implementation. It is interesting to note that in IBM the "problem ownership" role is eagerly sought by those executives who seek to demonstrate that they can manage their problems despite lack of formal authority and official resources, since senior management regards such skills as important indicators of promotion potential.

This completes the key questions that shape competitive organization design. More detailed design considerations are handled quite adequately by the conventional design approaches.

Adequate answers to the above list of questions lead to a design that addresses the need to compete as well as to seek efficiency. There is no question that such designs are somewhat more complex, and less efficient, than designs that focus primarily on efficiency. But in actuality, competitive design is concerned with effectiveness—after all, it is not essential to deliver a perfect design, but rather a design that is better than that of the best competitor.

Another way of looking at competitive design is to return to the military analogy with which we started. In designing the army to conduct the campaign, the general can ill afford to seek perfection on the parade ground. Rather, he must assemble his forces and materials to create an army superior to that of the enemy in the actual terrain. Our questions have consistently assisted managers in achieving this more modest, but pragmatic, purpose of designing competitive, if imperfect, designs. They go a long way toward delivering designs that are competitively superior—a key challenge of the 1980s.

REFERENCES

1. Kiechel, W., III. "Playing by the Rules of the Corporate Strategy Game," *Fortune,* September 24, 1979.
2. "The Future Catches Up with a Strategic Planner," *Business Week,* June 27, 1983.
3. Davis, S. Personal communication to author.
4. Galbraith, J. R., and D. A. Nathanson. *Strategy Implementation: The Role of Structure and Process.* St. Paul, Minn.: West Publishing, 1978.
5. Nadler, D. A., J. R. Hackman; and E. E. Lawler III. *Managing Organizational Behavior.* Boston: Little, Brown, 1979.
6. Rothschild, W. E. *Putting It All Together.* New York AMACOM, 1976; *Strategic Alternatives.* New York: AMACOM, 1979.
7. MacMillan, I. C. "Seizing the Competitive Initiative," *Journal of Business Strategy,* Spring 1982.
8. Peters, T. J., and R. H. Waterman. *In Search of Excellence: Lessons from America's Best-Run Companies.* New York: Harper & Row, 1982.
9. MacMillan, I. C. "Corporate Ideology and Strategic Delegation," *Journal of Business Strategy,* Winter 1983.
10. *Implementation Strategies.* AT&T, 1980.
11. Hax, A. C., and N. S. Majluf. "Strategic Organization," *Journal of Business Strategy,* Fall 1983.
12. Galbraith, J. R. *Designing Complex Organizations.* Reading, Mass.: Addison-Wesley, 1973.
13. Hayes, R. H., and W. J. Abernathy. "Managing Our Way to Economic Decline," *Harvard Business Review,* July/August 1980.

APPENDIX: Design Strengths and Weaknesses

First/Second Layer Groupings (examples)	*Potential Strengths*	*Potential Vulnerabilities*

Activity/Client
 	
Production
Purchasing · Assembly · Testing
 	
Marketing
Sales · Research
	Competitive Response
	• Good competitor intelligence
	• Rapid awareness of:
	  Competitive market initiatives
	  Technology change and new process introductions
	
	Market Response
	• Good total market perspective
	• Good market intelligence
	• High technical product quality
	• Good leverage with distributors
	• Efficient marketing
	
	Internal Functioning
	• High functional expertise
	• Good economics of scale, e.g.,
	  Equipment
	  Personnel
	  Physical plant
	• Good leverage with suppliers
	• Fast process and equipment innovation
	• Strong infrastructure, especially support services
		Competitive Response
		• Slow response to:
		  Competitive product and service initiatives
		  New products and services
		  Substitute products
		
		Market Response
		• System's focus on client may be low
		• Slow market response due to poor functional interfaces
		
		Internal Functioning
		• Poor integrative planning and development
		• Narrow divisional focus
		• Short-term perspective
		• High functional conflict
		• Develops functional managers

Activity/Output (see p. 328)	*Competitive Response*
	• Rapid response to:
	  Competitive moves in existing product market areas
	  Market and product expansion plans
	  Product enhancements
		Competitive Response
		• Slow response to:
		  Competitors' product innovations
		  Substitute products
		• Focus on existing rather than on new product/market areas
		• Integration needed across functions slows response to market actions by competitors

(continued)

APPENDIX *(continued)*

First/Second Layer Groupings (examples)	Potential Strengths	Potential Vulnerabilities
Activity/Output *(continued)* 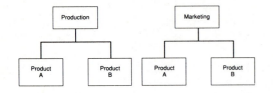	*Market Response* • Strong distribution channels • Strong integrated product and market intelligence • Some economies of scale due to functional centralization *Internal Functioning* • Strong supply channels • Functional and product expertise • Some economies of scale due to functional centralization	*Market Response* • Marketing inefficiencies, e.g., clients may have multiple contacts • Poorly integrated customer service • System's focus on client is low • Slow response to market changes *Internal Functioning* • Poor integrative planning and resource allocation across functions • Product synergies not considered • Economies of scale not fully realized

Activity/Client 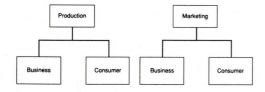	*Competitive Response*
	• Rapid resource allocation to existing functional and market areas
	• Rapid response to:
	  Existing market diversity
	  Competitors' moves in existing market areas
	• High competitive intelligence
	
	Market Response
	• Total market awareness
	• Good market intelligence
	• High leverage with distributors
	• Full-line sales
		Competitive Response
		• Slow response to:
		  New products
		  New technologies
		• Competitors' product initiatives
		• Innovation/growth restricted to existing market areas
		
		Market Response
		• Market inefficiencies, e.g.:
		  Product knowledge lessened
		  Possible product overlap
		• System's focus on customer needs is low
		• Possible variances in product quality

APPENDIX   *(continued)*

First/Second Layer Groupings (examples)	*Potential Strengths*	*Potential Vulnerabilities*

	Internal Functioning
	• High technical expertise
	• High leverage with suppliers
	• High economies of scale
	  Capacity
	  Facilities
		Internal Functioning
		• Poor integrative product planning and development
		• Economies in scale not fully realized, e.g., duplication of staff

Output/Output
 	
Product Group A — Product 1, Product 2
Product Group B — Product 3, Product 4
	Competitive Response
	• Good product planning and management
	• Rapid resource allocation to existing product areas
	• Rapid response to:
	  Competitive initiatives in existing product areas
	  Product and service enhancement
	
	Market Response
	Strong distribution channels
	• Tailored customer support systems
	• Sales force has high product knowledge
		Competitive Response
		• Lack of total market perspective
		• Diffused authority for critical functions
		• Divisional rather than corporate focus, leading to inability to perceive competitor in its totality
		• Low competitive intelligence
		
		Market Response
		• Distributors may face multiple contacts
		• Possible marketing inefficiencies, e.g., clients may have multiple contacts
		• Poor integrated customer service
		• Poor market intelligence
		• Poor technical product quality
		• System's focus on client is low

(continued)

APPENDIX   *(continued)*

First/Second Layer Groupings *(examples)*	*Potential* *Strengths*	*Potential* *Vulnerabilities*

Output/Output *(continued)*	*Internal Functioning*
	• Develops general managers
	• High product focus and morale
	• Possible product technology synergies
		Internal Functioning
		• Possible product synergies not realized
		• Functional inefficiencies
		• Low economies of scale
		  Capacity
		  Staff
		• Low technical expertise
		• Poor internal support systems
		• Corporate attention dissipated

Output/Activity	*Competitive Response* • Good product planning and management • Rapid response allocation to existing product areas • Product enhancement potential is high *Market Response* • High technical product quality • Tailored customer support systems • Sales force has high product knowledge • Strong product intelligence	*Competitive Response* • Lack of total market perspective • Divisional rather than corporate focus, leading to inability to perceive competitor in its totality • Focus on existing rather than new product areas • Possible product synergies not considered • Low competitive intelligence *Market Response* • Possible marketing inefficiencies, e.g., clients may have multiple contacts • Poorly integrated customer service • Poorly integrated market intelligence • Distribution and supply positions weakened by lack of total corporate approach

Product A — Production, Marketing

Product B — Production, Marketing

APPENDIX   *(continued)*

First/Second Layer Groupings (examples)	*Potential Strengths*	*Potential Vulnerabilities*
	Internal Functioning • Develops general managers • High product focus and morale • Possible product technology synergies within departments • High technical product expertise • High functional expertise	*Internal Functioning* • Functional inefficiencies • Inefficient capacity and staff utilization • Corporate attention dissipated • Conflicting goals (divisional versus corporate)

Output/Client
 	
Product A — Government, Business
Product B — Government, Business
	Competitive Response
	• Good product planning and management
	• Rapid resource allocation to existing product market areas
	• Rapid response to:
	  Existing market diversity
	  Competitive initiatives in existing product market areas
	  Customer needs
	
	Market Response
	• Good market intelligence and focus
	• Sales force has high product knowledge
	• Tailored customer support systems
		Competitive Response
		• Lack of total product market perspective
		• Divisional rather than corporate focus, leading to inability to perceive competitor in its totality
		• Focus on existing rather than new products
		• Diffused authority for critical functions
		• Possible product synergies not considered
		
		Market Response
		• Possible marketing inefficiencies
		  Sales force may compete for overlapping markets
		  Clients may have multiple contacts
		• Poorly integrated customer service
		• System's focus on client is low
		• Poorly integrated market intelligence
		• Weakened by lack of corporatewide approach

APPENDIX *(continued)*

First/Second Layer Groupings *(examples)*	Potential Strengths	Potential Vulnerabilities
Output/Client *(continued)*	*Internal Functioning* • Develops general managers • High product market focus and morale	*Internal Functioning* • Poor internal support systems • Functional inefficiencies • Inefficient capacity and staff utilization • Low technical product quality • Low functional expertise • Corporate attention dissipated
Client/Client East Coast → Business, Consumer West Coast → Business, Consumer	*Competitive Response* • Rapid response to: Existing market diversity Customer needs Existing market expansion plans • High market preemption potential *Market Response* • Strong marketing and sales • Good customer service • Facilitates client planning and coordination • High market intelligence • Particularly suitable for key account strategies	*Competitive Response* • Lack of total market perspective • May not have authority over all critical functions • Divisional rather than corporate focus, leading to inability to perceive competitor in its totality • Innovation restricted to existing markets *Market Response* • Over-response to client whims • Marketing inefficiencies, e.g., clients may have multiple contacts • Low product intelligence • Sales force faced with broader product line and consequently lower product knowledge • Weakened distribution channel position

APPENDIX   *(continued)*

First/Second Layer Groupings (examples)	*Potential Strengths*	*Potential Vulnerabilities*
	Internal Functioning • Develops general managers • High market integration internally	*Internal Functioning* • Corporate attention dissipated • Market overlap may cause internal competition • Low functional skills • Poor internal support systems and integration • Inefficient capacity and staff utilization

Client/Activity
 	
Business → Manufacturing, Marketing
Consumer → Manufacturing, Marketing
	Competitive Response
	• Rapid response to:
	  Existing market diversity
	  Customer needs
	  Market expansion plans
	  Competitors market initiatives
		Competitive Response
		• Lack of total market perspective
		• Divisional rather than corporate focus, leading to inability to perceive competitor in its totality
		• Slow response to:
		  Competitors' product innovations
		  Product expansion plans
		• Low competitive intelligence

	Market Response
	• Strong marketing and full-line sales
	• High leverage with distribution channels
	• High product quality
	• High market intelligence
		Market Response
		• Marketing inefficiencies
		  Product knowledge lessened
		  Product priority conflict
		  Possible market product overlap
		• Low product intelligence

	Internal Functioning • High function expertise • Good internal support systems • High leverage with suppliers	*Internal Functioning* • Product priority conflict (if multiproduct) • Low economies of scale (across divisions) • Poor integration between functions

(continued)

APPENDIX   (*concluded*)

First/Second Layer Groupings (examples)	Potential Strengths	Potential Vulnerabilities

Client/Output	*Competitive Response*
	• Rapid response to:
	  Customer needs
	  Market and product expansion plans
	  Competitive moves in existing product/market areas
	  Product enhancements
	• Rapid resource allocation to product market areas
	
	Market Response
	• Strong marketing and sales, e.g., sales force has high product knowledge
	• Good market intelligence and expertise
	• Good customer service
	
	Internal Functioning
	• Develops general managers
	• High product and market focus and morale
		Competitive Response
		• Lack of total market perspective
		• Divisional rather than corporate perspective leading to inability to perceive competitor in its totality
		• Low competitive intelligence
		• Slow response to competitors' product innovations
		
		Market Response
		• Marketing inefficiencies, e.g., client may have multiple contacts
		• System's focus on client is low
		• Possibly over-responsive to client whims
		
		Internal Functioning
		• Low functional expertise
		• Poor internal support systems
		• Low capacity and staff utilization
		• Product innovation/enhancement overlaps
		• Possible product synergies may be overlooked

What this article is about: Carrying out a radical strategy in a large firm is the acid test of corporate leadership. Yet, there are few models available to prepare and guide leaders to take unprecedented actions. The authors in this article address this issue and propose a framework for devising and implementing strategies that are discontinuous with the organization's present course of action. The framework considers four types of radical strategies: reorientation, turnaround, revitalization, and transformation.

4–3 How to Implement Radical Strategies in Large Organizations

Yvan Allaire and Mihaela Firsirotu

Yvan Allaire is Professor of Strategy, Marketing, and Research Methodology and Chairman of the Ph.D. program in the Department of Administrative Sciences at the University of Quebec at Montreal

Mihaela Firsirotu is Assistant Professor of Strategy in the Department of Administrative Sciences at the University of Quebec at Montreal

The business press has recently chronicled many corporations that are experiencing momentous shifts in strategic orientation. Reference is often made to a corporation's market repositioning, acquisitions and divestitures, structural changes, and so on. However, when reporting on such major strategic changes, the press has also begun to emphasize the softer dimensions, such as values, culture, and mind-sets. Thus, it is not entirely accidental that the topic of corporate culture has become a popular issue at a time when many corporations are experiencing major overhauls. Culture, and its resistance to change, provides an explanation for the insuperable difficulties a firm encounters when it attempts to shift its strategic criterion. Not only has the "right" corporate culture become the essence and foundation of corporate excellence, but it is also claimed that the success or failure of needed corporate reforms hinges on management's sagacity and ability to change the firm's driving culture *in time* and *in tune* with required changes in formal strategies, structures, and management systems.

SOURCE: *Sloan Management Review* (Spring 1985), pp. 19–34.

But while such observations are relevant, even though they are sometimes simplistic or faddish, they fail to inform corporate leaders on two critical issues:

1. What different type of radical strategies are available? And do different strategies call for different implementation procedures? For example, there has to be a difference between a radical strategy to turn around a moribund firm and a strategy to shift a corporation's resources to totally new markets and industries; or a strategy to prepare a healthy organization for major changes in its industry.
2. What lessons have been learned from the experience of corporations that have attempted, succeeded, or failed at radical strategies? Are there emerging frameworks, models, bits of wisdom that can guide corporate leaders facing such a task?

This article addresses these two issues by proposing clear, operational distinctions among four types of radical strategies: reorientation, turnaround, revitalization, and transformation. These four, well-demarcated radical change situations, which all call for very different actions, flow from a simple diagnosis of how the firm *fits* in its present and future environments. We then go on to describe a framework for thinking about, devising, and implementing strategies that are discontinuous with the organization's present course of action.

FOUR CASE SITUATIONS

No radical strategy will ever occur if the corporation's leadership is not convinced of the need for dramatic actions. Therefore, a critical first step is for a firm to arrive at an appropriate diagnosis of how the firm fits in its present environment. A prescription prevalent in the business policy and strategy field has been the need for fit[1] or alignment[2] between the firm's strategy and its environment. Still, the wise, but trite, prescription could be made more potent if more of a distinction were made between present and future environments: an assessment of a corporation's fit and adjustment to its *present* and *future* environments will reveal one of four possible situations, which are described below.

Case I: Harmony and Continuity

In this first case, the firm's strategy is well adjusted to its present environment, which results in the firm's sound economic performance. The future is an evolutionary, predictable version of the present, for which the firm will prepare in an incremental manner. In other words, the preferred state of affairs, whenever

[1]A. D. Chandler, *Strategy and Structure* (Cambridge, Mass.: MIT Press, 1962).
[2]J. Thompson, *Organizations in Action* (New York: McGraw-Hill, 1967).

FIGURE 1   Case I: Harmony and Continuity

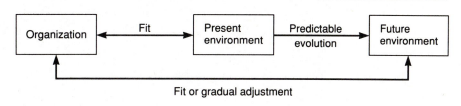

attainable, is for a firm to have a harmonious fit in its present environment while making synchronized, gradual changes to meet anticipated future requirements (see Figure 1).

Still, managers, and, for that matter, most people, have a strong tendency to cling to this approach even when there are warning signals indicating that a new approach is needed for the firm to cope with the future. (To the extent that the firm's management is not deluding itself into believing that a Case I strategy is the proper diagnosis, the textbook prescriptions and techniques for good management formulated for just such conditions are relevant and useful.)

A company's harmonious fit to present and future environments is most easily achieved in periods of easy economic growth and tranquil technology. However, periods of economic upheaval or economic transformation may disrupt and threaten the status quo of large businesses. If this happens, the business environment becomes "discontinuous," and becomes increasingly characterized by radical changes in the rules of the game. It is as if, in an ongoing game of chess, one of the players or some outside authority were to suddenly decree changes in the rules that govern the moves of chess pieces. Much of the players' past chess experience (and the hundreds of books offering advice on how to play chess) would automatically become obsolete. In the final analysis, if an organization finds that it has to adjust to radically changed circumstances, the Case I scenario is inappropriate, and even dangerous.

Case II: Preemptive Adjustment or Temporary Misfit

Preemptive Adjustment.   In this case, the firm is not well adjusted to its present market circumstances, which results in its immediate unsatisfactory performance. However, it is anticipated that the future will be fundamentally different from the present situation. The environment is expected to undergo a sudden breach of continuity or a sharp change from present conditions and trends: the firm is prepared and ready to reap rich rewards when this happens (see Figure 2).

A good illustration of this case is provided by Citibank's expenditures on technology and product development, which resulted in poor performance for some years in its retail banking operations. Nonetheless, this orientation has

FIGURE 2   Case II: Preemptive Adjustment or a Temporary Misfit

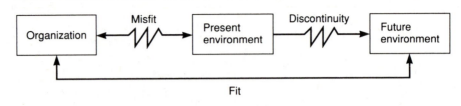

presently placed the firm in a favorable strategic position as deregulation of the banking industry has begun to take effect and radically change the competitive and market environments. Another example is MCI Communications. Its quixotic challenge at AT&T in the long-distance telephone market has been made more significant by successive changes in the regulations of the telecommunications industry in the United States.

Also included in this category are innovating firms that propose radically new products to presently unreceptive or undeveloped markets. Genentech's early foray in the gene-splicing and biotechnology field is a good example. Firms in this situation, if they are persistent and if their resources are sufficient, may eventually be vindicated; on the other hand, it may be that their ventures were ill-timed and ill-conceived.

Temporary Misfit.   Transient, short-lived phenomena may perturb the organization's present environment, thereby creating havoc and misalignment for the firm. Nonetheless, the future could bring a return to normal circumstances to which the organization will be well adjusted. The organization will then resume its past acceptable level of economic performance. Although this scenario may be plausible, it may also be one of wishful thinking, or what Abernathy, Clark, and Kantrow call the "transient economic misfortune" school of thought.[3]

The prevalence of this type of unfounded rationale is particularly evident in industries that are coming to the end of their growth cycle. For example, the leveling off in sales of kerosene heaters, cross-country ski equipment, video games, snowmobiles, and personal computers was characteristically attributed to transient phenomenon, such as bad weather or bad economic conditions. However, it was believed that as soon as these conditions returned to normal, sales would again surge at their previous rate. Of course, this did not happen. In these cases, sticking to this strategy was damaging as it led to a postponement of the kind of actions required to adjust these businesses to new realities.

---

[3]W. J. Abernathy, K. B. Clark, and A. M. Kantrow, *Industrial Renaissance: Producing a Competitive Future for America* (New York: Basic Books, 1983).

FIGURE 3 Case III: Transformation or Reorientation

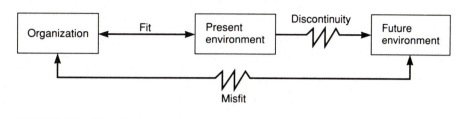

Case III: Transformation or Reorientation

Here, the firm is well adjusted to its present environment and turns in strong, respectable performances. However, its management forsees a future environment that is quite different from the prevailing one as a result of demographic, technological, regulatory, or competitive changes. To cope with, and thrive in, these upcoming circumstances, the organization must undergo a fundamental change (see Figure 3).

Transformation. Classic examples of major strategic *transformations* that have restructured whole industries include Boeing's shift to the production of jet engine commercial airplanes and IBM's immense wager on the integrated circuit technology of the 360. More recently, current and anticipated dramatic changes in computer markets and technology have called for major modifications of strategy at IBM and Digital Equipment. In the latter case, K. C. Olsen, Digital's president, "embarked upon a radical transformation of his engineering-oriented company into a tough, market-driven competitor."[4]

Reorientation. A reorientation scenario is one where a company, in anticipation of stagnation and even decline as its present markets mature, may *reorient* its resources into more attractive markets and industries. The business press is full of accounts of companies that are searching for renewed vitality through reorientation strategies. Below is a list of organizations that either have reoriented or are in the process of reorienting their operations.

In Canada, the Bank of Montreal has undertaken a major transformation of its structures and modes of operation. It is preparing for (and ushering in) an emerging banking environment that is thought to call for radically different operating technologies, management systems, and banking philosophy.[7]

---

[4]"A New Strategy for No. 2 in Computers: Will Digital Equipment Corp.'s Massive Overhaul Pay Off?" *Business Week,* May 2, 1983.

[5]"Black and Decker's Gamble on Globalization," *Fortune,* May 14, 1984.

[6]"Slimming Down: Beatrice Foods Moves to Centralize Business to Reverse Its Decline," *The Wall Street Journal,* September 27, 1983.

[7]G. L. Reuber, "Bits, Bytes, and Banking," *Business Quarterly,* Spring 1983.

The breakup of AT&T along with the heroic efforts of some of its components (Western Electric, Bell Labs, AT&T Information Systems, etc.) to shift from a regulated telephone monopoly environment to a competitive market context is perhaps the most striking example of a large-scale attempt at strategic transformation.[8]

Transformations may also result from a firm's resolve to change the "center of gravity" of the corporation.[9] For example, Monsanto's move downstream from commodity chemicals to proprietary, patented products illustrates a transformation strategy.[10] The displacement of a corporation's center of gravity often means that new skills and radically different modes of operation and styles of management must be brought into the organization in a short period of time. This kind of transformation may result in a company that is temporarily misaligned with its present environment.

Reorientation.   A reorientation scenario is one where a company, in anticipation of stagnation and even decline as its present markets mature, may *reorient* its resources into more attractive markets and industries. The business press is full of accounts of companies that are searching for renewed vitality through reorientation strategies. Below is a list of organizations that either have reoriented or are in the process of reorienting their operations.

- General Electric's shift from traditional electric products to high technology (computer services, factory automation).[11]
- Sears, Roebuck and American Express's invasion of the financial services market.[12]
- Philip Morris's aggressive entry into the beer industry (through Miller) and into the soft-drink industry (through 7 Up).
- Eaton's shift from reliance on trucks and other vehicle parts to electronics, factory automation machinery, and fluid power systems.[13]
- Pillsbury's shift to fast food and restaurant chains.[14]
- Gould's move from battery operations—the very foundation of the corporation which it recently and symbolically sold—to the production and selling of

---

[8]W. B. Tunstall, "Cultural Transition at AT&T," *Sloan Management Review,* Fall 1983, pp. 15–26; "Culture Shock Is Shaking the Bell System," *Business Week,* September 26, 1983; "AT&T Manager Finds His Effort to Galvanize Sales Meets Resistance," *The Wall Street Journal,* December 16, 1983; A. van Auw, *Heritage and Destiny: Reflections on the Bell System Transition* (New York: Praeger, 1983); P. Drucker, "Beyond the Bell Breakup," *The Public Interest* 77 (Fall 1984).

[9]J. R. Galbraith, "Strategy and Organization Planning," *Human Resource Management* 22 (Spring–Summer 1983).

[10]"Monsanto Slowly but Deliberately Shifts Emphasis to Research, Patented Products," *The Wall Street Journal,* January 13, 1983.

[11]"The $5-Billion Man: Pushing the New Strategy at GE," *Fortune,* April 18,1983.

[12]"Financial Forays: Sears Expansion Brings Increased Competition to Bankers and Brokers," *The Wall Street Journal,* October 12, 1981.

[13]"Eaton: Spinning Its Wheels on the Road to High-Tech Profits," *Business Week,* March 28, 1983.

[14]J. B. Quinn, *Strategies for Change* (Homewood, Ill.: Irwin, 1980).

electronic equipment. Gould Inc. now operates 57 electronic plants in 11 countries.

- Imasco's (a large Canadian cigarette manufacturer) move into the U.S.'s fast food restaurants and retail drug stores.[15]
- Philip's shift to high-tech products.[16]
- Cincinnati Milacron's shift from metal bender to supplier of new robotic technology.[17]
- U.S. Steel's redeployment of assets (Marathon Oil, etc.).[18]
- Singer's expansion into aerospace.[19]
- Johnson & Johnson's recent emphasis on high-tech medical hardware.[20]

Because the environments in which these firms presently operate do not provide a future with sufficient prospects for growth and profitability, they are seeking to move voluntarily to market environments offering more promise and potential. In such a reorientation of activities, the firm must manage a breach, or discontinuity, between its present and future state.

Case IV: Turnaround and Revitalization

The firm in this case is misaligned with its present environment: Its performance may range from mediocre to dismal. Furthermore, the company is ill-equipped to meet the future (see Figure 4). The business press reverberates with stories of dramatic efforts of companies salvaging and turning around large organizations, such as Chrysler, Massey-Ferguson, International Harvester, American Motors, Montgomery Ward, AM International, Geico, Clark Equipment, A&P, Braniff, Pan-Am, Boise Cascade, Allis-Chalmers, Dome Petroleum, Eastern Airlines, and Western Union.

But whether the situation calls for *revitalization* or *turnaround* actions hinges on the severity of the problems. There is, for example, a difference between a Burrough's or a Westinghouse's lackadaisical profit performance, sagging market share, and groping adjustment to changing markets on the one hand and, on the other hand, a Chrysler, Massey-Ferguson, or International Harvester on the brink of bankruptcy.

---

[15]"La Mauvaise Annee des Autres, une Autre Annee Record Chez Imasco," *Commerce,* July 1983.

[16]"Philip's High-Tech Crusade," *Business Week,* July 18, 1983.

[17]"High-Tech Track: Cincinnati Milacron, Mainly Metal-Bender, Now Is a Robot Maker," *The Wall Street Journal,* April 7, 1983.

[18]"Rousing a Giant: David Roderick Tries to Recast U.S. Steel by Redeploying Assets," *The Wall Street Journal,* February 7, 1983.

[19]"Singer: Sewing Machines Finally Take a Backseat as It Expands into Aerospace," *Business Week,* June 13, 1983.

[20]"Changing a Corporate Culture: Can Johnson & Johnson Go from Band-Aids to High Tech?" *Business Week,* May 14, 1984.

FIGURE 4   CASE IV: Turnaround and Revitalization

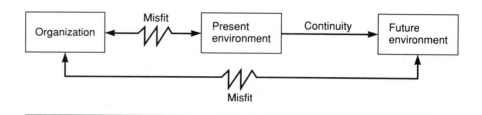

A company is in a *turnaround* situation if it has experienced such grave losses that its very survival is at stake if improvements are not achieved swiftly. However, a corporation may not be in any immediate danger but may show mediocre or below average results, calling for *revitalization* of its performance in the marketplace. Recent examples of businesses undergoing a revitalization are Prudential-Bache Securities,[21] Continental Corp.,[22] Corning Glass,[23] Burroughs,[24] Goodyear,[25] Sears's retailing division,[26] J.C. Penney,[27] Westinghouse,[28] and Sherwin-Williams.[29]

A FRAMEWORK TO DEVISE AND IMPLEMENT RADICAL STRATEGIES

Leaders faced with the challenge of transforming, reorienting, revitalizing, or turning around a large corporation will find few relevant models or useful prescriptions to guide their actions. Instead, they will most likely fret about culture and about how to create and sustain the kind of values they should want for their

[21]"New Bache Chief Pushes a Host of Changes, Including New Name, to Lift Firm's Image," *The Wall Street Journal,* October 29, 1982; "After a Year, Prudential's Takeover of Bache Mostly Causing Problems," *The Wall Street Journal,* July 16, 1982.

[22]"Continental Corp. Still Drifts despite Moves to Reorganize, Lift Its Insurance Earnings," *The Wall Street Journal,* April 19, 1983.

[23]"With New Chairman, Corning Tries to Get Tough and Revive Earnings," *The Wall Street Journal,* April 22, 1983.

[24]"Burroughs Tightens Up and Aims for IBM, but Many New Obstacles Stand in the Way," *The Wall Street Journal,* July 20, 1982.

[25]"Driving Ahead: Chief's Style and Ideas Help to Keep Goodyear No. 1 in the Radial Age," *The Wall Street Journal,* January 18, 1983.

[26]"Sears' Overdue Retailing Revival," *Fortune,* April 4, 1983.

[27]"J.C. Penney Goes After Affluent Shoppers, but Store's New Image May Be Hard to Sell," *The Wall Street Journal,* February 15, 1983.

[28]"Operation Turnaround: How Westinghouse's New CEO Plans to Fire Up an Old-Line Company," *Business Week,* December 5, 1983.

[29]"Sherwin-Williams Makes Big Turnaround under Chairman's Aggressive Leadership," *The Wall Street Journal,* December 14, 1983.

organizations. They may even be bullied by popular infatuation into a "search for excellence" that promotes specific and contingent observations as universal and compelling management principles.[30]

Based on the experiences of many leaders who assumed the role of corporate revolutionaries, we have devised a framework for implementing radical strategies. The framework is broken down into six basic steps: (1) making a proper diagnosis; (2) formulating a metastrategy for radical change; (3) assessing the company's culture and structure; (4) defining the goals of the company's culture and structure; (5) proposing a broad agenda for radical change; and (6) stabilizing the organization.

Step 1: Making a Proper Diagnosis

Perhaps the most pernicious role of a corporation's present culture and structure is in its shaping a *corporate mind-set* that makes its leaders and managers immune or oblivious to signals of danger.

For example, a leadership persuaded of its Case I situation of harmony, continuity, and incremental adjustments may be right. However, the leaders may be deluding themselves or they may be impervious to indications of dramatic industry changes. They may even deny the reality of their present difficulties and shortcomings, and they may cling to a Case II diagnosis of a transient, self-correcting phenomenon, thereby attributing the company's poor performance to factors beyond their control. They may, therefore, feel that no radical actions are called for on their part.

Obviously, the first step in implementing any radical strategy is to make sure that the diagnosis of the firm's state of adjustment to its present environment and its preparedness for future circumstances is based on a tough, lucid, and unbiased assessment. Radical strategies must be considered if the leadership concludes, on the basis of that assessment, that it must either transform, reorient, revitalize, or turn around the corporation. Each of these strategies has its own particular dynamics and set of considerations. Although the contents and rate of change will reflect each company's particularities, these four radical strategies (in particular, turnaround, revitalization, and transformation) should unfold in a pattern of steps and actions, sometimes sequential but often overlapping and concurrent.

The Four Radical Strategies

Reorientation.   Of the four radical strategies, reorientation is the easiest to implement. If a reorientation calls for the gradual divestment of present businesses and the acquisition of businesses in new fields—as General Electric and

---

[30]Quinn has provided a review of the tactics and processes used by leaders in their efforts to carry out far-reaching changes in organizations. See Quinn (1980).

Gould are doing—corporate management would acquire the cultures and structures of the newly acquired firms. On the other hand, if a reorientation calls for the addition of new businesses to a mature, but profitable business—as Philip Morris, Pillsbury, and Imasco have done—the culture and structure of these businesses should not be disturbed if they are functioning well. Nevertheless, there are a few pitfalls that a company should be aware of when implementing a reorientation strategy.

Corporate Management's Mind-Set.   The fundamental requirement of a successful reorientation is corporate leader's awareness that they are entering new territories, and, therefore, that their past experiences and specific skills may be of limited relevance, if not totally inadequate. It is tempting, but dangerous, to assume that what has made their companies successful in their present businesses will also make them successful in other industries. Such an attitude is sometimes reinforced by leaders emphasizing the similarities between the new and old businesses. For example, General Foods bungled in the fast food business (with Burger Chef) precisely because it first attempted to have this totally new business managed by people from its old business.

This trap is particularly dangerous when a corporation moves into new fields incrementally. For example, the chief executive of Johnson & Johnson challenged *Business Week's* cover story that stated that J&J would have to change its corporate culture as it moved more and more into high-tech medical hardware.[31] In his letter to *BW,* Mr. Burke retorted, "It is well known that Johnson & Johnson has been a high-technology company for decades. . . ."[32] Obviously, J&J's leadership diagnosed the situation as a Case I scenario (continuity), whereas *Business Week* concluded that it was a Case III situation (*reorientation*).

The Lure of Efficiency through Integration.   Even though corporate management may consciously acknowledge that a newly acquired or a newly formed business is different from the existing mature business, it may be tempted to integrate some of the new business's functions with the old one in order to take advantage of the cost savings. This temptation must be resisted, however, for the old business's culture may permeate the new business, thereby making it increasingly difficult for the new business to adjust to its own competitive environment. Woolworth is a case in point. When Woolworth, a successful, but mature variety store business, formed the discount store Woolco, it decided to integrate some of Woolco's functions (in particular, purchasing) with Woolworth's operations. This led to Woolco's ultimate failure in part because its operations were permeated by Woolworth's "five-and-dime" thinking. In contrast, Kresge managed its successful K mart division as a completely autonomous business.[33]

A successful reorientation, therefore, calls for a corporate leadership that

---

[31]*Business Week,* May 14, 1984.

[32]*Business Week,* June 18, 1984.

[33]"Counter Strategy, Woolworth, Defeated in Discounting, Aims at Specialty Markets," *The Wall Street Journal,* November 3, 1983.

knows it does not know how to run the new businesses it is either acquiring or forming. Every attempt should be made to keep the cultures and structures of both the new and old businesses separate and distinct.

Turnaround.   When a corporation's very survival is threatened, its leaders must carry out emergency actions that will stave off bankruptcy and buy them the time required to implement a radial strategy. The leadership must quickly find a new, more suitable market strategy that offers a compelling long-term solution to the firm's present plight. Often what is required to get the firm out of its rut is a new top management team that will challenge taken-for-granted "facts" and assumptions. Such a crisis provides top management with a formidable tool to carry out changes that would otherwise be impossible. However, the level of stress among managers and employees must be monitored and managed. Too much stress may well lead to counterproductive actions (e.g., rash decisions).

Revitalization.   Before a revitalization strategy can be implemented, an organization must first come to terms with two pervasive issues: (1) that there is no immediate evidence of crisis or threat to the firm's survival and (2) that mediocre performances are often justified by putting the blame on external factors that are thought to be beyond the control of management. Given this backdrop, it is up to corporate leaders to make a looming crisis tangible and to make known the dangers that the corporation faces. The leaders must make the case vivid and persuasive. Corporate management must also develop a sense of control and responsibility for the firm's performance.

Transformation.   Of all the radical strategies, transformation requires the most demanding and skillful leadership. What is needed is a genuine revolution initiated by a leader with a *vision* of the corporation's future and the *will* to achieve it. However, the typical scenario is one where the corporation's present performance is satisfactory—maybe even excellent—and thus there is no impetus and no obvious justification for change.

Transformation strategy also involves other risks. Top management frequently makes the mistake of focusing exclusively on the structural aspects of change and of assuming implicitly that an appropriate culture will emerge quickly and inevitably from the new structural arrangements. In addition, in the course of transforming the organization to meet impending changes, top management may bring about a misalignment that is similar to a Case II misfit situation. Corporate management must be aware that some degree of confusion and disarray among employees and clients may be unavoidable during the process of transformation and, therefore, may result in a lower level of economic performance for a period of time.

Step 2: Formulating a Metastrategy for Radical Change

To achieve radical change, the organization should be instilled with the new strategies, structures and systems, and supporting values deemed necessary to make such a change successful. Obviously, the leader, who is usually the CEO, must be able to distance himself or herself from the ongoing operations in order to set in motion the processes of change. This means that when present or anticipated events indicate that change in an organization's culture and structure is necessary, the leader must be able to formulate a *strategy* to implement a radically different strategy in the organization. This strategy is known as a metastrategy.

The leader's metastrategy is unwritten and communicated to very few people, at least in its early stages of implementation. At the beginning, the metastrategy may consist of a leader's tentative search for broad goals and directions. He or she will then set up or activate multiple (internal and external) channels to consult and discuss the goals and orientations.

When a leader becomes convinced—the sooner the better—that particular goals and directions are appropriate, he or she will then take the necessary steps to broaden support for the chosen direction through a well-thought-out sequence of symbolic actions and structural changes. The leader's metastrategy will reflect some hard thinking and firm conclusions about the kind of values that should be built into the organization. However, this does not mean that the leader should hold corporatewide seminars on the "culture we should have." (Culture is in the realm of feelings and sentiments, and does not develop well under clinical observation.) Rather, the metastrategy process is a formal, well-mapped-out strategy that leads to a new, formal, explicit strategy for the organization. In this way, the organization's future is dependent upon the quality of this present leadership metastrategy.

Presently, the business press is full of sagas of leaders going about the task of major corporate overhauls. The accounts of these struggles and our own research of specific cases lead to a firm conclusion: radical strategies have been successfully implemented only where corporate leaders were equipped with an effective meta-strategy.

Step 3: Assessing the Corporation's Present Culture and Structure

The objective here is to understand the organization as a sociocultural system, to chart the socialization that the corporation actually provides, and to get at the organization's mind-set. If the leaders emerge from the ranks of the corporation, this step requires that they examine the values, beliefs, and mind-sets (including their own) imparted by the organization. On the other hand, if the leaders are newcomers, this step calls for their fast and sensitive learning of the organization's tangible *and* occult properties. In either case, the process may be helped by finding answers to the following questions:

1. What are the tacit background assumptions and expectations in the corporation? Where do they come from?
2. What are the values and frames of mind that flow from the particular nature of the industry? How did the industry's peculiar technology, regulations, labor-management relations, nature of competition, and economics shape the

beliefs and behavior of the organization? These factors almost always play a critical role in shaping the mind-set of a corporation. Yet, this factor is generally overlooked in the recent crop of books and articles on corporate culture, which tends to view culture merely as the product of past or present charismatic leaders.

3. What stories, legends, myths circulate concerning the corporation's history, its past and present leaders? How are its successes and misfortunes explained?
4. What are valued behavior, promotion paths, and critical skills for success in the corporation?
5. What reinforcement of present culture is afforded by recruitment, training, promotion, organization structures, management systems?
6. What is the implicit or explicit process of socialization in the corporation? Who are the role models? What cues and messages are conveyed to new employees? What values are communicated in training sessions?
7. What is the degree of employee involvement in the corporation? Is there widespread commitment or calculative, limited participation on the part of management and employees? Are there groups (divisions, departments, etc.) with a subculture substantially at odds with the rest of the corporation?

The end product of this inquiry should be a statement of the basic values, assumptions, or expectations that have emerged from the organization's particular history, leadership, and contingency factors and that are supported by present-day management policies and practices. Below are brief examples of the set of assumptions that deeply permeated the operations of two large corporations.

AT&T.   W. Brooke Tunstall, assistant vice president of AT&T, found that AT&T's operations were deeply influenced by the following[34]:

- AT&T's role is to provide the best universal service at the lowest possible cost in a regulated environment.
- AT&T must be "one system," "one policy" throughout the organization to fulfill its role.
- AT&T is a three-legged stool: it must achieve a fair balance in the treatment of its employees, customers, and shareholders.
- Operational efficiency, technical skills, and a high level of effort to create a favorable regulatory climate are the keys for success.
- AT&T is a big family that cares for its employees.

Canadian National.   In her study of Canadian National (CN), a state-owned railway company (now diversified to a large extent), Firsirotu discovered the assumptions underlying the corporation[35]:

- CN has a public service responsibility to Canadian communities.

---

[34]Tunstall (Fall 1983).
[35]M. Firsirotu, "Strategic Turnaround as Cultural Revolutions" (unpublished Ph.D. thesis, McGill University, Montreal, Canada, 1984).

- Independence from government interference is a necessary condition of successful operation.
- CN has a degree of control over its market environments.
- Revenues for commercial viability are to a large extent dependent upon regulatory and political decisions and orders.
- Costing expertise and technical skills are critical to success in the corporation.
- Long-range financial planning is essential to successful management of the corporation.
- Additional volume of business is always good and will be sought through pricing actions rather than through better service offerings.
- CN is a big, patriarchal family with a top-down flow of authority and wisdom.

These two studies are instructive in that:

- They identify two sets of assumptions that have their roots in their respective industry's character, not in charismatic leadership. These assumptions are quite functional for the industry and context in which these organizations are operating; however, they would (and did) become very burdensome in different markets and context (e.g., AT&T in communication/information systems, or CN in the trucking business).
- Some assumptions may be conflicting, even mutually exclusive (e.g., independence from government and viability that depends upon political decisions), thereby creating tensions, variations in emphasis, and different means of reconciliation at various turns in the organization's history.
- These values and assumptions are shared and supported with different intensity in different parts of the organization. For instance, the union's leadership at CN is suspicious of the "big family" concept, but it stresses at every opportunity the "public service" role of CN as a functional rampart against the cutbacks and rationalizations that a strictly commercial role would impose on CN.

Step 4: Defining the Goals of a Company's Culture and Structure

A leader aiming to radically change the corporation must set up processes that lead to some definition of the company's goals in terms of its culture and structure. What would the transformed, revitalized, or turned-around corporation look like? What values, expectations, and assumptions are consistent with, and indeed necessary to, the effective implementation of the firm's changed strategic posture and new operating requirements? This determination must be respectful of the factors that have shaped the corporation and that continue to influence its development. Thus, in attempting to change an organization's culture and structure, the leadership should heed the following observations.

Coherence with Contingency Factors.   The values, strategies, and management systems that are proposed for the corporation should have an increasingly *functional* role in ensuring the survival and success of the firm as well as providing rewards to its employees. If contingency factors (e.g., regulations, competition, technology) are not changing, the proposed culture must build on the assumptions and expectations that flow from these factors. For example, despite repeated attempts, it has proved very difficult to instill a "marketing orientation" in banking firms operating in a regulated environment where the critical tasks, and, therefore, skills, consist of credit rationing, that is, of deciding which loan supplicants would be favored.

It will also be futile to, say, exhort the employees of a regulated monopoly offering a public service and requiring large capital investments to become "close to the customer," to show a "bias for action," to manage with "simple form and lean staff," and to preach "autonomy and entrepreneurship." The requirements for success, imposed by the economics and regulations of these industries, are pushing very hard in another direction, and attempts by management to install a culture that works against these forces will, therefore, be counterproductive.

However, when changes in contingency factors do occur, it is management's responsibility to ensure that these factors are quickly made visible to the organization's members and that these mutations are used as levels in working out changes in the organization's values and mind-set.

Multiple Linkages with the Present Culture. In the process of reviving or transforming a corporation, the leader must strive to preserve, emphasize, and build upon aspects of the present culture that are positive and compatible. The leader may even propose a culture that is a modernized version of old values and traditions that once made the corporation successful.

For example, Pistner, the CEO of Montgomery Ward, until very recently, declared his intentions of "replacing Ward's post-office mentality" and to "return to the homely, honest virtues that made Montgomery Ward a powerful retailing force fifty or seventy years ago."[36] Similarly, Warren, the CEO of the newly formed Canada Post Corporation, proposed to postal employees a return to the proud values of reliable service that once upon a time made their work honorable and respectful in the community.[37]

A present culture may exhibit inherent contradictions in values and assumptions which the proposed culture should then either build on, emphasizing some assumptions or values and downgrading others, or propose a novel reconciliation of these contradictions. Finally, aspects of a present culture and structure that are antagonistic to the proposed culture and structure should be identified and opposed directly. For example, in the overhaul of a Canadian bank, it was found that any reduction in the number of branches was resisted because the size of the network had become a measure of the institution's success and importance. Having recognized this, the leadership marshaled arguments in direct attack of that belief.

---

[36]"Weak Chain: Mobil Grows Impatient for Profit Turnaround at Montgomery Ward" *The Wall Street Journal,* February 16, 1983.

[37]P. M. Warren, "Canada Post Corporation's President: Address to the Canadian Club" (Montreal, Canada, March 28, 1984).

Step 5: Proposing a Broad Agenda for Radical Change

Figure 5 offers a useful schema for this step. The *aim* of radical strategies is to bring about required major changes in the structure—new goals and market strategies and new organizational designs and systems. But the *challenge* of radical strategies is to bring about the changes in culture and individual mindsets deemed necessary to support and reinforce the changes in structure. If this is not achieved, structural changes will be ineffective, or even counterproductive. However, it should be emphasized that the three dimensions of any organization (culture, structure, individuals) are not to be changed through the same mechanisms.

Table 1 summarizes the issues raised by radical, discontinuous, strategic change. It underlies the fact that management has a high degree of control on structural variables (formal goals, strategy, design, management systems). These may be changed at moderate to high speed, through the application of good *technical*, analytical management and competent *political* management of internal coalitions. In addition, if structural changes are legitimated by the present culture, management can implement such changes swiftly and easily.

However, when it comes to changes in cultural properties of the firm, management has, at best, only a moderate degree of control. Changes at that level tend to be slow and must be effected in part through *symbolic* management, accompanied by suitable structural reinforcements.[38] In order for this to happen,

TABLE 1   Dynamics of Strategic Change

The Organization	Degree of Control by Management	Rate of Change	Mode of Change
Structure	High	Moderate to high	Political and technical management plus cultural legitimacy
Culture	Low to moderate	Low to moderate	Symbolic management supported by structural changes
Individual	Low to moderate	Low to moderate	Conversion through replacement, training, reeducation, and restructuring of assumptions and world views

[38]T. J. Peters, "Symbols, Patterns, and Settings: An Optimistic Case for Getting Things Done," *Organizational Dynamics* (1978).

management must understand and make a conscious attempt to channel the complex social processes through which symbols, meanings, and values are created.

FIGURE 5   A Schematic View of the Organization

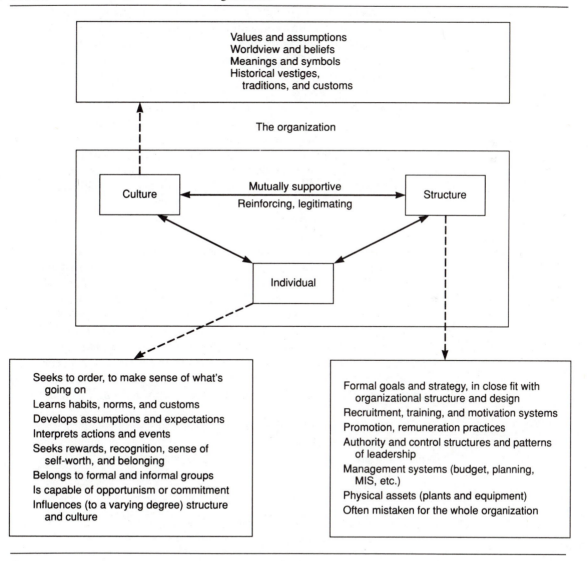

Effective changes in culture and structure must be carried out in a well-coordinated sequence of actions, which mutually reinforce, legitimate, and aim to cognitively reorient and restructure the mind-sets of management and employees. In the process, some tension between culture and structure is inevitable as changes at one level are not rooted in the other. However, this tension must be calibrated so that it does not reach a point where the linkage is severed and the present culture becomes antagonistic to the new structure. The resulting confusion, disarray, and disorientation among the members of the organization would be most disruptive.

To guard against a cultural clash, individual members should be provided with powerful symbolic materials and tangible structural evidence of a new corporate order. These should contain a compelling explanation of the corporation's present problems and future actions, as well as clear messages about the modes and norms of behavior that will be successful and rewarded henceforth. This agenda for radical change would typically include political and symbolic actions as well as recruiting change agents.

Political Actions.   (1) Broaden the political support for radical actions; (2) raise the level of dissatisfaction and discomfort with the present situation; (3) sensitize key actors to the need for change. If necessary, use outside consultants or research results to underline the risk of the present course and to offer a compelling case for change. For example, when Pistner took over as CEO of Montgomery Ward, he prepared a dramatic document that he called, "A Charter for Survival." Pistner wrote, "Survival is the right word. It implies that the company is in trouble and that its future is in doubt unless drastic measures are taken. The trouble is real, and an immediate change must be made."[39]

Symbolic Actions.   (1) Communicate forcefully a new image that captures the *external strategy and proposed culture* to be implemented; (2) use all available media channels to disseminate them (in-house journals, orientation sessions, training). Here the leader should become the articulate embodiment of the new goals, directions, and values. For example, Smith of GM is synthesizing the new spirit he wants in the corporation by embodying "the 3Rs—risk, responsibility, and rewards."[40] Similarly, Sullivan of Borden is trying to capture in an acronym, ROSE (return on shareholder's equity), his target for a revitalized company: "He sent ties with a ROSE logo to the top 200 managers. . . . He instituted incentive programs to reward executives for meeting financial goals, including bonuses tied in part to ROSE. . . ."[41]

Change Agents.   (1) Identify or recruit, train, and disseminate throughout the organizations change agents who are favorable to the new orientation and who explain and propagandize it; (2) maintain a liaison relationship.

---

[39]*The Wall Street Journal,* February 16, 1983.

[40]"GM's Unlikely Revolutionist," *Fortune,* March 19, 1984.

[41]"Borden: Putting the Shareholder First Starts to Pay Off," *Business Week,* April 2, 1984.

Step 6: Stabilizing the Organization

During periods of transition, more than any other time, the members of the organization will be looking out for signals—watching for clues, inferring intents and motives—to see which way the organization is going. Any discrepancy between the leadership's words and deeds will be spotted. Furthermore, any contradictory or ambiguous signal can sidetrack or slow down the process of change. For example, at AT&T, the former IBM executive Archie McGill had become the symbolic embodiment of the utility marketer and competitor in the information systems field. The ups and downs of his career at AT&T were interpreted as evidence of the leadership's real intentions concerning this new orientation. For this reason, his recent departure from AT&T created confusion and uncertainty, a feeling that the new style and spirit of management that had sprung up in parts of the corporation might be quickly uprooted.[42]

Therefore, when stabilizing the organization, the following steps should be taken: (1) ratify and reinforce the emerging world view in the organization with public decisions and announcements by promoting persons identified with the new vision; (2) establish tight consistency and coherence between words and actions; (3) use tactical decisions to support fundamental changes in orientation; (4) control and channel socialization processes; and (5) ensure that recruitment, selection, and training of employees are consistent with the new orientation.

CONCLUSION

Implementing a radical strategy in a large organization has proved to be an immensely difficult task, the acid test of a leader's skills. The difficulty of the task is compounded by a great deal of confusion about the very meaning of radical change and the paucity of models to guide management in such endeavors. However, we feel that the concepts and guidelines offered in this article provide a useful framework to think about and devise radical strategies and to manage strategic discontinuities.

Of course, in these matters, nothing can replace a leader's institutions, his or her experience, and natural skills. Nevertheless, these necessary attributes will work better when they are supported by a clear understanding of how one should go about transforming a social system and of how a corporation can be radically changed.

---

[42]*Business Week,* September 26, 1983.

What this article is about: Providing incentives for success requires that performance appraisal systems emphasize the strategic plan of the organization.

4–4 *Linking Strategy, Performance, and Pay*

R. Henry Migliore

*R. Henry Migliore is dean of the School of Business at
Oral Roberts University*

The appraisal portion of the strategic plan has long been a problem. How do you reward the achievement and performance of individuals as they operate the organization's strategic plan? How do you use the performance appraisal area to motivate the management team to achieve the objective in the strategic plan? How do you provide incentive for your people to stay with your organization? How do you develop a commonsense approach to salary and bonus rewards?

The keys to performance appraisal and salary administration within the strategic plan are profit and performance. This discussion focuses on two factors: (1) appraisal and reward for individual performance and (2) group bonus reward systems.

Figure 1 represents the various possible reward alternatives each individual faces. In the lower left-hand Section A, the low performer in an organization whose objectives were not achieved would receive low pay and a low bonus. At the other extreme, in Section C, where the individual has achieved his objectives and the organization has achieved its objectives, the individual would receive high pay and a high bonus. Sections B and D represent other situations. In Section B, the individual achieves his objectives yet the organization has modest success. Then he could receive high pay and a medium bonus. Section D is in a situation where a person didn't do as well on achieving his individual objectives but the organization did well, and he would receive medium pay and a high bonus. The rest of this column will discuss specific programs that contribute to individual rewards along with the group bonus reward.

FIGURE 1　Reward Alternatives

Individual objectives attained	10	High pay						High pay		
				(B)	(C)					
		Medium bonus						High bonus		
		Low pay						Medium pay		
				(A)	(D)					
		Low bonus						High bonus		
	1	2	3	4	5	6	7	8	9	10

Organization objectives attained

INDIVIDUAL REWARD

Ideally, the organization meets its broad overall purpose and reason for being. Specific measurable objectives in key result areas are largely met on a constant, sustaining basis. This success is based on a management team that has the motivation, ability, and insight to manage the organization's resources. The individual manager meets or excels his specific, measurable, key result objectives.

The successful organization rewards its contributors: stockholders, owners, managers, and employees. As a spin-off, it now contributes to society in its roles as taxpayer, employer, and so on. It encourages its suppliers to make long-term plans to meet its needs. The ripple effect of success works its way down.

The successful organization now must devote attention to rewarding its own managers and employees for their contributions. The organization's needs are met. Now how does the organization meet the extrinsic and intrinsic needs of its people?

Intrinsic needs are met through a properly functioning long-range planning/MBO philosophy. Organization members meet their higher-level needs of self-esteem, autonomy, recognition, and self-worth with this particular style of MBO.

The extrinsic needs have always been more difficult to deal with. Few salary and bonus systems do well over the long run. The big question mark among MBO scholars, students, consultants, and executives is: "How do you combine MBO with salary administration?"

In its simplest form, the person must be evaluated on how he performed against key objectives that were negotiated, thoughtfully considered, and obtainable. They usually number from 5 to 10.

The managers should also be evaluated. Then each year's pay increase should be based on performance of the 5-to-10 key performance objectives and the 10 criteria listed.

1. Use of long-range planning/MBO.
2. Developing people.
3. Contribution to morale.
4. Communication.
5. Creativity.
6. Emotional stability.
7. Job knowledge.
8. What kind of leader.
9. Problem solver.
10. Public image/social responsibility.

One method the author has devised would take already existing sets of objectives and turn them into appraisal forms as suggested in Figure 2. The individual's regular performance objectives are listed at the top of the sheet, and their final outcome is given a rating of 5 for excellent through 1 for poor performance. The 10 items listed above are then rated according to the same system.

These 10 items are nonmeasurable but should be considered. The main criteria should be the results of how the managers performed as compared to what they negotiated as their performance objectives. Each objective at year-end would have performance rated excellent through poor. Figure 3 might be followed in determining the specific pay increase. You would average the objectives and give them a 75 percent weight. The 10 nonmeasurable areas would get a 25 percent weight.

If the person fared well against these expectations and the organization has done well, he should receive a salary boost commensurate with the performance. In today's climate, this would be a 12 to 20 percent + pay increase.

Next, let's consider another circumstance: The organization hasn't done as well, but the individual performer posted a good record in all areas over which he had control. He should be paid by the same criteria. The organization has too much at stake to risk losing its high performers. Usually 20 percent of the people contribute 80 percent of the *key* results. Don't be niggardly with 20 percent. The same rule of thumb, 12 to 20 percent pay increase, holds if the organization does poorly. The other 80 percent receive pay in the third 10 percent range.

In the third possible circumstance, the organization does poorly but the individual does very well. In this case, the high-performance individual is not in a position to expect the kind of organizational rewards listed in the first two circumstances. A mature management system should realize this. My best suggestion is that the same five performance levels be recognized but that the pay scales be exactly half of what they normally would have been.

In the circumstance where the individual does poorly, it doesn't make any

FIGURE 2   MBO Performance Appraisal Form

	Excellent 5	Above Average 4	Average 3	Below Average 2	Poor 1	Discussion Notes
			Rating			
1. Operate within budget of $146,032 and cost per credit hour of $130	5					
2. Graduate 25 MBAs in May 1980	5					
3. Maintain enrollment of 100 FTE MBA students		4				
4. Publish in top third of the nation	5					
5. Average 35 aerobic points per week and reduce weight to 205			3			
	15	4	3			22 = Total
1. Use of LRP/MBO	5					
2. Developing people	5					
3. Contribution to morale	5					
4. Communication			3			
5. Creativity	5					
6. Emotional stability	5					
7. Job knowledge		4				
8. What kind of leader	5					
9. Problem solver			3			
10. Public image	5					
	35	4	6			45 = Total

Average of objectives = 22 ÷ 5 = 4.4.
Average of other items = 45 ÷ 10 = 4.5.
Weighted average = (4.4 × 75%) + (4.5 × 25%) = 4.425.

FIGURE 3   Pay Increase Determinants

Performance Level	Recommended Pay
1. Performance less than satisfactory (has not met all minimum acceptable performance standards and objectives for the position). Point average below 1.5.	Zero percent increase
2. Performance meets minimum standards and objectives but not up to average. Point average 1.5 to 2.5.	Not more than 5 percent increase (0–5)
3. Performance meets at least average standards and objectives and may excel in some areas. Point average 2.5 to 3.5.	Not more than 10 percent increase (5–10)
4. Performance is better than average overall and excels in a majority of standards and objectives for the position. Point average 3.5 to 4.5.	Not more than 15 percent increase (11–14)
5. Performance is outstanding because it excels in all of the objectives and conditions previously listed. Point average 4.5 to 5.0.	Not more than 20 percent increase (15–20)

difference what the organization did. The individual did not make the right kind of contribution and should not be rewarded. Rewarding for a poor performance is a guarantee to continue the same.

One complicating factor in this era of high inflation is what do you call a pay increase, and what do you call an adjustment for inflation? I know of no organization that has completely solved that problem. In reality, even with Figure 3, this past year with inflation at 15 percent, if a top performer received 20 percent, in effect he was receiving only a net 5 percent reward for his performance. This author believes the recommended pay percentages should be tied into the inflation rate. Theoretically, every organization should automatically modify its pay ranges based on the inflation level and then add the pay increase on top of inflation.

BONUS SYSTEM

Working hand in hand with salary rewards based on individual achievement is the bonus system. This is nothing new of itself. But how does it work with MBO? If the organization meets certain understood, agreed-upon objectives and criteria, every organization member shares in the harvest. Objectives such as sales, profit, manufacturing efficiency, quality, and safety could be the bases. Criteria could be set for these deemed to be of importance based on the individual organization. The bonus system must be simple, straightforward, and understood.

The most important objective is profit. Good, solid, long-term-oriented profit is the golden word of capitalism. It's simple: no profit, no bonus. Other objectives can be a factor but only after the profit objective is met.

The criterion for profit might be 15 percent before-tax profit on sales. A pool is set up with 20 percent of all profit above the minimum criterion of 15 percent going into the pool. For example, a $40 million sales company with $6 million profit would have no bonuses. One company provides a nice working vacation at a popular resort area if the minimum criteria are met. Another idea would be to give some percentage (e.g., 1 percent of all profits) if the minimum criteria are met. However, $7 million profit would put $200,000 into a pool. If there were 500 employees, this would be a bonus of $400 per person. All employees share equally in this pool. The bonus is a nonbudgeted item.

Another way the pool can be distributed is to give divisional managers shares of the pool to distribute as they see fit within their units. This method is of doubtful value because of the bias problem. This is one instance in which the author advocates treating everyone on the team the same. The bonus is the team reward. If the team wins the league championship, it goes to the Superbowl and everyone shares equally in the reward. If you don't win the league championship (in this case 15 percent profit before taxes), you stay home and everyone gets the same thing . . . nothing.

Under this system, a person has an opportunity to get ahead on his own and is also rewarded for being a team player.

This author still believes the most effective way to handle a bonus is to include everyone, including the management team, by setting up a bonus fund. The fund is not budgeted but comes out of after-tax corporate profits based on an audited financial statement. Another alternative is that funds should be available for bonus distribution unless the corporate performance exceeds all of the following: (1) 10 percent return on sales before taxes; (2) 5 percent return on sales after taxes; (3) manufacturing efficiency 80 percent; and (4) sales growth of 40 percent. The total fund available for distribution each year is not to exceed 10 percent of corporate after-tax net profit or 1 percent of sales. This sets some standards, is reasonably simple, and lets everyone in on the bonus if things go well. Another criterion is 20 percent of after-tax profit in excess of 8 percent gross revenue.

Again, pay particular attention to the 20/80 rules. Those 20 percent who contribute the 80 percent need to be rewarded. A rigid reward system that holds them back just encourages them to go elsewhere. The other 80 percent are not going anywhere anyway, so don't spend as much time worrying about them.

Some guidelines to keep in mind are:

The key is accountability, not activity.

Use job objectives instead of job descriptions as the focal point.

People who are committed to your organization are worth more than people who are not committed to it.

People who feel they are underpaid will act like it.

Don't give any kind of merit increase to someone not meeting his job responsibilities and objectives.

Bonuses should be paid only for beating an indicator.

Paying people below equitable market rates will assure you of marginal performance and high turnover.

Fair pay does not motivate, but unfair pay demotivates.

The higher the person is in the organization, the more you pay for strategies and creative thinking.

Performance appraisal and salary administration are part of the strategic planning process.

CONCLUSION

The performance appraisal approach outlined in this article is now being used in four organizations. Each adapted parts of it to fit particular needs in the organization. It has been in use for six months to two years. At this stage, this approach seems to be very positive. The management teams in all four organizations agree that this approach is superior to the one previously used. They now have a way of rewarding performance fairly, emphasizing the strategic plan, and providing a real incentive for people to see that they have a long-range future in the organization.

What this article is about: The human resource systems that developed in the 1960s and 1970s, that served Japan so well, are currently undergoing a transformation. This article assesses the magnitude and direction of the changes in the employment and promotion systems inside Japanese companies. The Japanese company of the future will be a hybrid that effectively combines the advantages of lifetime employment practices with some of the flexibilities of a Western-style horizontal labor market.

4–5 Continuity and Change in Japanese Management

Tomasz Mroczkowski and Masao Hanaoka

*Tomasz Mroczkowski is associate professor of international
business at The American University, Washington, D.C.
Masao Hanaoka is professor of management at
Daito Bunka University in Tokyo*

The relationship between tradition and change in Japan has always been complicated by the fact that change itself is a tradition.

—Edward Seidensticker

For Japan, the era of competing on the basis of being the low-cost imitator of the West and of using exports to stimulate its domestic economy came to a dramatic end with the rise of the yen. Japanese companies reacted by shifting the competitive battleground to a different plane. They have moved up-market to compete on the basis of quality, innovation, and product leadership while defending their cost structures against NICs and Western competitors by rapid automation. They have also sped up the process of multinationalization, moving lower value-added production offshore and locating production facilities close to consumer markets in Europe and the United States.

This strategy has required accelerated restructuring of the Japanese economy, including dramatic shifts in employment. It has also required that the Japanese management system be modified to make it more efficient. One of the most

SOURCE: *Human Resources,* Winter 1989, pp. 39–52.

important changes is that the "new" management system will have to encroach upon the traditional practices of lifetime employment and seniority-based wages.

Recent economic results indicate that after the shock of the high yen the Japanese economy has pulled off another "miracle"; and those in the West who saw an end to Japanese competitiveness have been proven wrong again. In 1987, Japanese industrial output was 4 percent higher than in the previous year. The profits of Japanese manufacturers grew by 25 to 30 percent in fiscal 1987 (after falling by 29 percent in 1986) and investment in new plants and machinery grew by a total of 33 percent in real terms in 1984–86.

Remarkably, Japanese manufacturing wage costs have been kept in check. After adding in productivity growth, Japanese firms now have lower unit wage costs than they did a year ago (while West Germany's have leapt by almost 5 percent). Japan has achieved all this while adjusting the size of its work force, shifting manpower out of sunset industries and into new industries and the service sector, and also moving production offshore. This remarkable achievement could not have been possible without major changes in Japanese companies' employment and reward systems—changes that many Western observers believed would be so disruptive and difficult that they would take a much longer time to implement.

This article assesses the magnitude and direction of the changes in the employment and promotion systems inside Japanese companies. An evaluation of these changes is crucial to understanding Japan's competitive strategy for the 1990s.

THE ROMANTIC MYTH OF JAPANESE MANAGEMENT

Almost all of the many books and articles on Japanese management published in the West have been written by non-Japanese observers. Frequently, these analyses have been used for the purpose of criticizing the shortcomings and failures of Western management. This practice has contributed to the creation of the myth of Japanese management. Until recently, this myth has gone largely unchallenged, especially in the United States.

The system of manpower management developed in the sixties and seventies that has served Japan so well is currently undergoing a gradual transformation. Even before economic and demographic conditions made it obvious, perceptive Japanese observers pointed out the inherent weaknesses of "Japanese management":

• The system of lifetime commitment and groupism encouraged employee dependency and suppressed individual creativity.
• The employment system discriminated against non-lifelong employees (temporary employees, women, part-timers, seasonal laborers, and employees hired midway through their careers) and prevented the formation of a free horizontal labor market.

- The seniority-based system of rewards created a promotion gridlock for middle management and especially for the younger outstanding employee.[1]

Japanese executives have long been aware of the disadvantages of their system but believed these were outweighed by its strengths. However, by the mid-1980s many companies found themselves unable to fully maintain the "old system." The search for a new Japanese management system was assumed with a great deal of urgency.

CONTINUOUS EVOLUTION AND THE CRISIS OF JAPANESE MANAGEMENT

In order to understand how it was possible to effect major changes in Japanese manpower management relatively smoothly and effectively, it is important to realize that Japanese management practices have never been static but rather have evolved through continual adjustments to new economic, social, and competitive priorities.

Prior to World War II, Japanese industry used a rigid form of status promotion *(shikaku-seido)*. Employees were divided into *shokuin* (white collar) and *koīn* (blue collar) workers, with simple seniority promotion ladders within each category and no possibility of upward mobility for *koīn* workers into the *shokuin* category. After the end of World War II, during the American occupation, a number of important changes occurred. A labor standards law was introduced and labor union growth occurred. The U.S. Army introduced management training programs, and wage systems were changed as the old employee status classification system collapsed. An attempt was made to introduce an American-style job classification system. While this attempt largely failed, companies, to varying degrees, began using ability and skills instead of seniority alone as a basis for job grade assignment.

During the 1950s and 1960s, Japan experienced labor shortages due to very rapid industrial expansion. Many of the familiar features of "Japanese management" were broadly introduced at that time: by the mid-sixties more than 70 percent of companies used employee suggestion schemes and almost a third used regular employee morale surveys. Companies used core groups of lifetime employees who were promoted using systems of grade ladders within integrated functions. Because of the labor shortages, part-time employment of women outside the lifetime system became widespread. The actual number of hours worked was reduced while efforts were made to prolong the retirement age from 55 to 60.

Japanese management scholars regard the seventies as marking a "peak" in the development of the practices which the world learned to regard as "Japanese

---

[1]Kunio Odaka, "Japanese Management: A Forward-Looking Analysis," *Asian Productivity Organization*, Tokyo, 1986.

management." However, in the seventies there were also a number of factors that demanded modifications in Japanese personnel management practices. Economic growth rates were, on average, only half that of the previous decade. With broad introduction of automation, Japanese companies began hiring significantly fewer recruits into entry-level positions. Over the years, this caused the average age of employees moving up the seniority ladder to increase, putting pressure on average wage costs. Real opportunities for advancement became increasingly limited, and attempts to boost sagging morale brought a proliferation of new titles empty of substance.

Japanese management reacted to these problems by increasing flexibility in the employment and reward systems. Temporary transfers of surplus employees and flex-time systems were introduced. Systems of "specialist" or "expert" posts with grades similar to those for managers were created to provide ways of promoting staff workers who had already reached the highest grade and for whom managerial positions were unavailable. Efforts were made to decrease the importance of seniority as the major condition for pay raises and introduce merit components into wage and bonus systems.[2]

The early eighties saw the sharp rise in the value of the dollar, making Japanese goods very competitive in the United States. The Japanese experienced an export boom which allowed them to postpone some of the inevitable changes in their economic policies.[3] The sharp rise of the yen in 1985 suddenly put enormous pressures on many Japanese companies. To remain competitive, they had to control costs, innovate, restructure, and often move offshore. In 1986, Japan's exports declined by 15.9 percent and the profits of Japanese companies also declined dramatically. Because of the strong yen, the number of bankruptcies shot up (since May 1986, more than 60 companies have gone bankrupt every month) and unemployment increased.[4] Capital productivity has been decreasing in Japan in the past few years. While total factor productivity in Japan grew more rapidly than in other countries in the 1960s and 1970s, in the 1980s the growth rate leveled off. Japanese productivity specialists forecast that under these conditions it will be very difficult to continue to make the kind of productivity improvements that Japanese companies made in the past.[5] The Japanese have reached a watershed in their economic policies.

By the mid-1980s, the entire system of Japanese management faced three major challenges:

- Japanese companies have mainly relied on the variable bonus and flexible benefits to control their wage costs. After the dramatic rise in the value of the

---

[2]Masao Hanaoka, *Nihon no Romukanri (Personnel Management in Japan)*, 2nd ed. (Tokyo: Hakuto Shobo, 1987).

[3]Peter F. Drucker, "Japan's Choices," *Foreign Affairs* (1987).

[4]Ministry of Foreign Affairs, "Background Statistics on the Japanese Economy," Japan, May 1987.

[5]Takao Watanabe, *Demystifying Japanese Management* (Tokyo: Gakuseisha Publishing Co., Ltd., 1987).

yen, the problem of cost containment became much more difficult. Average wages in Korea and Taiwan are now respectively eight times and six times lower than in Japan. The challenge many Japanese companies face is how to reduce labor costs, cut capacity, and restructure without resorting to massive layoffs.

- The second major challenge Japanese management faces is how to continue to *motivate* employees and managers in a new environment in which the system of evaluation and rewards, as well as employee attitudes and expectations, is changing.
- The third challenge for Japanese management is how to redesign employment relationships in a way that would blend the advantages of the older system of dependence on the company with the necessity to promote employee self-reliance, initiative, and creativity.

THE EMERGENCE OF A NEW MANAGEMENT PARADIGM

Restructuring: Methods of Employment and Wage Control

For many Japanese companies, especially those in mature industries, the most immediate problem is how to achieve significant reductions in employment levels as they reduce capacity and modernize. For example, over the next three years the three biggest Japanese steel companies plan to shed 40,000 jobs without firing anyone.

This process is being carefully monitored by the Japanese Labor Ministry as well as by the Japanese Confederation of Labor, which compiled a survey of how Japanese companies carried out employment cuts and what methods they intended to use for future reductions (see Tables 1 and 2). The tables reveal the lengths to which Japanese companies will go to avoid layoffs. All companies rely on hiring freezes and to a lesser extent on elimination of overtime. Both of these approaches are also commonly used in the West. What is peculiarly Japanese is the extensive use of job rotation and employee reassignments. In the case of larger companies (over 1,000 employees), almost half report using this as a major method of employment restructuring. Although part-time workers are indeed often laid off, firings and layoffs of full-time employees are reported by less than 10 percent of the companies surveyed (with the exception of the very small companies). Interestingly, in their plans for the future, the companies intend to continue the same policies by putting even greater emphasis on job rotation. Layoffs of full-time employees will continue to be rare.

Some of the methods used by Japanese management to control wage and salary costs differ even more from Western practices. Wage, salary, and bonus reductions are shared by all groups in the enterprise: directors and managers as well as employees. Even when temporary or permanent layoffs *are* used, they do not have the same implications for employees as similar practices in the West.

TABLE 1   1986 Employee Reduction
(in number of companies and percent of total responses)

	Size of Company (by number of employees)					
	1–99	*100–299*	*300–399*	*1,000–2,999*	*3,000+*	*All Companies*
Methods of Employment Control						
Hiring freeze	54	48	57	23	21	203
	36.5%	30.8%	42.5%	54.8%	51.2%	39.0%
Part-time workers terminated	36	24	22	10	14	106
	24.3%	15.4%	16.4%	23.8%	34.1%	20.3%
No overtime	23	19	21	8	6	77
	15.5%	12.2%	15.7%	19.0%	14.6%	14.8%
Shortening of working day	11	12	7	2		32
	7.4%	7.7%	5.2%	4.8%		6.1%
Job rotation	29	34	30	17	19	129
	19.6%	21.8%	22.4%	40.5%	46.3%	24.8%
Temporary layoffs	2	2		1	2	7
	1.4%	1.3%		2.4%	4.9%	1.3%
Planned employee reductions	9	3	5	2	3	22
	6.1%	1.9%	3.7%	4.8%	7.3%	4.2%
Employees fired	23	12	8	3	3	49
	15.5%	7.7%	6.0%	7.1%	7.3%	9.4%
Other	8	12	4	3	4	31
	5.4%	7.7%	3.0%	7.1%	9.8%	6.0%
Methods of Wage Control						
Overtime pay eliminated	46	66	64	23	22	221
	31.1%	42.3%	47.8%	54.8%	53.7%	42.4%
Director's/manager's pay reduced	45	32	31	6	9	123
	30.4%	20.5%	23.1%	14.3%	22.0%	23.6%
Postpone increases or reduce basic pay	55	44	38	12	13	162
	37.2%	28.2%	28.4%	28.6%	31.7%	31.1%
Director's bonus reduced	62	44	45	9	10	170
	41.9%	28.2%	33.6%	21.4%	24.4%	32.6%
General bonus reduced	56	45	39	11	9	160
	37.8%	28.8%	29.1%	26.2%	22.0%	30.7%
Other	6	3	8	2	3	22
	4.1%	1.9%	6.0%	4.8%	7.3%	4.2%
Total Number of Companies:	148	156	134	42	41	521

SOURCE: Susumu KoyōChousei, Ministry of Labor Employment Rationalization Survey, 1986.

TABLE 2 Future Reduction Forecast
(in number of companies and percent of total responses)

	Size of Company (by number of employees)					
	1–99	*100–299*	*300–399*	*1,000–2,999*	*3,000+*	*All Companies*
Methods of Employment Control						
Hiring freeze	57	60	57	22	15	211
	34.8%	36.8%	40.4%	51.2%	34.1%	38.0%
Part-time workers terminated	46	37	25	8	12	128
	28.0%	22.7%	17.7%	18.6%	27.3%	23.1%
No overtime	42	28	26	7	7	110
	25.6%	17.2%	18.4%	16.3%	15.9%	19.8%
Shortening of working day	23	12	12	4	1	52
	14.0%	7.4%	8.5%	9.3%	2.3%	9.4%
Job rotation	38	37	40	17	27	159
	23.2%	22.7%	8.4%	39.5%	61.4%	28.6%
Temporary layoffs	7	4	4	1	3	19
	4.3%	2.5%	2.8%	2.3%	6.8%	3.4%
Planned employee reductions	10	7	6	4	2	29
	6.1%	4.3%	4.3%	9.3%	4.5%	5.2%
Employees fired	20	8	9	2	2	41
	12.1%	4.9%	6.4%	4.7%	4.5%	7.4%
Other	6	9	5	4	7	31
	3.7%	5.5%	3.5%	9.3%	15.9%	5.6%
Methods of Wage Control						
Overtime pay eliminated	69	77	72	23	21	262
	42.1%	47.2%	51.1%	53.5%	47.7%	47.2%
Director's/manager's pay reduced	45	28	29	8	10	120
	27.4%	17.2%	20.6%	18.6%	22.7%	21.6%
Postpone increases or reduce basic pay	70	55	28	6	13	172
	42.7%	33.7%	19.9%	14.0%	29.5%	31.0%
Director's bonus reduced	74	49	43	8	8	182
	45.1%	30.1%	30.5%	18.6%	18.2%	32.8%
General bonus reduced	85	70	56	12	15	238
	51.8%	42.9%	39.7%	27.9%	34.1%	42.9%
Other	7	5	3	2	3	20
	4.3%	3.1%	2.1%	4.7%	6.8%	3.6%
Total Number of Companies:	164	163	141	43	44	555

SOURCE: Susumu KoyōChousei, Ministry of Labor Employment Rationalization Survey, 1986.

Japanese companies widely use intercompany manpower leasing and transfer. The system is run by company groups called *igyōshu kōryu*[6] and is organized on a territorial basis with local government and Chamber of Commerce support. According to a 1987 survey by the NHK *(Nippon Hosō Kyokai,* Japan Broadcasting Corporation), there are 471 local centers in which 17,000 Japanese companies participate. These centers exchange information on manpower surpluses and shortages and arrange for temporary or permanent transfers between the participating companies. They may also engage in joint new business/new product development. In effect, this system extends the lifetime employment principles while maintaining flexibility and economic rationality.

According to some Japanese manpower policy experts, Japanese companies will be moving toward more flexibility in their employment and wage policies. International and domestic competition may ultimately force companies to begin treating a larger portion of labor costs as variable costs rather than as fixed costs.[7]

THE NEW MOTIVATIONAL SYSTEM: PERFORMANCE-BASED EVALUATION AND REWARDS

The Changing Importance of Seniority

It is broadly believed that the principle of seniority governs the Japanese system of motivating employees, rewarding loyalty, and maintaining group harmony. In fact, the pure seniority principle has been systematically eroding in Japan, as evidenced by results of surveys carried out in Japanese companies by the *Romu Gyosei Kenkyujo* (a private research foundation). In the decade between 1978 and 1987, according to the personnel departments of the surveyed companies, the contribution of the seniority factor to pay raises systematically declined from an average of 57.9 percent to 46 percent while the contribution of the performance factor increased from 42.1 percent to 54 percent (see Table 3).

Low economic growth rates, which result in fewer recruits being hired, have made it uneconomical for companies to continue to pay ever higher wages to an increasing proportion of their senior employees. Japanese companies have reacted to this situation by remodeling the motivational system. While the retirement age in Japan has been extended, many companies are using various forms of early retirement incentives. Often, employees are finding their wage increases capped at age 40 to 45. In fact, in many companies average pay may drop by as much as 20 percent after age 50.

---

[6]*Igyōshu Kōryu* are groups or networks of small and medium-sized enterprises organized to exchange technical information, promote management development, and engage in manpower exchange.

[7]Hanaoka, *Personnel Management in Japan.*

TABLE 3   Relative Contributions of Seniority and Merit Factors to Pay Raises

	Seniority	*Ability (Merit)*
1978	57.9%	42.1
1983	54.4	45.6
1984	49.0	51.0
1987	46.0	54.0

SOURCE: Rōmu Gyōsei Kenkyūjo, July 8–September 11, 1987, (1,900 Japanese companies surveyed).

In order to gauge the magnitude of change taking place in the motivation systems employed by Japanese companies, it is necessary to understand the relationships between seniority and the other factors that affect employee promotion. However important, seniority has never been the only factor determining a wage or salary in a Japanese company. Assignment of an individual to a wage/salary grade depended largely on education and job-related skills. In intergrade promotions, both of these factors also played an important part. In the process of annual within-grade raises and bonus awards, however, it is general company performance which is the important factor in the increment negotiations. Under the traditional system, the final outcome in terms of a wage increment would typically incorporate a combination of the negotiated raise and seniority. The raise formula would thus look like this:

Individual base × Negotiated %   +   Distribution by   =   Raise
wage/salary   raise ("up rate")   length of service
within grade   years (expressed in
                                                              yen not as a %)

Loyalty to the company and peer pressure were judged to be sufficiently strong to motivate employees. The outstanding employee was not singled out for immediate large rewards but was kept motivated by interesting assignments, training opportunities, and eventual promotion to a higher grade or managerial position ahead of his peers.

According to a study performed by the authors at the Institute of Business Research at Daito Bunka University, this system has been undergoing substantial modifications. The personnel managers from 30 large and medium-sized companies representing a cross section of Japanese manufacturing and service sectors were surveyed and they felt without exception that the old seniority system could not be maintained without substantial change. On the other hand, only a handful of the managers wanted to abolish it completely. The majority of companies were planning and implementing gradual modification of the system, allowing them to keep some of its most useful features. Modifications usually started with the introduction of merit evaluation into the promotion/reward process.

Performance Appraisal Japanese Style

The *Shikaku* (position title) classification system used to form the basis of grading, promotion, wage, and bonus decisions in Japanese companies. This gradually has been giving way to performance appraisal and merit rating systems. Rather than replacing the old system with a new one, Japanese companies grafted performance evaluation onto the old system by incorporating it as a factor in the formulas used for pay increment calculation. In companies which have embraced the individual merit rating system, the formula would typically look as follows:

Individual × Average × Individual × Seniority = Raise
base salary/ "up rate" merit rating coefficient
wage within each
grade(%)

The actual impact of performance evaluations on pay varies from company to company and also depends on the position and grade of the employee. According to a 1985 study by the Japan Personnel Policy Research Institute, 35 percent of managerial bonus awards depended on the performance appraisal component, while for clerks this rate was only 22 percent.[8] Individual performance appraisal results can account for anywhere from 20 percent to 50 percent of the pay increment. The higher percentage is found in those companies that have pursued change most aggressively, including companies under Western management and joint-venture operations.

The Japanese concepts of performance and achievement are not the same as in the West and the relative importance of different components and ways of measuring and weighting them are different. The concept of personnel evaluation most widely used in Japan is the merit rating *(jinji kōka)*. This concept is based on educational attainment and job ability factors such as communication skills, cooperativeness, and sense of responsibility. *Jinji koka* is being gradually replaced by performance evaluation based on work results. The Japanese concept of performance *(gyō seki)* is distinct from the Western concept and includes not only the achievement of actual results, but the expenditure of good faith effort. New performance evaluation systems are currently being introduced in 75 percent of Japanese companies.[9]

Individual achievement-based rewards are likely to continue to grow in importance in the motivational systems in Japanese companies. One of the factors contributing to the problems of motivating Japanese employees is the erosion of labor unions. At one time, 56 percent of the labor force belonged to unions. As the Japanese economy matured, labor union membership declined, and union

---

[8]*Nippon Jinji Gyōsei Kenkyujo* (Japan Personnel Policy Research Institute) survey, February 8, 1985.
[9]*Nihonteki Koyokanko no Henka to Tenbo* (Ministry of Labor Research Center), Tokyo, 1987.

TABLE 4   Emphasized Factors of Wage System Around in 2000 (in percent)

	Management			Labor Union			Neutral			Total		
	Will increase	*Not change*	*Will decrease*	*Increase*	*Not change*	*Decrease*	*Increase*	*Not change*	*Decrease*	*Increase*	*Not change*	*Decrease*
Age	6.7	21.0	69.0	15.5	26.1	57.1	5.5	21.9	71.6	8.8	22.7	66.4
Service years	6.7	28.6	61.9	11.2	33.5	55.3	3.3	32.8	62.3	6.9	31.4	60.1
Educational background	5.7	17.6	73.8	10.6	18.6	70.2	4.4	19.7	76.0	6.7	18.6	73.5
Experience years	25.7	49.5	21.4	33.5	44.7	22.4	23.5	51.9	20.8	27.3	48.9	21.5
Job, occupational category	80.0	15.7	0.5	82.6	13.7	1.9	77.0	19.1	2.7	79.8	16.2	1.6
Ability for achievement	91.0	4.8	1.0	84.5	9.3	5.0	86.9	10.9	0.5	87.7	8.1	2.0
Amount of work done	50.0	35.7	11.0	34.2	42.2	21.1	38.3	48.1	13.1	41.5	41.7	14.6
Family size	2.4	45.7	47.1	7.5	47.8	44.1	7.7	49.7	40.4	5.6	47.7	44.0

SOURCE: Takao Watanabe, *Demystifying Japanese Management* (Tokyo: Gakuseisha Publishing Co., Ltd., 1987), p. 195.

participation rates have now fallen below 28 percent.[10] As Japan moves out of the smokestack industries and becomes a "service" economy, further declines in union membership are expected to occur. Company and work-group loyalties are being replaced by individualism.

The trend away from seniority and toward individual performance-based pay has been documented in a survey carried out by the Social and Economic Congress of Japan, which asked management and labor unions about changes in the factors that will determine Japanese wages by the year 2000 (see Table 4).

Redesigning the Employment Relationships

While maintaining considerable continuity with past practices, the system of lifetime employment is undergoing change. A 1984 survey conducted by the prime minister's office found that nearly half of all Japanese between the ages

---

[10]"All That's Left," *The Economist,* November 28, 1987.

of 20 and 29 expressed a preference for an "employment changing" job environment to the assurance of lifetime employment. In another survey conducted by a large job placement firm, a quarter of the college graduates interviewed had already changed jobs at least once.[11]

Most Japanese employers feel that it is advantageous to maintain the lifetime employment principle even if only in a modified form. Only a minority feel that the idea has outlived its usefulness. Most employers feel they must maintain lifetime employment for core employees in order to attract recruits of sufficient caliber. However, the group of "core" employees who enjoy lifetime employment can be quite small (it is only 10 percent in the fast-food industry).

While most companies have postponed the retirement age (as noted earlier), employees are now obliged to consider whether they will continue to stay with the company after the age of 40 or 45 or face the possibility of being transferred to affiliated companies. Companies are also using "specialist" positions for senior employees who are either being retired from managerial posts or are not considered promotable to managerial ranks.

The lifetime employment system is also being modified through increased use of diversified hiring methods. The routine hiring of school graduates is being more and more frequently supplemented by the hiring of contract employees and part-timers.[12] Hiring on the basis of skills for a specific, narrowly defined job opening is growing. For example, in 1988 Niko Shoken (Nikko Security, Co. Ltd.) started recruiting foreign-exchange traders at high salaries on a contract basis. These employees, in principle, cannot transfer to the lifetime employment track, and, if their performance is below expectations, their salaries may be cut or they may be fired. Similarly, Sumitomo Trust bank has been hiring security traders and economic analysts on a contract basis. As Mr. Osamu Sakurai, president of the bank, put it: "Under the lifetime employment system, we could not offer appropriately high salaries to obtain top talent. Nor could we hire on a short-term basis.[13] With these new hiring practices, labor mobility is rising and is expected to continue to increase gradually in the future (see Table 5). Mobility among Japanese managers and professionals is also increasing. According to a study performed by Nippon Manpower, a Japanese human resource development company, 75 percent of those surveyed declared that they would entertain a lucrative offer from a headhunter.[14]

While Japanese management clearly wants to continue to tap the advantages of lifetime employment for selected employee groups, there is growing evidence that a partial horizontal labor market is emerging rapidly. For years, Japanese

[11]Robert C. Christopher, *Second to None: American Companies in Japan* (New York: Crown Publishers, 1986).

[12]*Nikkei High Tech Report,* "Japanese Research Organizations Tap Foreign Technical Talent," April 13, 1987.

[13]*Nihon Keizai Shinbun,* (February 15, 1988.)

[14]Tomasz Mroczkowski, and Masao Hanaoka, "Japan's Managers Merit More Attention," *Asian Wall Street Journal,* October 29, 1987.

TABLE 5   The Prospect of Worker's Mobility in Future Japanese Society

	Management	*Labor*	*Neutral*	*Total Polled*
It will increase remarkably	3.2%	2.2%	3.3%	2.9%
It will increase a bit more or less	69.4	59.0	66.9	65.4
Unchanged	17.2	19.4	9.9	15.4
It will decrease a bit	0.6	1.5	0.6	0.9
It will decrease remarkably	0.6	—	—	0.2
No answer	8.9	17.9	19.2	15.2

SOURCE: Takao Watanabe, *Demystifying Japanese Management* (Tokyo: Gakuseisha Publishing Co., Ltd., 1987), p. 185.

employees demonstrated a preference for security over risk and opportunity. This attitude began to change after the oil shocks.

Japanese employees realized that they could not place all their reliance on their companies and that they would have to start relying on themselves. Today, the latest catchword among personnel specialists in Japan is "employee self-reliance." It is not only that the attitudes and expectations of employees—especially younger employees—are changing, but the companies themselves are creating programs designed to promote new attitudes of self-reliance. Career development programs have been among the most popular new personnel systems adopted by Japanese companies in the past few years.[15] Today, companies like Toshiba and Yamaha use extensive career counseling to help employees develop new skills and attitudes that would enable them to survive in a horizontal labor market.

THE MULTITRACK EMPLOYMENT SYSTEM

As they gradually redesign the employment and reward system in their companies, Japanese managers are trying to maintain the advantages of group harmony, employee loyalty, and cooperation (based on the lifetime employment principle) while both eliminating the burdens of employment hypertrophy and

[15]Masao Hanaoka, "Setting Up a Hypothesis of the Characteristics of Personnel Management," Institute of Business Research, Daito Bunka University, 1986.

enhancing flexibility by shifting more of the risk on a greater proportion of employees. At the same time, for many companies that base their strategies on product leadership and innovations, stimulating employee initiative and creativity is a high priority.

The way Japanese management hopes to reconcile these conflicting goals is through the creation of a multitrack employment system. Employees hired for "life" enter the general track and can be moved horizontally (job rotation) as well as vertically (grade promotion). In the past, vertical promotion was often restricted by rules governing the minimum and standard "staying years" within one grade—effectively ensuring promotion by seniority. As companies relax those rules, more-rapid promotion becomes possible. As job rotation and the hiring of specialists become more common, it becomes possible for a relatively junior employee to achieve a high grade. As companies choose to limit the percentage of lifetime employees, they expand hiring into the restricted tracks—which may include hiring more women, part-timers, and specialists.

As specific expertise becomes increasingly more important and seniority increasingly less, promotion grades become defined more precisely in terms of specific tasks rather than experience, general educational attainment, and general skills. Expanded flexibility can then also be applied at the higher (managerial) levels. However, promotion into these higher grades does not have to mean a managerial post. A variety of specialist positions offering high pay can be made available, which would allow for moving less-able managers into specialist positions and more-able specialists into management positions. A separate "subtrack" can be created for the failed or nonpromotable. This is the well-known *taigu shoku* or "window job" track.

Compared with the grade systems that were used in the sixties and seventies, the systems emerging today offer more flexibility and more options to personnel management. Hiring methods have diversified. Today, Japanese personnel departments use headhunters to fill managerial and specialist technical positions, they lease groups of needed employees from manpower agencies, they entertain "walk-in" offers from candidates, and they write a variety of contracts with employees on restricted tracks—including, to a greater extent, foreigners.[16] This is indeed a far cry from the standard practices in the past of relying primarily on school and university graduates. The flexibility of the system is being continually expanded. Many high-tech companies are diversifying grade denominations and promotion rules within particular tracks—especially research and development—to stimulate employment initiative and creativity.

CONCLUSION

Many of the critical practices on which the Japanese company bases its functioning depend on the principles of lifetime employment, company loyalty, and employee commitment. The Japanese will make every effort to maintain these

---

[16]*Nikkei High Tech Report.*

principles in the foreseeable future. The changes going on in employment practices and employee motivation are not designed to destroy the old system but to increase its flexibility. This is very much in keeping with the traditional Japanese approach to change; however fast and deep it is, continuity with the uniquely Japanese "essence" must be maintained. The new Japanese management paradigm will certainly be different, yet like the modern Japanese home which usually retains a Japanese style room among Western style rooms and furniture, the Japanese company will retain a core of Japanese practices.

Western assessments of Japanese capabilities tend to oscillate between total awe and serious underestimation. The difficulties in changing to a new management system should not be underestimated. Japanese company presidents find that responsibility for decisions that have to be made rapidly is being transferred to them, that they have to act boldly and quickly, and that often there is no time for gradual consensus building. Popular Japanese magazines have noted a large number of company presidents who have died in office during the past 18 months or so, blaming their untimely deaths on the pressures of diversifying, building offshore plants, cutting costs, and laying off employees.[17]

The Japanese have handled profound change in the past very well (during the Meiji era and after World War II). This suggests that they are in a good position to overcome the obstacles and difficulties. Research on the introduction of robotics and flexible manufacturing systems in Japanese and Western companies shows the Japanese to have superior capabilities in effective implementation of new manufacturing technology.[18] The Japanese appear very well positioned for the age in which competitive survival will depend on the ability of human groups to manage very rapid change. After the strains and difficulties of the current transformation, Japanese companies are likely to emerge in the 1990s as even more formidable competitors than ever before.

---

[17]Bernard Wysocki, "In Japan, Breaking Step Is Hard to Do," *The Wall Street Journal*, December 14, 1987.

[18]Ramchandran Jaikumar, "Postindustrial Manufacturing," *Harvard Business Review*, November/December 1986.

What this article is about: Corporate culture is more than just a business buzzword in the 1980s. It is often a key to the success or failure of business strategies. The authors give us a method of identifying a functional culture and some steps for keeping that culture from turning elitist.

4–6 Corporate Culture: Avoiding the Elitist Trap

Bernard C. Reimann and Yoash Wiener
*Bernard C. Reimann is chairman and professor, and
Yoash Wiener is a professor, both in the department of
management and labor relations
James J. Nance College of Business Administration,
Cleveland State University*

There can no longer be any doubt about it. Corporate America has a new buzzword. Just as strategy replaced decentralization in the 1970s, culture has replaced strategy in the 1980s. More and more managers and consultants are beginning to recognize that, while corporate strategy may control a firm's success or failure, corporate culture can make or break that strategy.

Not surprisingly, hundreds of articles and books published in the past few years have dealt with corporate culture. Several management books concerned with the topic have become best-sellers.[1] The message that comes through loud and clear is that strong corporate cultures have been major forces in the long-run success American business firms have enjoyed.[2] No wonder senior managers around the world want to improve their corporate cultures, preferably by tomorrow!

Just how valid is this popular belief that strong cultures are at the heart of corporate excellence? Is it based on systematic theoretical reasoning and supported by empirical evidence? We have found no such evidence. To the contrary, many strong-culture companies classified as excellent performers by Peters and Waterman were subsequently found to stumble badly.[3]

In the past few years, the literature has reflected a growing awareness that corporate culture is clearly a two-edged sword—and a very sharp one at that. A strong culture can be a vital asset to a corporation, but only if it is right for

SOURCE: *Business Horizons*, March–April 1988, pp. 36–44.

the firm's evolving mission and strategies.[4] If not, the strong culture can torpedo strategic thinking and action. It can create on the one hand a serious myopia among the top executives responsible for mapping new directions, and on the other hand, a subtle but powerful resistance to change among those who must execute new strategies. Yet, the systematic analysis of culture rarely seems to get much more than lip service from corporate strategists. Even for major strategic decisions, from diversification to mergers, corporate cultures are given relatively little thought—except after the fact, when problems start to surface.[5] The highly publicized difficulties associated with General Motors' acquisition of Electronic Data Systems provide dramatic illustration.

In this article we develop a value-based classification that can be helpful in the systematic analysis of corporate culture, discuss the implications of the resulting generic culture types for the firm's ability to change strategic direction, and examine the development of corporate cultures from an evolutionary perspective. This leads us to some practical suggestions for encouraging constructive culture transformations or avoiding destructive ones.

WHAT IS CORPORATE CULTURE?

Culture can be the social or normative glue that holds the organization together.[6] The corporate culture expresses the values and beliefs that members of the organization have come to share. Moreover, these values are typically manifested by symbolic devices such as myths, rituals, stories, legends, and specialized language.

One attribute distinguishes an organization with a strong culture from one with a weak culture: The high levels of commitment exhibited by its members. These strongly committed individuals accept their organization's goals as their own and tend to pursue these goals in a relentless, persistent, and often self-sacrificing manner.[7] What's more, member behavior is guided by innate senses of right and wrong and of moral obligation largely independent of any particular rewards or penalties. Clearly, a strong culture can be a powerful supplement to traditional motivational practices. It can be particularly effective in motivating behaviors whose outcomes are difficult to observe, measure, and reward. Examples include creativity, friendly customer service, or development of complex software.

Another important feature of a strong corporate culture is that corporate goals, policies, strategies, and action programs are rooted in and consistent with a relatively stable set of organizational values. This gives a thematic orientation and predictability to organizational life—that is, a clear corporate identity. Since weak cultures lack this set of stable values, they do not support a distinct corporate identity.

As foundations of a strong culture, then, shared values play a double role: They serve as powerful, built-in motivational forces for members, and they provide guides for corporate goals, policies, strategies, and actions. The nature of the value system is a crucial factor in the impact of culture on organizational effectiveness. If the prevailing values support appropriate goals and strategies, the culture will be an important asset. Conversely, the wrong values can make the corporate culture a major liability. Not only may the resulting strategies be misguided, but the highly committed members will be relentless in their pursuit of inappropriate goals.

A VALUE-BASED CLASSIFICATION

The two-dimensional matrix helps simplify the analysis of complex concepts and relationships. Not surprisingly, several of these kinds of classifications have been applied to the analysis of corporate culture. The problem is, these frameworks have typically not been based on the shared values that form the core of a corporate culture. Rather, they have been formulated with a broad range of variables, such as decision-making styles, organizational structures, leadership styles, and reward systems.[8]

A fundamental requirement of a classification of any concept is to base it on dimensions that reflect the central elements defining the concept. Since values are central to the concept of culture, the classification should be along value dimensions. Furthermore, a value focus will permit the examination of the likely effects of different types of value systems (cultures) on strategic orientation. The following two value-based dimensions are particularly useful for a two-by-two classification of culture types:

1. The content focus of corporate values.
2. The source and anchoring of these values.

The Focus of Values

Is the primary focus functional or elitist? *Fundamental* values concern functions performed for, and relations with, important organizational publics (customers, shareholders, suppliers, competitors, and employees). They reflect an outward orientation toward the creation of functional utility for the organization's environment. Functionally focused values deal with such issues as product quality, customer service, and innovation.

Elitist values view the primacy or superiority of the firm's membership, products, or services as an end in itself. They tend to be focused inward on characteristics of the organization. Elitist values are comparative in nature, such as: "We're number one!" or "Ours is better than theirs!" They emphasize a strong sense of pride in the organization, its membership, or its output. This preoccupation with organizational superiority can create a kind of corporate nationalism in which emotions tend to dominate rational thinking.

The Source of Values

Are the corporate values anchored in one *charismatic leader?* Or are they more broadly and permanently rooted in *organizational traditions?* When values are anchored in one powerful, charismatic leader, their acceptance by members is determined to a great extent by personal identification with this leader. When values are rooted in tradition, the same or similar values are transmitted from one generation of organizational membership to the next. They are not dependent on one powerful leader, but on multiple role models spread throughout the organization. Therefore, tradition-rooted values are likely to be far more stable, time-tested, and predictable than those anchored in a powerful leader.

The Problem of Classification

In practice it will often be quite difficult to classify the predominant value system in a corporation. It should be relatively easy to identify the source of values. The presence of a strong, charismatic leader is hard to miss. However, the focus of shared values is often far less obvious. Most strong cultures are likely to be based on a mixture of some functional and some elitist values. Nevertheless, we would expect to find a culture oriented predominantly in one direction or the other.

For example, IBM is famous for its emphasis on the functional values of outstanding customer service, respect for the rights of individuals, and the pursuit of excellence. This last value, in particular, has a strong elitist component, since IBM clearly stresses organizational primacy in its performance—whether in the stock market or in the competitive arena. However, IBM's leadership takes great care to keep its functional, mission-oriented values dominant. We would call IBM's value focus functional.

Generic Corporate Cultures

When the core corporate values have been classified according to the two categories of focus and source, the result is the four generic types of corporate culture shown in Figure 1. To reflect their predominant value orientations, we have named these cultures:

• Entrepreneurial.
• Strategic.
• Chauvinistic.
• Exclusive.

FIGURE 1   Generic Corporate Culture Types (based on source and focus of shared values)

		Source of values	
		Charismatic leadership	Organizational traditions
Focus of values	Functional	Entrepreneurial (external, short-term) 1	2 Strategic (external, long-term)
	Elitist	3 Chauvinistic (internal, short-term)	4 Exclusive (internal, long-term)

THE EVOLUTION OF CULTURE TYPES

Strong corporate cultures are not built up overnight. They evolve over considerable periods of time. Exemplary companies such as IBM, 3M, Delta, and Disney have taken generations to hone their cultures to their current levels of excellence. Moreover, these firms don't just let their cultures evolve in any old way. They spend much effort, time, and money to keep their cultures focused on their central, functional values. However, even these great corporate cultures had humble beginnings. Decades ago their founders—from the legendary Thomas Watson at IBM to the unforgettable Walt Disney—established most of the highly functional values that guide these enterprises today. There can be little doubt that the survival of their functional, time-tested central values has played a major role in the long-term success of these firms.[9]

A close look at each of the four generic cultures provides some useful insights into why relatively few firms have been able to develop strong and effective corporate cultures and maintain them over several generations of leadership. We propose that long-term effectiveness requires an orderly transition from the entrepreneurial to the strategic culture.

The Entrepreneurial Culture

The initial phase of culture development is usually the entrepreneurial one (Quadrant 1 of Figure 1). Here the source of the shared values is the charismatic leader/founder of the organization. It is quite rare for a strong corporate culture to emerge without the influence of charismatic prime movers.[10] The founder's initial value orientation tends, of necessity, to be functional: to create value for customers and other key publics.

If the founder is successful in developing a strong culture firmly based on functional, externally oriented values, the enterprise has a good chance for success, since its members will be committed to satisfying the changing needs of the environment. However, the entrepreneurial culture can be quite unstable and risky. It depends on an individual, charismatic leader. What will happen to the strong culture when the leader (inevitably) moves on? But a potentially even more serious danger is that, while the leader remains, his or her functional values may turn elitist.

The Strategic Culture

If an entrepreneurial corporate culture is to survive its leader's demise, its key functional values must somehow be institutionalized. The source of these values must shift to organizational traditions and multiple role models.[11] If the culture successfully negotiates the transition away from a single charismatic leader, it becomes the strategic type (Quadrant 2 of Figure 1). The value orientation is still functional, but it now becomes rooted in organizational traditions and plural leadership. We call this culture strategic because its stable core values have an external, long-run focus. It is a relatively rational culture without excessive dependence on charismatic leadership. The entrepreneurial, functional focus has been effectively formalized, and the culture has outgrown the more unpredictable and flamboyant tendencies of its entrepreneurial predecessor. The focus is on preserving corporate identity while still adapting to environmental changes.

The corporate culture in a typical Japanese company seems to fit this strategic category. Largely tradition-rooted values, such as the importance of quality, cooperation, effort, shared obligations, and loyalty, make for long-term, strategically oriented corporate cultures. The prevalence of this cultural type among Japanese firms is generally considered to be a major factor in their success.[12]

Among successful American companies fitting this category are Lincoln Electric, Dana Corporation, 3M, IBM, Caterpillar, and Walt Disney.[13] These companies have been successful in nurturing core values that are highly functional and "keep them constantly facing outward."[14] Moreover, these values are clearly focused on one or more critical success factors or competitive advantages. Examples of such overriding values are IBM's and Caterpillar's first-rate customer service and the scrupulous attention to quality control at McDonald's.

The Chauvinistic Culture

If the functional orientation of the entrepreneurial culture turns elitist, the culture becomes chauvinistic (Quadrant 3 of Figure 1). We use this designation to reflect a more internally focused, blind loyalty to corporate leadership and an overriding concern for institutional superiority. At the extreme, the chauvinistic culture may even exhibit many of the characteristics of a religious cult—strong loyalty to and identification with the values of a charismatic leader, and an exclusive, internally focused, we-they orientation. This type of culture tends to encourage efforts aimed at maintaining perceived institutional superiority at all cost. It may be particularly susceptible to the development of "groupthink," with symptoms such as the illusion of invulnerability, self-righteousness, and stereotyping.[15]

The Exclusive Culture

If the elitist value orientation of a chauvinistic culture survives its charismatic leader and becomes institutionalized, the culture becomes exclusive (Quadrant 4 of Figure 1). The name comes from its elitist but traditional, clublike orientation. As in an exclusive club, the elitist value focus is independent of charismatic leadership. Instead, it is anchored in well-entrenched organizational traditions.

Under some circumstances, exclusivity adds value to the organization's product or service. In knowledge industries, for example, where outputs are difficult to evaluate or define in operational terms, a purely functional focus may not be practical. In fact, the interests of knowledge industries such as consulting, law, or education may well be served best by developing and perpetuating an elitist cultural focus.

A case in point is the prestigious management-consulting firm. Most of the services this type of firm provides (especially in corporate strategy) are so complex and intangible that they cannot be evaluated in a rational manner. Therefore, these firms work very hard to project an image of superiority and exclusivity by hiring only top graduates of top universities and paying them exceedingly well (as well as charging very high rates for their services).

Another example is the big Wall Street law firm, whose socially elite clientele insist on dealing with an exclusive and prestigious firm. Similarly, a number of retailers have carved out extremely profitable niches with a strategy of exclusiveness. Among large universities we can see the same phenomenon with the Ivy League schools.

CULTURE AND STRATEGY CHANGE

The real test of the effectiveness of a corporate culture comes when the organization's environment changes, requiring an entirely new strategy. Management may find that the strong corporate culture that served it so well with the old strategy is no longer appropriate. Sometimes a strong culture can be like a millstone around the neck of a firm that is trying to respond to environmental changes.

The monumental task faced by Charles Brown and his management team at

AT&T after deregulation is a good example. Years (and many divestitures) later, the communications giant is still struggling to adapt its "service at all cost" culture to the demands of a fast-changing, highly competitive market. Similarly, Delta Airlines, one of Peters and Waterman's "excellent" companies, found that its strong but internally and operations-oriented culture did not prepare it well for the highly competitive post-deregulation climate.[16]

Both AT&T and Delta have relatively functional, strategic cultures, and it looks as though their cultures are successfully adapting to their changing environments and strategies. However, while a strategic culture is more likely to respond effectively to environmental changes, it is no guarantee of successful strategy creation. To be truly effective over the long term, the company must keep the focus on key values that promote critical success factors. However, the most serious obstacles to strategic changes are found in chauvinistic and exclusive cultures. An elitist orientation, especially when coupled with charismatic leadership, tends to produce some dysfunctions that can seriously hamper the strategy-formation process. Three of these are:

- Navel gazing.
- The "bozo" syndrome.
- Loose ethics.

Navel Gazing

The elitist orientation of a chauvinistic or exclusive culture can support a preoccupation with the superiority of internal processes, capabilities, or current outputs. As a result, potential environmental threats—from technological obsolescence to new competitors—are likely to be missed or ignored. Thus a strong elitist culture can help a firm become "incestuous and myopic."[17] This elitist myopia may be particularly likely in a chauvinistic culture, when the strong, chauvinistic leader becomes overly enamored of his or her creation. The chauvinistic organization is vulnerable to the single-minded pursuit of its leader's vision, even when that vision is seriously off the mark.

The sad fate of the upstart airline, People Express, is a particularly dramatic example of an excellent entrepreneurial culture which was eventually soured by an elitist preoccupation with its "superior" strategy and management system. People's charismatic founder, Don Burr, had a firm vision of creating a new, revolutionary kind of participative organization. His initial value orientation was highly functional: To create value for price-sensitive customers by deep discounts at the expense of unnecessary frills. At the same time, his participative management system helped keep his work force highly committed to the airline's goals of minimizing costs while giving excellent customer service.

The exemplary early success of People's strategy is well known. Low fares and convenient, friendly service brought in hordes of new customers, many of whom had never flown before. The media were full of praise for the firm's unorthodox management style.[18] Unfortunately, this heady success only reinforced Don Burr's conviction that his revolutionary management approach was the airline's key to success. The "superior" management system began to drive People's strategy rather than the other way around. As the fledgling airline's rapid growth began to strain its informal management system, Burr was reluctant to make needed changes. The results were rapidly deteriorating customer service, productivity, and employee commitment.[19]

Furthermore, Burr required continued rapid growth to prove to the world the superiority of the People management philosophy. It now appears that this single-minded pursuit of growth may have blinded Burr and his colleagues to the reality of the changing competitive environment. This blindness ultimately forced them to accept a takeover bid from Frank Lorenzo, Burr's former boss at Texas International Airlines.

The sudden reversal of fortunes at People Express illustrates the very real risk posed by an inward-looking, chauvinistic corporate culture. Here a highly charismatic founder espoused strong elitist values. He worked very hard to develop and maintain a culture that emphasized the company's superiority over its competitors. The resulting preoccupation with being successful mavericks may have blinded decision makers to the realities of the outside world.

A serious case of navel gazing can develop in exclusive cultures as well as chauvinistic ones. In fact, an exclusive culture may be even harder to move, because the elitist value orientation is, by definition, firmly entrenched in organizational traditions. This may occur, for example, if a firm has a sustained record of success. Success can carry its own seeds of destruction, if it strengthens the elitist orientation of an organization's culture until feelings of superiority and invincibility become widely shared.

Clifford and Cavanagh, in describing some of the reasons why "bad things can happen to good companies," give a number of examples in which once-successful firms stumbled badly. One is the Wall Street investment-banking firm of Donaldson, Lufkin & Jenrette. In explaining the reasons for a serious downturn in its performance after years of record profits, DLJ's president, John Castle, is quoted as saying: "Our overwhelming success during the first 15 years led to overconfidence—a sense of invincibility—that proved part of our undoing in the mid-1970s."[20] To regain its effectiveness, DLJ had to work very hard to recapture the more externally oriented, functional focus it had gradually lost over the years.

The Bozo Syndrome

In some instances, an elitist focus can go beyond mere navel gazing. Rather than simply not seeing environmental changes, organization members become downright belligerent in their rejection of information that does not fit their own view of the world. We call this the "bozo syndrome," in which organization members actually begin to consider outsiders who do not share their values inferior "bozos." Such arrogance can be spawned easily by a value system focused on organizational superiority—especially if this value focus has been reinforced by early and dramatic success. The shared feeling of invincibility can become so strong that members begin to belittle competitors. The feelings sometimes even extend to suppliers and customers.

The consequences of this syndrome can be quite damaging. Executives may come to feel that they know what's best for the company and disregard, or block, all inputs that are inconsistent with their beliefs. As a result, they are likely to underestimate competitors, scorn the advice of experts or consultants, and even ignore customers' real wants. The company's performance clearly will suffer in the long run if real customers and competitors do not conform to the executives' stereotypes.

Apple Computer provides a recent illustration of this syndrome. Apple's strong, cultlike culture was centered around the strongly antiestablishment, "we know better than those bozos" values of its co-founder and CEO, Steven Jobs. The major value focus in this culture was the superior technical elegance and sophistication of the firm's products with the shared belief that this was just what the market needed.

When Apple virtually owned the market it had created, this elitist orientation did not stand in the way of its excellent growth in sales and profits. However, Apple's strongly chauvinistic culture proved to be a real hazard in the large and growing market for business and professional computers. These sophisticated and conservative new customers were looking for a dependable, standardized product that could communicate with other computers, printers, and other equipment. The last thing most of them wanted was a technically elegant but noncomformist product like the Macintosh.

Apple's disappointing performance in this growth market was a major reason for Jobs' ouster.[21] The present CEO is John Scully, a former top executive with PepsiCo, who has brought more externally and functionally focused values into the corporate culture (especially into marketing). Apple Computer's basically chauvinistic culture, therefore, appears to be changing to a more strategic one.

In fact, Scully has reemphasized Apple's commitment to being an alternative to IBM, and he is wooing customers with the ease of use and graphics capabilities of Apple's products. The focus is shifting from technological elegance to effective implementation and marketing. To quote Scully: "Implementers aren't considered bozos anymore!"[22]

Loose Ethics

The strong chauvinistic culture is preoccupied with maintaining an image of superiority. The pressure on members to live up to this image can be intense. In addition, chauvinistic cultures foster the view that the end justifies the means. The result is a climate in which the temptation to bend ethical and legal principles to achieve a given goal becomes both hard to resist and easy to rationalize.

Loose ethics can be illustrated by the legal problems encountered by Tandem

Computers. Deal and Kennedy describe in vivid detail the strong commitment felt by Tandem's executives toward their organization and its flamboyant founder, Jim Treybig.[23] It appears that their commitment to produce profits was so great that some employees may have resorted to unethical misbooking of revenues. The SEC recently has charged Tandem with violating the securities law by overstating its fiscal 1982 revenues.

ORGANIZATIONAL SUBCULTURES

So far, we have been discussing corporate culture as though it were one homogeneous organizational characteristic. This, of course, is rarely the case except in relatively small firms. The typical corporation includes many subunits and groupings, and members of each of these units may share beliefs that differ from the values shared by members of other units. This raises the possibility that organizations can be characterized not only by a central corporate culture, but also by many subcultures. In our conceptualization, the definition of an organizational subculture is the same as that of corporate culture, except that the focus of analysis is either on organizational units (departments or divisions) or on cross-organizational groupings (occupational and professional groups or project teams).

A multiplicity of divergent subcultures may be divisive, especially when no strong central corporate culture exists. In the absence of a unifying central culture, it is possible for an organization to be pulled in different directions when various units in the organization have incompatible value systems.

On the other hand, when both a central corporate culture and individual units' subcultures exist in an organization, the likelihood of conflict is small. While various units may be characterized by different cultures, these are not likely to be incompatible as long as most of the organization's members still share similar core values, especially if the core values are functional rather than elitist. These values can be superordinate goals that take precedence over local subunit values in cases of conflict, acting like glue to bind together and integrate otherwise highly differentiated subunits. In contrast, an elitist value focus may be more likely to encourage interdepartmental competitive rivalries.

General Electric is a good example of a large, extremely diverse firm that has a long tradition of central core values overcoming the often quite different corporate cultures of its individual businesses. As CEO Jack Welch put it recently: "For GE to have one culture makes no sense. We have a lot of different cultures. But we try desperately to have one company with one set of values."[24]

COUNTERCULTURES

The most critical problem with subcultures is not the one created by natural differences in orientation of different divisions. A far greater danger is posed by a strong counterculture. This is the all-too-common situation in which management has (or espouses) one set of values, and the rank and file have another, often conflicting set of beliefs. This unfortunate state of affairs can come about in several ways.

A common type of counterculture, likely to be found in highly formal, bureaucratic organizations, is one based on a "civil service" mentality—minimal effort and protection of the status quo. Try as it might, top management will not be able to instill a strong work ethic or innovative thinking into this type of culture (except with drastic measures, such as mass firing).

An even more troublesome counterculture may arise if an elitist, competitive culture pits management against its employees—a familiar situation in labor-management relations in industries from steel to health care. Harold Geneen's reign at ITT illustrates the dangers of letting such a value gap develop between the CEO and lower management. His emphasis on competition and challenge fostered a very cohesive subculture of managers focused on their common fear and hatred of their boss rather than the good of the company. When this powerful leader left, the culture collapsed, leaving a cultural vacuum.

Perhaps the most sudden (and often painful) way to create countercultures is through mergers or acquisitions. One of the major reasons mergers frequently fail is a clash between the cultures of the two (or more) organizations involved.[25] Here, two strongly exclusive cultures would probably cause the most problems. A serious clash between the two is almost inevitable, unless they can be made to focus on their joint superiority. We would predict the combination of two strategic cultures to allow the easiest transition because of their external, functional value orientations. This would be particularly true, of course, if the key functional values were similar or complementary. Elitist values, on the other hand, tend to be mutually exclusive.

SHAPING THE EVOLUTION OF THE CULTURE

Cultural transformation in an organization cannot easily be accomplished in a purely mechanical fashion. Value internalization by members reflects processes of influence and persuasion that are largely evolutionary and emergent. Thus, cultural changes cannot depend solely on formal management decisions and systems. On the other hand, management isn't totally helpless in the face of cultural evolution. Appropriate actions can help shape that evolution. The most serious danger is the transformation of an entrepreneurial culture into a chauvinistic one. Instead, management must concentrate on facilitating the evolution toward a strategic culture. We have pointed out that the main source of influence is the founder/leader. What can the leader do to shape the desired cultural evolution?

First, of all, leaders must develop self-awareness. They have to recognize that any charismatic leader can be tempted to equate his or her own identity with that of the organization. They must avoid the elitist trap of seeing their organizations, products, philosophies, and memberships as superior and most important in comparison to all else. To develop this kind of self-awareness, leaders need to take the following steps:

- Strongly discourage the development of personality cults or excessive hero worshipping.
- Practice delegation and participation to encourage the development of enduring management structures independent of the influence of an individual, charismatic leader.
- Encourage constructive dissent to wean individual decision makers from the strong influence of charismatic leadership.
- Promote functional values, such as cooperation, discipline, self-sacrifice, fairness, initiative, creativity, and customer service.
- Be willing to step aside or move on if their staying involved inhibits the transition to a more stable, strategic culture.

In addition to steps that the leader can take directly, the following general management actions can facilitate the development of a strategic culture:

- Recruit and select people whose personal values are consistent with functional organizational values.
- Institutionalize the proper functional values by extensive socialization and orientation, including the use of symbols such as rituals, myths, and special language. Make every effort to discourage the emergence of a leader's personality cult.[26]
- Prevent the development of countercultures by promoting a strong central culture based on cooperation and by avoiding moves such as mergers that bring together incompatible cultures.
- Remove the charismatic leader if he or she is blocking the effective transformation of the entrepreneurial firm into a strategic culture, unless the leader takes that step voluntarily.

This last step is the most drastic and should, of course, be undertaken only as a last resort. For example, Apple Computer's board took this difficult action only after the firm's performance had deteriorated badly and the president, Scully, had recommended it.[27] Since the removal of the charismatic Jobs, the fortunes of the company have improved dramatically. At Lotus Development, on the other hand, Mitchell Kapor saw the light himself and resigned before his presence could damage the company's needed transition to a strategic culture.[28]

CONCLUSION

A better understanding of their corporate cultures can give top executives some important clues about possible biases that may adversely affect their strategic choices. It can also help managers anticipate or even avoid strategy-implementation problems. Furthermore, the analysis of culture should not be limited to their own corporations and subunits. An appreciation of the dominant culture of a competitor can be extremely useful in anticipating future moves and competitive responses.

The main lesson for managers is to make every effort to establish and maintain an externally oriented, functional value focus while avoiding the natural tendency to develop elitist values concerned with the firm's superiority. The resulting strategic culture tends to support, rather than inhibit, strategic change and adaptation to environmental realities. It will support the implementation of corporate strategies from entering new markets or adapting new technologies to mergers and acquisitions. While a strong strategic corporate culture is no guarantee of success, a keen awareness of the importance and fragility of cultural processes is essential to the long-run strategic management of the corporation.

REFERENCES

1. See Deal, T. E. and Kennedy, A. A., *Corporate Cultures* (Reading, Penn.: Addison-Wesley, 1982); R. Moss Kanter, *The Change Masters: Innovation for Productivity in the American Corporation* (New York: Simon & Schuster, 1983); T. J. Peters and R. H. Watersman, Jr., *In Search of Excellence,* (New York: Harper & Row, 1982); and W. G. Ouchi, *Theory Z* (Phillipines: Addison-Wesley, 1981).
2. Deal and Kennedy (note 1), p. 5.
3. *Business Week,* "Who's Excellent Now?" November 5, 1984, pp. 76–78.
4. See: Kilmann, R. H., Saxon, M. H., and Serpa, R. (eds.), *Gaining Control Of the Corporate Culture* (San Francisco: Jossey-Bass, 1985); H. Schwartz and S. Davis, "Matching Corporate Culture and Business Strategy," *Organizational Dynamics,* Summer 1983, pp. 30–48; or N. M. Tichy, "Managing Change Strategically: The Technical, Political and Cultural Keys," *Organizational Dynamics,* Autumn 1982, pp. 59–80.
5. Prokesch, S. E., and Powell, Jr., W. J., "Do Mergers Really Work?" *Business Week,* June 3, 1985, pp. 88–91.
6. Tichy (note 4).
7. Wiener, Y., "Commitment in Organizations: A Normative View," *Academy of Management Review,* 7 (1982): 418–28.
8. See, for example: Deal and Kennedy (note 1); L. D. Ackerman, "The Psychology of Corporation: How Identity Influences Business," *The Journal of Business Strategy,* Summer 1984, pp. 56–65; and N. K. Sethia and M. A. Von Glinow, "Arriving at Four Cultures by Managing the Reward System," in Kilmann, et. al. (note 4), pp. 400–420.
9. Wiener, Y., "Forms of Value Systems: A Focus on Organizational Effectiveness and Cultural Change and Maintenance," *Academy of Management Review* (forthcoming in 1988).
10. Kanter (note 1).
11. Kanter (note 1).
12. Ouchi (note 1).
13. See: Peters and Waterman (note 1); Ouchi (note 1); and H. J. Martin, "Managing Specialized Corporate Cultures," in Kilmann, et. al. (note 4), pp. 148–62.
14. Pascale, R. "Fitting New Employees into The Company Culture," *Fortune,* May 28, 1984, pp. 28–40.

15. Janis, I. L., *Victims of Group-Think* (Boston: Houghton-Mifflin, 1972).
16. *Business Week* (note 3).
17. Pascale (note 14), p. 10.
18. *Time,* "Super Savings in the Skies," January 13, 1986, pp. 40–45.
19. Bennett, A., "Airlines's Ills Point Out Weaknesses of Unorthodox Management Style," *The Wall Street Journal,* August 11, 1986.
20. Clifford, Jr., D. K., and Cavanagh, R. E., "When Bad Things Happen to Good Companies," *Management Review,* January 1986, pp. 5–10.
21. Uttal, B., "Behind the Fall," *Fortune,* August 5, 1985, pp. 20–24.
22. Wise, D. C. and Lewis, G., "Apple part 2: The No-Nonsense Era of John Scully," *Business Week,* January 27, 1986, p. 98.
23. Deal and Kennedy (note 1).
24. Hamermesh, R. G., "Making Planning Strategic," *Harvard Business Review,* July–August 1986, p. 118.
25. Prokesch and Powell (note 5).
26. For a good description of socialization practices, see J. P. Wanous, *Organizational Entry, Recruitment, Selection, and Socialization of Newcomers* (Reading, Mass.: Addison-Wesley, 1980).
27. Wise and Lewis (note 22).
28. Ehrlich, E., "America Expects Too Much from Its Entrepreneurial Heroes," *Business Week,* July 28, 1986, p. 33.

What this article is about: Managerial thinking on the relationship between strategy and organizational culture tends to be informed by a static perspective. Culture is viewed as normative values and beliefs which enforce a relatively homogeneous, fixed set of behaviors—"the way we do things around here." Because culture is fossilized in habit, it resists change and frustrates strategy formulation and implementation. This article develops an alternative, dynamic, and process-based model of culture. Culture is redefined as "the significant shared meanings which allow managers collectively to make sense of what they and others do." Strategy constitutes an important constellation of these meanings, and strategic management is a cultural process aimed at altering managers' interpretations about the fundamental nature and purpose of their organization and their roles within it. It is argued that senior executives seeking strategic change need to pay more attention to what messages they are seeking to communicate and how these messages are likely to be received. In this way, they can more readily hit on the right language and symbolic action to influence strategy.

4–7 *Strategy, Organizational Culture, and Symbolism*

Sebastian Green

Dr. Sebastian Green is Senior Lecturer at Victoria University,
Wellington, New Zealand. He was previously Research
Associate at the Centre for Business Strategy,
London Business School

Corporate culture is one of those grand concepts which, since bursting onto the intellectual landscape in the early 1980s, has captured the interest of academics, journalists, and businessmen alike. In fact, the concept has a rich ancestry, stretching back at least as far as the writings of Mayo and Barnard in the 1930s. This time, corporate culture has emerged from the chrysalis to orchestrate the reevaluation of the attributes of organizational success which are not part and parcel of the "orthodox" rationalist paradigm.[1-4]

This paradigm has been sorely tested by the failure of formal strategic management systems in large organizations to deliver their promised cargo. Though not necessarily instituted to cope with increases in economic turbulence, these

Source: *Long Range Planning* 21 (August 1988), pp. 121–29.

systems have proved unworthy of the task. In particular, formal rational scientific models of strategy have come under increasing criticism on the grounds that managers cannot, or will not, behave in appropriate fashion.

The reason, as Salmans[5] has pointed out is that:

> Management is an art not a science, and that while a carefully shaped strategy may make or break a company, the corporate culture may make or break the strategy.

Although the cultural path ought to lead away from a technical model of organizational life, cultural engineering, as the term suggests, frequently steers us back to it. Managerial concern tends to center on culture as a critical variable[6] which determines how well the organization copes with its strategic imperative: the need to remain or become competitive in the face of changing economic circumstances. If culture blinds people to the need for change or causes them to resist it, then cultural blocks have to be eliminated. All too often, the tools for so doing—structure, systems, and procedures—are conceptualized in technical rather than symbolic terms. If culture represents the irrational, then the challenge is to control it rationally.

Yet, culture, like art, does not succumb to pushbutton control: It is far too complex and multifaceted. You do not control culture, at best you shape it. What is true of culture is also true of its products, one of which is strategy. Analysis is rarely value-free; we bring a whole host of prior assumptions, received wisdoms, learned ways about perceiving and interpreting the world—in a word culture—to any strategy analysis.

The insight of the cultural approach is that strategy is viewed as emerging out of culture even while it has the power to change it. It is no longer a manipulable and controllable mechanism that can be changed at the drop of a hat. Rather, as Greiner[7] points out, strategy making is a "shaping process that gradually moves the organization along a particular path."

In this article we compare two different models of corporate culture and its relation to strategy. The first, termed the structural static model, predominates among "culture practitioners." The second, termed the interpretive model, has wide currency in social science, yet has, as yet, had relatively little impact on management. We consider the strengths and weaknesses of the structural static approach to culture before moving on to consider what interpretive theory has to offer.

THE STRUCTURAL STATIC PERSPECTIVE

Ignoring its many varieties, the dominant model of culture as it relates to strategy sees strategic change being constrained through rigid behavioral patterns. These patterns are underpinned by strong social sanctions (norms, rules, values, and collective mental programming) which constitute the normative glue[8] of corporate culture. Three related issues occupy center stage: social morphology—what is culture and how can it be classified; social physiology—how does an organization's culture affect its strategic alignment with the environment and, hence, its performance; and social engineering—how can corporate culture be changed to improve strategic alignment and performance. This normative orientation is in line with what Salaman and Thompson[9] have termed the orthodox approach where the focus is on "managerial priorities and problems, and managerial concerns for practical outcomes."

Social Morphology

It has become a virtual *rite de passage* for writers on corporate culture, irrespective of theoretical persuasion, to proffer a new definition or construct a new taxonomy. This is not surprising considering the experience of social anthropology where no shortage of definitions occur—Kroeber and Kluckhohn's[10] study of culture listed 164 definitions. Kluckhohn himself variously defines it as the total way of life of a people; the social legacy the individual acquires from his group; a way of thinking, feeling, and believing; an abstraction from behavior; a theory on the part of the anthropologist about the way in which a group of people in fact behave; a storehouse of pooled learning; a set of standardized orientations to recurrent problems; learned behavior; a mechanism for the normative regulation of behavior; a set of techniques for adjusting both to the external environment and to other men; a precipitate of history; a map; a sieve, a matrix.

Writers within the structural static perspective tend to focus on culture as a mechanism for adjusting collective behavior within the organization to the exigencies that confront it. One definition which has widespread currency, runs as follows:

> Organizational culture is the pattern of basic assumptions that a given group has invented, discovered, or developed, in learning to cope with its problems of external adaptation and internal integration, and that has worked well enough to be considered valid, and, therefore, to be taught to new members as the correct way to perceive, think, and feel in relation to those problems.[11]

There are a number of problems inherent in this definition. First, it is less a definition of culture than a theory about how culture is created and transmitted so as to solve problems of adaptation. Second, the environment is considered to be external to and independent of the organization rather than a product of managerial design. Third, Schein's definition implies that culture is a "thing" which has been successfully established by an undifferentiated group of managers solely to meet their recognized needs for internal order and external responsiveness. This view reduces the notion of culture—people have many diverse needs; it construes a greater degree of adaptive balance and harmony between organization and environment than is ever likely to exist; it ignores subcultures within the organization; and it exaggerates managerial ability to fine-tune internal processes to external ones.

Criticism can also be leveled at the noticeable tendency to classify whole cultures as: strong or weak, innovative or staid, traditional or modern, and so on. The test of any classification scheme should be whether it is useful (rather than whether it is "right"). These categories, with their emotive overtones of good and bad contribute to what Whyte described as "the vain quest for utopian equilibrium, which would be horrible, if it ever came to pass."[12] They ignore conflict, subcultures, and the complexity of organization life. One only has to talk to people working in unicultural companies to recognize that different people attach different significance to rules about what is expected; that there are limits to conformity; that people often only pay lip service to cultural imperatives; and that, frequently, adherence to espoused values relates to status and nationality. Corporate culture buffs would do well to heed Geertz's warning[13] that *nothing has done more to discredit cultural analysis than the construction of impeccable depictions of formal order in whose actual existence nobody can quite believe.*

For example, IBM is generally held up as an exemplar of a strong, distinctive culture which maintains its core values irrespective of the economic circumstances it faces. Yet the IBM personal computer was developed by an independent business unit, separate from the parent company's "giant bureaucratic tangle and granite-set rules."[14] One reason for spinning off the development of the PC was, as David Bradley, one of its designers, put it, "If you're going to compete against five men in a garage, you have to do something different." Two of the hallowed pillars of IBM's culture are "IBM means excellence" and "respect for the individual." If these values are indeed as widespread as commentators suggest, then why was it necessary to free individuals from IBM's culture in order to facilitate their development of an excellent product?

Most large organizations have their high-fliers, young turks, dead wood, team players, rebels, specialists, and administrators. Each has a different view about the world and a different way of playing the game. Organizations are multicultural,[15,16] to such an extent that the imposition of a core-value complex on a plurality of subcultures requires "a manipulative process, based on propaganda and procedure."[17] Inevitably, this process breaks down when the complexity of social life defies managerial intentions. Or new leaders or situations emerge which require subtle, but nonetheless fundamental, changes to the existing core-value complex. Different and opposing sets of values can well coexist, indeed it is often through such differences that change is catalyzed. For example, a brief sortie to Marks and Spencer's flagship Oxford Street branch reveals little of the famed, family-oriented corporate culture. The increase in the number of part-time workers and the diversification into furniture and more fashionable clothes (many manufactured overseas) indicates that meanings are on the move at M & S following the advent of Sir Derek Rayner.

The art of cultural analysis is to capture these complexities through rich description, to go behind stereotypes and make explicit different social viewpoints. The method long favored by anthropologists is fieldwork where the goal is to "grasp the native's point of view, his relation to life [in order] to realize his vision of the world" (Malinowski quoted in Reference 15, p. 359). In this way, one can begin to shed light on the key cultural question: What manner of people are these? For anthropologists, the hidden agenda is to foster tolerance and respect for others and to reflect on one's own idiosyncracies. For managers, there is a somewhat different agenda, to see what is admirable in others and seek to emulate it.

Social Physiology

The structural static perspective takes as axiomatic the proposition that an (effective) organization is a unitary system bound together by a common task and common values. The overwhelming concern is with order, consensus, and control and the trick is to get people to eschew personal agendas for corporate objectives. Ouchi,[18] for example, suggests that culture is a way of reconciling divergence in interests between individuals and the organization which is not adequately handled by the market or by a bureaucratic structure.

Because culture is separate from the rest of the organization's social system (formal structure, systems, and strategy), it is capable of a wide range of modes of integration within it. A key management task, therefore, is to enhance system integration. This requires that different sets of norms, values, and beliefs be brought into alignment both with each other across the organization and with other parts of the system such that together they fit the demands made by the environment. Culture's specific role is to allow the organization to survive as an integrated, ordered community in its (various) environments.

The need for organization change is generally signaled through changes in strategy. However, the most brilliant strategy is worse than useless if it cannot be implemented because it is socially unacceptable. This may happen when intended strategy calls for new ways of doing things which either conflict with traditional ways, or which lead to changes in (relative) power. While formulation of strategic options may be an analytic process, strategy choices and implementation are behavioral processes. The implicit assumption here is that, once established, corporate culture becomes relatively resistant to environmental, and hence to strategic, change.

Alternatively, if we recognize that the whole strategic management process is rooted in people, then "cultural blinkers" may also constrain strategy formulation.[19,20] People bring their own intellectual baggage to bear on new problems, part of which has been conditioned not only by intrinsic cognitive limitations,[21] but also by traditional or habitual ways of doing things: "the way we do things here." Because of the "taken for granted" nature of assumptions underpinning traditional ways of doing things, people are frequently unaware of their cultural blinkers or regard it a heresy to challenge them. This affects their ability to contemplate new options and new solutions. At the same time, the normative, prescriptive element of culture circumscribes acceptable ways of doing things.

As such, it is corporate culture rather than strategy which is the key to understanding organization success. If the culture is right, then the "right" strategy can be implemented. While strategic alignment is the functional imperative, it is corporate culture which is the organizational lubricating oil or, more generally, the spanner in the works. Reminiscent of the arguments in the field of economic development about whether economic growth can proceed without profound social (cultural) development, so too in the literature of strategic management, culture is seen primarily as a constraint to deep-seated organization change. This has led Schwartz and Davis[22] to develop the notion of cultural risk as a means of establishing when a particular strategy is likely to meet stiff resistance. They argue that it often makes sense to change the strategy to the existing culture (although in some cases, though extremely difficult to accomplish, culture can, and in some instances must, be changed).

Social Engineering

Hence the search for excellent cultures which avoid the problems of a culture/ strategy mismatch. Peters and Waterman,[1] Deal and Kennedy,[2] Ouchi,[3] Athos and Pascale,[4] and Wilkins,[23] all argue that the possession of an appropriate, widely shared and acted-on belief and value system is an essential prerequisite for successful strategy implementation. If the reverse causality is the case— successful performance leads to excellent culture—then culture loses much of its appeal as it can no longer be invoked to promote organization success.

The key problem for organizational architects, therefore, is how to lever culture into excellent shape. This requires a good appreciation of one's own culture. Unfortunately, insight is frequently blurred because: "The task of comprehending a particular culture becomes more formidable the more one becomes acquainted with it: one's initial model is little more than an amalgam of the observer's own prejudiced presuppositions."[24]

The second dilemma emerges from the requirement for contingent cultures (i.e., those that fit strategy and hence the external environment). Excellent cultures are excellent only if they are contingent upon their respective environments. Applying the model of a particular excellent culture to companies in other circumstances will not necessarily bring success. Importing inappropriate cultural practices such as the best of Japanese ways of managing (e.g., group-style management) may be as disastrous as importing inappropriate technology. Consultants frequently pay lip service to the need for a contingency framework while searching for universal attributes of excellence. Peters and Waterman's[1] eight golden rules of excellence and Deal and Kennedy's[2] advocacy of strong cultures and powerful leaders locate their authors within the classical management school far more than in the relativist, contingency school.

The third problem is that managers seeking to change corporate culture must have the legitimacy to do so. How can people who are reared within a particular value and belief system and who are judged according to their adherence to the rules, then turn round and overthrow the system that in nurturing them has also enchained them? Leaders who change direction run the risk of being regarded as heretics, turncoats, or plain incompetents. External change agents or new-comers may be ignored or won over. Consultants' views are rejected on the grounds that "they don't really understand the problems," and new leaders succumb to the culture once an initial "honeymoon period" is over.[25]

Finally, practitioners are themselves culturally blinkered by Western management practice to favor "a restricted set of organizational change levers . . . which limit contemporary change-management practice." Formal structure, human resources management systems, information systems, and budget systems are inadequate tools for changing culture. At best, they have only partial success and at worst, wholly unintended results. Perhaps people do not have the skills necessary to visualize the necessary changes[17] or there may well be significant political opposition to changing formal structure or procedures.[26] Even when the necessary changes are well understood, the tools prove inadequate as, for example, when conventional reward systems fail to promote innovative behaviour.[25]

No wonder, therefore, that Schwartz and Davis,[22] writing about AT&T's change of strategy in 1978, state that:

> Despite the major changes in structure, in human resources, and in support systems, there is a general consensus both inside and outside AT&T that its greatest task in making its strategy succeed will be its ability to transform the AT&T culture. It will probably be a decade before direct judgements should be made as to its success.

Inappropriate Metaphors

Our own view is that culture cannot be managed if this means pressing buttons or pulling levers so as to shift it to some desired state where culture, strategy, and environment fit together like pieces in a jigsaw. If culture could be levered into shape, by now someone would have discovered the method. The metaphors of fine-tuning and fit which abound in much of the (structural static) literature on culture and strategy are altogether inappropriate for something as complex as human social systems.

Nor is culture in essence static: What appears to be uniform and stable at any point in time, from a longer time horizon can be shown to be processual and multidimensional.[27] Preoccupation with means/ends instrumentality, the heritage of Western Rationalism, has tended to eclipse the need to understand process: how actions and events are made meaningful over time. In the following section we develop a model of culture and strategy which addresses these problems.

THE INTERPRETIVE MODEL

Instead of viewing culture in terms of social control (values and norms predicating behavior), or as static behaviors constraining change, interpretive theory redirects attention to the way people collectively make sense of the world in which they live and their own position within it. It recognizes that "We tend to be blind to our own assumptions when we are locked inside them."[4] Yet it recognizes that these assumptions do change in response to novel situations and to social inter-action. Through working with, talking to, and socializing with other people across organizational boundaries, individuals make sense of, that is, they attach meaning to, events, actions, words, and things. "Knowledge is never a matter of the lone individual learning about an external reality. Individuals interacting together impose their constructions on reality. . . ."[28]

Shared significant meanings affect how managers collectively interpret their roles, the nature of the business, competitors' actions, strategic data and required strategic action, and so on. These meanings are in the first instance created by interacting individuals. Yet, once established they are only sustained and ex-perienced by later generations by reaffirmation in everyday actions.[29] Weick[30] has suggested that there is a preexisting reality at the core of most organizations which "consists of small grains of truth that are enlarged into constructions by interdependent action." It is the shared meanings about what is important in organizational and personal life which lie at the heart of culture. A good definition of culture which captures this orientation is given by Geertz[13]:

> Believing with Max Weber, that man is an animal suspended in webs of significance he himself has spun, I take culture to be those webs, and the analysis of it to be therefore not an experimental science in search of law but an interpretive one in search of meaning.

An example will help clarify.

> The newly appointed CEO decided that a key requirement for turning around the company was to improve product quality. People paid lip service to quality control but it held no real meaning for them. His aim was to elevate quality consciousness to the keystone of the new organizational reality, so translated the value: "Thou shalt pay attention to quality," more or less, into a veritable article of faith informing everyday action.
>
> In the past, quality had been the responsibility of quality inspectors, something to be bolted on at the end of the development process. He now proclaimed: "Quality is the be-all and end-all of my company's existence and I take personal responsibility for it." He identified every recurrent defect on the product and created a taskforce of executives to deal with them.
>
> To endow the process with significance (i.e., give it meaning) he took on the biggest problem personally.
>
> A few people in the company saw his actions as merely another management ploy for increasing productivity, a way of further exploiting the work force. They interpreted the creation of a taskforce as at best, a new management gimmick, and at worst, closer scrutiny. However much it was proclaimed, they did not believe that lack of product quality lay at the root of the company's problems. The minority carried on as before.
>
> Then the whole process of improving quality received an unplanned fillip. Due to fortuitous circumstances, a staff buy-out was concluded and many of the dissidents found themselves part owners. Although the individual stakes were insignificant in quantitative terms, ownership had strong symbolic appeal for most people. Not sur-

prisingly, people throughout the company took more care and attention over their work and thought about how improvements could be made.

When a sales increase followed on the back of a rise in consumer spending, people saw it as vindication for their CEO's actions and words. Faith in the new philosophy became even more contagious and quality improved further. In retrospect, the easiest explanation was that the CEO had brought about the changes. A further shared meaning was thus created. "Our leader saved the company."

The shared meanings which comprise culture are just such as those relating to quality, ownership, and the abilities of the CEO. They provide the categories and models which people use to steer through the exigencies of social and economic life.[31] It is important to point out that these categories and models are quite different from the "collective mental programming" (Hofstede) view of culture favored by structuralists. As the anthropologist, Mary Douglas, has aptly put it:

> . . . we think of ourselves as passively receiving our native language and discount our responsibility for shifts it undergoes in our life time. The anthropologist falls into the same trap if he thinks of a culture he is studying as a long-established pattern of values.[32]

Theorists writing in this vein do not see organizations as static entities resisting change, but as "impressively imaginative" processes, continually changing in response to endogenous pressures, with such changes being only loosely coupled to managerial intentions.[27,33,34]

While people "modify, change, and transform social meaning,"[35] the crucial question for managers is whether they can do so intentionally and proactively. Meanings reside in the minds of managers and you cannot control what people think. Moreover, beliefs (significant meanings about what is) and values (significant meanings about what ought to be) frequently emerge out of action inspired by a novel situation: the "If I hadn't seen it with my own eyes, I would never have thought it possible" syndrome. Going back to our example, could quality be improved through the CEO's ability to make the concept of quality meaningful to his staff, or was it just circumstances—the buy-out and an autonomous upturn in sales—which did the trick?

The intentional shaping of culture's web of shared meanings is inevitably a hazardous process. It can be made less so by recognizing that changing meanings is a communication process. While shared meanings cannot be arbitrarily controlled, they can be "tweaked" by those who have a clear sense of what it is they are really trying to say, who seek to convey their message in a variety of mutually reinforcing ways, and who are continually sensitive to the constructions that others place on their words and actions.

This may, however, not be sufficient. Communication is a two-way process, and if people are locked into particular ways of thinking about the world, then all attempts at changing this are likely to fall on deaf ears or be misunderstood.[36,37] For example, Peter Bonfield, one of the people responsible for the revival of ICL, accounts for the early difficulty in changing the organization from being production to marketing led, put it in the following terms: "Basically it was a problem of our not understanding the animal we were training . . . our words and the nodding heads didn't mean the same thing."[38]

In such cases, it may be essential to appeal to a stronger, deeper set of symbolic meanings, in order to get people to listen.

The Symbolic Side of Strategy

> Much strategic activity is devoted to bringing about a shared vision and shared interpretations of experience, that is, who we are and who we are not.[6]

The traditional view of strategy sees its function as matching internal resources to environmental opportunities and threats, in order to promote present and future competitive advantage. Irrespective of whether actual strategy is largely deliberate or largely unintentional,[39] the focus is on the economic and instrumental functions of strategy.

Apart from its role in improving a business's economic competitive advantage, both intended and realized strategy also have social functions in terms of adjusting and reproducing organizational shared meanings and the social relations which they articulate. Strategy is "good to think with" about a whole range of social phenomena: It makes firm and visible a particular set of judgments in the fluid process of classifying persons, businesses, markets, and events; it redefines the past and preempts the future in terms of the present, thus linking past, present, and future within an organizational context; and it is a means of separating, placing boundaries around, and making visible statements about organization and organizing.

This author is not aware of any definitions which capture this aspect of strategy but if there were one, it would probably read something like:

> Strategy is, at its most powerful, a process for generating and encapsulating significant meanings about the nature, direction, and purpose of organization, which enables members to make intelligible their organizational worlds and explain to others that what they are doing makes (collective) sense.

In this sense, both a company's mission statement and its business philosophy statement are essential parts of corporate and business strategy. In the best scenario, they create a corporate identity which gives managers a sense of belonging, which allows managers to assess new initiatives, and which explains why the current identity is adequate or inadequate for the future. In the worst scenario, these statements are just lists of words which hold no meaning for managers, and which reflect a meaningless corporate existence where managers feel lost and disconnected from their task environment.

The symbolic power of strategy draws attention to how the strategic management process enacts culture and, in giving it visible expression, modifies it in much the same way that speech gives meaning to language. Its effectiveness in motivating people and bringing about organization change depends crucially on the extent to which people know about it, understand it, and have faith in it. The creation of such knowledge, understanding, and faith through the strategic management process transforms strategy from a sophisticated economic plan into a potent social symbol signifying change.

The symbolic content of strategy highlights the role of senior management and especially the CEO in the strategic management process. Their visibility; the extent to which other organization members interpret their actions; their control over internal resources; and the ritual adulation of leaders, founders, exemplars, and heroes in organizational stories, myths, and legends, places them at the epicenter of the cultural arena. More than anybody else, therefore, they have to understand their organization's structure of shared meaning in order to manipulate its symbols and create new ones in the furtherance of (their perceptions of) organization purpose.

Tweaking Meanings: Symbolic Management.   It has, of course, long been recognized within the literature that leaders are continuously involved in a wide range of diverse symbolic activities. For example, Pettigrew[40] argues that entrepreneurs may be seen "not only as creators of some of the more rational and tangible aspects of organizations such as structures and technologies but also as creators of symbols, ideologies, languages, beliefs, rituals, and myths . . ."; Brown[41] maintains that the organization is a system of shared meanings in which much of the organizational work consists of symbol manipulation and the development of a shared organizational paradigm; Goffman[42] elaborates the view that individuals in organizations are involved in a continuous theatrical performance whereby, through adroit use of symbols, they aim to shape the impressions that people form of them; Smircich[6] suggests that leadership can be viewed as the management of meaning and the shaping of interpretations; and Trice and Beyer[43] argue that managers need to use symbolic means to encourage innovation and change so that existing structural arrangements can be dissolved without their occupants being degraded.

The problem, however, is how to manage meanings symbolically through the strategic management process, for here the literature is somewhat silent. Two rules are important. The first is that the distinction between different levels of meaning requires explicit attention. All too often it is merely the surface, literal meaning of strategy which is considered: for example, a cost-cutting strategy requiring redundancies and rationalization. There are, however, deeper levels of meaning arising from the way people interpret phenomena as if they signify more than that to which they directly refer. There are those meanings that force themselves on the recipient by being intentional (what the author wanted to say), and by being taken from a common, general lexicon of symbols.[44] An example, would be the CEO giving up his chauffeur-driven Rolls-Royce as part of the cost-cutting strategy. They have obvious meaning. Then there are the disguised, unintentional, elliptic meanings which depend upon idiosyncratic interpretation. For example, lights burning in the CEO's office late into the night, the arrival of external consultants, the cancellation of the Christmas party.

Managers involved in trying to accomplish strategic change need to be constantly aware of the way their actions and words communicate messages which may or may not be received as intended. For example, the message that cost reductions are required so as to maximize returns to shareholders is likely to evoke quite a different response to the message that cost "leadership" is essential to show competitors who is best.

The symbolic side of strategy reveals to organization members the "true" hierarchy of values to which its architects subscribe. Compare, for example, two CEOs faced with an urgent need to turn around their respective companies. One announces that in order to survive growing international competition, costs have to be reduced. However, he fails to get rid of the company aeroplane which is used to ferry senior executives around the world. The other CEO tells his staff that the only way to attract more business is for punctuality to improve. He then gives every one of his staff a new wrist watch. In the first case, there is a clear conflict of messages, in the second, the message is symbolically reinforced.

The second rule is that changes which go against the status quo need legitimizing in terms of a more forceful set of shared meanings. The nature of symbols is that they lend themselves to such reinterpretation. The power of symbols resides in the ambiguity surrounding what it is they signify, allowing people to reinterpret old symbols in new and more appropriate ways. For example, where the dominant structure of meaning in the organization is that of traditionalism, strategic change may be facilitated through framing it in terms of rediscovering roots, "sticking to the knitting," reverence for the past, and pragmatism. Alternatively, where an aura of modernism prevails, change needs to be garbed in rationality, progress, and idealism.

Although such verbal sleight of hand serves to legitimize change, it will often be necessary to look outside the organization for validation. Griswold[31] argues that in order for a system of meaning to have the leverage to legitimize social change, it must be, or appear to be, external to the system of action. As an example, she provides a fascinating account of how the rehabilitation of the Trickster in the late 17th century legitimized acquisitive economic practice. Such practice had long been regarded by the Church as damnable, and by the English elite as contemptible. Through reworking familiar cultural materials in a new theatrical and social context, the Jacobean City Comedy transformed the Trickster, a universal character in folklore, to the Gallant. A cunning, greedy, erotic, duplicitous, often unsuccessful, yet never wholly defeated and immensely entertaining character became a resourceful, penniless, young gentleman in London seeking his fortune and free to enjoy the full economic and social rewards of his cleverness. By engineering a conceptual somersault, a cultural virtue was made of an economic necessity. And in the process, the entrepreneurial activities suitable for early capitalism were thereby made legitimate.

Strategy can act to legitimize such "conceptual somersaults" in culture through its imagery of external threats, combat, and survival. The importance of this language to the legitimation of change emphasizes the need for leaders to make ideas tangible and real to others through their choice of metaphors, words, or models.[45] All too often the strategic management process is seen merely as marshalling the facts. The prime task is to make meaning speak through facts, to make strategy a powerful cultural symbol, rather than a weak one.

While leaders rarely have the time, the inclination, or the detailed knowledge to become involved in the minutiae of strategy, their revealed affirmation of this process, and their ability to endow it with meaning, not only enhances commitment to it but strongly shapes interpretation of strategy's multiple meanings.

CONCLUSION

The structural static perspective divides up the organization and its external environment into separate bits: culture and organization lagging behind strategy, lagging behind environmental change. The task of the strategic management process is to overcome this by engineering a better fit between culture, strategy, systems, structure, and so on. In this way, the organization can be made to adapt to the exigencies created by environmental change. The essential problem is that managers' ability to fine-tune culture into balance with other parts of the organization and with the environment is likely to be frustrated through an inherent inability to grasp the complexity of systemic interdependencies within and beyond the organization; misinterpretation of actions aimed at shaping people's perceptions; the difficulty of devising an appropriate (contingent) culture; and a failure to recognize the political dimensions involved.

Richer insights can be obtained through seeing strategy as an integral part of culture, not something that stands outside it, and in recognizing that culture can be shaped through symbolic means rather than by technical levers. For culture and strategy are intertwined, they are neither design nor outcome but both. The interpretive approach leads us to view strategy as a distinct phase in the cultural process whereby certain groups of people attempt to create symbols which drive people in certain directions and influence their interpretation of situations and of past and present events.

By being aware of and encouraging sensitivity to the way strategy communicates messages to organization members, by framing these messages so as to strike a chord with what organizational members hold dear, and by recognizing strategy's potential for unifying disparate meanings across the organization, the way to a more effective strategic management process is opened. But always the caveat remains: Because meanings are located in people's minds, all attempts to manage them can, to use Eco's phrase, at best be tentative and hazardous acts of influence.

REFERENCES

1. Peters, Thomas and Waterman, Robert. *In Search of Excellence*. New York: Harper Row, 1982.
2. Deal, Terence E. and Kennedy, Allen A. *Corporate Culture: The Rites and Rituals of Corporate Life*. Reading, Mass.: Addison-Wesley, 1982.

3. Ouchi, William G. *Theory Z*. Reading, Mass.: Addison-Wesley, 1981.

4. Athos and Pascale, *The Art of Japanese Management*. New York: Penguin, 1984.

5. Salmans, Sandra. "New Vogue: Company Culture." *The New York Times,* January 7, 1983.

6. Smircich, Linda. "Concepts of Culture and Organisational Analysis," *Administrative Sciences Quarterly* **28** (1983).

7. Greiner, Larry E. "Senior Executives as Strategic Actors," *New Management* **X**(X) (1984).

8. Tichy, Noel. "The Essentials of Strategic Change Management," *Journal of Business Strategy* **3,** no. 4 (Spring 1983).

9. Salaman, Graeme and Thompson, K. (eds), *People and Organisations*. New York: Longman, 1974.

10. Kroeber, A. L. and Kluckhohn, C. *Culture: a Critical Review of Concepts and Definitions*. Cambridge, Mass.: Harvard University Press, 1952.

11. Schein, Edgar H. "Coming to an Awareness of Organisational Culture," *Sloan Management Review,* Winter 1984.

12. Whyte, Jr, William H. *The Organization Man*. Touchstone Books, 1972.

13. Geertz, Clifford. *The Interpretation of Cultures*. London: Hutchinson, 1975.

14. *Business Week,* October 3, 1983.

15. Gregory, Kathleen L. "Native View Paradigms: Multiple Cultures and Culture Conflicts in Organisations," *Administrative Sciences Quarterly* **28** (1983).

16. Martin, Joanne and Siehl, Caren. "Organizational Culture and Counterculture: An Uneasy Symbiosis," *Organizational Dynamics,* Autumn 1983.

17. Hunt, John. "The Shifting Focus of the Personnel Function," *Personnel Management,* February 1984.

18. Ouchi, William G. "Markets Bureaucracies and Clans," *Administrative Sciences Quarterly* **25** (March 1980).

19. Child, John. "Organizational Structure, Environment, and Performance: The Role of Strategic Choice," *Sociology* **6** (1972).

20. Miles, Raymond E.; Snow, Charles C.; and Pfeffer, Jeffrey. "Organization-Environment: Concepts and Issues," *Industrial Relations* **13** (1974).

21. Schwenk, Charles R. "Cognitive Simplification Processes in Strategic Decision-Making," *Strategic Management Journal* **5** (1984).

22. Schwartz, Howard and Davis, Stanley M. "Matching Corporate Culture and Business Strategy," *Organizational Dynamics,* Summer 1981.

23. Wilkins, Alan L. "The Cultural Audit: A Tool for Understanding Organisations," *Organisational Dynamics,* Autumn 1983.

24. Leach, Edward. *Levi-Strauss*. London: Fontana Modern Masters, Fontana Books, 1970.

25. Kanter, Rosabeth Moss. *The Change Masters*. London: Allen and Unwin, 1984.

26. Bower, Joe and Doz, Yves. "Strategy Formulation: A Social and Political Process," in *Strategic Management,* ed. Schendel, Dan and Hofer, Charles. Boston: Little, Brown and Company, 1979.

27. Weick, Karl. *The Social Psychology of Organizing*. Reading, Mass.: Addison-Wesley, 1969.

28. Douglas, Mary and Isherwood, Baron. *The World of Goods*. London: Routledge and Kegan Paul, 1978.

29. Giddens, Anthony. *Studies in Social and Political Theory*. London: Hutchison, 1977.

30. Weick, Karl. "Organizational Communication: Toward a Research Agenda," in *Communication and Organisations: An Interpretive Approach,* ed. Linda L. Putnam and M. Pacanowsky. Beverly Hills, Calif.: Sage Publications, 1983.
31. Griswold, Wendy. "The Devil's Techniques: Cultural Legitimation and Social Change," *American Sociological Review* **48** (1983).
32. Douglas, Mary. *Purity and Danger: An Analysis of Concepts of Pollution and Taboo.* London: Routledge and Kegan Paul, 1966.
33. March, James G. "Footnotes on Organizational Change," *Administrative Sciences Quarterly* **26** (1981), pp. 563–97.
34. March, James G. and Olsen, John P. *Ambiguity and Choice in Organisations.* Universitetsforlaget, Bergen, Norway, 1976.
35. Silverman, D. *The Theory of Organisations.* London: Heinemann, 1970.
36. Starbuck, W. H. "Organizations as Action Generators," *American Sociological Review* **48** (1983).
37. Nystrom, Paul C. and Starbuck, W. H. "Theoretical Observations on Applied Behavioural Science: Managing Beliefs in Organisations," *Journal of Applied Behavioural Science* **20,** no. 3 (1984).
38. *Financial Times,* May 14, 1986.
39. Mintzberg, Henry and Waters, James. "Of Strategies Deliberate and Emergent," *Strategic Management Journal* **6** (1985), pp. 257–72.
40. Pettigrew, Andrew M. "On Studying Organizational Cultures," *Administrative Sciences Quarterly* **24** (1979).
41. Brown, Richard Harvey. "Bureaucracy as Praxis: Toward a Political Phenomenology of Formal Organisations," *Administrative Sciences Quarterly* **23** (1978).
42. Goffman, E. *The Presentation of Self in Everyday Life.* New York: Doubleday, 1959.
43. Trice, H. M. and Beyer, J. M. "Studying Organizational Cultures through Rites and Ceremonials," *Academy of Management Review* **9,** no. 4 (1984).
44. Barthes, Roland. *Image-Music-Text,* Stephen Heath taken from French, Hill and Wang (1978).
45. Bennis, Warren. "The Four Competencies of Leadership," *Training and Development Journal,* August 1984.

FURTHER READING

Johnson, Gerry. *Strategic Change and the Management Process.* Oxford: Basil Blackwell, 1987.

Pfeffer, Jeffrey. "Management as Symbolic Action: The Creation and Maintenance of Organisational Paradigms," in *Research in Organisational Behaviour,* ed. L. L. Cummings and B. M. Straw. JAI Press, 1981.

Pondy, Lou; Frost, P.; Morgan, G.; and Dandridge, T. C. (eds). *Organizational Symbolism.* JAI Press, 1983.

Acknowledgments—Thanks are due to Professors John Hunt and Dean Berry and Dr. John Roberts, all of the London Business School, for their helpful comments on an earlier draft of this paper.

What this article is about: The process by which HRM policies influence strategy formulation is explored. Studies of General Motors and Hewlett-Packard are used to illustrate the possible roles of HRM in business strategy.

4–8 *Human Resource Management as a Driving Force in Business Strategy*

John E. Butler

John E. Butler is a professor of management at the University of Washington

Early strategic management research was quite explicit with respect to the value of links between human resource management policies and strategic considerations.[1] This early research recognized the impact that managerial philosophy, roles, and prescriptions might have on the strategic plan that emerged. Although human resource considerations have not been the main highlight of strategy formulation research, they have received some attention in human resource management (HRM) research, especially as an agent of implementation,[2] and some attention from strategic management researchers.[3] In developing a strategic HRM model, an attempt is made to explain why an exclusive focus on implementation limits the long-term theoretical benefits, which are available to the area of strategic management. In the process, the focus will be directed toward discovering and explaining the important underlying factors that link HRM and strategy by offering a preliminary explanation of the process by which HRM policies actually influence strategy formulation.

The concept of an emergent strategy as part of an incremental formulation process was first popularized by Mintzberg.[4] When viewed in a market context characterized by disequilibrium, this notion of emergent strategy helps clarify the HRM-strategy linkage. Using both concepts, a model is developed that

SOURCE: *Journal of General Management* 13, no. 4 (Summer 1988/89), pp. 88–102.

Acknowledgment. Special thanks to Lee Dyer, Gerald R. Ferris, Ian C. MacMillan and Randall S. Schuler for their helpful comments and suggestions.

examines HRM in a marketplace characterized by constant opportunity, which appears as suited for spontaneous action as deliberate planning. HRM policies appear capable of playing a major role in influencing this emergent component through the encouragement of action on market opportunities. In this manner they can directly affect strategy formulation and help the firm gain competitive advantage.

EVOLUTIONARY DEVELOPMENTS

Because of the applied focus of both HRM and strategy, it seemed natural that HRM researchers sought ways to tie their interests with those of strategic management. Strategy implementation was a natural point of convergence because HRM researchers have proven adept at designing systems to accommodate corporate goals and policies. Once this implementation focus was established, predictable but not time-ordered patterns became evident in the evolution of this research stream. This pattern of development, for new research groups, usually involves the identification of relevant problems and an attempt to interest others in the research area. Three distinct stages can be identified in strategic HRM research, which help us understand why most current HRM research has an implementation focus.

The first stage, a "call to action," made a strong case for the importance of strategic HRM. Its value as part of the strategy implementation process was emphasized, and prescriptions were made to include human resource managers in the strategy-making process. Broad sweeps tended to characterize some of this research, which were designed to encourage others to enter the problem area.[5]

Following this initial effort, a somewhat more normative body of research emerged. Staffing, training, appraisal, and reward systems were linked to successful strategy implementation. General and philosophical prescriptions for practicing managers also emerged. In some cases these related a firm's HRM policies, culture, and corporate success in more general ways.[6] Much of this research attempted to accentuate how selecting the appropriate combination of human resource options facilitates the successful implementation of a chosen strategy.

The development of mid-range and contingency-type theories gives evidence of the emergence of phase three research. The HRM options, identified in phase two research, were related to strategy-influencing factors such as organizational structure, technology, market structure, and a variety of exogenous influences. This resulted in both general and specific frameworks for matching human resource policies to strategic choice. The accommodation of human resource policies to organizational goals, environmental conditions, organizational life cycles, control requirements, and specific responses to decline all served as central themes.[7]

Each of these stages was important to the development of a following for this area, but to achieve long-term viability a theoretical base related to formulation may be needed. This will directly relate HRM to strategy at the inception stage, and should encourage researchers to make a more permanent commitment to this area. HRM/strategy-formulation theories must extend beyond developing appropriate human resource menus, which are designed to fit any contingency or deliberate change in strategic direction. Because the current focus has stressed the importance of HRM due to its ability to facilitate implementation, it has become an accommodating rather than a driving force in strategic management theory.

NEW CONCEPTS OF HUMAN RESOURCE MANAGEMENT

Opportunity Creation

The first step required to support an enhanced position for strategic HRM involves development of direct linkages between human resource policies, profit, and strategy that extend beyond a facilitating function. A theory of less perfect market dynamics, developed by the economists of the Austrian School, provides a useful theoretical basis for hypothesizing a direct link.[8] It provides a means to link HRM to the dynamics of the marketplace and thus relates it directly to profit.

The economic theory of perfect competition leads to the conclusion that markets are in equilibrium because no one buyer or seller can influence prices and all are accurate in assessing that market price. This constrained view has some limitations and seems to imply that the market must be forced into disequilibrium if advantage is to be gained. The driving of markets into disequilibrium was an entrepreneurial role envisioned by Schumpeter[9] as occurring when new products are introduced or firms exploit new technology. This resulted in temporary market imperfections, which allowed these individuals or firms to achieve entrepreneurial profits. This view is consistent with the dominant view in strategy that suggests that managers take advantage of environmental opportunity through a careful assessment of firms' strengths and weaknesses. This view of the market process is also consistent with the belief that strategy helps create its own opportunities and suggests that other factors within the control of management should be designed to accommodate intended policy. HRM is often seen as fitting into this accommodating position.

While it is comforting to be able to view equilibrium as a "point of tranquility" that establishes both the price charged and the quality of a product or service offered, our knowledge of decision making suggests other viable alternatives.

FIGURE 1　Model of Market Dynamics

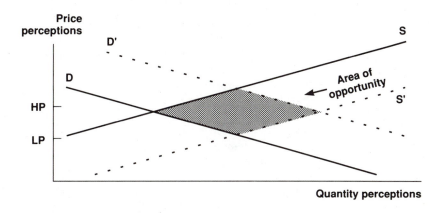

For instance, Hayek[10] believed that the imperfect nature of both information collection and processing resulted in a situation in which multiple beliefs existed about both the prices charged and the quantities of products and services offered. Thus, like other members of the Austrian School of Economic Thought, he was more comfortable with the belief that markets are never in equilibrium. They believed that great uncertainty exists about prices and that the opportunity to earn above-average returns was always available and did not require unique effort to drive markets into disequilibrium.

This arbitrage view of market adjustment is less widely accepted, probably because it admits environmental influences, but it provides a basis for a rethinking of the strategic impact of HRM. Figure 1 has been developed to clarify these market concepts. It depicts a market in which a range of perceptions exists about both the price asked and the quantity of products or services offered. It is within this "area of opportunity" that HRM policies can be a major force in formulating emergent strategy, which in turn helps shape the strategic direction of the firm.

The market dynamic process, depicted in Figure 1, suggests a process more amenable to direct manipulation by HRM policies. The distance between points D and D′ represents a range of estimates about demand and, although not pictured in this figure, there would also be a range of estimates about the appropriate shape of these curves. Similarly, the distance between points S and S′ represents a range of perceptions about supply conditions. The "area of opportunity," shaded in Figure 1, indicates the magnitude of opportunity-identification possibilities with respect to any particular market. HRM policies can be directed toward influencing managers to act on these opportunities and thus can have a more direct impact on the strategy formulated by the firm.

Capitalization On Opportunity

The ability to benefit from the market dynamics process, depicted in a very simplistic way in Figure 1, depends on the firm acquiring inputs at lower prices (LP) than that at which it sells them (HP). We should think of inputs in the broadest possible sense because, in most cases, they will involve multiple inputs that go through some type of transformation process. As firms notice and take action on these opportunities, the distance between points D and D' or S and S' will be reduced, as will the area available for opportunity exploitation, because the flow of information produces a convergence of perceptions. The market may temporarily reach an equilibrium position, but these periods of limited opportunity will be temporary and short-lived because new applications and uses will result in distortions. In this respect the planned and intentional components of strategy help restore the market to a position more suitable for emergent action. This theory of the market adjustment process helps explain how human resource policies act directly to create profit and thus help formulate strategy for the firm. It is because the awareness of opportunity involves individual action that the selection, training, appraisal, and reward policies of the firm can influence opportunity detection to such a great extent. To the extent that HRM policies

FIGURE 2   Model of the Dual Functions of HRM in the Strategy Formulation Process

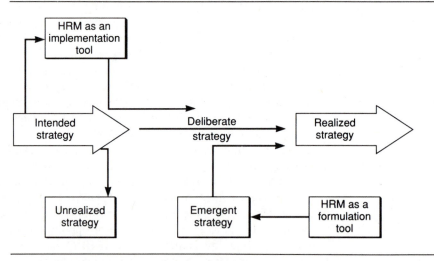

Adapted from H. Mintzberg and J. A. Waters, "Of Strategies Deliberate and Emergent," *Strategic Management Journal*, 6, p. 258. Copyright 1985. Reprinted by permission of John Wiley & Sons.

influence the norms, culture, and behavior of individuals within the firm, they also influence the level of opportunity identification and the unintended components of strategy. As depicted in Figure 2, HRM can facilitate certain planned and intended components while also encouraging particular unintended components related to strategy formulation.

STRATEGY FORMULATION

While strategy formulation should be forward looking, one problem with research in this area is that it requires one to focus on past action. For instance, Hambrick's[11] definition of strategy as "a pattern in a stream of decisions (past or intended) that (a) guides the organization's ongoing alignment with its environment and (b) shapes internal policies and procedures"[12] reflects the historical perspective often required of strategy researchers. This definition is adapted from Mintzberg,[13] who makes a distinction between intended and realized strategy. The concept of strategy being partially emergent is gaining increasing support and is useful in supporting the linkage between HRM and strategy formulation.

Traditional views of strategy formulation have focused on the planning process, making specific statements about the firm's strategy at the functional, business, and corporate levels. Like the current research in strategic HRM, and following the lead of Chandler,[14] other factors have been generally viewed as adapting to intended strategic policy. By viewing the strategy formulated as both intentional and emergent, this process can be seen somewhat differently. HRM systems can be examined to determine their ability to help formulate strategy through emergent, profit-generating action.

Beyond Intention to Behavior

Mintzberg's[15] depiction of formulation fits well with the market-adjustment process concept (see Figure 2) and the enhanced role for HRM. His conceptualization portrays strategy as something that emerges as a function of intended plans, unrealized elements of intended plans, and certain nonintended elements. By viewing strategy as both intentional and emergent behavior, HRM policies designed to create or encourage certain types of profit-generating action become more directly related to the strategic process. Earlier prescriptions for a more formalized planning process are being gradually adjusted to reflect these views and concepts. For instance, the new concept of Model Four-type planning advocates high levels of initiative at all levels of the organization.[16] Notions about strategies being changed on a scheduled basis are being replaced by the realization that strategic direction tends to be stable and the process of change is long term and very complex.[17] The value of this ability to respond was supported in an observation made recently by Dave DeBusschere, when he was dismissed as the general manager of the New York Knicks professional basketball team. Reflecting on how strategy should emerge in his organization, he stated:

> Upon reflection, no team has ever been successful when operated as part of a big business. This is true in all professional sports. The way it works inhibits and prohibits immediate action, quick decisions, and the necessary decision making that has to be done on one level and one level only.[18]

In his own way DeBusschere was making the point that a basketball team owned by Gulf and Western Corporation was resting too much on a totally intended strategy and was not able to benefit from the emergent components, as might a team owned by a sportsman-entrepreneur. In this case, HRM policies might have been a better tool to use, for it would have allowed managerial flexibility at the local level while providing some controls on the strategy that emerged.

A series of studies by Mintzberg provided systematic support for the existence and value of unintended strategy. In one study, of a small food store that eventually evolved into a large retail chain, over 50 distinct strategies, both opportunistic and planned, were identified.[19] Planning often seemed to involve less formulation activity and more publicizing of the existing strategy. As the firm was tracked from its early entrepreneurial stages to a more formalized state, it was found that the culture at the top had a major impact on the strategic behavior that emerged. Thus, like Starbuck and Hedberg,[20] Mintzberg and Waters[21] found that the strategy influencing behavior of managers, while affecting the organization, was also affected by it.

Another study, investigating the notion of adhocracy, sought to determine the effect of this organizational design on strategy formulation. In a study of the National Film Board of Canada, Mintzberg and McHugh[22] found that this form of management was especially suitable for organizations with unique outputs facing dynamic and complex environments. The role of managers in affecting strategy through their behavior was observed directly in the adhocracy configuration. Ideas for films emerged from the bottom and structure was adapted to satisfy production needs. Consistent strategies seemed to emerge because the organization sought to take advantage of the knowledge and skills of employees as well as the current norms of the organization. External events, financing, and some intended top-down plans also affected the strategy that emerged. In this case, the adhocracy appears to be especially suited to take advantage of the 'area of opportunity' (see Figure 1). Mintzberg and McHugh used this study to provide a modified view of the formulation process.[23] They depicted strategies as growing like weeds and not as a cultivated crop. Fortunately, strategies are capable of growing as long as the organization provides an environment in which managers can learn. Consistency results from the proliferation of certain patterns of behavior, which often are preceded by periods of divergence. Most importantly, management of the process requires an appreciation of its workings.

The concept of an emerging strategy fits in well with the disequilibrium view of the market adjustment process. Advantage lies in the ability to formulate strategy via both unintended and intended action. The firm must be capable of acting on those opportunities, which may be lost if subject to the time delays inherent in using more formal planning processes. Action on these opportunities publicizes their availability, which also results in their dissolution and thus maintains "first-mover advantage." Over time, the pattern of action on selected opportunity, for any firm, helps define its emergent strategy.

THE ROLE OF HRM

The theoretical connection proposed suggests that firms use their HRM policies to develop managerial action profiles capable of exploiting market opportunities. The HRM-Strategy model, depicted in Figure 3, is designed to depict the role of HRM as a facilitator of intended planning as part of its strategy implementation role, and as an encourager of flexibility and independence of action as part of its strategy formulation role. The proper balance between these functions ensures that emergent behavior is not smothered by controls, but neither does it work at variance with top-down plans. Two recent studies of firms noted for their HRM involvement, General Motors and Hewlett-Packard, are useful in illustrating how this dual function might work.

General Motors

The new General Motors compensation plan highlights the problem of trying to use a human resource tool in an isolated implementation sense.[24] GM wanted to use its bonus plan as a vehicle for rewarding strategic recovery by developing rewards that were less affected by periods of poor performance. The new plan created a larger bonus pool, lowered the level of profits needed to activate the plan, reduced the payout period, included more managers, and raised the minimum bonus.

It was felt that the majority of the managers penalized during periods of poor performance were not the ones who either had failed to recognize important external events or were responsible for formulating the inappropriate responses that had led to the poor performance. The new compensation scheme was designed to facilitate the attraction and retention of good managers. It was also intended to act as an immediate signal to those employees of management's intention to reward executives on the basis of long-term expectations of improved performance. Ultimately, union opposition postponed and diluted the plan but its perceived impact on strategy may have been somewhat illusionary.

FIGURE 3   Unified Model of HRM, Strategy Formulation, and Market Dynamics

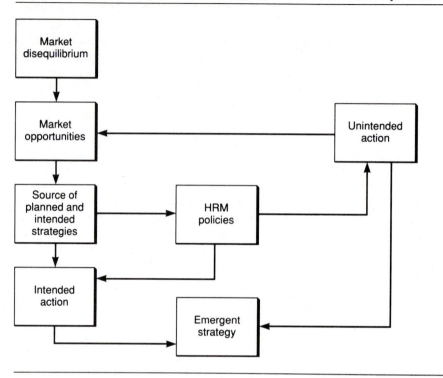

The GM approach assumed it could improve performance by rewarding appropriate strategies while it essentially ignored the pervasiveness of the formulation process. A few powerful individuals at the top may have ignored certain aspects of competition in their deliberate strategies, but the unintended components that emerged from the rest of the management pool did little to alleviate their current competitive situation. The notion that a cost disadvantage, relative to the Japanese or other U.S. manufacturers, could be overcome through a totally intended strategy using HRM as a tool for implementation, ignores some of the dynamics of unintended action.

Cost reduction is a dynamic process, and other firms are not going to sit idly by while competitors attempt to catch up. To the extent that you want appropriate behavior to emerge from the firm, you have to change the pattern of managerial behavior. By allowing the exodus of current managers dissatisfied with the current bonus situation, the opportunity is provided to infuse the organization with new managerial talent. This might produce more competitive advantage because HRM policies could then be used as a vehicle to encourage the emergent behavioral component.

The selection, training, and appraisal policies could be modified to encourage independence of action, which is necessary for the emergence of a differentially advantageous, unintended strategy formulation component. A compensation scheme based on this type of individualistic and opportunistic behavior might be more advantageous, in a competitive sense, than one designed to retain and reward the same manager who had produced and implemented the plans, over a long time frame, of what is now being viewed as an undesirable situation.

Hewlett-Packard

A recent study conducted at Hewlett-Packard provides some insights on the interplay between the prevailing culture, HRM policies, and unintended strategic components.[25] Hewlett-Packard appears to be more conscious of the link between HRM policies, corporate culture, strategy, and success. Recognizing the role of HRM on emergent strategy, Harris noted:

> Successful companies guide and shape their company's culture to fit their strategy. One of the tools used to accomplish this shaping is the reinforcing of certain ideas, values, and behaviors and discouraging others by means of human resource management activities: selection and placement, appraisal, rewards, and training and development.[26]

The importance of matching these various components is increasingly being recognized.

Hewlett-Packard uses values and objectives as guides to encourage individual action because it believes this helps to shape the firm. Obviously there is some top-down strategy and direction reflected in HRM policies, but these are designed to facilitate rather than constrain managerial initiative. Managers are selected based on their ability to operate in this environment, and "management by walking around" is a notion that implies that opportunities exist for those who look. This is consistent with the disequilibrium notions of the marketplace and the use of HRM policies as a force in the formulation process, as depicted in Figures 2 and 3. Individual managers are encouraged to shape their own goals, and it is on this basis that they will be evaluated. Unlike GM, Hewlett-Packard pays above-average salaries, and bonuses represent real increments in salary. Because independence of action is stressed, managers actually develop in the job and each position serves as a training ground for the next. This undoubtedly helps explain why so many firms seek to hire Hewlett-Packard managers.

Care obviously should be taken when contrasting case studies, especially in the context of this research. Normative suggestions are not being made about the appropriateness of any particular HRM policy, but rather about the advantages of having policies that allow strategy formulation to be affected by managerial actions. The particular form of that action cannot be known precisely but the use of appropriate action can be influenced. Environmental, industry market structure, and organizational characteristics will also influence the development of appropriate policies, but their influence does not minimize the value of the HRM impact on strategy.

UNIFIED NOTIONS FOR FORMULATION

With the array of strategy topologies that have been offered for consideration, it would be impossible to map the effects of altering HRM policies on each of them. Because Mintzberg's[27] concept of emergent strategies has been incorporated into the theoretical approach taken here, it seems appropriate to use his topology of strategy types in relating HRM, strategy, and market dynamics.[28] A strategy almost totally deliberate (planned), one almost totally emergent (environmentally imposed), and one between these extremes (process) have been selected for examination.

On the one extreme, a perfectly intended strategy requires shared intentions, or at least the willingness to accept corporate leadership. A "planned strategy" is described as one in which "leaders at the center of authority formulate their intentions as precisely as possible and then strive for implementation . . . with a minimum of distortion."[29] While this focus on planning is desirable, most, if not all, organizations lack the power to control all environmental influences. Even organizations that desire institutional controls to ensure that imposed guidelines are followed need a certain amount of flexibility. HRM policies will be especially important here because, in an opportunity-embedded market, too many controls may inhibit managerial action. For the HRM manager, a fine line must be drawn because a system that encourages both initiative and compliance must be constructed. This often requires strong controls but with a minimum of punitive consequences.

At the other end of the spectrum, an "environmentally imposed" type of strategy can be classified as one that is completely emergent. Here, the "environment can directly force the organization into a pattern in its stream of actions, regardless of the presence of central controls."[30] The desirability of responding to environmental influences is best demonstrated in extreme cases such as Baldwin Locomotive Co. or the Esterbrook Pen Co. These firms continued to produce products long after the environment attempted to force them to adapt and change. Emergent strategies can also go awry, as independence of action leads to no strategy, because managerial action lacks direction. HRM policies must be designed to help ensure that managerial initiatives are sensitive to the general trends of the organisation.

The "process" type strategy is one of the types Mintzberg and Waters characterized as between these two extremes. With this type of strategy:

> . . . the leadership functions in an organization in which other actors must have considerable discretion to determine outcomes, because of an environment that is complex and perhaps also unpredictable and uncontrollable. But instead of trying to control strategy content at a general level, through boundaries or targets, the leadership instead needs to exercise influence indirectly.[31]

Here the needs of the organization require managers who are suitable for all domains; emergent, control, and balanced. Selection becomes a far more complex process because multiple policies are needed across all HRM functions. The balanced mode is more typical and represents best the dynamics depicted in Figure 3.

CONCLUSIONS

It should be clear that this research has not attempted to discard or minimize the efforts to include HRM in the strategy implementation process. That effort has been rather successful and its impact should be broadened. The notions about market adjustment, strategy formulation, and HRM have been connected in a preliminary manner so that HRM can be seen as a driving force in the strategy formulated by the firm. In this respect, HRM policies must be viewed as both producing action and affecting implementation. Rather than simplifying life for those responsible for HRM, this suggests a more complex decision-making environment because policies designed to support implementation or intended strategies may be at variance with those needed to encourage emergent action. Thus, the model suggested here, with respect to strategic management considerations, implies an HRM research agenda far more complex than the current one.

Notions about how certain HRM policies lead to opportunistic behavior should be traced to determine the nature of the relationship to profit. More attention should be given to relating strategy to HRM within the confines of current and future strategic models in the same way that technology, market structure, or marketing policies are examined. This balance between HRM policies, emergent and intended behavior, and the degree of market opportunities also suggests that HRM policies may be useful in guiding emergent behavior designed to make the firm more responsible to both planned and environmentally influenced action.

REFERENCES

1. Learned, E. P.; Christensen, C. R.; Andrews, K. R.; and Guth, W. D. *Business Policy*. Homewood, Ill.: Richard D. Irwin, 1965.

2. For example, see Fombrum, C. J., Tichy, N. M. and Devanna, M. A. *Strategic Human Resource Management.* New York: John Wiley & Sons, 1984.

3. For example, see Guth, W. D. and Macmillan, I. C. "Strategy Implementation versus Middle Management Self-Interest," *Strategic Management Journal* 7 (1986), pp. 313–27.

4. Mintzberg, H. "Patterns in Strategy Formulation," *Management Science* 24 (1978), pp. 934–48.

5. Kanter, R. M. "Frontiers for Strategic Human Resource Planning and Management," *Human Resource Management* 22 (1983), pp. 9–22.

6. For example, see Peters, T. J. and Waterman, R. H. *In Search of Excellence.* New York: Harper & Row, 1982.

7. For example, see Ferris, G. R., Schellenberg, D. A. and Zammuto, R. F. "Human Resource Management Strategies in Declining Industries," *Human Resource Management* 23 (1985), pp. 381–94.

8. Kirzner, I. M. *Perception, Opportunity, and Profit.* Chicago: The University of Chicago Press, 1979.

9. Schumpeter, J. A. *The Theory of Economic Development.* Cambridge, Mass.: Harvard University Press, 1934.

10. Hayek, F. A. "Economics and Knowledge," *Economica* 4 (1937), pp. 33–54.

11. Hambrick, D. C. "Some Tests of the Effectiveness and Function Attributes of Miles and Snow's Strategic Types," *Academy of Management Journal* 26 (1983), pp. 5–26.

12. Hambrick, D. C., p. 5.

13. Mintzberg, H., p. 935.

14. Chandler, A. D., Jr. *Strategy and Structure: Chapters in the History of the American Industrial Enterprise.* Cambridge, Mass.: The M.I.T. Press, 1962.

15. Mintzberg, H., pp. 934–48.

16. Chakravarthy, B. S. and Lorange, P. "Managing Strategic Adaptation: Options in Administrative System Design," *Interfaces* 14, no. 1 (1984), pp. 34–46.

17. Mintzberg, H. and Waters, J. A. "Of Strategies, Deliberate and Emergent," *Strategic Management Journal* 6 (1985), pp. 257–72.

18. Vecsey, G., "DeBusschere: The Last Shot," *The New York Times* 135 (46648), January 8, 1986, pp. A19–A20.

19. Mintzberg, H. and Waters, J. A., "Tracking Strategy in an Entrepreneurial Firm," *Academy of Management Journal* 25 (1982), pp. 465–99.

20. Starbuck, W. H. and Hedberg, B. L. T. "Saving an Organization from a Stagnating Environment," in *Strategy + Structure = Performance,* ed. Thorelli, H. B. Bloomington: Indiana University Press, 1977.

21. Mintzberg, H. and Waters, J. A., pp. 934–48.

22. Mintzberg, H. and McHugh, A. "Strategy Formulation in an Adhocracy," *Administrative Science Quarterly* 30 (1985), pp. 160–97.

23. Mintzberg, H. and McHugh, A., pp. 194–95.

24. McGill, A. R. "Applying Rewards and Compensation Theory to the Real World of Business: A Case Study of General Motors Corporation," in *Strategic Human Resources Management,* eds. C. J. Fombrun, N. M. Tichy, and M. A. Devanna. New York: John Wiley & Sons, 1984.

25. Harris, S., "Hewlett-Packard: Shaping the Corporate Culture," in *Strategic Human Resources Management,* eds. C. J. Fombrun, N. M. Tichy, and M. A. Devanna. New York: John Wiley & Sons, 1984.

26. Ibid, p. 218.

27. Mintzberg, H., pp. 934–48.

28. Mintzberg, H. and Waters, J. A., pp. 257–72.

29. Ibid., p. 259.

30. Ibid., p. 268.

31. Ibid., p. 264.

What this article is about: The Post-it Notes' success was the result of the creative vision of man and a corporation renowned for innovation. This article is an interview with that man.

4–9 Lessons from a Successful Intrapreneur

An Interview with Post-it Notes' inventor Art Fry

Art Fry is no household name, but ask any office worker for a Post-it Note, and you're sure to get exactly that. Fry's invention, the self-sticking pieces of note paper from 3M, have become a standard part of the office, appearing every-where—on computer screens, memos, telephone receivers, and desk lamps. Once people have used Post-it Notes, they can't imagine how they ever got along without them.

Actually, the idea for the Post-it Note began to take shape in Fry's mind in 1974, when scraps of paper he used for bookmarks fell out of his hymnal book in church. As a result, he started to think about a movable, adhesive marker.

Fry remembered an adhesive that had been discovered several years earlier at 3M. It was strong enough to hold, yet it was easily removed. As an adhesive, it was perceived as being of little value. At church one morning, however, Fry suddenly thought of at least one use for this "failed" product that was "temporarily permanent."

He took advantage of a 3M policy that allows scientists to spend up to 15 percent of their time on personal projects. In fact, 3M had institutionalized a corporate culture that encourages intrapreneurship.

After more than a year of experimentation and refinement, Fry was ready to show samples of his pad to those at 3M. It was difficult at first to convince them that people needed a sticky note pad that would sell at a premium compared to scratch paper.

In 1977, however, Post-it Notes saw the light of day when they were test-marketed in four U.S. cities, using normal advertising and promotional methods. The results were mixed. When free samples were handed out, however, people

SOURCE: *The Journal of Business Strategy* (March/April 1988), pp. 20–24.

began to realize the many benefits of the product. In 1979, 3M began to distribute Post-it Notes in 11 western states. They were introduced nationwide in mid-1980.

The rest, as they say, is history. By early 1981, Post-it Notes were introduced in Europe, where their reception paralleled the results in the United States.

The product continues to be a dramatic success. Although 3M does not release sales figures for its individual products, one can only imagine the financial benefits the company has reaped over the years.

As for Fry, he was promoted to the position of corporate scientist and continues to work at 3M. The success of the Post-it, he admits, has been immensely gratifying. "As an inventor," he says, "developing a successful new product is about as close as you can come to achieving immortality."

In the following interview with *The Journal of Business Strategy,* inventor and intrapreneur Art Fry explains how an environment of creativity and innovation at 3M allows him and his fellow inventors to develop unusual—and ultimately successful—products such as the Post-it Note. He also explains how intrapreneurial companies must handle the delicate balancing act of fostering and encouraging the intrapreneurial work force.

EARLY EXPECTATIONS

The Journal of Business Strategy

The Post-it brand note pad is a standard piece of office equipment for almost every business person in the United States. When you first thought of the idea for this product, did you ever envision that it would become so popular?

Art Fry

Right from the start, I was extremely excited about it because all the pieces seemed to fit, as far as our division at 3M was concerned. Everything just seemed right. I knew how many pads people used when they were able to get them for nothing. When I was giving them away, people were using astounding amounts in a valid way. And I said to myself, I know how much Scotch brand Magic Tape people use when they can get it for nothing, and I know what the sales figures are for Scotch brand Magic Tape (our company's companion product), so the Post-it Note had to be a winner. This gave me a lot of courage. However, even though my estimates were 6 to 7 times as high, even 10 times as high, as earlier estimates concerning the potential for it, they were still low.

A HOTHOUSE OF CREATIVITY

JBS

Could you describe the business climate at 3M, which allowed a product such as the Post-it Note to be developed?

Fry

We have three modes of management. In one mode, we have people who can manage innovation and creative functions that allow new, long-range projects to be developed. We have so-called habitats set up for these people. Once you get a product to the second phase—that of a developing business—you need more technical people who are good at building. There is higher overhead in this building phase and, often, it requires different sorts of people than those who originally conceived the product idea and who were the original entrepreneurs. Finally, you get into the third phase— the mature phase—where it's highly competitive. In this phase, you have to become extremely efficient to slim down your operation in the production of the product to get lower overhead and a higher return on capital.

Over the years, 3M has been extremely careful to develop a remarkable habitat for its creative people. At 3M, each division is run as a separate company with its own profit and loss statements. A division vice president here would have the same responsibility as a CEO in many other companies. As a matter of fact, some of our divisions would be considered major corporations if they were separate companies. Within the division, you're never far from either the top or the bottom. So what you do really has an effect on the total success of a project. You feel responsible and empowered by the situation, and it takes away the feeling that "it really doesn't matter because somebody else will pick up the ball if I drop it." You feel that you've got the ball, and you can run with it. This has a remarkable effect on people.

JBS

Did you have to "champion" the idea of the product's value?

Fry

Yes. If you develop something that's new, one of the problems often is that there aren't words to describe it. Many times, a big part of the problem is in communicating things about the idea and keeping the same vision within the whole team. If the product idea had been the sort of thing I was pursuing on my own as an entrepreneur on the outside, there wouldn't be this problem. But here, you are in an organization. Of course, the strength of the organization was what made it possible for the development of the Post-it Note. I couldn't have developed it on the outside. Developing it on the inside means that 80 percent of what is needed is already there—in systems, equipment, people. The 20 percent that doesn't fit requires changes in our technology, in manufacturing, and in how we market it. It's a matter of convincing people that the product is needed in the first place. In any organization, you can get the money and the teams of people, but you need the right people. One person can't do it all.

JBS

Is a corporate bureaucracy a necessary control for the development of new products, or does it tend to be a stumbling block to creativity?

Fry

It's a necessary thing. Bureaucracy represents accumulated know-how, which will really test you before a product is released. Once you get your product out in the field, you have suppliers, distributors, and everyone else all lined up, ready to go. There's inertia in the system, and it's really hard to change course. So when your competition, which is starting fresh, scrutinizes this product, it can leapfrog you with any needed improvements, and come along and destroy your market share. One of the things that a bureaucracy can do is help make sure you don't make those major blunders.

FOSTERING A CREATIVE VISION

JBS

Would you describe the success of the Post-it Notes as a prime example of corporate intrapreneurship?

Fry

I really would. There is a kind of a classic way that things happen when you're at 3M. First, you need a product champion to get that core vision going. Then, you need the facilities that 3M has and a willingness to pull the concept together. Most of the technology was already there. The company had enough people to determine the things we didn't know and to make most of those things happen. Almost by definition, an intrapreneur is someone who doesn't have all of the skills to do the things that need to be done. Therefore, he has to work within the organization, making use of its skills and attributes.

JBS

What do you think motivates corporate intrapreneurs?

Fry

Mostly to make something happen, to make something take shape, and to come alive as a result of the excitement and the satisfaction of success. All of us want to make our lives count for something. I was just talking to a chemist here a few minutes ago. He has had many technical successes, but none have become a commercial success. If he were just satisfied with being paid by the hour, he wouldn't necessarily be dissatisfied, but his goal in life is to make his work count for something.

JBS

Did a specific marketing strategy pave the way for the product's success?

Fry

In this particular case, the marketing strategy of sampling was a key factor. We started marketing the product in four cities. We put it on the shelves of stores and sent out brochures, but it didn't sell too well. The people that did buy it, however, were tenacious. They kept on buying it. We asked ourselves, why weren't there more of them?

At that point, our division vice president and our technical director went out in the field and talked to people who were using the product. They tried selling it themselves and realized that for most people, the words weren't describing what it really was. The Post-it Note is a product that elicits creativity in people. What could encourage more creativity than a blank piece of paper with adhesive on it? Most people received a sample, played with it, and started to find applications for it in their own work. So we changed the marketing strategy. We not only gave out brochures and a description of the product, but included a ten-sheet pad as well. We tried this in Boise, Idaho. As a result, the sales for Post-it Notes took off in Boise. We found that for new things, especially tactile things that require touch, taste, feel, and so forth, you've got to start out with a product and then determine what the words mean.

JBS

Has the success of the Post-it Note at 3M resulted in the company's encouragement of other intrapreneurs?

Fry

3M has always encouraged its intrapreneurs. We just didn't know what to call them before Gifford Pinchot (author of *Intrapreneuring*) came along. At times, we had a lot less complimentary words for them because intrapreneurs are often burrs under the saddle of management. But we've always encouraged and supported product champions and set aside budgeted money for research and development. However, the success of the Post-it Note has encouraged others at 3M to be product champions and intrapreneurs. They can see that it can be done by people who have skills similar to mine, and I'm not superhuman. Therefore, if I can do it, they can do it, too.

JBS

Because of the Post-it Note's incredible success, do you feel increased pressure to develop other new products?

Fry

Oh sure. There's always some pressure because people will always want to know what's next. They expect more from proven performers. The main motivation is always internal, however. I think once you've had success and seen something take shape and work, you want to do it again or to try to help others to do it.

JBS

Let's discuss the other side of success. How do corporate inventors and their companies deal with the failure of a new product?

Fry

It's a percentage game. Failure is the most common thing; success is the least common. That old saying is true: You have to kiss a lot of frogs to find a prince. In building a new product, you are really building a business. The idea might start with a new technology, or it might start with an idea for a product itself. However, it has to match a need for the customer. Then your company must have the ability to produce it. You need adequate staff, technology, suppliers, and raw materials. You must have sufficient supply to deliver it to the customer on time and to give him quality. It's like a jigsaw puzzle, and all the edges have to match. You can work on a project for a long time, and there might be just one or two edges that do not match. Sometimes, you're lucky enough to find those things out early; other times, you go a long way in the development cycle before you finally discover you can't force fit them, and so they fail.

SUPPORT FROM THE TOP

JBS

What about senior management's role in supporting a new product? What part did 3M's former Chairman Lew Lehr play in the success of the Post-it Note?

Fry

Lew had his secretary send out some samples of the pads to the CEOs in the *Fortune* 500 and to their secretaries as well. That helped to percolate Post-it Notes down through organizations because every pad contains 100 sheets—so there were 100 people getting exposed to this. In addition, if a CEO was using them, you felt empowered to use them yourself. That really helped us. Also, Lew Lehr came up through the laboratory. He was an excellent intrapreneur himself and had an ability to spot this trait in others and to provide encouragement. A favorable notice by a CEO or a highly placed person can do a lot to smooth out some of your political problems and get all the troops moving in the same direction. Lew helped to provide that.

JBS

Can companies institute intrapreneurship as a business strategy and also as a way to attract creative people to an organization?

Fry

They must do it. They must hire intrapreneurial types and seek them out within their organization. In addition, companies must allow these people their freedom. Sometimes, after companies have gotten what they want out of intrapreneurs, they get rid of them. If a company does that just once or twice, the signal is sent out to the rest of the troops that creativity doesn't pay. This effectively kills corporate intrapreneurship. Intrapreneurs are often a different sort of a breed. You have to first hire them and then provide sanctuary and budgets for them. You've got to expose your business to them and allow them to look not only at the established directions but in other directions as well.

JBS

One final question: What advice would you give to corporate inventors and corporate intrapreneurs?

Fry

Everything is doable. Generally, the thing that stops us is ourselves. Choose the things that you like to do. You'll work hardest at it, and you'll have more successes. Don't consider anything either below or above you. It's amazing what you can do then, because a lot of things aren't going to get done unless you do them. Try to be a servant and a steward in life, because we all have just so much time on this earth. If we try to do things that will improve the quality of people's time and lives, we're going to be successful. If our goal is just to achieve stature or to make money, we'll fail. But if we leave something behind that's valuable for people, we'll be successful.

Part V

Business Ethics

The final section takes an in-depth look at business ethics. The first of six articles explores the issue of codes of ethics and ethical business behavior. The next two articles, one by a CEO and one by an academic, provide an interesting perspective on the current debate about business ethics. Doug Wallace and Julie Belle White then discuss an integrity audit and lessons learned from using such an audit. The next two articles explore two U.S. companies' approach to ethics and values—Johnson & Johnson and the Boeing Company. This section concludes with Patrick Murphy's article on implementing business ethics.

What this article is about: Management has responded to business scandals with company "codes of ethics." But these codes have little to do with ethics and may not be able to mandate an ethical business climate. This article discusses clusters of categories found in various corporate codes of ethics.

5–1 A Different Look at Codes of Ethics

Donald Robin, Michael Giallourakis, Fred R. David, and Thomas E. Moritz

*Donald Robin is a professor of marketing at
Louisiana Tech University, Ruston
Michael Giallourakis is an associate professor of management
at Mississippi State University, Mississippi State
Fred R. David is an associate professor of management at
Auburn University, Auburn, Alabama
Thomas E. Moritz is an instructor in the School of Business and
Finance, Hardin-Simmons University, Abilene, Texas*

Organizational codes of ethics are: (1) very different, (2) often similar, (3) not connected with ethics, (4) perceived as an important tool for fostering ethical conduct, and (5) not very effective in a broad ethical sense. A welter of contradictions? Indeed, all of the above statements are true—and this fact makes an analysis of ethical codes extremely difficult. However, in order to understand why codes are not very effective (point five), we must be able to analyze them. And in order to perform any kind of analysis, we must deal with points one through four.

Point one frustrates the analysis of ethical code because the differences seem to prevent us from classifying the items found in them. We are then faced with the problem of analyzing codes one at a time, which reduces our ability to offer any general means of improvement. Point two, however, offers some hope. If there are any important similarities, they can form a basis for our grouping activities. With clusters of code items to analyze, we can make statements about their ethical content (point three); attempt to determine why they haven't been very effective (point five); and suggest what might be done to improve them. If codes were not used by organizations as important tools for fostering ethical

SOURCE: *Business Horizons*, January–February 1989, pp. 66–73.

conduct (point four), none of this discussion would be interesting or important. But businesses do seem to perceive them in that way.

One of the similarities among the codes is their tendency to be legalistic. The first title in Motorola's summary of their "Code of Conduct" is "Improper Use of Company Funds and Assets," with the following two entries:

1. The funds and assets of Motorola may not be used for influential gifts, illegal payments of any kind, or political contributions, whether legal or illegal.
2. The funds and assets of Motorola must be properly and accurately recorded on the books and records of Motorola.

Under "Dealings with Distributors or Agents," one finds, "Motorola shall not enter into any agreements with dealers, distributors, agents, or consultants which are not in compliance with U.S. laws and the laws of any other country that may be involved; or which provide for the payment of a commission or fee that is not commensurate with the services to be rendered." The other two titles, "Customer/Supplier/Government Relationships" and "Conflict of Interest," contain similar legalistic statements, all of the form "Thou shall. . . ." or "Thou shall not. . . ." Motorola's approach is far from unique. It appears in almost every code that we studied.

The headings in the code of the Coca-Cola Company are also narrow and legalistic, but they can be compared to Motorola's code as an example of the *differences* that occur between code items from various companies. The Coca-Cola "Code of Business Conduct" contains nine, rather than Motorola's four, major headings. These titles include, among others: "General," which begins: "The Company, its employees, and agents shall comply with all applicable legal requirements . . ."; "Political Campaign Contributions"; "Payments, Gifts and Entertainment Involving Customers and Suppliers"; "Accuracy and Completeness of Company Books and Records"; and "Business Conduct Inquiries." While Coca-Cola's code is different from Motorola's in important ways, there are several similarities in the *content* of these two codes. For example, the use and recording of company funds and dealings with persons outside the firm appear in both codes. Thus, although substantive differences existed between codes, important similarities in their character and content also could be discerned.

In order to use the similarities in the codes as the basis for analysis, some form of classification was necessary. Classification involves the division of items into groups that are homogeneous with respect to some criteria. There are two approaches to classification, both of which are used in this study. With groups established, it becomes possible to suggest what characteristics of codes aren't working, why they aren't working, and what might be done to improve them.

ORGANIZATION OF CODE BY CATEGORY

In a survey of the organizations appearing in the *Business Week* 1000, firms were asked for a copy of their code of ethics, if one existed. They returned 84 codes, while 168 responses to a separate and additional questionnaire were also received. The difference in the two figures is due to either the nonexistence of a code or the company's unwillingness to send one to the authors. The 84 codes came from some of the largest service and manufacturing organizations in the United States.

A two-step process was developed to provide an initial grouping of the code items. The first step used the personal judgment of two reviewers to evaluate the items listed and group them under broader, more descriptive headings where appropriate. The second step involved a third reviewer to test the results of the first two. The lists generated by these reviewers were then compared and titles composed for the groupings. The final list contains 30 categories.

It was also desirable to statistically group the 30 categories based on their usage by the different companies. Three clusters of items from codes of ethics resulted from this analysis, accounting for 24 of the 30 categories. Table 1 is a presentation of all 30 categories with suggested labels for the clusters.

TABLE 1   Clusters of Categories Found in Corporate Codes of Ethics

Cluster 1
"Be a dependable organization citizen."

1. Demonstrate courtesy, respect, honesty, and fairness in relationships with customers, suppliers, competitors, and other employees.
2. Comply with safety, health, and security regulations.
3. Do not use abusive language or actions.
4. Dress in business-like attire.
5. Possession of firearms on company premises is prohibited.
6. Use of illegal drugs or alcohol on company premises is prohibited.
7. Follow directives from supervisors.
8. Be reliable in attendance and punctuality.
9. Manage personal finances in a manner consistent with employment by a fiduciary institution.

Cluster 2
"Don't do anything unlawful or improper that will harm the organization."

1. Maintain confidentiality of customer, employee, and corporate records and information.
2. Avoid outside activities which conflict with or impair the performance of duties.
3. Make decisions objectively without regard to friendship or personal gain.
4. The acceptance of any form of bribe is prohibited.
5. Payment to any person, business, political organization, or public official for unlawful or unauthorized purposes is prohibited.
6. Conduct personal and business dealings in compliance with all relevant laws, regulations, and policies.
7. Comply fully with antitrust laws and trade regulations.
8. Comply fully with accepted accounting rules and controls.
9. Do not provide false or misleading information to the corporation, its auditors, or a government agency.

(continued)

TABLE 1   *(concluded)*

Cluster 2 (continued)

10. Do not use company property or resources for personal benefit or any other improper purpose.
11. Each employee is personally accountable for company funds over which he or she has control.
12. Staff members should not have any interest in any competitor or supplier of the company unless such interest has been fully disclosed to the company.

Cluster 3
"Be good to our customers."

1. Strive to provide products and services of the highest quality.
2. Perform assigned duties to the best of your ability and in the best interest of the corporation, its shareholders, and its customers.
3. Convey true claims for products.

Unclustered Items

1. Exhibit standards of personal integrity and professional conduct.
2. Racial, ethnic, religious, or sexual harrassment is prohibited.
3. Report questionable, unethical, or illegal activities to your manager.
4. Seek opportunities to participate in community services and political activities.
5. Conserve resources and protect the quality of the environment in areas where the company operates.
6. Members of the corporation are not to recommend attorneys, accountants, insurance agents, stockbrokers, real estate agents, or similar individuals to customers.

ETHICAL TOOLS TO EVALUATE CLUSTERS

To assess the clusters, we must first define the tools of evaluation. The most important of these tools is philosophical ethics. Philosophers have been struggling for centuries to provide us with approaches for defining right and wrong. Unfortunately, philosophical ethics is often viewed as nonspecific in character by people who aren't familiar with it. However, the discipline actually offers very specific advice about how to behave ethically. The study of ethics existed long before the business disciplines were formally developed; over that time period it has generated several philosophies that can be used to direct our behavior. These philosophies are similar to those in economics in that they sometimes disagree over the approach that should be used to solve a problem. Nevertheless, like the economic philosophies, the ethical philosophies can provide us with considerable guidance.

Of the several ethical philosophies that have been developed, two major traditions currently dominate the literature—deontology and utilitarianism. Deontology is probably favored over utilitarianism by moral philosophers today, although both are popular. Many of the attacks on business come from a deontological tradition, but utilitarianism has historically been used to provide most of the ethical justification for the modern economic systems found in capitalistic democracies. Each philosophy is briefly described in the following sections.

Deontology

This branch of moral philosophy focuses on universal statements of right and wrong, concerning the duties and rights of individuals. The most telling criticism of deontology is that exceptions to universal statements can almost always be found. Some deontologists have dealt with the problem by suggesting that there are prima facie universals that allow exceptions in certain situations. Thus, while we may believe the universal statement, "It is wrong to lie," a little thought should produce instances where lying can prevent major harm for an individual or society. To deal adequately with these necessary exceptions, the burden of proof is shifted to the individual who breaks the universal, and anyone who does so must be prepared to justify his or her action.

Immanuel Kant provided much of the background for modern deontology. He formulated what he called the "categorical imperative," which states that "one ought never to act unless one is willing to have the maxim on which one acts become universal law." Thus, we would ask whether we would be willing to live in a world where everyone lied whenever it was in his or her best interest to do so. If we would not like to live in that way, then, according to the categorical imperative, we must consider lying unethical. Further, it becomes our duty not to lie. In fact, the term deontology is derived from the word "duty."

Many of the ethical judgments attained by using a deontological approach are the same as those developed by utilitarianism. However, the two approaches differ in important ways.

Utilitarianism

There are many variations of utilitarianism, just as there are of deontology; however, the key concepts are not difficult. The utilitarian ideal can be summarized as "the greatest good for the greatest number." Reaching this ideal involves performing a social cost/benefit analysis of the action in question and acting on the results. The individual is required to identify and somehow measure all social and economic benefits deriving from the action. A similar approach is used for all of the social and economic costs, and these costs are subtracted from the benefits. If the net result is positive (favors the benefits), the action is considered ethical. If two actions are compared, then the one with the largest positive result is preferable. The problems of trying to quantify all social and economic benefits and costs should be apparent. However, utilitarians might respond that if a person does the best that he or she can, then that person is acting ethically.

The concepts of utilitarianism are easy for business to understand and accept because of their ties to the justification of capitalism. Adam Smith and others have argued that capitalism provides the greatest *economic* good for the greatest number. The concept of "utility," the core term in utilitarianism, is also familiar to modern economists. However, in ethical analysis, utility includes social as well as economic benefits and costs.

The most important criticism of utilitarianism, for the purposes of this presentation, is its proposed "unjust" distribution of utility. Severe harm to an individual or to small groups can be offset by small gains to a large number of other individuals. This result is viewed as unethical by the critics of utilitarianism. If utilitarianism is to be useful to business, this issue must be dealt with. For example, it is possible (but by no means ensured) that in the case of Nestle's sale of infant formula to Third World mothers, a utilitarian analysis would have suggested that it was acceptable to continue the sale. However, the outcome of that case favored a deontological analysis, resulting in very severe restrictions on the sale of infant formula in Third World countries. The telling arguments revolved around the severe harm incurred by individuals, even though the sale also did considerable good. Although this case emphasized deontology, many ethical decisions lend themselves to a utilitarian analysis. Thus, both philosophical systems can be useful in evaluating corporate codes of ethics.

EVALUATION OF CLUSTERS

In the current study of codes of ethics, one cluster was labeled, "Be a dependable organizational citizen" (Table 1). The categories included in this cluster all direct the employee to be a nice, dependable person. Such dictates may or may not describe desirable outcomes for the organization, but they have very little to do with ethical conduct. Deontology and utilitarianism have little or nothing to say about these dictates, and their appearance in a code of ethics suggests a lack of understanding or a mislabeling on the part of those organizations that use them. Furthermore, these rules are very specific, providing only limited direction for employees. Service organizations such as banks and utilities were heavy users of categories in this cluster. Examples include Bank of Boston, City National Bank, Wachovia Corporation, Wisconsin Electric Power, ITT, Northeast Utilities, and Texas Utilities. However, a few large producers, such as Dow Chemical, Monsanto, Sara Lee, Du Pont, and Celanese, have also used these categories. Exact quotes from the items in this cluster appear in Table 2.

Another cluster is entitled, "Don't do anything unlawful or improper that will harm the organization." This cluster contained the largest number of categories and was by far the group most subscribed to. Over 50 companies included some

TABLE 2 Selected Direct Quotes from Codes

Cluster 1

"Demonstrate courtesy, respect, honesty, fairness, and decency in all relationships with customers, competitors, the general public, and with other emplyees."—Bank of Boston.

"If an employee reports for work improperly dressed or groomed, the employee will be instructed to return home to change clothes or take other appropriate corrective action."—Bank South.

"Wachovia will not tolerate any alcohol or drug use or abuse which is or may be detrimental to your job performance or the reputation of Wachovia."—The Wachovia Corporation.

"All employees of the Company are expected to perform efficient work and service at all times and avoid any activities which might compromise or conflict with the best interests of the Company."—Atlantic City Electric Company.

Cluster 2

"It is the policy of Exxon Corporation that all its directors and employees shall, in carrying out their duties to the Corporation, rigidly comply with the antitrust laws of the United States and with those of any other country or group of countries which are applicable to the Corporation's business."—Exxon Corporation.

"Employees of R. J. Reynolds shall avoid situations where their personal interest could conflict with, or even appear to conflict with the interests of the corporation and its stockholders."—R. J. Reynolds Industries.

"All Company activities are to be conducted in compliance with all applicable federal, state, and local laws, regulations, and judicial decrees."—Northeast Utilities.

"No bribes of any type may be paid to anyone."—Texas Instruments.

"A payment is prohibited if: (A) It is illegal; (B) No record of its disbursement or receipt is entered into the accounting records of the Company; or (C) It is entered into the accounting records of the Company in a manner which is false or misleading."—Hercules.

Cluster 3

"Manage our human, capital, and other resources to achieve excellence in service to our customers at the lowest attainable cost, consistent with reliability, quality, safety, and environmental standards"—Arizona Public Service Company.

"To deliver to customers only products of proven high quality at fair prices and to serve them in such a manner as to earn their continuing respect, confidence, and loyalty, both before and after the sale."—Texaco.

"Advertising used by the Company is legally required to be true and not deceptive in any manner."—J.C. Penney Company.

of these categories in their codes of ethics. The legalistic character of the items in this cluster make it a set of rules designed to protect the organization, rather than a set of values to guide behavior. Examples of specific quotes from this cluster also appear in Table 2.

The ethics literature does deal with some of the issues raised in the second cluster, but in the context of ethics, these issues lead to reasoned and rational decisions based on certain central values. For example, two of the categories in this cluster deal with bribery. Within the context of this cluster, the issue seems to be one of prohibiting bribery because it is against the law, and the organization could get into trouble if bribes are given or taken. The message is actually "Don't break the law." This message, while certainly desirable, is substantially different from a deontological value that might, for example, state: "Always act in such a manner that you would be willing to live and work in a world where everyone acted as you do." This latter statement effectively prohibits bribery just as well as the rules that are part of this cluster, but it does many other things as well. The organizational value suggested above is a restatement of Kant's categorical imperative and obviously goes far beyond merely obeying the law. Thus, this cluster also seems to lack ethical thought or content.

The final cluster was entitled "Be good to our customers." It contained only three categories, which roughly dealt with ways in which the behavior of employees could satisfy customers (see Table 2 for examples). While these three categories lack the breadth of say, Peters and Waterman's "Close to the Customer" from *In Search of Excellence*,[1] the intent is somewhat broader than in the other clusters. The first item from this cluster in Table 1 was adopted by only 10 companies, item two by 15, and item three by 24 out of the 84 companies represented in the study. There was no obvious tendency toward one or more particular industries. The cluster is somewhat more suggestive of ethical thought, since both deontological and utilitarian reasoning could be used to justify the statements. For example, the marketing concept suggests that following cluster three suggestions is efficient and will produce utility for all. The approach also satisfies deontological requirements. However, all of the clusters need a more thoughtful and organizational use of ethical study for the final result to be called a true code of "ethics."

The six unclustered items also appear in Table 1. Item one of this group was adopted by 31 companies. It is not an ethical dictate and could be confusing to individuals attempting to apply it, since personal integrity and professional conduct can mean different things to different people. The second item, dealing with harassment, could be the result of an ethical analysis, or it could simply be a reaction to societal concerns. Of the 84 codes that were analyzed, this item appeared in 19.

Item three also appeared in 19 codes, but it simply supplies directions on how to deal with perceived unethical occurrences. Directions about reporting such

---

[1]Thomas J. Peters and Robert H. Waterman, Jr., *In Search of Excellence* (New York: Harper & Row, 1982).

occurrences ought to be in every code, but they probably should not be part of the ethical statements in the code itself. The most popular of these six unclustered items was number four, dealing with community and political service, which was adopted by 46 companies. It would be difficult to fit this item into any of the most popular moral philosophies, but it does have social responsibility connotations.

Item five, conservation of the environment, again reflects social responsibility issues rather than ethics, but it could be the result of an ethical analysis. Only 12 companies used this category in their codes. Finally, item six lacks both ethical and social responsibility ties. It was adopted by three financial institutions and was the only one of the six that suggested any specific usage.

Before moving to the second grouping effort, we need to examine the expectations for, and effectiveness of, codes of ethics. The following discussion sets the stage for selection of appropriate categories in the second grouping and for evaluation of the results.

MANAGEMENT EXPECTATIONS FOR CODES OF ETHICS

It was argued in the preceding sections that current codes were for the most part not ethical statements, but dictates or rules that either prohibited or demanded specific behaviors. It is suggested in this section that, despite the fact that codes are currently not very effective, business has high expectations for them.

A considerable amount of work has been spent in analyzing codes of ethics. However, two relatively recent articles summarize the general feeling by many (not all) researchers that codes lack much impact. Cressey and Moore, in an elaborate analysis of corporate codes of ethics, are convinced that "Any improvements in business ethics taking place in the last decade are not a consequence of business leaders' calls for ethics or of the codes themselves. We believe that, instead, any changes have stemmed from conditions imposed by outsiders."[2] Further, an empirical study by Chonko and Hunt involving marketing managers found that "The existence of corporate or industry codes of ethics seems to be unrelated to the extent of ethical problems in marketing management."[3]

Both results suggest that codes of ethics are not a major factor in important decisions involving ethical questions. Codes may communicate the specific rules suggested by the three clusters in the last section, but they have little impact on

---

[2]Donald R. Cressey and Charles A. Moore, "Managerial Values and Corporate Codes of Ethics," *California Management Review,* Summer 1983, p. 73–77.

[3]Lawrence B. Chonko and Shelby D. Hunt, "Ethics and Marketing Management: An Empirical Analysis," *Journal of Business Research,* August 1985, p. 356.

what might be considered the *important* problems of business. Unfortunately, corporate management seems to expect more from them. The Center of Business Ethics at Bentley College published the results of a study in which they inquired whether the respondent's company had been "taking steps to incorporate ethical values and concerns into the daily operations of [its] organization" and, if they had, what they hoped to achieve by doing so. About 80 percent of the 279 respondents said that they had taken such steps, with five major objectives. In order of perceived importance they were: "to be a socially responsible corporation"; "to provide guidelines for employees' behavior"; "to improve management"; "to comply with local, state, or federal guidelines"; and "to establish better corporate culture." The first two were substantially more important, while the last three were seen as about equal in importance. Codes of conduct were used by 93 percent of the respondents to achieve these objectives. The next most popular approach, employee training in ethics, was used by only 44 percent of the respondents.[4]

In a study published in January 1988 by Touche Ross, respondents again cited the adoption of business codes of ethics as "the most effective measures for encouraging ethical business behavior." In this study, 39 percent of the respondents selected codes of ethics as most effective, 30 percent selected a "more humanistic curriculum in business education," and 20 percent selected "legislation." Interestingly, 55 percent selected "legislation" as *least* effective.[5] Thus, codes are still seen by managers as the most viable approach for dealing with ethical problems.

However, there is a gap between what managers hope to accomplish with corporate codes and what is actually accomplished. Compliance with local, state, or federal guidelines might be achieved based on the categories in cluster one. Also, *very specific* guidelines for employees' behavior might be set based on the character of the categories, but broad guidelines and other objectives seem to be beyond what is currently attainable. To the degree the codes analyzed in this article are representative, their content and apparent intent lack the ability to truly aid in ethical decision making.

Cressey and Moore, in their analysis of corporate codes of ethics, believe that these documents "tend to imitate the criminal law and thus contain few innovative ideas about how the ethical standards of a firm, let alone of business in general, can be improved."[6] A quick review of the 30 categories listed in Table 1 and the examples presented throughout this article should verify that our findings confirm this belief. Rule-based statements dominate, while broad, shared values are almost absent.

---

[4]Center for Business Ethics, "Are Corporations Institutionalizing Ethics?" *Journal of Business Ethics,* October 1986, p. 86.

[5]Touche Ross, *Ethics in American Business* (Detroit: Touche Ross, January 1988).

[6]Cressey and Moore (see note 2), p. 73.

FIGURE 1   A Partition of Code Items

Degree of Guidance

Low (little specific guidance)   *High (very specific guidance)*

	Low	High
Rule-based	Cell 1 (None of the rule-based statements were weak enough to be placed in this cell)	Cell 2 Cluster 1 (all items) Cluster 2 (all items) Cluster 3 (items 2 and 3) Unclustered items 2, 3, 4, and 6
Value-based	Cell 3 Cluster 3 (item 1) Unclustered items 1 and 5	Cell 4

Type of Guidance (vertical axis label)

LOGICAL PARTITION OF CODES BY DIMENSION OF GUIDANCE

Since ethical guidance of employees is the desired outcome of adopting a code, two dimensions of guidance were used in another grouping effort. Figure 1 employs the second grouping approach, logical partition, to evaluate the degree of guidance provided by current codes of ethics. The horizontal categories identify the degree of specificity in the code items, while the vertical categories classify the code items according to type of guidance—rule-based or value-based. All of the code items seem to fit easily into two of the four cells, with all of the items in clusters one and two falling into the same cell.

Many of the early attempts at developing codes of ethics were broad, value-based statements of the "Be good!" type. They tended to be altruistic and unattainable, to confuse rather than aid understanding. Cell three in Figure 1 is designed to cover these statements. The problems that occur with cell three statements revolve around whose values are used in describing "personal integrity" or determining "quality" and what is meant by these broad, ill-defined value statements. Only three items were placed into cell three—item one of cluster three, and items one and five of the unclustered group.

Historically, the critic's reaction to the ineffective cell three statements is a call for more specificity. The reaction of business to this call is cell two—specific guidance statements. All of the items in clusters one and two, two of the items in cluster three, and four of the unclustered items have been placed in cell two. In all, this cell accounts for 27 of the 30 items. Cell one has been left blank, but arguably some of the rule-based items in cell two could be classified as providing a relatively low level of guidance. However, since rules are supposed to provide very specific guidance, and since the item labels were composites created by the authors, the companies using them have been given the benefit of the doubt. It is the *intent* of the companies in creating the code items that is important in this article, and the intent seems to have been the creation of cell two statements.

Perhaps the most interesting part of the partition is cell four. If very specific guidance could be combined with a value-based approach to social responsibility and corporate ethics, it could have an important impact on performance. There is simply no way to create enough rules to cover even the most ethically important occurrences, even if they could be identified before they occurred. Perhaps this situation helps explain why most of the code items, including all of those in clusters one and two, are turned inward toward the firm itself. Creating rule-type statements to deal with all of the important issues from the organization's environment is simply too massive an undertaking to be handled effectively. However, if core values could be created to direct organizational behavior—values felt and understood by everyone in the organization—they could be the basis of a very effective code of ethics. This approach seems to call for the study and development of a specific corporate culture. The principal determinant of any culture is its values or guides to behavior. If such values were established as part of a corporate culture to guide the ethical behavior of an organization, many unforeseen events could be dealt with ethically. Unfortunately, cell four is void. It may be that some firms are using a cell four approach without recording it, but this study and recent literature on the subject does not find pervasive use of such an approach.

What would a cell four code look like? What role would it play in directing corporate behavior? A cell four code of ethics would be a statement of the company's ethical and socially responsible values. These values could be derived from an evaluation of potential threats and opportunities using both deontological and utilitarian reasoning. It would be a document that is open to all of the organization's publics and a constant reminder to employees about the expected approach for conducting all activities. Such a code would be a tool in the training program for new employees and part of the broad effort to enculturate all employees. Eventually, it would become an aid in spreading the folklore of the organization, providing the themes around which corporate myths and heroes are created. However, only if the code is used in conjunction with strong enculturation efforts would it reach the high level of guidance that is part of cell four.

Some progress in this direction seems to be occurring. A February 1988 document by The Business Roundtable made the following observation:

> In the growing movement among major U.S. corporations to develop and refine mechanisms to make their ethics effective, there are two interrelated purposes:
>
> First, there is the aim to ensure compliance with company standards of conduct. At work is the realization that human consciences are fragile and need the support of institutions.

Second, there is the growing conviction that strong corporate culture and ethics are a vital strategic key to survival and profitability in a highly competitive era.[7]

We believe that the most effective results will occur when these two purposes are combined. When standards of conduct become ethically determined values and are integrated into a strong corporate culture, then corporate behavior will become more ethical.

---

[7]The Business Roundtable, *Corporate Ethics: A Prime Business Asset* (New York: The Business Roundtable, February 1988), p. 6.

What this article is about: This article is based on remarks to an Executive Forum on ethics and management, given at the Indiana University School of Business on November 7, 1986. In it, the author stresses that ethics isn't a matter of law or public relations or religion. He gives his thoughts on managing ethics and recommends four principles for managers.

5–2 A CEO Looks at Ethics

Vernon R. Loucks, Jr.

Vernon R. Loucks, Jr. is CEO of Baxter Travenol Laboratories, Inc.

It's not often that a top executive gets to talk about ethics even though his company hasn't done anything wrong. My guess is that it's a lot easier to take a reasoned view of the subject without a bunch of TV cameras and subpoenas waving around in your face.

The topic of ethics is an important one. It's a part of management that balances ideals against reality. During a business career, every manager can be virtually certain that he or she will have to make some rugged ethical decisions.

ETHICAL ISSUES: TIMELY AND TIMELESS

As tempting as it might be to think that ethical issues are modern and exciting, they're really not all that new. It was about 560 B.C., for example, when the Greek thinker Chilon registered the opinion that a merchant does better to take a loss than to make a dishonest profit. His reasoning was that a loss may be painful for a while, but dishonesty hurts forever—and it's still true.

Others down through history (Greeley and Gandhi are two examples)[1] have talked about the immorality of taking money without earning it. And let's face it: When there's something going on that reasonable people would agree is unethical, there's usually an amount of cash on hand. There's nothing at all modern about that.

---

[1] Horace Greeley wrote, "The darker hour in the history of any young man is when he sits down to study how to get money without honestly earning it."

SOURCE: *Business Horizons*, March–April 1987, pp. 2–6.

John Galbraith may have put it best. He once said: "There are no new forms of financial fraud; in the last several hundred years, there have only been small variations on a few classical designs."

But to say that ethics is an old subject is not to say that it's worn out. Much to the contrary, there seems to be a wave of interest in it lately—and I think that's healthy.

For one thing, there's a lineup of blue-chip companies that have been called on the carpet for some serious ethical flaws over the past year or two. G.E. was in the headlines for illegal billing and E.F. Hutton for wire fraud. The problems at Manville, General Dynamics, Union Carbide, and Morton-Thiokol have ranged from scandalous to shocking.

Those can't all be bad companies full of bad people. In a large company (and especially an international business), periodic ethical problems are all but predictable. It was reported in the *Harvard Business Review* recently that, over the past 10 years, two-thirds of America's 500 largest corporations have been involved in some type of illegal behavior.[2]

So virtually no one is exempt from concerns about ethics—and some aspects of business today present added opportunities for unethical behavior. We have deregulation, merger mania, computerization, electronic transfer of funds, and growing international trade. Each of these presents opportunities for variations on Galbraith's classical designs.

Let's also not forget that it really isn't companies but people who are ethical or unethical. Corporate charters and bylaws take no action, right or wrong. They just sit there, leaving it to individual people to act properly or not. In this area as well, the record shows room for improvement. A survey of personnel vice presidents across the country showed that one out of every seven job candidates these days is likely to tell a lie about his or her background.[3]

People or companies are not necessarily less ethical than in the past. If anything, we work under a hotter spotlight than ever before. Mike Wallace, George Gallup, and the SEC are watching almost every move we make. So there is reason to care, and there is some good evidence that managers do care. The Conference Board is conducting a nationwide study about ethics as viewed by chief executive officers. Although the report won't be issued until later this year, the study has found a high level of concern among top executives for many current ethical issues: employee privacy, sexual harassment, product safety, and a host of others.

---

[2]Saul W. Gellerman, "Why 'Good' Managers Make Bad Ethical Choices," *Harvard Business Review,* July–August 1986, p. 85. Gellerman reports on the conclusions of Amitai Etzioni, a professor of sociology at George Washington University.

[3]According to a September 1986 survey reported by Robert Half International, New York. The findings were based on interviews with vice-presidents and personnel directors of 100 of the nation's 1,000 largest corporations.

WHAT IS ETHICS?

Ethics is a real concern. Though by no means new, it will be with us always, limited only by the imaginations of those inclined to be unethical. But what *is* ethics?

Ethics is not law. Nor is it public relations, with all the associated worries about corporate image. Nor is it religion or apple pie. It's not something you get from a consultant or from a course in business school.

So what is ethics? It somehow relates to law *and* to moral codes of conduct. For example, the dictionary defines ethics in terms of morality, and morality in terms of ethics. But if we as managers are to come to realistic grips with this subject, we need a more specific concept of just what it is.

In his book *Business and Society,* George Steiner defines business ethics as behavior "that is fair and just, over and above obedience to . . . laws . . . and regulations."[4] Steiner goes on to say:

> Corporations . . . have moral responsibilities which are not necessarily matters of law and which are not necessarily identical with the personal moral codes of the executives who run them. These may be internal (i.e., deciding matters connected with stockholders, customers, employees, creditors, and officers) or they may be external (such as matters affecting the interests of communities, competitors, government, and society).[5]

I like that definition for a number of reasons. It accurately points out that ethics relates to law but can also transcend the law. It's realistic in saying that collective ethics cannot satisfy everybody's views (although it seems to me that, in most cases, the majority should agree).

Perhaps most important, the definition reflects the fact that a corporation needs to satisfy a diversity of groups: employees, customers, investors, and others. No one group ought to benefit while the others suffer. Therefore, corporate priorities—including ethics—must always consist of a balance of interests.

It's because of that need to balance the interests of various constituencies that business ethics is so vitally important. Ethics is simply and ultimately a matter of trust. People act in their economic self-interest. But a system based on that fact must also be grounded on mutual trust, among individuals and among organizations. A buyer needs to trust a manufacturer, a lender needs to trust a borrower, and so on.

The problem with a breach in ethics is not that it violates some natural or heavenly law—even though, in fact, it may do that. The practical problem is that an ethical violation makes continued trust difficult or even impossible. That

---

[4]George A. Steiner, *Business and Society: Cases,* 2nd ed. (New York: Random House, 1972), p. 211.
[5]Steiner (note 4): pp. 224–25.

formulation puts business ethics on a plane different from religion, philosophy, or politics. A view of ethics based on matters of trust also helps make the subject more practical and manageable.

MANAGING ETHICS AT BAXTER TRAVENOL

Business ethics, after all, is a concern of management. It's something that managers, from the top on down, must properly deal with every day in any organization.

Is ethics qualitative and philosophical and gray around the edges? It certainly is. It's impossible to computerize. You can't delegate accountability for it, if you intend to be a truly responsible and effective manager.

Of course, it's easier to say you *should* manage ethics than to tell *how* to manage it. I don't pretend to have a cookbook. The issues are far too interdependent for such an easy approach. I do have some thoughts on the matter, however, and some examples from within Baxter Travenol.

Baxter is a $5 billion manufacturer and marketer of health products. We have about 60,000 employees and operations around the world. We also work in a field where topics such as product safety can be matters of life and death.

We place a high priority on ethical behavior. We're among the many *Fortune* 500 companies that have definitive codes of conduct. Ours covers conflicts of interest, insider trading, and that sort of thing—and we take it very seriously.

But that's not enough. In fact, it's far from being enough.

When you start talking about ethics or anything else, the plain fact is that a few things happen among 60,000 employees and a few million transactions a year that the CEO doesn't know about. I'm sorry, but that's the way it is.

As an example, we have between three and four hundred issues pending at any given time in the area of product liability. It's far more than I should even try to track or monitor personally. The cases are extremely diverse, and they range from the serious to the ridiculous. I understand we have one now where a customer claims that he wrenched his back while unscrewing a bottlecap.

At the same time, we might also have 150 cases where employees say they've been aggrieved in some way. Although all of those cases don't deal with ethical matters, each of them needs to be taken seriously.

So how do we manage this? Beyond maintaining a large staff of lawyers, beyond spending millions every year in legal fees and regulatory activities, what can we do about managing properly in an area like product liability or employee relations or ethics in general?

We do what I've said already: We work to balance interests that often seem to be in conflict. We judge ideals against reality, and we realize that it's never easy. The issues are sensitive. There are few, if any, automatic answers.

MORE QUESTIONS THAN ANSWERS

Think about a specific product, manufactured and marketed internationally by Baxter Travenol: the artificial heart valve. We make a range of valves with various designs. They're surgically implanted to replace patients' own natural valves when, for any number of reasons, they happen to fail. The artificial valve is truly a lifesaving device. It's been around for a couple of decades, and it's used almost routinely today.

Of course, heart valves present more critical tolerances than many other products—lawn chairs or donuts, for example. For that reason, they also present some hard ethical questions along several dimensions. Perhaps the most basic question is whether it's ethical to make a profit on such a product.

A debate has raged across our industry for some years about the emergence and great success of for-profit hospitals. Some say to leave them alone; they have the same right as anyone else to succeed or fail. Others say it's wrong to make a profit from human illness or injury.

There's not much of a logical leap from the hospital to the heart valve. Yes, the company supported the development of the product and shepherded it through 8 or 10 years of regulatory reviews. And, yes, the company runs all the risk of failure in a competitive market.

But what about it? Is it right to make a profit when someone's survival is involved?

There are plenty of other questions. For example, if a profit is proper, then how much profit? And is it acceptable to increase the risk of the valve's malfunctioning by a tenth of 1 percent in order to reduce manufacturing costs (and maybe ultimately the price) by, say, 25 percent? Or is any increase in risk simply unconscionable?

This really gets at the issue of balancing interests. Certainly, the patient's interest is in the area of safety. But what is a reasonable level of safety when you consider a shareholder's legitimate interest in a reasonable return on investment?

The question that fascinates me is liability—for example, the patient whose artificial valve fails after five years' time. Does he (or do his survivors) have a legitimate grievance against Baxter Travenol? Many feel they do have a grievance, even with all the waivers that were signed before the operation and even with the realization that a new valve was necessary only because the valves that God makes tend to fail sometimes.

Heart valves are among 120,000 products that we market at Baxter Travenol. Not all of them are so critical, but many others carry just as much reason for concern. Our blood products, at a time of national concern about AIDS, are an excellent example.

The point is, it's not easy. To talk about business ethics with any degree of honesty means grappling with some tough issues in the real world.

Another example is not a product example but an issue we've shared with some big corporations, including IBM, GM, and Coca-Cola. The issue is whether to stay in business in South Africa.

On September 30, 1986, Baxter Travenol completed the sale of our operations in South Africa. We'd been there for almost 40 years, making lifesaving products. We were growing and highly profitable.

As to apartheid, we have nothing to debate. It's absolutely intolerable. As humans, as citizens of the world, and as businesspeople, we should do anything we can to wipe it out. But my question is whether running away is the best we can do.

Again, look at the balance of interests. Is the government in Pretoria harmed by the pullout of U.S. corporations? If so, who else is hurt? What about the customers who were relying on us? What about the people we were employing? And what about the investors in Baxter Travenol? Can and should a corporation fight a problem like apartheid on its own ground? Would that be more effective in the long run than trying to starve the problem by pulling out?

I realize that I'm providing questions without answers. But the problems I've cited are real—and it's the job of management to solve them.

FOUR PRINCIPLES FOR ETHICAL MANAGEMENT

If I won't suggest easy answers to the questions I've raised, I will offer some principles that, in my experience, ought to guide our ethical decisions as managers. There are four of them.

1. *First, hire the right people.* Employees who are inclined to be ethical are the best insurance you can have. They may be the only insurance. Look for people with principles. Let them know that those principles are an important part of their qualifications for the job.

2. *Second, set standards more than rules.* You can't write a code of conduct airtight enough to cover every eventuality. A person inclined to fraud or misconduct isn't going to blink at signing your code anyway. So don't waste your time on heavy regulations. Instead, be clear about standards. Let people know the level of performance you expect—and that ethics are not negotiable.

3. *Third, don't let yourself get isolated.* You know that managers can lose track of markets and competitors by moving into the ivory tower. But they also can lose sight of what's going on in their own operations. The only problem is that *you* are responsible for whatever happens in your office or department or corporation, whether you know about it or not.

4. *Fourth and most important, let your ethical example at all times be absolutely impeccable.* This isn't just a matter of how you act in matters of accounting, competition, or interpersonal relationships. Be aware also of the signals you send to those around you. Steady harping on the importance of quarterly gains in earnings, for example, rather easily leads people to believe that you don't much care about how the results are achieved.

Mark Twain once said: "Always do the right thing. This will surprise some people and astonish the rest." I'm saying that it will also motivate them to do the right thing. Indeed, without a good example from the top, ethical problems (and all the costs that go with them) are probably inevitable within your organization.

History shows that, in the long run, the ethical course of action is the profitable course as well. That hasn't changed since 560 B.C. or so, and I don't believe it will. I also don't think we've ever really improved on the Golden Rule.

What this article is about: When the capacity to make ethical decisions becomes faulty, quality may take a dive, careers may be ruined, and lives may even be lost. When the dust settles and the fingers stop pointing, the next big question is, "Can we prevent this?" The author traces the cause of corruption in the business world to corporate culture itself.

5–3 An Ethics Roundtable: The Culprit Is Culture

William C. Frederick

William Frederick is a professor at the University of Pittsburgh's graduate school of business

"One bad apple spoils the whole bunch" is a popular explanation for business scandals. From the unethical excesses of Ivan Boesky to the Yuppie Five, we are urged to believe that it is a failure of personal character, not of the corporate institution, that causes employees to go astray.

The bad-apple theory takes the heat off the organizations that hire such wrong-doers: "Our company's policies would never condone this kind of misbehavior" is the generic response to a scandal. It also enables top-level managers to protest their innocence.

The theory even seems to provide an easy, if uncomfortable, solution: Discard the offenders and the rot won't spread. If problems recur, corporate shoulders shrug—some bad ones are bound to slip through even the most vigilant personnel screening and succession process.

But this theory avoids the root of unethical behavior. A growing body of research suggests that the source of ethical problems in business is the organization's culture, especially when the culture intersects with managers' values. Ironically, the meshing of culture with managers' values can also be the secret of improving a company's ethical performance.

Ethics research tells us a great deal about the value systems of managers:

- A study of over 200 corporate managers by Frederick and Weber reveals that managers' *individual* value preferences are about the same as those of most adults in the United States.

- But Weber demonstrates that three-quarters of the managers show a preference of *person*-centered values rather than *society*-centered values; and an even larger percentage give a higher score to *competence* values than to *moral* values.
- Earlier studies by George England showed the same result. Six out of ten U.S. managers took a pragmatic, results-oriented approach to problems; only three in ten typically asked themselves, "Is it ethical?"
- England also demonstrates that the values that really count at work are those that promote the goals and purposes of the company: efficiency, ability, achievement, high productivity. Such values as tolerance, equality, compassion, trust, loyalty, and honor have far less chance of being used in making management decisions.
- A large-scale survey of managers' values conducted by W. H. Schmidt and B. Z. Posner for the AMA confirmed this general tendency of managers to focus their professional energies on organizational effectiveness, high productivity, efficiency, leadership, organizational growth, and organizational stability. The organization's value to the community and its service to the public were given lower priority.

These research findings are no surprise. We want and expect professional managers to promote the goals of their companies in pragmatic ways. Their on-the-job values—the ones they really use while working, as opposed to those values they admire and may use at home or among friends—drive them to act in ways that promote the company's interest. That's what they are paid to do. When they do it well, they are rewarded—or move on.

"WHAT CONFLICT?"

But pragmatism carries a price. When faced with moral dilemmas at work, the managers in one Fortune 500 corporation, according to researcher Robbin Derry, rely almost exclusively on the embedded traditions and established rules of the company's culture as their ethical guide. For these managers, following the organization's rules *was* the ethical thing to do. Fully one-third of the managers claimed never to have faced a moral conflict at work—a pretty neat trick, if you think of the complexities of most managers' jobs. They figured since they never broke company rules, they never acted unethically. Others simply believed that ethics and morals have no place at work, so it just never occurred to them. Still others thought that ethical concerns were not a part of their job description or their responsibility. The buck did *not* stop with them.

Here one can see the powerful grip an organization's culture can exert on its members. The pragmatic manager intent on promoting the company's goals takes a dangerous step when he or she begins to equate ethics with "how we do things around here." The two may go together very well—as when Johnson & Johnson promptly recalled those Tylenol capsules. But culture and ethics may clash tragically—as when Firestone stubbornly refused to recall its Radial-500 tire that was subject to failure.

A SEEDBED OF MISBEHAVIOR

Recently, researchers have been studying the links between corporate culture, ethical standards, and the behaviors that result. Victor and Cullen have begun to define the basic components of the ethical climates that typically permeate business firms. Their findings: Economic efficiency, a reliance on organizational rules, and the use of law or professional codes (that is, accounting or engineering standards) dominate the ethical climate in the companies studied. Largely left out of these climates: personal morality, friendship, and social responsibility. That is likely to mean that a manager or an employee with a strong sense of personal morality, social responsibility, or a caring attitude will not be encouraged to express those values in making business decisions because the company's climate dictates otherwise. The result? The company increases its chances of taking actions considered by the public to be morally objectionable, socially irresponsible, and uncaring about others.

Cochran and Nigh, by studying more than 400 Fortune 500 companies, discovered that illegal practices are most likely to occur under four conditions: when profits are low, when the company is large, when higher growth rates are experienced, and when the company has a more diverse product line. Under these conditions, they found a tendency for a company's standard operating procedures to permit, encourage, or overlook lawbreaking. Once again, research carries this message: A company's culture is the seedbed of misbehavior.

FRAIL DEFENSES

Corporations have taken various measures to correct undesirable practices. Along with tossing out the bad apples, codes of ethics come most readily to mind. Michael Hoffman found that some 75 percent of the companies he surveyed had such codes. But their effect on corporate misbehavior is coming into question. In a study of 200 codes, Cash Mathews discovered that they are designed primarily to protect the company against its own employees, rather than to protect the public against illegal practices indulged in by the company. Worse still, having a code of ethics is linked to more, not fewer, legal infractions. The same is true about "read-and-sign" affidavits that so frequently are part of company efforts to curb undesirable behavior; along with a greater emphasis on "employee integrity" and "company reputation," such code provisions have no apparent deterrent impact on illegal practices. What makes a difference between corporate lawbreakers and law-abiding companies is the type of industry and the size of a company. Codes of ethics are frail defenses against the potent blend of corporate culture and managers' on-the-job values.

Another popular reform has been directed toward the makeup of a company's board of directors. But Gautschi and Jones took a careful look at these efforts and found a less-than-rosy picture. In 100 leading corporations, their research shows that corporate lawbreaking is more likely to occur if the company has a large board, a large number of outside members, a large proportion of inside company officers on the board's executive committee. Reformers, take note! These are the very conditions that were supposed to produce a higher ethical standard for decision making.

The research evidence is highly suggestive, though not conclusive. Ethical lapses in business may well be a function of the inertial forces present in a company's culture. These forces can work for desirable outcomes, as well as producing tragic ones. Knowing a company's true values and where they tend to drive the company and its managers is a good first step to take. Lasting reform may have to deal directly with this tougher realization. "Throwing the rascals out" (or in jail) may bring feelings of righteousness, but such a strategy may only cloak the nature of the real problem. Take a look at your organization's culture. *That*'s where you are likely to find the culprit.

What this article is about: The authors develop an integrity audit and reveal that there are common gaps between desired behavior and actual practice. They identify nine lessons for organizations and seven dangerous myths.

5–4 Building Integrity in Organizations

Doug Wallace and Julie Belle White

*Doug Wallace is director of the Center for Ethics, Responsibilities and Values
at the College of St. Catherine, St. Paul, Minnesota
Julie Belle White is an associate professor of ethics and leadership at the
Colleges of St. Catherine and St. Thomas, St. Paul, Minnesota*

"Shortly after the Tylenol incident, an individual claimed that his eyes had been damaged by some sort of acid that was in a bottle of eye drops that he had purchased at one of our Target Stores. We talked with him, and found reason to believe that he might not have been telling the truth. In fact, an analysis of the drops he had used did not indicate that there was acid in them. We believed that he might have been seeking a monetary reward from us, or that he wanted to get his name in the news.

"So the issue was: 'What do we do with the eye drops that are still on the shelf?' We weren't convinced he was telling the truth, so why should we pull the product off the shelves and take the chance of losing sales? But we also have a contract with out customers that, although it's not a legal contract, says 'We'll sell you products that are safe'. We let our customers know that we test our merchandise and that we believe it to be safe. We unconditionally take merchandise back if customers don't want it, if it is broken or doesn't work, or whatever.

"Because of that drive to serve the customer, we pulled the stuff off the shelves. We felt that, on the balance, our customers would feel better knowing that we took the extra step to assure them that the products in the stores were safe. We could have tried to explain that we thought this individual might have been playing games, but we didn't feel the customers wanted us to depend on our analysis of one individual. We felt our customers would want us to act in

SOURCE: *New Management* 6, no. 1 (Summer 1988), pp. 30–35.

everybody's best interest until we were assured that we could put the product back on the shelves."

The Target story is about integrity, that elusive but highly desirable attribute in people and organizations. Our own journey into understanding organizational ethics started with a few questions we asked ourselves about integrity: "What does it take to maintain integrity in a business?" "Can we picture a successful business that celebrates wholeness (the root word for 'integrity' means wholeness)?"

Tired of bad-news ethical cases, we began our search by looking for organizations in which employees successfully worked through tough, conflicting ethical challenges. Such stories don't usually make headlines, but we did find them; 15 such stories as a matter of fact (including the Target one summarized above).

Next, we turned to several managers with excellent reputations both for their work and for their reflectiveness about the management of ethical issues. They each read some of our 15 stories, and (in focus groups) they identified the factors they judged made these good-news solutions possible: In all, they identified some 50 factors that we then grouped into five clusters.

Subsequently, these factors were put into a survey that was completed by 239 respondents—recognized leaders in their organizations whom we called "informed observers."

They were asked to rate each of the 50 factors two ways: (1) the extent to which the factor was *actually* practiced in their own organizations; and (2) the extent to which they believed the factor was *desirable* as an important ensurer of integrity.

We put the raw data from the surveys through typical statistical analyses and identified 40 of the original factors that were deemed "very important and desirable." For each of the factors, we measured the significant statistical difference between *actual* and *desired* ratings (*t*-tests for those of you who are researchers), giving us a "gap" score which profiles the extent to which people see ethical discrepancies in their organizations.

These 40 factors now make up the items in a diagnostic questionnaire we call the *Integrity Audit*.

What have we learned from this *Audit?* We feel we've identified the most important factors that determine an organization's climate of integrity. Below, we've grouped our conclusions into nine *lessons* for organizations (which we've linked to illustrative factors from the *Audit*), and seven commonly held assumptions that turn out to be *dangerous myths*.

LESSONS FOR ORGANIZATIONS

1. Lesson: *Having people with integrity in the organization is necessary but not sufficient*. Two audit factors ("*The organization has an individual who has a sense of, and commitment to do, the right thing*" and "*The president holds a* *clear position about ethical values*") turned out to be highly desired. But, surprisingly, there is fairly high agreement that these *already exist* in most organizations. At the same time, many other key items that are as highly desired were judged to be woefully absent in current practices. Thus, our audit shows that, without clear visible commitment from top management, integrity is obviously at risk but, by themselves, leaders with integrity are not enough if the organization lacks the other eight essential characteristics listed below.

2. Lesson: *Mutual trust and openness are absolutely essential.* This comes through like a sledgehammer in our audits. People are clear that trust and openness must characterize relationships in their organizations. Some of the greatest gaps occur on such audit factors as: "*Mutual trust and respect exist within the organization and among groups*" and "*Honesty and openness characterize relationships among affected parties and key players.*" These items are important because if people don't trust and respect each other they probably won't surface the ethical dimensions of management issues (and they certainly will be reluctant to solve problems with one another). This lesson is reinforced by another high gap item, "*There is a willingness to ask for help and consultation when a problem arises.*"

3. Lesson: *The best way to work through ethical problems is by involving others.* Another way of saying this is that people believe that several heads are better than one. In our work with organizations, this dynamic goes to the top of the list in ensuring a chance for integrity. We all know from management research that participatory problem solving is superior to unilateral, autocratic decisions. This knowledge also needs to be applied when addressing ethical conflicts.

Further, once a group of people knows about a problem stemming from a conflict of values, that problem can never be treated the same again: Too many people who know about it will now have become accountable. Indeed, once several people know of an issue—and recognize each other's awareness—ignoring the conflict imperils both the leaders and the organization itself.

An entire cluster of audit factors reflects this insight, for example: "*An ongoing commitment to joint discussion and resolution among the parties involved is evident*" and "*Time is taken to resolve the problem.*"

4. Lesson: *Responsibility is the key organizing concept and principle.* The word *responsibility* has been used in the English language since about the time of the French and American revolutions. "Response-ability" only exists when we have choices—based on principles of right and wrong—along with the capacity and obligation to take action. When people are responsible for ethical conduct, accountability pervades the entire organization. To be accountable means that one has the means to act appropriately and ethically, that people are empowered to act, and that they are supported in their actions.

Audit factors that illustrate this point are typically rated as highly important and desirable. Here are a few such items: "*Individuals within the organization assume responsibility for ethical decision-making,*" "*A search for options is encouraged,*" and "*Alternative choices of action are perceived as available.*"

5. Lesson: *Ethical principles exist and are shared by all.* Two audit factors are rated as highly desirable: "*The principles of the organization are integrated into the work of the organization*" and "*There is a desire for (and a sense of) fairness.*" People in an organization know if there are ethical principles that really count. If standards of acceptable behavior are unclear (or articulated only at the top), people can ignore them.

Another audit factor deals with what happens to these principles when the going gets tough: "*There is a willingness to sacrifice and pay a price in order to do the right thing.*" Johnson & Johnson's response to the Tylenol catastrophe is one highly visible illustration of the meaning of this audit factor: J & J's "credo" was believed and shared by those in the organization, and thus served as the basis for successfully meeting an unprecedentedly tough choice.

6. Lesson: *Planning for integrity has a high value.* In a climate of integrity, people explore the possible ethical consequences of all policies and decisions. Since they know that not every consequence can be anticipated, they plan for how they are going to take the heat for unexpected outcomes. This is reflected in such audit items as, "*The organizational structure provides for adequate planning and participation*" and "*The organization anticipates and plans for the consequences and conflicts resulting from a decision.*"

7. Lesson: *The decision-making process needs to take into account the perspectives of stakeholders.* Listening to the views of *all* constituents who may be affected by the actions of an organization is critical to maintaining an environment of integrity. By extension, narrowing an organization's frame of reference when under stress often leads to tragic consequences. "*Stakeholders who are affected are involved in the decision-making process*" is rated as a highly desirable factor and reflects the importance of considering competing perspectives. Even if constituents cannot be involved directly, role-taking by managers can contribute to balancing various ethical claims.

8. Lesson: *A clear sense of mission and stewardship is shared throughout the organization.* The importance of this comes through loud and clear in the audit, as well as in our work with organizations. These items, all rated as highly desirable, make the point: "*A firm sense of mission is shared throughout the organization,*" "*The organization's mission and goals are clear and ordered in priority,*" and "*The organization has assumed an ethical posture or mission.*"

It's significant that the first two of these items say nothing directly about integrity or ethics; instead, they address clarity of mission and its integration into the consciousness of employees. For example, Cray Research has one of the corporate world's clearest missions: "Designing and developing the fastest, most powerful computer systems there are." This mission statement, articulated by everyone in the organization, clearly contributes to Cray's highly hospitable environment for integrity.

We think the factors of mission and stewardship go hand in hand because they indicate an attitude of reciprocal trust among clients, employees, and the public. The audit statement, "*The organization has a sense of stewardship; a sense of obligation toward others*" underscores this lesson. Note, too, that a firm sense of mission should not be confused with "having a mission statement." The latter is often an artificially constructed statement that is not "owned" by the organization.

9. Lesson: *Living models need to show the way.* Leadership emerges throughout organizations without regard to formal roles or titles. Sometimes the best modeling can come from a "follower"—a manager of a unit who unconsciously sets a pattern for those who respect her. One of the most important items in the audit puts it this way: "*Leaders in the organization are intelligent and sophisticated in analyzing ethics, and serve as models in the ethical decision-making process.*"

DANGEROUS MYTHS

As we have gone back to review these lessons, we have been struck by the fact that several popular assumptions about how integrity can be achieved in organizations just don't hold up. In light of our audit, some common beliefs actually appear to hold out false promises and, in that sense, they are alarming because they can mislead leaders/managers. Here are some of those dangerous myths.

1. Myth: *Ethical problems can be remedied without much time or effort.* *Reality:* This isn't possible! It's comforting and easy to fall into a pattern of believing that integrity is subject to a quick fix. But, in fact, the organization must be willing to commit time, money, and information to ethical problem solving. Literally, it must put its resources where its mouth is when it comes to demonstrating the importance of integrity.

2. Myth: *What a company needs is a well-communicated code of ethics.* *Reality:* Any code (or credo) which isn't supported by the culture—and isn't correlated with a supporting reward structure—will be viewed by employees as a sham. If the reward structure has not been altered when adopting a code of ethics, there will always be problems. Thus, an isolated code is worse than none at all because it becomes a source of cynicism.

3. Myth: *Someone at the top is needed to champion an ethical position.* *Reality:* This perpetuates the myth of individualism—of Lone Ranger Ethics—and depowers people by suggesting that nobody need do anything until someone on a white horse comes in and saves the day. In fact, every manager and employee must accept responsibility to make integrity real. This often begins with, and is sustained by, the aggregate of small initiatives and the daily practice of good ethics.

4. Myth: *All one really needs is a set of good ethical principles.* *Reality:* Both principles *and* processes are needed. Principles alone, without processes that help people to wrestle with competing stakeholder claims, are never sufficient. Although principles can take on the appearance and promise of delivering ethical answers, they do not foster development of the critically needed skills that enable the organization to cope with ambiguity. Principles without process will be ineffectual, at best, and destructive, at worst. Response-ability integrates both processes and principles.

5. Myth: *There is only one right way to solve an ethical dilemma. Reality:* Options are essential. The ability to make choices and to see things from a variety of perspectives is critical to developing the capacity to "work through" ethical issues in management. Seeing things from only one point of view (which is common under stress) has the effect of putting blinders on us and causing us to overlook critical facts that optional frameworks would have helped us to uncover. The search for options incorporates all stakeholders and nurtures healthy communications.

6. Myth: *Experts can tell us how to handle ethical problems. Reality:* That's an effective way to incapacitate an organization! Leaders/managers need to learn that, within every important operational and planning decision, there are ethical assumptions that need to be surfaced. That fact is central to what it means to manage. In contrast, relying on experts keeps people imprisoned; they won't learn how to identify, understand, and resolve issues in concert with colleagues. Empowerment is central to moral leadership (as John Gardner pointed out in his article "Leadership and Power" in the Fall 1987 issue of *New Management*).

7. Myth: *If one had clear rules, one wouldn't have any problems. Reality:* Rules deal only with specific applications and instances. When people run into situations for which rules don't apply—which is to say most of the time—they get frustrated and stuck. Empowering people with the ability to think for themselves is essential. Yes, this is difficult. But there is no substitute for cultivating ethical habits of mind (for example, the senses of "fairness" and "respect for people") which can serve as guiding principles when sticky and complex problems inevitably surface in an organization.

POSTSCRIPT

Some surprising and intriguing conclusions have been drawn from the research that led to the *Audit,* and we intend to continue evaluating the results and assessing the conclusions. Planning is now underway to use the *Audit* within several more industries and organizations over the next few years as a way to provide some comparative yardsticks. We are also looking at what differences gender, age, and other demographic variables may make in the way people weigh various factors.

While the *Audit* is still in its infancy, we are encouraged because it seems to be useful in several ways:

• It can assist management to see how employees evaluate the ethics of the company. If there is high congruence between actual and desirable factors, that can be a source of celebration (and most organizations need things to celebrate these days!). If, on the other hand, there is a great amount of variance between actual and desired practices, the *Audit* serves to point the way for needed corrective initiatives.

- It can help provide a benchmark (and, later, a measure of the effectiveness) of initiatives designed to improve the climate of integrity. Often, it is difficult to demonstrate that changes have made a difference, and the *Audit* can offer an important measure from the point of view of stakeholders.
- It pinpoints within each of its five clusters (ethical habits, mission and structure, leaders and constituents, communications patterns, and problem-solving process) where the organization's strengths and weaknesses lie. In larger companies, it can indicate how consistently employees rate the climate for integrity between divisions or departments. In the case of a recent merger or acquisition (or even a pending one), it can point out how well the two cultures match up.

The *Audit* is only one among a growing number of tools and models that provide realistic and doable steps in assessing organizational integrity. In creating the *Audit*, we have learned that developing and maintaining organizational integrity isn't easy, *but it is possible*. The lessons from the *Audit* can encourage managers and employees, strengthening and enabling them to make, in Barbara Toffler's words, the "tough choices."

What this article is about: This article is a description of the Boeing Company's system for managing values. The authors also identify nine principles from the Boeing experience.

5–5 The Boeing Company: Managing Ethics and Values

Kirk O. Hanson and Manuel Velasquez

Kirk O. Hanson, Stanford Graduate School of Business
Manuel Velasquez, Santa Clara University

BACKGROUND

The Boeing Company today has a reputation as one of America's best-managed, most successful, and most ethical large corporations. In its most recent annual survey of corporate ratings, *Fortune* magazine reported that Boeing was considered by other executives to be one of America's three best-managed companies.

Founded in 1916, the Boeing Company has become one of the world's major aerospace firms. Its principal operations are distributed among three industry segments: Commercial Transportation Products and Service, Military Transportation Products and Related Systems, and Missiles and Space. Four divisional companies conduct most of the Company's operations: Boeing Commercial Airplane Company, Boeing Aerospace Company, Boeing Military Airplane Company, and Boeing Helicopter Company. In addition, a small portion of the Company's total activities are conducted in diversified areas including computer services, electronics, and operational support services. These activities are concentrated in two divisional companies, Boeing Electronics Company and Boeing Computer Services Company. Corporate Headquarters are located in Seattle, Washington, with other major operations in Wichita, Kansas, and Philadelphia, Pennsylvania.

To date the Company has built over 27,000 airplanes, including 5,000 advanced multiengine jets. Net earnings for the Company were $566 million in 1985 and $665 million in 1986. In 1986 about 67 percent of the company's total

SOURCE: *Corporate Ethics: A Prime Business Asset, A Report on Policy and Practice in Company Conduct* (New York: The Business Roundtable, February 1988), pp. 11–20.

revenues of $16.3 billion were from commercial operations and 33 percent from sales to the U.S. government.

Frank A. Shronz has been President and Chief Executive Officer of Boeing since 1986. T.A. Wilson is Chairman of the Board and was Chief Executive Officer from 1969 to 1986. Malcolm T. Stamper serves as Vice Chairman and was formerly President. Stamper also serves as chairman of the company's Ethics and Business Conduct Committee.

ORIGINS OF BOEING VALUES

Every discussion with company executives and managers about the origin of Boeing's strong values starts with an emphasis on the leadership of former chief executive William Allen. Having served as company lawyer for 20 years and as a director for 14 years, Allen was asked in September 1945 to resign from his law firm to take over Boeing as it shifted out of wartime production into peacetime activities. Allen is remembered as a man of great sincerity and honesty who "exuded integrity." On the eve of his acceptance of the company presidency, Allen jotted down a list of resolutions that reflected his personal values:

- Be considerate of my associates' views.
- Don't talk too much . . . let others talk.
- Don't be afraid to admit that you don't know.
- Don't get immersed in detail.
- Make contacts with other people in industry.
- Try to improve feeling around Seattle toward the company.
- Make a sincere effort to understand labor's viewpoint.
- Be definite; don't vacillate.
- Act—get things done—move forward.
- Develop a postwar future for Boeing.
- Try hard, but don't let obstacles get you down. Take things in stride.
- Above all else, be human—keep your sense of humor—learn to relax.
- Be just, straightforward; invite criticism and learn to take it.
- Be confident. Having once made the move, make the most of it. Bring to the task great enthusiasm, unlimited energy.
- Make Boeing even greater than it is.[1]

Under Allen, the Company acquired an enduring reputation as a highly ethical and reputable company whose employees shared his strong sense of values and integrity. To ensure continued attention to ethical standards, Allen formed an Ethics Committee on May 5, 1964, that would report to the Board and would be composed of members of the Board and upper management. In addition, he

---

[1]Harold Mansfield, *Vision,* 2nd ed. (New York: Madison Publishing Associates, 1986), pp. 250–51.

had an ethics policy drafted and put in place as an expression of the Company's commitment to high values. The "Allen Era" is remembered by employees to this day as a period of uncompromisingly high standards and *squeaky-clean-ethics*. "You never had a question where he stood," commented one senior executive, "he always emphasized that we would do the right thing."

Allen was succeeded by T. A. Wilson, an executive with an engineering background and similar high standards. Under Wilson the airplane company expanded until a disastrous collapse in 1969–1970 of both the military and commercial airplane markets. Within a few years, the company was forced to reduce its labor force from 150,000 employees to about 55,000.

Consumed with financial and operational problems as he struggled to keep the Company viable, Wilson was caught off-guard when in 1974 several Boeing employees were caught up in the foreign payments scandals that rocked the airline industry. Their actions directly violated Boeing standards. Wilson personally went before Congress where he openly and honestly admitted everything that the Boeing employees had done. Wilson accepted responsibility for their actions, apologized, and vowed to ensure that it would never happen again. In a powerful way, the embarrassing incident brought home to Wilson the extent to which the company had neglected to ensure continued adherence to the high standards of the Allen era. The lesson was clear: The proper procedures for marketing people had to be clearly formulated, adequately communicated, and effectively enforced. Upon returning to Seattle, Wilson launched a complete review and overhaul of all sales policies in the Boeing airplane companies, instituted training programs for all their sales people designed to communicate the Company's standards, and put auditing mechanisms in place to ensure their compliance.

REEVALUATION OF BOEING SYSTEMS FOR MANAGING VALUES

Boeing went well beyond the pattern of ethics codes and other relatively modest efforts of the late 1970s to address questions of corporate ethical behavior. Its staff began to work with top executives in 1981 to reassess and improve the overall ethics effort. Senior management began to research policies and techniques for managing values at other companies, management literature, and the attitudes of Boeing's executives.

These efforts led to a presentation to the Executive Management Group in April of 1984 at which the Vice President-Contracts and General Counsel discussed "Pressures on Your Ethics Barometer" of company employees with the senior management group. The presentation candidly assessed the competitive and internal organizational pressures that could lead to inadvertent or incidental ethics violations. He predicted that "some of you and your employees may become deeply involved in criminal or related investigations in the near future." The presentation directly addressed the need to distinguish between situations where "risk-taking" and "get-it-done" behavior, two strengths of the company, were appropriate and where they were inappropriate. The presentation also highlighted the responsibilities of the Executive Group to *manage* the company's ethical culture.

This presentation presaged a major incident which was about to break and, due to its timing, framed the task of managing values and ethical behavior in a way that strongly shaped future Boeing efforts.

THE BOEING COMPUTER SERVICES INCIDENT

Days after the "Ethics Barometer" speech, and 10 years after the overseas payments incidents, the company was again surprised by an incident of unethical behavior. On May 29, 1984, the Boeing Computer Services Company (BCS) was notified by the Department of the Interior that before submitting a proposal to construct a financial system for the National Park Service, BCS had access to government inside information that was not available to other bidders for the same project. This constituted a violation of federal procurement rules. The Federal Systems Group (FSG) of BCS was suspended from doing any business with any branch of the federal government. Because BCS FSG personnel worked on many of Boeing's government contracts, impact was felt across the total company.

The president of Boeing Computer Services acted quickly, going to the location of the incident and the customer's headquarters. The employees were identified, disciplinary action taken, and a pledge made to initiate a major program in business ethics. As a result, the suspension was lifted in 10 days.

The business ethics program in BCS was intended to ensure that the squeaky-clean ethics of the Allen era remained alive and strong. Boeing Computer Services revised its marketing procedures, established an ethics training program for its employees, set up a means for employees to report any ethics violations to an "Ethics Advisor," and established internal audit procedures to review all future government proposals.

A BCS employee was appointed to design the training program and to serve as Ethics Advisor who would be reached by phone to handle any questions or concerns BCS employees might later have about an ethics issue. Questions that the Ethics Advisor might not be able to handle were referred to the Secretary of the Corporate Ethics Committee.

The training program was based on BCS's *Business Conduct Guidelines,* which included sections dealing with "Marketing to the Public Sector." The training program consisted of training sessions for all BCS employees aimed at impressing upon employees the importance of adhering to ethical standards, particularly those standards found in the BCS *Business Conduct Guidelines.* The training sessions made use of a BCS-developed video tape that presented several cases illustrating potentially troublesome ethical dilemmas. During the two and one-half hour training sessions the tape was stopped several times and the approximately 30 employees in each session were encouraged to identify, discuss, and resolve the ethical dilemmas posed by the tape. A revised BCS *Business Conduct Guidelines* booklet was distributed during the sessions and its contents were briefly reviewed. The revised version included common questions and answers and concrete illustrations that provided practical guidance for employees. Employees were informed of the existence of the Ethics Advisor and given the phone number through which he could be reached.

The choices BCS made in designing the ethics training program were to have significant impact on the way ethics was approached at Boeing. Two characteristics were significant: The training was focused both on rules and on broad principles and the training was to be delivered by line managers and not by professional trainers. Line managers were chosen because it was felt that employees would take the program more seriously if it was led by their own supervisors, even if that manager was not a practiced trainer.

CORPORATEWIDE EFFORTS

The BCS suspension has been termed by some Boeing employees as "one of the best things that happened to the Company." Although the suspension was relatively short, it and the foreign-payments incidents combined to ensure that Boeing executives recognized the need to manage ethics actively. It also initiated a sequence of actions that have situated Boeing as one of the most forward-looking and skilled companies in the field of ethics management. Three specific lessons emerged from the suspension. The first was the importance of recognizing the special ethical demands of dealing with government agencies as distinct from those of dealing with commercial enterprises. The second was that those employees who deal with external parties are in ethically sensitive positions and require special attention if they are not to become future ethical liabilities. The third was that attending to ethical standards is not mere "window dressing" but can be critical to a company's very survival.

In the fall of 1984, the Vice President-Contracts and General Counsel returned to the Executive Management Group and used a unique technique for dramatizing the need for the ethics programs. He had the executives review a questionnaire consisting of some 20 "gray areas" issues in conflict of interest, gifts and gratuities, and other areas. The results indicated there was a wide range of views on the propriety of certain behavior and the interpretation of some policies. This in itself dispelled any further question of the need to deliberately define and communicate Boeing's values and standards. The support for the program from this point forward was extraordinary, and was critical in securing rapid implementation of the program.

The following year, 1985, the Company elected to capitalize on the experience of BCS by implementing a voluntary program to encourage similar programs in the other Boeing operating companies, both commercial and government-related. The program consisted of five elements.

First, in August 1985 the Company revised and brought together the Company's ethics policies into one booklet entitled *Business Conduct Guidelines*. The booklet covered five main areas of proper business conduct: marketing practices; offering of business courtesies; conflict of interest; acceptance of business courtesies; use of Company time, materials, equipment, and proprietary information. It consisted of a short informal summary of basic company policies in each of the five areas, followed by a series of questions and answers to clarify, interpret, and apply the principles identified. The booklet struck a balance between listing just a set of rules and identifying broad principles. At the end of the booklet, the formal policies were all reprinted in full together with other formal policies related to business ethics considerations such as political contributions, company records, antitrust compliance, and business expense reimbursement. Each division decided for itself how and to what levels to distribute the booklet. In BCS and in many of the government contracting divisions, all employees received it.

Second, in the Fall of 1985 various operating divisions of the Company began to conduct training programs in business ethics. The programs used the new booklet as their centerpiece, and most were largely modeled on the BCS training sessions. Each division assigned one of their employees to develop the training program. Most companies elected to adapt the two and one-half hour BCS program, customizing the BCS training video and cases to fit their own particular circumstances. Also in most companies, the first training sessions were given to the company's top managers, who then proceeded to give the training sessions to their subordinates, who then trained their own subordinates in descending levels. Again, each operating company decided for itself what type of training was appropriate and to whom it was delivered.

Third, again following in the footsteps of BCS, each of the operating companies typically assigned an employee—usually the person charged with designing the company's training program—to serve as the main "Ethics Advisor" for the company. In addition, some of the companies also organized a system of "Ethics Focal Points" to serve as ethics advisors to each *functional* area. Employees with any ethics concerns were encouraged to take them first to the person serving as their area's Ethics Focal Point. Should the issue require further attention, it would then be communicated to the operating company's Ethics Advisor. Should it still require further attention, it would then be sent to the Secretary of the Corporate Ethics Committee.

Fourth, in June 1986 Boeing added to its Corporate Headquarters the Office of Business Practices. The new office was to serve as a direct channel which could be contacted by any employee through the corporation who was concerned that misexpenditures of taxpayers' or shareholders' funds had occurred. As director of the office, the Company picked a 30+ year executive who had substantial experience in the government contracting process. The office was charged with determining the facts relating to all reports and concerns raised and keeping the caller advised on its findings. While the ethics advisors were to interpret the corporation's ethics policies and provide advice and clarifications before employees acted, the Office of Business Practices was to handle employee calls relating to perceived infractions. The office could be reached from any place in the country through a toll-free 800 number or through the Boeing Telephone Network.

Fifth, the Corporate Ethics Committee was renamed the "Ethics and Business

Conduct Committee," with the responsibility to oversee all the ethics programs of the Company as well as respond to any questions referred by the Ethics Advisor or the Corporate Office of Business Practices. The four-person committee consisted of Boeing's Vice Chairman, who chaired the committee, and the senior Corporate executives for the legal, controller, and human resources functions.

While Boeing has maintained the autonomy of its operating companies, there has been since 1985 a gradual tightening of the guidance given to the companies for the design of their ethics (now generally called "business practices") programs. The programs are still not dictated by the Corporate Director of Business Practices or by the Ethics and Business Conduct Committee, but increasingly more detailed guidelines and guidance have been given to the operating companies.

One of the forces leading to the standardization has been Boeing's signing of the Defense Industry Initiatives on Business Ethics and Conduct (DII) in June 1986. The Boeing ethics program was already well underway prior to the launching of the DII, but the reporting requirements of the DII highlighted the need to be able to show substantial progress in *all* government-related divisions. From the first, Boeing has gone beyond that requirement by implementing the business practices or ethics programs companywide, including in the two-thirds of Boeing which is commercial and not directly government-related.

In 1986 the training done by the operating companies was more extensive than in 1985, and in early 1987 Boeing Computer Services produced a new training program, making more extensive use of cases, which is being more rapidly copied by the other operating companies. This program is still principle- and value-oriented rather than rule- or policy-focused, is still designed to be delivered by line managers, and now focuses more directly on techniques for ethical decision making and on balancing the various principles which are articulated.

Also in 1987, the corporation revised and reintroduced the *Business Conduct Guidelines*. The booklet includes more rules and policies, but maintains a principle focus in the question-and-answer format. It is expected the operating companies will do a more extensive job of distributing the new booklet.

HOW DID ETHICS LEADERSHIP EMERGE?

The most important question for other companies is how did Boeing's management decide to take such an early and leadership role in ethics and how did corporate leaders get strong backing from relatively autonomous operating companies.

There are several answers, but the following stand out to us as key to understanding Boeing's experience:

- *Tradition of Strong Values and Ethics*. There is no doubt a history and tradition of a strong commitment to ethical management gives a company a strong base to build on. All of Boeing's leaders, but particularly Bill Allen, gave the corporation a tradition of integrity that makes every Boeing employee aware that the corporation has been committed to good business practices.

- *Strategic Importance of Integrity.* Because Boeing is so strongly situated in and dependent on the commercial airplane market, it has long been aware that it cannot afford, from a business standpoint, to have airline passengers or airline company executives consider it anything but highly ethical and well-managed.

- *Initiative of Staff.* At crucial moments in the past 10 years, Boeing has been blessed by staff who took extraordinary initiative to develop and implement an effective ethics program. The aggressive efforts of key top executives and staff far exceed that seen in most companies. The key executives and staff consistently identified effective strategies for ethics efforts.

- *The Boeing Computer Services Incident.* The BCS suspension certainly sensitized Boeing at an early date to the need for more aggressive action. It led the BCS president to set a pattern in BCS that other operating companies have learned from.

- *Effective Efforts to Win Divisional Support.* The 1984 "gray areas" questionnaire dramatized the need for all units of Boeing to take ethics and business practices seriously. Since that time, CEOs T. A. Wilson and Frank Shronz, and Boeing's group executives, have found a good balance between being directive and letting the operating companies do as they please. There is no doubt in the units that they must effectively manage their ethics and values.

PRINCIPLES FROM THE BOEING EXPERIENCE

It is now possible to enumerate several key principles at work in the Boeing experience:

1. *Every chief executive recreates the ethical culture of the corporation.* It is not enough for a CEO to assume the company is ethical or that employees know they are expected to act with integrity. Employees wait, even in the most ethical companies, for a new CEO to give clear signals on what balance of priorities is expected. At Boeing, the assumption that everyone knew they were to be ethical led to unpleasant surprises.

2. *Top management must secure the active support and commitment of divisional or operating company executives.* Management theory has emphasized the value of autonomous or lightly managed units. The CEO must find a way to win their support without destroying that autonomy and its benefits. Occasionally, a unique technique such as the "gray areas" questionnaire must be used to dramatize the need for active management efforts. Top management must also, at times, be willing to violate the autonomy of the divisions on critical issues.

3. *Ethics should be approached as a systems issue and not as a problem of "bad" individuals.* The April 1984 talk by the Vice President-Contracts de-

veloped a view that the ethics problem must be addressed by managing various systems in the company: the clear formulation of company policies, the communication of those policies; rewards and incentives given to employees; and resources available to employees for the resolution of difficult and "gray area" issues.

4. *Each succeeding level of management must make creation of an active ethics program and maintenance of ethical behavior a central part of management performance evaluation.* At Boeing, CEOs Wilson and Shronz have made it clear that ethical scandals in one's operation will result in severe reductions in bonus, and that ethics training and other program elements were being measured as a part of management performance.

5. *The corporation must identify an effective training strategy.* In the Boeing case, the focus on rules *and* principles, on line management delivery, and on the discussion of real cases was sophisticated and effective, and appropriate to the Boeing environment.

6. *Training and other program elements should be tailored to each division or operation.* There is no single structure in most companies that ensures success in ethics programs. Boeing let each division, commercial and military, design the program, within guidelines. This also helped create divisional buy-in and support.

7. *Ethics programs should be rolled out from the top down.* The effectiveness of Boeing efforts and the efforts in each operating company were greatly aided by the fact that top management and then the senior management of each division had addressed the issue and been through the program first. This also made each manager a more effective leader of the training sessions for his or her staff.

8. *Programs should have multiple upwards-communication channels.* Boeing has created no fewer than five resources available to the typical employee who has an ethics or business-conduct question. They can go to their own boss, their functional "ethics focal point," their divisional "ethics representative," the Corporate Director of Business Practices, or even the Corporate Committee on Ethics and Business Conduct. There should be no question in any employee's mind that the company wants these issues aired.

9. *Ethics programs are best implemented across the entire corporation.* The Boeing program is stronger because it is implemented in both commercial and government-related divisions. There should be no doubt among employees that the program reflects genuine corporate commitment and values.

What this article is about: The history of the well-known Johnson & Johnson credo is discussed, along with its current impact. The author identifies the critical factors of the credo's success.

5–6 *Johnson & Johnson's Credo*

Laura L. Nash

Laura L. Nash, Ph.D., Nash Associates
Cambridge, Massachusetts

DEVELOPMENT OF THE CREDO AND SUBSEQUENT CREDO PROGRAMS

There are only a few "movie star" elements in the world of business that are able to capture public affection and recognition in a way that anonymous executives and large corporate entities do not. A well-known brand-name product, for example, can carry this celebrity status. Catch a glimpse of one on a store shelf in unfamiliar surroundings, such as in a foreign country, and it is like seeing Katherine Hepburn at the table next to yours in a public restaurant. You instantly feel you know her and love her and that basically you are both of the same stuff.

If any business ethics code could be said to have obtained celebrity status in America, it would be the Johnson & Johnson Credo. During the two nightmare incidents of Tylenol poisonings and in the subsequent press reports of the product's stunning recovery, the J & J Credo was frequently referred to as *the* contributing factor in the company's exemplary behavior. The American public became familiar with its name and many people personally identified with the tragedy which the company was being forced to confront.

Despite the Credo's high profile and the company's obvious public-spiritedness during Tylenol, the actual content of Johnson & Johnson's Credo or how it has become a significant part of management's thinking have been unknown to the general public and even to executives in other large corporations.

SOURCE: The Business Roundtable, *Corporate Ethics: A Prime Business Asset, a Report on Policy and Practice in Company Conduct* (New York: The Business Roundtable, February 1988), pp. 77–104.

469

And yet the impact of the Credo is undeniable. Already over 40 years old, the Credo is the "glue" that holds Johnson & Johnson together. So strongly is it believed in by top management that, as chairman James Burke has often remarked, "The Credo is the unifying force for our corporation."

The following report outlines the development of this remarkable document, its content, and the many ways in which its force is evidenced at the company. The Johnson & Johnson Credo and the beliefs which it represents have evolved over a long period of time. Because the Credo was the product of an existing culture rather than an attempt to deliberately start a program in ethics, it takes more information to gain an understanding of how it works. The ways in which the Credo is communicated and given practical meaning in the company are at times less refined than in some other companies and certainly more difficult to describe coherently without sounding like a faith believer.

For the fact of the matter is that the Credo gains its effectiveness in a thousand different and informal ways as well as in a few deliberate programs. Thus this report is not so much a formulaic prescription for companies that want to improve their ethics as it is a study of how a strong ethical stand like that which marks the Credo can have a profound effect on the way in which an entire company thinks about its responsibilities.

Many aspects of Johnson & Johnson's experiences and programs are capable of generalization and are clearly relevant to other companies—even to those which aren't willing to wait the 40 years which have cemented the Credo's significance at J & J.

BRIEF DESCRIPTION OF THE COMPANY

Johnson & Johnson is a widely diversified international health-care corporation which has divided its operations into three major business segments: consumer, professional, and pharmaceutical. Founded in the late 1800s by three brothers, the company is perhaps best known for its original businesses in baby and sterile bandage products. Today the company operates over 160 businesses in over 50 countries. Its products range from baby powder to toothbrushes, pain relievers to intraocular lenses.

With 1986 sales totalling over $7 billion and net earnings and earnings per share increasing 15.6 percent and 18.5 percent, respectively, before a one-time charge, the company has shown consistently strong growth over the long term (average compound sales growth over the past 100 years: 11.6 percent). Before its one-time write-off, return on stockholders' equity rose 21.6 percent in 1986.

Both the outstanding performance and the one-time charge against earnings are typical of Johnson & Johnson. The write-offs included $140 million in costs associated with management's decision to withdraw and no longer manufacture consumer capsule products after a second case of criminal tampering with Tylenol. This action reflects management's strong emphasis both on service to the consumer and to the stockholder over the long term. By Forbes's estimate, the 1986 EPS of 3.98 (before extraordinary charges) should jump to 4.57 in 1987. The 1986 profit on sales would have been a record 10.1 percent without the one-time charges. In corporate president David Clare's opinion, it is Johnson & Johnson's high PE which benefits the stockholders and provides validation for the Credo.

The corporate headquarters, located next to the original J & J site in New Brunswick, New Jersey, is but a small part of an organization which is separated from its home in both distance and culture. So autonomous are the many J & J companies that Brazilians will regard Johnson & Johnson as a Brazilian corporation, and many Britishers assume it began in the United Kingdom.

Each company is headed by its own president (called a managing director in most overseas locations), who has his or her own board of senior managers to help set policy in that business or businesses. Each president reports directly or through a Company Group Chairman to the powerful Executive Committee. Company presidents, however, are usually left very much on their own in terms of the way in which they will manage their particular company. The Executive Committee, located in "the tower" of the new corporate headquarters building, is composed entirely of insiders with long-term operating experience at Johnson & Johnson. Because most senior managers are moved frequently and end up having headed many different J & J businesses, there is less distinction by function within the committee itself than in most large corporations.

THE JOHNSON & JOHNSON CULTURE

One cannot begin to understand the contents and lastingness of the J & J Credo without first looking at the business culture in which it was born and continues to thrive. There are two major factors influencing the Johnson & Johnson way of doing business, both of which are extremely powerful. The first is the Credo. The second is the almost fanatical emphasis on decentralization which exists throughout the company.

Johnson & Johnson's unique form of decentralization places great emphasis on individual autonomy and initiative. It is nothing to hear that the corporation has decided to enter a new market by giving a company president no more direction than "to set up a new business"—no specification of product or market provided.

Some programs such as employee safety are mandated by the executive committee but corporate programs as widely varied as quality improvement or employee health are offered as services rather than imposed from the top. Indeed, recent attempts to respond to end-user needs by centralizing the marketing of certain products (such as the hospital services businesses) are taking years to gain broad acceptance by the managing directors and company presidents.

The Credo itself, however, is an important exception to decentralization. Says

James Burke, "The Credo is our common denominator. It guides us in everything we do. It represents an attempt to codify what we can all agree upon since we have highly independent managers."

If at first glance decentralization and the Credo appear to be contradictory notions, it is nevertheless important to keep the two simultaneously in mind in trying to understand how this company approaches its business. If you just looked at the pervasive influence of the Credo and other centralized control methods such as financial auditing, you would think that the company was highly autocratic. On the contrary, in operation the Credo supports decentralization. It depends on personal commitment and great personal autonomy in deciding what is the best way to proceed. These are the very qualities which decentralization and a loosely structured organization are meant to encourage.

Decentralization also implies certain ethical values which are fundamental to the Credo. The greatest of these is trust: trust in an individual manager's ability to make the right decisions from both a business and a moral point of view. This same focus on trust is emphasized in the Credo's strong protectiveness over the J & J brand franchises. No policy or decision should be allowed to undermine the consumer's trust in the company.

Such concerns, which are defined in the tenets of the Credo, are not at all hostile to the principles of decentralization if—and it is an important provision— managers are consistently committed to the values which the Credo implies. Some of these are inherent to decentralization, but building that kind of consistency can call for occasional autocracy. On those infrequent occasions when "the best way" is not obvious to everyone, Johnson & Johnson's top management has no hesitation in determining the "spirit of the Credo" for the company. To understand how the Credo gains its strength, one has to accept that the Credo is both an autocratic force and a means of furthering decentralization.

Top management acknowledged the distinctive relationship between the Credo and decentralization in its recent Statement of Strategic Direction. According to David Collins, Vice Chairman of the Corporation and formerly responsible for McNeil Consumer Products Company at the time of the first Tylenol crisis, this statement summarizes *how* the company will succeed in the future based on three distinctive factors of its success in the past.

These are:

- Managing with a view to the long term.
- Decentralization.
- The Credo.

1945: PUBLICATION OF THE FIRST CREDO

This constant tension between decentralized power and centralized control over the basic *way* of doing business harks back to the early days of the company. Johnson & Johnson's first business in baby powder and wound dressings placed a high emphasis on product quality and brand reliability. In wound dressings

Our Credo

- We believe our first responsibility is to the doctors, nurses, and patients, to mothers and all others who use our products and services.
- In meeting their needs, everything we do must be of high quality.
- We must constantly strive to reduce our costs in order to maintain reasonable prices.
- Customers' orders must be serviced promptly and accurately.
- Our suppliers and distributors must have an opportunity to make a fair profit.
- We are responsible to our employees, the men and women who work with us throughout the world.
- Everyone must be considered as an individual.
- We must respect their dignity and recognize their merit. They must have a sense of security in their jobs.
- Compensation must be fair and adequate, and working conditions clean, orderly, and safe.
- Employees must feel free to make suggestions and complaints.
- There must be equal opportunity for employment, development, and advancement for those qualified.
- We must provide competent management, and their actions must be just and ethical.
- We are responsible to the communities in which we live and work and to the world community as well.
- We must be good citizens—support good works and charities and bear our fair share of taxes.
- We must encourage civic improvements and better health and education.
- We must maintain in good order the property we are privileged to use, protecting the environment and natural resources.
- Our final responsibility is to our stockholders.
- Business must make a sound profit.
- We must experiment with new ideas.
- Research must be carried on, innovative programs developed, and mistakes paid for.
- New equipment must be purchased, new facilities provided, and new products launched.
- Reserves must be created to provide for adverse times.
- When we operate according to these principles, the stockholders should realize a fair return.

especially, the provision of a reliable sterile product, itself the first practical technological response to new theories of antiseptic treatment of wounds, established the company's reputation among medical people and led to increasing business success.

When General Robert Wood Johnson, the son of the founder with a 22-year stint at the company under his belt, became head of the corporation in 1932, he decided that the corporation was failing to thrive under heavy centralization. It had become inefficient and out of touch with its markets. Under "the General's" direction, the businesses were broken up into independently operating companies, and the company diversified both in terms of product and geography.

The company's subsequent growth and success confirmed Johnson's conviction that in most business circumstances "two plants, like two heads, often worked better than one" [Source, *Or Forfeit Freedom*, p. 250]. So strong was this ethos that Johnson wrote an article for Colliers entitled "Break It Up," which ran counter to then-current wisdom of management science favoring centralization to achieve economies of scale. His attitudes toward employee treatment, which included supporting proposals for a minimum wage, were equally revolutionary at the time, and placed him at odds with the industry as a whole (he was even thrown out of the National Manufacturers Association).

In his book, *Or Forfeit Freedom*, the General outlines a list of general principles for business success. They began as follows: "Accept attainment of a decent living for all as the fundamental goal of business." He dedicated the work "to those men and women who have worked with me through the years. From them I have learned the lesson that business must and can do its work for the good of humanity."

Taken together, General Johnson's belief in fair employee treatment, decentralization, and product quality formed the backbone of principles which are formalized in the Credo. In 1944–45 he published these ideas in a single document, entitled "An Industrial Credo" for the enlightenment of other business people in the trade.

Richard B. Sellars, chairman of Johnson & Johnson in the 1970s, points out that although the General probably did not author the precise words of the Credo, the philosophy was his own, and that he was "really attempting to define for his associates and for the business community and for his peers some of the things he felt very seriously about."

Four central responsibilities were identified in the Credo, to which a fifth, the community, was added in 1947. A full text of the current Johnson & Johnson Credo appears in the boxed illustration. The document is remarkably succinct and somewhat surprising in comparison to most ethics codes. Whereas most codes state a set of rules, "Our Credo" states a set of relationships, four to be exact:

1. Customers.
2. Employees.
3. Communities in which they work and live.
4. Stockholders.

As a philosophical tome or a minisummation of company torts and contracts, the Credo fails miserably. Unlike most codes, it does not even include the word "honesty." Other ethical principles such as fairness or justice appear haphazardly in several places.

And yet in this author's opinion, the Credo is an extremely powerful document for several reasons. First and foremost, *the Credo is at all times tied in to the regular concerns of business management:* product choice, delivery times, costs, employee compensation, corporate taxes, maintenance of company property, research and innovation, new equipment, and financial reserves. Equally important, profit is not a dirty word. The Credo puts forth a world view in which profit is obtainable through just and ethical behavior.

In commenting on the Credo's contents, John Heldrich, a member of the executive committee, pointed out this constant integration of business and ethical concerns: "There's no separation in the responsibility we have to the four key components of the Credo. Our philosophy is that if we do them all well, the stockholders (the last on the list) will benefit."

One indication of the Credo's ongoing importance at Johnson & Johnson is the changes in text which have occurred over the years. Though the Credo is still true to the General's basic tenets, it has by no means been a one-shot effort. In 1948 the title was changed simply to "Our Credo," which it remains today. Later in the 1950s Jim Burke was among those who worked closely with the General to modernize and refine the document's wording so that it was better adapted to in-house use. Among the changes made at that time was the substitution of the words "of highest quality" for the former "good quality" in reference to products. "Make them better at lower cost" was changed to "reduce the cost of these products." During the fifties and sixties there were no distinct programs about the Credo, perhaps in part because the General was still actively running the company. In 1972 the Credo was the theme for the J & J annual report. During that same year a series of 10 Credo dinner meetings, headed by then-chairman Philip B. Hoffmann, was conducted for more than 4,000 management employees to reinforce these beliefs.

1975: THE CREDO CHALLENGE MEETINGS

The next major step in the Credo's evolving programs occurred in 1975 when then-president James Burke decided to hold a series of meetings with top management to test the validity of the document. The Credo, now over 30 years old, was still significant to top management, but was it really as meaningful a statement of responsibility for all managers, as it had once been intended to be?

Origins

Several events led up to Burke's asking this question at this particular time. First of all, there was the general emphasis on corporate misconduct by the American public. These were the years when many American companies were facing investigations for improper political payments and corporate ethics codes were being proposed in many a board room. When the idea of an ethics code was discussed at Johnson & Johnson, top management saw no need. The company already had its Credo, and any kind of rulebook code would be unnecessary.

Nevertheless, a few incidents were discovered during this period which, though minor, caused top management to wonder whether the Credo was being supported as automatically as they all assumed. An improper payments scheme was uncovered in a few of the foreign operations. It had been going on for several years and though the sums of money were relatively trivial, they had nevertheless involved falsifying records in order "to protect the Company." James Burke summed up his own reactions to these incidents as follows:

> We got some humility. None of us felt these incidents were indicative of the overall ethics of the Company, but clearly our view of ourselves as lily-white had to be revised.

But the Credo Challenge Meetings were not simply a housecleaning effort after the discovery of a few dust bunnies. Jim Burke's own belief in the document was singularly strong, and he was personally bothered to think that it might lose visibility and meaning in the company over time. Ever since he had become president, one of the company's top industrial relations executives whom Burke highly respected had been pushing him about the same issue. This man argued that even though top management fervently believed in the Credo, little was being done to actively promote it throughout the company.

Program Design

Given his own personal commitment to the document and his previous work with the General, Burke was quite determined to pursue the matter further. However, he did not like the idea of simply imposing the document top-down. When one manager suggested that the Credo be published once a week for a year in the company newsletter, Burke rejected the idea as "too pompous." When someone else suggested that each senior manager be allowed to sit in on one meeting of the executive committee in order to get a feel for the values which drove their decision making, Burke felt it would be "too confusing." The extreme emphasis on give and take, the evolution of policy over time, and the lack of rigid territorial boundaries in the executive committee's comments would fail to provide any meaningful leadership to the operating managers.

Burke decided instead to hold a series of "discussions" with top managers about the validity of the Credo in their own business climate. The idea itself was in true J & J style. They would start with the one unifying standard the company had, the Credo, and then turn over to the operating managers the responsibility for understanding the document. Out of this notion developed the Credo Challenge Meetings.

The suggestion to hold the meetings among the top management groups met with resistance. Burke recalls the strong reservations of Richard Sellars, then chairman and CEO. Sellars felt that neither Burke nor anyone else had the right to challenge the Credo. Its authority was above any individual in the organization. Moreover, what if the presidents really did reject the document? That was the only serious fight he and Burke ever had. Burke, however, continued to press for the meetings, arguing that the Credo could never be dictated, that it needed more visibility, and that if it really wasn't meaningful to the thousand-plus managers in top positions around the world, the document was a farce. Better to take it off the walls than have it stand for hypocrisy.

The Credo Challenge Meetings took place over more than three years, beginning in 1975, with a total of over 1,200 managers attending. Company Group Chairmen and their immediate reports, the company presidents and managing directors (overseas equivalent to a company president), gathered together in groups of 25 or less to discuss the Credo over a two-day period. Either James Burke or David Clare presided.

They began by asserting their own belief in the Credo and their insistence that the company have a basic philosophy that was reflective of the real beliefs and needs of the corporation. They read through the document, discussing their own interpretation of individual points in it either by telling war stories or simply explaining the words in more detail. Then they turned the discussion over to the other managers.

Three challenges were issued: Was the Credo still applicable in whole or in part? Were there any changes which should be made? And most importantly, how should it be implemented in the management of Johnson & Johnson companies?

Burke and Clare continually emphasized their determination to take a hard look at the Credo. The mere fact that they were holding these meetings (very few centralized meetings are held) indicated their seriousness, and equally important to the final impact of the process, they encouraged an open discussion. This may have been easier to achieve in the J & J culture, but the emphasis on openness cannot be taken for granted. Richard Sellars, for example, had to remove himself from these meetings. In his words, he "breathed too heavily on the process." Burke confirmed: "Dick was not autocratic about many things, but he was on this one thing."

Burke helped encourage open discussion by observing at the outset of the meeting that the Credo was hanging in J & J offices around the world, but if the people in that group were not committed to it, it was "an act of pretension and should be ripped off the walls."

Results

What resulted was, in Burke's words, "A turn-on. A genuine happening." As managers struggled with the issues of the Credo, two things became clear:

1. Balancing all the responsibilities outlined in the Credo was very difficult and required discussion.
2. Most managers were intensely committed to the tenets of the Credo.

While managers came into the meetings with their own beliefs and did not leave with a totally new set of beliefs, the meetings seemed to spark a greater intensity of commitment and exploration.

One of the most effective aspects of the Credo Challenge Meetings, according to company group chairman James Utaski, was the voice of collective experience.

When, for example, some managers questioned whether it was really the case that top management would not allow stock price to override other considerations of the Credo, many others told of specific experiences which they had had where this was clearly the case. The general consensus was that though the values were "somewhat idealistic," they were not far off from reality.

Another company president confirmed this opinion:

> *At the Credo challenge meetings you discover, listening to your peers, that it {the Credo} has crept into everyone's value system. Finding that out is really beneficial. You come away with a healthy respect for the document and what it says, and you pass that on in your own companies.*

I found that this observation held true repeatedly in my own interviews, that the meetings brought the Credo principles out of the closet, as it were, so that managers further down in the organization felt as comfortable about referring to the Credo or its principles as did those at the top of the organization.

Carl Spalding, now president of the Dental Care unit, recalled his Credo Challenge Meeting with mixed emotions. At the time of these discussions he was head of the largest South African J & J company. Many of those in attendance seriously questioned whether J & J was indeed being fair in its operations there. He was able to discuss this issue in detail before the group and personally welcomed the opportunity—despite his personal discomfort—of telling in his own words why he felt that he and the company were acting responsibly.

Burke and Clare both feel that the challenge meetings demonstrated that they had in the Credo a set of guiding principles which were even more powerful than they'd imagined.

Such affirmation by the already-believers may sound self-deluding to an outsider, but it is possible to get a good sense of what they are referring to by viewing the edited video tapes of some of the meetings. [Author's note: I have also looked at some unedited tapes, and feel that the edited versions are true to the general tone of what went out.] These are available from Johnson & Johnson and are quite powerful in demonstrating the conviction in the Credo which the Challenge Meetings elicited. A comment from those meetings gives a flavor for the kind of insight and discussion which occurred. Discussing profit in relation to the other responsibilities of the Credo, one manager said:

> *We are playing with four white balls, and the fifth is red (referring to the Credo's fifth responsibility which is to shareholders). Now everyone knows better than to drop the red one, but no one knows what to do with the white ones.*

Other managers countered this cynicism by suggesting that the question should be viewed the other way round: the issue was not profit in order to secure these other things (such as high quality or decent wage for all employees), but rather the issue was profit not at the expense of these things. Burke pointed out that the cynicism was not new, that there were always new generations at J & J and that they always challenged the Credo.

A general conclusion of the meetings and references to the Credo in my interviews with J & J managers is that most people in top management feel that the Credo is a driving, motivating force over time, that it is possible to integrate all five (now combined to four) principles over time, and that it has no meaning unless it is being lived.

The last point is particularly significant. Most managers emphasized that the Credo has an indirect but nevertheless powerful influence on their decision making and behavior. It is not that they constantly refer to it by pulling out the document whenever they have an important decision to make. Rather, it stands for values that are being lived out every day and that are important to maintain in the future.

This view is both a matter of personal belief and business sense. David Collins made this point emphatically when he stressed that the Credo does not describe "an eleemosynary organization" but rather a way of doing *business*. As Burke concluded when asked why busy executives should bother with a Credo, "It tells us what our business is about."

FOLLOW-UPS TO THE CREDO CHALLENGE MEETINGS

There have been two major follow-ups on the Credo Challenge Meetings, which are still held twice a year for new top managers.

Company Challenge Meetings

Company presidents are encouraged to hold their own Credo Challenge Meetings with their own top management groups. A kit has been provided for this purpose, which includes very general guidelines for the discussion (including the original challenge questions).

The fact that many of the presidents have held these sessions (in the J & J culture no manager would be ordered to hold them) is an indication of how useful they have felt the discussions to be and how committed they themselves are to the Credo. As one company president remarked to me:

> You feel pretty awkward getting up in front of your people and saying, "Now I'm going to read through the Credo." But when you've seen Jim Burke do it and how it inspires you, well you just go ahead.

Revision of the Credo

A second major development of the Credo discussions was another revision of the Credo itself. This process involved discussion in the executive committee and much personal commitment from the top two officers of the company. Jim

Burke estimates that he spent at least 50 to 60 hours on the wording of the revisions, some of which are major changes in format, while others are simply a matter of fine-tuning the document to the current business environment.

Whereas the original Credo had five paragraphs, of which numbers two and three distinguished between the company's responsibility to management and to employees, the updated version combines these. Now it simply speaks of the corporation's responsibility "to our employees," meaning management and hourly employees alike. Product quality was again redefined; it now reads "of high (rather than highest) quality" in acknowledgment that the company was not intending to market only the highest cost products in the uppermost market segments. There were also some deletions, the most controversial being the phrase, "with God's grace," while others were added. For example, responsibility for a working environment that is healthy and safe as well as clean was spelled out, while responsibility to the environment and natural resources was added to the definition of good community citizenship.

Most of these changes could be said to reflect major social issues in American society as a whole during the late 1970s, but two were purely a result of the corporate worldview: "products" was changed to "products and services," and the phrase "our dealers must make a profit" was altered to read "our suppliers and distributors must have an opportunity to make a fair profit." The change reflects an insistence by many managers that the original wording was unrealistic in that no one could guarantee a profit for another.

Such revisions may seem minor to outsiders, but they are important reflections of the significant seriousness with which J & J managers regard the Credo: this is not a document intended for hypocrites. The words cannot be empty.

Introduction of the Revised Credo

In 1979 Burke's Credo revisions were completed and managers from the 150 J & J companies were brought together at a Worldwide Managers Meeting in New York City. (As one of the few times in which top managers are brought together, these sessions often signal the most important issues facing the company.) The centerpiece of this particular session was the new Credo. Jim Burke described the new document within the context of the completed Credo Challenge Meetings. He called it "a revitalized Credo—a statement of purpose that everyone now not only understands, but has had the change to contribute to."

Burke's intention to have everyone own a piece of the Credo is reinforced by the form of the document itself, which was somewhat simplified in the last revision. Deliberately generalized to describe "what everyone can live with," it continues to leave ambiguous how exactly to implement its tenets. Burke feels that any attempt to supply the answers would destroy the very process which gives the Credo its strength—the commitment and discretion of individual managers to see that it is lived out.

1986–1987: THE CREDO SURVEY

The most recent generation of Credo activity at Johnson & Johnson has been the Credo Survey, which began in 1986 and is just being conducted overseas as of this writing. The survey is a 240-item confidential questionnaire about the company's Credo performance. It is organized around the four principle responsibilities defined in the Credo, and asks employees to rate how well their company, their company's management, and their immediate supervisors are meeting specific aspects of the Credo.

Origins

In the words of Peter Dinella, who heads the program, the idea of conducting such a survey was a natural evolution in the life of the Credo. The Challenge Meetings had been designed primarily as a way of testing the Credo's relevance among the top echelon of managers at the company. Once their commitment was established, it was only a matter of time before they asked all employees, "How are we doing?"

Jim Burke traces the origins of the survey back to the "Live for Life" program, an employee wellness effort which began 10 years ago. He wanted to get a sense of whether employees felt that this and other J & J efforts were really carrying out management's responsibility to employees. On the other hand, he did not like standard attitude surveys, which he felt were too big brotherish in their own way. When it was suggested that employee responsibility be expanded to a general survey of Credo performance, Burke became enthusiastic. He introduced the Credo Survey at the company's 1985 Worldwide Management Meeting, just as he had presented the revised version of the Credo four years earlier. As Peter Dinella remarked, the Credo is such a part of the fabric at J & J that no one really required any rationale for a survey about it even though nothing of this sort had ever been conducted previously at the company. (Confidentiality—who sees the results—was really the only question managers raised to Dinella when he first introduced the program at meetings around the world.)

Design

The survey program itself has been designed in the spirit of the Credo and the J & J culture. All Johnson & Johnson employees, from Jim Burke to the floor sweeper at the smallest plant, are sent a questionnaire. The results are tabulated in Dinella's office and kept strictly confidential.

Each company president or corporate department head receives the results for his or her own company only, along with the figures for the corporation as a whole. It is then the responsibility of these managers to present the results to their own management boards and develop an appropriate response to the information thus obtained.

The program is deliberately intended to encourage participation at the company management and employee level, and there is even a training video developed by the Credo survey program to help managers in this task. According to one manager with whom I spoke, the feedback meetings have had more interaction than most company discussions, and people are taking the survey results quite seriously. A second round of questionnaires must be distributed no sooner than 12 and no later than 24 months after the first survey has been conducted. While the company results will eventually be reviewed once a year by the executive committee (and thus by a company president's direct boss), in the short term only the company president and the tabulator knows the results. According to Peter Dinella, if a group chairman calls and asks him for a specific company's results, he is told to call the company president directly for the information. Reports Dinella, "I haven't received many calls recently after the first few refusals."

The extremely decentralized execution of the survey mirrors its purpose, which is not to punish managers with relatively poor Credo performance, but rather to serve as a resource for the managers themselves to align various aspects of their companies more closely with the Credo. The questions are highly specific and range from how much management strives to reduce costs to one's personal sense of job satisfaction. The document is heavily weighted toward the second responsibility in the Credo, which is toward employees. This is partly due to its being an employee (as opposed to say a customer) survey, and partly due to the fact that for a long time Jim Burke had the sense that employee responsibility was probably the weakest area of Credo performance for the company. This orientation also reflects the history of the company culture, and the General's pioneering policies on employee welfare. In fact, when Dinella held initial meetings with various managers to discuss the potential design of the survey, there was great unanimity to weight the questions toward the second paragraph of the Credo.

Results and Evaluation

The overall results for the domestic companies confirmed this suspicion. In the areas of customer, community, and stockholder responsibilities, the companies received on average a "very good or good" from between 72 percent and 82 percent of the employees. Employee responsibility was assumed to be good or very good by about 60 percent.

The results of the survey within the domestic companies have been very interesting. According to Dinella, at the very least, no one has complained that the profile of his or her company has been inaccurate. In many cases the feedback has been that the survey has proved to be a tremendous source of information. Not only does the survey provide feedback on performance, perhaps more importantly it has offered a way of encouraging further questioning and understanding of the Credo throughout the organization.

The survey program has sparked an overt discussion between management and employees on topics which are often taboo in the day-to-day operations of a large organization. At one company, for instance, there was some problem with the ratings on management trust. The president wanted to pursue this, so he ran a small blurb at the back of the company newsletter soliciting anonymous comments about what trust meant at J & J. The response was enormous and has already led to several changes in employee communications. For example, the company goals are now communicated more frequently and further down the line than before.

At another company, where management received unsatisfactory ratings on open communications and several other aspects of employee relations, the president decided that the next time a problem came up for management, the very first discussion of it would occur in front of the line supervisors and some employees. This was a dramatic shift toward participatory decision making without any directive from on high. This same company recently ran its second round of the survey and showed significant improvement in the areas which had been of concern.

Unfortunately for this report, the international companies have not yet completed the first round of surveys. How Dinella and top management deal with the differences in cultural values which will inevitably be revealed should provide a fascinating insight to the ethics of a diversified multinational company. At this point, Dinella can only say that he will be looking for the commonalities of viewpoint and performance first, and he predicts that the opening of the Credo—that the customer comes first—will have the greatest consistency worldwide.

However, he has found one commonality already in the survey process itself: The exercise serves to stimulate people's awareness of their own commitment to the Credo. One president in the United Kingdom, for example, had initially been quite negative at the start of the survey process. He recently called Dinella to report that the questionnaire process was nearly completed and that he had been surprised to discover that his employees were intensely committed to filling out the questionnaire, that they had done so with "purpose, intent, and good will."

THE IMPACT OF THE CREDO TODAY

The Credo is a living document at the company today. It is given high visibility through a variety of communication channels. You see it constantly appearing in company publications and in-house policy statements.

The Statement of Strategic Directions refers to the Credo in its first line along with the philosophy of decentralized management and emphasis on long-term growth.

The company recruiting brochure for college graduates and MBAs, entitled

"The Johnson & Johnson Way," begins as follows: "The Johnson & Johnson Credo—a statement of corporate responsibility—spells it out. . . . Everything we do must be of high quality. And whether it is in manufacturing a product or in developing human resources, quality is the Johnson & Johnson way." The Credo is printed in toto on the back cover.

In the annual report Burke and Clare make regular mention of the Credo, their obligation and intention to see that its principles are upheld, and cite specific instances of that when they are material to the company's performance (as in the second Tylenol incident in 1986).

In short, as a symbol of company identity and of the commitments of the people in it, the Credo is an extremely effective document. (Recently, other companies, such as Campbell's Soup, have modeled their own statements of principles after the J & J Credo contents and format.)

In my own experience, I found copies of the document everywhere, from the great bronze reproduction of it in the lobby of Old Kilmer House (the previous headquarters of the company) to the brochures produced by various departments in the company.

But the Credo is not just a PR document for outsiders. Most of all, the Credo is an employees' document. I was particularly struck by the obvious pride and pleasure which J & J people take in the document itself. Like the colorful felt college banners which grace so many undergrad and alumni's walls, you will find copies of the Credo framed and unframed in many employees' offices.

For example, I was talking to Jack Begley, head of internal auditing, and he mentioned that the Credo had been translated into many languages for the international companies. I expressed mild interest over this piece of information. Instantly I found myself swept out the door and into the main office. Among a maze of modular cubicles which housed the auditors, Jack was dodging from desk to desk, ripping Credos off the walls and promising to return them after he'd make a copy for me. Everyone tolerantly pointed him to "John" or "Rosa's" cubicle for yet another foreign language Credo. The sense of team spirit in this room about the Credo itself was incredible. For these employees, the Credo was clearly a symbol of their own business achievement and company identity. Similarly, when James Burke accepted the Advertising Council's Award of the Year he took obvious pride in reviewing the Credo and the set of responsibilities which it outlines, and attributed the success of his company to its influence.

THE ROLE OF TOP MANAGEMENT IN MAKING THE CREDO A LIVING DOCUMENT

Obviously it takes more than PR, a discussion group, or a survey—however good—to made a document like the Credo meaningful in a company as large and diverse as Johnson & Johnson. One cannot understand how the tenets of the Credo are given credibility at the company without looking at the role which Chairman and CEO James Burke and President David Clare play in the process.

There is no doubt that the impact of the Johnson & Johnson Credo depends heavily on the two top officers of the company. Even though the culture itself has been shaped by the General's tenets for over 40 years and the top officers are a product of that culture, it is Burke's and Clare's visible commitment to the Credo which managers mentioned most frequently in our interviews. They are reminded of this commitment continually in formal speeches, in the course of executive committee meetings, and of course in the Credo programs mentioned in this report.

In talking about the Credo with Jim Burke and David Clare, their personal impact becomes clear immediately. Sincerity is as impossible an emotion to measure as altruism, but surely the word "genuineness" would have to be applied to these leaders when they discuss the Credo. They both grew up with the Credo, and as Burke says, "The more I live with it, the more impressed I become with its power."

Although Burke has a strong Jesuit education and wryly states that his course in Thomistic philosophy at Holy Cross was one of the best experiences in his college education, his orientation toward the Credo is decidedly not pop-philosophical. He avoids three syllable abstractions and keeps the Credo grounded in actions. As he put it, ethics is really not the issue. The Credo is very simple in terms of ethics, it is the common denominator which everyone can believe in. When asked whether he thought the Credo represented an unusually high ethical standard of business conduct, Burke disagreed. He felt that it was an excellent standard, but he also felt that it described accurately the practical values of this society. Moreover, in recalling his own MBA classmates at Harvard Business School, Burke felt that most business leaders of his generation agreed with the tenets of the Credo. He remembers picking out in his own mind who would become the most successful members of his unusually successful class (MBA '49), "In every case," he recalls, "I admired their ethics."

The real issue, says Burke, is not ethics. It is trust.

David Clare agrees: "When a consumer buys a box of BAND-AID brand adhesive bandages, he or she trusts that it will be the same quality as the last box, and the box before that. Our employees should be able to trust that we will provide safe working conditions and fair treatment. Without trust, we can't be a good business."

Trust is also at the heart of Burke's and Clare's management style and how they enforce the Credo. In most instances managers are trusted—and expected—to figure out for themselves what is the right way of doing business.

In Burke's opinion, everyone has to live and work from his or her own values. He feels that a highly detailed set of rules would not be as effective as the General's tenets in ensuring commitment to basic company responsibilities. "The law libraries are full of texts about the codification of laws. As soon as you make a rule, people argue about it. What is so powerful about the Credo is that the document is so simple. You have to decide what is the right course in a specific instance."

There are, however, real arguments over how managers execute these responsibilities. To quote Clarke, "Like most whitewater situations, there is a lot of learning in the turmoil."

This is not, however, an open-ended invitation to moral relativism. Burke feels that, no matter how international, the company has a right to expect certain overall responsibilities from all its managers. The Credo offers managers the opportunity to reflect on these responsibilities as well as what they personally believe in, and to make a commitment to both. However, when an issue is singularly controversial, Burke and Clare will assume direct responsibility and control over deciding what is the true spirit of the Credo.

Certain Credo issues are considered sacrosanct. Safety is one, quality control another. Financial reporting, certainly. As an example of how far ethics and Credo will invite an extraordinary breach of the company's cultural norms, Vice Chairman David Collins told me of the time when a quality assurance auditor uncovered a leakage at one of the company plants in Latin America. She was not reassured that there would be immediate recognition of the problem by the manager responsible, and so she went directly to Dave, who headed the Latin American division at that time. He agreed that it was an emergency situation, and intervened at once. He also backed the auditor when her boss objected that she should have gone through all the channels for a disputed audit first. He stressed how extraordinary the occurrence was. "Ordinarily," he explained, "if you try to go above your boss to a company president or group chairman and there is no emergency, you get your head served to you by both people."

In Collins' mind, the episode illustrated that people know that if an ethical issue is involved they will be supported for working against plan.

It does sometime happen, however, that Burke and Clare will be challenged by their own team on a Credo issue. One manager, for example, told of the time he approached Clare on a promotion case. He felt that to promote someone above someone else in line was against the Credo. Clare's response was to agree and to add jokingly, "Don't forget to write your resignation before you go home."

In most cases, however, there is more information sharing and give and take than there is autocratic control. As one manager commented, Burke and Clare are pivotal in making the Credo meaningful in the company, but they do not give the Credo its high impact in a commanding way. Rather, they take a rational approach. They'll review its history; they'll discuss what it actually means. In this manager's words, "They're not just doing a sell job."

Take, for example, product quality. The company believes in high quality and this is explicitly stated in the Credo. In Burke's words, if there are 2 percent defects in a given company, the executive committee will ask the product manager what is going wrong. They'll give the product manager a chance to explain; they'll also summarize their own position. In most cases, the manager will initiate the corrections—he or she will spend more money than was allocated in the plan or contact the quality assurance department for help on the problem. "But the overriding value," according to Burke, "is that we all make sure that you (the consumer) can trust that we are going to deliver on what we say, package by package."

GENERAL COMPLIANCE AND VIOLATION PROCEDURES

To give a document teeth, there must be some monitoring of performance against its stated objectives. At the outset of the Credo Challenge Meetings, Jim Burke wondered aloud whether managers out in the 150 companies and in the company's functional departments really believed in the Credo and were supporting it in their own activities. Ironically, despite top management's tremendous commitment to seeing the Credo upheld, there are very few formal monitoring mechanisms of compliance. The strategic plans of the individual companies do not usually mention the Credo. The Credo survey results are reviewed only once a year.

Not surprisingly, the explanation lies in J & J's decentralized culture. Vice Chairman Dave Collins explained: "This is a company that relies on individual initiative, high personal ethics, and common sense. Any system that diminishes those qualities isn't right for this company."

This is not to imply, however, that there is no monitoring of Credo performance. The following three examples give a good flavor of how other aspects of managing the company provide checks and balances on Credo performance.

The Executive Committee

The many indicators of Credo performance, such as the recent survey, the quality audits, or safety performance records, are taken very seriously by the executive committee. For example, twice a year every member of the executive committee receives a report on consumer/customer complaints from all the companies in Johnson & Johnson. These are reviewed very carefully, as are employee safety reports. In the latter case there are very strict procedures for cited managers to account for safety lapses.

Company presidents are in attendance when such reports are reviewed, and they must be prepared to talk about the results. According to one company president, such meetings "can't be faked. Because it's on the mind of our leaders, it (the Credo) is made important."

There is also the constant and explicit self-monitoring which occurs within the Executive Committee itself, where the statement, "I'm not sure this is in the spirit of the Credo" commands immediate attention.

Internal Auditing

Part of the success of this system, if it can be called that, is the communication process within the company. Decentralization could in theory present tremendous obstacles to monitoring Credo compliance if the executive committee relied only on self-reported violations from the company managers. This is not in fact the case. There are several important corporate monitoring functions. Safety and quality auditing have already been mentioned. One of the most important monitoring mechanisms is the internal financial auditing function. Johnson & Johnson makes every attempt to ensure that records are kept as accurately as possible. So dedicated is it to this task that, unlike most public corporations, the company had an internal independent auditing department long before it had outside auditors.

According to Jack Begley, who heads this division (which Dave Collins jokingly calls "the eyes of the company"), his job is made very easy because of the total commitment to accurate reporting and management integrity at the top. "There is no guessing," says Begley. "I don't have to play a double standard."

Such a posture is not always so comfortable. For example, during the Foreign Corrupt Practices Act discussions, Begley was called in by Burke and Clare and asked if he felt that all members of the executive committee operated in the same way concerning facilitating payments and reporting. Begley gulped and answered, "No." When questioned further, he named two names. Later another member of the committee who had received the same grilling compared notes with Begley and thanked him wholeheartedly for speaking honestly: "Thank God you answered the way you did, for I'd named the same two names." The executives in question were not fired because the international business standards at the time were so ambiguous, but top management's position had been made clear to them on this point.

Concludes Begley, "We're puritanical in this respect." When some expense account improprieties were uncovered among very senior executives in the recent past, their position and the fact that the dollar amounts were not very big had no influence on Burke's and Clare's decision: The executives were immediately fired. Clare then sent what was in Begley's mind "a very clear letter on the subject of management impropriety." To Begley, the letter was important in that it set the record straight and discussed the precise policies which had been broken. "It sent the message that management is just."

I reviewed this letter, which was written within the past year, and found it to be a fascinating insight into just how tough-minded top management can be. Not only did it specify that it was senior management which had committed "serious improprieties," but it listed the specific incidents to which "all of our management should be sensitive." These included the use of frequent flyer coupons, personal expenses on company expense reports, changing one's own approved benefits, and charging expenses of an outside business venture to the company. While such incidents are infrequent, they are not covered up. Clare reminded all the senior officers to whom the letter was sent that "these situations represent unethical behavior in contravention of the Credo, and are grounds for termination of employment. . . . Most of these situations could have been prevented if appropriate review and approval had taken place."

Performance Assessments

One item in the Credo is management integrity—managers must be "ethical and fair" in all their dealings with employees. Clearly this kind of tenet is impossible to quantify, and there is no attempt to "audit" managers' ethical performance directly. Nevertheless, managers are personally assessed on a number of factors which are expressly mentioned in the Credo, from the safety record of their plants to support of the local community.

Informally, the way in which a manager approaches the business and discusses plans is an important access of how well the Credo is being fulfilled. If a manager should suggest a cost-cutting plan which would displace a large number of employees without accounting for their needs or the community's needs, his or her direct supervisor will ask questions about these responsibilities and suggest that they be addressed before going any further. For instance, when a company manager suggested closing down an older unprofitable plant in a small southern town in the United States, the executive committee had a long discussion with him about possible alternatives and the responsibilities which they felt J & J had to the people in that town. They altered the plan substantially, suggested to another J & J company which was seeking to expand that it use part of the old facility and some of the employees. Two hundred jobs were retained as a result. The committee also altered the severance and relocation programs which the company manager had recommended and help set up a local recruiting service for the industries in that region. At no time was the company manager's judgment about closing an unprofitable business in question, but the executive committee broadened the balance of his plan to bring it more into line with the way in which the Credo describes treating employees and communities. It also expected him to learn from this experience.

What of the manager who really does not share the worldview of the Credo, whose personal business values are at odds with the document's tenets? In few cases there will be a direct firing on this basis. First there will be the informal feedback and education mentioned above. The first assumption is that he or she needs help in understanding the principles. As Jim Burke commented, it is a matter of education and exposure to the J & J way of doing things and to how top management expects things to be done. This includes not only a negative response to avoiding the responsibilities of the Credo, but also a working knowledge of what management will not punish you for (as in, say, the recall of a questionable but profitable product if there are doubts as to its safety). In such matters the Credo is not always mentioned, but frequently does enter the discussion. If, for example, a company manager is reluctant to reserve funds for purchasing equipment that would significantly improve product quality or the safety of the operation, it will be pointed out that this is not really in the spirit of the Credo. These observations usually have a significant impact over time.

If an employee continues to be at odds with the Credo, he or she will be counseled more formally about his or her performance on these issues. If it appears over time that a manager simply cannot operate in accordance with the principles of the Credo, there will be a move to separate.

SAMPLE ILLUSTRATIONS OF HOW THE CREDO AND MANAGEMENT'S BUSINESS DECISIONS ARE INTEGRAL TO EACH OTHER

In assessing the role of the Credo at Johnson & Johnson, it is impossible to draw a neat line between cause and effect. The Credo is the product and the cause of management's way of taking on the responsibilities which it describes. It evolved out of the practicing values of the General and of those who worked at the company for many years. At the same time, the Credo inspires the inclusion of these values in management's thinking by articulating the company's responsibilities and providing a reference point for expected behavior.

The programs directly related to the Credo which are described above are important attempts to enhance the document's importance. It is equally necessary, however, to look at the many indirect ways in which the Credo is evidenced at the company in order to understand the full force of the document on managerial responsibility.

Below are a few brief descriptions selected from the many programs, policies, and incidents which illustrate the effectiveness of the Credo at Johnson & Johnson.

Product Recalls

There have been hundreds of incidents every year to demonstrate the exercising of Credo responsibility at J & J, from the decision to keep corporate headquarters in New Brunswick, New Jersey, to the conduction of a Credo Survey this year. But one of the most dramatic demonstrations of commitment to the Credo has to be the consideration of a product recall. When, for example, the first Tylenol tragedy engulfed the company in 1982, many employees and the public at large watched the company not only out of concern for public welfare, but to see whether a large multinational company really cared about its customers.

David Collins, who was responsible for McNeil Consumer Products Company at the time of the tragedy, and James Burke both feel that in retrospect there was not one decision made during that crisis which was not in accordance with the Credo. To quote Collins:

> *It was astounding. Here you had all these people, outsiders and insiders, running into Burke's office with information, opinions, and no pat answers. Sometimes people would be shouting at each other across the table. Meanwhile, out in the company, people*

were making hundreds of separate decisions which in retrospect I feel completely supported the Credo.

The story of the J & J response to Tylenol cannot be told here in the detail which it very much deserves. It should be noted, however, that Jim Burke has often stated that the guidance of the Credo played the most important role in management's decision making during these crises.

But in the end the Tylenol tragedy may have been most significant for its effect on people within the company itself.

Every war has its significant battles, every policy has its significant tests, and Tylenol was clearly that for Burke's and Clare's long-term program to revitalize the Credo at Johnson & Johnson. Nothing could confirm top management's seriousness about committing to the Credo more strongly than its performance on Tylenol, and clearly every J & J employee around the world was watching to see what his or her company would stand for. To quote one manager who was discussing his own belief in top management's commitment to the Credo, "Tylenol was the tangible proof of what they had said at the Credo Challenge Meetings. You came away saying, My God! You're right. We really do believe this. It's for real. And we did what was right."

Day-to-Day Decisions

If Tylenol represented the extraordinary nightmare under which a company would probably respond (depending on its basic moral posture) either heroically or with total demoralization, it is important to look at the less dramatic decisions for an insight into the Credo's influence at J & J. My favorite story is about Baby Oil, and it is one which both the former product manager and corporate president, Dave Clare separately recalled as a good illustration of how the Credo will override normal patterns of decentralized decision making at J & J.

Over a decade ago the Company ran a very successful campaign to market their famous baby oil as a tanning product (Remember "Baby, Baby! Turn on the Tan with Johnson's"?) At this time there was little sensitivity to the sun's harmful effects on the skin. But a medical friend of Clare's had happened to point out to him that there was beginning to be gathered some evidence that tanning might be harmful. Since baby oil actually sped up the burning–tanning process—truth in advertising!—it might actually be the case that J & J was indirectly harming consumer health. When the baby oil product manager made his next presentation and happened to use the phrase, "healthy tan," Clare jumped all over him. What did he mean by healthy tan? Could he prove it? The manager was totally taken by surprise. Clare suggested he have his people take a look at the reports before going on with the campaign.

Carl Spalding, then manager of baby oil and now president of the entire Dental Care group, recalls the incident with a shudder. He had been in charge of baby oil for only a few weeks and was totally excited to take over and continue what had been a creative and profitable campaign. This was his first presentation—or rather, half completed presentation—to the executive committee. He went back and reviewed the medical evidence with his people, and initiated the suggestion to the executive committee to "pull the plug," to borrow his still-dramatic recollection of his decision. Clare agreed. There was no way the company could ethically continue to promote baby oil as a tanning product. As Clare put it in our interview, "It simply would be wrong to entice people to harm themselves."

Sales immediately fell from $10 million to $5 million. Spalding then launched the highly successful campaign to market baby oil as a cosmetics remover.

Spalding feels that the incident was highly significant for his own training, because it steered him toward a way of thinking which he would never forget. "It told me that the Credo meant something to the people at the top, and that it should mean something to a product manager too."

He feels that he has this same responsibility to educate younger people in the company about the values of the Credo, and he initiates that process in several ways. He holds his own challenge meetings for new managers, refers to the Credo in employee communications, occasionally sends people copies, sometimes in a special frame, and most importantly, works at setting the right example.

Johnson & Johnson's Quality Assurance Program

Another good example of how the Credo gets lived out at the company is in the new companywide quality assurance program. Herb Stolzer, assistant to the chairman and the person responsible for customer complaints, product quality, operations, "etc.," feels that the fit between this activity and the Credo "is almost too good to true." He argues that the program should give the customer higher quality and save substantial amounts of money, which is the kind of balancing act which the Credo describes:

> Our message is totally consistent with decentralization and with the Credo. We are saying that it is important to get it right the first time whether we are talking about the text of a letter which would otherwise have to be retyped or a product specification for the research department. Once you are able to impress on a top manager that he or she is responsible for whatever directions issue from that office, things begin to change at every level.
>
> We're beginning to hear of better planning and communication between research and product managers. Research directors are beginning to feel more inclined to say, "Hey! You haven't told me enough. If you don't have the answer, you need to do more marketing homework before I go to the lab." And then they'll wait a month before ordering an expensive research test.
>
> Now no one says, "Oh this is being done because the Credo says to do it." But it's in the spirit of the Credo, and I think that makes it easier to institute.

Not only do such changes improve costs, they also result in greater honesty overall.

James Utaski, a company group chairman, has been very active in pushing the lesson of the quality assurance program down through his own company. He uses the Credo as a chief point of access to the program. For example, in a recent speech to employees and managers at a plant in Puerto Rico, he introduced his quality program as a "celebration" of quality, and referenced what the Credo said on this and several other responsibilities as a way of showing how the program is both a personal and company commitment.

The Quality Assurance Program is also a good example of how the company and the Credo change. As Sal Romano, head of the internal quality auditing function put it, "The Credo is not a memorial to the General. It changes and we change."

The wording on quality has changed several times in the Credo revisions, from the addition of the phrase "highest quality" to its subsequent revision to read "high quality." Attitudes on how to execute this responsibility also change. The new program is deliberately trying to move the responsibility for quality away from manufacturing inspectors and make it everyone's job.

Quality is also audited on a regular basis by a corporate team of 14 people, headed by Sal Romano. Their job is to ensure that the products produced meet the given specifications, which are at a minimum up to good manufacturing standards. Romano does not try to draw a direct relationship between his daily activities and the Credo, and yet he credits the Credo for the existence of his department and the mission it has.

Living out a philosophy of cooperation between corporate and the individual businesses while trying to ensure quality standards requires a fine discretion on the part of the auditors and the committee which reviews the reports. On the one hand, if a company president is repeatedly skimping on quality, a senior manager who is a member of the executive committee will persist in asking him or her very tough questions about the way he or she is running the company. On the other hand, no one wants to make the audit too rigidly attached to numerical judgments. The categories are "Acceptable, Marginal, and Unacceptable."

Employee Welfare

"Life for Life" program. In the late 1970s Jim Burke had a vision of Johnson & Johnson employees being "the healthiest in the world." The unique wellness program that was eventually created was devised, however, not only on some devilish notion of Credo consistency, but out of management's personal concern for employees and a strong business rationale: Healthy employees cost less in terms of absenteeism, general productiveness, and benefits claims.

To date the program is available to approximately 33,000 employees at about half the J & J sites. The results are impressive. For example, the average smoking rate among employees is now 15 percent (10 percent at some companies), as compared to the national average of 27 percent. Such figures are deemed by outside reviewers to have a clinically significant effect on the health of J & J employees, and hence on their medical costs.

Community Responsibility

Johnson & Johnson is extremely sensitive to good community relations. Managers are not only monitored for their company's contribution to local causes, but these are reported in great detail in several in-house publications. One of the greatest commitments to community was the decision to keep company headquarters in New Brunswick. John Heldrich, who heads many of the personnel functions at J & J, recalled how the Credo played a role in that decision:

> *I was probably the only member of the executive committee who had been born in New Brunswick. I felt that the health of that community was totally dependent on what we did, and that if we pulled out it was very likely that the downward spiral of urban disintegration would continue here. To leave was inconsistent with the Credo.*

Richard Sellars, chairman, agreed and proceeded to lead a turnaround in the New Brunswick area which is still continuing.

As in most J & J activities, community support is executed not only with good conscience but with good business sense and initiative. To Heldrich, an improvement in community health—from the local education process to housing to a healthy industrial tax base—is the best way to prepare for the predicted labor shortages of young workers two decades from now. Rather than be content with a contribution to a scholarship fund, Heldrich has been instrumental in institutionalizing a public/private partnership with local community representatives and elected officials to help plan New Brunswick's comeback. A major figure in the program, called "New Brunswick Tomorrow," he and other J & J managers have been personally involved in the planning and financing of the area's redevelopment and employment efforts. Their work has already paid off not only in terms of physical improvements to the area around J & J headquarters, but in public goodwill toward the company. A recent poll by the Eagleton Institute at Rutgers University revealed that J & J had a 74 percent approval rating in the local community (only 22 percent could name their own state senator).

Once again it is difficult to trace a direct connection between the Credo and New Brunswick Tomorrow. Comments Heldrich:

> *What we are doing here is not specifically mentioned in the Credo, but it is definitely generated by the Credo. You cannot get commitment either at the top or down the line to programs as innovative as these unless managers have a substantial level of interest in society at large and in their own communities. And that commitment is spelled out in the Credo.*

J & J's community activities are a reminder to outsiders not to conclude that the Credo is all about charity. As in all Credo issues, this one remains tied to basic economic and ethical considerations at the same time.

International Operations

One of the most frequent questions about ethics codes is whether they are realistic in an international context. Can a company overcome pervasive differences in culture around the world and achieve a consistent way of doing business in all its divisions? Clearly Johnson & Johnson's top management feels that it should do so, that in counterbalance to the extreme independence of the operating companies there should be a general ethical approach that ties everyone together.

One of the ways in which this is accomplished is by frequent relocations of the company's managers. All the top officers have initially had extensive experience throughout the J & J companies and usually in many parts of the world. They are aware of country-specific cultural factors which may present problems for the managing directions who report to them.

Moreover, the American managers bring the Credo's value system with them, and there is a strong communication process between Americans and foreign nationals at the operating level. Because top management is so serious about the Credo, company managers carry an unquestionable authority to see that it is carried out. "That's not the way J & J does business" is a real negotiating factor overseas. As one senior manager with extensive overseas experience told me:

> There are some countries where they now know that it is not worth holding us up for a bribe, because we won't pay it. To get this message across takes tremendous patience in a company manager. It takes stockholder patience, too.

In some instances, the gap between value systems is inevitably too great, and Johnson & Johnson has abandoned certain businesses for this reason. As in most multinationals, the most problematic international issues concern payments to minor foreign officials to get services which are supposedly already due them. Given the ambiguity on "facilitating payments" in the FCPA, there is a constant reinterpretation of these instances, and they are carefully monitored at the corporate levels. All such payments must be legal and accounted for accurately, and the internal auditing mechanisms are very strict throughout the Company.

South Africa.   This issue is an intensely private one for the company. Because of the great complexity and controversy surrounding South Africa in general, the company's decision to remain in South Africa is not described here. An official policy statement is available from the company. It should be noted, however, that of the several people with whom I spoke on this topic, all were totally convinced that the company's policy and behavior are politically unpopular both here and in South Africa, but that they are in conformance with the tenets of the Credo.

CONCLUSION

In the final analysis, I feel that outsiders have to accept that the Credo is indeed the success which Johnson & Johnson's managers believe it to be, and that its strength rests on a paradoxical set of factors. James Burke's remark, that Johnson

& Johnson has always tried to manage the business out of conflict, sets up the conditions under which the Credo is effective. The Credo is a very strong document which is capable of maintaining its strength under extreme questioning and in the face of highly conflicting demands on the company. Because the values of the Credo are so deeply ingrained in the culture of the organization, decentralization is a support, not a threat to its tenets.

Openness and questioning marked the way Tylenol was handled, when the attitude was that any and every idea should be entertained if the company were going to make the right decisions. It marks the way meetings are run, and the way extreme differences of style within individual companies are tolerated at corporate headquarters.

On the other hand, conflict at J & J has a stable reference point, a set of values in place which is summarized by the Credo. As the Credo's chief representatives, Burke and Clarke take final responsibility for deciding what should be done in such controversial cases as Tylenol, and they looked to the Credo for guidance.

The principles of the Credo and the way in which managers are given responsibility for seeing that it is maintained assumes that there is a common reservoir of decency within every office at the company. This is an assumption which is made real in the commitments and culture of the organization. The widespread skepticism which the General encountered and which many new managers continued to demonstrate cannot be overcome by force. The belief and experience of top management is that time, consistent behavior, and rational exploration of the content and benefits of the Credo will cause it to take hold.

As John Heldrich pointed out, "As soon as you get here your first learning experiences are that there is a right and wrong way to do business in this company. Say you have had a bad batch of material. Your supervisor will tell you to drop the batch—we don't use marginal materials here. This is what the Credo is about and you learn it on a day-to-day basis. You might say you grow up with it."

If you asked Johnson & Johnson, "How do you bottle the Credo?," the superficial answer would be frustrating. "Well, first you have to have it in place for 40 years. . . ."

In other words, the process of making an ethics statement meaningful is both subtle and cumulative over a long period of time.

One cannot really learn from the Credo simply by looking at the bare bones of the document and the challenge meetings. There are thousands of incidents which demonstrate the many ways in which the Credo's message is communicated, its responsibilities are assumed by managers, and decisions are affected by its existence. This report has tried to recount as wide a variety of examples as possible in order to increase our learning process about how this document works and why. At the risk of grossly simplifying what is in this report, here follows a list of the critical factors contributing to the success of the Credo over time:

Johnson & Johnson's Credo Critical Factors of Success

- A document that is succinct, clear, easily made visible.
- Tenets that are closely integrated with practical business concerns.
- Responsibilities are held in balance, not in priority.
- Close relationship between idealistic words and reality as seen in the history of the company and its culture. The document is not anonymous; it gives an idealized character portrait of the firm.
- A high value on trust—having it and earning it—in the document and in the organization.
- Strong communication programs.
- Strong educational efforts: both learning through example and through discussion of the document.
- Willingness to challenge the tenets.
- Willingness to test whether compliance is really there.
- Maintaining a constant tension between the absolute authority of the document and great personal discretion on how it can be applied.
- Top management is personally committed to the document.
- Top management is not shy about explicitly referring to the document and taking a stand on ethical issues.
- Top management is ready to act as final arbiter on the really hard calls.
- The existence of many indirect checks and balances on compliance (safety policies, financial accounting system, consumer complaint reviews, employee recruitment, etc.).
- Informal consideration of management performance on Credo compliance.
- Sustained attention to the document over time; updating its relevance and meaning.
- Consistency. The document describes every major aspect of the business and every major aspect of the business is expected upon examination to be consistent with the document.

It would be foolish for an outsider to suggest that after reading this report the Credo and the company are now fully understood. Ironically, even though its products are known the world over and Tylenol is perhaps the one piece of corporate history which most Americans would be able to identify, Johnson & Johnson remains the very private company which it always has been. It held its first and only meeting for outside analysts in 1972. Insiders attribute this privacy to the General himself, who is said to have kept a very low corporate profile in order to discourage outside interference. Only gradually has this self-protectiveness dissipated.

In compiling this report, I felt that although everyone at J & J was very supportive of the effort, I was like a stranger who attends a very intimate family gathering. Inquiring after the details of the Credo was like inquiring why someone's honored grandmother always wore purple: It was not a question of exploring why so much as having the honor of being able to observe a beloved tradition.

In this spirit, I did not try to "prove" the sincerity of what people claimed about the Credo, but rather have tried simply to describe as much of its influence as I could gather.

Does Johnson & Johnson really mean it? The answer is, I feel, already obvious from the tone of this report. Management's commitment to the Credo is explicit, frequently articulated, and often considered and debated. As one member of the executive committee stated, "Part of management's responsibility is to convince the doubters inside the company that, in fact, following the Credo is the best way to manage our business." On the other hand, the company shies away from any outside advertisement of the Credo which might appear to be self-aggrandizement.

The recall stories are a good example of management's commitment to the tenets of the Credo. Most of the recall incidents have been controversial within the company because the product served a need originally. Dropping it means a disservice to some portion of the market and probably some penalty to stockholders in the short term.

In resolving such conflicts of responsibility, top management is usually conservatively cautious. If the decision is between minimal injury or greatest benefit to the greatest number, management will tend to lean toward the former. What is also clear, however, is that their thinking is not restricted to a simple moral cost-benefit analysis. James Burke and David Clare and other J & J managers repeatedly stressed that the Credo demanded the simultaneous consideration of many responsibilities and a balance over time. As Burke remarked, "Tylenol knocked the stuffing out of us," but it did not for a moment cause management to hesitate to face its responsibilities once again when Zomax came up.

A continual phrase which popped up during my interviews was, "If we hadn't done such and such." Apparently this is a stock way of thinking through problems at J & J, and it is one which is especially applicable to the Credo itself. Says Jim Burke, "If we hadn't had a Credo, we would have had to invent one."

For more information or a copy of the Johnson & Johnson *Credo,* please write Dept. of Public Relations, One Johnson & Johnson Plaza, New Brunswick, NJ 08933. Telephone: 201/524-6819.

What this article is about: This article outlines an approach for *implementing* business ethics. A company should both organize for ethical business policies and execute them. The organizational dimension refers to structural components including codes of ethics, conferences and training programs, and an ethical audit. The corporate culture must support these structural elements with top management playing a central role in implementing ethics. The execution of ethical business policies includes implementation responsibilities and tasks. These responsibilities are leadership in ethics, delegation, communication, and motivation of the company's ethical position to employees. Execution tasks are delineated for the marketing function. Although many company examples are provided, a program in place at McDonnell Douglas is highlighted as a model of ethics implementation.

5–7 *Implementing Business Ethics*

Patrick E. Murphy

Patrick E. Murphy is an associate professor of marketing in the College of Business Administration at the University of Notre Dame

INTRODUCTION

Most organizations have learned that it is not enough to have a well-designed corporate strategy in place. Equally important is to be able to *implement* this strategy. In fact, one projection is that only about 10 percent of all strategies are effectively implemented. If implementation is to succeed, the entire organization must be committed to the strategy and even the smallest detail should not be overlooked. The same is true with ethics. Implementing ethics is not just a concern of managers setting the firm's overall strategic direction, but should pervade all levels of the business.

The author would like to thank Gerald Cavanagh, S. J., Stephen Greyser, Gene Laczniak, Lee Tavis, Clarence Walton, and Oliver Williams, C. S. C., for their helpful comments on an earlier version of this article.

SOURCE: *Journal of Business Ethics* 7 (1988) 907–15. © 1988 *by Kluwer Academic Publishers.*

Recent events concerning unethical business practices, not only on Wall Street, but also in many other places, appear to highlight the lack of attention to implementation of ethical policies. The existence of a carefully defined ethical code does not guarantee ethical behavior. A good example is General Electric (GE). The company has long had a formal, written code of conduct that is communicated to employees and perceives itself as a leader in subscribing to ethical business practices. Yet, GE ran into trouble in 1985 for having time cards forged at a Pennsylvania defense plant. This situation caused a suspension of new defense contracts for a time and much embarrassment for the firm. More recently, their Kidder Peabody subsidiary was implicated in the insider-trading scandal even though GE was assured before their June 1986 acquisition of Kidder that the firm faced no major problems with the SEC or Justice Department. These events lead to a management shake-up at Kidder. GE found that it is quite difficult to implement ethics in their far-flung range of businesses.

What can be done to make sure that ethical policies are implemented and that the firm will steer clear of wrongdoings that result in legal problems and/or bad press? The answer is not an easy one. This article outlines steps that companies might use in carrying out ethical business practices. Implementing business ethics involves organizing for and executing ethical policies.[1] The organizational aspects of implementation are covered initially and then we turn our attention to executing ethical strategies.

This paper takes a pragmatic, rather than a philosophical, approach to examining ethics. The manager is pulled from several directions—personal, organizational, and market—in reconciling ethical dilemmas.[2] Making good moral judgments requires frank discussions and ethical sensitivity. This point was well articulated by B. H. McCoy (1983): "In contrast to philosophy, business involves action and implementation—getting things done. Managers must come up with answers to problems based on what they see and what they allow to influence their decision-making process."

ORGANIZING FOR ETHICAL BUSINESS POLICIES

Figure 1 lists the organizational dimensions of business ethics and procedures that will bring about the implementation of ethical company practices. *Structure* refers to formal organizational mechanisms that foster ethical decisions. *Culture* pertains to the informal organizational climate.

---

[1] This definition and format of the article are partially adapted from "Marketing Implementation," in Murphy and Enis (1985).

[2] The following discussion of implementing business ethics relies primarily on structural or organization procedures. An alternative approach which focuses on individual responsibilities is outlined by Nielsen (1986).

FIGURE 1 Implementing Business Ethics

Organizing for Ethical Business Policies

Structure: the formal organization	*Culture: the informal organization*

Corporate codes
  Specific
  Public documents
  Blunt and realistic
  Revised periodically
	Open and candid
	
	Management role

Committees, conferences, and training	
Ethical audit questions	

Executing Ethical Business Policies

Implementation responsibilities	*Implementation tasks*
Leadership	Product alteration
Delegation	Price negotiation
Communication	Place determination
Motivation	Promotion presentation

Structure

Corporate codes have long been viewed as the major organizational structure in which to implement ethical policy. Research indicates that approximately 90 percent of *Fortune* 500 firms and almost half of all companies have codes in place (Center for Business Ethics, 1986; Murphy, 1986). Several writers, the first being the late Ted Purcell, S. J. (1978), have viewed ethical codes as the cornerstone to "institutionalizing" ethics. However, codes of conduct continue to be criticized as being too general, containing too many platitudes, serving purely as public relations ploys, or being designed strictly to avoid legal problems (Berenbeim, 1987; Wartzman, 1987). Cressey and Moore (1983) found that codes give more attention to unethical conduct likely to decrease a firm's profits than to conduct that might increase profits. After closely examining over 50 corporate code of ethics, several observations can be offered.

If codes are to serve as a foundation for implementation, they should possess the characteristics listed in Figure 1. Corporate codes should be *specific*. Employees need guidance in interpreting their actions. Motorola gives specific examples (i.e., A Motorolan traveling on Motorola business may accept the courtesy of free lodging in a customer facility so long as properly noted on the Motorolan's expense records) after each of the sections of its code. IBM lists three types of activities—mandatory, acceptable, and unacceptable—in its Business Conduct Guidelines.

An area needing specificity is gifts and entertainment. Several companies state that employees can give or receive gifts of "nominal," "token," or "modest" value. However, it is very difficult to determine what is nominal or token and when a gift becomes a bribe. A number of companies have made their codes more specific in this area. Ford and GM stipulate that employees cannot give or receive gifts exceeding $25. Waste Management defines nominal value as "not exceeding $100 in aggregate annual value." Donnelly Mirrors gives the following guidelines: "If you can't eat it, drink it, or use it up in one day, don't give it or anything else of greater value."

Second, codes should be *public* documents. Some corporate codes are exclusively for internal corporate use. If a code is worth developing, it should demonstrate to customers, suppliers, stockholders, and others interested in the company the organization's commitment to fair and ethical practice.

Corporate codes should also be *blunt* and *realistic about violations*. For example, Baxter's code states that violators will be terminated. Gellerman (1986) indicated that the most effective deterrent is not to increase the severity of the punishment, but to "heighten the perceived probability of being caught." Therefore, active enforcement of existing codes should enhance compliance. Firms also need to consider how employees should react when confronted with violations of the code. Several codes instruct them to talk to their supervisor. Marriott tells employees to "see your manager or department head" if the issue cannot be resolved with the immediate supervisor.

Finally, codes should be *revised periodically*. That is, they should be living documents and updated to reflect current ethical problems. Caterpillar has revised its code three times since 1974. Investment banking firms likely would want to revise their codes in light of recent events. Specifically, Goldman Sachs now lists 14 business principles and the last one states: "Integrity and honesty are at the heart of our business. We expect our people to maintain high ethical standards in everything they do, both at work for the firm and in their personal lives." This point probably should be placed much higher on the list and given greater emphasis in future revisions.

Ethics committees, training, and conferences are a second structural method for implementing ethical business policies (see Figure 1). Only 15 percent of firms have ethics modules in their training programs and about 30 percent discuss ethics in management or policy sessions (Murphy, 1986). Motorola has a Business Ethics Compliance Committee that is charged with interpreting, clarifying, communicating, and adjudicating the company's code. Some firms have used ethical consultants or speakers at dealer meetings on ethics. Cummins Engine for a time had an in-house ethicist. Polaroid held day-long in-house conferences on ethics in 1983 and 1984 as part of a major ethics program.[3]

The Drackett Company, a subsidiary of Bristol Myers, recently implemented an ethics module in their 1987 Market Research Conference. Attendees at the

---

[3]For a discussion of Polaroid's program, see Godfrey (1987) and Godfrey and Williams (1985).

meeting submitted in advance their responses to 16 ethical scenarios. During the meeting, small groups met to discuss 3 of the 11 scenarios where there was the greatest disagreement. According to the manager who led this activity, it was enthusiastically received. Many of the participants were surprised by their colleagues' judgments, but enjoyed the interchange in analyzing these issues.

Another structural suggestion for implementing business ethics listed in Figure 1 is an ethical audit. Just as financial and marketing audits seek to gain information about these functions, an ethical audit would pose questions about manufacturing practices, personnel policies, dealings with suppliers, financial reporting, and sales techniques to find out if ethical abuses may be occurring. It might be argued that the answers to such questions are less important than raising and grappling with the issues.

Dow Corning instituted a face-to-face audit in their firm over 10 years ago at company locations throughout the world. The agenda has shifted over the years from a standard one of 8 to 10 items for each site to a tailored discussion of specific questions about functional areas. At sales offices, issues such as kickbacks, unusual requests from customers, and special pricing terms are examined. John Swanson, who heads this effort as Manager of the Corporate Internal and Management Communications Division, explained that the benefit of their innovative audit approach is "to make it virtually impossible for employees to consciously make an unethical decision."[4] Swanson (1987) indicated that 21 meetings were led by one of the four Business Conduct Committee members in 1986–87 and a report was prepared for the Audit Committee of the Board. He emphasized that there are no shortcuts to implementing this program and it requires time and extensive interaction of the people involved.

Culture

The informal organization or corporate culture is the second component of the organizational dimension of ethics implementation (see Figure 1). Some commentators have indicated that the informal organization is much more important in the development of the firm's ethical posture than the formal organization. The informal organization creates the culture, and formal policies are then a reflection of that culture. It works well at Hewlett-Packard, where the firm allows policies of liberal health benefits and no layoffs, because Bill Hewlett and David Packard want to remain true to the ideals on which the firm was founded. On the negative side, the recent revelations of nepotism and bribe taking by executives at Anheuser-Busch was at least partially explained by observers who criticized the Busch family for perpetuating a corporate culture that condoned these activities. Therefore, the informal organization must reward ethical activities and give signals to managers that the company is committed to integrity in all business dealings.

---

[4]For more detail on this program, see Swanson (1984) and ("Dow Corning" . . . 1986).

A candid and ethical culture is one where communication freely flows within the organization (Serpa, 1985). This type of culture can help to reduce "moral stress" (Waters and Bird, 1987) and achieve "moral excellence" (Hoffman, 1986). A number of individuals, including a CEO of a Big Eight accounting firm, have advocated this approach to dealing with ethical problems. A climate where ethical issues can be openly discussed can lead to this type of culture. Spending time in management meetings is one avenue that has been used effectively. This sort of ethical training should ideally occur before problems arise and not after the fact, such as the instance of E. F. Hutton and General Dynamics contracting with the Ethics Resource Center for ethics training after running into serious problems.

The role of top management is crucial in creating the culture of an organization. The tone starts at the top. The CEO and other Vice President-level executives are extremely important in setting the ethical tenor of the firm.

EXECUTING ETHICAL BUSINESS POLICIES

Figure 1 also shows the two components of the executing phase of business ethics implementation. It is not enough to have the structure and culture that support ethical decision making. These organizational dimensions must be combined with implementation responsibilities and tasks so that a firm is ethical in its execution of strategies.

Implementation Responsibilities

Although there are four execution responsibilities listed in the figure, the overarching one is leadership. As Bennis and Nanus (1986) have stated: American corporations are overmanaged and underled. Leadership is important in all aspects of the business, but it is critical in the ethics area.[5] Horton (1986) examined characteristics of CEOs and listed integrity as an "indispensable ingredient." A good example is James Burke of Johnson & Johnson who had managers evaluate the J & J credo (which is often given as the reason for the swift and ethical reaction to the Tylenol poisonings). Basically, they reaffirmed the company's long-standing commitment to ethical business practice. A recent illustration is Lee Iacocca's stance regarding Chrysler's questionable practice of disconnecting odometers during testing by executives. He admitted that the company made mistakes in judgment and set forth a program to rectify them and promised that they would not happen again in a two-page national ad. Mr. Iacocca did not view this as a product recall, but added "the only thing we're recalling here is our integrity."

---

[5] A recent in-depth examination of the ethical leadership issue appeared in Enderle (1987).

Delegation follows from leadership, but is an essential responsibility for effective implementation to occur. Middle- and lower-level managers are sometimes placed in difficult ethical situations because high-level executives are unclear in their delegation of ethical responsibilities. Statements such as "I don't care how you do it, just meet or beat your quota" or "Ship more to that customer this month than you did last" or "Find a way to fire that person" often give subordinates the impression that any tactic can be used to reach organizational objectives. Several years ago managers in a truck plant installed a secret control box to override the speed of the assembly line because they felt it was the only way to achieve production objectives set by upper management. If the delegation responsibility is to be dispatched properly, executives must be more explicit about what are acceptable and ethical practices.

Communication is an essential responsibility if ethical policies are to be executed in any organization. Formally, this communication can happen in many ways through the ethical code and seminars/training programs that deal with ethical issues. New employees of most companies are asked to read and sign the ethical code upon their employment. In many instances, however, little communication follows the initial exposure. To overcome this potential problem, Caterpillar requires its managers to report annually about its implementation of the code within the division/department. Similarly, Michigan National Bank requires that employees sign off on the ethical code every year.

Informal communication is also a potentially effective implementation responsibility. The grapevine can disseminate information that formal vehicles cannot. For instance, the fact that a salesperson lost his/her commission for padding the expense account may not lend itself to discussion in the company newsletter. However, the word can get through informal channels and consequently influence future behavior.

The last, but certainly not the least important, implementation responsibility is motivation. If companies are to be successful in executing ethical marketing policies, individuals must be motivated to do the right thing. This means that higher-level executives must look closely at how performance is measured. Managers who engage in exorbitant entertaining of clients or informally practice discrimination should not be rewarded for these activities. One of the problems with the Wall Street scandal was that top managers did not look closely at the large profits their firms were earning. How did these large returns happen? Unfortunately, we know the answer in many cases. Employees are motivated by higher-level executives and their expectations regarding ethical business practices.

Implementation Tasks

Implementation tasks relate to specific functional areas within the firm. One area that has received much attention in the academic and popular press is marketing implementation (Bonoma, 1984; Enis and Murphy, 1987; Peters and Waterman,

1982). Since marketing is charged with external relations with customers where many ethical issues arise, it will serve as the focal point for this discussion. Other functional areas could be treated similarly. For example, if human resources were the focus, tasks relating to hiring, training, and promoting employees would be relevant.

Figure 1 lists the relevant implementation tasks for the marketing-mix variables of product, price, channel, and promotion. Product alteration is intended to get the consumer to make the intended exchange. Ethical issues result when minor adjustments are promoted as being significant changes to the product. Furthermore, the development of me-too products could be questioned from an ethical standpoint. One other product alteration issue relates to the product manager. Does this person, who is usually on the fast track, make needed modifications to a brand to ensure its long-term marketplace staying power or only perform cosmetic changes to improve next quarter's market share or profit picture?

Price negotiation is often at the heart of marketing implementations. Those sales executives and marketing managers who can effectively negotiate on price win many contracts. An ethical problem occurs in this process when one of the participants has much more power than the other. An example is a large Midwestern department store chain which dealt with a small candy producer and told the company that they would pay 70 percent of the negotiated price and the small firm could keep the account or pay 100 percent and they would lose the account. These types of practices are unethical, but not illegal. They possibly might be curbed by the small firm taking its case to the top echelon of the larger company.

Place determination refers to getting the product to the place it is demanded in an expeditious manner. Here marketers often promise more than they can deliver. It becomes an ethical issue when there is economic or psychological harm to the client/consumer. In health care or life-threatening situations, execution of place determination is critical. Greater emphasis on marketing by these organizations may heighten the ethical problems they face. Furthermore, large retailers may coerce other members of the channel to achieve their objectives in getting products to the market.

Promotion presentation is often viewed as a crucial function of marketing. Both selling and advertising have persuasive, informative, and reminding components. The persuasive area is most often associated with ethical abuses. In selling, ethical problems often arise when persuasion is too intense or competitors are unscrupulous in their appeals. What the ethical salesperson should do is to ensure that the buyers are making decisions on what he/she believes are the most important evaluative criteria. If the unethical marketer cannot deliver on its promises, the ethical firm has a good chance to gain the business. Even if the business is lost once, there is sometimes an opportunity to gain it later. For example, a communications firm sought a contract with a defense contractor, but found the defense company only wanted entree to newspaper editors. The consultant indicated that he could not meet these unrealistic goals and " . . . walked out. Several months later he got a $50,000 contract" (Davidson, 1986).

Some companies even identify the types of sales tactics that are acceptable in their firm's code of ethics. For instance, ADP, a computer software company, states: "Aggressive selling should not include defamation of competition, malicious rumors, or unsupportable promises." IBM's code makes a similar point: "It has long been the company's policy to provide customers the best possible products and services. Sell them on their merits, not by disparaging competitors."

The advertising area is one where persuasion is often criticized for being unethical. If the message includes puffery, but not deception (which is illegal), then it falls into an ethical gray area. One type of advertising that is receiving growing criticism is advertising to children, especially for war toys and highly sugared products. Furthermore, the current debate about advertising beer and wine on television centers on free speech versus potential negative effects of product usage on consumers, especially teenagers who find the lifestyles portrayed in these commercials to be rather desirable.

In examining a number of codes of conduct, it was surprising to find that very few list a specific posture with respect to advertising. An exception is Ford, which provides explicit policies for the use of comparative advertising. This might be an area where consumer-products marketers consider developing explicit guidelines. Some have ad hoc policies regarding sponsorship of shows dealing with sensitive subjects or containing large amounts of sex/violence. It appears that thought should be given to appropriate advertising messages and possibly even media in implementing the ethical policies of the firm.

AN ILLUSTRATION OF BUSINESS ETHICS IMPLEMENTATION

In 1987 one firm, McDonnell Douglas, engaged in an extensive business ethics implementation program.[6] Their effort even has a theme—"Always take the high road." The corporate code has been revised for the third time in the 1980s. A series of three ethics books were distributed to all employees at their home address in June. The "Code of Ethics" book features ethical decision-making guidelines, a short version of their code and the ethical decision-making checklist. The latter two are also available in pocket-size cards and are shown in Figure 2.

The "Standards of Business Conduct" book lists five overriding standards and several areas pertaining to each of them. Discussion of these standards is treated in three sections—*In General* (states the overall principle), *Specifically* (contains specific rules, laws, and requirements applicable to each standard), and *Where to Go* (where to turn for help). This book concludes with a section on procedures

---

[6]McDonnell Douglas is a participant in the eighteen-point voluntary industry agreement, "The Defense Industry Initiatives on Business Ethics and Conduct." The company's commitment to ethics is the driving force for this program, not industry or governmental pressure.

FIGURE 2 McDonnell Douglas Ethical Code and Checklist

Implementing Business Ethics

McDonnell Douglas Code of Ethics

Integrity and ethics exist in the individual or they do not exist at all. They must be upheld by individuals or they are not upheld at all. In order for integrity and ethics to be characteristics of McDonnell Douglas, we who make up the Corporation must strive to be:

- *Honest and trustworthy in all our relationships.*
- *Reliable in carrying out assignments and responsibilities.*
- *Truthful and accurate in what we say and write.*
- *Cooperative and constructive in all work undertaken.*
- *Fair and considerate in our treatment of fellow employees, customers, and all other persons.*
- *Law abiding in all our activities.*
- *Committed to accomplishing all tasks in a superior way.*
- *Economical in utilizing company resources.*
- *Dedicated in service to our company and to improvement of the quality of life in the world in which we live.*

Integrity and high standards of ethics require hard work, courage, and difficult choices. Consultation among employees, top management, and the Board of Directors will sometimes be necessary to determine a proper course of action. Integrity and ethics may sometimes require us to forgo business opportunities. In the long run, however, we will be better served by doing what is right rather than what is expedient. (From MDC Policy 2, *MDC Policy Manual*).

Ethical Decision-Making Checklist

Analysis

- *What are the facts?*
- *Who is responsible to act?*
- *What are the consequences of action? (Benefit-Harm Analysis)*
- *What and whose rights are involved? (Rights/Principles Analysis)*
- *What is fair treatment in this case? (Social Justice Analysis)*

Solution development

- *What solutions are available to me?*
- *Have I considered all of the creative solutions which might permit me to reduce harm, maximize benefits, respect more rights, or be fair to more parties?*

Select the optimum solution

- *What are the potential consequences of my solutions?*
- *Which of the options I have considered does the most to maximize benefits, reduce harm, respect rights, and increase fairness?*
- *Are all parties treated fairly in my proposed decision?*

Implementation

- *Who should be consulted and informed?*
- *What actions will assure that my decision achieves its intended outcome?*
- *Implement.*

Follow up

- *Was the decision implemented correctly?*
- *Did the decision maximize benefits, reduce harm, respect rights, and treat all parties fairly?*

for reporting possible violations including employees' obligation to report, confidentiality, and absence of reprisals.

The third book, "Questions and Answers," shows how selected standards apply in potentially difficult work situations through a question and detailed answer format. This publication is written in layman's terms and cross-referenced to the longer standards book. The company also has a corporationwide ethics training program that all management and blue collar employees attend. A seven-person ethics committee is formally charged with implementing all facets of the program.

The informal organization is involved in several ways. An extensive ombudsman program is operational as well as a number of instructions to employees to openly discuss and air ethical abuses they see occurring. At the end of the "Questions and Answers" book, employees are asked for their comments or questions on ethical issues. These informal responses are to be returned directly to the Corporate Ethics Committee. Another alternative for responding about ethical problems and violations is a hotline number used exclusively for reports to this committee.

The role of top management is instrumental in making the program work. S. N. "Sandy" McDonnell, the former CEO, has been on the forefront in advocating ethical practices in the aerospace industry. He has taken a leadership role as evidenced by the following comment made in 1984:

> A company has to go beyond just tacking an ethics code up on the wall. You have to make sure that everyone knows and understands it—from the chairman on down through supervision (Miller 1984).

and this statement which appeared in a 1987 company publication describing his commitment to the current ethics program:

> What I hope all this will lead to is a business environment in which the issue of ethics remains in the forefront of everything we do. If we always make the ethical choice, if we always take the high road, we will be doing not only what is right, but also what is best for McDonnell Douglas and ourselves as individuals.

A procedure is delegated and communicated throughout the organization in the form of the company's "ethical decision-making" checklist in Figure 2. The steps outlined are analysis, solution, development, selection of the optimum solution, implementation, and follow-up parallel closely those advocated by Nash (1981) several years ago. These mechanisms have motivated employees to become more active in providing comments and suggestions on how ethics can be improved in the firm. This complete ethics-implementation program can serve as a model for other companies.[7]

---

[7]Although McDonnell Douglas was implicated in recent U.S. Defense Department contract problems, the company feels that its policies are sound and set up a high-level task force to determine whether additional guidelines are needed. The CEO stated: "We want to leave no doubt that McDonnell Douglas believes in and acts in accordance with the highest ethical standards" (Schachter 1988).

CONCLUSION

The major premise articulated here is that firms can ethically implement their business strategies. Several conclusions can be drawn.

1. Codes of ethics must be more than legal or public relations documents. They must provide specific and useful guidance to employees. Firms are urged to rethink their codes to make them more viable by including specific practices, examples, or answers to often-asked ethical questions.
2. Visible signs must exist that ethics matters to the firm. This can be accomplished by spending time in formal meetings discussing ethical issues and working through the corporate culture. Both the carrot and stick methods should be used. Employees should be rewarded for making ethical choices and at the same time the code must be enforced. These actions must be communicated throughout the firm, so that the commitment is understood.
3. Top management must pay attention to detail on how results are accomplished. The same scrutiny should be employed when examining profits as costs. Similarly, management should not give vague or unrealistic goals to subordinates without some explanation of how they are to be attained.
4. Ethics implementation needs a champion. Someone must make it happen. It is essential that the CEO be in support of it, but in companies like McDonnell Douglas and Polaroid the ethics cause had a champion. This is likely most effective if the job title is not solely related to this task.

In implementing business ethics, attention must be paid to both the organizing and executing components (see Figure 1). Only if managers and top executives are consciously committed to carrying out ethical policies will implementation actually occur. Tough questions must be asked and appropriate answers should be given at all levels of the organization. We can improve the ethical posture of business, but everyone must be committed to it.

REFERENCES

Bennis, Warren and Nanus, Bert. *Leaders*. (New York: Harper & Row, 1985).
Berenbeim, Ronald E. *Corporate Ethics*. (New York: The Conference Board, 1987).
Bonoma, Thomas V. "Making Your Marketing Strategy Work", *Harvard Business Review*, March–April, 1984, pp. 69–76.
Center for Business Ethics: 1986, "Are Corporations Institutionalizing Ethics?," *Journal of Business Ethics* **5,** pp. 85–91.
Cressey, Donald R. and Moore, Charles A. "Managerial Values and Corporate Codes of Ethics", *California Management Review*, Summer 1983, pp. 53–77.
Davidson, Jeffrey P. "The Elusive Nature of Integrity," *Marketing News* (November 7, 1986), p. 24.
'Dow Corning Corporation, Ethics, "Face-to-Face" ': *Ethics Resource Center Report*, Winter 1986, pp. 4–7.

Enderle, Georges. "Some Perspectives of Managerial Ethical Leadership," *Journal of Business Ethics* **6,** (1987), pp. 657–63.

Enis, Ben M. and Murphy, Patrick E. "Marketing Strategy Implementation", in *Contemporary Views on Marketing Practice*, ed. G. L. Frazier and J. N. Sheth (Lexington, Mass.: Lexington Books, 1987), pp. 159–73.

Gellerman, Saul W. "Why Good Managers Make Bad Ethical Choices," *Harvard Business Review*, July–August 1986, pp. 85–90.

Godfrey, Joline. "Ethics as an Entrepreneurial Venture," *Training News* (June 1987).

Godfrey, Joline and Williams, R. "Leadership and Values at Polaroid Corporation," unpublished paper, (1985).

Hoffman, W. Michael. "What Is Necessary for Corporate Moral Excellence?" *Journal of Business Ethics* **5** (1986), pp. 233–42.

Horton, Thomas R. *What Works for Me: 16 CEOS Talk About Their Careers and Commitments* (New York: Random House, 1986).

McCoy, Bowen H. "The Parable of the Sadhu," *Harvard Business Review*, September–October 1983, pp. 103–108.

Miller, William H. "Business' New Link: Ethics and the Bottom Line," *Industry Week*, October 29, 1984, pp. 49–53.

Murphy, Patrick E. "Marketing VPs Views Toward Marketing Ethics", Working Paper, University of Notre Dame, 1986.

Murphy, Patrick E. and Enis, Ben M. *Marketing* (Glenview, Ill.: Scott-Foresman, 1985).

Nash, Laura. "Ethics without the Sermon," *Harvard Business Review,* November–December 1981, pp. 79–90.

Nielsen, Richard P. "What Can Managers Do about Unethical Management?" *Journal of Business Ethics* **6** (1987) pp. 309–20.

Peters, Thomas J. and Waterman, Jr., Robert H. *In Search of Excellence* (New York: Harper & Row, 1982).

Purcell, Theodore V., Jr. "Institutionalizing Ethics on Corporate Boards," *Review of Social Economy,* December 1978, pp. 41–53.

Schachter, Jim. "McDonnell Douglas to Probe Use of Defense Officials as Consultants", *Los Angeles Times,* August 5, 1988, Part IV, 3.

Serpa, Roy. "Creating a Candid Corporate Culture," *Journal of Business Ethics* **4** (1985), pp. 425–30.

Swanson, John E. "Developing a Workable Corporate Ethic," in *Corporate Governance and Institutionalizing Ethics*. ed. W. M. Hoffmann, J. M. Moore, and D. A. Fedo (Lexington, Mass.: Lexington Books, 1984), pp. 209–15.

Swanson, John E. Personal communication with the author, June 21, 1987.

Wartzman, Rick. "Nature of Nurture? Study Blames Ethical Lapses on Corporate Goals," *The Wall Street Journal*, October 9, 1987, p. 21.

Waters, James A. and Bird, Frederick, "The Moral Dimension of Organizational Culture," *Journal of Business Ethics* **6** (1987), pp. 15–22.